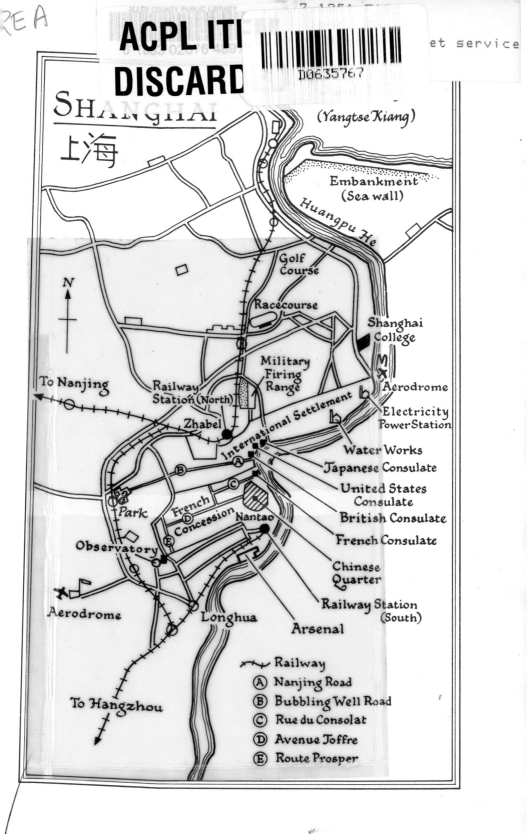

REA

ACPL ITE
DISCARD

ALLEN COUNTY PUBLIC LIBRARY

D0635767

et service

SHANGHAI
上海

(Yangtse Kiang)

Embankment
(Sea wall)

Huangpu He

N

Golf
Course

Racecourse

Shanghai
College

To Nanjing

Railway
Station (North)

Military
Firing
Range

International Settlement

Aerodrome

Electricity
Power Station

Zhabel

Ⓐ

Water Works

Japanese Consulate

Ⓑ

Ⓒ

United States
Consulate

Park

French
Concession

Ⓓ

Nantao

British Consulate

French Consulate

Observatory

Ⓔ

Chinese
Quarter

Aerodrome

Longhua

Arsenal

Railway Station
(South)

To Hangzhou

⊰⊱ Railway

Ⓐ Nanjing Road

Ⓑ Bubbling Well Road

Ⓒ Rue du Consolat

Ⓓ Avenue Joffre

Ⓔ Route Prosper

THE CHINESE SECRET SERVICE

THE CHINESE SECRET SERVICE

Roger Faligot
and Rémi Kauffer

Translated from the French
by Christine Donougher

William Morrow and Company, Inc.
New York

Allen County Public Library
Ft. Wayne, Indiana

To André and Sylvie

Copyright © 1987 by Editions Robert Laffont, S.A., Paris

Translation copyright © 1989 by Christine Donougher
Maps copyright © 1989 by Peter McClure
First published in Great Britain in 1989
by HEADLINE BOOK PUBLISHING PLC

All rights reserved. No part of this book may be reproduced or utilized in any form or by any means, electronic or mechanical, including photocopying, recording or by any information storage and retrieval system, without permission in writing from the Publisher. Inquiries should be addressed to Permissions Department, William Morrow and Company, Inc., 105 Madison Avenue, New York, N.Y. 10016.

Recognizing the importance of preserving what has been written, it is the policy of William Morrow and Company, Inc., and its imprints and affiliates to have the books it publishes printed on acid-free paper, and we exert our best efforts to that end.

Library of Congress Cataloging-in-Publication Data

Faligot, Roger.
    [Kang Sheng et les services secrets chinois. English]
    The Chinese secret service / Roger Faligot and Rémi Kauffer ;
translated from the French by Christine Donougher.
        p.   cm.
    Translation of: Kang Sheng et les services secrets chinois.
    ISBN 0-688-09722-7
    1. K'ang, Sheng, 1898-1975.   2. Intelligence officers—China—
Biography.   3. Intelligence service—China—History—20th century.
4. Secret service—China—History—20th century.   I. Kauffer, Rémi.
II. Title.
UB251.C6K36413   1989
327.1'251—dc20
[B]   90-30786
                                                                    CIP

Printed in the United States of America

First U.S. Edition

1 2 3 4 5 6 7 8 9 10

The International had no choice . . . I have said that its objective was to give to the Chinese proletariat, as quickly as possible, the class consciousness it needed to make a bid for power . . . I have to recognise that a secret service on the Russian model, but stronger, would have been a possible solution.

André Malraux

Nouvelle Revue Française

April 1931

Contents

Foreword

This book was published as a hardback in Britain just as the pro-democracy demonstrations were crushed in Tiananmen Square, Beijing. The ten-year process of reforms and modernisation put into operation by ageing leader Deng Xiaoping was thus temporarily halted. Dreams of a more democratic society vanished. Inside the Chinese Communist Party, the factions fought on.

Unfortunately, among other things, this development confirmed what the authors had predicted in the initial French edition of this book in 1987: that the security and intelligence community had become a real political force in the People's Republic of China.

As information flowed to the West from mainland China, the extent of the repression following the May/June 1989 events became clear for all to see. Its perpetrators were the Chinese state security forces and the disciplinary commission of the Communist Party, both of which are headed by key Politburo member Qiao Shi.

Qiao Shi's importance and his strength lies in his peculiar relationship with the inner circle at the top of the Party: he is Deng Xiaoping's *protégé*, deposed reformist leader Zhao Ziyang's friend, and yet he is also conservative Prime Minister Li Peng's ally. He went with Zhao to talk to the Tiananmen students, yet he had no qualms later about leading the repression and acting as interim General-secretary after Zhao's downfall. As head and symbol of the security lobby, Qiao Shi strikes a careful balance between conservatives and moderates, and thus asserts his own power.

But the security community in China also encompasses intelligence and counter-espionage operations abroad, the monitoring of democratic countries' response to repression in the People's Republic and, most notably, their reactions over trade and crucial questions such as the fate of Hong Kong or the rebellion in Tibet. Beijing's Big Brother has also increased surveillance on students and other Chinese nationals overseas.

After fifty years of rule by Mao's *eminence grise* Kang Sheng, the Chinese secret service has, over the last decade, undergone extensive modernisation. Today, Chinese spies use computers and video cameras.

Oddly enough, the mid-eighties saw the birth of not only a Soviet-inspired, KGB-like Ministry of State Security (the *Guoanbu*), but also a US-type National Security Council, known as the International Studies and Research Centre, whose director, diplomat Huan Xiang—formerly a *chargé d'affairs* in Britain in the fifties—died unnoticed during the Tiananment events.

The tradition of secrecy and ruthlessness of Chinese spies, as described 2,500 years ago by Sun Zi in his *Art of War*, shows no signs of abating.

Roger Faligot and Rémi Kauffer
September 1989

Acknowledgements

Many witnesses wished to remain anonymous. For Chinese from Red China or Taiwan, indeed even Hong Kong, it is often a question of protecting themselves from all kinds of trouble. One also knows that confidentiality is always a strong notion amongst the Chinese community in general, never mind during an historical inquiry on secret services. This extends to the officers of the security services in Tokyo, Taipei and Hong Kong who were willing to answer the authors' questions.

Many Europeans, university fellows, businessmen, journalists have preferred not to be named, in the fear of jeopardising any subsequent trips to the People's Republic of China. Thanks to them all.

Since the original French edition of this book, we have been saddened by two pieces of news from Hong Kong. Firstly, the death has been reported of the last of the great reporters of the *Far Eastern Economic Review*, David Bonavia, who was most helpful to us during our quest. Secondly, the Universities Services Centre will have to close down as a consequence of the Sino-British agreement over Hong Kong. All China-watchers have been indebted to the documentary treasures to be found there. We would like to thank warmly the Centre's charming director, John Dolphin, and wish him good luck for the future.

Our thanks in particular to:

The journalists of the Japanese daily, *Yomiuri Shimbun*, for their friendly help throughout our investigation and in particular to Yamada Hiroshi (Paris correspondent) Tobari Haruo (Hong Kong correspondent) and to Maruyana Masuru, assistant editor-in-chief of Foreign Affairs in Tokyo.

The linguists who have helped us work with the records and documents in the original language beginning with our Chinese teacher, Christophe Landry.

The team at the Centre de Recherches et de Documentation sur la Chine Contemporaine of the School of Further Studies in Social Sciences (Faculty of Human Sciences in Paris) whose writers also edited the indispensable *Dictionnaire biographique du mouvement ouvrier chinois* (under the direction of Lucien Bianco and Yves Chevrier). Without forgetting Jean-Luc Domenach.

The dynamic team of the Tokyo *China Directory* and posthumous thanks to Inagawa Jiro, Chairman of Radiopress Inc., who passed away recently.

David Bonavia, great reporter of the *Far Eastern Economic Review*, Hsia Chiy-yen, author of *A Winter in Peking*, the experts of the Institute of International Relations, Taipei, K.L. Mo from the *Mingbao*, Hong Kong.

In Hong Kong:
To Yeung Man Lee, second-hand bookseller of the Sun Chau Book Company, Ding Wang, author of numerous works on the contemporary history of China, Thomas K. Lu (Lu Keng), editor of the magazine *Pai Hsing* (*Baixing*), Xu Xing, economist, Li Wen (Li Ping Huang), editor-in-chief of the magazine *Jingbao*; James Yi, chief public relations officer at the British Trade Commission, and to Michel Legras, adviser at the Centre Culturel Français in Hong Kong, driving force behind the *Bulletin de sinologie*.

In Taiwan:
Prof. Guan Shuzhu who knew Kang Sheng well; Augustin Hoo Cheshy, former ambassador in Latin America; Jen Chi-yeuan, director of Studies in Communism, Diachaju; General Wu Li-chun, former member of the SACO, General Cheng Wei-yuan, chairman of VACRS, David S. Chou, assistant director of the IIR, Hsing Kuo-chiang of the IIR, Ku Chen-kang, chairman of the WACL, who knew Zhou Enlai very well, as well as Tang Ying and Chung-shen Thomas Chang; the experts of Section 4 of the *Fawbu Diaochaju* at the Alliance Française of Taipei, one of whom is Bernard Martial.

In Tokyo:
Imagawa Eiichi, director of the Department of Research at the Institute of Economics and Development, and Mitsumasa Uchino from the Institute of Economic Research and World Politics, to the employees of the Naicho and of the Bureau of Security in the National Agency of the Police.

In France:
To Marc Berge, Mrs Combe and Mr Hamaide of the Service Historic de l'Armée de terre, A.M. Cuer and Mrs Denis of the Library of the Quai d'Orsay (records of the Ministry of Foreign Affairs), and the various correspondents of the AFP who helped us in our research.

To Mr Peron of the Citroën public relations office, Father Richard of *Échanges France-Asie*, Pierre de la Robertie, teacher of Chinese, and Alain Kervern, teacher of Japanese and author of *La Lumière des bambous*, and to Mr Étienne Manac'h, former French ambassador in Beijing and author of *Mémoires d'Extrême-Asie* (*Memoirs of the Far East*).

To Mrs Jobez, at the Friendly Society of French People Formerly in Shanghai, and to all its members who invited us to their annual dinner (in particular Mr Georges Bouvier), Yves Gignac, Secretary General of the ACUF and his many Chinese friends, Colonel Paillole, chairman of ASSDN, Colonels Cantais, Duaghreilh, Germain, de Saint-Hilaire, formerly of the SDECE. To Regis Bergeron and Jacques Jurquet, former senior members of the pro-Chinese movement in France who were very willing to answer our questions and give us their accounts of meetings with Kang Sheng. To Jean Pasqualini, author of *Prisonnier de Mao*, Yves Bossuet, Edward Behr (author of *La Transfuge* (*The Renegade*), Pierre Broué, Stephane Courtois, Maurice Ciantar, Pierre Kergoat, Annie Kriegel, Pierre Laurin, Georges Le Bigot, Constantin Rissov; Philippe Robrieux, Annette Wieviorka.

In Belgium:
Jacques Grippa, former chief of the Communist Resistance, founder of the pro-Chinese movement in Belgium, was very willing to answer our questions regarding his meetings with Kang Sheng and to pass on to us numerous unpublished documents.

André Moyen, 'Captain Freddy' in the Resistance, is in a very different area. His encyclopaedic knowledge of the world of intelligence and Asia as well as the advice he has given to us have been invaluable.

Colonel William Ugeux, Mrs Réné Cliquet from the Belgian-Chinese friendship societies and Ambassador Chou, as well as their friends in the Ministry of Foreign Affairs in Taiwan.

In Switzerland:
Alain Campiotti from *L'Hebdo de Lausanne* (*Lausanne Daily*).

In the USA:
David Campbell, formerly of the IOSS, Joseph Bukholder Smith, formerly of the CIA in Singapore and Mr Roger K. Haley and the US Congress Library.

In Great Britain:
Duncan Campbell (*New Statesman*), Anthony Grey (author of *The Prime Minister was a Spy*), Alex Hendry (of the *Daily Express*), Nigel West, author of *M15* and *M16*.

In Mauritius:
Paul Perrier, as well as several friends in Asia who, without helping us directly in our research for this book, have welcomed us warmly.

Chronology

1898 Start of the Boxer Rebellion. Birth of Kang Sheng.

1911 First Revolution. End of the empire.

1912 First Chinese Republic with Sun Yat-sen as president.

1919 Fourth of May Movement, protesting against the Treaty of Versailles' endorsement of Japanese territorial claims on China.

1921 Founding of the Chinese Communist Party.

1927 The communist–nationalist alliance collapses. Communist insurrections put down by Chiang Kai-shek.

1929 Mao Zedong founds the first Chinese soviet republic.

1931 Japan invades Manchuria, in north-east China.

1934 Beginning of the Long March, organised by Mao.

1936 The Xi'an Incident: Chiang Kai-shek is kidnapped and forced into an alliance with the communists against Japan.

1945 Defeat of Japan.

1947 Beginning of the civil war between nationalists and communists.

1949 Mao seizes power. The nationalists take refuge in Taiwan (Formosa).

1950 Korean War.

1961 Rupture between China and the USSR.

1964 De Gaulle recognises the People's Republic of China.

1965 Beginning of the Cultural Revolution.

1969 Triumph of the Cultural Revolution. Ninth Congress of the Chinese Communist Party.

1971 China becomes a member of the UN. Lin Biao, Mao's heir-apparent, is assassinated.

1972 Richard Nixon visits Red China.

1975 Death of Kang Sheng.

1976 Deaths of Zhou Enlai and Mao Zedong. Gang of Four arrested.

1978 Hua Guofeng becomes Prime Minister.

1980 Return to power of Deng Xiaoping. Trial of the Gang of Four, including Mao's widow, Jiang Qing.

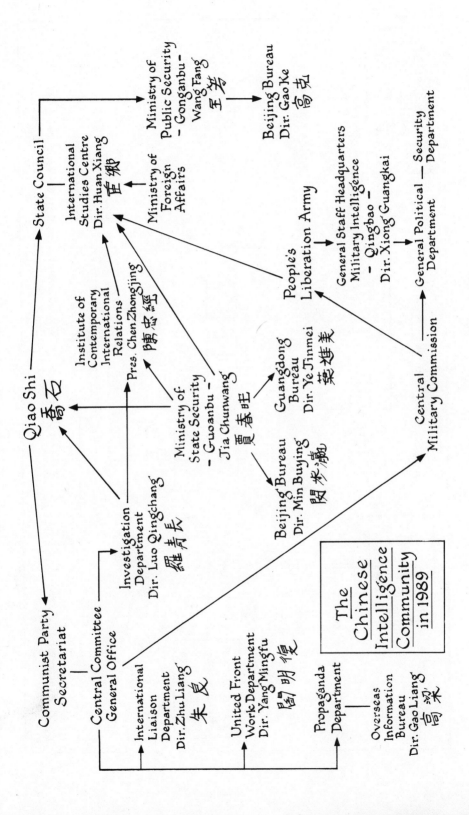

The
Chinese
Intelligence
Community
in 1989

Qiao Shi 喬石

Communist Party Secretariat

State Council

Central Committee General Office

International Studies Centre Dir. Huan Xiang 宦鄉

Ministry of Public Security – Gonganbu – Wang Fang 王芳

Beijing Bureau Dir. Gao Ke 高克

Ministry of Foreign Affairs

Institute of Contemporary International Relations Pres. Chen Zhongjing 陳忠經

Investigation Department Dir. Luo Qingchang 羅青長

Ministry of State Security – Guoanbu – Jia Chunwang 賈春旺

Guangdong Bureau Dir. Ye Jinmei 葉進美

People's Liberation Army

General Staff Headquarters Military Intelligence – Qingbao – Dir. Xiong Guangkai

General Political Security Department — Department

Beijing Bureau Dir. Min Buying 閔步瀛

Central Military Commission

International Liaison Department Dir. Zhu Liang 朱良

United Front Work Department Dir. Yang Mingfu 閻明復

Propaganda Department

Overseas Information Bureau Dir. Gao Liang 高粱

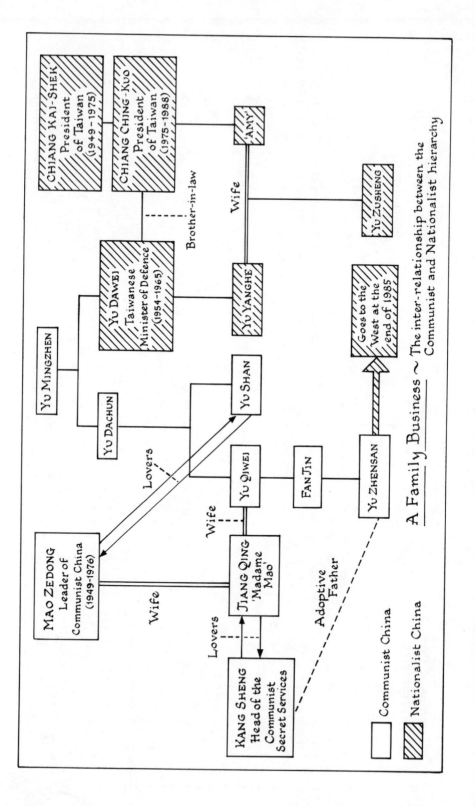

A Family Business ~ The inter-relationship between the Communist and Nationalist hierarchy

CHIANG KAI-SHEK
President of Taiwan (1949–1975)

CHIANG CHING-KUO
President of Taiwan (1975–1988)

Brother-in-law

'AMY'

Wife

YU ZUSHENG

YU DAWEI
Taiwanese Minister of Defence (1954–1965)

YU MINGZHEN

YU DACHUN

YU YANGHE

YU SHAN

Lovers

MAO ZEDONG
Leader of Communist China (1949–1976)

YU QIWEI

FAN JIN

YU ZHENSAN

Goes to the West at the end of 1985

Wife

JIANG QING
'Madame Mao'

Wife

Lovers

Adoptive Father

KANG SHENG
Head of the Communist Secret Services

☐ Communist China

▨ Nationalist China

Preface

Beijing, December 1975. All along the avenues of the capital of the People's Republic of China, the passers-by, covered from head to foot in thick padded cotton garments, ward off as best as they can the biting cold on which the warm rays of sun make little impact. As usual, winter in the old city is harsh, but the sky is amazingly blue. A foolhardy person might venture out without a jacket but, in a country making a painful recovery from the turmoil and excesses of the Cultural Revolution, the foolhardy are a disappearing species . . .

'May those accursed days never return!' the street murmurs silently, a seething mass of inscrutable faces and carefully concealed hopes.

In the small colony of foreigners in the northern capital, expectations have reached fever-pitch. They know from what people are saying, they sense from the attitude of Chinese officials, that important events are about to take place. For months now, no one has seen President Mao Zedong, an old man of more than eighty, at any of the formal ceremonies; the Prime Minister, Zhou Enlai, scarcely five years his junior, has made no public appearance; there has been no sighting of Field-Marshal Zhu De, the Red Army's Chief of Staff, who has just turned ninety – three representatives of the old guard in imminent danger of extinction through natural causes; the most eminent figures in the Chinese leadership; founding fathers of the communist regime.

'What is really going on?' is the question worrying the foreign diplomats whose embassies are like so many fortresses permanently under siege by the men from 'Public Security', the *Gonganbu*, who follow their every move, listen shamelessly to their telephone conversations, vet their telexes, open their mail and interrogate their domestic staff daily.

China, as they well know, remains what it was at the time of the Emperors: a country where mystery is a cult, secrecy a religion. How do you penetrate the bamboo wall? The Westerners' means of investigation are terribly limited, those of the Soviets almost non-existent. But the Soviets do not complain! For the diplomat-spies of the KGB, Beijing is a paradise on earth: accustomed to the fact that nothing important ever comes out of the Chinese capital, Moscow Centre does not expect miracles of them.

Russians and Westerners eye their Japanese colleagues with envy.

Refined and courteous, they always seem to know what is going on. And the fact is that very often they do!

Tea-time brings recollections of humiliations suffered. The Tenth Congress of the Chinese Communist Party in 1973, for instance. Western diplomats only found out about it afterwards – in the columns of the *Daily Telegraph*. They all grouse about their chanceries' insistence – from Washington, Paris, London – on accurate reports, detailed notes. As though it were possible to cheat a bit, to make a lot out of nothing at all, or virtually nothing.

'Still nothing on television?'

Nothing. Yet television is the only means of becoming a little better informed about the state of health of the dignitaries of the regime. Every time they appear in public, the cameras are there, recording for history their marble smiles, their handshakes, their mechanical embraces. The embassies' video-recorders consume these official pictures screened in abundance by Chinese television. In the peace and quiet of their offices, the diplomats replay the tapes in slow motion and comment: that one looks in pretty bad shape; this one looks more alert; so-and-so has vanished from the scene – is he ill, or dying?

It is not much, admittedly, but what else is there to get your teeth into? Nothing: unverified rumour, gossip, 'confidences' that are no more than indoctrination ploys. So you keep your eyes on the *People's Daily*, examine photographs with a magnifying glass, watch television, listen to the radio.

The radio! The first sign will come across the airwaves. Suddenly, on the afternoon of 16 December, broadcasting is interrupted. The first notes of a funeral march replace the monotonous chatter of presenters, then an anonymous, impersonal, sinister voice makes the announcement: '. . . the Central Committee of the Chinese Communist Party, the Standing Committee of the National People's Congress, the State Council of the People's Republic of China . . .'

The litany goes on, interminably. But from the very first notes of music, everyone understands: someone important has died. A top official, maybe *the* top official, Chairman Mao perhaps. In the streets, offices, workshops, army barracks, universities, everyone holds their breath. This is suspense on a colossal scale in the most densely populated country in the world.

'And what if it were Prime Minister Zhou Enlai?' is the most anguished worry. Because he avoided the worst excesses of the Cultural Revolution, because he strikes everyone as being the only bastion against a return to the 'bad days', Zhou Enlai enjoys enormous popularity in China. If he is dead, what will happen? Are Mao's wife and her extremist friends who make up the Gang of Four going to seize power? Will the wind of madness blow again?

Some people start sobbing. Others wring their hands or bite their nails while the voice of the anonymous speaker continues its recitation: '. . . and the State Council of the People's Republic of China deeply regret to announce that Comrade Kang Sheng, member of the Central Committee of the Chinese Communist Party, member of the Politburo of the Central Committee of the Chinese Communist Party, Vice-President of the National People's Congress, died, after an illness, on 16 December 1975 at 06.05 hours.'

It isn't Mao Zedong or Zhou Enlai! Straight away, there is an incredible sense of relief, one might even say of release. People suddenly stop holding their breath. Their tears dry, or, with all due discretion, flow less freely. Were it not for the fact that these people are Chinese – that is, expert in the art of disguising their emotions – foreign observers would notice on more than one face signs of a curious well-being. The sudden death of Comrade Kang Sheng, 'top-ranking member of the Chinese Communist Party, great combatant and theoretician of the people', is certainly not plunging his compatriots into grief.

And yet it does have some effect. The very next day, the leadership of the Party and of the Chinese State pay solemn homage to the deceased. On 19 and 20 December the days open with formal mourning ceremonies. Smitten by the still-biting cold, delegates of workers, peasants, students, diplomats and Western residents take part. Coaches covered in white carnations – white being the colour of mourning in China – have been leaving the universities and factories since dawn. They converge on the Workers' Palace of Culture where the people of Beijing are invited to mourn their dead comrade.

In front of the building, the masses march very slowly in time to the gong-like beat of two funeral marches, one Chinese, the other by Chopin. Everyone holds a white flower in their right hand. As always in communist China, particular attention has been paid to creating an impression. This production is imposing, compelling, capable of making the most indifferent, the most hostile observer feel as deeply stirred as everyone else. Even the 'foreign devils', these Westerners with their incorrigibly critical attitude, cannot help succumbing eventually to the collective emotion. The Central Committee's Propaganda Department and the senior members of the committee responsible for organising state funerals have done good work.

Beijing's municipal employees too! A platform has been raised. A giant portrait of Kang Sheng – thin face, inscrutable eyes hidden behind thin-rimmed glasses – hangs over it, surrounded with flowers. And beneath, as though protected by the dead man's spirit, about ten people have taken their places. Naturally everyone recognises Chen Yonggui, the most famous member of this little cohort. Chen is a media star: a little man with an emaciated face whose merits Chinese television is constantly lauding. A 'hero of the proletariat', he is happy to play a Stakhanov-like role to the Chinese peasantry, as a champion of productivity who has been propelled into the Party's Politburo. But who among the people of Beijing crowded around the

Workers' Palace of Culture recognises Cao Yi-ou, a shrunken little woman with almost white hair?

Kang Sheng's widow stands motionless, silent, almost frozen to attention, despite the few tears trickling down her face. Perhaps she is already worrying about the fate that lies ahead of her, now that her husband and 'comrade-in-arms' is dead. Without a word, she shakes hands with these thousands of strangers, while countless numbers of funeral wreaths, sent by State and Party bodies, by foreign governments and 'fraternal Marxist-Leninist parties', pile up.

Incontestably one of the finest is the wreath sent by the Albanian president, Enver Hoxha. A personal friend of Kang Sheng, the leader of this tiny pro-Chinese enclave in Europe wants to make a strong statement of his grief. No doubt for this reason, the cameramen working for Chinese television spend some time filming the delegation from the Balkan mountains. For several days afterwards, a spectacular sequence, showing a dishevelled young Albanian woman in tears, is screened repeatedly, additional proof of the 'indestructible friendship' between the two parties, and therefore between the two peoples.

Proofs of friendship, too, are the wreaths sent by Sekou Touré's Guinean government and the Communist Parties of Burma, Malaysia, Thailand and Indonesia. Then there is the conspicuous presence of the head of the PLO Bureau in Beijing, of delegates from the extreme left-wing Chilean movement, MAPU, of several dignitaries from North Korea and, to complete the picture, a handful of British and American 'visitors'.

And all this is just the beginning. For a comrade of the historic stature of Kang Sheng, the funeral ceremony has to be conducted with extreme care, so as to impress indelibly on people's minds the image of Red China's omnipotence and that of 'the Marxism-Leninism of our time, Mao Zedong Thought'.

On 21 December all the flags are at half-mast. This is the big day, the day of final homage to the deceased revolutionary combatant. In the big hall of the People's Palace of Congress, an imposing edifice situated close to the famous Tian'anmen Square, are several thousand hand-picked cadres. Over the entrance, a huge banner says it all: 'May the memory of Comrade Kang Sheng, great revolutionary of the Chinese people and glorious militant in the anti-revisionist struggle, live eternal!'

With this reminder of the eminent role played by the deceased in the merciless struggle against the socialist enemy brother, the USSR, the message is loud and clear. The rest is in keeping with the occasion, a mixture of sobriety and grandiloquence. At the back of the hall has been placed a portrait of Kang Sheng, framed in black cloth, and the urn containing his ashes, covered with a red flag.

Wreaths of flowers are piled on top of each other, among them one from Chairman Mao – Mao himself, of course, is not here; already very ill, he does not attend any of the funeral ceremonies of his comrades-in-arms. Mao's own imminent death will mark the end of a regime.

Jiang Qing, though, is here! The wife of the Chinese Chairman waits, impassive, stiff, all buttoned up in her proletarian uniform, practically standing to attention. Behind her glasses, her eyes are scornful and defiant. Suddenly they become misty: the man who has just died is one of the very few who really mattered in the life of this actress of stage and screen who, through intrigue, boldness and determination, became the wife of one of the world's most powerful heads of state. Much more than a mere comrade-in-arms . . .

Now, at the end of 1975, Madame Mao seems to be at the height of her power. With the help of Kang Sheng, her lifelong ally, she has disposed of all her most dangerous enemies one by one – either getting them downgraded in the hierarchy, interned or quite simply executed.

All? Perhaps not. There's Deng Xiaoping – an indomitable little man with a crewcut and sharp roguish eyes. The groundswell of the Cultural Revolution almost swept him away like a wisp of straw, along with his comrade Liu Shaoqi, 'the Chinese Khrushchev'. But Deng was a survivor. Like a reed, he yielded when necessary but never broke. For several months now, he has been moving to the fore on the Chinese political stage, capable as ever, with his inimitable way of calling a cat a cat and correctly maintaining that it doesn't matter whether a cat is black or white; as long as it catches rats it's a good cat!

The struggle between the Deng Xiaoping camp and the Gang of Four, over which Madame Mao presides with a rule of iron, will be merciless, as everyone knows. Perhaps it is for this reason that the silence is even heavier than usual. As the interminable funeral orations begin, everyone wonders which side to back. The Gang of Four and all-out revolution or Deng Xiaoping and his die-hard pragmatism? For those in the know there is also a middle way already shaping up: that embodied by Hua Guofeng, Vice-Premier since January. With his slicked-back hair and inexpressive face, Hua looks like a Soviet apparatchik – an unflattering comparison.

'When the fox dies, even the rabbit weeps. There's sympathy between fellow creatures!' according to one Chinese proverb. This is especially true on this 21 December 1975. In the midst of the ceremony, another ritual is being observed: pupils paying homage to their master. Gazing on the portrait of the man who, during half a century of undercover warfare, has shaped them all are the men from the intelligence services, from the secret police, from 'Special Affairs': Chen Yun, now an economist, once an underground collaborator of Kang Sheng when they were exiled together in the Soviet Union; Wang Dongxing, Chairman Mao's trusted aide, the feared head of the regime's Praetorian Guard, the 8341 Detachment; Liao Chengzhi, a 'young' man of sixty-seven with a mandarin smile, whose youth had all the ingredients of an adventure story; Ling Yun, a grey bureaucrat and Public Security professional; Luo Qingchang, the counter-espionage ace, Zhou Enlai's protégé. All these men whose names recur throughout the history of Red China's secret services listen attentively, their faces set like masks, their bodies immobile.

'. . . Let us unite in order to bring about the triumph of the communist cause. Let us unite in order to achieve even greater victories!' the orator concludes in a fine flight of lyricism that fools no one: unity was never less likely . . .

It is over now. Soon all that will remain of Kang Sheng will be a heap of ashes in the small urn that Wang Dongxing and Wu De, the Party's First Secretary in Beijing, will accompany without any great ceremony to the cemetery for revolutionary leaders at Babaoshan.

Soon Zhou Enlai and Mao Zedong will also die. The storm will break, wiping out the Gang of Four. And the official version of Chinese history, ever treacherous, will assert that Kang Sheng was not white but black, that he was not a man but a monster.

1

A Child of Shandong

At nightfall, girls and boys would gather at the temples adorned with tormented-looking sculptures which appeared all the more terrifying in the darkness. It was the same every evening. These young people with drawn features and emaciated faces would recite their mysterious incantations, their monotonous murmurings mingling strangely with the smell of incense.

Having fasted for several days, they felt as light as could be. The master of ceremonies offered them a cup containing a bitter-tasting strong beverage. He also gave them a magic formula written out as four characters on a scarlet or saffron piece of paper. Most of them could not read. This heightened the mystery. A few words were whispered in their ear, and each of them in turn came up to burn their secret message in a little earthenware bowl. The ash was mixed in a liquid resembling tea and imbibed with deep reverence.

And suddenly everything would change for these Chinese zombies. The 'celestial warriors' would begin to quicken inside them. With heads held high and chests thrown out, they became invincible. No one could stop them. Deep in a frenzied trance, performing a thousand contortions, and simulating combat, they juggled with words more powerful than bullets or cannonballs:

> This is the dawn of the millennium
> Blood will run
> By autumn
> The ground will be strewn with bleached bones.

A vision of the end of the world, and of the century. For it was indeed the end of the century: 1898, the Year of the Dog.

That year thousands of similar secret ceremonies unfolded in the remotest corners of the Shandong peninsula, on the east coast of China, 850 kilometres south of Beijing.

Up in the northern capital, the Emperor on the Dragon Throne was no more than a child of thirteen, and since he was weak and vulnerable the rebellious peasants believed that they would be able to overthrow the Manchu dynasty.

This movement swathed in incense and mystery was born in Shandong under the name of *Yi He Tuan*, the Society of Harmonious Fists - the fists of justice and equity. Europeans, intrigued by the ritual and fighting methods of this Brotherhood of the Apocalypse, called them the Boxers.

Shandong, as its name – meaning 'eastern mountains' – suggests, lies on the eastern seaboard. This rocky promontory into the Yellow Sea was once an island. But the Yellow River brought down such large deposits of alluvium that the island became part of the mainland, a mountainous peninsula dominated by the legendary mountain Tai Shan of which the Chinese are so proud. The magnificent harbours were perfect for fishing, the hills rich in coal and iron but also numerous underground springs, while to the west lay a large agricultural plain. And yet, at that time, the people of Shandong suffered great privation, not least because of the density of its population.

Shandong has always been a rebellious, and indeed indomitable, province. Twenty-one centuries ago, it was the last small state to hold out against the unification carried out by Qin Shihuan, the emperor responsible for building the Great Wall of China, and who had all books destroyed. There was an endless series of peasant uprisings, such as the rebellion under the Song dynasty immortalised in the great classic novel *The Water Margin*. Shandong was also one of the places where the great Tai Ping Rebellion of the nineteenth century originated.

But China is a country of contrasts and legends: Shandong was also a fount of wisdom. Two of the greatest Chinese philosophers, Confucius and Mencius, were born there, in the sixth and fourth centuries BC.

Kong Zi, better known as Confucius, preached respect for an immutable order, yet foresaw great upheaval: 'The big mountain falls away. The main beam breaks. The wise man withers like a plant.'

Mencius was closer to the sentiments upheld by the Boxers. 'Fish is what I want. Bear's claws are what I want. But if I cannot have both, I forgo the fish and content myself with bear's claws. Life is also something I want, so too is justice. If I have to choose, I forgo life and content myself with justice.'

The Boxers wanted justice, and at the end of the nineteenth century Shandong seemed to suffer every scourge imaginable. The Yellow River had broken its banks. The Qing government – the Manchus who ruled from Beijing – neglected the maintenance of the dikes. The floods caused terrible damage everywhere. Fifty sub-prefectures were destroyed, and hundreds of thousands of Chinese drowned.

As if this were not enough, the 'foreign devils' chose that year, 1898, to attack China. In Paris, the Great Powers divided the cake between them. Japan, who had just won a war against China, was given suzerainty over Korea. The island of Taiwan also became Japanese territory. The Russians took Port Arthur; the British got the New Territories opposite Hong Kong island, and also the port of Weihaiwei; while Port Bayard, which the Chinese call

Guang Zhouwan, was ceded to the French.

The Germans chose Shandong. They, like their partners, expected the colony to remain theirs for at least ninety-nine years. The murder of two German missionaries shortly before gave them the necessary pretext. In mid-November 1897, the famous Admiral von Diederichs took possession of the bay of Jiao Zhou and the town of Qingdao, one of China's best harbours, crucial to control of Chinese waters. Then, in March 1898, the Germans forced the Qing empire, already very weak, to concede to their exorbitant demand: the right to build the railway from Qingdao, later to become a seaside resort, to Jinan in the west, capital of Shandong. In addition, they obtained exclusive mining rights to the land lying fifteen kilometres either side of the railway track. This was the ruination of all those Chinese who made their living trading on the river.

Then Shandong was faced with another foreign imposition: 1,000 Christian churches, 20,000 missionaries and converts, who represented a world completely different from that of traditional China. The Chinese hated the missionary leaders. The German Cardinal Anzer, a personal friend of Emperor Wilhelm II, whom he advised to send troops into Shandong, was detested. Even more hated was Alphonse Favier, the fat French monseigneur with the flowing white beard of a Russian priest who was Bishop of Beijing and Vicar-General of the Lazarists. He was credited with the most sinister designs, including stealing thousands of works of art for his own personal collection. The Boxers who tried to kill him couldn't believe it when he successfully warded them off with an axe. They went home disappointed, without the Bishop's head stuck on the blade of a halberd.

As far as the Boxers were concerned – and their rebellion soon spread across the whole of North China – the 'long-nosed devils' were the cause of all their misfortunes. Their banners and flags bore terrifying legends calling for revenge. At first their hatred was directed as much against the Manchu dynasty as against the foreigners, against whom they bore countless grudges: the telegraph poles erected by the soldiers in pointed helmets cast baleful shadows over the tombs of venerated ancestors. Furthermore, the Germans (called *De Guoren* in Chinese, meaning 'People of the Land of Virtue') desecrated the land, hacking at it with picks to extract the coal . . . Their railway sleepers cut through the rings of the tutelary dragons . . . And they themselves were even rumoured to steal Chinese children and tear out their eyes, which they supposedly used to make photographic equipment – camera lenses and film gelatine. German optics were obviously already renowned . . .

Driving out foreigners became of such overriding importance that the rebels neglected to storm the Forbidden City in Beijing. Instead, the Empress Dowager, the cunning Ci Xi, even managed to form an alliance with the Boxers against the foreigners. In China, xenophobia was a powerful unifying force. So much so that the Boxers changed their rallying cry to '*Fu Qing mie yang!*' 'Support the Qing dynasty and drive out the foreigners!'

In 1900, the Boxer rebels besieged the foreign legations in Beijing for fifty-five days until an expeditionary force arrived, crushed the Boxers and occupied the Forbidden City. At the time, Western journalists were surprised that the traditional image of Chinese womanhood did not correspond with what they saw during the uprising. Chinese women, armed with hatchets and knives, fought on the front line. They formed special commando groups, carrying lanterns as a means of identification: red lanterns for young girls, blue for older women. The important role of women in the movement was particularly evident in Shandong. But in this region women were generally said to be taller, bolder and more liberal in their ways than elsewhere in China.

In that year of 1898, at the same time as this great movement of revolt sprang up, a woman gave birth to her third son, an event not of any obvious significance compared with the misfortunes being visited upon the region of Jiao Nan, a small town on the coast, some thirty kilometres from Qingdao, south of the bay of Jiao Zhou.

The happy father, Mr Zhang, was considered a rich landowner, but in those troubled times it was unwise to invite envy. How many peasants did not dream of seeing his magnificent red-brick house, with its beams of camphor wood and its solid red-lacquer wooden door, go up in flames? The Zhang residence exuded prosperity and comfort inherited from a bygone age: delicate wood panelling; nests of tables; ebony wardrobes inlaid with mother-of-pearl; a master bed piled high with mattresses, and with a silk brocade canopy; a twelve-panel tortoiseshell-lacquered screen.

As any Chinese father would, Mr Zhang noted that it was the Year of the Dog, that his third son would therefore be a pessimistic, not to say rather tortured, human being, doubting everything. On the other hand he would be honest, confident of his rights, capable of manipulating men and always concerned for the general good even at his own expense. The Chinese, connoisseurs of the horoscope, attribute one particular predilection to the Dog: he adores everything mysterious, occult, underground, secret. Moreover, he falls into the Yin category in Taoist philosophy, which embraces the feminine principle and darkness. Among some of the more famous individuals born under the sign of the Dog are two past masters of more or less secretive diplomacy: the French statesman Talleyrand and the Chinese statesman Zhou Enlai.

The Zhang family name is one of the most common in the world: in 1987, it belonged to 120 million people. The given name, which in Chinese follows the family name, required some thought, and depended as much on the stars as on Mr Zhang's preference. He originally called his son Shaoqing, 'He Who Continues His Father's Work Fittingly', but when the boy started school, he was given his courtesy name, Shuping, which means 'Calm Child, Third-born of Four Brothers'. Who could have predicted, seeing this rather puny infant, that under the name of Kang Sheng he would one day be one of the grand masters of the Chinese Revolution and perpetrator of its black deeds? That the mere mention of his name would set millions of men and women trembling?

He was a quiet child, who played little with others of his age, preferring learning to read and write. He would shut himself away for hours on end copying out characters. He ruined his eyesight reading the great classic novels by the light of a soya-oil lamp. If he had had his way he would have spent his whole time at the elementary school at Shaonan Xian. He was always the first to arrive for classes and the last to leave. Shuping led the quiet studious life of a future scholar.

Though the Zhangs' existence seemed a peaceful one, appearances were deceptive. As the years went by, the red dragon that slumbers in the earth's womb began to stretch its limbs once more. In 1911 another revolution broke out. It marked the collapse of the Qing dynasty, and the success of a huge nationalist movement with socialist aspirations. Sun Yat-sen, the father of modern China, wished for this upheaval more than any man alive. Since the turn of the century he had been travelling the world, rallying the Chinese overseas to the cause of democratic China, raising funds, making frequent propaganda tours to drum up support. Then, in 1905, together with some friends who, like him, had taken refuge in Japan, he formed the Revolutionary League of China. 'What we want,' declared Dr Sun, 'is to drive out the Manchu barbarians, restore China to the Chinese, create a republic, distribute the land equally . . .' At the time his small party spanned modernist scholars, socialists in mandarin clothing, but already, inside the golden chrysalis, a great purple butterfly was struggling to emerge – the Guomindang, the People's Nationalist Party.

When the Revolution broke out, Sun Yat-sen was still in France fund-raising. He took a passage on the first ship bound for China and arrived in Shanghai on Christmas Day 1911. The Qing dynasty, the Manchus he so detested, collapsed majestically. Four days later, delegates from the seventeen provinces, summoned to Nanking, elected the bowler-hatted, stiff-collared, moustachioed rebel provisional president. On 1 January 1912, Dr Sun proclaimed China a republic, and the Emperor Pu Yi abdicated. Feudal China, unchanging and unshakeable, had had its day – in principle, at least. In 1913, a 'very treacherous and very cruel' warlord, Yuan Shikai, led a *putsch*. A former governor of Shandong, he dreamed of taking his place on the throne of the deposed Son of Heaven. Sun Yat-sen tried unsuccessfully to oppose Yuan Shikai, then once again went into exile where he met the daughter of one of his supporters, also in exile in

Japan. Exquisite as jade, the very beautiful, very young and very rich Song Qingling tenderly ministered to a broken man. . .

Another revolutionary in exile was celebrating the one-hundredth issue of his newspaper *Pravda*, in which there was a report on events in China: 'Despite the grave shortcomings of its leader Sun Yat-sen (who has a meditative and indecisive spirit, due to the absence of proletarian support), the revolutionary democracy in China has done a great deal to awaken the people, to win freedom and the democratic institution that goes with it.' In putting his signature to this article, Lenin was staking a communist claim to Chinese nationalism.

Meanwhile, as always, the revolution raged in Shandong. And with it came anarchy and chaos. As Confucius said: 'The main beam cracks . . .'

Highwaymen, landless peasants, starving vagrants and warlords swept through the countryside in bands, like wolves, terrorising the population. In 1913 bandits kidnapped a member of Kang Sheng's family and demanded a large ransom. Repeated uprisings, looting and insurrection all contributed to the downfall of the house of Zhang. The kidnapping was the last straw. Mr Zhang decided to move to the town, taking with him his family and most loyal servants – it was common at the time for landowners to fall back on the protection of the fortified towns. The Zhang family chose to move to Zhucheng, south of the river Wei, further inland. A sub-prefectural town of 25,000 inhabitants, it was still prosperous, although it did not benefit from the advantages of the German railway line, the famous Jiao Ji, linking the future seaside resort of Qingdao with Jinan, the capital of Shandong. Closed in on itself, isolated behind high walls, like a tortoise in its shell, Zhucheng was situated in the middle of large fertile plains growing tobacco, wheat and maize. But this haven of tranquillity did not remain untouched by the disturbances. The boldness of the pillagers increased daily. Civil guards had to be organised. Decapitated heads, dripping with black blood, stuck on bamboo poles, their faces twisted into the silent sardonic smile of triumphant death – these were what greeted children on their way to school every morning. Bandits and rebels who had been caught plundering awaited their hour of execution in crowded gaols.

Shuping went to the Guanhai school for boys. His passion for literature grew with every passing day, but he also became interested in politics. At the end of the First World War, his province, Shandong, was at the heart of a great controversy. At Versailles, the victorious powers divided the spoils of the German Empire between them. Under the terms of Articles 156 and 157 of the Treaty of Versailles, Germany surrendered 'its rights and interests in the Shandong peninsula' to Japan.

The Chinese were filled with dismay. Their delegation, not wanting to lose face, refused to sign the treaty. An enormous wave of protest spread throughout the whole of China. Had she not sent 200,000 coolies to the arms factories in Europe in order to help the Allies defeat Germany? Was she not entitled to justice and recognition for this help?

On 4 May 1919, there was a new uprising. The Fourth of May Movement was a protest against the voraciousness of the foreigners, of the Japanese in particular, but it also marked popular weariness with the warlords whose infighting had been tearing the country apart since the death of the Empress Ci Xi and the fall of the Manchu dynasty. It gave one man cause to rub his hands: Dr Sun Yat-sen observed the growing influence of his nationalist revolutionary party, the Guomindang.

In Beijing, and throughout China, there were strikes, demonstrations and rioting, involving workers and students. The Fourth of May Movement marked the arrival on the Chinese political scene of a fully-fledged intelligentsia, heavily influenced by the West and by socialist ideas. A boycott of Japanese goods was organised. Among those who took part was Kang Sheng, who spent the whole summer distributing leaflets and putting up posters, banners and flags in Zhucheng, but also in Qingdao and throughout the province. This inevitably brought him into conflict with the authorities at the school where he taught.

'Zhang Shuping, you are required to teach *Xiu Shen*, the cultivation of the self, obedience to authority, filial piety, stoic resignation, as propounded by our venerable Master Kong, and not to preach rebellion,' Kang Sheng was told regularly. But to him, the moral philosophy of 'Master Kong' – in other words, Confucius – seemed an oppressive survival of feudal China. He had just turned twenty-one and despite his austere, almost monk-like, manner, his reserve and slight obsequiousness, Kang Sheng was burning with impatience. He was a perfect example of the young nationalist intellectuals, born into the landowning gentry, who, as a result of the Fourth of May Movement, would join Dr Sun's Guomindang party or otherwise the nascent communist movement.

The education system in Shandong was in a constant state of turmoil, and the province led the way in educational reform. The governor of Shandong at the time of the Boxer Rebellion, Yuan Shikai, developed a plan for reform. The Empress Ci Xi believed she could save the Manchu dynasty by listening to the reformers, and although this did not prevent her downfall – nor did it prevent Yuan Shikai from coveting the Dragon Throne – the new educational system was adopted: there was an administrative restructuring of schools, but most important was the introduction, in addition to traditional and classical studies, of courses in science and politics, imported directly from the West and from Japan, where Shandong nationalists, exiled in Tokyo, encouraged modernism.

Yuan Shikai also founded a military academy in the capital, Jinan, and a technical college for orphans and children of the poor. At the same time, the landowning gentry were encouraged to finance their own private schools. A new race of modern civil servants was produced by these schools. At the beginning of the century, there was great upheaval, with the abolition of the old system of Mandarin examinations, the opening of schools to a huge population of children, and the emergence of a new idea: education for the masses. The State contributed to the financing of education on a regional and prefectural level. This huge wave of reforms did not come without resistance, but at the same time it gave rise to the Fourth of May Movement, and Jinan found itself at the centre of the anti-Japanese campaign. Students, elementary school teachers and those responsible for the education of the younger generation received the unexpected support of industrialists, merchants and men like Jin Yunpeng, former governor of Shandong and future leader of the government of Beijing.

It was in this climate abounding with new ideas that Kang Sheng attended the teacher training school at Qingdao. After that, he began teaching at the Yuying elementary school, in Zhucheng.

But the Fourth of May Movement had another effect on education: among the protesters' demands was a new equality between boys and girls.

A little girl aged six, from a very humble background, was one of the beneficiaries of this. She was born in 1914 and her name was Shumeng, which means 'pure and simple'. An extremely rebellious child, one day, to the surprise of her playmates, she unwound the bindings on her feet and vowed never to wear them again. Since she tied her hair in a single pigtail and dressed in her brothers' cast-off clothes, she had a reputation for being a tomboy. Her father, Li Dewen, aged sixty, twice her mother's age, behaved like a tyrant. In his moments of madness, under the influence of alcohol, he would beat his wife terribly. But Shumeng's mother was not prepared to put up with it. One fine day, she packed her bags and left, taking the little girl with her. A landowner by the name of Wang allowed them to move in with him. The young woman became a general help – this included nocturnal duties, which old Wang favoured despite his concubines, who were in no position to complain since they had failed to provide him with a male heir.

It may have been here, at Wang's house, that a local gentleman-scholar, Xue Huangdeng, felt sorry for the little girl and decided to take her under his wing and sponsor her entrance into elementary school. Whatever the facts of the matter, she was given a new name, Yun He, 'Cloud Crane', and started attending the sub-prefectural school. But, impervious to lessons in Confucian morality, the other children refused to make friends with her, on account of her humble circumstances. She in turn became aggressive and belligerent. The children's parents complained about the endless pranks Yun He got up to and, after a term, she was expelled. To make matters worse, she quarrelled with one of Wang's daughters so Wang dismissed her mother – no doubt he had grown weary of her charms . . .

A young man who often visited Wang's house offered the weeping servant a modest job. With his hair drawn back, little pince-nez on his nose, a slim figure in his black robe, everyone knew who he was: Kang Sheng. This apparently insignificant episode was to have amazing repercussions lasting half a century. Yun He changed her name often but history would remember her by the name she finally adopted, Jiang Qing, as the woman who became Mao Zedong's wife. So it was that she and her mother found a home with the Zhangs, who, though poor themselves, could still spare a crust and give them a servant's room to sleep in, a *kang* to lie on and a sweet sense of being part of the family.

It was a run-down place. When it rained heavily, great gusts of wind would sweep through the room via the dilapidated windows that lacked their paper coverings. The little girl would sit up all night waiting for her mother to come home, sometimes setting out to look for her in the darkness of the neighbouring streets. Often Yun He's mother would return exhausted at dawn, bringing only a biscuit or, better still, a *man tou* – a small hot roll – to eat. Sometimes, she would burst into tears. Because, in order to put bread in their mouths, Yun He's mother not only made herself available to Zhang, she also went selling her charms from door to door.

As for Kang Sheng, he had married a rather retiring young girl who had all the traditional virtues. She bore him a daughter, Yu Ying. This unexceptional marriage was just another of the secret episodes in the life of Kang Sheng, when he conformed to family tradition rather than obeying his own instincts. During that time, he continued to teach and soon became headmaster of the school in Zhucheng. One of his pupils was little Yun He.

Kang was torn in different directions: for him, educational reform was a necessary upheaval and yet he considered the traditions of ancestral China to be important. He would spend whole evenings, brush in hand, copying extracts from the classic novel *The Dream of the Red Chamber* (*Hong Lou Meng*). A love story written in the eighteenth century, this great work by Cao Xueqing depicted the inexorable decline of four great families, the Jia, the Wang, the Shi and the Xue, who are treated as symbols of the disintegration of a feudal society. The detailed description of dazzling luxury, of intrigue and the dissolute behaviour of these families and the tragic fate of their slaves and subjugated peasants had a great topical resonance for the young Shandong teacher. There was a striking resemblance between the decadence of these great families and the behaviour of the landowners of his own era, such as his father, Zhang, or Wang, at whose house he still spent evenings discussing philosophy and literature.

All through his life Kang Sheng was to display the same morbid fascination with what he was about to destroy – the art of destruction and the destruction of art. As he saw it, the *Red Chamber* was the purple banner of revolution, adding fuel to his passionate desire to help the poor and organise them into overthrowing the immutable order of things.

For, while Kang taught children the great virtues of Chinese humanism and its rules, he knew that they were confronted daily with poverty, famine, rioting, murder, treachery. While the young Yu Ying slept quietly in her cradle, he liked to copy out whole passages of the novel, such as the lament of the young Lin Daiyu, its tragic heroine whose death follows inexorably on the birth of her forbidden love:

> Why blame me if my soul
> Suffers a double agony?
> For spring that is generally welcomed
> I love and hate at the same time
>
> I love it for coming so quickly
> I hate it for departing so soon.
> Without a word it leaves us,
> Having arrived without a word.

As the years went by, Kang Sheng became a veritable expert on *The Dream of the Red Chamber*. He would seek out rare editions, and was thrilled by an edition illustrated with several hundred lithographs published in Shanghai in small volumes. Of course, he was also very interested in the *Romance of the Three Kingdoms* and the adventures of the fearsome Cao Cao, or *The Water Margin*, stories of uprisings and banditry in ancient Shandong, but he could match the most eminent literary critics on *The Dream of the Red Chamber*, writing several essays about it, some of which were published. And so it was that Kang Sheng entered the ranks of gentlemen-scholars.

One day he went to the capital to sit his promotion exams. He made his way to Jiaoxian and took the train to Jinan, 250 kilometres away. This old city of some 400,000 inhabitants built under the Ming was a place of both culture and perdition. People came here to sit exams; they also visited the courtesans in their 'flower houses'. A large number of prostitutes lived in the capital anyway, but when students from all over the province came to Jinan to sit their exams, hundreds of young girls would invade the city, joining the young men in their lodgings. The women of Shandong were renowned for their easy virtue. One day a judge decided to carry out a huge police raid and the young prostitutes were sold to the peasants for the price of a pig.

An ancient Chinese city with brick-built houses, Jinan lies at the foot of the Li Shan mountains, south of the Yellow River. Seventy-two springs supply its numerous canals and lakes with fresh water. To the south-east, below the ancient wall, are the Pearl spring and the magnificent Black Tiger spring. The lake inside the city walls, the Daming ('very sparkling'), was popular as a meeting-place and cultural centre, its tea houses and theatres on its small islands popular with scholars, merchants and civil servants.

It was not only the rich who lived in Jinan; in the mid 1920s, unable to cope with life in Zhucheng any more, Jiang Qing's mother arrived with her daughter. The little girl continued her studies at the First elementary school and before long, as a young adolescent, she turned to one of the chief activities in the Shandong capital: the theatre. Whether Kang Sheng enquired after her when he stayed in Jinan, history does not relate. But their paths were soon to cross again . . .

Kang Sheng, it is true, had a great many other things on his mind. By the early twenties he was being inexorably drawn to communism. His instructor and mentor, Huang Chongwu, guided his first steps as a teacher and as a militant. He gave Kang Sheng the works of several German authors to read. Kang knew a little of the language of Goethe and of the invaders of Shandong before 1919, but not enough to read these books in the original. Fortunately, Karl Kautsky's *Class Struggle*, and *Gonchandang Xuanyen*, otherwise known as *The Communist Manifesto*, by Marx and Engels, had just been translated into Chinese.

Huang introduced him to his friends Wang Jinmei and Deng Enming, who, as early as 1920, had founded a Marxist study group. Though forgotten today, they were at the time pioneers of the Chinese communist movement. Kang Sheng also met a third man who made a great impression on him. This man did not live in Shandong but travelled a great deal around China, in order to promote interest in the movement of which he was secretary, the Socialist Youth Corps. Three years Kang's senior, Yun Daiying, who came from Hubei, was, like Kang, a young intellectual born into a rich landowning family. It was he who translated the book by Kautsky that Kang found such compulsive reading. His Marxism had a tint of black, though, for he proclaimed himself an anarchist. But he had developed techniques for creating unrest in the countryside with which young men like Kang Sheng and his new friends Wang Jinmei and Deng Enming could readily identify. They would talk long into the night about their dreams for a new China, while Yun went from town to town, telling young people to return in the vacation to their homes in the countryside in order to spread the word. Soon he was even publishing a newspaper, with an avid readership, called *Chinese Youth* (*Zhongguo Qingnian*). And, like all his peers, he moved closer every day to the communism inspired by the distant echoes of the new Soviet republic that lay beyond Mongolia.

The Socialist Youth Corps became communist even before the founding of a Chinese Communist Party. All over China, and even overseas, groups of young people were springing up like the famous Ningbo mushrooms. In Shanghai, in August 1920, Chen Duxiu, a prominent intellectual, set up the first Youth Corps, while another university revolutionary, Li Dazhao, founded a similar group in Beijing, and at Changsha a very young man called Mao Zedong formed a circle of his own. Thousands of kilometres away, in February 1920, Zhou Enlai was laying the foundations of a similar movement in France. All these groups were a direct product of the Fourth of May Movement, with a natural inclination to come together.

In May 1922, the First Congress of the Socialist Youth Corps took place in Canton. It already consisted of seventeen sections and had a membership of 5,000.

A smiling, affable man, whose name, according to his passport, was Mr Petersen, arrived in the southern city, weary after the long train journey from Siberia. He had come to attend the Youth Corps congress. Although he had wanted to remain incognito, he was cheered by the young Chinese as soon as he arrived. For Sergei Dalin – his real name – came from the Far Eastern Bureau of the Communist International, the Comintern, and furthermore he represented the Youth International, the KIM.

Peng Shuzhi, one of the organisers of the Youth Corps who later met him, remembered him well: 'Although he was about thirty, Dalin seemed to have lost none of his youthfulness . . . He was intrigued by China – and more than intrigued, fascinated . . . And the way in which he talked about it, and encouraged me to talk about it, showed me that he was as much a deep thinker as he was a man of passion. Why did China fascinate him? Because it was for him the ultimate enigma, because he didn't know quite how to approach it in order to unravel the complex web to which he compared it.'

French counter-espionage, which was at that time deeply rooted in China, noted the comings and goings of Dalin, alias Petersen, to Canton, Shanghai and Beijing. According to well-placed informers, Dalin was also a 'special services official' and soon an 'organiser of special detachments', the famous *Tchon* commandos of the OGPU, recruited from among the Chinese communists.

But a much more important event took place after the Youth Corps congress, which had voted to join the Communist International. Giving his Chinese friends the slip, and trying to shake off anyone who might be following him, the man from the KIM paid a visit to Dr Sun Yat-sen, the uncontested leader of the Guomindang.

'Do you not think that an alliance, a united front, between the Guomindang and the communists would change the face of history?' was the substance of what he said. Dr Sun dismissed the possibility of such an alliance. Naturally, it would entail an alliance with the USSR, for whom he had great admiration, but the Chinese communists numbered no more than a handful of intellectuals, admittedly brilliant but without any great influence. Dalin was ushered out with typical Chinese courtesy, but the lines of communication were still open; it was up to Dalin to think of a new formula. They would have occasion to speak again, thought Sun Yat-sen.

How right he was. A year earlier, the inaugural congress of a tiny Chinese Communist Party had taken place in the utmost secrecy. It was attended by a mere thirteen delegates representing a total of fifty-seven communists in the whole of China. The person elected General Secretary, the elderly Chen Duxiu, was not even one of those present. And how were the two Comintern delegates sent by Moscow to foresee that scarcely half of these few Chinese gathered in a small cramped room in the French concession would remain faithful to communism? Or that the nice young man seated near the window, a certain Mao Zedong, would one day become the USSR's most formidable enemy?

Besides, this mini congress that took place at the end of July 1921 almost came to grief. During one session in a smoke-filled room, while the Chinese listened open-mouthed with admiration to the convoluted translation of an interminable report delivered by a delegate from Trade Union International, the door suddenly opened behind them.

'I'm looking for Mr Chen . . . Forgive me for disturbing you.'

And before anyone could get a good look at him, the stranger had turned on his heels and disappeared.

'The French secret police!' hazarded a delegate from Shanghai. Within five minutes, all the delegates had scattered without even returning to the girls' school where they were staying to pick up their suitcases. They left just in time. The French police arrived in force. One zealous inspector notice the presence of six ashtrays and a dozen teacups on the rectangular table – no detail is considered too small in counter-espionage. And the congress was resumed further south, on a charming pleasure boat on Lake Nanxu.

Wang Jinmei and Deng Enming, Kang's friends from Shandong, attended the congress. They went home full of hope, and from them Kang Sheng learned what had been decided at the meeting. He did not yet belong to the Party, of course, but his group was to join the big family at the Canton congress. And he was a trusted comrade.

At the beginning of 1922, Wang and Deng went to Moscow and attended the Congress of Far Eastern Communist and Revolutionary Organisations. It is hard to describe the enthusiasm of these two Chinese, the feeling of power that came from belonging to a major historical movement that would change the world. There were not only Chinese communists at this congress but also representatives of the Guomindang. The hour of the much-desired alliance was at hand.

Later, Kang Sheng was to follow the path forged by these two men, but Wang Jinmei, who was exactly the same age as Kang Sheng, and Party Secretary for Shandong, suffered delicate health and died in Qingdao in July 1925. His friend Deng Enming took his place. In 1925 he organised the strike by railway workers on the famous

Qingdao–Jinan railway line. A dynamic individual, full of energy, he was eventually captured by his enemies and executed.

While a state of ferment continued to prevail in Shandong, Kang Sheng disappeared. He had attracted the attention of the police on several occasions and thought it best to keep a low profile for a while. At the time, most of the students who went abroad, either to Japan or the West – mainly France and Germany – were from Shandong. Germany, the country formerly in control of Shandong, was the obvious place for someone like Kang Sheng to go. During the course of 1922, according to several testimonies, he studied at a technical institute in Berlin. He learned German, which he would speak haltingly all his life. His father no doubt sent him to stay with German friends, made when Shandong was still a colony of the Reich.

In those days, there was a revolutionary who travelled regularly between Berlin and Paris, and ran the European section of the Chinese Communist Party. His name was Zhou Enlai. Kang and Zhou were to become comrades for half a century, first of all running the underground Communist Party together, and then, after 1949, collaborating on Red China's foreign policy. Lifelong companions, inseparable rivals, often joined in friendship, sometimes in hatred, they both crossed the threshold of death at the same time.

Legend would have it that they met in Berlin, then capital of the Revolution in Europe. In July 1922, Zhou Enlai settled in Paris, at 17 rue de Godefroy in the 13th *arrondissement*. There were many Chinese already living in the area, which has since become the French 'Chinatown'. The place d'Italie was the centre of revolutionary activity directed against the 'Middle Empire'. This was where the newspaper *Youth* (soon to change its name to *Red Dawn*) was printed for the 500 Chinese communists in France. A young French communist woman would regularly bring the 300 francs, wrapped in a little canvas bag and hidden in her blouse, sent by the Comintern to 'Mr Chen', at 5 rue Thiers. Another woman, Suzanne Girault, was in charge of the transfer of funds to the 'Chinese comrades'; she was a key figure, trained by the OGPU, Russia's secret service. Paul Coupette, a 33-year-old communist, used his café on rue de l'Amiral-Mouchez at Chaumont as a letter-drop for his Asian brothers' secret correspondence. A little fellow, a student-worker at La Garenne-Colombes, was responsible for printing the newspaper. He was nicknamed 'Doctor of Mimeography'. A long time afterwards he would be known throughout the world as the leader of China during the eighties under the name of Deng Xiaoping.

Kang Sheng, who was then known by the name of Zhang Shuping, was a familiar figure in the Chinese hang-outs in Paris – the restaurants of Billancourt and the 13th *arrondissement*, the cafés of the Latin Quarter, the meetings in smoke-filled rooms where the talk was of preparing the way for the Revolution and of dreams of a new world, of a modern China. He also took part in the development of the secret infrastructure of the Communist Party. And, so legend has it, he took a close interest in the methods of the French police who kept watch on these strange 'worker-students', information that would prove extremely useful in the future . . .

The Sûreté Nationale (the French equivalent of the British M15 or the American FBI) was in fact closing in on them. In 1924, the Revolution recalled its expatriates. Zhou Enlai returned to China at the end of the year and went to Canton. Kang Sheng must have returned no later than the following summer, for there is documentary evidence that in September 1924 he entered the new university of Shanghai, known as Shangda. His friend and mentor in the youth movement, Yun Daiying, invited Kang to join him there. Yun had joined the communist movement as early as 1921. He was generally admired for his pedagogical skills and was the most senior teacher at Shangda.

Shangda had been founded as a revolutionary university in 1923 as a result of an agreement between Dalin and his friends from the Comintern and Sun Yat-sen. For, at last, their approaches to the venerable doctor had borne fruit: he agreed to an alliance with the communists, on the express condition that they should become members of his party, the Guomindang. Officially, the Guomindang financed the university. The rector had been a member of Sun Yat-sen's party since its inception. Shangda was supposed to be like a Guomindang nursery, but in fact it became a formidable communist breeding-ground. Sergei Dalin made sure of it. The university was situated in the International Concession, on Ximo Street, an interconnecting group of little Western-style one-storey houses. In September 1924 some 300 students enrolled, including Kang Sheng's future secretary, as well as his future wife.

The man actually responsible for this revolutionary institution had just returned from Moscow; his name was Qu Qiubai. Called upon to fulfil numerous different tasks for the Party, he left the running of Shangda to others. The university was divided into two large departments, social sciences and literature, and it became an extraordinary centre of learning and education for future communist cadres, just like the Sun Yat-sen University in Moscow. Students were taught political economy, philosophy of history, history of philosophy and the history of the communist movement in China and elsewhere. A great many of the teachers were communists, but some were anarchists, socialists and left-wing nationalists. The flower of all those who had broken with the Mandarin education system were here. Amongst the books studied was Bukharin's *The ABC of Communism*, which Qu Qiubai claimed to have translated himself.

In an adjoining room, a Hunan playwright would enthral students with his classes on the literature of fantasy. The big cultural department at Shangda tried to combine the study of foreign literatures with that of the Chinese classics. Naturally, the literature of the USSR figured large. 'Socialist realism' was the order of the day. A teacher at Shangda, the writer Jiang Guangci, even tried to adapt the famous school of Russian proletarian culture, the *Proletkult*, to China. This tubercular novelist gave a blow-by-blow account of the history of the revolutionary movement in Shanghai in his book *The Party of the Sans-Culotte* – the novel that André Malraux was to draw on when he wrote *La Condition Humaine* (*Man's Estate*), in particular for the description of his hero, the Chinese Kyo, who was based not on Zhou Enlai but on Qu Qiubai.

Yun Daiying, Kang Sheng's mentor, had recruited students for Shangda from the cream of the communist youth movements. Naturally, when he was doing so, he thought of the young school-teacher from Shandong and tried to contact him through his old teacher, Huang Chongwu. 'Yes,' replied Huang, 'I had thought of encouraging him to work with you in Shanghai, but he is studying in Europe, in Germany or France – I'm not sure where exactly . . .'

When the young man returned to China, Kang Sheng learned that highly placed members of the Communist Party he had secretly joined wanted to send him to Shanghai.

Peng Shuzhi, Dalin's friend, who had also returned from Russia, started teaching at Shangda in September 1924. Later he recalled some of his pupils from that period, including this one: 'Zhao Yun, a very taciturn young man quite lacking in appeal, unfortunately destined to figure prominently in the history of the Chinese Communist Party and of the People's Republic of China under the name of Kang Sheng.'

For Kang Sheng finally agreed to attend the university, which was already famous, adopting the new pseudonyms of Zhang Zhen and Zhao Yun. And so it was that he went to Shanghai, city of shadows and of a thousand snares.

2
Red Shanghai, White Shanghai

'Beneath the windows of the house flows a tributary of the Blue River, the Huangpu, all waves and smoke and cargo boats and sampans. For this city, the largest on the shores of the Pacific, larger even than San Francisco, is an enormous port where hundreds of heavy-tonnage steamers dock every day, an enormous open wound through which the blood of China is pumped out via the Blue River, a breach in the wall giving access to British cannons and dreadnoughts, as well as universities, knowledge, workers' committees and the revolutionary dawn . . .'

Such was Shanghai, the vast mysterious metropolis that greeted the astonished gaze of the young militant newly arrived from Shandong, where he had left his wife and child to follow his demanding mistress: the Revolution. A teeming multitude of more than two million people, a veritable tower of Babel in Central China, a paradise for adventurers, prostitutes, gangsters, opium, illicit gambling and secret societies, where the rising Chinese bourgeoisie were concentrated, with their banks, their money, their merchant vessels, their cotton mills, factories, shops and warehouses. And at the same time a hell on earth for the thousands of half-starved human beings that were picked up from the streets amid general indifference. In short, a world that cried out for change . . .

Several worlds rather! In Shanghai, Gateway to China, East and West rubbed shoulders, sharing a mutual fascination for each other. Though the white man had the upper hand in the Concessions, seized by force from the Manchu emperors whom he intimidated with the threat of modern weaponry, he knew that his area of influence was bounded by Chinese-controlled quarters and suburbs. More than a million men, women and children clothed in rags were crowded into an indescribable maze of tiny shacks and buildings filled to bursting, built along narrow streets and dark passages and dangerous back-alleys. There was virtually no electricity and no running water, and a perpetual smell of squalor, sweat and smoke, of Chinese noodles, spicy cooking and open-air markets.

In the streets of the Chinese part of the city, there was frenetic activity, with people buying, selling, begging and hurling abuse at one another. The craftsmen worked outside, carving mahjong pieces, umbrella handles, pipes and cigarette-holders out of ivory, or, more modestly, out of pig's bones. They would carve chandeliers and abacus beads out of wood. Some carded, or sewed silk, others sold brightly coloured perfumed sweetmeats: strange-shaped caramels and soya cakes. Yet passers-by scarcely spared them a glance, preferring to admire the canaries and swallows on the bird-sellers' stalls.

On the quayside, an army of dockers unloaded the huge freighters and countless junks to a cacophony of steamships' sirens. Harnessed to carts in teams of eight or ten, they would haul their load, shouting out slogans to encourage themselves in their task.

'. . . *lai le* . . . *hui le*!' chanted the foremen.

'. . . *hui le* . . . *hang le*!' responded the dockers.

They were thin but indefatigable, since their lives depended on it. Many pinned their hopes on the unions that militant communists, anarchists and nationalists were trying to set up.

In the mills, the noise of the machines drowned everything. Women and children laboured ten hours and more a day. They plucked ducks' feathers, sorted waste and separated silk from cotton. Coolies carried the bales of raw material on thick bamboo poles.

Everyone eyed the two Concessions with bitterness and envy, both the French Concession and the larger Anglo-American Concession, the 'International Settlement'. The French Concession had its own laws, judges, courts, police and guards. The Settlement had its own police, laws and army. Situated on the eastern coast of China, European Shanghai was nothing less than a state within a state, and wounding to the self-esteem of the Chinese, these 'Sons of Heaven' who suffered the daily humiliation of the 'unequal treaties' signed under constraint.

No matter! Here economic dynamism was the law. Modern buildings, big stores and warehouses sprang up virtually overnight on the banks of the Huangpu. His heart filled with hatred for the 'foreign devils', Kang Sheng discovered that 300,000 of his countrymen lived under the French administration and 750,000 in the International Settlement. English, Americans, French, Germans, Belgians, exiled White Russians, Portuguese, Swiss and Japanese – the non-Chinese of Shanghai numbered less than 30,000 but they controlled at least half of the city . . .

Many of the Shanghai Europeans were children of the 1914–18 war, drawn to the mystery and romance of Asia after the terrible destruction suffered by their middle-class families on the Old Continent. There was no future for them at home, where they counted for nothing. Here they were the élite, a race apart: the 'Shanghailanders'. The best among them believed in Europe's civilising mission; they wanted to build, nurse, administer. The worst were just like Gibbons, the fat brutish arrogant fellow ridiculed by Hergé in *Tintin and the Blue Lotus*. 'Chop-chop . . . savvy?' they would shout disdainfully in pidgin at the thin-limbed rickshaw coolies. In exchange for a handful of rice they could travel their domain, the Concessions. They would parade along the Bund, the seafront promenade, and the quai de France, the rue du Consulat, Nanking Road or Bubbling Well Road, a little enclave of Old England on Asian soil. In the clubs and dance-halls, they could get drunk on the latest cocktail, called 'A Million Dollars'. For a few Chinese dollars they could put their arms round a dancer wearing a *qipao*, the Chinese dress with a high collar, slit up the side to the thigh. And for a few dollars more, they could spend the night with her. This was an Asia of dreams: of adventure, eroticism and buckets of money.

At the beginning of the century, it was a Frenchwoman, Anne Ballard, who ran the finest brothel in Shanghai. One day she was found stark naked sitting astride the French consul, to whom she was gently giving the whip to the cry of 'Gee-up there, pig!' After that mini scandal, affairs were conducted more discreetly. Any Shanghailander who knew the score would keep a 'sing-song girl'. If he could not afford this, he would buy a book of tickets from his favourite dance-hall: for every ticket, he got one dance. The rest had to be negotiated directly, between man and woman – sometimes between man and man.

'Poluski girls! Poluski girls!' Chinese children, acting as pimps, would call out in pidgin. In Shanghai, the most highly esteemed girls were Russian. They would all claim to be the daughter of an officer, or of one of the Tsar's high-ranking officials, who had been driven out of the country by the Bolshevik Revolution. 'Some of them are,' old Shanghailanders would confirm. 'In any case, these White Russians are very valuable. They make the best police auxiliaries in the Concessions – take that Yakolev, in the French Concession, for instance . . .'

And while the Slavic charms of the Russian girls broke many hearts, so too did those of young Chinese girls from Suzhou, a town in the interior. What drew attention to them were their astonishingly blue eyes. Their talent supplied the rest: from a very young age, they were groomed for their future 'profession'. Half geishas, half prostitutes, they conducted their business from a brothel. The daily lot of the other girls – Chinese, Malay, Indian, even Portuguese from Macao – was to solicit custom on the streets, on the North Szechuan Road, or elsewhere. And the money that changed hands went mostly into the pockets of the underworld bosses. For Shanghai, Paris of the Orient, Gateway to China, was also the realm of the secret societies.

It all happened very discreetly. The steamship slowed down as it approached the city and the sailors lowered strange oilcloth bags into the water and floated them down the Huangpu, a tributary of the Chang Jiang, known by the Europeans as the Blue River. As the ship sailed on, the lighter for having unloaded some of its cargo, a flotilla of sampans and junks then descended on the bags, fishing them out of the water with long bamboo gaffs. The bags contained kilos of opium. The drug was then taken to the depots on the boulevard des Deux Républiques, at the intersection of the French Concession and the Chinese town. There was enough to supply the hundreds of clandestine opium dens in Shanghai, enough to make a lot of money.

An all-powerful gang controlled the opium traffic. And everyone feared the terrifying 'godfather' of the gang, Du Yuesheng, a man hard, pitiless and cruel, such as a poverty-stricken youth often produces. His name alone was enough to inspire terror. From a distance, Mr Du, in his traditional Chinese robes in which he nearly always kept his hands hidden, seemed to be an honest tradesman, not a crook. Those lucky enough to get close to him and survive unscathed came away with a completely different impression: with his close-cropped hair and cold piercing eyes, he was a diabolically clever killer.

Born in 1887 in the little town of Gaoqiao, he suffered a destitute and unhappy childhood – he lost his parents when he was nine – that turned him into an adolescent prepared to do anything. In 1902, fascinated by the mirage of the big city, he came to try his luck in Shanghai. The place was teeming with freemasonries with strange and complex rituals and with secret societies: the Tong, the Red Gang, the Green Gang, the League of Heaven and Earth. Most of them, formed for the struggle against the Manchu emperors, supported the republican cause, a tendency that the nationalist leader Sun Yat-sen, himself a member of the Society of Three Harmonies, greatly encouraged.

A republic – and why not? Like the vast majority of the Sons of Heaven, Du Yuesheng hated the Manchu dynasty. In Shanghai, the Green Gang at that time was much less powerful than the Red Gang. Originally a peaceful association of boatmen, it sought, like this young man, to create for itself a place in the sun. Du Yuesheng successfully underwent the initiation tests for admission as early as 1908. It took him ten years to transform the Green Gang into a formidable institution in the service of organised crime.

Republicanism and Chinese nationalism have a lot to answer for. Under cover of these more idealistic notions, Mr Du and his associates controlled most of the prostitution and drug-trafficking in Shanghai with an iron grip. Their accomplices were everywhere, even among those in positions of authority in the Western Concessions, and their henchmen constituted a veritable militia. Armed to the teeth, they patrolled day and night the opium dens and brothels controlled by the Green Gang.

For some time already, Du Yuesheng had thrown in his lot with another big shot, Huang Jirong – the Chief Inspector of the Chinese police in the French Concession. Fat and completely without scruples, 'Pockmarked Huang' had a hold over several of the senior administrators of the French Concession, based either on corruption, fear or cowardice. No ordinary cop, Huang, influenced by his young wife, considered it preferable to come to some agreement with the ambitious godfather of the Green Gang, a decision that neither partner would have cause to regret: within a few years, their turnover had quintupled.

In his splendid residence at 26 avenue Paul-Doumer, Du Yuesheng added ever younger concubines to his collection, smoked opium in finely carved pipes and, in his spare time, meditated. A man of action, he harboured enormous ambitions. Mr Du had plans for his Green Gang to start trafficking in a new drug: heroin. He also dreamed of eventually playing a political role.

After having for a long time cold-shouldered him, the very dynamic Shanghai bourgeoisie was at last gradually beginning to recognise him as one of their own. In order to become their spokesman, the one-time urchin from Gaoqiao decided to play the nationalist card. Du had his reasons. A young officer very close to Dr Sun Yat-sen, called Chiang Kai-shek, a protégé of the Shanghai mafioso, was secretly affiliated to the Green Gang and would refuse him nothing. Despite his leftist talk, Chiang was no *bona fide* left-winger in the Guomindang Nationalist Party. 'Chiang is clever. Perhaps I will have need of him one day, as he has need of me today!' thought Du Yuesheng, who was worried about the progress the communists were making in his domain. The Reds still numbered no more than a handful, but they were working long term, and Mr Du had profited by the knowledge that success is born of sustained persistent effort. And of course there was the flirtation between the Guomindang and the Chinese CP.

'. . . Dr Sun Yat-sen thinks that communism or even a Soviet system cannot be introduced into China because the conditions for the establishment of communism or Sovietism do not exist. Mr Joffe entirely shares this point of view.'

It had all begun with this joint declaration signed in January 1923 by Dr Sun Yat-sen and Adolphe Joffe, a high-ranking Soviet diplomat and personal friend of Trotsky. This constituted a spectacular first step towards the alliance between the Guomindang and the communists that had been advocated for a considerable time by the most sensible cadres of the Communist International, the Comintern, and by Sergei Dalin in particular.

And indeed, the Sun Yat-sen/Joffe declaration signalled the beginning of a period of close collaboration. In October 1923 the Comintern sent a notable emissary to China: Mikhail Markovich Grusenberg. He made a discreet entry into Canton, capital of South China and a fief of the Guomindang, aboard a livestock barge. For his new mission in the service of Lenin, he adopted the *nom de guerre* of Borodin.

Who was this Bolshevik whom the Chinese were soon calling Bao Luo Ding? To some of his Russian comrades, he was an adventurer pure and simple. To others, a genuine professional revolutionary. Borodin had been everywhere: the United States, England, Scotland, Ireland, Chile, Mexico. He had daring, a good dose of cynicism and indisputable talents as an organiser – enough to win over Sun Yat-sen, who was conscious of the efficacy of Bolshevik methods and impressed by Lenin's personality.

The flirtation seemed about to lead to marriage. In 1924 the Reds won the right to dual membership: they could join the Guomindang while remaining militant communist card-holders. In June, Sun Yat-sen, Borodin and Chiang Kai-shek, just back from a trip to the USSR, set up the military academy of Huangpu, on a little island near Canton. Here, Soviet advisers would help train the nationalist officers required to implement Sun Yat-sen's grand design: the leader of the Guomindang wanted to create a proper nationalist army, capable of successfully taking on the warlords, which would set out from Canton and march up to Shanghai, and then on to Beijing, uniting China by force of arms. Sun called this manoeuvre the *Beifa*, the Northern Expedition.

Each of the two allies immediately advanced all their pawns into the heart of the new academy. Sun Yat-sen appointed Chiang Kai-shek to run it. This was a clever move: the Comintern could not but be aware of the young officer's reputation for being a leftist. Meanwhile, Borodin appointed alongside Chiang, whose association with the Green Gang he was unaware of, a cadre in the Far Eastern Red Army, Vassili Galen alias Blücher. A strange partnership indeed: Galen shamelessly encouraged the Chinese communists to infiltrate the 'officer factory' of Huangpu, while Chiang Kai-shek took advantage of his position as commander-in-chief to admit secretly a great many of his friends in the Green Gang. But in public everybody congratulated one another on this wonderful alliance so completely devoid of ulterior motives.

'Together, Guomindang and communists will pursue the *Beifa* to the end! United as the fingers on one hand, we will take Nanking, Shanghai, then Beijing. We will crush our common enemies: the Western imperialists, the feudal landowners and the warlords . . .'

At the end of the year a left-wing leader of the Guomindang, Liao Zhongkai, became the representative of the Nationalist Party at Huangpu. He was a personal friend of Sun Yat-sen and a keen supporter of the alliance with the USSR and the communists. His opposite number among the Reds was none other than Zhou Enlai, a brilliant young cadre educated in France, where he was a militant activist among the Chinese expatriate community. Until his death in January 1976 Zhou's name was to remain inextricably linked with the history of the Chinese Communist Party.

Under the auspices of the alliance between the Guomindang and the Chinese CP, the future of communism seemed radiant. At the end of 1924, Kang Sheng finally took the decisive step and officially joined the Party. Until then he had been only an associate member – in practice, unofficially carrying out the duties of secretary of a student cell. What was to be done with this young intellectual torn between his taste for calligraphy and fine arts and his passion for the revolutionary cause? Judging that the young man had given ample proof in Paris and at Shangda of his devotion and discretion, the committee for the city of Shanghai appointed him one of the labour organisers. In a movement that entertained a quasi-mystical cult of the working class, this was indeed an honour: despite his social origins, Kang Sheng obviously enjoyed the full confidence of his comrades.

Although hounded by a particularly aggressive police force, the Reds in Shanghai had the wind in their sails, as the godfather Du Yuesheng himself had sensed. Hand in hand with their leftist friends in the Guomindang, they had enough influence to organise strikes and demonstrations.

'In union there is strength,' says the proverb. In the eyes of the workers, the alliance of the two parties was indissoluble. Their abiding hope was that soon the nationalist army, that of Chiang Kai-shek and his friend Bao Luo Ding, would march northwards, towards Shanghai, crushing the warlords and the foreign devils. Then a new era would begin for the Sons of Heaven . . .

The Shanghai communist leadership was completely won over to this idea. However, Kang Sheng was told to avoid joining the ranks of the Guomindang, despite the agreements reached between the two parties that enabled him to do so. Too many valuable communist cadres had already been taken up by the demands of working with the nationalists. Some would even lose their precious 'party-mindedness' in this close collaboration, a risk against which this new recruit, destined, it was felt, for a brilliant career within the communist movement, had to be protected.

Labour organisation was in the hands of experienced militants: Li Lisan, younger than Kang Sheng but already a rising star; Deng Zhongxia, formerly dean at the revolutionary university of Shangda; and Liu Hua, founder of the Workers' Club of West Shanghai. From the beginning of 1925 Shanghai was overtaken by a wave of serious strikes. The city was in turmoil, with the men and women working in the mills in a state of virtual revolt. Under Li Lisan's leadership, Kang Sheng and his comrades tried, not unsuccessfully, to organise this spontaneous but promising protest movement. They set up a system of workshop and factory delegates and general assemblies, culminating in a central strike committee, on which Li Lisan figured prominently, with a young militant from Hunan province, the future 'Chinese Khrushchev' of the Cultural Revolution, Liu Shaoqi, running him a close second. In his own way, a great deal more discreetly but no less efficaciously, Kang Sheng won his spurs on the committee as an agitator and mass militant.

Tension mounted daily. In the Concessions the Westerners anxiously followed the course of events. Everything came to a head when a young worker at the Japanese Naiga Wata factory was killed by police. In the International Settlement the British opened fire on student and worker demonstrations, causing casualties, both dead and injured.

On 4 June the strikers numbered 75,000. By 13 June they were 160,000.

A wealthy Chinese shipowner tried to mediate. Founder of the Sanbei Steam Navigation Company and, at Dr Sun Yat-sen's personal request, of the Shanghai Stock and Commodity Exchange, Mr Yu Qiaqing was a leading financial figure very close to the Guomindang. He volunteered his services in the fear that the anti-Japanese protests would turn to revolutionary action. This was the first time he crossed paths with the young communist Kang Sheng. The two men were to meet again five years later under very strange circumstances . . .

Having started out as an apprentice, Yu Qiaqing was now a big businessman of the same metal as Mr Du – cunning and completely without scruple, beneath an affable exterior. He cleverly played for time, going through the motions of negotiating while the protest movement began to lose momentum, despite the desperate efforts of Kang Sheng and his communist comrades to sustain it. When the demoralised workers finally returned to work, the executioner's sword suddenly came down on the Reds: in September, Liu Hua was arrested and put to death under atrocious circumstances. The Shanghai General Labour Union was disbanded.

The class struggle in Shanghai was no empty formula. The communists had to choose between going underground and fleeing the city. Kang Sheng was among those who decided to stay . . .

The limousine came to a halt just opposite the building. As soon as they set eyes on the car, five men emerged from heaven knows where, took up position behind the pillars and drew out their weapons. Like all Chinese killers, they had large-bore pistols, Brownings or Mausers. The car's passenger had no sooner begun to climb the steps than they simultaneously opened fire. The man collapsed in a pool of blood. Their deadly work done, the killers kept the angry crowd at bay, then turned on their heels and fled.

That day of 20 August 1925, it seemed that China's destiny might take a different turn: the five killers' victim was none other than Liao Zhongkai, Dr Sun Yat-sen's faithful friend and most trusted adviser. Minister of Finance in the nationalist government, Liao had been the Guomindang representative at the 'officer factory' at Huangpu, the communist Zhou Enlai's opposite number, a task worthy of his capabilities. As leader on the left wing of Sun Yat-sen's party, Liao Zhongkai advocated the continual strengthening of ties with the USSR and the Chinese communists, and his policies had been crowned with success at the time of the big strikes in Shanghai, when Red militants and nationalist agitators had joined forces against Western and Japanese imperialists. He left a wife and a seventeen-year-old son, Liao Chengzhi, who was to become a leader of clandestine communist activity in Shanghai, alongside Kang Sheng, and later a senior official in the People's Republic of China.

The tragic death of Liao Zhongkai was just one more bloody episode in the battle of succession after the death in March of the founder of the Guomindang, Dr Sun Yat-sen. His spectacular funeral had been the occasion of a particularly hypocritical display of unity between the leaders of his party. Since then, the three main factions of the nationalist movement – the left; the centre, led by the charming but superficial Wang Jingwei; and the conservative wing, secretly led by Chiang Kai-shek with the support of the Green Gang – had been engaged in a covert but ruthless struggle for supremacy.

Was Du, the Shanghai godfather, behind the killing on 20 August? Rumours were fuelled when one of the leaders of the extreme right of the Guomindang fled to Hong Kong. In any event, Du's secret protégé, Chiang Kai-shek, made the most of this opportunity: under pretext of conducting an investigation into the death of Liao Zhongkai, he launched a campaign of terror that enabled him to silence several of his rivals. Ever attracted by expediency, Borodin, the Comintern representative in China, made a show of congratulating the young officer on his determination to strike against counter-revolutionaries. This was either far too subtle a ruse or a gross error of judgement for which he was to pay dearly in the future: Borodin knew full well that Chiang was distancing himself day by day from Sun Yat-sen's policy of alliance with the USSR but he was literally enthralled by Chiang's audacity and cynicism. After all, the nationalist leader had personally shot and killed one of those presumed guilty of the murder that took place on 20 August before the man could say anything – or perhaps so that he should never again say anything . . . 'I was overcome with anger. I couldn't help myself!' he said by way of explanation.

Cynicism, audacity, cunning and duplicity – such things found favour with Du Yuesheng. The bloody Canton incident made him decide to play the Chiang Kai-shek card for all it was worth. The man had obviously gained in stature. He seemed to Du the only Guomindang leader capable of silencing the Reds, whose unbridled activism in Shanghai clearly demonstrated that they were potential candidates for power, at least in the medium term.

What did the communists in that great Chinese sea port know of the secret dealings between the young nationalist leader and the boss of the Green Gang? Very little. Valuable though their alliance with the Guomindang was, it nevertheless diminished their room for manoeuvre. Caught between Borodin's politicking and Chiang's ambition, they could not see their way clearly any more, and were counting above all on a continued expansion of the workers' protest movement to put them in a commanding position.

In 1926 Kang was judged sufficiently seasoned to become head of the Organisation Department for the Shanghai CP. This was a key post since, in Leninist thinking (then taken as the absolute authority), organisation was essential. This flattering appointment led him on to particularly treacherous terrain: that of intelligence matters. The young militant began to work for the Party's Political Security Bureau, a body with basically technical functions, responsible for locating safe meeting-places for Party leaders, protecting their clandestine quarters and providing them with the liaison agents indispensable to their needs.

His two new jobs brought Kang Sheng into contact with Wang Kai, a former railway navvy responsible for the Party's communications system. Wang Kai had established his headquarters in the working-class suburb of Zhabei. He too had to find meeting-places for the leaders. Kang Sheng and Wang Kai performed this difficult task to everyone's satisfaction. The young militant from Shandong soon came to know every alleyway in the city. For the Political Security Bureau he rented 'clean' rooms, using shops and trading stalls as letter-drops for his liaison agents. He favoured the French Concession, where repression was less brutal on account of the authorities' more liberal attitude. The key word in this complex organisation was compartmentalisation. None of these countless intermediaries was supposed to know the identity of any of the other links in the chain, so as to avoid the risk of collective exposure.

As for the CCP's Soviet comrades, they could not but be interested in the clandestine achievements of this Chinese militant whose literary background and natural discretion rendered him singularly fit for delicate tasks . . .

A huge red-brick construction, the Soviet consulate in Shanghai was situated in Huangpu Road, not very far from Garden Bridge and the Central Post Office, nearly opposite that 'Temple of Imperialism', the United Kingdom consulate-general. It was a strange place, more like a revolutionary headquarters than a peaceful diplomatic mission. It was allowed, under international law, to fly the red flag in the midst of Settlement territory.

By day and by night, police look-outs or informers for the Westerners watched an army of Chinese shadows slip in and out of the building: agents who had infiltrated the Chamber of Commerce, leaders of the Seamen's Union, Chinese police with flexible professional ethics, labour agitators such as Li Lisan, whose star had been in the ascendant since the anti-Japanese strikes of May–June 1925.

'In order that the revolutionary cause may triumph in China, we need money, more money, and yet more money!' The Soviet vice-consul Wilde and his right-hand man, Golenovsky, in charge of propaganda, never tired of repeating their messages to Moscow. They were listened to. For the second half of 1925 the consulate had originally been allocated the sum of 100,000 Chinese dollars; in October of that year it was granted an additional 150,000 dollars.

The funds were sent via the Dalbank, a Soviet company set up in April 1922 in Harbin, a town close to the border between China and the USSR. In Shanghai the titular director of this curious banking establishment was a man called Course. In actual fact, his deputy, David Frumberg, shouldered most of the responsibilities of the job. The Dalbank also financed the military academy at Huangpu, by order of the Comintern and under the tight control of the OGPU, that huge espionage machine, half intelligence service and half secret police, which had succeeded the Cheka as the 'sword' of the Russian Revolution.

At the consulate in Huangpu Road, Comrade Babitsky was in charge of military matters. In other words, he belonged to the Red Army's secret service, the *Glavsnoie Radzdivatelnoie Oupravlenie*, commonly known as the GRU. Founded by Trotsky, the GRU functioned as a very special kind of secret service. Not only was it supposed to spy on the enemy but also – and more importantly – it was to train communist cadres in every country of the world in armed insurrection. Faithful to Lenin's theories, the leaders of the Comintern believed that insurrection was an art and that its management could be entrusted only to carefully selected specialists. Recruiting these specialists and then training them was the principal task of the military section of the GRU.

Babitsky had several officers to help him. The two most important were Chusov and Kojenikov, each of whom had his own area of operation. To Chusov fell the unremitting task of bribing Chinese military personnel, particularly important in a country where people sold themselves quite shamelessly to the highest bidder. Kojenikov's job was the infiltration of the European communities in the Concessions, and that of the White Russians, and the establishment and maintaining of contact with the Chinese communists. A former officer in the Tsar's army who had joined the Bolsheviks after 1917, he had been attached to Borodin's personal staff in Canton. He was a fair-haired young man, pale-skinned, with darting eyes. Protected by his cover as a 'journalist', Evgeni Kojenikov liked to keep changing his identity. The Europeans in the Concessions knew him as a likeable journalist, Mr Morsky. To his colleagues at the consulate and to the Chinese communists, he was simply Comrade Pik.

Impatience was rising at Huangpu Road. The time for action seemed to be fast approaching in the shape of those soldiers in the nationalist army who had left Canton in the summer of 1926 on the Northern Expedition so close to the heart of Dr Sun Yat-sen. Since the death of the latter, Chiang Kai-shek was directing operations, with the aid of the chief Russian military adviser, Vassili Galen alias General Blücher. But Chiang did not have great freedom of action: whilst he dreamed of marching directly on Shanghai in order to anticipate the risk of a successful rising on the part of the Reds, Borodin and Blücher managed to set his rivals in league against him. A more cautious strategy was decided upon: a direct offensive on the north, circumventing Shanghai.

The nationalist army made methodical progress, repulsing the war-lords' troops as they went. Each new victory for Chiang Kai-shek and Borodin gave rise to an enthusiastic response among the workers of Shanghai. The unrest in the factories and poor suburbs continued, to the great displeasure of the head of the Chinese police, Gui Zengyang; of his French counterparts, Mallet and Fiori; and of the chief of the Settlement police, the Englishman Patrick Givens. But the fate of Shanghai now lay in the hands of a new warlord, Sun Chuanfan. He had long thin moustaches and wore richly coloured uniforms. He was known to be cruel to the weak, and servile to the strong, like most of his men. In fact, Sun Chuanfan had limited confidence in his troops' ardour for war. He trusted only his Praetorian Guard, composed of soldiers from Shandong or White Russian mercenaries.

Meanwhile, the Reds were mustering their forces. Strikes were spreading in the mills and on the docks, and while the police came down on union organisations, the students began to play a part in proceedings. Moscow sent reinforcements. On 7 October, Sergei Dalin reappeared in Shanghai, the man who first proposed to Sun Yat-sen an alliance between the Chinese CP and the Guomindang. But he did not remain in the city; he was to meet up with Borodin in Canton in order to give him the latest instructions from the Comintern, whose policy for China varied from one day to the next, depending on factional infighting between Stalin, Zinoviev, Bukharin and Trotsky.

A few days after Dalin's return, a representative of the OGPU came to inspect the Soviet operation in Shanghai. Sorely disappointed in what he found, Comrade Sidorkin called together the consular cadres, whom he considered defeatist: 'To retreat would be a counter-revolutionary crime! The nationalist army is marching north. Let us prepare for the armed insurrection of the Shanghai proletariat . . .'

Those at Huangpu Road were not in the habit of questioning orders from the Kremlin. On 19 October 1926, three Russian militants – Achin, Merner and Chusov – met at the consulate to con-sider by what means a victorious uprising might be achieved. Chusov, as an officer in the Red Army's secret service, was responsible, together with Kojenikov, for the combat sections of the Chinese Com-munist Party, which consisted of between 150 and 200 militants, armed with a disparate assortment of weapons, known as *Tchon – Tschasti Osobavo Nasnatcheniia*, or Special Operations Units. They could count on the support of their colleagues in the Guomindang shock troops.

But on 23 October, the day chosen by the communists and their allies as a day of action, the *Tchon* did not show up. The men must have had a more clear-sighted appreciation of the situation than their leaders or Soviet advisers. Only a few thousand strikers attempted to demonstrate. They were dispersed by Sun Chuanfan's White Rus-sians, who shot down like rabbits a few workers and a dozen communist militants. The uprising ended in complete fiasco.

A few days later a new communist leader arrived secretly in Shanghai to give support to his comrades. He had been the Party official at the Huangpu military academy, Zhou Enlai. This revolutionary with Mandarin ways also came to prepare for 'the insurrection of the Shanghai proletariat'.

On 26 October, the Communist International, presided over only latterly by Nikolai Bukharin, Stalin's closest ally, sent a telegram to the Chinese CP. The Komintern 'advised' them to do everything possible to expedite the march northwards of the nationalist army, even if this meant restraining the revolutionary aspirations of the peasants in order to retain the sympathy of the conservative wing of the Guomindang.

Moscow was still backing the alliance.

'Armed insurrection is no game!'

It was because they had failed to take heed of this fundamental axiom of Leninism that the 'strategists' who had planned 23 October met with failure. Guilty of having been too faithful to the ever-changing orders emanating from Borodin and the Soviet advisers, the communist bodies in Shanghai were now reorganised from top to bottom. Kang Sheng, who was still in charge of the Political Security Bureau and the Organisation Department, was closely involved in this initiative. He was now directly answerable to Luo Yinong, secretary of the CP for the whole province, and to the 'revolutionary mandarin' Zhou Enlai. In a strong position as founder of the Communist Party in exile, and as political commissar at the Huangpu military academy, Zhou had become one of the most prominent leaders in the movement. He set up his headquarters in the communist section of the Third District, in an apartment on rue Lafayette, which had been found by people working for Kang Sheng – once again, right in the heart of the French Concession.

Convinced that a victorious uprising had simply been delayed, the Soviets were still trying to speed things up. At the end of November a new consular agent, Kondratenko, with a Chinese interpreter at his side, summoned the leaders of the *Tchon* to the High Society. For a clandestine meeting of such importance, this was a well-chosen venue: a huge six-storey fun palace situated on the edge of the two Concessions, the High Society was a busy place with a lot of people passing through. One could meet just about anybody there. There were gaming rooms and slot machines, tight-rope artistes and theatre troupes, whores and pickpockets, quacks and false prophets, bearded masseuses, melon-seed vendors and bird-sellers. Distorting mirrors, shooting galleries, lucky draws and Aunt Sallies completed the picture. All the languages of China were spoken here, and most of the European ones as well, but most predominant was the language of money, for the place belonged to the ubiquitous Mr Du.

'At the High Society only one thing is absolutely impossible to find: an honest woman!' so it was commonly said. This was so much the case that the prostitutes themselves did not solicit for custom unless accompanied by their madames – and even then, only on brothel premises!

Naturally, the meeting was largely devoted to the disgraceful showing the combat units had made on the twenty-sixth. 'A veritable disgrace to communist militants!' said Kondratenko. 'Armed action is a matter for professional revolutionaries. We're going to have to send for some from the Soviet Union.'

These were not empty words. On 15 December, Massur arrived in Shanghai. This robust fellow, a former seaman, had commanded the militia at Vladivostok, the great Russian port of the Sea of Japan, where the headquarters of the OGPU Far Eastern Section were located. He brought with him an old acquaintance of the Shanghai communists: Gu Shunzhang. A handsome man from the lower depths of the city, Gu had begun life as an ordinary labourer. Originally a railway worker, then employed in the Nanyang cigarette factory, where the communists had established one of their first factory cells in the summer of 1924, he joined the Party almost immediately – prompted either by a taste for adventure or by the fierce desire not to end his days on a production line. The new recruit at once proved to be very talented in the ways of clandestine life. Without any false modesty, he explained to his new comrades the reason for this unusual facility: Gu Shunzhang belonged to Mr Du's Green Gang. It was among the criminal fraternity that he had learned to give police tails the slip, to find undetectable hiding-places, to strangle noiselessly a bothersome adversary or a dangerous witness . . .

'But all that's in the past! Now I'm with you,' he said self-assuredly. After having completely repudiated his former allegiances, Gu was chosen by Li Lisan himself to maintain Party discipline and organise strike pickets during the unrest of May–June 1925. He gave his new bosses complete satisfaction, to the extent that he was sent for training to Canton, where he was Borodin's bodyguard for a while, along with one of the future chiefs of the Chinese communist special services, the seaman Deng Fa. Borodin, who had an expert eye for men of action, deemed Gu to be promising material and put him in contact with the local OGPU agents. By October 1926 Gu was judged sufficiently mature to make the great leap: he was sent to Vladivostok to follow a full training programme of initiation into methods of espionage and armed insurrection. And this was the élite individual whom the Soviets were now sending back to China to run the communist shock groups in Shanghai, accompanied by a Latvian specialist, Comrade Kugol.

At the beginning of February 1927, the troops commanded by the moustachioed warlord Sun Chuanfan, having been seriously trounced in skirmishes with the nationalist army, began to evacuate

Shanghai in order to retreat slowly northwards. Was this the moment at last?

'Certainly it is. And right now, comrades . . .' was the verdict of Remissov, Borodin's personal emissary, who had come to Shanghai bringing his boss's orders. Snapping his fingers at the reserved response from the diplomats at the consulate, he deliberately urged them on, once again.

On 17 February a pamphlet in English was distributed among the British reinforcements who had come to defend the Settlement in the event of a Chinese rebellion: 'You have been sent here to combat our revolution. The Chinese workers and peasants will not tolerate this. They will fight all the more spiritedly for their independence. Do not think that the Chinese masses are "Chinagos" whom you can massacre like cattle. Those days have gone for ever . . .'

On the nineteenth the strike began. By the twentieth it had become total, to the great surprise of the communist leaders, who did not dare hope for so much. But an unforeseeable turnaround by Sun Chuanfan threw everything into question: backed by the French and English soldiers from the Concessions, his troops invaded the Chinese town and proclaimed martial law. The warlord had been handsomely paid by the Shanghai rich to restore order! Before the horrified gaze of a few foreign observers, the revolt was submerged in blood, with two hundred Chinese decapitated in the streets, their heads stuck on bamboo poles or displayed on kitchen platters . . .

This was the rule of law and order!

'We must wait longer,' decided the communist cadres. 'Sun Chuanfan is not going to stay for ever: he's far too scared of the nationalist army. Soon our hour will come.'

They were unaware that the warlord had for a long time been negotiating his withdrawal from Shanghai – to the benefit of Chiang Kai-shek.

In the early afternoon of Saturday 26 March 1927, General Chiang Kai-shek entered Shanghai. But the leader of the nationalist army did not come marching in at the head of his troops. On the contrary, it was with the utmost discretion that he came ashore at Huangpu, accompanied only by a few bodyguards; Chiang came not in triumph but to negotiate.

He was taken through the barricades and spiked barriers blocking the streets of the city to a building situated on the edge of the French Concession: the former Ministry for Foreign Affairs. In this rather outmoded setting, the General received some very strange visitors. The first was none other than 'Pockmarked Huang', the chief of Chinese inspectors in the French police force and Mr Du's associate in opium-trafficking. After a fairly brief chat, the corrupt fat official was succeeded by another policeman, an Englishman this time: Patrick T. Givens, head of the Political Branch of the Settlement police, and a highly respected agent of the Secret Intelligence Service.

The commander-in-chief of the Guomindang army explained to this representative of the British Crown that he had come to Shanghai to reassure the Westerners. In a few days' time his troops would arrive. Far from considering themselves the avant-garde of some kind of revolution, they would prove to be intent upon re-establishing order – in other words, eliminating the communists. To carry through successfully this work for the public good, he asked the Settlement authorities to grant his soldiers the 'right of pursuit'. Givens needed some persuading, but only for form's sake. In fact everything had already been arranged with the President of the International Concession's Municipal Council, the American Sterling Fessenden.

Chiang was not lying. For months he had been planning this fantastic overthrow of the alliance, progressively asserting his authority over the nationalist army and reducing the influence of his rivals and of the Soviet advisers. An affiliated member of the Green Gang, he was now in control of the Guomindang.

It was in this dual capacity that he then received Yu Qiaqing. Since the strikes of 1925, in which he had played the role of intermediary between the workers and their Japanese employers, the honourable Mr Yu had become the standard-bearer of Shanghai's bourgeois rich. A mere handful of the initiated knew of his close links with the Green Gang and its formidable godfather, Du Yuesheng – a secret better kept to yourself if you wanted to live to grow old. Yu assured Chiang of the support of the business community he represented, asked for a few details about the planned operation, promised that very large sums of money would be paid to the Guomindang army and to its leader for their good and loyal service, then went home to his wife, son and three daughters.

With Mr Du the conversation was even briefer. The two men knew each other well. Chiang Kai-shek had been sponsored within the Green Gang by Chen Qimei, one of the secret society's most eminent members, assassinated in 1916. On the death of his benefactor, Chiang had adopted Chen's three nephews, one of whom, the very cunning Chen Lifu, now acted as his personal secretary. The talk was exclusively of concrete problems. Mr Du promised the young general the support of the Green Gang henchmen.

Patrick Givens, Sterling Fessenden, 'Pockmarked Huang', Yu Qiaqing, Du Yuesheng – why were these men of influence, all so very different from one another, and sometimes representing conflicting interests, now turning in unison to the head of the nationalist army? The answer can be given in three words: the Communist Party.

The situation in Shanghai had changed since the end of February and it was the Reds who now had control of the city. On 20 March a new general strike had totally paralysed the docks and factories. Half a million workers sat idle. The walls were covered with vengeful slogans. One after the other, police stations had been attacked by poorly armed but very determined groups.

'This time we cannot go back: we must throw all our forces into battle,' was now the opinion of the communist leaders Luo Yinong, Zhou Enlai and Chen Duxiu, that renowned intellectual who for the past year had been calling for a break with the Guomindang, thereby earning himself the reputation of being a Trotskyite.

Almost with relief, Zhou Enlai gave the green light to the combat detachments, of which his assistant, Gu Shunzhang, was in charge. The former member of the Green Gang had done fine work, putting to good use the lessons he had learned from his Soviet OGPU instructors in Vladivostok. His men had hardly any firearms, but this was no cause for worry, they could use whatever came to hand: hatchets, bamboo poles, hammers, tools, butcher's knives. He showed the strike-picket militia how to make 'machine-guns' out of barrels filled with petrol. These did not cause much harm but they did make a lot of noise – enough to frighten troops lacking in fighting spirit. This idea was inspired by Soviet techniques of street warfare, and put into practice *à la chinoise*. For reasons that will become clear later, Popular China's official history prefers to credit Zhou Enlai with this invention rather than Gu Shunzhang.

Under leadership of this kind, the communist combat detachments turned in a more commendable performance, spearheading the insurrection. 'Through his remarkable work, Comrade Pik is largely responsible for the Chinese *Tchon*'s good showing,' Chusov, the Shanghai head of the Red Army's secret service, the GRU, declared publicly. He decided to maintain close contact with Yu Denong, the military head of the 'special committee' of the left-wing faction of the Guomindang, which was hostile to Chiang Kai-shek. Indeed, Yu Denong paid several visits to the Russian consulate in Huangpu Road.

The insurrectionists had the upper hand. On 22 March, four days before Chiang Kai-shek's clandestine visit, the uprising held sway over the city and the suburbs, with the exception of the International Concessions, which were bristling with barbed wire and machine-gun emplacements.

On 25 March the militants in the Organisation Department, run by Kang Sheng, set up a meeting at the Wuzhou Pagoda of five hundred communist cadres. Luo Yinong chaired the meeting. In the midst of all the shouting and the chanting of slogans, he won agreement on three important decisions:

'If the Chamber of Commerce and the Chinese Millowners Association do not accept the twenty-two demands of the General Labour Union, a new anti-capitalist general strike will be called.

'A militia of 50,000 armed "worker-supervisors" will be created to protect the Revolution. All will receive full politico-military training.

'The Party will call on the nationalist bourgeoisie of Shanghai and its representative Yu Qiaqing to set up, together with the workers, a revolutionary municipal council. . . .'

This programme was just what Yu Qiaqing and the rich Chinese of Shanghai did not want to hear! Confusion reigned: Luo Yinong was appealing to a 'nationalist bourgeoisie' that was primarily concerned with its own interests. Workers and craftsmen had risen up to help the Guomindang troops gain victory; however, these troops were now preparing to march against them in full agreement with the 'imperialists' in the Concessions and with the Green Gang villains. As for the Soviets in Huangpu Road, caught between their orders from Moscow and counter-orders from Borodin, they did not know which way to jump.

There was no doubt that there was chaos in the making.

On Sunday 9 April 1927, the godfather Du Yuesheng invited He Songling to visit him at his new house in rue Wagner, an old-style building that today houses a Chinese secondary school. He Songling hesitated, then accepted the invitation. Mr Du certainly had an appalling reputation. But in a town where the communists were now very powerful, what had he to fear from the head of the Green Gang? On the contrary, if Du Yuesheng was making overtures to the Reds, it must mean that he recognised their supremacy. The godfather was sufficiently cunning to want to come to some Chinese-style arrangement, even with his worst enemies . . .

Undisputed leader of the Shanghai General Labour Union, a post in which he had succeeded Li Lisan, now head of the Party's City Council, He Songling, alias Wang Shouhua, felt like a victor. That evening he went to rue Wagner, without any escort. This was fatally unwise: hardly had he entered the sumptuous dwelling than two thugs from the Green Gang tried to pounce on him. He Songling suddenly realised the enormity of his error. Determined to sell his life dearly, he began to fight back and repelled his aggressors. Suddenly Mr Du himself appeared at the top of the staircase, with a vacant expression in his eyes, his voice sounding disembodied. Under the influence of opium, he was obviously in some kind of trance.

'Not here! Not in my house!' he shouted.

Other gangsters appeared, carrying weapons. They dragged He Songling outside, where the union leader was thrown into the back of a car, which took off at top speed in order to get away from the French Concession as quickly as possible. He was found several days later, having been buried alive . . .

This dreadful death acted as a catalyst. On 11 April, British soldiers cleared the perimeter of the International Settlement, using bayonets, as had been agreed between Patrick Givens and Chiang Kai-shek. The next day at dawn the Green Gang henchmen entered the fray. There were several thousand of them, organised into veritable civil-war commando units, armed with guns, hand grenades and the latest model of machine-guns, Vickers or Hotchkiss. In the heart of Shanghai they joined up with crack squads from the nationalist army who had entered the city in small waves under cover of darkness. The Guomindang soldiers were commanded by former cadets from the Huangpu 'officer factory' who were themselves affiliated to Mr Du's secret society.

Relying on the effect of surprise, Chiang Kai-shek and his sleeping partners had decided, come what may, to eliminate the strike pickets and the communist armed groups led by Gu Shunzhang – if need be, by absorbing the remains of the warlord Sun Chuanfan's army. As long as they were paid, the Shandong mercenaries were always ready to switch their allegiance. As for the White Russians, they had been decimated by the communists a few days earlier and had a score to settle . . .

The *Tchon* courageously opened fire on their assailants with a resolution that plunged the Russian diplomats into confusion. In Huangpu Road the most compromising files were already being destroyed, but disagreement was rife, since not everyone appreciated the calls for moderation coming from Borodin and from Moscow.

'The worker detachments of the Chinese Party must not under any circumstances fire on Chiang Kai-shek's troops: it will jeopardise our policy of alliance with the Guomindang!' Achinin, the consular secretary, had explained to his comrades shortly before the attack. So, having fired the Chinese communists into action, the Russians were now abandoning them overnight in the name of *Realpolitik*!

Achinin was not joking. Putting his words into action, he had charged his Chinese liaison officer, Wang Zichian, and two Soviet advisers, Vassiliev and Maximov, to see that his orders were carried out: the *Tchon* were to be sent into hiding and instructed to bury their weapons.

Those militiamen who had followed the two Soviet comrades' instructions were now regretting it. The rest were fighting for all they were worth. It cost the nationalists ten hours of fierce fighting to overcome the desperate resistance of the worker combat units led by Zhou Enlai and Gu Shunzhang, with which Kang Sheng and the militants in the Organisation Department were responsible for maintaining contact. It was around the union headquarters, in Zhabei, and in the modern office building of Boashan Lu's Commercial Press, where several thousand communists had gathered two days earlier, that the fighting was most bitter. Zhou Enlai and Gu Shunzhang both fell into the hands of Chiang Kai-shek's soldiers. They were more fortunate than their militants, and escaped: Zhou because one of his former pupils at the Huangpu military academy recognised him, and Gu through the intervention of friends connected with the Green Gang.

The third Shanghai uprising, which had started in hope and elation, ended in a bloodbath.

Chiang Kai-shek was in an insuperable position. His soldiers controlled all of Shanghai and its suburbs. They arrested people on the streets, they searched houses, they readily turned to violence and torture. In the suburb of Longhua, mass executions took place at night, under the headlights of military trucks. Twenty-five members of the 'Revolutionary Municipal Council' fell into the hands of their mortal enemies. The others were in hiding. To save their lives, the captive militants talked. They denounced their best comrades.

'Down with the communists!' 'Throw out Borodin and Galen!' 'Death to the criminals!' 'Resist the plan to make women common property!' 'Kill the avant-garde of the Russian Soviets!' proclaimed pamphlets, newspapers and banners. But the General Secretary of the Party, Chen Duxiu, the regional leader, Luo Yinong, and the head of the Military Department, Zhou Enlai, had fled, while the leader of the *Tchon*, the former gangster Gu Shunzhang, was actively being hunted down, with a price on his head of one thousand Chinese dollars.

Kang Sheng also managed to slip through the nationalist net and immediately went completely underground. For him, as for his surviving comrades, the 'lyrical illusion' of the worker insurrection had ended in failure. The exhilarating period of strike pickets and combat units was over. They had to prepare themselves for a long struggle, a battle in the dark. They had to suppress once and for all the adolescent that lies within every revolutionary; they had to harden themselves to win, to become inhuman. And worse . . .

Chiang Kai-shek's victory threw the Soviet diplomats into panic. Were the nationalists going to be so bold as to come and flush them out too? With little wish to create a pointless incident, Chiang decided against this. The Soviets' defeat now conclusive, they now resumed their internal quarrelling. Chusov, who had opposed Secretary Achinin's orders, was recalled to Moscow. Evgeni Kojenikov, the former officer of the Tsar, was entrusted with an important mission.

'Chiang Kai-shek has dropped his mask: he's nothing but an agent of the bourgeoisie and of imperialism! He must be neutralised at all costs, killed if necessary. Considerable funds will be made available within the next few days . . .' announced Borodin, making a 180-degree turn.

Kojenikov obediently conveyed the order to his OGPU friend, the Azerbaijani Georges Melamed, known to the Chinese by his pseudonym, Comrade Troyanov. Melamed was in contact with Luo Yinong, the local Party chief and a senior Political Security official. Knowing from experience that the ways of Borodin and of Moscow were as impenetrable as those of General Chiang Kai-shek, Melamed complied with the order. Through the Political Security Bureau, he recruited a Chinese employee at the Japanese consulate as an intermediary to approach the ultra-clandestine cadres of the Japanese Communist Party in Shanghai with a request for the 'loan' of two comrades to keep watch on the comings and goings of the leader of the

Guomindang army, reasoning that the Japanese were able to circulate more freely than the local population and were keen to play an active part in the victorious uprising in China.

At the end of April everything seemed ready. The former USSR vice-consul in Shanghai, Wilde, who had become one of Borodin's personal advisers, brought the cash, as promised, together with new orders: 'Stop entrusting terrorist acts to anarchist elements or mercenaries, as you have done until now. Everyone must assume their own responsibilities: the onus for this important task lies with the leaders of the Chinese Party . . .'

His mission accomplished, Wilde left for Hangzhou, a Chinese town to the south of Shanghai, not far from the mouth of the Blue River.

And it was from Hangzhou that a telegram bearing Wilde's signature arrived several days later. In coded language, he invited the Soviets of Shanghai to 'moderate' their actions against the commander-in-chief of the nationalist army. In plain words, this meant: cancel the operation against Chiang.

Once again, Borodin had changed his mind.

Luo Yinong and the Chinese communists took it very badly: the Guomindang were assassinating their comrades and they did not even have the right to retaliate any more. As for the Soviet comrades' advice, it changed from one day to the next. However, discipline required them to submit to this new directive, and so they did.

Evgeni Kojenikov, meanwhile, received orders to report to Hangzhou as a matter of urgency. The OGPU chief in that town, the Pole Gloud, had just intercepted a telegram from 'Comrade Pik' to his real employer – who was none other than the head of the Settlement police in Shanghai, Patrick Givens. Kojenikov, the former White Guard converted to Bolshevism, the intrepid mentor of the combat sections of the Chinese CP, was in reality a mole working for the British.

The affair caused quite a stir within the GRU, the Red Army's secret service. On learning of this betrayal, Russian secret agents questioned how long it had been going on. Since at least 1926, several military intelligence officers believed.

'Remember when our OGPU colleagues in Vladivostok sent one of their agents to Shanghai to infiltrate Givens' police force? He was immediately identified. Pik must have informed the English . . .'

Those in the know were able to name the agent concerned: Comrade Sima, the young Ukrainian militant who, under her real name of Seraphina Krivetz, had accompanied Hendricus Sneevliet, the Comintern envoy, to the Chinese Communist Party's First Congress, when he came to Shanghai in July 1921.

On 18 May 1927, Evgeni Kojenikov narrowly escaped capture by the OGPU. Considering this no mean feat, the double agent awarded himself three pips and under the pen name of 'Captain' Pik started to write a book about his exploits. No more was heard of him until May 1929, when he found himself in the news again, this time for attempted fraud. Kojenikov had tried to sell for a small fortune confidential information to a left-wing American journalist – information, it was later learned, concerning the activities of Patrick Givens and the British Intelligence Service in China, no less.

Comrade Pik certainly had eclectic political tastes. Perhaps it was inevitable that this bloody shambles, which American writer Harold Isaacs called 'the tragedy of the Chinese Revolution', should comprise, alongside the horror, an element of farce. But neither Kang Sheng nor those of his communist comrades who managed to escape the massacres of April 1927 were in a position to appreciate the black humour of the situation. The failure of their Shanghai endeavour, the victory of Chiang Kai-shek and his secret ally Mr Du, their own incompetence and that of their Soviet advisers led to them to the following brutal conclusion: 'We need an OGPU for China. The setting-up of a proper Chinese Communist Party secret service is an immediate priority.'

3
The Birth of the *Tewu*

'. . . Detectives must be attached to all branches of our organisation to keep watch on suspect persons. The Party must rid itself secretly of all traitors or agents of the opposing party . . .'

This was certainly spelling it out. On 31 May 1928, the Organisation Department of Chinese Communist Party headquarters circulated an odd underground pamphlet for the exclusive use of cadres and confirmed militants. Kang Sheng, who seems at this point to have already completed an initial training course in Russia with the OGPU, is thought to have been the man behind this rather exceptional publication. His aim? Simple: the pamphlet was to inform Party leaders of various precautionary measures to be taken in the underground struggle against the Guomindang, now the Party's deadly enemy. It listed a series of elementary pieces of advice, deliberately written in a very simplistic style. The intention was to make an impact on comrades' imaginations, putting a few key concepts into their heads, rather than giving a detailed picture of all possible security measures.

The pamphlet's conclusion makes its point very clearly, stating that the precepts in this 'little red book for underground revolutionaries' should command the full attention of Party members, being 'the result of our organisation's secret agents' experience'.

So, it was good advice, based on reliable sources. (The pamphlet strongly resembles the instruction manuals distributed by OGPU cadres in the USSR to their pupils.) It was imperative to try and get sound – that is to say, loyal – agents into the enemy camp. Each secret agent should only be in contact with a single Party militant, to whom he should submit his reports direct. In the event of its being impossible to infiltrate government bodies, there should be no hesitation in having recourse to bribery in order to cull information. Bribery was an effective measure, but nevertheless certain precautions were to be observed: any rendezvous with a paid informer must take place only in a public place or on waste ground, never at the private home of the militant, which should remain secret.

If the communist leaders were hammering home the need for security measures in this way, it was because the Party, having been bled white in Shanghai by Chiang Kai-shek and his allies, had also suffered two other very serious setbacks in the course of 1927: the suppression of the so-called Autumn Harvest Uprising – the name was poetic but the results were disastrous – and the bloody liquidation of the Canton commune, on direct orders from Joseph Stalin, for internal Soviet political reasons.

These three abortive uprisings considerably weakened the Party, with cadres and militants being tortured to death by Chiang Kai-shek's soldiers, and the rank and file disillusioned by the fecklessness and irresponsibility of their communist leaders prepared to fall in line, on no matter what conditions, at a mere word from Moscow.

Only a few peasant resistance groups survived, such as that led by the 'fringe' leader Mao Zedong, who tried to give himself room for manoeuvre by taking advantage of circumstances. Already, the future leader of China no longer believed that there was anything to be gained by repeated urban insurrections: they all ended in massacre. But he was still far from forming his theory of 'the encirclement of towns by the countryside'.

For those in the towns, the most important thing that had to be saved was the Party apparatus. Having learned from the disasters in Shanghai and Canton, the communist leaders now had one priority: to know at all times what plot their *bête noire* Chiang Kai-shek was hatching next. The nationalist leader was in fact occupied on other fronts: he had to contend with the rival government that Wang Jingwei and the leaders of the centrist faction of the Guomindang had established – with full Soviet backing – in Wuhan, the big industrial city situated at the confluence of the Blue River and the River Han.

The man in charge of restructuring the Party in Shanghai was Zhou Enlai. In all confidence he gave new responsibilities to the former gangster Gu Shunzhang: had Gu not proved his loyalty and revolutionary capabilities during the Shanghai uprising? However, this confidence was not shared by everyone. Quite a number of comrades were worried about Gu Shunzhang's past association with the Green Gang, and held against him his stormy private life and his taste for money, violence and manipulation. Zhou Enlai had to defend his appointee every inch of the way, reminding his comrades that Gu Shunzhang was a son of the people and, even more important, he enjoyed the support of the Soviets, who had trained him in secret service methods at Vladivostok.

As head of the Department for Special Affairs, the *Tewu*, Zhou Enlai did not take kindly to interference from his comrades. Besides, his job was not an easy one: he had to build up an effective security apparatus to protect Party headquarters in Shanghai, and get his spies into Nanking, where Chiang Kai-shek had set up government – all this in the context of a weakened and hounded clandestine party.

Yet Zhou Enlai did score some successes, notably within the Guomindang itself: under the leadership of Li Kenong, future head of Chinese special services and Vice-Foreign Affairs minister, several *Tewu* agents were operating right in the heart of the enemy camp, as members of Chiang Kai-shek's secret services! They were able to furnish valuable information on planned anti-communist round-ups;

thanks to them, the Party was no longer deaf or blind.

In Shanghai, Zhou Enlai entrusted Gu Shunzhang with a dual mission: he was to recruit agents within the three police forces – Chinese, French and British – and he was also to deal with the physical elimination of presumed traitors, a task which the former gangster fulfilled with undisguised pleasure, aided by a team of henchmen that he recruited himself from among his friends in the criminal fraternity or among the dockers.

One incident illustrates his methods. At the beginning of 1928, Zhou Enlai's protégé eliminated a couple who were informers for the Chinese police, He Jiaxing and He Jihua. While they were sleeping peacefully in their beds, Gu Shunzhang and several of his men got into their house and riddled them with bullets where they lay. To cover the noise of gunfire, one of them set off some fire-crackers outside. Their crime accomplished, Gu and his comrades calmly left the scene, leaving behind the bodies of the two ex-communists.

Although, like Zhou Enlai, Kang Sheng considered these procedures indispensable, he did not greatly appreciate them. Besides, he did not get on well with Gu Shunzhang, who was too crude and brutal for his taste: a born killer of undeniable skills, but with dubious political motives. And perhaps a future rival.

Unlike Gu, Kang Sheng chose to operate with subtlety. Under Zhou Enlai's orders, he continued to deal with 'matters of organisation' and clandestine unions, working in tandem with Li Weihan on the former and Liu Xiao on the latter. But Kang Sheng did not restrict himself, as before, to ensuring the security and protection of the Party's secret places and the running of clandestine meetings. Experience had already taught him that in order to survive it was important to make himself indispensable, to 'rely on his own strength'. So he set up a small spy network of his own, recruiting agents among fellow natives of Shandong. Although, as a good communist, he advocated the overthrow of traditional hierarchies and long-established customs, he nevertheless recognised the great weight they carried: in this vast country, family ties and regional allegiances played a major role in the system of social relations.

In order to get about incognito – he had a price on his head – Kang Sheng lighted upon an original solution. Being thin, he was easily able to pass himself off as a rickshaw runner. The 'jinrickshaws' of Shanghai, whose work was extremely hard and conditions of existence wretched, did not have much chance to get fat. They were all as thin as rakes and were not expected to last more than six years in the job. There were two thousand of these poor wretches running the streets of Shanghai for the convenience or pleasure of their clients, and among them one of the most important communist leaders in the city.

Whenever he ran through the Western Concessions under cover of this strange disguise, Kang Sheng was revenged for the insults he had to bear, and the weariness of the day was lifted from him as he rejoiced internally. For the rickshaw was an Anglo-French creation, invented by an Anglican pastor, the Reverend Bailey, and a Frenchman, Ménard. Now their invention served as a *laisser passer* to one of the worst enemies of the Western imperialists.

A clandestine life is hard on the nerves. Although tuberculosis at one point forced him to take several months' rest in his native province, Kang Sheng daily succumbed a little more to a vice he would never be able to give up: tobacco. He chain-smoked as an antidote to an existence that consisted of great physical exertion, permanent insecurity, underground meetings and ruthless factional infighting. Unlike their Bolshevik mentors, who did not start tearing each other to pieces until after they came to power, the Chinese communist leaders were already at each other's throats. In order to get rid of anyone standing in their way, they would not hesitate to accuse him, without a shred of evidence, of being an informer for the Guomindang. The rise of Stalinism in the Comintern and in the USSR only aggravated this legacy of traditional Chinese society.

Discreet but terribly efficient, Kang Sheng did not escape calumny. Since he could not be attacked on the issue of his loyalty to the Party, which was incontestable, those who wished him ill suggested that he did not keep very good company – his friend and Shandong compatriot Li Puhai, for instance, who, having been captured by the police in Beijing, denounced several comrades in order to save his own skin.

Indifferent to the quarrelling, unless he was putting on a very good act, Kang Sheng just lit up yet another cigarette. Behind those glasses that gave him an intellectual air, he would smile mysteriously and think of the strange French proverb he had one day happened to overhear: 'The dogs bark but the caravan passes.'

For a communist, what more grandiose a caravan, in that year of 1928, than that of the Revolution on the march?

> Arise, proletarians/Leave the machines,
> Strike a blow and march/Line up for battle!

It was like a pilgrimage, a return to where it all began. In July 1928 revolutionaries from all over the world converged on Moscow, their hearts full of hope. The Comintern was summoning its children to the Soviet capital, where the great red flame had been lit eleven years previously, for its Sixth Congress. It was time to take the offensive. Everywhere – in the countries of old Europe, in Latin America, in Asia – the revolutionary mole was emerging from the soil before the terrified gaze of the capitalists and their despicable lackeys.

Joseph Stalin and Nikolai Bukharin, the grand organisers of the ceremony, had completely different things on their minds than naive idealism – especially Stalin, who hoped to be pulling the strings at this Communist International high mass. In association with Bukharin, he had managed to get his rival Trotsky exiled to Alma-Ata. Together, they had removed the inseparable pair Zinoviev and Kamenev. But their alliance, they knew, would not last very long.

It was in this portentous context that the Chinese CP came to Moscow for its Sixth Congress. Proof of the Party's weakness was the fact that, for the first time, it was taking place in exile. Contrary to legend, the delegates – seventy-five militants from each region of China – did not meet in the Soviet capital but in a convalescence home near by.

A convalescence home for a very sick party – Stalin did not lack a sense of irony. Especially as it was no ordinary rest home: it belonged to the OGPU and usually served as a holiday place for tired heroes of the secret services. As was to be expected, the Soviet hosts had wired up the Chinese's assembly rooms, if not their bedrooms, with microphones. For Stalin, who was partly responsible for the errors committed on the Soviet side during the abortive uprising in Shanghai, was not keen on any over-bold delegate asking embarrassing questions with impunity. As far as he was concerned, the Sixth Congress provided the opportunity to settle the thorny problem of the 'Chinese question' once and for all.

Chinese meetings always take place against an extraordinary din. No one waits their turn to speak. There is constant muttering and interruption. The OGPU eavesdroppers must have been very surprised. But the main thing was that the compromise settled upon in advance by Stalin and Bukharin should go through unopposed.

Naturally, that is what happened. It was decided to support the alternative Wuhan government against Chiang Kai-shek, to call a halt to all the wildcat uprisings, to win back the confidence of the masses and to pay more attention to the development of rural communism – this being Bukharin's hobby-horse, which in the event turned out to be perfectly justified. It was this Bolshevik theoretician and not Mao Zedong who first put forward the hypothesis of an encirclement of the economically advanced countries by those of the Third World.

Stalin, who, true to character, wanted a strengthening of the Chinese CP apparatus, was also given satisfaction. It was formally decided to create a secret service, the *Tewu*, for which the Soviets would train the best recruits in intelligence work.

Finally, a new Politburo line-up was appointed: a figurehead general secretary, three of Bukharin's men and three of Stalin's – not to mention the ex-gangster Gu Shunzhang, who was elected *in absentia*, having been kept in Shanghai by his 'special work'. Zhou Enlai remained in charge of the Military Department and the running of the *Tewu*. But Stalin was counting on Li Lisan, who had organised the strikes of May–June 1925 in Shanghai, to carry through the restructuring of the communist apparatus.

Kang Sheng did not take part in the Moscow Congress, but he came out of it well: after some debate, his name was added to the list of members of the new Central Committee. When Li Lisan returned to

China, bursting with self-importance, Kang Sheng immediately realised that Li was to be the new boss and that, for the time being at least, it would be wise to fall in under his banner.

Dynamic but unmethodical, courageous but swollen with vanity, intelligent but sectarian, Li Lisan had a strong tendency to treat his political adversaries like hotheads who must be made to toe the line. He was convinced he was the 'Chinese Lenin', but had absolutely none of the qualities of his Russian model. At the age of twenty-nine, his future looked rosy and he was raring to confront the extraordinary destiny that he thought lay in store for him.

He immediately tried to remove his potential rivals and to 'Bolshevise' the Party to excess, to turn it into an ultra-centralised, ultra-disciplined, ultra-hierarchical, ultra-militarised instrument. Completely lacking in any subtlety, these notions provoked a predictably violent reaction.

'Li Lisan hasn't got his feet on the ground. His policy, if followed, would only end up by cutting the Party off from the masses! It's out of the question . . .' In substance, this is the heretical language that Xu Xigen used. He was expressing the opposition of union leaders to the line adopted by the Sixth Congress, as revised and corrected by the new Party chief. Born in 1903, he had embraced communism in 1925 and occupied the post of secretary of the Shanghai section. He was well known for his plain speaking.

Though by this time Kang Sheng was engaged in 'special operations', he had not yet completely left behind him his past work as a leader in the labour section. To everyone's surprise, he threw his good intentions to the wind and aligned himself with Xu Xigen and the Party's Provincial Committee.

The confrontation began to gather pace in November 1928. Xu Xigen led the Provincial Committee in a public censure of the measures for reorganisation imposed by Li Lisan. A letter was addressed to the Politburo in the name of the militants of Shanghai, that bastion of the Party. 'The implementation of new ideas will only serve to turn the workers against communism for good,' it said.

Li Lisan took it all very badly. It was inconceivable that anyone should try to give him lessons in politics. In the name of Comintern discipline and Party spirit, he increased his pressure on the Provincial Committee. More discreetly, he attempted to turn Xu Xigen's main supporters against him, promising to pardon him if they toed the line – his line.

Kang Sheng was among those who declared publicly in February 1929 that Li Lisan was after all right and that Xu Xigen was in grave error. His friends in the Xu Xigen camp were deeply shocked by this volte-face and bitterly reproached him for abandoning them. Very few understood his real motives. By siding with the strongest, and eating humble pie, Kang Sheng was only observing the motto of all great secret service chiefs the world over: first and foremost, survive.

His long career would be marked by a hundred more 'betrayals', a hundred more changes of direction, a thousand complete turn-arounds.

'A clever bird chooses the tree in which to perch': a skilful man chooses his master carefully. In order to avoid jeopardising his future, Kang Sheng reluctantly resigned himself to following what communists would later call the Li Lisan line. Like his comrades, Kang Sheng then almost immediately turned his attentions to his own concerns, to 'special operations'.

The junk sculled away from the quayside. It was only when it had reached the middle of the Huangpu that the crew hoisted the sails, sewn on to bamboo laths. The vessel then headed for the open sea, giving way to heavy-tonnage steamers and countless sailing ships.

Once out at sea, far from prying eyes, there was a sudden transformation. This was not some innocuous trading boat. These were no ordinary seamen. The crew revealed themselves for what they were: shock militants of the Chinese Communist Party. On the bridge of the junk, they set up bamboo targets and got their weapons – large-bore automatic pistols – out of the hold. Gu Shunzhang then distributed the ammunition and conducted the shooting session.

Gu struck upon this somewhat unorthodox method of training as a way of allowing the *Tewu* assassins – the 'Red Guard' specialists – to learn how to use their weapons out of the hearing of inquisitive eavesdroppers and away from a city entirely under the control of enemies, be they Guomindang or Westerners. The men would practise for hours on end, then throw the spent cartridges into the sea, only returning to port after nightfall. Without exchanging a word, they would then head back for their separate hideouts. Gu Shunzhang and two of his men would collect the pistols for safe-keeping. Gu was never short of ideas. So that the Red Guard – a killer élite of about twenty hand-picked men – could get even better practice, he also came up with the idea of taking advantage of traditional Chinese festivals. These provided a golden opportunity: with all the shouting and the noise of firecrackers, who would hear the firing of an automatic pistol?

It was at the end of 1927 that Gu had recruited the first members of his 'special team'. Almost immediately, he suffered his first setback: the arrest of his assistant for the southern area of the city, Li Kesang. But this had not quelled his spirits. Thereafter, Gu selected his killers from the Surveillance Groups, responsible for protecting the distribution of tracts and Party posters. The Political Branch of the police in the French Concession, run by Étienne Fiori, maintained that these 'volunteers' were hired assassins handsomely paid out of the funds of a Comintern subsidiary, International Red Aid.

Determined and utterly without scruple, Gu Shunzhang had won over Li Lisan. By now more and more convinced of his national destiny, Li would not tolerate any criticism from his comrades. He was 'Bolshevising' the Party in his own way, imposing his authority by any means available, including the physical liquidation by the Red Guard of rank and file opponents. With senior members, he preferred to get rid of them by putting them in charge of particularly exposed sections. Chiang Kai-shek's secret police could then deal with them.

Li Lisan's methods were not particularly fraternal, but in a country where the Guomindang maintained a climate of manic anti-communist terror, they were extremely effective. As in the USSR, where Stalin was imposing himself, the dictatorship of a single man was gradually taking hold in the Chinese communist movement. As ever, Zhou Enlai kept his counsel, while Mao Zedong, the undisputed leader in his rural base of Jiangxi, preferred to keep out of factional quarrels. However, the increasing authoritarianism of Li Lisan was undermining the Chinese Communist Party. The least dispute between individuals would degenerate into a full-blown affair of state: a dangerous paranoia was contaminating even the most level-headed militants.

So it was in Tientsin, in May 1929. A leader called Wang Qaowen was firmly opposed to the majority on the Provincial Committee. Convinced that this was purely and simply an enemy ploy, his own comrades decided to do away with their opponent. Without the slightest scruple, they cabled Shanghai: 'Please send to Tientsin at once special agents assigned to eliminate rebels . . .' They could not have expressed themselves more clearly: the Provincial Committee was asking for assassins! As soon as Gu Shunzhang received this call for murder, he sent two killers to Tientsin. On 1 June, the *Tewu* men opened fire on an opposition meeting. Wang Qaowen and one of his friends were killed in the attack.

'Once on the back of the tiger, it is difficult to get off,' says the proverb. The two killers sent by Gu Shunzhang were arrested by the Chinese police and, in an attempt to save themselves from their predicament, they betrayed their comrades. Twenty-three communist cadres, including those who had asked for the murderers, were in turn arrested. Large numbers of CP files were seized: both account books and reports on meetings about propaganda, the press, pamphlets and military organisation. Worse still, the police found the record book detailing movements of liaison agents and a register of the dispatch and receipt of correspondence for the whole province. The investigators learned a great deal from a close reading of these highly confidential documents – notably, that the Chinese Communist Party was already suffering from a surfeit of paperwork.

As this incident well illustrates, the settling of scores between majority and opposition communists was playing straight into the hands of their adversaries. The police in the International Concessions rubbed their hands in glee. In April 1928, Sikh agents working for Patrick Givens captured Luo Yinong in Gordon Road. This was a prize catch: in the summer of 1927, Luo, together with Evgeni

Kojenikov, alias Comrade Pik, had planned an attempt on Chiang Kai-shek's life, called off at the last minute by Borodin. Since then, as a member of the Central Committee, he had been responsible for various counter-espionage operations. The Guomindang, on hearing of his seizure, began clamouring for him to be handed over to them.

'The leader has been caught! The communist scourge will soon disappear,' ran the newspaper headlines. A French publication, the *Journal de Shanghai*, announced that the Chinese had paid a reward of one thousand dollars to the English Settlement police for their captive – and no one seemed to find this shocking. In exchange, the poor wretch was handed over by Givens to the Guomindang torturers, who, after having thoroughly worked him over, shot him.

As for the French, they had laid hands on a close collaborator of Kang Sheng, Liu Xiao. Taken in by his false identity, however, they let him go. No sooner had he been released than he fell into the clutches of the British police, in the shape of the inevitable Givens. In the Ward Road prison, Kang Sheng's friend stoically endured torture, but did not talk, thereby probably saving the life of his boss. Kang Sheng vowed him eternal gratitude for his courage.

Despite this run of bad luck, the underground communists continued to consider the Concession zones less dangerous than the Chinese town or the suburbs, ruled by the close alliance of Mr Du's Green Gang and Chiang Kai-shek's police – the latter, in fact, being run by two longstanding members of the Green Gang, the Chen brothers. Each as ruthless as the other, Chen Guofu and his younger brother, Chen Lifu, had a lot to live up to: they were the nephews of Chen Qimei, Chiang Kai-shek's mentor in the Green Gang, who had been assassinated in 1916. After that, Chiang had made Chen's nephews his own adoptive sons and trusted aides.

On 20 March 1928, Chen Lifu became head of the Guomindang's Organisation Department: in other words, Kang Sheng's opposite number on the nationalist side. Without delay, he set up a political espionage body, the *Diaocha Tongzhi*, or Central Bureau of Investigation and Statistics of the Central Executive Committee, a very special service indeed, more concerned with investigation than statistics. Like a gigantic octopus in the service of the Guomindang, the tentacles of the Central Bureau reached everywhere: into elementary schools, secondary schools, universities, cultural bodies, newspaper offices, banks, even the civil service. Chen Lifu and the nationalist leaders had not forgotten the counsel so freely given by the Soviet advisers during the 'honeymoon' period of 1923–7. They had been happy to adapt Soviet methods of totalitarian training to the Chinese mental outlook.

Chiang Kai-shek's protégé was no mere thug, though. Like his adversaries Zhou Enlai and Kang Sheng, he was an intellectual who had done well at Shanghai University and had then gone on to study at the University of Pittsburgh in the United States. As soon as he returned to China in 1925, he had put himself at the disposal of the nationalist leader, and was appointed his private secretary. Ever since then he had kept up numerous contacts with the Chinese abroad and employed in his Central Bureau a fair number of his compatriots who had returned from exile. In exchange, they pledged their loyalty to Chen Lifu, on the heads of their own families. These were no empty words: the Central Bureau chief, as a member of the Green Gang, had many overseas contacts and no one was beyond the reach of his vengeance. Otherwise, he was an affable fellow, married to an artist, who prided himself on his knowledge of poetry and Taoist philosophy.

'Tall, thin, pale, with long, already greying hair brushed back' was how he was described twelve years later by an emissary of the Free French movement, Pierre Laurin, as he sat installed in his room which resembled a monk's cell more than a virtual ministerial office. At the end of the 1920s he was already a key personality in the Guomindang, and an outstanding exception in a nationalist movement steeped in corruption. Chen Lifu was not actually interested in money; he was driven by his ideas. He was a 'reactionary monk' fanatically dedicated to a cruel, fierce anti-communism. The Europeans in the Concessions hardly knew him – he lived mostly in Nanking, Chiang's capital – and they did not like him. Too much a law unto himself, Chen did not fit into their framework of understanding.

Chen had adopted the Russian concept of an omnipresent secret service capable of sounding hearts and minds like some pitiless god. But to this he added a typically Chinese dimension: the use of psychological manipulation. Like his communist enemies, he did not distinguish between intelligence gathering and working on his adversaries' minds. In his eyes, it was not simply a matter of stopping the Reds or even of killing them. They had to be broken morally and be made to admit, through the application of a subtle balance of force and persuasion, the superiority of Sun Yat-sen's 'Three Principles of the People' over Marxist ways of thinking. The more resolute preferred death. The rest, who were numerous, humbly made their 'submissions' to the Guomindang and grassed on their former comrades in order to win pardon for their past errors. Better still, some were 'turned' and made to hunt down their erstwhile friends like dogs, with all the faith and ferocity of the newly converted.

Gradually the sickly sweet opium of betrayal would spread throughout the Communist Party, which was already reeling from the violence of its internal battles and the summary logic of Li Lisan. No one would trust anyone else. Everyone would live in doubt and anxiety. The enemy would be destroyed, as it were, from within.

Who could be a proper match against this formidable opponent? A man of action like Gu Shunzhang? Intellectuals like Zhou Enlai or the guileful Kang Sheng, who had broken with the intricacies of Chinese philosophy? The question was of concern not only to the Chinese communists, but also to Moscow's secret services.

*   *   *

It was the Year of the Snake.

On 10 January 1930, a strange-looking man, dressed in a new but already crumpled suit, set foot for the first time in his life on Chinese soil. It was cold that day, exceptionally cold. In Shanghai the thermometer registered less than seven degrees Celsius, the lowest temperature recorded in the city since 1893.

The stranger came from far away: Berlin via Paris. His companion had joined him in Marseilles, where they had both boarded a Japanese steamer bound for Asia. Two days before reaching Shanghai they were still in Hong Kong, where they crossed paths with another subversive, Nguyen Ai Quoc – a borrowed name, of course, for a Vietnamese communist who was trying to bring together a few revolutionaries from his own country in the slums of Kowloon, the Chinese town in the British colony, and who would one day bear a much more famous name: Ho Chi Minh.

Like the Comintern Vietnamese agitator, the stranger well deserved the title of 'professional revolutionary'. He was tall, well built and handsome, despite a scarred face that bespoke past fights and ordeals. He was very attractive to women and, his unexpected changes of mood notwithstanding, men liked him too. Richard Sorge had joined the German Communist Party the moment it was founded, in 1919. Having survived the difficulties of the early days, this élite militant had been admitted to the heart of the *Otdyel Mezhdunarodnoi Sviazi*, the OMS, the Comintern's International Liaison Section. Now entrusted with a special mission to China by the Red Army head of intelligence, the Latvian General Jan Karlovich Berzin, Sorge and his companion, Vassili Borovich, had come to Shanghai to set up an espionage network independent of the one run by the Russian diplomats from the consulate in Huangpu Road – and more efficient, too.

After the bloody failure of 1927, the Soviets had restructured their spy network in China from top to bottom. Having learned from the unfortunate experience of the suborning of their Comrade Pik by British Intelligence Service agents, operating under cover of what was supposedly a municipal body in the Settlement, the Russians had resigned themselves to giving absolute priority to counter-espionage. A new face appeared in Shanghai: that of Zaprudsky. He was responsible for the surveillance of Soviet nationals in the city. Using the services of the press agency Tass – a traditional cover for the OGPU – when necessary, he was supposed to infiltrate the police in the Western Concessions to find out what their plans were.

'The lodging house run by our friend Tarassov at 15 Tsongchow Road has been identified by Givens' agents,' he trumpeted as soon as he started the job, proud of his efficiency as the harbinger of bad news: Mrs Tarassov belonged to a network of former White Russians who had been 'turned' by the Soviets. But, as it turned out, the fact that she had been identified did not put an end to the activities of this group, later to be joined by several colourful characters, among them, the dancer Volsky, Lantzov (who was charged with infiltrating artistic circles in Shanghai), Madame Bulgasky-Belsky, wife of a senior officer in the Red Army, and of course the exuberant Hungarian woman Bambero, alias Wambeira, married to an Argentine revolutionary and an expert in modern dance and arms dealing.

Counter-espionage was essential, if only to avoid any 'unfortunate mistakes'. During the Canton uprising, organised by the Comintern and turned into a bloodbath by the Guomindang, the USSR vice-consul, Abram Ivanovich Hassis, and five other Soviet diplomats were gunned down in the street by Chiang's soldiers. To make sure that this kind of bloody incident did not happen again, it was decided that the consular premises in Huangpu Road would never again be used to shelter espionage activities or secret contacts with the Chinese communists. In Shanghai there were other less compromising possibilities – the Soviet Merchant Navy branch office, for instance, whose director, Rotfield, was in fact a member of the OGPU. His apartment at 71 Range Road had already been the venue for more than one clandestine meeting and without any hesitation he agreed to the plan. In January 1928, a Soviet agent from the economic department, Delbich, replaced Zaprudsky at the head of the OGPU counter-espionage section. Delbich lived at 29 Medhurst Road, right in the heart of the International Settlement. His best agents were Gapanovich, who specialised in British affairs, Chaparov and Lipov. Worried about this superactivity, Patrick Givens' men put a tap on their telephones.

The deputy director of the local office of Chinese Eastern Railways, Gorbatiouk, also lived within the International Concession, at 6 Carter Road. He was an astonishing fellow who claimed to have been in command, in 1924, of a Red Army brigade, no less. Since the end of 1927 he had actually been in charge of the GRU in Shanghai. He had one real obsession: he relied less on agents of Soviet nationality and more on 'comrade spies' from Eastern Europe – Poles, Czechs or Latvians – who, if they were exposed, would not compromise the USSR. General Gorbatiouk went about setting up his own network, quite separate from that of the OGPU. He was chiefly interested in the activities of foreign armies and of arms dealers, of whom there were a great many in Shanghai.

Gorbatiouk also happened to appreciate the true value of feminine charm – its value as something to be traded. At the end of 1928, he moved into the very busy shopping street of Avenue Joffre, in the heart of the French Concession, where the police began to notice his numerous meetings with the seductive Natalia Valouev, a very unconstrained young woman who assiduously frequented foreign military personnel passing through Shanghai. Natalia was not the only woman in Gorbatiouk's network. Madame Missandrov, alias Zuesman, and Ronia Liberman also took their orders from him. Ronia, a charming scatterbrain, would invite dashing British and American officers to visit her apartment at 135 Route Grouchy, which just happened to be rented in the name of an employee of the Chinese Eastern Railways.

No one is perfect, however, and the head of the Shanghai OGPU was suddenly accused of two sins. One was venial: the misappropriation of funds. The other was tantamount to mortal at the end of the 1920s: a strong tendency towards Trotskyism. Gorbatiouk defended himself tooth and nail against the accusation, but the verdict had already been decided. After a certain amount of confusion, he was recalled to the USSR, never to be seen again in Shanghai.

The lifeblood of war continued to flow, with Soviet funds passing through a new front, the Metropolitan Trading Company. (This import–export business could guarantee discretion: it had been set up by a former colleague of Borodin's, the German Arthur Schmidt.) However, attached to the funds that reached Shanghai came stricter and stricter orders. Stalin was now absolute master in the Kremlin, having got rid of his last serious rival, Nikolai Bukharin, and was on the offensive against 'traitors', 'social fascists' and 'renegades' everywhere. In short: against everything that was not Stalinist.

Now completely under his control, the new Comintern decreed a one-day general strike for 1 August 1929. To have gone back on this would have been to invite an accusation of cowardice. At the beginning of July, a meeting took place at 30 Wankashan Gardens, the home of Babintsev, an unofficial representative of the Comintern. There, two GRU officers, Mosse and Stroyanov, showered 'advice' on the leaders of the Chinese Communist Youth League: 'The trial of strength is at hand! The Chinese Party must reactivate its combat groups as a matter of urgency. The GRU and the Comintern's military apparatus will provide new instructors . . .'

It was decided that the fateful 1 August would be a great 'Red Day'. The local organisers of the CP would lead the way, while the two satellite movements, the League of Oriental Peoples and the Pan-Chinese Federation of Labour, would follow on, drawing in the masses. It all looked very good on paper. But in China there are always hundreds of middle men. The two hundred Mauser pistols destined for the shock groups simply vanished somewhere along the way, while the strikes attracted little support and the street demonstrations were insignificant. In short, Shanghai's great 'Red Day' turned out to be only vaguely tinted pink.

Moscow was losing patience. The OGPU chiefs decided that the secret services had to be 'sinicised' to make them efficient, so at the end of August a Soviet agent called Neptusky escorted to Shanghai three Chinese spies, trained, like the ex-gangster Gu Shunzhang, in Vladivostok. Was it sheer coincidence that they all happened to come from Shandong, Kang Sheng's native province?

As for the legendary boss of the GRU, Jan Berzin, he decided to professionalise his Chinese networks, and immediately thought of his German agent Richard Sorge. Another agent in the Red Army secret service, Haan, was instructed to prepare the ground for Comrade Sorge. His mission accomplished a few days before the arrival of Sorge, Haan returned to the USSR and, so that there should be no danger of anyone giving the game away, a rumour was put about that he had fallen out of favour.

Sorge now set about the business of building up a Shanghai network. His agents were all out of the ordinary: Ozaki Hozumi, a Japanese journalist; Ursula Hamburger, alias Sonia, a German adventuress who played a key role in several major GRU operations in China, and then in Switzerland during the Second World War; 'Mr Wang', who, it can now be revealed, was in fact Chen Geng, one of the best military experts in the Chinese CP, known and appreciated even in the ranks of the Guomindang for having saved the life of General Chiang Kai-shek during the Northern Expedition.

Another Chinese who was very actively associated with the German from the OGPU went by the pseudonym of Chung. Although there is no concrete proof, there are grounds for wondering whether Chung's real name was not in fact Kang Sheng. The description later given of him by Sorge, when the latter fell into the hands of the Japanese security services, would seem to corroborate this identification. For the young communist from Shandong, who had become a formidable 'professional revolutionary' after a five-year struggle in the shadows, 1930 was in any case to prove extremely eventful.

The 'White Terror' reigned in Shanghai, shrouding the city in a cloak of fear. Chen Lifu, the brains behind Chiang's secret police, cast his net wide in the Chinese part of town and the working-class suburbs, and even into the heart of the Concessions. His catches were prodigious: every day, communist militants fell into the hands of the 'reactionary monk'. Expertly tortured and subjected to clever psychological manipulation, many agreed to tender their 'submission' to their captor, betraying their closest comrades to the Central Bureau. Then, having turned traitor in order to save their lives and those of their families, they became targets for the Brownings of the Red Guard crack assassins. They were left with no option but to sink deeper into treachery and join the ranks of the Guomindang.

This drain on manpower gave Kang Sheng additional responsibilities. He became executive secretary of the Central Committee's Organisation Department. His was a gruelling task: on him and him alone rested the security of the Party leaders, who themselves were often prostrated by the extent of the repression. It was up to Kang to confront the subtle and perverse manoeuvres of Chen Lifu – a challenge he took up.

Kang issued draconian orders to Party cadres, imposing a ban on leaving their hideouts during the day, the setting-up of a network of ultra-clandestine liaison agents, a restriction on meetings to an absolute minimum, a withdrawal into the International Concessions. He himself did not set a very good example, going out all the time, running around all over the place, from one secret contact to another.

But he had a very good cover. Through some fellow natives of Shandong – yet again – the impassive Kang had now become a ticket-seller for the British Tramways Company. Under this guise, he could circulate fairly freely by day in the streets of the Settlement. At night, he would return to the French Concession, where his 'safe houses' were located. He organised nocturnal meetings for the Party leaders, and never slept in the same place two nights running.

The head of the Organisation Department a ticket-seller! Perhaps he thought of that bombastic poem written in 1928, in exile in Japan, by the communist writer Guo Moro, under the deadly dull social-realist title 'The tramways have returned to work'. Perhaps Kang was most worried about the rise to power within the underground organisation of his rival Gu Shunzhang.

Gu ruled over the thugs and assassins of the *Tewu* with rather perverse pleasure. The fear that gripped the other Party leaders, holed up in their safe houses by Kang Sheng, seemed to lend him wings. What could be more exciting to this arrogant and violent man, who made no secret of his contempt for 'bureaucrats', than this deadly game of hide-and-seek with the Guomindang police? What could be more exhilarating than pitting himself against his former friends in the Green Gang at the risk of his own life? A veritable Frégoli of communist espionage, he drew with the greatest facility on an incredible range of disguises: sometimes a pedlar, sometimes a policeman, an actor or magician, he could become unrecognisable.

It was at the High Society, that paradise of gaming, entertainment, prostitution, of perversions of every kind, that Gu liked to arrange meetings relating to his work. In the innocuous guise of a ticket-seller out for a good time, Kang Sheng would sometimes slip into this den of the Shanghai criminal underworld in order to hand over to him the names of traitors to be executed.

Kang Sheng, on the other hand, was also anxious to concentrate on properly political tasks. With no very clear mandate from the Central Committee – but does not necessity create its own laws? – he had assumed responsibility for relations with the Party's 'communist brothers' among the Korean, Vietnamese and Japanese communities in Shanghai. Korean and Japanese revolutionaries had some difficulties in getting along together, as their respective countries had been at war with each other since the beginning of the century, when Japanese troops had invaded Korea and raised the Mikado's flag over it. Since then, in 1919, a Korean government in exile had been established in the International Settlement, which was supported by the communists and their Chinese 'big brothers'.

Kang Sheng did not underestimate the strength of the Korean CP in Shanghai, which was in contact with the Comintern through a Hungarian in the city, Franz Szekely, alias Comrade Sekel. The Korean communists supported other groups: the League of Partisans of Korean Independence, the Union of the Korean Youth of China, the Young Korean Girls' Club. And, an obvious sign of their excellent organisation, they had their own OGPU run with an iron fist by Comrade Kim Miang-wei.

Since the involvement of several of their leaders in the plot against Chiang Kai-shek that had been called off by Borodin in 1927, the Japanese communists in Shanghai had strengthened their organisation: in August 1928, Tamari, one of their agents responsible for liaising with the Vietnamese revolutionaries, had organised several secret meetings; in November 1929, three militants from the Nippon archipelago, Murata, Ushida and Taiseido, had met the USSR 'unofficial consul' Rotfield; and a Japanese OGPU agent, Miama had had several meetings with Franz Szekely, the Comintern's contact with the Koreans.

In Shanghai the Japanese militants had to be especially cautious. Their country's leaders kept a close eye on this great Chinese port, which they dreamed of annexing. Consequently, their secret services were there in force. They had no less than four separate organisations: Major-General Sato's military intelligence service, whose presence at 637 Dixwell Road was scarcely concealed; the Governor-General of Korea's intelligence service, located in the same street in the Settlement and run by the honourable Mr Ono; the secret bureaux of Manchurian Railways and of the Ministry of the Interior, which were actually based on the premises of the local Japanese consulate, under the firm rule of the very energetic Mr Okagi.

For the Vietnamese revolutionaries, Shanghai, together with the British Crown Colony of Hong Kong, was more or less a necessary base. In Shanghai, Nguyen Ai Quoc, the future Ho Chi Minh, retrieved the anti-imperialist propaganda pamphlets printed in France by the 'Colonial Section' of the French CP, and which communist seamen such as Paul Cermolacce brought secretly into China on board merchant ships.

Kang Sheng intended to impose Chinese supremacy over this group of Asian communists crowded into Shanghai, and to make his party a real 'head of the family'. On the threshold of the 1930s the leaders of the Chinese CP did not know what they know today: that ideology is often less important than the most elementary geographical facts. Not one of them, however intelligent, could have suspected at the time that their natural inclination to assume revolutionary leadership in the Far East contained the seed of an amazing historical change of direction: the rupture between Beijing and Moscow. They all shared a deep faith in the historic destiny of the Comintern, and a boundless admiration for the supreme leader of the Soviet people, Joseph Stalin, which overcame any doubts, questioning and protests of self-esteem in the face of Russian agents' transgressions or ineptitude.

Nothing, absolutely nothing, suggests that Kang Sheng was any exception to this rule. But, immersed as he was in nurturing relations with the Chinese communists' Asian 'brothers', perhaps he sensed unconsciously the contradiction between the Soviet alliance and the future development of China. However, life underground in Shanghai did not allow him much time to ponder on international political issues.

Then the newly appointed secretary of the Chinese Communist Party Organisation Department fell into the hands of his Guomindang enemies. Through carelessness? Or because he was betrayed? To this day it remains impossible to decide, owing to a lack of detailed information on the exact circumstances of his arrest. All that is known is that it occurred during the early months of the year, and that it is now clearly a great source of embarrassment to the nationalist Chinese of Taiwan, who hate any allusion being made to it, but also to the communists, who remain very close-lipped about it too. It is as though Kang Sheng's capture concealed facts that are as uncomfortable to one party as to the other.

And so the mystery remains. There is no doubt that it strengthens the case of those who believe that the two-way embarrassment is explained by the inadmissible role of liaison officer between the Guomindang and the Chinese CP played by Kang Sheng at that time, but unfortunately there is no decisive proof of this. A mystery? Two mysteries, in fact. For equally little is known of the precise conditions under which Kang Sheng was simply set free.

Who in 1930, in the midst of a struggle of the most incredible bitterness between communists and nationalists, could have rendered such a service to a key figure in the enemy's secret service? Evidently it must have been someone of equal importance: a pillar of the Guomindang called Ding Weifeng. A companion of Dr Sun Yat-sen in the very early days, he, like Kang Sheng, was from Shandong. Although now in Nanking, where he held the office of head of the Guomindang's Central Political School, he had maintained numerous links with his native province. Born into a family of intellectuals and public officials, Ding at the age of fifty-five was a predominant figure on the Central Executive Committee of the Guomindang. He delegated a great many of his responsibilities as director of the Political School to his deputy, Ku Chen Kang, formerly a student in Soviet Russia who, today ensconced in Taiwan, belongs to the most extremist faction of the Guomindang and is honorary president of an organisation as mysterious as it is controversial: the World Anti-Communist League. He too prefers to remain silent on the precise activities of his boss at that time.

The fact is that Ding Weifeng exerted his influence, which was considerable, to obtain Kang Sheng's release. Simply through solidarity with a fellow native of Shandong? Certainly not. It seems that his own nephew was arrested at the same time as Kang Sheng, for he too was a communist cadre. But the least that one can say is that this explanation is not in itself sufficient to account for the strange deal that must have been concluded to result in the freeing of the head of the communists' Organisation Department.

After this brief stay in the Guomindang prisons, whereas many others would have become *personae non gratae* and suspected of now working for the nationalist Chen Lifu and his secret police, Kang Sheng was not. In a party riven by internal strife, he immediately went back to work as though nothing had happened.

Among the Reds, the atmosphere was worse than ever. Despite directives for caution coming from Moscow, and the reservations of Mao Zedong and the leaders of the Party's rural bases, Li Lisan continued to press his *putsch*-ist strategy of insurrections, a stubborn pursuit of a 'left-wing' policy that even Stalin thought no longer appropriate, and which Zhou Enlai, on a liaison mission to Moscow, declared himself incapable of explaining.

As soon as he got back from the Soviet capital, Zhou Enlai gradually started to transfer his allegiance. The tone of his discussions with the 'Soviet comrades' had convinced this astute politician that Li Lisan's days were numbered, so, judging Li's cause to be hopeless, Zhou abandoned him. In the autumn, the so-called 'twenty-eight Bolsheviks' returned to China: they had all been students at the Sun Yat-sen University, set up in the USSR to train Chinese CP cadres. Their leader was just twenty-five years old. His name was Wang Ming and his arrogance knew no bounds. All Moscow's hopes were placed in this young intellectual who had received his whole training in Russia from the Ukrainian Pavel Mif, director of the Sun Yat-sen University and Stalin's favourite expert on Chinese affairs. Wang Ming was to take over from the uncontrollable Li Lisan as leader of the Party.

Then, in November 1930, Pavel Mif himself arrived secretly in Shanghai, to supervise personally the takeover by the new Moscow-designated leaders.

With actors and set now in place, the performance could begin – of a tragi-comedy that could well have been called *Comintern Parade*.

4
A Matter of Betrayal

Pavel Mif was an impatient man, one of those ideologues who light-heartedly dispatch others to the Gulag, not even realising that they themselves will one day end up in Siberia. This, however, is where he died, some time between 1937 and 1954.

Hardly had he arrived in Shanghai than he feverishly set about trying to get the Chinese CP to fall into line. Despite the optimistic view taken in Moscow, it was not an easy task: opposed to Li Lisan were not only the usual Comintern yes-men but also the leaders of the very rebellious 'working-class faction'. Led by Xu Xigen this lobby had already stood up to Li Lisan in his days of glory, Kang Sheng's last-minute turnaround notwithstanding. Now it rose from the ashes, like a phoenix with anarchistic ideas, to refuse any overly strict demand on allegiance. Its new leader, an intellectual with an impressive union track record, was none other than He Mengxiong.

Mif and his devoted 'twenty-eight Bolsheviks' decided that a plenum of the Party's Central Committee should be called without delay, and obligingly undertook to organise it, down to the smallest detail.

The secret meeting took place on 16 January 1931. There were two matters on the agenda: the winding-up of the ill-fated 'Li Lisan line' and the designation of new leaders. Summoned at the last minute for a 'routine meeting', the supporters of the working-class faction fell into a real trap: everything had been decided beforehand by Pavel Mif and his young protégé Wang Ming. For anyone who failed to understand that the Comintern's wishes were orders, the Party's strike force was at hand: *Tewu* henchmen, armed with pistols, under the command of their boss, Gu Shunzhang.

In these circumstances discussions could not go on for ever; in fact they lasted less than four hours. The die was already cast: Li Lisan was ousted, the working-class faction completely outmanoeuvred, and Wang Ming and his comrades installed in positions of command.

Kang Sheng did not so much as open his mouth during this veritable *putsch*, and was rewarded for his silence with a new appointment: he was named director-in-chief of the Organisation Department, with a secretary, Kong Yuan, to assist him. Better still: not without some satisfaction, he saw his rival Gu Shunzhang removed from both the Central Committee and the Politburo. Despite the fact that Gu had agreed to terrorise the plenum, Pavel Mif could not forgive him his former links with Li Lisan. The extremely arrogant head of the Red Guard took it very badly, but he had to bow to it.

He Mengxiong and his friends in the working-class faction were bolder and actually raised the flag of revolt, recklessly calling for a Party congress to be held immediately and for Pavel Mif to be recalled to Moscow. The very next day, about twenty of these dissidents, led by He Mengxiong, met in a reception room in the Eastern Hotel, fully determined to set up their own central committee. Hardly had they begun their discussions than a whistle sounded and suddenly armed Chinese police, flanked by some of Chen Lifu's agents and a few thugs from the Green Gang, came bursting into the room. Not a single member of the working-class faction escaped this providential round-up, which, it was quickly rumoured, owed a great deal to a calculated indiscretion on the part of Wang Ming that had been opportunely picked up by Mr Du's allies.

The amputation having been accomplished with very Stalin-like energy, it was important to prevent it giving rise to a gangrene fatal to the Party. On 20 January, one of the foremost communist leaders, Zhang Guotao, arrived in Shanghai from the USSR and in all innocence checked into the Eastern Hotel. He was quickly recovered, then taken to one of the Organisation Department's 'safe houses'. It was here that he learned from Kang Sheng himself, and from his secretary Kong Yuan, of the arrest of the dissidents. The two men seemed very distressed by the tragedy that had taken place at the Eastern Hotel and extremely worried about the terrible danger to which it exposed the Party apparatus.

Completely in his element, Pavel Mif was scornful of these 'petty-bourgeois' fears. He immediately made the most of his advantage. At the end of January the new leadership sent Kang Sheng round the cells in the western quarters of the city to root out any partisans of the working-class faction that might be lurking there.

In February the new man of power in the CP, Wang Ming, learned two important things. The first did not greatly affect him – which was the execution of the leaders of the working-class faction. The second irked him enormously: under the leadership of the former General Secretary of the Party, Chen Duxiu, the Chinese Trotskyists, who were not very numerous and dispersed in many chapels, had decided to embark on a process of unification.

'Will there never be an end to this permanent tendency towards indiscipline and this taste for dissidence!' he thought.

Difficult days lay ahead for the Party of which he had finally just taken control.

'Ladies and gentlemen, a big hand, please, for the great Oriental magician Hua Guangzi . . .'

The Year of the Horse had succeeded the Year of the Snake. The winter of 1930–1 was milder than that which had greeted the GRU agent Richard Sorge on his arrival in Shanghai the year before. On the terraces of the big department store on Nanking Road, the Sincere Company, the inhabitants of the city could, without any fear of the cold, marvel at the most astonishing fairground spectacle, the 'Master of Mystery' Hua Guangzi, a brilliant illusionist who had been appearing for several months at the High Society.

If only they had known. Hua Guangzi was none other than Gu Shunzhang, head of the Red Guard and Zhou Enlai's trusted aide. Gu Shunzhang actually felt terribly bitter. He had not come to terms with his removal from office. With no illusions as to what lay ahead, he lived a life of semi-retirement under this unexpected and particularly well-chosen disguise, content despite all with still finding a way to deceive the world.

Idleness poisons the body and the mind: acting on this principle, Zhou Enlai interceded in favour of his right-hand man. He eventually got the Central Committee to entrust the former gangster with a mission worthy of him. He was to go to the neighbouring town of Hangzhou, where Chiang Kai-shek, the self-styled Generalissimo of the Guomindang, had established his winter quarters in preparation for the final assault against the rural soviets of Jiangxi, Mao Zedong's stronghold.

Gu Shunzhang was supposed to find out Chiang's secret plans and maintain contact between Shanghai and the 'Red bases' at all costs. Delighted with this return to favour, Gu changed his false name but not his cover. He became Li Ming, the leader of a troupe of actors and jugglers, all of them communist, and took a room in the Hotel Pacific.

When Zhang Guotao, the Chinese militant who had returned from Russia and innocently checked in at the Eastern Hotel, received orders to go to the rural base of Eyuwan, on the edge of the three provinces of Hubei, Hunan and Anhui, he quite naturally asked Gu to organise his safe-conduct. 'Li Ming' cheerfully agreed to do so.

On 31 March 1931, one of Gu's men came to fetch Zhang Guotao and his wife from their secret apartment and took them to the New World Hotel in Nanking Road, often used as a hideout by *Tewu* agents, where the couple spent the night.

The next day, another of Gu's men, disguised as a taxi driver, took Zhang Guotao to the boat on which a cabin had been booked for him under an assumed name. A young *Tewu* militant met him at the Hangzhou landing stage and took him to Gu Shunzhang, who found two hideouts in town for his 'guest'. In a few days' time a guide was to come and fetch him and take him to Eyuwan. Gu had made all the necessary arrangements: Zhang was to take a bus and someone would meet him in a little village where the communists had a secret radio transmitter, and where a Red Guard detachment was resting; the Eyuwan militants would come here to take delivery of their 'consignment'.

On 8 April, towards eight in the evening, Zhang Guotao did indeed leave Hangzhou by bus, escorted by a *Tewu* guide as planned. That same day Gu Shunzhang was stopped in the street and arrested by agents from the Central Bureau of Investigation and Statistics controlled from Nanking, the Guomindang capital, by Xu Endeng, who had returned to China from the United States and had recently been appointed Chen Lifu's lieutenant. Gu Shunzhang was immediately transferred by plane to Nanking, where he was initially interrogated by Xu Endeng. But this catch was too big to be taken lightly: the head of the Red Guard was very soon taken to Chen Lifu's office.

Once captured by the Guomindang head-hunters, the only choice available to a left-wing militant was between immediate abjuration and a dreadful death, as a young Trotskyist, Xie Ligong, learned from bitter experience. Xie was the right-hand man of Chen Duxiu, the great Chinese intellectual who was the first General Secretary of the Communist Party before being expelled for not toeing the line.
    'If I make my submission and acknowledge the Three Principles of the People, if I betray my comrades as a gesture of good faith, will my life be spared?' asked the young man, lost to all sense of shame.
    He was given a solemn promise that this would be so. Furthermore, in order to overcome his final reservations, it was arranged for him to meet Chiang Kai-shek in person. Dazzled at having exchanged a few words with such a powerful personality, Xie Ligong plunged headlong down the path of betrayal and renunciation. After some sordid bargaining, the young man gave away the secret addresses of Chen Duxiu and most of his Trotskyist friends. He abased himself before the Generalissimo and betrayed his own mentor. In exchange for this total 'submission', he was promised a choice post within Chiang Kai-shek's secret police.
    'That Judas sold his friends with the utmost readiness! We aren't under any obligation to honour our agreement with him!' the Generalissimo told his colleagues. Xie Ligong was indeed given a job with the Guomindang police, but a very unimportant one.
    Gu Shunzhang was obviously altogether different. He was no mere footsoldier but one of the enemy's top men. His meeting with Chen Lifu was private, between one secret service chief and another.
    No one has ever found out exactly what the two men said to each other. In Taiwan today, people say that Gu Shunzhang was so annoyed at being ousted from the Politburo, and so demoralised by the violence of the internecine struggles he had witnessed, that he was literally captivated by the strength of Chen Lifu's convictions. Speaking from experience, they will tell you that a man admitted into the antechamber of death is one hundred times more malleable than any other. They will try and prove to you that Sun Yat-sen's Three Principles . . .
    In short, they will discreetly gloss over the inadmissible.
    The inadmissible being the close links between the Guomindang

establishment and the Green Gang, together with its godfather Mr Du; the very simple observation that Gu and Chen Lifu spoke a common language, that of the secret society into which they had both been initiated. Despite their differences, they could find common ground in the memory of shared rites and the vow they had both taken to be ready at all times to obey the orders of the Green Gang. It was this, even more than fear, that took Gu Shunzhang down the path of abjuration. In siding with the strongest, he was returning to the world of his adolescence; he was coming home. When he left Chen Lifu's office, he was already a different man.

There was just one thing that worried him after his renunciation: the fate of his family. His wife, son, parents-in-law and brother-in-law all lived together in an apartment on Weihaiwei Street in Shanghai, a place where he sometimes stayed, and the address of which was known to Party leaders.

'We'll take care of them,' said Chen Lifu and his lieutenant Xu Endeng, full of solicitude for their new recruit. Taking one of Gu's shirts with him as a token of identity that would be recognised by Gu's family, one of their agents took off for Shanghai, but by the time he got to Weihaiwei Street he was already too late.

On Zhou Enlai's orders, several Red Guard militants had kidnapped the 'repentant's' relatives. The Party leadership intended to use them to exert pressure on Gu Shunzhang and prevent him from giving away any major secrets to Chen Lifu. Gu understood perfectly what this blackmail threat meant. But it was already too late for him as well. He had started to talk, and there was absolutely no going back with a man as formidable as Chen Lifu.

So, for the first time in his life, Gu broke down, realising that in his haste he himself had signed his loved ones' death warrant. Despite Chen Lifu and Xu Endeng's somewhat hypocritical words of encouragement, the former Red Guard chief knew that he was right. This violent, even barbarous man was better placed than anyone to anticipate the course of events.

Gu Shunzhang was not mistaken. Zhou Enlai too was caught out by his ex-comrade's haste and was no longer in any position to backtrack. For the sake of the Party's survival, these innocent lives had to be sacrificed on the altar of discipline. An impression had to be made on the minds of any militants who might be tempted, through weariness or disillusionment, to follow Gu Shunzhang down the path of submission; they had to be chilled with fear, terrorised. Zhou Enlai, the Dr Jekyll of Chinese communism, suddenly turned into an abominable Mr Hyde. Opting to dirty his hands in expiation of his misplaced confidence in the traitor, he ordered Wang Shide, one of Gu's colleagues, to execute the ex-gangster's family.

In Nanking, Xu Endeng was interrogating the former head of the Red Guard without giving him time to draw breath. Chen Lifu's lieutenant was amazed to discover just how important his catch was:

Gu Shunzhang knew everything and was telling all. Overwhelmed by this flood of revelations, the agents of the Central Executive Committee's Bureau of Investigation and Statistics were running around from one place to the next in order to take advantage as quickly as possible of this providential source of information. They missed capturing Zhou Enlai, Li Weiha, Kang Sheng and Qu Qiubai, whose main hideouts Gu had given them, by only a few hours. Less fortunate were the rank and file militants left to carry the can for their leaders who had fled. The Guomindang police struck everywhere, making arrests, interrogating prisoners and torturing them.

Within a few months this exceptional betrayal led to the capture of eight hundred rank and file militants and communist cadres, and the ruin of the major part of the clandestine infrastructure. His family killed, and he himself condemned to death by his ex-comrades, Gu Shunzhang plunged ever deeper into treachery. He sold out on the communist writer Yun Daiying, arrested more than a year before but not identified until then; the head of the Department of Peasant Affairs, Luo Qiyuan; the weak General Secretary Xian Zhongfa; his former right-hand men in the *Tewu*, Zhang Songsheng and Cai Fei. He gave away several dozen militants in the security network, Red syndicalists, underground printing presses, hideouts, stockpiles of revolutionary literature, the location of two radios, meeting-places, the names of tradespeople and hotel owners who were communist sympathisers, the families of comrades. Worse still for a party on the edge of the abyss, he revealed the channels of communication between Shanghai and the rural bases, which he himself had set up.

Deprived of the cover and assistance provided by the Chinese CP, the international apparatus of the Comintern was in turn affected. While the French police pulled off a sensational coup in Saigon, partially robbing the newly founded Indochinese CP of its leadership, a Vietnamese cadre, Le Quang Dat, was captured in Shanghai. There was a succession of other major setbacks: the arrest in Singapore of a French Communist International agent, Joseph Ducroux, alias Serge Lefranc; the 'fall' of Ho Chi Minh, trapped by the English Special Branch in Hong Kong; the Franco-British search of an apartment at 49 Nanking Road in Shanghai, for which the upkeep was paid by a so-called teacher of English and German, Hilaire Noulens, who was also a Comintern man. Duly interrogated by Generalissimo Chiang Kai-shek's secret police, he categorically refused to make any confession, remaining silent on his true identity and on his true nationality. His wife was no more ready to talk than he. But full accounts for a year's activity of the Comintern's Eastern Bureau had been found in their safes (the head of the Bureau, Pavel Mif, having returned to Moscow once his protégés had been placed in command of the Chinese Party).

Only Richard Sorge escaped this huge round-up. His compatriot Otto Braun, a Comintern secret envoy, left his base in Manchuria and came to Shanghai. A future military adviser to the rural soviets, and a rival of Mao Zedong, Braun eventually met Sorge at the Astor House Hotel and handed over to him the sum of 20,000 dollars to be used to grease the palms of the Chinese judges of the Noulens couple.

However, figures and anecdotes cannot fully convey the extent of the damage caused by Gu Shunzhang's betrayal. Apart from the wholesale massacre of militants, there were political consequences to be taken into account. These were decisive: the destruction of the bastions of Party apparatus weakened the Chinese CP to such an extent that it was unable thereafter to regain a proper foothold in the towns, where it was reduced to going almost totally underground with virtually no worker support. As for the rupture of communications between the rural soviets and the Shanghai central leadership, this had incalculable consequences, favouring the experiment of building up 'Red bases' in the country that Mao Zedong and his team were conducting. Since orders from the Comintern or the central Party leadership only trickled through to him, the future Chairman of Red China could pursue his own strategy without risk of reprimand or disgrace.

Chiang Kai-shek and Chen Lifu were quite wrong to rub their hands after Gu Shunzhang's betrayal and the dismantling of the communist urban apparatus. The weapon that would later destroy Guomindang China was quietly being forged far from Shanghai, with its fascination for the West and its shady criminal underworld, in the Red maquis of Jiangxi.

In Shanghai, Zhou Enlai, reacting with terrifying calm to the succession of setbacks, decided to build up the communist secret service again, stone by stone. As far as the Party was concerned, this was a matter of life or death. He appointed Guang Huian head of the Red Guard, the Chinese CP's armed wing. He then gathered round him a team of seasoned militants, courageous men capable of organising the work of infiltration and espionage now more dangerous but also more indispensable than ever before. These men of iron were Chen Yun, Pan Hannian, Ke Qingshi and, naturally, Kang Sheng.

In August, Wang Shide, the assassin of Gu Shunzhang's relatives, fell into the hands of the Guomindang. Like his former boss, he humbly made his submission to Chiang Kai-shek. Trembling like a leaf, he led his interrogators to a very quiet building in the French Concession.

'That is where they are,' he said in a choked voice, pointing to the ground in the cellar.

With the aid of a mechanical digger, the four bodies were unearthed: Gu Shunzhang's wife, both his parents-in-law and his brother-in-law. The *Tewu*'s vengeance had spared Gu's son, the young An Sheng.

Professor Guan Shuzhu is an old man who has been living since 1949 in

Taiwan, to which he retired, like many others, after the defeat of Generalissimo Chiang Kai-shek. But he has not always been a member of the Guomindang. At the beginning of the 1930s, after studying in the USSR at the Sun Yat-sen University, he was one of the leaders of the student movement within the Chinese Communist Party. In 1931 he was hiding in a French restaurant, called the Normandie. And it was in an apartment in the French Concession in Shanghai that he met Kang Sheng. He still retains a favourable impression: Kang appeared to him to be above all a distinguished-looking comrade, elegant, with only one weakness – for cigarettes. In short, anything but a killer.

There was good reason for Kang to look distinguished in those troubled times. For, incredible though it may seem, he had become the personal secretary of one of the most powerful members of the Shanghai bourgeoisie, the very honourable Yu Qiaqing.

How did Kang manage to land himself this unlikely post? Quite simply, by playing his trump card again: the Shandong connection. Yu Qiaqing's staff, whether by design or accident, happened to be entirely composed of fellow natives of his province. Several of them were already working on occasion as informers for Kang's personal network. Through them, he was admitted into Mr Yu's residence, and Yu, impressed by his breadth of knowledge and fine manners, treated him as his favoured confidant.

'Unless one goes into the tiger's den, how is one to catch the cubs?' as a Chinese proverb so aptly puts it. By insinuating himself into Mr Yu's confidence, the communist leader was taking this advice to heart.

Yu Qiaqing was the wealthy shipowner, the proprietor of the Sanbei Steam Navigation Company, who had offered his services as a mediator between Chinese strikers and Japanese employers in May–June 1925. In April 1927, in concert with Du Yuesheng, the godfather of the Green Gang, he had rallied the Shanghai bourgeoisie round Chiang Kai-shek. Two years later, to the month, he had crowned his rise to the top by becoming head of the Chamber of Commerce in a veritable *coup d'état* orchestrated by Mr Du and his mob.

In becoming Yu's zealous servant, Kang Sheng had indeed ventured right into the tiger's den – and penetrated to the heart of the all-powerful gang that ruled over the lower depths of Shanghai.

In the eyes of the owner of the Sanbei Steam Navigation Company, Kang Sheng had one great skill: his remarkable calligraphy – precisely the kind of thing that would appeal to a Chinaman so attached to traditional values. Yu Qiaqing had started out at the very bottom of the social ladder, first as an apprentice then rising to become Boy Number One with an English family in Shanghai. Now one of the most powerful compradors in China, he had boundless admiration for scholars, artists and intellectuals.

Zhou Enlai learned with satisfaction of Kang's new job. He himself had several personal contacts among those close to Du Yuesheng. One of these contacts, the very eccentric Yang Du, ostensibly a die-hard

monarchist, secretly worked for the information and 'public relations' network over which Zhou Enlai jealously retained control. The
communists clearly appreciated the necessity for infiltrating the formidable gang that held sway over the city and was hounding their
comrades.

So, without even having really consulted each other, Kang Sheng
and Zhou Enlai had reached the same conclusion: to ensure the survival of the clandestine apparatus of their party, to prepare for the
second round against the Guomindang, they had to be shameless
about using people above suspicion, either with their consent or without their knowledge. The two militants were hereby inaugurating a
long tradition of manipulation of 'fellow travellers' by the *Tewu*, a
tradition that reached its height in the 1960s and early 70s, and continues to this day.

Kang Sheng could rejoice: the Shandong connection was turning
into a real gold-mine! The same could be said of Mr Yu's friendship.
Completely won over by his secretary's many talents, the shipowner
decided to introduce him to Commissioner Fiori and his French
friends in the Concession police force. This was of course like letting
the wolf into the sheepfold – except that this sheepfold was more like
a foxes' lair . . .

'A Chinese group had total control of our territory, with most of the
French senior officers taking bribes and the group in the position of
appointing all Chinese personnel, who were paid by them and were
entirely under their orders . . .'

This is an eloquent picture of what was going on. Captain Louis
Fabre could not have spelled out more clearly to what extent the police
in the French Concession were blighted by corruption and completely
infiltrated by the Green Gang. This honest police officer was not the
only one to think in this way: it would have been impossible to find
anyone in Shanghai prepared to wager so much as a dollar on the
integrity of the French police. And not many would have laid a cent on
the honour of the Settlement police.

Certainly not Jacques Reclus, in any case. A libertarian with deeply
held convictions, he had already crossed swords with the French police
in Shanghai in 1928, and exposed their corruption. The young man
had something to live up to: he was the son of Elie Reclus, a French
writer banished for being a Communard, and the nephew of Elisée
Reclus, who was also condemned to exile after 1871. Jacques Reclus
first set foot on Chinese soil on 2 May 1928, arriving on a cargo ship
from Marseilles, accompanied by his friend Pascal Mugnier, a left-
wing lawyer who had already been expelled from Vietnam for 'inciting
unrest'. On the advice of his Chinese anarchist friend We Kesang,
Reclus had come to Shanghai to teach French. Horrified by the bla-
tant corruption that everyone seemed to take for granted, he decided
to denounce it publicly. One of his cousins was a senator. The young

teacher sent him a detailed report on the venality of the Corsican police in the Concession and their links with the criminal underworld. This really set the cat among the pigeons and led to a complete change of senior staff.

'Reclus is in fact supported by the Russian agent Rover. He's working for the communists,' said the police without the slightest shred of evidence. Those who had lost their cushy jobs because of his moral crusading joined forces against him and forced him to leave for Nanking.

The two new men of power in French Shanghai, Consul-General Koechlin and Commissioner Étienne Fiori, resumed the usual practice of making deals with the Green Gang. This went a very long way: on days of unrest in the city, Mr Du's men would turn up in the French Concession to be issued once again with armbands conferring on them the status of 'law enforcers'. It is true that nothing had been denied to their boss, Mr Du, who was President of the General Association of Businessmen in the French Concession (a body completely dominated by his own men, such as the lawyer James Wu), and a member of the Ratepayers Association of the French Concession in Shanghai, two groups that were very keen on law and order, who, in the words of Commissioner Fiori, 'spontaneously put themselves at the disposal of the police department' in the event of any trouble.

Fiori was a colourful character, who became an agent with the French intelligence services having had a 'very good war' in 1914–18. Tall, elegant, urbane and impulsive, he had an inimitable accent, half French and half Corsican, brown hair fashionably plastered down on to his head and a mocking lop-sided smile. This was the head of the French police, whose headquarters were situated in rue Stanislav-Chevalier. His assistants in the political department, Sarly and Yakolev (a naturalised White Russian), worked on the fourth floor of the building at the back of the courtyard. The three men were in regular contact with 'Pockmarked Huang', who was still head of the Chinese inspectors in the French police force, but also with Mr Du and the honourable Mr Yu Qiaqing, and consequently now with Kang Sheng.

How could anyone refuse such an intelligent and astute young man anything? At the request of the owner of the Sanbei Steam Navigation Company, he was accorded a very rare privilege: a personal *laisser passer*. This document, duly stamped by the official departments, gave him access to the five police guardhouses in the Concession and even to the cells in which his comrades who had been arrested by the French were languishing.

To insinuate himself, like a poisonous snake, into the very midst of the enemy – this is what would have delighted the child of Shandong with such a fascination for the complex and subtle games of betrayal in the war of the *Three Kingdoms*; this is what delighted the ruthless adult he had become. After the elimination of his comrades in April

1927, after Gu Shunzhang's treachery, Kang Sheng had lost any shred of innocence for ever.

In one sense it was better for him that it was so, because this was no child's play. The double or indeed triple game that Zhou Enlai's right-hand man was playing with the French police was terribly dangerous. Kang had to display at all times a truly exceptional sang-froid and ability to dissimulate. The least mistake could have proved fatal.

It was a deadly game, and a perverse one, too. It would not have suited a sensitive soul. In order to gain the confidence of Fiori and his colleagues, Yu Qiaqing's protection alone was not enough. Sometimes it was necessary to give pledges. This meant supplying the French with information, as a token of good faith. Kang Sheng seized this opportunity to rid the Party of certain unwelcome elements by informing on several militants.

All these denunciations were, of course, presented as the result of information obtained by those working for Yu Qiaqing or his friends in the Green Gang. Delighted with such efficiency, Fiori and his friends would then tell Kang Sheng about action they themselves were taking against his own party. Several planned raids were foiled: Kang Sheng lost no time in tipping off the communist leadership.

More than ever before, the French Concession had become the final refuge of those few leaders of the CP who remained in Shanghai after the defection of Gu Shunzhang. A Red guardian angel, Kang Sheng looked after the security of his peers. He had completely changed his appearance: the days of the rickshaw runner or the ticket-seller on the trams were long past. Like his boss, Mr Yu's personal secretary now wore traditional Chinese robes. He had his own room, in Mr Yu's home, and took advantage of his rare moments of leisure to paint or practise his calligraphy.

But 'no amount of gold will buy you time'. And in Shanghai, time passed so quickly . . .

There was hardly any moonlight on the docks that evening in 1932. Crouched behind the cranes, bales of cotton and mooring posts, the *Tewu* men lay in wait, their weapons at the ready. Kang Sheng was also waiting, furious at not being able to light the cigarette he so much craved. But naturally a leader must set a good example. Besides, the least carelessness could well have cost them very dear, and there could be no question of jeopardising the rendezvous with Comrade Wang Lanyin.

Wang Lanyin was a Cantonese militant who specialised in labour organisation; a former student at the Sun Yat-sen University, she had worked in Moscow as a secretary at the Chinese CP Congress in the summer of 1928. She had returned to China with her husband the following year, living first in Tientsin and then moving to Shanghai. Eventually, after suffering serious health problems, the young woman had been posted to Hong Kong. It was there that the British Special

Branch had questioned her with regard to subversive activities.

Not at all anxious to have responsibility for any undesirable political detainees, the British police were sending Wang Lanyin and another comrade back to Shanghai, where, according to Kang Sheng's informants, the ship transporting them was due to dock at any moment.

However, several hours had already passed and no boat had yet appeared at the place where the two communists were supposed to disembark. And with good reason: Special Branch had discreetly tipped off their Guomindang counterparts about the transfer of Wang Lanyin and her companion in misfortune, hoping that agents from the Bureau of Investigation and Statistics would intercept them, leaving the honour of the British police above suspicion.

Naturally, Chen Lifu's men did not intend to let slip such a wonderful opportunity. Rightly fearing that the communists might attack, they had boarded the steamer just as it was about to sail up the Wusong River, which flows through the International Settlement. Wang Lanyin's comrade had managed to escape by jumping into the water, but she had been less fortunate and, not being able to free herself, had fallen into the hands of her enemies.

Kang Sheng could not expose his special team of militants to risk any longer. With a heavy heart, he gave the signal to withdraw. And so one of the last operations of the communist secret services in Shanghai ended in miserable failure.

With the appointment of the new leadership team for the *Tewu* after the defection of Gu Shunzhang, Kang Sheng was once again given a thankless but perilous task. He had to act, at the risk of his own life: he had to warn endangered militants before it was too late, evacuate those hideouts that remained undetected, move important documents, destroy others. In short, save anything that could still be saved . . .

In this difficult task, Chen Yun proved to be a great help to him. Kang was well acquainted with this very loyal militant who had been trained in hardship. They had already worked together within the context of labour organisation and Kang had been amazed by the vitality of his comrade, who in 1987 was to be the only member of the 'Five Musketeers' of the *Tewu*, 1931–2, to occupy a senior post in the People's Republic of China.

Wang Ming, Pavel Mif's protégé, had shamelessly taken advantage of the power vacuum created by Gu Shunzhang's denunciations to get himself appointed General Secretary of the Party. To find a hideout worthy of his new status, he naturally turned to Kang Sheng and Chen Yun. The two *Tewu* bosses found him a superb place, in a private clinic on the outskirts of Shanghai.

'It's all right, but my wife, Meng Qingshu, and I cannot be expected to live in such a cramped apartment. We'll have to rent the whole floor!' said the new Party leader haughtily.

The two militants were rendered almost speechless by this, but it did not take them long to work out the reasons for Wang Ming's attitude: the Moscow-trained communist considered himself far too important to go running around after the Party membership. He intended to run the Party from his apartment, transforming it into a real head-quarters, and using couriers to deliver his *ex-cathedra* messages. The two comrades tried in vain to impress upon him that an over-luxurious lifestyle was likely to attract attention to the couple. Wang Ming remained intransigent. Meng Qingshu and her husband got the whole floor, with the exorbitant rental paid by the Central Committee.

As it turned out, Wang Ming and his wife did not remain long in Shanghai. As early as October 1931, Kang Sheng and the Party's security apparatus secretly got them back to Moscow, at their own request. The scheming of the pro-Soviet camp served only to drain the CP of its lifeblood and to give Pavel Mif's protégé six months' illusion of power.

Zhou Enlai also had to leave the city, a month before Wang Ming. Since the arrest of the man who had murdered Gu Shunzhang's rela-tives, there had been a price on Zhou's head and a photograph of him, wearing the cadet's uniform of the Huangpu 'officer factory', adorned the walls of both the eastern and northern railway stations in Shanghai. In short, his life was hanging by no more than a thread. Kang Sheng and Chen Yun got him to Mao Zedong's Jiangxi maquis, using a hastily worked-out route: Zhou left the city disguised as a priest. Neither he nor Kang Sheng were unaware that since Chiang Kai-shek's much-publicised conversion to Christianity, priests were in saintly odour in Guomindang China.

Gradually, the whole of the Central Committee fell back on Mao's Red base, renouncing for ever all hope of an urban revolution on the Russian model of 1917. At the beginning of 1932, only two members remained in Shanghai: Kang Sheng and Li Zusheng, one of the 'twenty-eight Bolsheviks'.

On 28 January 1932, a new calamity befell the city. At ten-thirty p.m., Japanese marines began to attack the districts surrounding the International Settlement. The Japanese wanted their own concession and were making it known through armed force.

The Japanese soldiers found the 19th Route Army in their path, shabbily dressed and equipped with ancient rifles, and even blunder-busses. Some were still wearing armour, like medieval warriors. Yet they held their own against the Imperial marines, who were justly considered an élite force.

The battle was fought along a 25-kilometre front beneath the curi-ous gaze of the Westerners in the Concessions. Though the Japanese had reckoned on an engagement lasting no more than four days at most, it went on for six weeks. Moored fore and aft on the Blue River, Japanese cruisers and destroyers bombarded the Wusong zone with naval guns. Advancing up the Huangpu River, they systematically crushed the Chinese quarters, while General Chiang Kai-shek made no move to come to the aid of his compatriots.

Only the 19th Army attempted to resist the onslaught. On 4 March, its leaders had to admit defeat: they could no longer hold out. In a gesture of despair, Chinese soldiers blew up their last fortifications before taking flight, with rage in their hearts and a taste of bitterness in their mouths at the total inertia displayed by the head of the Guomindang. Primarily concerned with his anti-communist struggle, Chiang Kai-shek had never imagined that the sight of the Japanese would so stir the Chinese population.

A few hours later, the Japanese soldiers marched through an area of devastation to the thin applause of their Shanghai compatriots. The Empire of the Rising Sun had conquered its share of the city through a hard-fought struggle and now had its own concession. But, apart from the reports filed by the great French journalist Albert Londres, little was heard of the affair in Europe. The Old Continent's interest in China was confined to the fantastic trans-Asian automobile expedition by Citroën tracker vehicles.

It so happened that this daring driving feat was to have a great influence on Kang Sheng's personal destiny . . .

The 'Pamir Group' had left Beirut on 6 April 1931 in an attempt to establish a link between the Mediterranean and the Sea of China by following Marco Polo's silk routes. After a genuine odyssey covering more than twelve thousand kilometres, the Group entered Beijing less than a year later, on 12 February 1932.

This extraordinary technical and human achievement sparked the enthusiasm of Westerners and Chinese alike. To celebrate the event, the ever courteous Du Yuesheng invited the leader of the Citroën team, Georges-Marie Haardt, and several of the notable French personalities of Shanghai to dine at his house.

In so doing, Mr Du was showing great indulgence towards the French, because they had in fact given him cause for complaint. The root of the problem was a very honest seaman, Vice-Admiral Herr: scandalised by the fact that the Green Gang's drugs had been brought into the city on board two coasters sailing under the French flag, he had ordered them to cease trafficking on pain of incurring severe penalties. Like all Chinese, Du set great store by the notion of 'collective culpability' and considered Consul Koechlin and Commissioner Fiori – who only the day before had been regarded as friends – responsible for the 'narrow-mindedness' of their compatriot. This did not prevent him from offering his guests some tasty Chinese dishes, and notably the particularly choice dish of Ningbo mushrooms.

As the assassination of the Red syndicalist He Songling showed previously, invitations from the godfather of the Green Gang often turned out to be invitations to a murder. Nor did the Ningbo mush-rooms, which had a taste of death, fail in this tradition. Three of the affable Mr Du's guests died shortly after this banquet in more than suspicious circumstances: Consul Koechlin, the French Colonel Macair and the unfortunate head of the Citroën team, Georges-Marie Haardt, even though he had nothing to do with any of it. He died on 16 March 1932, in the Repulse Bay Hotel in Hong Kong, officially of pneumonia.

Journalist Albert Londres, who was in Shanghai investigating the burning issue of drug-trafficking, died two months later in the fire on board a modern steamer, the *Georges-Philippar*, somewhere off the coast of the Somali. 'I'm bringing back dynamite!' he had rashly confided to some friends before leaving Saigon for Europe – the dynamite, in all probability, being too much accurate detail about Mr Du's activities, which cost the over-curious journalist his life.

Two men survived the strange evening at the home of the Shanghai godfather: the banker Louis Bouvier – no ordinary fellow, he was something of an adventurer who, born into a modest family from Burgundy, had worked his way up the hard way; and the Corsican Commissioner Etienne Fiori. They were both entitled to special treat-ment because they had saved the godfather's life by warning him of a plot against him hatched within the Green Gang. Du Yuesheng on that occasion had even declared Bouvier his 'blood brother', vowing that, as long as he lived, the Shanghai underworld would never lay a finger on the young French banker.

Fiori, though, was extremely ill. In fact he very nearly died and, taking heed of the warning, he hastily returned to France. Koechlin and he were immediately replaced by men who could not be bribed: the French Consul, Henri Meyrier, Commander Louis Fabre and Commissioner Robert Jobez, the future Free Frenchman. In so far as they were able, they tried to make life more difficult for Du Yuesheng and the Green Gang, and won the support of the diplomatic authorities.

This upheaval did not exactly suit the Green Gang but it suited the *Tewu* even less, for, with Fiori's departure, the illustrious Yu Qiaqing lost his main contact with the French police. Just when the Japanese invasion and the reinforcement of the Guomindang's secret police started to make Kang Sheng's task considerably more difficult, the tragic episode of the poisoned mushrooms deprived him of his most useful source of information.

The nationalists, however, adopted a tougher line. Anxious to get rid of the Reds once and for all, Chiang Kai-shek was seeking new measures. The Generalissimo, who considered Chen Lifu and his brother were becoming too powerful, had decided to divide his special services into several more or less rival departments, whose bosses, having proved successful against the CP, would spend more time spying on each other than politicking – this being an old technique of those seeking to retain power within secret societies.

In 1932 a new department emerged out of Chen Lifu's organisation, which became known as the Military Council's Bureau of Investigations and Statistics, or more simply BIS, when the wave of pro-American hysteria overwhelmed the Guomindang.

The head of BIS, Dai Li, was born in 1895 in the village near Chiang Kai-shek's family house. The orphaned child of a father considered a wastrel by his relatives, Dai had been raised by his mother who was unable, despite all her appeals, to curb the young man's taste for adventure. At fourteen, he left family and school to join the army of a warlord, and eventually ended up as a cadet in the Sino-Soviet Huangpu military academy, where he met the Russian Vassili Galen and the communist Zhou Enlai. He clashed with them right from the start, to the point where he set up a kind of surveillance network in the academy to spy on the Reds and denounce them. A supporter of the Guomindang, he, like Chiang Kai-shek and Chen Lifu, had very close ties with the Green Gang.

Captain Dai Li, head of the nationalist secret police, met with his hour of glory during those bloody days of April 1927, when he distinguished himself by a display of savagery that earned him the unflattering nickname of 'The Butcher'. Some credit him with being the author of a particularly inhuman method of execution: acting on his orders, the Guomindang soldiers are supposed to have thrown several thousand communists alive into the boilers of locomotives.

Whatever the case, Kang Sheng's new enemy was a real masterspy. Affable, courteous, extremely active, and good company to his friends, in actual fact, this merciless individual said he was prepared to do anything to destroy the resistance of the Guomindang's opponents – forcibly injecting them with doses of heroin, if need be. Incurably addicted despite themselves, the victims of this treatment became for the most part human debris capable of the basest act in the service of their new master.

He never tired of telling his men, 'Always be very polite to the Reds who have come over to our side. But treat them for what they are: lackeys. Never let them raise their voices or make any demands! Never trust them, because we are masters and they are cowards who have betrayed their friends to save their wretched skins!'

As well as the BIS and its chief, Dai Li, Generalissimo Chiang Kai-shek gave his full support to another, more directly political, movement. The idea of creating the 'Blue Shirts', based on the European fascist model, had come to him during meetings with the German advisers to the nationalist army, and notably with Lieutenant-Colonel Hermann Kriebel, who was with Hitler at the time of the abortive *putsch* in 1923 in Munich and an early member of the Nazi Party.

This new movement, which brought together the extremist wing of the Guomindang, was born in April 1932. Among its leaders were the inevitable Chen brothers, but also their erstwhile captive Gu Shunzhang. Since his defection in April 1931, the former head of the Red Guard had not wasted any time: a member of the Guomindang's Central Executive Committee in August 1931, a personal adviser to the Generalissimo, the former pupil of the Soviet OGPU retained his expertise after having changed sides. The assassin-in-chief of the Communist Party had become assassin-in-chief of the Guomindang. Under his orders, the clandestine terrorist cells of the Executive Department of the Blue Shirts of Shanghai, Beijing, Canton and Hong Kong hunted down the communist leaders in order to shoot them on sight, killing them like rabbits. According to the French intelligence service, the Deuxième Bureau, one of the men on the Executive Department's black list was none other than one Zhao Yun – the pseudonym Kang Sheng was using at that time.

But Gu Shunzhang was living dangerously. His barely concealed political ambitions attracted the anger of Chen Lifu and his brother, who disliked such fierce competition. They did everything they could to oust him, and, according to the official version, managed to have him shot in 1935 on the somewhat unlikely pretext of his 'reversion to communist ideas'.

And so ended the astonishing career of the former head of the communist secret services? Nothing could be less certain. In 1987 a rumour was still circulating in Taiwan that Gu Shunzhang's execution was just a sham, allowing the communist traitor to go totally underground in order to conduct the anti-communist struggle in the utmost secrecy, in collusion with the Green Gang. He is said to have died long after 1935, under a false identity. This would perhaps explain the attitude of Guomindang officials today who react with considerable embarrassment when asked to give details of the circumstances of the death of the man whose defection delivered such a decisive blow to the urban apparatus of the Chinese CP.

'The Generalissimo could no longer tolerate the impertinence of Ding Ling. He lost patience with her. The Blue Shirts have abducted her and buried her alive!'

This rumour flashed round the humble streets of the Chinese sector and round the literary salons. On 14 May, a Sikh patrol of the International Settlement police had found a body lying behind 7 Quisan Road: it was that of the former provincial secretary of the Communist Party.

Number 7 Quisan Road was just where Ding Ling lived, and the young woman had disappeared. This non-conformist writer, a communist with libertarian ideas, was one of the *bêtes noires* of the hard-line Guomindang, whom she particularly annoyed with her rejection of social conventions and her denunciations in the press of the regime's corruption. No one was really surprised that she should have been assassinated. In 1931, the Generalissimo's assassins had already shot five young writers of the extreme left who had been handed over by the Settlement police, including another very talented woman writer, Rou Shi. Other artists had 'disappeared', either buried alive or smothered under blankets.

Happily, this time the rumour of death turned out to be false. The Blue Shirts had indeed abducted Ding Ling, but in order to transfer her secretly to Nanking, together with her communist lover. Beyond all shame, the Judas who betrayed the couple had gone to collect his thirty pieces of silver: his name was Feng Da, a former lover of Ding Ling who had been spurned by the fiery young woman.

The person responsible for organising the joint abduction from 7 Quisan Road was Chen Qihun. Known by his code name of Mao Shaowu, he was a former communist *Tewu* agent who had been captured and 'turned' by his comrade Gu Shunzhang. 'Special delegate to the Guomindang's Central Executive Committee responsible for seeking out communists in the Shanghai region', he was in the vanguard of the struggle against communism. A few days after the disappearance of Ding Ling, Mao Shaowu and Dai Li sent a team of killers to shoot down Yang Xingfo, rector of the Sinica Academy and a leader, together with Dr Sun Yat-sen's widow, of the Chinese League for the Protection of Human Rights, which was very hostile to the regime.

This was too much for the communist secret services. After these two blows delivered by the Guomindang heavies, some reaction was called for, otherwise there would be a total loss of face. The 'Stray Dog Extermination Squad', which came into being on 7 January 1933, at a secret meeting held in an area close to the docks, probably under the chairmanship of Kang Sheng, was mobilised. This strangely named body, under the rule of Guang Huian, one of the 'Group of Five' appointed by Zhou Enlai after the defection of Gu Shunzhang, replaced the former Red Guard.

A month after the abduction of Ding Ling, Mao Shaowu visited his mistress, a 'sing-song' girl who lived with several of her friends in a brothel in Chekian Road, the Diang Xing Hotel. The Guomindang's special agent had asked the young woman to organise a good party for him and his Chinese colleagues from the Settlement police or Public Security. Confident of his mistress's talents, he walked gaily down the narrow alleyway leading to the Diang Xing Hotel. Suddenly, five assassins from the Stray Dog Extermination Squad appeared out of nowhere, armed to the teeth. Mao Shaowu barely had time to regret his lack of caution before he fell to the ground, riddled with high-calibre bullets. He died shortly afterwards in hospital.

Who had betrayed him? The Blue Shirts were furious. A 'repentant' ex-communist, Lao Yuan, was accused of having secretly returned to his first allegiance and of having informed the *Tewu* of his boss's movements. Several of those who had 'repented' left Shanghai at that time, feeling as much threatened by death at the hands of their Guomindang employers as by their former friends in the CP. With the Blue Shirts on the one hand and the Red exterminators on the other, they felt their chances of survival were remote.

Determined to strike hard before the Guomindang finished off their few surviving partisans, the Reds went on to the offensive once again. On 12 August, they killed Mao Shaowu's successor on his way to the Hotel Sun-Sun. A month later another 'penitent' was shot down. Bombs were placed in police stations in Tientsin and Beijing.

Negotiations then began between Xu Endeng, Chen Lifu's lieutenant, and the European police. Xu obtained authorisation for his men to enter the International Concessions. Better still, the French and Anglo-Americans agreed to come to his assistance in eliminating the Reds. This was almost unheard of. The Guomindang launched Operation Red Guard, which led to the capture of some thirty exterminators of 'stray dogs', including a compatriot of Kang Sheng known as 'Little Shandong', and also the wife of Guang Huian, the leader of the group. They also recovered a large cache of firearms.

At the time when Adolf Hitler was assuming power as head of the Nazis in Germany, Chiang Kai-shek's followers, inspired by the SA's methods, were emerging in the fight against the communist *Tewu*.

But never again would they succeed in capturing the elusive Kang Sheng.

Chiang Kai-shek's relentless campaign against rebel intellectuals and non-conformist artists was turning against him. Shanghai cinema circles, a flourishing cultural centre at the beginning of the 1930s, began to lean more and more to the left, indeed towards communism. Always quick to seize an opportunity, the head of the *Tewu* decided to take advantage of this to extend his intelligence and logistics networks into the very heart of the studios and laboratories dedicated to filmmaking. Hounded in the working-class suburbs by the Blue Shirts and the dictator's secret police, the communist apparatus managed to survive even after it had lost almost its entire working-class base.

This close acquaintance with the film world proved to be very useful to the underground leader of the CP, and not only for political reasons. Kang Sheng had someone he wanted to push in front of the cameras. On one of his trips to his native province of Shandong he had met up in Qingdao with his young female compatriot, Cloud Crane. He had been amazed by the changes that had taken place in her over the years, and could not but admire the result. Cloud Crane was no longer the rebellious little girl he had once known. Now she was a very attractive young woman, confident of her charm and passionately interested in the theatre. He recognised at once in the future Madame Mao an extraordinary ambition, and this attracted him ever more strongly to her.

At some point they became lovers, probably as early as 1931. Kang Sheng occasionally visited Shandong for both political and family reasons – he had left a daughter and three brothers in the province. (The Party took advantage of his visits to entrust him with secret liaison missions – as was the case with all trusted militants connected with the clandestine operation.) The affair between Cloud Crane and Kang Sheng was, then, as intermittent as it was passionate. However, it played a decisive role in the lives of both of them.

It was through Kang Sheng that Cloud Crane met Yu Shan, an elegant young woman who specialised in traditional Chinese opera. Through her husband, Yu Shan got Kang Sheng's young compatriot into the University of Qingdao, where she had been refused admittance when she had previously applied.

But Cloud Crane was beautiful, too beautiful. The very aristocratic Yu Shan began to fear that her own husband might in turn fall under the young woman's charm. To avert this danger, Yu introduced Cloud Crane to her own brother, Yu Qiwei. As it happened, Yu Qiwei was a Communist Party militant and a comrade of Kang Sheng, and he too maintained ambiguous relations with artistic circles, working in their midst for the triumph of the Red cause.

Despite her youth – she was eighteen – Cloud Crane had already taken numerous lovers. But Yu Qiwei was only the second underground communist militant – after Kang Sheng – that she had ever known. Rather tall for a Chinese, he appeared slightly untidy in his long traditional robe. He had a fine expressive face and obvious natural authority. Soon, he and Cloud Crane fell in love. Qiwei could not conceal from his lover for long his secret revolutionary activities. Far from cooling Cloud Crane's ardour, his political commitment only increased her admiration for him.

It was Yu Qiwei, even more than Kang Sheng (whose relationship with Cloud Crane had always contained an element of complicity derived from their shared memories) who introduced her to Marxist theories and to politics in art. Before long, they were living together, and could be seen on spring or summer evenings strolling along the beaches of Qingdao, hand in hand, discussing philosophy, politics, theatre, feminism and free love.

Cloud Crane had lost none of her passion for acting, or of her fascination –.fostered by Kang Sheng's descriptions of the city – with Shanghai, the great metropolitan centre for arts, letters, Chinese cinema. Yet her love for Yu Qiwei kept her in Qingdao. This was the first time in her eventful life that she accepted the idea of sacrificing her ambitions to a man. But fate – in the shape of the Guomindang police – intervened. The underground communist Qiwei was arrested.

Cloud Crane felt impotent and useless. Although a recent recruit to the CP, she was not sufficiently politically motivated to follow in her lover's footsteps and abandon for ever her passion for the theatre, her fascination with the cinema. Hoping that Qiwei's family, some of whose members were well connected at the highest level of the Guomindang, would be best placed to negotiate for the release of her lover, the young woman decided to succumb to the siren-song of

Shanghai, embodied by Kang Sheng. She left Qingdao with no hope of ever returning.

Kang was thirty-five by then, and had spent more than ten years fighting the militant cause. Cloud Crane, who adopted the name of Lan Ping at that time, meaning 'Blue Apple', was just twenty. While the communist leadership was already considering transferring the head of the *Tewu* to a less exposed position, they became lovers once again for a few days – an extremely brief liaison, marked by the climate of tension and violence that reigned over Shanghai, the battleground of a fight to the death between Reds and Whites. Blue Apple threw herself headlong into the affair, as though to smother the burning memory of Yu Qiwei, and Kang Sheng almost sacrificed the love of the woman who shared his underground life with him, Cao Shuying, a young militant from Shandong.

Also from Shandong was the journalist and art critic Cui Wanqui, to whom Kang Sheng entrusted the important task of making Blue Apple a celebrated screen actress. Meanwhile, the pressure exerted by the Guomindang in Shanghai was becoming unbearable as they closed in on the leader of the *Tewu*, the only one of the leaders of the 'Three Uprisings' still living in the city, despite the treachery of Gu Shunzhang. He figured on every wanted notice, every blacklist. In agreement with the remains of the Comintern's secret apparatus, the decision was taken to send Kang to the USSR before his amazing luck ran out. He knew too much for the Party to be able to risk keeping him where he was.

A communist is not his own man. Even if he had wanted to, Kang Sheng could not have refused an order of this kind – no more than he could have refused to take with him Cao Shuying, his real companion in the eyes of the Party.

Before leaving Shanghai, he handed over what remained of the *Tewu* apparatus to his two trusted aides, Li Shiqun (alias Slavin) and Ding Mocun, who had just returned from Russia, where they had been trained in espionage techniques by OGPU agents.

The Li Shiqun/Ding Mocun partnership did not long survive the Shanghai heat. Arrested in May 1934, their cover – the Agency for Social Information – blown, they submitted to the Guomindang, betraying as a sign of good faith the head of the Comintern liaison office, the person in charge of maintaining radio contact with the Russians, and his seven technicians. Chiang Kai-shek's secret services thus laid hands on seven secret transmitter-receivers, enabling them to cut the umbilical cord still joining Moscow to Shanghai, Chinese communism to Russian communism.

For Kang Sheng, his exile from Shanghai marked the end of an era. A new chapter in his story was already beginning in Moscow, where the Chinese militant, now fully initiated, hoped to assume the status of a major leader in the world revolutionary movement. He had in fact discovered in himself another failing: ambition.

5

A Chinese in Russia

Drifting off the Isle d'Ouessant, opposite Lizard Point, was a ship sailing under the Dutch flag. A few days before, she had still been in Rotterdam, her port of registry. She was now supposed to be well on her way to New York. The ship's name was the *Rotterdam*. She was the finest vessel in the Dutch merchant fleet.

Aboard the vessel a tragedy was being played out which as the hours went by assumed a farcical dimension. The crew had mutinied and wanted to divert the ship's course – and sail back to Holland.

For the small communist cell that had started this mutiny, the objective was simple: to return to port, with the captain in irons in the hold and red flags flying from the rails. For this mutiny would serve as a timing device, set to cause a delayed-action explosion: the general insurrection of workers, seamen and dockers in Rotterdam, no less. In short, a replay of the Battleship *Potemkin*, the Russian vessel that mutinied in 1905, thereby triggering off the first revolution against the Tsar.

Brave Captain Van Dulken had very strict instructions from the ship's owners. In case of rebellion, he was to do all he could to quell it. So began an incredible battle of wits. At first the mutinous sailors got what they wanted: Van Dulken turned his ship round. But in the night, with the help of some loyal crew members, he returned to the helm and set the ship on course for America. In the early hours of 5 September 1932, the vessel, once more under the control of the mutineers, changed course for the third time and headed for Rotterdam . . .

In the old Dutch port, the biggest in the world in terms of tonnage, a tiny revolutionary council was in feverish activity. Its intentions were to put the town to fire and sword, to stir up the 'down-trodden' all over Holland, blow the wind of revolution as far as the Dutch East Indies, the jewel in the colonial crown, where two rebellions led by the Indonesian Communist Party had already been put down by the Dutch army in 1927 and 1928. Moscow intended to avenge the injury, and strike hard at Dutch imperialism.

For this special task, the Port and Docks International, the Comintern's maritime subsidiary, mobilised its most effective revolutionary element, including the Rotterdam conspirators – three communist militants with an extraordinary future ahead of them. The first of the three, Hamburg seaman Richard Krebs alias Jan Valtin, was to break with the Comintern after being interned by the Nazis. The second, diamond merchant Paul de Groot, the Russian special services' man in the Dutch CP leadership, would end up general secretary of his country's Communist Party. The third was Chinese, and for him adventure and legend were nothing out of the ordinary: he was the son of Liao Zhongkai, the long-standing associate of Dr Sun Yat-sen who had been assassinated by Green Gang killers in Canton in 1925.

Liao Chengzhi, as he was called, joined the communist underground movement immediately after completing his studies in Japan. A liaison agent for the Ports and Docks International and its secret apparatus, he came to Europe in 1928, sharing the fate of 30,000 exiled Chinese seamen. He was seen in Marseilles, rehearsing plans for insurrection in the Seamen's International Club in rue Fauchier, but the city's political climate did not suit him. A sordid squabble had set the communist leadership against several of its own members, who stood accused of transforming the dockers' union into a criminal gang full of traffickers and gangsters. A thorough investigation conducted by the Sûreté Nationale had resulted in numerous arrests of underground Comintern cadres. So Liao Chengzhi left Marseilles and mostly likely met Paul de Groot in Anvers, centre of the secret apparatus of the Ports and Docks International. Between the two of them they hatched the Rotterdam operation.

The ultimate failure of the operation led to Liao Chengzhi being imprisoned by the Dutch for two weeks. He was then expelled to Germany, where he was soon picked up by the police and expelled yet again. Whereupon he went to Moscow, staying only a few days before returning to Shanghai.

In Shanghai Liao Chengzhi was assigned by Kang Sheng to organisation work within the communist group in the seamen's union. On the famous Shanghai *Bund*, his new base became the Seamen's Club, run by an Italian working for the Comintern, Comrade Fessino. Now Liao Chengzhi really came into his own, organising the huge system of clandestine messengers, as well as the union's 'special' liaison network which extended all over Asia, beginning with Singapore and Hong Kong . . .

On 28 March 1933, the Comintern 'sailor from nowhere', Liao Chengzhi, fell into the hands of the Guomindang and only escaped torture and death because of Dr Sun Yat-sen's past friendship with his father. At the same time another 'Red sailor' left Moscow for Holland. This thirty-year-old syndicalist, like Kang Sheng a native of Shandong, was called Liu Changsheng. He arrived in Rotterdam to continue the work of his predecessors. Having previously been employed first in a tea factory, then as a seaman-docker at Vladivostok, he was passionately interested in the thorny problem of the simplification of the Chinese language and its transliteration into Roman characters.

In Moscow he and his Soviet masters had taken stock of the failure of the mutiny organised by Krebs, de Groot and Liao, and he had come up with a new plan to incite rebellion in the Dutch fleet. Liu Changsheng's Battleship *Potemkin* would be the Dutch warship *Zeven Provinciën*, the pride of the royal fleet. The French Deuxième Bureau kept a close eye on this second attempt, bearing in mind the 1919 mutinies in the French fleet. Fifty years later, the yellowing pages of the reports filed by France's intelligence agent in the Netherlands, Colonel Lespinasse Fontegrive, doubtless drawing on information supplied by his colleagues in the Dutch intelligence service, give an extremely detailed account of Liu Changsheng's initiative and its results.

'The majority of the naval squadron was at that time off the island of Celebes,' he wrote on 16 February. The *Zeven Provinciën* was in Olehleh (Sumatra) with a crew of 27 officers, 26 European non-commissioned officers, 37 corporals and European seamen, and 246 native non-commissioned officers and men. During the night of Saturday to Sunday, while a large number of officers were ashore attending a reception given by the civil authorities, the crew of the *Zeven Provinciën* took command of the ship, raised the anchor and set sail in a south-easterly direction.

'The captain of the vessel, Commander Eikeboom, gave chase aboard a small government craft, the *Aldebaran*, which was not even armed.

'The fleet, alerted while off Celebes (three thousand kilometres as the crow flies from Olehleh), dispatched the cruiser *Java*, the destroyers *Iiet Hein* and *Evertsen*, as well as several other vessels and a squadron of Dornier Wall sea planes to head off the mutineers who had announced they were heading for Surabaya, and progressed at a speed of seven knots in order to conserve fuel supplies.'

The mutineers in fact denied, in a wireless message, having mutinied at all, but claimed to have wanted simply to protest against the reduction in their wages. They then undertook to return the ship to its commander and to welcome him aboard with a presentation of arms. From Sunday the fifth to Friday the tenth was a period of waiting, but nothing could happen before the vessels sent by the fleet and the mutinous ship had made contact.

'In response to questions in parliament, the government at once declared that there could be no question of anything but unconditional surrender, and that this would be achieved by force if necessary, even if the ship were to be sunk in the process.'

The government at The Hague was not joking. The whole Indies fleet, backed up by six Dorniers, went after the *Zeven Provinciën*. After the customary warnings, the sea planes dropped their bombs on the rebel ship. Panic ensued: the sailors hurled themselves into the lifeboats as though the ship were sinking.

They quickly surrendered. Nine months later, on 15 November, the Batavia court-martial condemned those it judged to be the leaders of the mutiny to between one and sixteen years' hard labour.

The Comintern journal, *Inprecorr (International Press Correspondence)*, to which Kang Sheng had begun to contribute that year, published a long report on the *Zeven Provinciën* mutiny. Being a piece of propaganda, it naturally failed to acknowledge that the mutiny had been planned.

'The tragedy of the *Zeven Provinciën* sailors who rebelled was to trust in the moral effect of their action. They reckoned they could force the authorities by their action to recognise finally the wretched conditions of seamen. The bombs dropped on the *Zeven Provinciën* will compel many seamen to abandon these hopes for ever. Only a policy of strife, boldly conducted, and taken to the utmost extreme, is likely to lead to victory.'

Immediately after the mutiny, Liu Changsheng returned to Moscow, where Kang Sheng was awaiting him.

Now thirty-five years old, Kang was a slim man; dressed in a close-fitting dark suit and coat, only his stiff collar and a garishly striped tie broke the monotony of his outfit. With his high bared forehead, thick brushed-back hair, prominent nose, fleshy almost feminine lips, bright malicious eyes magnified by the thick glass of his steel-rimmed spectacles, he was already cultivating a scholarly look. Only his face betrayed contradictory impulses: sometimes an impassive coldness, and at other times nervous tics brought on by his endless consumption of tobacco.

This was not his first visit to Moscow, so he did not share his companion Cao Shuying's wonder when, as they approached the OGPU headquarters, she set eyes on Kitaî Gorod, the Chinese area that lay to the east of the Kremlin, where, in the Middle Ages, Asian merchants had sold their furs and spices.

If Kang Sheng had taken the young Shuying with him, it was because he was intending to remain for some time in the USSR. For a girl from Shandong, she was smaller than average, and the mutinous fringe that fell on to her little face reddened by the bitter cold made her look even more like a student. Only twenty-three, and having just graduated from the Jinan Girls' School, she had enrolled at Shanghai University, where she had met Kang Sheng, twelve years her senior.

Cao changed her given name: from now on she would be known to the Party as Ciao Yi-ou. No doubt Kang Sheng chose the name Yi-ou, meaning 'she who strikes and attacks by surprise'. A political allusion or an erotic one? Kang Sheng liked to hold sway in both realms.

Kang Sheng's first lightning visit to the Russian special services had taken place in 1928, at the time of the Chinese Party's Sixth Congress, during which it had been decided, in the presence of Zhou Enlai, to found a Chinese secret service modelled on the OGPU. On that occasion Kang Sheng had learned the rudiments of counter-espionage. His former companions in Shanghai laughed at his enthusiasm, especially for learning how to use and crack codes – for the Chinese, this was not something to be taken lightly, but an ancestral art, perfected by the Mongols.

At the end of 1932 Kang was again invited to work for a short time in the USSR, alongside the German Otto Braun, as secretary of the underground Party in Manchuria, organising resistance to the Japanese army. Then, in March 1933, bowing beneath the onslaught of repression, the Chinese Communist Party of Shanghai decided to appoint him its representative to the Comintern in Moscow. In principle, he was to replace Chen Shaoyu, alias Wang Ming, in this post, but Wang did not return to Shanghai, due to the arrest of his entire 'reception committee'. Kang Sheng therefore settled for the number two job with the Comintern. This was no cause for loss of face: he was becoming the number one authority in the realm of espionage.

As soon as he arrived that winter in snow-covered Moscow, Kang went and knocked on the door of the secret services. It was a matter of assessing the situation in consultation with the experts in Chinese affairs in the rival organisations: the OGPU (soon to be renamed the NKVD) and the Red Army's Fourth Bureau (the GRU). Colonel Beremeny, responsible for the surveillance of the Chinese community in Moscow on behalf of the OGPU, alerted Kang to the virus that continued to wreak havoc: Trotskyism. Lordly, smiling, warm, Colonel Oscar Antonovich Stiga, in charge of GRU operations in the Far East, was concerned about something else entirely: he wanted to know all about the Japanese army, and about the likelihood of an attack against the USSR. As deputy to General Berzin, he controlled another great secret agent, the German Richard Sorge, who, as we have seen, became involved in Shanghai, returning to Moscow in January 1933. In May 1933, Sorge went to Japan, in order to gather information on the Japanese intentions.

Long afterwards, the rumour circulated that in April 1933, the two greatest communist spies of the century, Kang Sheng and Richard Sorge, had lengthy discussions on the situation in Asia.

For four years, the 'Old Man', Leon Trotsky, had been isolated with his small entourage, on Princes Island, an hour by boat from Constantinople, where the Byzantine emperors used to exile those members of their families most given to conspiracy. Whenever the old Bolshevik's family went to the city to shop, they were closely watched by the OGPU, who were ready to pounce at the slightest cause for alarm.

But, despite this isolation, the former head of the Red Army received visits from loyal supporters from all over the world. He also wrote thousands of letters, messages, proclamations, pamphlets and books, beginning with an early autobiography entitled *My Life*. What was even more extraordinary was that the Comintern felt beholden to reply to his arguments, so great was his influence still, particularly in Asia. Though unfamiliar with China, he had correspondents there, including one of the great leaders of Chinese communism who had opposed Stalin and allied himself with Trotsky's cause: Chen Duxiu.

Since 1927, Trotsky had been criticising Stalin in no uncertain terms: the Georgian's sympathy for the Guomindang, at the expense of the Chinese Communist Party, left no room for doubt; Trotsky probably feared that, because of the Japanese offensive, the Soviets would again force an alliance with the Guomindang against the Chinese communists. So he took up his pen in October 1932 to write 'A Letter to His Peking Friends', attacking Wang Ming's slogan of a 'nationalist revolutionary war against Japanese imperialism'. For Trotsky, as long as the USSR herself was not in danger, the important thing for the Chinese Communist Party was to do away with the Guomindang dictatorship:

'Today, through force of circumstance, the revolutionary unrest is directed primarily against the Guomindang government. We explain to the masses that Chiang Kai-shek's dictatorship remains the main obstacle to the creation of a constituent assembly and that we cannot rid ourselves of militarist cliques in China except by armed insurrection. Voiced and written protests, strikes, meetings, demonstrations, boycotts – whatever the concrete ends for which these are organised – must take on as a corollary the slogans "Down with the Guomindang!" "Long Live the Constituent Assembly!"'

'In order to achieve genuine national liberation, it is right that the Guomindang should be overthrown. But this does not mean that it is necessary to wait until the Guomindang is overthrown in order to fight. The more widespread the struggle against foreign oppression becomes, the more difficulties the Guomindang will face. And the more we mobilise the masses against the Guomindang, the more the struggle against imperialism will develop.'

This article was published at the beginning of 1933 in Paris, in the Trotskyist magazine *Class Struggle*.

In December of the same year Kang Sheng replied violently to it:

'In his article in *Class Struggle* the counter-revolutionary Trotsky, in February 1933, accuses our Party of speculation because it has issued the slogan of nationalist-revolutionary war against imperialism; he claims that this slogan can only be used in the case of a Japanese imperialist war against the USSR. Some Chinese communists also claim that this slogan is at odds with the defence of the USSR. Events have demonstrated the opposite and also refuted the Trotskyist calumny. Trotsky's arguments and those of opportunist elements in the Party are basically directed against the nationalist-revolutionary war. They constitute in effect a betrayal of the genuinely revolutionary struggle of the Chinese people against the Japanese imperialist offensive directed against the USSR and have also rendered this imperialism an inestimable service in its planned intervention against the Soviet Union.'

This polemic was important, the stereotypical posturing

notwithstanding. It paved the way for the great turning-point, that of 1935, when the Chinese CP, acting on the advice of the Comintern, would seek another alliance with Chiang Kai-shek.

Kang Sheng was not deaf to certain rumours that accused him of being a Trotskyist sympathiser. What better way of purging himself of this reputation than by launching a blistering attack on Lenin's former companion? By taking this stand, the young Chinese communist appeared for the first time in a new light: as a militant politician of international stature, in whom an inordinate taste for polemic and for ideological dispute was already evident.

The occasion for doing so presented itself in December 1933 during the Thirteenth Plenary Assembly of the Comintern's Executive Committee. A small book published in Paris in 1934, entitled *Revolutionary China Today* and signed 'Van Min' (Wang Ming) and 'Kang Hsin' (Kang Sheng), contains the speeches made by the two men. Wang Ming painted a broad picture of the situation in China, concentrating in particular on 'the consolidation, expansion and unification of the Republic of Soviets' and of the 'Red Army'. In passing, in order to please Kang Sheng, Wang Ming paid homage to the special services: 'Our political state leadership [OGPU] has latterly improved and strengthened its organisation and its operations very appreciably. Despite all its efforts, the Guomindang has not succeeded as in the past in organising any serious counteraction at our rear. [Applause] The Guomindang and imperialist intrigues and counter-revolutionary plots have all been thwarted.'

Kang Sheng, in his turn, spoke for an hour, during which he pilloried Trotsky and his friends. But the body of his statement, contrary to that of Wang Ming, turned on his personal experience: 'the expansion of the revolutionary movement in non-soviet China and the work of the Communist Party', touching on 'the partisans' struggle against the Japanese in Manchuria'. While congratulating himself on the progress of his party ('Since the International's last executive meeting, it has gained 110,000 members, of whom 30,000–60,000 are in non-soviet territory'), Kang Sheng underlined its weaknesses: 'The fight against provocation, the observation of the rules of conspiracy still leave something to be desired, despite repeated appeals from the Central Committee to all Party members and the few successes we have recently scored in this area.'

How could they forget the intrigues, the defections, the treachery in Shanghai, the perfidy of his predecessor Gu Shunzhang? For those Comintern members who might have forgotten what the Stalinist policy of 1927 had led to in China, Kang twisted the knife in the wound:

'Let us emphasise that in non-soviet China, we are militating in an atmosphere of White Terror. People are executed not only for belonging to the Communist Party but even to Red unions, to International Red Aid, and to other mass revolutionary organisations. However, despite all this, our Party is developing largely because it is constantly advancing along the path of Bolshevisation, because its CC conducts the struggle not in any abstract way but in an effective, efficient and concrete manner.'

Citing his own experience in Manchuria, Kang Sheng emphasised how important it was:

'1. To organise anti-Japanese agitprop groups among the soldiers and the people and to train political sections within military units;

2. To organise armed detachments to eliminate Japanese agents, spies and informers;

3. To grant the people freedom of assembly, freedom of the press, freedom to strike, etc.;

4. To refuse to pay rent to landowners, and so on.

This organisation achieved some great successes in the struggle against Japanese imperialism.'

Kang Sheng explained in passing how his native province, Shandong, 'by relying on the revolt of the peasants in the Communist Party, had organised soviets and confiscated landowners' property' (including that of his father, old Zhang).

Finally, the international dimension was not forgotten. Abroad, among the overseas Chinese, a 'society for the salvation of the fatherland' had been founded. 'Popular and anti-Japanese, this society would fight to achieve the aforementioned demands and to prosecute the war for national liberation.'

Kang Sheng had little trouble winning applause for rendering homage to the Comintern, though he did so without obsequiousness and with less condescension than the unctuous Wang Ming: 'The Chinese CP delegation proposes a contract of emulation to its fraternal communist parties with the aim of accomplishing the task of which Piatnitski has spoken to us, a contract whose fulfilment will be verified at the Seventh Congress of the Communist International.'

There was a ripple of applause, but everyone noted that Kang Sheng was talking of a 'contract' between partners. There was no subordination in the language he used. And that throughout his long speech, instead of giving everyone the title of 'comrade', he referred to the Comintern dignitaries simply by their names (unlike Wang Ming).

As he made his entry into the arena of international communism, on the eve of Christmas 1933, Kang Sheng gave the Soviets the very clear impression that they would be wise to pay attention to his services and reckon on having to deal with him in future.

But how did these Chinese in Moscow live, whom Kang Sheng was in charge of, as guardian of their consciences, political warder and talent-spotter? Rather badly. Especially during the 1930s. Having arrived in the USSR in successive waves, the 'Chinese comrades' had become the 'Comintern coolies'. Words like 'proletarian solidarity' rang out loud and clear in official speeches, but in practice the communists from the Far East discovered the harsh truth – the Russians did not like the Chinese. And the feeling was reciprocated.

'The main leaders of the Comintern were all smiles, but the opportunities for meeting them were pretty rare,' recalls Professor Guan Shuzhu, a student in Moscow in 1931. 'Underneath was a teeming mass of bureaucrats. It was all administrative pettinesses, corruption, back-handers, contempt for these young people, these "egg-faces" who had come from a different planet.'

The accommodation they were given consisted of insalubrious small bedrooms, several to a room. The Hotel Lux and other Comintern establishments were reserved for the Party leaders. The Russians were sparing with the food in the canteens and with ration tickets. No opportunity was lost to force the Chinese to part with their few kopeks' pocket money. And worst of all, the OGPU watched them as though they were thieves. Not to mention the suspicion that began to emerge at the end of the twenties, when it was realised that a good half of the Chinese inclined towards Trotskyism.

The Chinese had come to study. To learn to cast themselves in the mould of the perfect Bolshevik (*Bu-er-shi-wei-ke* in Chinese). In 1921 the Russians had opened the Communist University for Toilers of the East (KUTVa), a kind of elementary school for Asians. Gregori Broïdo was its first director. The teachers at the KUTVa figure among the great names of Bolshevism and the Asian revolution: the Tartar Sultan Galiev, the Iranian Sultan Zade, the Dutchman Henrikus Sneevliet (alias Maring), and the Indian Mobendra-Nath Roy. Ironically, all these men would to a greater or lesser extent break with communism, soon considered to be an obstacle to the national liberation of their respective countries. This was equally the case for another eminent pupil of the KUTVa, Tan Malaka, President of the PKI, the Partai Kommunis Indonesia. Moreover, at the Comintern's Sixth Congress in 1928, an Indonesian delegate created a scandal by issuing a denunciation from the platform of the International's position in China and supporting Trotsky on this issue.

In 1925 the Sun Yat-sen University opened, run by Karl Radek and subsequently by Pavel Mif. Its name clearly indicated that it was open to the non-communist elements of the Guomindang, the most famous of whom was Chiang Ching-kuo, Chiang Kai-shek's son, who even married a Soviet blonde (on becoming President of the Republic of Taiwan he would quickly take steps to conceal this embarrassing marriage). There were, however, some genuine communists who wore out the seats of their pants on the benches of the Sun Yat-sen University: the future Premier of the People's Republic of China, Liu Shaoqi, and the Mongol leader Ulanfu, a friend of Liu. A French communist, 'Henri Ségalla', taught these six hundred Chinese – two hundred of whom were women – the 'ABC of Communism', all the ins and outs of revolution: how to organise the coolies of Tientsin, the peasants of

Shandong, the seamen and dockers of Shanghai; how to train Party cells, union sections, etc.

The Russian counter-espionage people snooped everywhere. They went through notebooks with a fine toothcomb, gathered information from informers, incited jealousy, kept battalions of young Russian women to seduce the students. Primarily to test them. For these universities constituted excellent reservoirs of talent. Some of the students selected to fulfil the Comintern's most delicate missions were sent on to the special services' schools. One graduate of the KUTVa, Luo Yinong, became, as we have seen, responsible for counter-espionage in Shanghai before being captured and shot by the Guomindang in 1928.

Until 1928, a GRU man, Stoyanov, had been detailed to oversee the Chinese students at Sun Yat-sen University and pick out the best to train as special agents. Then in 1929 he went to Shanghai as a GRU representative. His role, like that of all the OGPU watchdogs, was also designed to nip in the bud the Trotskyist epidemic that was wreaking havoc among the Chinese ex-patriate community.

In fact, hardly had the Chinese Communist Party's Sixth Congress taken place in the summer of 1928, than Trotsky supporters at the Sun Yat-sen University formed a secret group around An Fu and Fan Jinbiao. Their demands smacked of heresy: 'We want the Chinese Party to discuss the opposition problem . . . and the Comintern to re-evaluate the Chinese question . . . and Trotsky to be restored to his rightful place in the leadership, especially as he predicted the disastrous outcome of the Chinese Revolution in 1927, due to the Comintern's advice.'

The first purges began. Yueh Sheng, then a student at Sun Yat-sen University, later recounted in his memoirs:

'The first purge meeting of the Party at Sun Yat-sen University took place, as I remember, in October 1929. Representatives of the Comintern, of the Russian Party's Central Committee, of the Russian Party's District Committee and others were present. After a brief statement explaining the method of purge, delivered by General Pavel Ivanovich Berzin, President of the Party's purge committee at Sun Yat-sen University and an old Boshevik who was at the time, I believe, head of the Red Army's intelligence service, I stood up to give my second important speech in Moscow. I openly accused Qu Qiubai and his like of being guilty of opportunism. Qu Qiubai was guilty of opportunism of the left, I said, while Zhang Guotao was guilty of opportunism of the right.'

The crazy machine was in motion. One day, a student doubtless affected by the 'virus' denounced all his room-mates. When the leather-coated OGPU men caused them to disappear, he fell into a deep depression. At bottom, the poor fellow was good-hearted. That evening he could not stand finding himself all alone with those empty beds. The next day he was found hanging from the latch on one of the windows.

A third school, the Leninist School, which was reserved for the élite, the Comintern leaders, was located in a big Le Corbusier-style building in the heart of Moscow. It belonged to the Comintern secret apparatus, the Department of Overseas Relations (OMS). A longstanding revolutionary, Klaudiia Ivanovna Kirsanova, wife of the famous Yaroslavsky, ran it. Students were taught Marxist economy, Leninist methods of organisation, the history of the Russian Revolution, the infiltration of unions. The aim was to Russify the International as it became increasingly under the control of the Russian Party and of Stalin.

The Leninist School trained many communist leaders: the Yugoslav Tito, the Vietnamese Pham Van Dong and Ho Chi Minh, the Pole Gomulka, and the Frenchman Waldeck Rochet. Its most famous Chinese pupil was none other than tubby little Deng Xiaoping, who had narrowly escaped arrest in France and, with the Sûreté Nationale close on his heels, had taken refuge in Moscow.

The final elements in the Comintern's political education system were the special services schools, whose students were selected for special technical training. The young Li Chinyung, for example, a brilliant student, was given radio training. The technical course at the Comintern's school for radio in Verkhovnoie, near Kazan, was undoubtedly very good. In 1933 Lin was sent on an ultra-secret mission to Shanghai, where he was to set up a radio link and prepare for the return of Wang Ming to the mother country. But security was not all that it should have been: the poor radio operator was captured and his head filled with grand ideas was sent rolling into the sawdust.

On 1 May 1935, a group of Chinese men and women and their radio-school teachers marched in the Labour Day parade in Red Square in Moscow. At their head were two teachers whose names were to become legendary: Seppel Weingarten and Max Klausen, who became Richard Sorge's assistants in Asia.

'I must add that some Chinese did not follow the official classes in the Soviet schools,' Professor Guan remembers. 'This was the case for men like Zhou Enlai, Chen Yun, Peng Zhen and of course Kang Sheng. In fact the OGPU trained them directly. We knew this at the time. They had separate status. They enjoyed a great many advantages that were accorded to the leaders of the foreign communist parties. Naturally, these leaders were also kept under surveillance, but Kang Sheng was freer than the others for the simple reason that it was he who was watching his comrades on behalf of the OGPU and the International.'

This was true. The OGPU (soon to be renamed NKVD) and the GRU had their own schools with stations erected on the Chinese border.

In Khabarovsk, at the confluence of the rivers Amur and Ussuri, above Manchuria, future secret agents (including Kang Sheng in his time) attended the Vostokskaia school. Until the 1930s, the 'Dalbiouro', the Comintern's Far East Bureau, was located in the same town, before being transferred to Vladivostok.

In the mid 1920s, Stalin had given the go-ahead for the training of Chinese agents, or Comintern agents operating in Asia, at the Kitaiskaia, the Chinese university. This impregnable citadel was situated one hundred and twenty kilometres south of Irkutsk, between Lake Baikal and the Mongolian frontier. Chinese, Koreans, Japanese, and Mongolians were all trained there in the art of subversion, the subtleties of double-dealing, the mechanisms of counter-espionage. By about 1930, three hundred Chinese had received their secret agent's diploma. They knew how to set up a network, control agents, brainwash the enemy, use invisible inks, make dead-letter drops, set up clandestine radios, infiltrate enemy services, detect double agents. It is no accident that numerous words in the Chinese espionage vocabulary came from Russian. Sometimes they are even transcribed phonetically into Chinese – OGPU for instance becoming *Ge-po-wu*. But the Chinese had their own tradition, dating back twenty-five centuries, to the period of the warring kingdoms, when in his *Art of War* Sun Tzu wrote: 'There are five types of secret agent to use: local, inside, double, dispensable, flying. When these five types are all in operation simultaneously and no one knows what they are doing, they are called "the divine web" and they constitute a sovereign's treasure.'

Kang Sheng's 'divine web' was gradually taking shape, while the Soviets for their part hoped to set up Chinese, Korean, Japanese, Indonesian and Annamite affiliates of their own special services.

On the borders, the OGPU even organised paramilitary troops. So it was that on 23 December 1932, Lieutenant-Colonel Bonavita, the French military attaché in Beijing, sent a surprising dispatch to Paris: 'The presence of numerous OGPU "special detachments" equipped with machine-guns has been reported among the Soviet troops stationed in Mongolia. And these include cavalry troops belonging to the OGPU.'

A short time later, Kang Sheng himself, from secret bases in Khabarovsk, Harbin and Vladivostok, organised special troops in Manchuria. According to a report written by Kang Sheng concerning the period June 1932 to December 1933, 'as a result of our work, recently organised anti-Japanese partisans are operating under our direct orders. These detachments have achieved some great successes. Originally numbering 4,000 to 5,000 men, they are now more than 10,000.'

Then, in 1935, with the aid of the Comintern, Kang recruited some four thousand students and Chinese workers in Russia, as well as Korean and European revolutionaries. Organised into cavalry and tank regiments and mechanised units, and stationed in Outer Mongolia, these volunteers received the order to link up with Mao

Zedong and Zhu De's troops, who were marching on North Shanxi.

Kang was not content with political or theoretical initiatives. The art of espionage had led him to become initiated in the art of war. He was at the same time learning languages. He already had a rudimentary knowledge of French and German. But he improved his Russian and English in order to perfect his talents as an 'internationalist'. Kang did not have a natural gift for foreign languages. He had to work assiduously, with a lot of perseverance and determination, in order to acquire a whole vocabulary that was totally useless in daily life: the Comintern 'newspeak'.

After four years' regular language practice, Kang Sheng could hardly form sentences in Russian. Instead he spoke a 'pidgin' version, without conjugating the verbs, making mistakes in his declensions, and was unable to pronounce the 'sh' sounds. But he could read newspapers or political reports. And his Soviet hosts appreciated his linguistic efforts, which were uncommon among the other international leaders of the Revolution.

For the next half-century, the names of Mao Zedong and Kang Sheng were to become closely linked. The first opportunity for Kang Sheng to associate himself with Mao came in February 1934. In January, the Second All-China Soviet Congress was held in the Red base of Ruijin, at which Mao had had to yield to the pressure of the 'internationalists', in other words of the Comintern as represented by the German Otto Braun. The composition of the Central Executive Committee consisting of 175 members, elected on 1 February, reflected this. Wang Ming and Kang Sheng were, of course, on it, although resident in Moscow.

Kang wrote the preface for the Russian edition of Mao's speech: 'Report of the Central Executive Committee and of the Council of Representatives of the People's Soviet Republic of China on the occasion of the Second All-China Soviet Congress'. His signature now appeared increasingly often at the bottom of political texts, foreshadowing the eminent role reserved for him at the Comintern's big world congress, in the summer of 1935.

1935 was extremely eventful. In January, ration cards for bread were abolished in Russia. On 15 April, the Paris daily communist newspaper, L'Humanité, carried the headline: 'USSR HAPPIEST COUNTRY IN THE WORLD'. A week earlier, on 8 April, the daily paper Izvestia had illustrated this by publishing the decree: 'Measures to combat criminality among children', which introduced the death penalty for crimes ranging from theft to treason for anyone over the age of twelve. A pharmacist called Henri Yagoda became the head of the new secret service organisation NKVD and the first head of a new penitentiary system known for short as the Gulag. The five-year plan was in full swing, and Pierre Laval, the French Prime

Minister opened the first subway train in Moscow on his visit there in May. In the summer, the miner Alexei Stakhanov dug out 102 tons of coal with a pneumatic drill in a single day – fourteen times the usual amount. This great socialist triumph allowed other more sordid events to be kept out of the limelight: in July, in Leningrad, two old wounded lions of Bolshevism, Zinoviev and Kamenev, were tried *in camera*. They stood accused of having planned to assassinate Stalin. Yagoda had mobilised five hundred NKVD officers, drawn from all the republics, to be present, in uniform, while these new methods of conducting the defence of socialism were pursued.

The trial date had not been randomly selected by Stalin. At exactly the same time, the biggest international gathering of communists was taking place in Moscow, the Comintern Congress. It was hot that summer, but the reception extended to those attending was rather cold. For this, the seventh and last Congress, the Muscovites no longer showed their usual warm curiosity in the 510 delegates, who had come from all over the world. Exoticism was no longer acceptable. The enthusiasm, the brotherly reunions, the verbal sparring and amazing plans to change the world were not there.

Confined to the Hotel Lux and the area around it, under the close watch of the NKVD, the delegates were shocked to discover that they were barred from the Kremlin. This only served to fuel rumours of hidden repression. Some of the delegates of the sixty-five Communist Parties affiliated to the Comintern actually living in Moscow passed on information to their comrades from outside the country. Among those living in the capital were, of course, Kang Sheng and Wang Ming, but also the unfortunate Brazilian leader Carlos Prestes, who had arrived in 1934 for the Seventh Congress that was supposed to take place then (the Sixth was held in 1928). Stalin had postponed it. Thereupon, the Russians had forcibly detained Prestes in Moscow.

On 25 July the Palace of Nobility opened its doors to those attending the Congress. Standing on Voroskovo Street, this palace built at the beginning of the last century had served as the setting for many of the scenes in Tolstoy's great novel *War and Peace*. The scarlet standards embroidered with gold cyrillic characters, the giant portraits of Marx, Engels, Lenin and Stalin contrasted oddly with the cold pink- and mauve-veined marble. Having walked past the iron guard of NKVD robots armed with fixed bayonets, the delegates waited in silence for the performance to begin. Then came the ovation, with everyone on their feet. The applause was deafening, Kang Sheng clapping as enthusiastically as anyone else. Stalin walked towards the platform with a heavy tread, followed by Molotov and a few others. On the platform, in the place of honour next to Dimitrov, the 'Bulgarian Lion', the new head of the Comintern, who had just emerged from the Nazi gaols, sat the heads of two communist parties: the French and the Chinese. Maurice Thorez wore a light-coloured short-sleeved sports shirt, casually unbuttoned at the neck, it was so hot, while Wang Ming, with his waxy porcelain-doll face, his wavy black gypsy-like hair combed back, his fine features reminiscent of those of a Sha'anxi puppet, wore a muzhik shirt under his wide-lapelled grey-striped suit.

And between the two, looking dramatic, solid and triumphant, sat the 'leader of the proletarian world', the 'little father of the people', the 'red sun in the hearts of communists', the 'kindly' Joseph Stalin.

Renewed applause. Anthems rang out on all sides, the *Rotfront* from the Germans, *Avanti Populi* from the Italians, *La Jeune Garde* from the French.

Stalin lit his pipe, gazing possessively over his little world. The debates began, but everything had been fixed in advance.

Wearing shirtsleeves, his hair already turned white by the hardships he had endured, the German Wilhelm Pieck started on his speech of self-criticism: 'The class-against-class line has led to regrettable sectarian errors,' he said contritely, letting the blame fall on the inept Central Committee. And yet the Soviet Party had imposed this line of action. But this time it was proposing a completely different magic formula: popular fronts.

The French delegation, which was the largest, was in favour of this approach. Heading their delegation were Thorez, Cachin, Guyot, Waldeck Rochet. Only the previous day, on 24 July, the French section of the Communist International had transformed itself into the French Communist Party, and for several months now its leaders had been engaged in negotiations with their fraternal enemies, Léon Blum's socialists. The Seventh Congress was to sanction this new policy of alliance.

To justify this new policy of union with the socialists in Europe and with the Guomindang in China, Georgi Dimitrov saw fit to refer to a legend that revealed a great deal about the communists' ulterior motives:

> Comrades, remember the ancient legend of the Trojan horse; the city had protected itself against enemy attack by surrounding itself with an insurmountable wall. The army trying to take the city had suffered serious losses, without being able to penetrate its defences, until the day it managed to get inside the walls, right into the enemy's midst, by means of the Trojan horse.
>
> It seems to me that we revolutionaries ought to use the same strategy against the human wall with which our enemy fascism has surrounded itself as a protection against the people's violence.

On 7 August the Chinese delegation had the floor, Wang Ming being the first to speak. Smoking a cigarette, Kang Sheng observed his companion with a sardonic eye, like a producer auditioning a young student from the Academy of Drama. As usual, Kang had written a major part of his speech: 'On the revolutionary movement in colonial and semi-colonial countries, and the tactics of the communist parties', focusing in particular on 'the promotion of a policy of a united anti-Japanese national front'.

Kang Sheng in his turn gave a speech, delivered more quickly, in a more staccato style. Its theme was not very different: an alliance with the Guomindang on the basis of Sun Yat-sen's three great principles: 'Democracy, the People's Livelihood and Nationalism'. Seven Chinese in all addressed the Congress.

Liu Changsheng, the organiser of the *Zeven Provinciën* mutiny, was sent back to China to communicate to Mao the content of their speeches. Without even waiting for Mao's response, Wang and Kang tried, without success, to start negotiations with Chiang Kai-shek's military attaché in Moscow, Deng Wenyi.

At the close of the Congress, forty-five leaders were elected to the International Executive Committee (IKKI), including four Chinese: Wang Ming, Zhang Guodao and, in absentia, Mao Zedong and Zhou Enlai. This new leadership also included the NKVD watchdogs: Yezhov, who was soon to replace Yagoda as head of the NKVD; Mikhail Trilisser, who took over the Comintern's Department for Overseas Relations (OMS), thereby sealing the downfall of the veteran Ossip Piatnitski. The consequence of this was that from now on members of the Comintern's special section would be spying directly on behalf of the USSR.

Wang Ming was also elected to the Praesidium and became an 'alternative member' of the Secretariat. 'Kon Sin', better known as Kang Sheng, was elected 'alternative member' of the Executive Committee and the Plenum, along with thirty-three others, including Bo Gu, the former general secretary of the Chinese Communist Party, with whom he had worked in Shanghai. This was in accordance with the rules of precedence and seniority, but even more important was the fact that Kang Sheng was so overburdened with special activities and the increasing amount of travel his job entailed that it was impossible for him to participate in the regular activities of the IKKI.

Nevertheless, the Seventh Congress conferred on Kang Sheng the status of a political militant of international standing. Those who knew him in Moscow at that time have observed how much he fraternised with numerous personalities in the Comintern. Many perished in the Stalin purges, but several of those who escaped ended up after the war as heads of state and senior officials in Eastern Europe, or at the head of powerful communist parties. With hindsight, one would be justified in thinking that even then Kang Sheng was spinning his web.

A circle of Asians gravitated around the Chinese Party; for them, this 'big brother' provided even more of a model, if not a figurehead, than the Russian Party. Caught between the two, even as early as the 1930s, they cleverly played them off one against the other. Take the Indochinese, for instance: their Communist Party was new and held its First Congress in Macao that year, without even informing the

Comintern. Kang Sheng spent a long time talking with the three Indochinese delegates to the Comintern Congress: Le Hong Phong was elected secretary of his party; and the one who called himself 'Chayan' was none other than Nguyen Ai Quoc, the future Ho Chi Minh. The third member of the Vietnamese threesome was Nguyen Thi Minh Khai (who did not like people to dwell on the fact that she was the wife of comrade Le). An ardent feminist, an unrivalled militant who had been imprisoned for a long time by the French, she was responsible for maintaining clandestine relations between the Indochinese groups and the Chinese Party in Hong Kong from 1927 to 1928. Her feminist address on behalf of the women of Asia had shaken the Comintern Congress:

The women of heroic China, the women workers of Japan and India, the women workers and peasants of Indochina are becoming a real force in the revolutionary ranks of the colonised peoples of the Far East . . . For hundreds of years, feudal customs and the prevailing moral order have transformed the women of the Far East into silent and docile slaves of their parents and their husbands. This moral order has paralysed their will, repressed, stifled and obscured their soul. Fellow women comrades! By following the path of revolutionary struggle, we are freeing ourselves from this moral order . . .

Then this radiant Indochinese woman returned secretly to her country to carry on the struggle there. She evaded the French for a long time, until her arrest after leading an insurrection. She screamed at the violence done to her, on the Sûreté's premises, but did not give away a single name. When she was thrown into a communal grave, no one could recognise her broken body.

Among Kang Sheng's friends was the head of the Japanese movement, known as 'Okano'. His real name was Nozaka Sanzo. A key figure in the Japanese Communist Party (Nihon Kyosanto) until his arrest in 1928, he escaped three years later and took refuge in Moscow. On the death of Katayama Sen, who was also in Moscow, Nozaka Sanzo became Party leader and at the Seventh Congress was elected to the Comintern's Executive Committee. Meticulous, with a keen interest in the detailed work of analysis and synthesis of intelligence on the Japanese war machine, Nozaka fascinated Kang Sheng. For Stalin's men, the Japanese Communist Party's numerous sources happily supplemented the messages sent by Sorge's network working in the heart of the Nippon Empire. Five years later, like Ho Chi Minh, Nozaka met Kang Sheng again at Yan'an and together they organised huge operations against the Japanese army.

Despite his close friendships with fellow Asians, Kang Sheng did not scorn the Europeans. He frequently ran into the French delegates in Moscow, Guyot, Vassart or Marty. André Marty and Kang Sheng met at the Comintern Plenum in December 1933, after which the Black Sea mutineer returned to France. On 6 November 1936, Kang Sheng and a small group of fellow members of the Comintern sent him a message of congratulation on his fiftieth birthday, a unique testimony to a brief encounter.

Kang Sheng struck up relationships with some communists from Eastern Europe whom he was later able to turn against Moscow. Among them were the Rumanian cavalry officer Émile Bodnaras, a student at the Leninist School and at the special services training college; the Hungarian Sandor Nogradi, a fellow student of Bodnaras, a secret agent in France under the name of Kellerman, and a guerrilla fighter in Slovakia during the Second World War, then Hungarian ambassador to Popular China; and another future ambassador to Beijing, the German Richard Gyptner, secretary of the Comintern's Western Bureau in Berlin until Hitler came to power. Finally, in February 1935, Josip Broz alias Tito arrived in Moscow to represent the Yugoslav section. He met Kang Sheng at this point, when rumour already had it that Kang had 'Trotskyist' sympathies.

It is understandable that Kang Sheng, in view of his role, should have made some unshakeable enemies. But forty years later, the accusation resurfaced. In August 1977, Tito visited China for the first and only time. He was accompanied by Stane Dolanc, head of the Yugoslav secret services. Welcomed by Hua Guofeng, Li Xiannian and Deng Xiaoping, Tito recalled his stay in Moscow (Deng had been there ten years before Tito). Addressing himself to Hua, the former head of Public Security who had become Premier after the death of Mao, Tito created a sensation:

'It can be said without any shadow of doubt that at that time Kang Sheng was playing a multiple game. On the one hand, he was humouring Stalin, but at the same time he was betraying his confidence. Similarly, he had made contact with the Trotskyists, and had considered joining their movement, but he had also taken steps to infiltrate and sabotage their Fourth International . . .'

Could it be that the Yugoslav head of state wanted to please his hosts, knowing they were keen to efface the role played by Kang, who had died two years earlier? Was it a matter of vengeance against the man who had given him such a rough ride during the 1950s? In any case, Tito certainly got the measure of Kang's psychology: a multi-faceted game of mirrors was entirely his style, even in the 1930s. Trained in Chinese clandestinity and then cast in the OGPU mould, Kang had inherited the art of the turnaround, which was as old as the Russia of the Tsars and the Chinese millennium.

Wang Ming said the same thing a hundred times in his memoirs: Kang Sheng would leap up from his chair in order to be the first to applaud whenever Stalin or Dimitrov addressed a meeting. And in

1933, the reader will remember, he was first in line to attack Trotsky. But it was quite logical that he should be on good terms with the Trotskyists: at the time they still believed they would win the game, and even in Stalin's entourage there were those who feared this might actually happen. Had anyone reproached Kang for his behaviour, he would simply have replied that his job, his 'work in special affairs' as they say in Chinese (*Tewu gongzuo*), required him to infiltrate opponents, starting with the Chinese community. Hence his reputation for being a Trotskyite, which has gained credence since his death.

'His leftist policy during the Cultural Revolution had its roots in Moscow,' maintains Professor Li, archivist and meticulous historian of the Taiwan special services at Fawubu Diaochabu. Did Kang Sheng not bear some of the responsibility for the arrest in Moscow, in 1934, of the Korean Kim Zaen, head of a 'diversional espionage organisation', to quote the expression used in *Izvestia* in its 24 September 1934 edition? There is no doubt that Kim was a genuine secret agent, since Japan interceded on his behalf and obtained his release.

In fact, the hunting of potential dissidents, of those who might oppose the Comintern line, that is to say the Wang Ming line, was a continual process within the Chinese community. Under cover of counter-espionage, Kang Sheng also excelled at running political opponents to earth. The example of one-time seaman Chen Yu from Canton, who arrived in the USSR in 1931, is often cited. He had undoubtedly been talking to people suspected of Trotskyism, for Kang Sheng brought the merciless weight of 'proletarian justice' to bear upon him. Chen had his Party card taken away from him, and Kang had him sent to Stalingrad to work as a labourer in a smelting works.

On another occasion Kang Sheng whispered to Wang Ming that there were dreadful goings-on at the Leninist School: 'Those old rogues Zhou Dawen and Yu Xiusong are infecting the foreign community in the Leninist School. And the director is apparently protecting them . . .! It's disgraceful. Can we not do something?'

Wang Ming understood the message. As always, he passed Kang Sheng's ideas off as his own, in order to shine before Stalin or Dimitrov. He requested an interview with Stalin and explained the facts: 'It's all the fault of Kirsanova, protectress of those two Trotskyite louts . . .'

The next day Zhou and Yu were arrested and sent to Siberia and Xinqiang. Klaudiia Ivanovna Kirsanova, the courageous wife of Yaroslavsky, did not benefit this time from her status as a Bolshevik veteran, companion of Lenin. She disappeared . . . to be replaced by her deputy Vulko Chervenkov, brother-in-law to Dimitrov and future Prime Minister of Bulgaria.

In 1936, despite his Chinese preoccupations, Kang Sheng, acting for the Comintern, began to follow the situation in the West. It was in any case with great enthusiasm that he and Wang Ming spent most of the time during the historic Seventh Congress organising international propaganda in favour of a united anti-Japanese front.

Living in Moscow at the time was Wu Yuzhang, and elderly linguist passionately interested in the problems of modernising the Chinese language. Wang Ming and Kang Sheng decided to send him to Paris in 1935, in order to establish his newspaper *The Time of National Salvation* (*Jiuguo Shibao*) in the French capital. Impressed by the growing influence of the French Communist Party, and convinced that for some while yet France would remain the great cradle of democracy, Kang and Wang felt that the venerable scholar would be well placed there to inspire the Chinese in Europe with the spirit of alliance. Furthermore, they published a robust article in his paper denouncing those who were proposing, as Lenin had done with the Brest–Litovsk treaty, to sign a separate peace with Japan.

In the summer of 1936 Kang was given a secret mission. In the turbulent Europe of those days, he passed virtually unnoticed, disguised as a sales representative, through Scandinavia, the Netherlands and Belgium to France. In Paris in 1935 a woman calling herself Étienne Constant founded the Association of Friends of the Chinese People, based at place de la Trinité, in the 11th *arrondissement*. A pretty brunette with fiery eyes, 'Étienne Constant' was really a Rumanian called Sofia Jancu. She was soon to become the mistress of the communist leader Gabriel Péri, who had just returned from a long trip to Indochina, where he had been investigating the repression. Prompted by the Comintern, 'Étienne Constant', together with General Ching Minshu, organised a huge conference for Chinese living in Europe on 29 August 1936. There were 450 delegates from England, Germany, Switzerland, the Netherlands, as well as some who lived in France. And thus was born the Federation of Chinese Associations in Europe for the Salvation of China. Some of the most eminent French intellectuals lent their support to the initiative: the art historian Elie Faure, the Breton socialist Augustin Hamon, the lawyer Henri Levy-Bruhl, and not least André Malraux.

This conference, like the Congress of Overseas Chinese in Europe that took place on 20 September 1936, provided an opportunity not only to gauge their strength, but also to exert external influence on the policy of the Guomindang, to mobilise a vast swell of public opinion against Japan. Furthermore, Kang Sheng learned to build up a huge network of contacts among the Chinese diaspora.

In the interval between these two events, a vast forum opened in Geneva, which Kang Sheng attended, along with many other young Chinese. This was the First World Youth Congress, held under the auspices of the League of Nations from 31 August to 7 September 1936 to attempt to avert the dangers that were gathering on the horizon, across the border. The League of Nations, like the International Labour Bureau, was already crawling with communist agents or offi-

cials who could be counted on to support the cause of countries hostile
to Fascism. Seven hundred delegates from twenty-five countries had
made the journey to Geneva: members of Christian associations,
youth hostel associations, the world peace community, and the Communist Youth International, the KIM. The Chinese, at war with
Japan, and Republican Spain, by force of circumstance, were under
the spotlight. They would happily have forgone this privilege.

Two KIM leaders, who would spend their whole lives steeped in the
murky world of special operations, were responsible for the brilliant
but behind-the-scenes organisation of this assembly: the Frenchman
and Comintern representative Raymond Guyot, and the Hungarian
Mihaly Farkas alias Wolf, who became famous after the war as head
of the bloodthirsty Hungarian political police, the AVH.

Strife-torn Spain was Kang Sheng's third destination in his European odyssey that autumn of 1936. After his stay in Switzerland, the
Communist Party of Pierre Nicole, close friend of Gabriel Péri, had
helped the Chinese revolutionary to get to Paris, where he stayed a
fortnight – the time it took for Arthur Dallidet (whom Kang had met
in Moscow in 1934) and Maurice Tréand, the two men in control of
the secret apparatus of the French Communist Party, to make suitable
arrangements for his onward journey.

Imagine the Comintern's Chinese envoy wandering the streets of
Barcelona on the eve of war, with the Republicans mobilising, and
hundreds of Comintern representatives arriving, trying to swell the
numbers of the small Spanish Communist Party. There were the military experts who would train the International Brigades, men such as
Manfred Stern, the future General Kleber, with whom Kang had
worked in Manchuria three years earlier; the NKVD secret police
agents who were beginning to open files on the anarchists the easier to
eliminate them afterwards; Stalin's emissaries who packed up 7000
cases of gold ingots – the Republic's gold – and sent them for safe-
keeping; and Ambassador Antonov-Ovseenko, who was already
lavishing advice on the Republican government. But what precisely
was Kang Sheng's mission in the midst of this motley crowd of
enthusiasts, the first Internationalists ready to form their own
brigades for the defence of the Republic?

On 22 September Maurice Thorez went to Moscow to beg Stalin to
help Spain. On the way back his path crossed that of the Chinese
Comintern leader, who was convinced that in Spain, as in China, in
the face of the forces of evil, the achievement of unity would be no
simple matter.

6
The Kidnapping of Chiang Kai-shek

The drama took place on 12 December 1936 – in China this time. Kang Sheng had returned from Spain and followed events from Moscow with bated breath. In Xi'an, in Shanxi province, the former capital of the emperors of China, two Guomindang generals kidnapped their own commander, Generalissimo Chiang Kai-shek. They were Zhang Xueliang and Yang Hucheng, and had until this time been leading the armies of the north-east and the north-west. The abduction could not have come at a better time for the communists, for the Generalissimo was about to launch a huge military offensive against them, while the Japanese were intensifying their conquest of China.

But what did Zhang and Yang want?

Simply to impose on their leader an alliance with the communists, to unite the population against Japan. And for a year the Comintern had actually been urging the Chinese Communist Party to form a united front against the foreign aggressor.

Without any delay, the Guomindang officers approached the communist leadership, offering them the chance to participate in tripartite negotiations to seal the alliance. Mao hesitated. He was not the only one who thought this an excellent opportunity to dispose of Chiang, his lifelong enemy. But Zhou Enlai did not share this opinion. He had had dealings with numerous nationalist officers at the Huangpu military academy and was more familiar with their psychology than this peasant Mao.

On 13 December, General Zhang Xueliang's personal plane was sent to fetch him.

Wang Ming, in Moscow, later claimed that Stalin himself wrote a telegram to the leaders of the Chinese Party: 'Attribute the Xi'an incident to the Japanese secret services, saying they penetrated Zhang Xueliang's entourage in order to weaken China. Pursue the idea of a national anti-Japanese front and, above all, no matter what the cost, obtain the release of Chiang Kai-shek, who will be able to lead the alliance we desire.'

Once again Stalin wanted to keep Chiang in power. His intervention was understandable but perfectly pointless. For the Chinese communists themselves had for nearly a year been conducting a whole series of operations aimed at forcing Chiang Kai-shek to negotiate. It was a strange business, with Zhou Enlai and the communist special services masterminding the initiative. Because, first of all, there was a mole in the immediate entourage of the rebel general Zhang Xueliang.

This unwittingly influential agent was called Li Puhai. In 1927 he had been head of the Party's propaganda machine when the Guomindang captured him in Beijing. Threatened with execution, he gave away details of the Party's organisation, leading to the arrest of sixty of his comrades. He then changed his name, no doubt to save his skin. Under the name Li Tiancai, he eventually became a member of Zhang Xueliang's staff.

A renegade can always change sides a second time . . . or he might never have changed sides in the first place. Was Li playing a double game? Advising General Zhang to ally himself with the communists? The Guomindang thought so because they shot him the day after the Xi'an incident. There was one damning piece of evidence against him: a native of Shandong province, Li had been a close friend of Kang Sheng in the 1920s. This was enough to lend credence to the suspicion that Li had continued to work for the communist secret services.

And then there was Deng Fa. In 1931 he had become head of the secret services in the Soviet Republic of China, while Kang operated in the 'White zones'. The department was then called the Bureau for Political Protection (*Zhengzhi Baohuju*). Aided by Li Kenong, Deng Fa fiercely suppressed any 'counter-revolutionary activities' in the 'Red zone'.

In 1936 the American journalist Edgar Snow met Deng Fa, 'the head of the Red Army's OGPU', in the course of his reporting:

> This Deng Fa, a Cantonese, was the son of a working-class family and had been a Western-style chef on a steamer on the Canton–Hong Kong line. He had been one of the leaders of the big seamen's strike in Hong Kong, and on that occasion had been beaten up and had most of his ribs broken by a British policeman who did not like strike pickets. Then he had become a communist, entered the military academy at Huangpu and taken part in the nationalist revolution until, in 1927, he joined the Red Army in Kiangsi!

Snow forgot to mention – but perhaps he did not know? – that Deng Fa, formerly Borodin's bodyguard, had been trained for five years by the Russian secret services in Vladivostok. The two men warmed to each other, and did a little sightseeing together. Then, when the time came for them to part, the journalist could not resist one final question:

'Do you not fear for your life?'

'No more than Zhang Xueliang fears for his,' replied Deng Fa with a chuckle. 'I live in his house.'

And this is the puzzling question in this baffling affair: what on earth was a leader of communist intelligence doing in the home of the great Guomindang general?

And now for the third man: at the centre of preparations for the

Xi'an incident was a fellow accomplice of Kang Sheng and Zhou Enlai during the Shanghai period, Pan Hannian.

Pan met Zhang Xueliang in a European restaurant in the outskirts of Shanghai. Prepared for this meeting, Zhang got straight to the point: 'I am ready to co-operate with you communists and especially to stop the civil war . . .'

They ended their meal in good spirits, drinking to the future of China, but no decision came of their conversation. Only one of Zhang's associates, Wang Izhe, remained in contact with the communists, and arranged another meeting. This time Li Kenong, a comrade of Pan Hannian (and of Kang Sheng), an expert in devious plots, and Deng Fa's deputy, met the rebel officers. The meetings in Luochan became regular occurrences throughout February and March 1936, the Year of the Rat. A local ceasefire was tacitly observed by the North-Eastern Army of the Guomindang and the Red Army. For the first time since 1927, nationalists and communists were no longer shooting at each other. In General Zhang's view, this was already considerable progress, a genuine first step towards total peace. He wanted to negotiate at the highest level: 'I want to meet either Mao Zedong or Zhou Enlai!'

Zhou Enlai was of course appointed to attend this meeting.

On 9 April Zhou, accompanied by Li Kenong, arrived in Yan'an, which was still under nationalist control at the time. The meeting that would change the fate of China took place in a small Catholic chapel, beneath the shadow of a large crucifix.

There could be no question of Zhang acting prematurely against his leader Chiang, and yet his plan and that of the communists was one and the same: to gather all the Chinese forces under the same banner.

The machine was set in motion. But Chiang Kai-shek was beginning to worry. There were reports of fraternisation between his troops and Mao's. By temperament, he would have been tempted to have several officers shot, just to set an example.

But, unknown to his generals, as he himself would later relate, Chiang Kai-shek was already planning to negotiate with the communists. Chen Lifu, the head of Chiang's political secret service, was entrusted with this mission.

On 5 May 1936, the Chinese communists published a telegram calling for an end to internal hostilities and for peace negotiations. Shortly after, Zhou Enlai, the CCP representative, and Pan Hannian, representing the Communist International, arrived in Shanghai to meet Chang Chun, the government representative. At first, I was intrigued by Pan Hannian's precise status. But in investigating the matter more deeply, Chen Lifu discovered that Pan was in possession of a Morse code to communicate with the Communist International and I enquired no further. When Pan came to Nanking to negotiate with Chen Lifu, the government asked the communists to accept the following four points: 1. To adopt the Three Principles of the People (of Sun Yat-sen); 2. To obey the orders of Generalissimo Chiang Kai-shek; 3. To disband the Red Army and to integrate into the National Army; 4. To abrogate the soviets and to reorganise them into local governments.

According to Chiang Kai-shek, Pan Hannian accepted these proposals. On whose behalf was he actually negotiating – that of the Chinese CP or of the Comintern? For this plan was tantamount to surrender. But Zhou Enlai did not take part in the second meeting; he had left Pan to negotiate on his own.

Today, Pan Hannian's biographical note in Popular China is not very flattering. It consists of only a few words: 'He betrayed the Revolution in 1936 and became a secret agent for the Guomindang. He remained a spy hidden within the Chinese Communist Party for a long time . . .'

A seasoned Comintern militant, trained by the special services in the USSR, Pan Hannian had lived through the dark hours of carnage in Shanghai, alongside Kang Sheng and others. One interpretation of his actions was that he had simply obeyed 'the voice of his Master'; another that he had simply shown himself to be a hopeless diplomat. It did not occur to anyone that in fact it was all a subtle ploy on the part of Zhou Enlai to keep the Guomindang and the Comintern occupied by getting them to talk to each other, while he used his knights, and even those of his opponent, to checkmate the enemy, encircling the king, Generalissimo Chiang Kai-shek.

And on 12 December Chiang was indeed kidnapped. On 7 December, Zhou Enlai, accompanied by Bo Gu and Ye Jianying, the chief of staff of the Eighth Route Army, arrived in Xi'an. Shortly afterwards, they were joined by the heads of their intelligence services, Li Kenong and Luo Ruiqing. Ruiqing, a tall well-built fellow from Sichuan province, was deputy director of foreign intelligence. He had been trained initially in France, by the special section for which Raymond Guyot worked in the Comintern's Western Bureau (WEB), then in the USSR, like Kang Sheng, by the Moscow secret services, from 1932 to 1935.

The various parties present negotiated on every detail: the cessation of hostilities, the release of political prisoners, collaboration between the two armies, the setting-up of an anti-Japanese front.

After many sleepless nights, once the supplies of English cigarettes had filled the ashtrays and the large bottles of bourbon had been emptied, an agreement was reached on 24 December. Basically, it was no more than an interlude. For the special services the war never ceased, as even the most optimistic realised as soon as liaison missions were established in 1937. Dai Li, the most formidable of Chiang Kai-shek's spies, had vowed to sabotage the CCP–Guomindang agreement.

At number 1 Qixianzhuang, in Xi'an, was a dentist's surgery; and, as was common practice with the Comintern, the surgery in question – that of the German Herbert Wunsch – served as a cover for the clandestine Communist Party. At the start of the Xi'an affair, Wunsch had been killed by a stray bullet so his house was selected to become the official premises of the communists' Guomindang Liaison Office. Two former students at the Russian universities ran the political side of it. In July 1937 a youth who was not yet twenty arrived as secretary to the committee. But beneath his harmless appearance as a junior office boy, this Luo Qingchang was already working in the realms of darkness. Soon, under Kang Sheng's orders, he would become, even to this day, one of the great masters of Chinese espionage.

Agent 0.63 had been working for the Russians for a long time. Without ever having visited the USSR, he was filled with the deepest admiration for the vast country bordering his own region of Xinjiang. And besides, the NKVD paid for his silence and his complicity in cash. This was the period when Stalin harboured the secret dream of completely annexing Xinjiang, a big desert area rich in resources such as petrol and uranium.

0.63 was an important man, none other than the governor of Yarkand.

At the beginning of September 1937 a new head of the cipher department, attached to the NKVD, arrived in Urümqi, the capital of Xinjiang province. His name was Vladimir Mikhailovich Chorokov alias Petrov. His boss was the terrible Lavrenti Beria, who remained his master until 1953. Petrov was then attached to the Soviet Embassy in Australia. Terrified by the purges taking place within the services at that time, he decided in April 1954 to defect to the West, and knocked on the door of ASIO, the Australian Security and Intelligence Organisation. He revealed to them, among other things, the strange fate of 0.63, the Chinaman from Xinjiang.

I entered the OGPU (later to become the NKVD) in May 1933, I was twenty-six. I wanted a job that would allow me to eat my fill. I couldn't have found better: the OGPU restaurant was the best in the whole of the Soviet administration. At the OGPU, we enjoyed privileges that were not available to anyone else . . . I was assigned to the signals department. One day, my boss Iliyne announced that our armed forces in Xinjiang wanted a cipher officer at their headquarters in Urümqi. And that was how irrefutable proof of a vast secret organisation came my way. Our agents' telegrams told of subversive intrigue on the part of Japanese agents and Anglo-Saxon missionaries, who were depicted as dangerous propagandists and smugglers. So when the pro-Soviet puppet government of Urümqi was threatened by a rebellion of officers and local tribal chiefs, an additional detachment of NKVD border troops, backed up by tanks and aircraft, was sent to conduct a bloody purge against anti-Soviet elements . . .

One of my primary tasks was to monitor coded messages relating to a secret operation in the course of which the general of the rebel Chinese at Hotan had been captured. This incident had been organised by an NKVD agent in that sector, a Chinese who was on good terms with the general. This agent was directly controlled from Moscow by radio contact.

This Chinaman, Chen Yun, who had been sent to Moscow, became a senior official in Deng Xiaoping's regime half a century later. We have already come across him in Shanghai, in 1931, with Kang Sheng; he was with Kang again in 1935 at the Comintern Congress in Moscow.

One morning Petrov decoded a telegram marked 'Top secret and most urgent'. It was addressed to the chief of staff General Kraft and to the local head of the NKVD, Colonel Voitenkov: 'Neutralise agent 0.63 identified as a British agent!'

0.63 had until then been a source of first-class information, thanks to all the people he met in his capacity as governor. He now received a message inviting him to Urümqi. He was at once shown to Colonel Voitenkov's office. His puffy face, his elephantine appearance, everything about his physiognomy, which was that of a greedy sensualist, condemned him as a traitor from the moment the suspicion was raised. It was true there were British Intelligence Service agents covering Xinjiang, such as Peter Fleming, brother of the famous Ian Fleming, creator of James Bond, 007. But Moscow was mistaken: 0.63 had never betrayed his Soviet friends and innocently thought he had been summoned in order to be congratulated and given a new mission.

'We have proof that you are an Intelligence Service agent!' screamed Voitenkov at the outset.

From an adjoining room, Petrov could hear the yelling and the shouting and the sobbing of the poor governor, who defended himself like the very devil. In front of the door two NKVD bodyguards drew their Tokarev pistols . . .

'. . . and English spies must be treated accordingly, like the wretched rabid dogs that they are!' concluded the Colonel by way of delivering a verdict.

The two NKVD men had dug a grave under the floorboards in the corridor. 0.63 came out of the office in a daze. Outside darkness was falling. He lay face down in the grave. In the yard the engine of a lorry started up. One of Voitenkov's assistants put his Tokarev to the back of 0.63's head and fired three shots at point-blank range. The governor's flabby body tensed. His corpse was doused with petrol and set alight. The grave was filled in, the floorboards replaced and the bamboo matting laid out on top. 0.63 had been neutralised . . .

Chen Yun could rub his hands with satisfaction. Once again, the rule of Moscow had prevailed. And the murder of 0.63 was just one incident among countless others in the secret war of Xinjiang.

Civil war had been raging in this desert region for years. Xinjiang is a multi-ethnic province in which the *Han* population (the native Chinese) are a minority. The largest region in China, Xinjiang has a population of only four million. The Muslim Uygurs remain the most numerous, but thirteen other minorities also live there, such as the Kazakhs, the Mongols, the Russians, the Uzbeks, the Hui, the Kalka . . . Apart from its considerable mineral wealth, one only has to look at a map to appreciate the strategic importance of the region. Situated to the south of Mongolia, it is surrounded by Turkestan – and therefore by Russia – and lies not far from Iran, Afghanistan, Baluchistan, the Punjab, North India and Tibet.

Soviet strategy hardly changed over the years. The NKVD encouraged ethnic conflict in Xinjiang, even going so far as to intervene at the request of its allies. This was a secret operation, for Chiang Kai-shek, a friend of the USSR, could hardly take much delight in seeing an area that had traditionally been part of the Chinese Empire disappear to a neighbouring state's advantage.

The Soviet's man was a Manchu adventurer called Sheng Shicai. The officer responsible for protecting the north-east frontier, he was based in Urümqi. Advised by a White Russian general, Antonov, he conducted a constant war against the Muslim General Ma Shiming. After a *putsch* in April 1933, Sheng was appointed governor.

An enlightened soldier, Ma had crossed the whole stretch of the Gobi Desert with five hundred men and a single objective: to deliver the Muslims from Chinese domination. His headquarters were at the Caves of a Thousand Buddhas at Dunghuang. His plan was to capture all the oases along the silk route, including major cities like Kashgar and Urümqi. He found many Muslims ready to respond to his call, but they were poor soldiers. Enraged by their failure to overthrow the Chinese garrison at Hami, they massacred every living being in the area.

In 1933, despite his disorganised and bloody tactics, Ma and his troops, galvanised by a fanatical reading of the Koran, seriously threatened to take Urümqi. All that year Sheng Shicai had been conducting negotiations with Stalin via his consul-general. Stalin feared lest the Japanese should take advantage of the disturbances in Xinjiang to move into the province; following their takeover of Manchuria, they had also recently annexed Jehol. A Japanese agent, Onishi Tadashi, was acting as adviser to General Ma. The governor of Xinjiang decided to call Stalin to the rescue. At Christmas 1933, Red Army units of some three thousand men belonging to NKVD special units, in unmarked vehicles, but also armoured cars entered the Chinese province. The impact they made was not only psychological.

Soviet aircraft bombed the routed Muslim army. Some time later, General Ma, having negotiated his safe conduct with the Russians, took refuge in the USSR. Rumour has it that he, like 0.63, was liquidated by the NKVD.

Stalin had won. Sheng declared, to the great displeasure of the central government in Nanking, which he theoretically represented, that he had made 'indestructible friendship with the USSR' a part of his platform. His party called itself the 'Anti-imperialist Society', and his troops formed the 'Anti-imperialist Army'. The Japanese were of course the prime targets. And the annexation of a part of Chinese territory was well under way. On 16 May 1935, Sheng signed an agreement binding him to the USSR for technical assistance, mineral and oil exploitation, the construction of roads leading through the Karakorum passes, giving access to India. In the region of Borthala, Soviet engineers discovered uranium deposits. In Kuldja, construction of a military airfield, with an adjoining training centre, was under way. And five thousand more Soviet soldiers arrived in Xinjiang in May 1937. General Ma's Muslim successors, having been bribed by the Japanese, were attempting a new uprising – which only served to bring Sheng a little closer to Moscow.

At that point Chen Yun arrived in Xinjiang. With him came new NKVD experts. This young fellow with a square face and a determined chin was one of the few workers to attain leadership rank. His real name was Liao Chengyün, and he was born in the slums of Shanghai in 1906. A teacher noticed the child's shrewdness and helped him, enabling the boy to learn several thousand characters, as many as a young scholar would be familiar with. He trained as a typesetter, a job requiring precision and an attention to detail, becoming a skilled worker. Moreover, Chen worked in the famous Shanghai printing company, the Commercial Press, which was set up at the turn of the century and was the largest in the whole of the Far East. With its ultra-modern machines, this company was the pride of the Shanghai bourgeoisie. The reader will recall that in 1927 the big Commercial Press building was the last bastion where Zhou Enlai had taken refuge, with four hundred Red Guards, in the face of a thousand Green Gang hitmen. Chen Yun was the president of the unions in this great hive of activity in Baoshan Lu. In fact, for several years he had distinguished himself as a pioneer of the union movement alongside Liu Shaoqi, Zhang Hao (Lin Biao's uncle) and Deng Fa, the 'Red bandit'.

At Zhou Enlai's request, made before he fled in 1931, Chen Yun joined Kang Sheng to rebuild the secret services in Shanghai. His experience and his many contacts in the union world were of great help. However, at the end of 1934, Chen joined Mao's Long March. He did not remain with it until the end: in January 1935, on the occasion of the Congress of Chinese Soviets in Zunyi, Mao sent him to the USSR to explain his policy to Stalin.

Travelling via Shanghai, Chen Yun went to Moscow, where he was welcomed with open arms by Kang Sheng and Wang Ming. Despite his militant activities, Chen Yun had a different vision of the Revolution from that of Kang Sheng. They did not share the same objective: the well-being of the Chinese or power . . . They had both been cast in the Stalinist mould. Kang the taciturn, Chen the jovial. Kang the son of a landowner, Chen the son of a proletarian. Come evening, Kang Sheng, in his OGPU cadre's apartment, would untangle the 'divine web' of intrigue, while Chen Yun, in his dormitory, would study the works of Varga, the Comintern economist, by the light of a candle.

Nevertheless, during his two-year stay in the USSR, Chen – according to several testimonies – attended classes at the NKVD schools. He specialised, so it is said, in economic intelligence. And in the spring of 1937, Beria, the head of the NKVD, and Dimitrov, the Comintern leader, with Kang Sheng's agreement, sent Chen to Xinjiang, as an emissary to the Manchu Sheng Shicai. To avoid friction with his Chinese comrades, Stalin was initiating tripartite negotiations between Sheng Shicai, the Chinese Party and himself.

Kang Sheng and Wang Ming remained in Moscow another six months, then considered their mission accomplished. The time had come for them to return to China. In mid-October, as they sat drinking Turkish coffee, the lion-like Dimitrov, the Comintern's strong-arm man, congratulated Wang Ming, Kang Sheng and the third member of the band, Wang Jiaxiang, the future Chinese ambassador to Russia.

'Congratulations on your tremendous work! The setting-up of a united anti-Japanese national front is no small achievement. You have done noble work for your country, for the International, for world peace . . . Comrade Stalin is personally grateful to you . . .'

Kang Sheng felt rather well disposed towards this fine fellow Dimitrov (and towards his vivacious wife, Helena Dimitrova, who taught cipher and deciphering techniques at the Leninist School). But, unlike Wang Ming, he was not taken in by him. His stay in the USSR, which had been such a practical education, had also taught him to be suspicious. Wang Ming had become a devoted follower of Stalin, Kang Sheng an attentive pupil already covetous of his master's position. In public Kang Sheng always agreed with Wang Ming – especially as he often repeated things that had been communicated to him by Kang only the day before and took the credit for himself. Kang had helped Wang to forge a security apparatus of great efficacy in rooting out unreliable elements within the Chinese community in the USSR. In exchange, Wang had introduced him to those in the highest echelons of the Comintern. At first this was very valuable . . . Almost bordering on obsequiousness, Kang Sheng was always of the same opinion as the person he was speaking to. In order to reach the summit of Taishan mountain, and the ultimate ecstasy, it was necessary to suffer. Every time he bowed and scraped, his hatred increased. But Stalin, Beria and the other had started out this way . . .

Right to the very end, he seemed to be Wang Ming's man. Wang Jiaxiang will always remember a final meeting with Stalin, a few days before the departure of Kang and Wang for China.

Stalin, in the presence of Dimitrov, was talking of this and that. Suddenly he asked Wang Jiaxiang:

'Well then, how many men are there in the Red Army?'

'Of those who have arrived north of Sha'anxi, about 30,000,' was the reply.

'But not at all, that's a gross underestimation,' said Wang Ming, looking exasperated. He was well aware of Stalin's obsession with the Japanese menace: 'There are 300,000, isn't that so, Kang Sheng?'

The head of the secret services, by definition, ought to have known. Kang nodded sagely, like some connoisseur who cannot be taken in, and quoted a lower figure . . .

During the course of his stay Kang Sheng had also observed the constricting influence of the NKVD men on the Comintern, its complete penetration by them. He had worked with these stony-faced men in the dispatch of mysterious messengers, the circulation of special funds, the transfer of arms and of pamphlets. The spark of revolution had died in them. On the other hand, he had noted the efficiency of these networks during his trip to Switzerland, France and Spain.

He had seen the Revolution devour its own sons. At the beginning of 1937, for instance, the elimination of Bela Kun, the old Hungarian revolutionary, had created a sensation. Wang Ming gave Kang a detailed account of this. Bela Kun was the historic leader of the Hungarian Revolution of 1919. At the Seventh Comintern Congress in 1935, he naturally had a seat on the Executive Committee. This former companion of Lenin was a legend in his own right. Oddly, he was sent on a mission to Latin America, then recalled to Moscow, where he was accused of 'Zinovievism' . . .

At the beginning of 1937, at a meeting of the Executive Committee, Manuilsky accused him of every evil:

'You have always been a deviationist, even as leader of the Hungarian Republic in 1919. You were already a spy for Rumanian State Security . . .'

'This is provocation! Slander!' shouted Béla Kun. 'You want to assassinate me! I shall complain to Stalin . . .'

A heavy silence descended on the meeting. The delegates present – Wang Ming, Togliatti, Pieck, Gottwald, Florin, Varga, Kuusinen, Tuominen – lowered their eyes. The old Hungarian was suspended from all his duties. He left the room, slamming the door behind him. In the corridor outside, an NKVD squad was waiting for him.

'You call yourselves communists? You're nothing but miserable assassins!' His cries grew fainter in corridors that reeked of damp and fear. He was shot shortly afterwards.

In the autumn of 1937 Kang Sheng and Wang Ming flew to Xinjiang. They were on their way to Yan'an, the revolutionary capital, and had to land at Urümqi to refuel, a stopover for which there was a strong political motive as well: to strengthen ties with the famous Sheng Shicai.

Sheng explained to the two Comintern delegates what he had already explained to Chen Yun, who was still in the city on a liaison mission:

'Now I would like to join the Chinese Communist Party!'

The Manchu adventurer seemed to want to take out an insurance policy against the future. The two Chinese visitors could not take such a decision without consulting Moscow, which had developed a very special relationship with Urümqi.

Stalin's response was final: it was completely out of the question. As far as Sheng was concerned, he wanted to create a kind of equilibrium between the Russians and the Chinese. He suggested that when the two delegates got to Yan'an, they should send him technicians to build the new Xinjiang.

That day Sheng Shicai confronted Kang Sheng for the very first time with the concrete problem of dual allegiance to the Comintern (under Stalin's iron rule) and the Chinese Communist Party. In this instance, Stalin's interests were quite contrary to those of Mao and of the Chinese in general.

Kang Sheng, Wang Ming and Chen Yun, who were about to leave Urümqi after a two-week stay, promised to deal with the matter.

And indeed, some time later, Deng Fa, 'the Red bandit', was sent to Sheng Shicai. That was the beginning of a rivalry between the Russians and Chinese in Xinjiang – a rivalry between 'comrades', of course – that was to go on for thirty years and which, in a certain manner of speaking, continues even to this day.

Shortly afterwards, Sheng became furiously angry. A young Chinese courtesan called Liu Yin, who had made her way into his entourage and from there into his bed, revealed to him details of a plot against him 'concocted by those gentlemen in the Kremlin'.

'The NKVD planned to poison you and then to blame the Japanese for the crime. Stalin will annex the whole of Xinjiang . . .'

'But how do you know these things?'

'Because I'm the person they assigned to carry out this mission . . .'

Sheng began to nurse a deep hatred for the Russians. More expert in the ways of war and lovemaking than in the noble art of espionage, it never occurred to Sheng to wonder whether the Chinese communists were not trying to discredit Stalin.

Obviously Sheng had no reason to suspect that Kang Sheng and Wang Ming were not loyal disciples of the 'kindly little father of the people'. They had even demonstrated this loyalty in the most sinister fashion.

The reader will remember Yu Xiusong, the student leader considered to be too close to the Trotskyists, whom Kang and Wang had had deported to Siberia, at the same time obtaining from Stalin the removal from office of the principal of the Leninist School. Well, unfortunately for him, Yu Xiusong managed to escape the Siberian Gulag, by some bureaucratic means, and was assigned a mission to Xinjiang. And there he came face to face with Kang Sheng . . .

On the morning of 29 November 1937, the Soviet plane took off, carrying Kang Sheng, Wang Ming and Chen Yun back to Yan'an.

Not far away, in the desert, the snow was dirty. With hands and feet tied behind their backs Yu Xiusong and a dozen of his friends lay on the ground, their faces already frozen into the ice, with a small red hole in the backs of their necks.

7
Kang Sheng the Matchmaker

The Tupolev bomber TB3 began its descent, flying in concentric circles. Yan'an, capital of the Revolution, lay dormant in the icy cold
that afternoon of 29 November 1937. The droning of the four-engined
Soviet aircraft shook the valley. It sounded like a Japanese bombardment. Mao Zedong had been warned by telegram of the arrival of
the mysterious plane. He had been expecting it even earlier: but
because of the violent snow storms in Xinjiang, the plane's Russian
pilot had not been able to take off until very late morning.

Mao quickly pulled on his sheepskin-lined coat, his scarf, his hat
with ear-flaps, and rushed out of his cave at the foot of Mount
Fenghuang. His bodyguards followed hot on his heels, and the three
men all jumped into the old banger and raced down the hill to the tiny
runway. Zhou Enlai, who had also been informed of the Russian
plane's arrival, had spread the word round the valley. He too hurried
over to meet the plane, accompanied by Zhang Guodao. Some hundred people were already waiting, among them the Comintern's secret
adviser, the German Otto Braun.

It was the first time a plane had ever landed at Yan'an, which the
communists had chosen at the beginning of the year as their capital,
just after the Long March. There was considerable surprise when the
four men came down the gangway: Chen Yun, Wang Ming, followed
by Kang Sheng and Zeng Shan, like Kang a former rickshaw runner.

'Your arrival is a pleasure that surpasses all expectation,' said Mao,
visibly impressed by the imposing transmitter-receiver and the anti-
aircraft guns supplied by Stalin, which were being unloaded from the
hold.

That same evening there was a joyous welcome party. While
numerous bottles of wine were being uncorked, Zhang Wentian, then
general secretary, greeted the newcomers.

'We must first of all congratulate Comrade Chen Shaoyu, otherwise known as Wang Ming, on the way in which he has implemented
the Comintern line, particularly in the face of the rightists and the Li
Lisan clique . . . and on the immense amount of work he has done in
the name of our Party within the Communist International, putting us
on an international footing. As for Chen Yun, he deserves our praise
for the missions he so energetically carried out in Moscow, and more
recently while the remnants of the Red Army's Fourth Front based
themselves in Xinjiang. Comrade Kang Sheng has also played a decisive

role with his special work. Need I remind you of his critical contribution in protecting the vital organs of our Party in Shanghai?'

Mao was smiling deep down inside. He had not greatly approved of Wang Ming's activities in Moscow. After all, if the Chinese CP could pride itself on Stalin's friendship, it was no thanks to Wang Ming ensconced in the Kremlin, but on account of Mao, historic leader of the Revolution. It was Mao Zedong who, like Moses taking his people across the Red Sea, had led his troops on the exhausting Long March. Of course, the fact that Stalin had sent the Chinese delegation from Moscow to Yan'an showed that the Russian leader hoped to exert greater influence through the intermediary of Comintern loyalists trained in Russia. But once the latter had returned to China and the umbilical cord with Moscow had been severed, were they not likely to become absorbed? In any case, from now on it was in China, and in China alone, that the strategy of the Chinese communists would be decided. But with his innate sense of intrigue, Mao gave no indication of his aversion towards these comrades returned from Russia. That evening, he even praised to the skies the activities of those whose influence he wanted to lessen.

'It is good to drink water while thinking of its source,' he said, raising his glass and quoting a Chinese proverb. 'For what is the source of our success, the establishment of a united front with the Guomindang? It is of course the declaration of 1 August 1935, from which the united front derives. And who is responsible for this declaration? Comrade Wang Ming, whom we welcome this evening . . .'

Zhang Guotao, who attended the reception, later recalled that someone had referred to the consignment of heavy arms in Wang Ming's aeroplane.

'Why does the Russian air force not bring us arms more often?'

In the eyes of this naive individual, Wang Ming represented the omnipotence of the USSR and the Comintern.

'Because, officially, there is a treaty between Chiang Kai-shek and the Soviet Union,' he replied, 'it is impossible to fly over this territory without Chiang's agreement. As it is, we had to fly here in secret on this occasion.'

Mao drove the point home with a question that remained dramatically unanswered: 'But Moscow supplies Chiang Kai-shek with such a great quantity of arms? Is it not possible for them to supply us with some too?'

Mao was wrong-footed. Exploiting the awe in which he was held, Wang Ming reported the criticisms of the Chinese that were voiced in Moscow, in an attempt to put Mao in his place, for all that he was the undisputed leader of the Chinese Revolution.

Mao had to be diplomatic and concede considerable importance to these newcomers to the political leadership. And he was happily surprised to note that it was not long before Kang Sheng and Chen Yun, although trained in the Stalinist school, chose his camp. Both men, being realists, realised who was the real leader of the Revolution and rallied to his red flag.

A meeting of the Politburo was held ten days later to consider the military situation; also on the agenda was the matter of consolidating the alliance with the Guomindang. After some discussion, on 13 December the composition of the new leadership was settled upon. There was no longer a general secretary but a whole host of secretaries: Mao Zedong, Wang Ming, Zhu De, commander-in-chief of the Red Army, Zhou Enlai, Zhang Wentian, the outgoing general secretary, soon to be exposed as a Trotskyist, Zhang Guotao, Bo Gu, Chen Yun and finally Kang Sheng, who became head of the secret services: the Bureau for Political Protection (*Zhengzhi Baohuju*). This information, which in principle was classified *nei bu*, highly confidential, did not remain so for long, as documents in the archives of the French secret services show. Louis Fabre, head of French counter-espionage in Shanghai, sent to Paris, in the form of a secret report, No. 4508, a list of the new Chinese Central Committee. He conscientiously noted down: 'Kang Sheng alias Chao Yun, head of the OGPU'.

Kang Sheng began to establish himself in the job and to review the running of the secret services. Not only did he have to consider operations in the outside world, his first priority was to secure the protection of Yan'an itself. For this strange town, surrounded by hills, that stands on the River Yan, a natural citadel with its caves cut into the cliffs, was growing rapidly. Anyone who might be considered an adventurer or revolutionary intellectual of any kind seemed to converge on the communist-held city. Before the arrival of the communists, a local population of some 5,000 inhabitants lived in the clay houses and in certain magnificently decorated caves.

But this dusty little town, where the yellow earth clings to the skin, was invaded by a huge war machine, the Revolution's high command, its logistical resources, its training schools. Within ten years the population had increased twentyfold. Who could say with any certainty that Japanese spies or Guomindang informers had not infiltrated the place? Kang Sheng's task was a tough one. First of all, it involved protecting the senior officials of the Party. Later Mao was to organise his own Praetorian Guard, but in the meantime Kang Sheng surrounded him with a team of élite soldiers armed with heavy Mauser pistols. Then Mao was moved out of his three adjoining caves in Mount Fenghuang, where he had written his theoretical book *On Contradiction*. In 1938 he joined Liu Shaoqi, Zhou Enlai and Zhu De on the outskirts of town, in Yangjialing at the foot of Mount Qingliang. Kang Sheng had a base there, so that he could keep Mao informed at all times, but he chose the western suburb of Zhaoyuan as the nerve centre of his services.

*   *   *

Shortly after the December 1937 meeting, Kang Sheng got an odd surprise. He was told there was a young woman from Shanghai come to see him.

She was waiting at the Fishermen's Garden, an old house situated on the hillside that had belonged to a former landowner; it had an underground passage leading to a bunker that led into one of the deepest caves. Kang had insisted on this arrangement in order to safeguard his radio networks and his files that were expanding daily. He closed one of these files and had the young Shanghai woman sent in.

The head of the secret services had no difficulty in recognising this radiant starlet who had abandoned her *qipao*, with its slit up to the thigh, for the kind of military tunic worn by the Red Army. Despite her cropped hair and fringe, she had not changed. It was Cloud Crane, formerly his young pupil in Zhucheng, whom he had later known as Lan Ping, or 'Blue Apple', his mistress in Shanghai.

She scanned his face but also found him unchanged. He had the same emaciated face, the same thin lips, that eternal rawboned wolfish smile, that habit of breathing deeply to mark a pause. But there were deeper wrinkles on his forehead and his hair was receding. She was only twenty-four and he was already forty.

Nevertheless, the two natives of Shandong were together again. It was a moving reunion. He behaved like an old Taoist master; she put on a little girl act. In their inimitable Zhucheng accent they talked of the school in Qingdao, of Shandong, of the theatre in Jinan, the cinema in Shanghai. She told him all about that dazzling, sordid world, and about the fall of the city. She told him about her films, about the part she had played in Ibsen's *The Doll's House*, but also about the terrible quarrels and rivalry among the actors, made worse by political factionalism and the underground war. And she described how, in August, during the bombing of Shanghai by the Japanese, she had fled, intent on reaching Yan'an, in order to be able to offer her services to the Revolution more directly. In Xi'an, the Guomindang capital, she had met another theatre actress, Li Lilian, who was also making her way to Yan'an, where she hoped to meet her lover and marry him – her lover being Otto Braun, Moscow's adviser to the Chinese. The two young women had travelled together.

Every time she met Kang Sheng, Lan Ping noticed how he was climbing ever higher up the Party ladder. Within a few days, she had already heard that he was working in Mao's immediate entourage. And that he was widely feared, because of his enormous power. The people of Yan'an were beginning to fear the Master of Zhaoyuan, who was always accompanied by his four bodyguards. Sometimes, like some feudal lord wearing a fur cape and gleaming boots, Mao would ride out with a few others, chosen from his seraglio, to hunt bear or shoot duck. Would Lan Ping one day be part of this seraglio? Would Kang Sheng help her to enter this magic circle, as he had helped her in Qingdao and in Shanghai, when she was living with Yu Qiwei?

And as they had then, during that time of adventure, the two children of Shandong now rediscovered each other. The day after they were reunited in love, Lan Ping, a cunning vixen, confided in Kang Sheng: 'There's something I must tell you. After you went to Russia in 1934, I was captured by the Guomindang. I made my submission! Of course I signed under duress, but there is certainly a written document with my signature on it, in which I renounce communism . . .'

Kang lit his second cigarette of the morning. 'Who's going to hold it against you? At present, we are allies of Chiang Kai-shek . . . Of course, it could become known and go against you!'

But it was also in Kang Sheng's interests that it should not become known. Might he not be accused of having been her mentor, her sponsor? There was one woman who knew all about their relationship; she was formerly in charge of the communist youth movement, and her name was Xu Yigong. It was up to Kang to keep her quiet. Comrade Xu, who had also come to Yan'an, was duly admonished by the head of the secret police in a terrifying ordeal; she forgot everything she knew about Lan Ping and testified to her moral integrity whenever called upon to do so.

Thus began a genuine complicity between this amazing couple that over the next thirty years involved them in the constant rewriting of Lan Ping's story, and in getting rid of people and documents that might testify to the whirlwind – and not very proletarian – life of the Shanghai starlet.

Then Lan Ping decided that she ought to polish up her political knowledge. She entered the Party's Central School, housed in an old converted Catholic church, where three hundred male students focused all their attentions on ten poor students of the opposite sex. Kang Sheng had supreme control of the school, for a simple reason: as in all communist parties, the section responsible for counterespionage dealt with the selection of cadres and the education they were to be given. Moreover, it was a very rich breeding-ground for recruiting agents. Kang had allies there: Li Weihan, the director, had been known as Luo Mai in Shanghai when he worked under Kang's orders in 1932. As for Liu Ren, the deputy director, he had joined Kang Sheng's team in Moscow . . .

Lan Ping had little difficulty in following the courses. She was already acquainted with Mao's favourite great classic novels: *The Romance of the Three Kingdoms, The Water Margin, Journey to the West* (like Kang, she preferred *The Dream of the Red Chamber* or the erotic *Jin Ping Mei*). The students also copied out whole passages from basic Marxist texts, and from Mao's great essays. It was traditional Chinese practice to learn by faithfully copying out the works of the great master-thinkers, and soon the whole nation would be reproducing characters from the Chairman's works. In fact, while Lan Ping was applying herself to her studies in the spring of 1938, he was writing two more texts that won him universal renown: 'Strategic Problems of the Anti-Japanese War' and 'On Protracted War'. These two essays at once met with an astonishing international fate: bound together in a single volume, this guerrilla manual was secretly published in Russian by Beria's NKVD. Some time later, an agent with Roosevelt's secret service, the OSS, got hold of a copy in the USSR. A Russian prince, Serge Obolensky, and a former Soviet consul who went over to the West in 1937, Alexander Barmin, translated it into English for the Americans. Inculcated with Chinese strategy, Obolensky was parachuted into France in 1944 at the head of an OSS commando unit. He led the maquis in the liberation of Châteauroux and discovered to his horror that they were communist when they marched past with raised fists saluting him – and he a White Russian and a naturalised American who had come to teach them guerrilla warfare according to Mao's dicta.

Despite appearances, this strategy did not really interest Lan Ping. She was now hoping to enter the Lu Xun School of Arts and Literature, named after the great libertarian writer who died in Shanghai in 1936. The communists had appropriated his intellectual heritage while at the same time taking the edge off its real import. Foremost in this 'revisionist' campaign was an old acquaintance of the young actress, the supreme literary ideologue, Zhou Yang. But an obstacle arose: the decision lay with the then Secretary of the Organisation Department, Chen Yun. Since his return from Russia with Kang Sheng, this veteran of the secret services in Shanghai had not yet turned to the realm of economics in which he was to excel. He was still part of that greyer world in which the key words are: organisation, discipline, control over biography, the rise of cadres, security . . .

Chen Yun detested the young actress. She was the protégée of Kang Sheng, whom he had grown to hate, having spent so much time with him. She was only 'a depraved little starlet ready to perform any base act' in order to gain prominence. And, despite her reputation as a woman of easy virtue, Chen Yun was not allowed to take any liberties with her.

At that stage, no unfavourable information seemed to have followed the young woman from Shanghai. Her travelling companion Li Lilian had been authorised by Chen to attend the Lu Xun School and, on top of that, to marry her beloved Otto Braun. Under pressure from Kang Sheng, who was in any case deputy director of the school, Chen Yun had to give way: Lan Ping could study drama and opera in order better to serve the people.

Nor did nepotism stop there: hardly had she been admitted to the school than young Lan Ping was appointed assistant teacher in the Modern Drama Department. In order to gain his revenge, Chen circulated spiteful rumours and even openly criticised her acting.

The spring of 1938 had already set in when delightful news reached the ears of Lan Ping. One fine day the theoretician Zhou Yang came to her, all smiles, and announced: 'Comrade Mao is going to come and give a lecture at Lu Xun. I've no qualms about telling you this, but don't mention it to anyone else for security reasons . . .'

In any case, the young actress would not have shared this secret. She dreamt of approaching the revolutionary leader, especially as strange rumours were circulating: Mao had sent He Zizhen, his third wife, to 'convalesce' in the USSR. The whole of Yan'an was whispering about it. For this was only an excuse. Mao had actually got rid of his wife after some terrible domestic rows.

As if it were not enough that he had to conduct the war, lead the Party and write philosophical manuals, Mao still found time for endless romances.

The 'free love' advocated by the revolutionaries did not tally very well with certain old Chinese principles. He Zizhen, who had loyally stood by Mao since 1928, including during the harrowing Long March, would not accept her husband's infidelity. 'It's not a question of petty bourgeois jealousy,' Comrade He would shout tearfully, 'on the contrary, it's a matter of revolutionary comradeship. I am entitled to your respect because I have always stood by you during the most difficult times of the revolutionary struggle.' Deng Yingchao, Zhou Enlai's faithful companion, and all the wives of the senior officials agreed, but they knew that Mao could not resist the lure of the senses.

There was that American woman Agnes Smedley, for instance. For Mao, the most important quality in this woman's character was her sense of adventure. She was born before the turn of the century in Colorado, and as a young journalist had become involved in the Indian nationalist movement, for which she ended up in prison.

When she came out, she militated on behalf of that other British colony, Ireland. In Germany, as a result of meeting a magnificent Brahmin, Virendranath Chattopadhyaya, she became a communist and, according to French counter-intelligence, 'for seven years she was the mistress of the revolutionary Hindu, before they parted in 1929, when she left Germany'. Meanwhile, the young woman made a marriage of convenience with a Chinese communist, Wu Shaoguo, in order to provide him with an American passport. During the same period, she went to Moscow to report on the great anti-imperialist councils. This was no mere cover: Agnes Smedley was a remarkable investigative journalist, a writer of the modern age, one of the many gifted writers – including Albert Londres, André Malraux, Harold Isaacs, Edgar Snow – who made China and its passions known to the world. In 1929 she became a correspondent for the great liberal newspaper the *Frankfurterzeitung*. (This daily could boast another exceptional correspondent in China: Richard Sorge.) That same year, under the name of Mrs Peter Petroïkos, she arrived in Shanghai. As she saw it, the Comintern defended above all the poor, the oppressed, the landless peasants and the coolies. She was in Xi'an in the autumn of 1936, where she had a ringside seat at Chiang Kai-shek's abduction. A year later she arrived in Yan'an and began writing a major book on the war being fought by the communists.

Smedley and Mao were fascinated by each other. Their relationship was the talk of the town. Mao would meet her at the home of another American, a strange doctor of Lebanese origin, George Hatem – whom the Chinese called Ma Haide – who was a friend of Kang Sheng, and married to a beautiful actress called Su Fei. Smedley had taken on as her secretary another actress, Lily Wu, who refused to conform to the 'Yan'an fashion' of short hair and military tunic and instead kept her hair in a chignon and dressed in gossamer. One night when the leader of the Revolution was visiting Agnes Smedley and 'the Sarah Bernhardt of Yan'an', Lily Wu, Mao's wife He Zizhen came bursting in. The bodyguards stood rooted to the spot as their leader and the two women were shamelessly harangued. The judgement of Solomon? Agnes Smedley was expelled from Yan'an and He Zizhen sent to Russia.

Lan Ping was no feminist. In fact, all her life she seemed to set herself against her sisters.

She was above all an individualist and a go-getter. Power was the only thing that mattered to her – the power to seduce and hold sway over the men in Shanghai, in Yan'an, perhaps one day over a kingdom. Anything but to return to the poverty of her youth. If she joined in the growling of tigresses against Smedley and Lily Wu, it was not because she shared the prudishness of the senior officials' wives, but because she wanted them out of the way. For her, the recent farce meant two things: Mao liked actresses, and Mao no longer had a lady friend . . .

The big day at the Lu Xun School came, and she elbowed her way through the crowd to the front row, where she sat, notebook in hand, lapping up the words of the great leader. Mao appeared like a luminous red sun buttoned up in his freshly laundered pearl-grey tunic. On several occasions, unlike her petrified comrades, she asked bold questions, with a radiant elegance that was reflected in Mao's eyes.

'I still have a lot to learn, but, thanks to you, I see that it's possible for me to deepen my knowledge,' she confided to her hero at the end of the lecture, flattering him with a raw recruit's deference.

'If there's anything you don't understand, don't hesitate to come and see me in my office . . .'

The incident was the talk of the school. When Lan Ping entered the classroom the room fell silent. Seducing the master meant attracting hatred.

One did not just enter at will into Mao's cave. All things considered, only one man could help her, once again: Kang Sheng.

Lan Ping telephoned him in his cave.

'Comrade Lan Ping, I've heard that you've been very successful at Lu Xun. Several eminent cadres have spoken to me about you. As long as you are determined enough . . . You are immensely talented and you will go far . . .' Kang's words carried a hint of knowingness.

'Thank you, minister, if one day I should prove successful, you can be sure that I shall never forget your help . . .'

Kang had the whole network of senior officials' field telephones tapped, which was why it was impossible to show any familiarity. So, before long, the actress called on Kang in person. 'I've come to see you because I have certain questions I want to ask Comrade Mao on the relationship between political consciousness, art and literature. How should I go about it?'

'Well, now . . .'

As usual when presented with a seemingly insurmountable problem that he was none the less sure of being able to resolve, Kang scratched his chin. 'He told you to go and see him. Well then, go ahead. But he's very busy. So it's not that simple. I have a suggestion: write to him, explaining that the day after the seminar it occurred to you that you would like to put a few additional questions to him. Then I will go and find out what mood he is in. If he agrees to see you, I shall arrange a date with his personal secretary, Chen Boda. But don't whatever you do take up too much of his time at your first meeting. The Revolution has need of him.'

It was best to take this one step at a time.

Lan Ping wrote her note. Her mentor corrected it and gave it to Xiao Li, his secretary, who rewrote it calligraphically.

Two days later, Kang Sheng presented his young friend's request.

Shortly afterwards, Lan Ping entered Mao Zedong's cave. In August 1938 he appointed her a secretary in the archives of the Military Commission, the high command prosecuting the anti-Japanese war, of which he was chief. His office adjoined hers. In the autumn she became his mistress. Kang Sheng encouraged this liaison by every means at his disposal. Better still, he conducted a valiant campaign to get Mao to divorce poor He Zizhen, who was confined in Russia. The head of the secret services put together a file on the remarkable achievements of Lan Ping in Shandong and Shanghai. He had to act quickly because the senior officials of the Chinese CP were beginning to voice their disapproval: Zhou Enlai, Zhu De and Liu Shaoqi hated these palace intrigues. Was it desirable that their leader should compromise his prestige on account of this starlet, this little madam?

They conducted their own enquiry in Shanghai. The head of the underground Communist Party, Liu Xiao, formerly Kang Sheng's deputy, delivered an implacable verdict: 'Lan Ping associated with the nationalists. As suspected, she was even a Guomindang spy!'

In the paranoiac world of communism, this suspicion could lead to the worst. But Lan Ping was already pregnant by Mao. A solution had to be found . . .

Kang Sheng dispelled the suspicion hanging over her.

'Mao and I have decided to live together,' declared Lan Ping, a gleam of defiance in her eyes. Legend has it that Mao threatened to give up fighting for the Revolution and to return to Hunan to work the land.

Kang had done well. He had won Lan Ping the support of Mao's two eldest sons by Yang Kaihui, the heroine shot by the Guomindang. Skilfully manipulated by Kang, they criticised their evil stepmother He Zizhen and sang the praises of the woman who might replace her. It was decided to accept Mao's divorce and his marriage to Lan Ping, on condition that she never got involved in politics.

And Lan Ping changed her name. Henceforth, she was known as Jiang Qing, meaning Azure River. (Qing was also an abbreviation for Qingdao, the town in Shandong where she had met Kang Sheng.) In 1941, she gave birth to a daughter, Li Na. Destiny had made Jiang Qing the first lady in the communist world and the name of that destiny was Kang Sheng. She never forgot it.

Kang Sheng devoted the year of 1938 not only to court intrigues worthy of the great classic novels he so much enjoyed; the war against the Japanese was raging, the alliance with the Guomindang was in a shaky condition, and Kang Sheng had been entrusted with the task of building up the greatest secret service of the century in this strife-torn country. In reshaping the *Tewu* he drew on his varied experience as head of the Party's secret service in Shanghai, as a pupil of the Russian OGPU, as an admirer of the British Intelligence Service and the French Deuxième Bureau; not to mention as a student of the two-thousand-year-old tradition of Chinese espionage based on Sun Zi's classic treatise on the art of war.

On 6 November 1938, the sixth Plenum of the Central Committee adopted a resolution calling on the Party as a whole 'to increase its vigilance and be on its guard against plots by the Japanese and their fellow travellers – Trotskyists, traitors and anti-communists – who are engaged in subversive activities within the Party as well as outside it.' The Party also called for the liquidation of spies to be organised.

Kang Sheng was confirmed in his position as head of the secret services. But these were dependent on three naturally rival leaderships: those of the Party, the government of Yan'an and the Army. But the Party was to take precedence over the others, and its secret service, Kang Sheng's base of operations, would gradually gain ground over the whole of the empire of shadows.

That November, Kang renamed the former Political Security Bureau and called his new agency the Department of Social Affairs (*Shehuibu*), 'Social Affairs' being a euphemism for disinforma-tion, counter-intelligence, internal repression, the rooting-out of dissidents, central archives, radio transmissions, contacts with other politico-military bodies and foreign secret services.

Basically, the Social Affairs Department was run by Kang Sheng, assisted by a deputy and his general secretary. Section 1 dealt with organisation and personnel; section 2 with intelligence properly speaking; section 3 with counter-espionage; section 4 with the analysis of intelligence; and finally there was a General Affairs section, connected with the agents' training corps. Two special sections did not appear in the official organisation chart: the security section and the section for special operations, *Zhisibu* in Chinese, which was headed by the deputy director of the whole Department . . .

A Manchu who became one of the Department's most important figures, Zhou Dapeng was at that time head of the political section in the omnipotent Military Commission over which Mao himself presided. He became Kang Sheng's point of contact with this body. The Social Affairs Department set up local, regional and technical branches throughout China, in both White and Red zones. Each region had a department with its own representatives, and at the level of the *xian*, the smallest geographical unit and a legacy of the Manchu Empire, Social Affairs' officers detailed to collect information as well as supervise the proper functioning of the underground Party were thick on the ground. But the *Shehuibu* exercised control over foreign relations.

Two men who both fell victim to the political purges of the 1950s were responsible for this area of *Shehuibu* activities: Rao Shushi and Pan Hannian, the one based in Yan'an dealt with the Comintern, the other in Hong Kong liaised with expatriate comrades. Pan, the reader will remember, played a central role in the incredible Xi'an Incident . . .

Kang believed that the training of his secret agents left a lot to be desired. He called in an expert, Wu Defeng, who remained a wholehearted supporter of Kang all his life. In 1936 Wu was in charge of communist intelligence in Xi'an, then, after the declaration of war against Japan, he was entrusted with a delicate mission: that of supervising Party intelligence in the two key northern provinces of Jehol and Liaoning. So when he arrived in Yan'an he took charge of the first communist intelligence school, in collaboration with Kang Sheng. As many future cadres had already been given some training by the Soviets, Kang Sheng wanted to sinicise his service.

'Forget what you've learned in Moscow. You're in China now. You must now do things the Chinese way. You were corrupted over there, and you can't have learned how to do the work as it should be done.'

This was not very complimentary to his former friends in the NKVD or the OGPU, but Kang Sheng was already seeking to sever the umbilical cord. The instruction given in this special school was multifarious: Wu De, for instance, mayor of Beijing during the Cultural Revolution, who became Kang's henchman, specialised in economic intelligence at the school.

In Zhaoyuan, in the Fishermen's Garden, the 'Minister of High-level Works', as he was soon nicknamed, not without an element of awe, organised his think-tank, surrounded by myriad secretaries, foremost of whom were Fu Hao, future communist ambassador to

Japan, Xiao Li, his personal secretary, and Zhao Yaobin, his principal private secretary. Kang's wife, Cao Yi-ou, who bore him his first son, Zhang Zishi, did the filing and kept the team supplied with black tea and Manchu cigarettes.

Kang Sheng took pleasure in establishing what he called 'invisible relations' (*Touming Guanxi*), which meant winning the personal loyalty of men and women within the communist apparatus, either by means of seduction or blackmail. It was sometimes said he did not hesitate to recruit female spies in the beds of their husbands away on missions in the White zone. His aim was to spin a 'divine web', to quote the expression of the father of Chinese espionage, Sun Zi; a network of agents who would lie dormant sometimes for whole decades before being activated.

There were three bodies dependent on the Social Affairs Department: the Committee for Work in Enemy Territory (that dominated by the Japanese), the Committee for Work in Friendly Territory (that of the Guomindang), and finally the United Front Work Department.

The Work in Enemy Territory Committee was actually set up by the Central Committee in September 1944. A voluminous document gives details:

> The Central Committee has established a Committee for Work in enemy-occupied zones, to oversee operations in enemy-occupied cities. Comrade Zhou Enlai has been given overall responsibility for this, assisted by Kang Sheng as his deputy. Chongqing is the centre of operations for South China, and Yan'an for Northern China . . .
>
> Operations will begin with the purpose of: 1. Gathering the intelligence necessary to an understanding of the situation and to a study of past experience; 2. Cultivating the social relations necessary to conceal residences, operations and communications in order to bring these operations to a successful conclusion; 3. Recruiting and supporting cadres capable of working in enemy-occupied territory thanks to their social contacts; their past experience in the cities from the point of view of secret service work; cadres with the experience to provide covers for undercover work and to assist in secret communications; and comrades capable of finding jobs in the industrial sector in cities. The Party must exercise caution in the selection of these comrades.

Another important organisation was the United Front Work Department. Traditionally, the concept of a united front implied an alliance between the Communist Party and another social, political, ethnic or religious force.

This could be the Guomindang, or a church, an ethnic community, or the Chinese overseas communities. The United Front made it possible to gather intelligence through contacts, as well as through infiltration of groups outside the CP. Zhou Enlai himself was for a long time in charge of it: which explains his central role in negotiations with the Guomindang in 1938. He was then replaced by Li Weihan, who had just handed over the running of the Party's Central School to Kang Sheng. He joined that section of the special services responsible for meeting the huge need in time of war for publicity and propaganda.

The New China News Agency, or *Xinhua* in Chinese, turned to a cadre highly qualified in secret warfare to run it. And so it was that Liao Chengzhi, 'the Red seaman', the man behind the Dutch mutinies in 1932, became a journalist. He had been applauded in Yan'an in the summer of 1937 for playing the leading part in a play inspired by the Spanish Civil War, entitled *The Spy*. On the opening night, Kang Sheng had clapped furiously: he was after all the only Chinese the Comintern had sent on an official visit to the Spanish Republicans, a year earlier.

As soon as it was set up, the New China News Agency established close links with Chinese intelligence and subsequently provided Chinese secret agents with cover jobs. And of course it was in direct contact with the Zhaoyuan Information Department.

But Liao was an adventurer. He could not stay put. He was sent to Guangdong, better known to Westerners as Canton, which was in the hands of the Japanese, to organise the underground Party. Incredibly – and this serves to illustrate the pragmatism of the English – the Hong Kong authorities, on the Canton border, helped him to recruit volunteers to train his guerrilla troops in Huibao, and to harass the Japs. The Intelligence Service did well out of it, getting very useful information in exchange. Ironically, the Intelligence Service made an arrest in the colony in early 1941 and sent back a report to London: 'We are holding the leader of an intelligence organisation modelled on the German Gestapo, with strong pro-German sympathies.' This was Dai Li, the head of the Guomindang secret service, who was inspecting his network in Hong Kong. Chiang Kai-shek had to intervene personally to get him freed. Hence, Dai Li's deep-rooted hatred of the English. He never forgot this incident.

One little man followed these strange comings and goings with a smile. Mr Suzuki, a barber working for the British, shaved all the colony's eminent personalities – the governor, the generals, the head of Special Branch who had just expelled Dai Li, the directors of the Hong Kong and Shanghai Bank. He was greatly liked. One day a British officer expressed surprise that he had not learnt a word of English. Suzuki replied with that eternal smile of his: 'I'm an intelligence officer, I don't have time to learn the language!'

The British wrote one report after another concerning this affair, asking London what attitude to adopt. Meanwhile, Colonel Suzuki – to give his correct rank – was running round Hong Kong taking notes. In December 1941 it was decided that he should be expelled. One month later, on Christmas Day 1941, he was back, in uniform. Hong Kong was taken by surprise and fell to the Japanese . . .

At the same time, in Singapore, the English were encountering similar difficulties. There was a waiter who served whiskies in the officers' mess at the Hotel Shawan, with a big smile. After the Fall of Singapore, he revealed his true identity: he was Colonel Kadomatsu Tsugunori, head of the Japanese secret services.

Meanwhile, Liao Chengzhi, who had found refuge in Hong Kong, returned to China. He took over command of some guerrilla units under Kang Sheng's orders. But in 1942 Dai Li's police eventually captured him in Zhuqiang. Once again, because he was the son of the deceased Guomindang dignitary Liao Zhongkai, the life of this communist masterspy was spared.

As the years went by Kang Sheng's empire extended, not least through the influence of Jiang Qing. In the early 1940s a security bureau was formed, the mere mention of whose name still sets Chinese today trembling: the Chinese OGPU, the *Gonganbu* . . . The eradication of traitors, of double agents, started to become a major preoccupation. On 29 April 1941, he delivered a speech to a class of Yencheng security personnel and defined the most salient features of secret service work: 'Working against subversion is a special mission, a secret war of minds, a job carried out with no immediate check in order to deal solely with counter-revolutionaries. In short a task of indefinite duration, no doubt among the most difficult but also the most glorious . . .'

Kang Sheng no doubt had his eye on the Army, with a view to controlling its secret services. Through the history of Chinese communism, an eternal battle rages between the Party services and those of the armed forces, despite intermittent truces. On 3 December 1943, the head of the Political Department of the Eighth Route Army, General Luo Ruiqing, during a lecture, defined the role of the communist secret services against the enemy as 'a new expression of the class struggle'. However, he continued, it was not just a question of fighting the 'cruel Japanese' but also of considering the role of the Guomindang, who were theoretically allies, but not actually to be trusted.

Luo, thin-faced with an aquiline nose, arched eyebrows and thick hair, was all smiles when he wanted to emphasise a particularly important point, as though trying to nudge his audience towards his own conclusions, allowing them to believe that this clever idea was their own. 'We cannot cleave to the simplistic idea that there is a primary enemy and a secondary enemy . . . In one sense, the subversive policy of the Guomindang could become a greater threat to us than the Japanese secret services' sabotage work . . .'

Who was this Comrade Luo, who in the course of a lecture lashed out at several of Mao's key concepts? Born in 1906, the son of large landowners in Sichuan, at the age of twenty he was admitted to the famous military academy at Huangpu. A Party member, he took part in the armed uprising in Nanchang on 1 August 1927; 1 August has since been celebrated in the People's Republic of China as marking the birth of the Popular Liberation Army. He was sent to Russia, where he studied counter-espionage techniques with the OGPU and conceived a boundless admiration for his boss, the legendary Polishman Dzerzhinsky, whose virtues of revolutionary integrity and moral rectitude he liked to stress. Luo would have willingly compared himself to the terrible Pole or to some public state prosecutor of the French people in 1793 . . . As a matter of fact, he visited France in the 1920s: the Comintern's Western Bureau, headed by Raymond Guyot, sent him there to learn about espionage at first hand, with a communist party in a capitalist country.

In 1930 Luo became political commissioner of the Sixth Army, in other words Lin Biao's deputy. Wounded in 1932, he went again to the Soviet Union, but two years later he was in charge of security in the First Army Corps, again with Lin Biao. He took part in the Long March and, having worked with Political Security as deputy director of foreign intelligence, became deputy to the director of the anti-Japanese politico-military university in Yan'an (*Kangda*) – who happened to be Lin Biao. Kang Sheng was often to encounter Luo subsequently, and sometimes in battles that were almost homeric in scale, worthy of the Three Kingdoms . . .

There was of course rivalry between politicians and the military, but even within the political camp there were those who wanted to curb the excesses of Kang Sheng by imposing a watchdog deputy on him.

'Li Kenong really is a strange customer!' the inhabitants of the Red bases would whisper with a shudder whenever he passed by. A little man, moustachioed, potbellied and fleshy, with thick-lensed glasses, he also caused people to smile. He hardly ever went out without a squad of Young Pioneers of the Revolution who served as errand boys, messengers, valets, servants, 'companions'. The best-known of his little darlings, Zhang Qibang, a boy of fifteen who came from Shaanxi, was always beautifully dressed, with gleaming belt and gold buttons, impeccable tunic and spotless shirt. He was derisively nicknamed *Qiba*, which means 'little penis'.

In Yan'an there was one woman to every thirty men, and only the cadres enjoyed the good life. The Chinese, traditionally, allowed themselves some sexual latitude. And Kang Sheng had no choice: the appointment of Li Kenong as his deputy was forced upon him. Now approaching forty, Li recalled with melancholic nostalgia his youth in Anhui, his studies in France, the Fourth of May Movement of 1919, which brought him into contact with numerous writers and poets. Li, like Kang, was fond of poetry. In 1926 he was working in Shanghai under Gu Shunzhang, and even managed to infiltrate the

Guomindang's secret service. Then followed the obscure events surrounding Gu's betrayal in the spring of 1931. According to one malicious rumour, he 'grassed' on Li Kenong, who was captured in Wuhan, and supposedly betrayed, in his turn, the hiding-place of Xian Zhongfa, the only worker who ever became general secretary of the Party, an appointment imposed by Moscow simply in order to create some kind of harmony among the various factions opposing each other at the time; in other words he was something of a figurehead secretary . . .

'All this is a great farce. It was Gu Shuzhang who betrayed Comrade Xian . . . I was never arrested. I fled to Jiangxi province at once and continued working there, is that not true, Zhao Rong?' was always Li's response to his detractors. Addressed by the name he used to go by in Shanghai, Kang Sheng, as always in such cases, would bat his eyelids like some timid virgin and nod knowingly, as though he knew a great deal but didn't want to talk about it, effectively silencing critics and assuring Li of his protection, but at the same time giving him to understand that he would be well advised to adhere faithfully to the precepts of the master, otherwise some nasty file might be dug up and gone through with a fine toothcomb.

Luckily for him, Li Kenong had other supporters, among them Zhou Enlai, who in 1931 had suggested replacing Mao's old friend from Hunan, He Shuheng, a syndicalist unskilled in matters of security, as head of the Department of Political Protection with Li Kenong. Mao opposed the nomination. The two men agreed on Deng Fa, Borodin's former bodyguard, who became head of the services. Li Kenong nevertheless became the number two, as administrative director.

In 1932 he became general secretary of the United Front Work Department, responsible for spying mainly on nationalist organisations, duties which he continued to pursue after being appointed, the following year, head of the Bureau of Investigation in the Political Security Department of the First Front Army (whose political commissioner was Zhou Enlai). During the Long March, Li pursued his activities under Deng Fa's supervision, and in 1936 he took part in the strange diplomatic to-ing and fro-ing in Xi'an at the time of Chiang Kai-shek's abduction.

His abilities always brought him back to Zhou Enlai and the hypersensitive Communications Bureau, linked to the embryonic Department of Foreign Affairs. Then Li was sent back to Shanghai, from where he extended his influence over the whole of China, maintaining contact with Hong Kong and abroad. He was, therefore, vastly experienced when he came to help Kang Sheng, and also to keep an eye on him, at the Social Affairs Department.

Well-groomed right down to his fingertips, Li was an astute politician, like his friend Zhou Enlai. But he threw himself into the most sordid schemes, the most monstrous machinations, the most devious operations. Kang entrusted him with the section devoted to very special activities (*Zhisibu*), including physical eliminations, relations with the underworld, the secret societies, and even opium-trafficking, which was used to fill the Department's coffers.

From the Social Affairs Department, Kang's horizons were limitless. He was already contemplating an assault on all the diplomatic and military intelligence services.

Mao was in agreement: the Party, and therefore his service, should dominate the rest. From 1940, he had his say in the *Qingbaoju*, the military intelligence service run by his friend Ye Jianying. Several times a week, if not every morning, Kang or one of his deputies held an open briefing session on the military situation. For this kind of intelligence also came to him eventually for the purposes of analysis. Political leaders, military leaders as well as foreign representatives, from the Comintern, and sometimes Koreans or Japanese, also attended. From 1943, although very taken up with the struggle against internal dissidents, Kang headed the operational intelligence service of the Eighth Route Army in Chen Yi's New Fourth Army.

But this tendency of Kang's to seize upon everything now began to arouse jealousy, anxiety and a good deal of animosity, even among his best friends. Even Zhou Enlai realised how ambitious Kang was. Subtly and forcefully, he put the point to Mao that the whole security system should not depend on a single person. Basically the Chairman agreed; he organised his own bodyguard. But otherwise, he had too great a need of Kang Sheng to remove him from the Fishermen's Garden.

As head of the embryonic Ministry of Foreign Affairs, Zhou Enlai held a trump card: he could quite legitimately ask his contacts, in China or abroad, to supply him with political and diplomatic intelligence, and so was able to build up his own team, outside Kang Sheng's sphere of influence. He had a good contact within the Social Affairs Department in the shape of Li Kenong. In the military realm, one of Li's men, Liu Shaowen, belonged to the same lobby, which was run on a day-to-day basis by Zhou's personal secretary, Chen Jiakang, who had studied in Moscow and of whom a great deal more will be said later.

The two Gong sisters are a good illustration of the system Zhou set up that was one day to provide China with a great diplomatic corps. Their father was a brilliant general in the 1911 Revolution and a friend of Sun Yat-sen. The younger sister, Gong Peng, who was born in Yokohama but brought up in Shanghai, went to Yan'an in 1935, drawn there by a romantic fascination with distinguished bandits, such as one finds in the great Chinese classic novels.

She worked with the local peasants, and one day attracted the attention of General Peng Dehuai. For her, Peng was the incarnation of the great warriors of the Three Kingdoms. She became his secretary. Then she became Zhou Enlai's secretary and, after the Xi'an pact, she accomplished dozens of missions as a diplomatic liaison agent assigned to foreign delegations.

The elder sister, Gong Pusheng, distinguished herself as a brilliant student at Columbia University in the USA; then, like her sister, she became a leader of the non-communist student movement in Shanghai. At the age of twenty-one, a dedicated feminist, she was appointed to the United Nations' Human Rights Committee. In New York she met a woman with whom she became close friends, Eleanor Roosevelt, the wife of the President of the United States.

Pusheng was not a political activist. She was careful to conceal her true nature as a secret member of the Communist Party, all the more so because Eleanor was known to have left-wing sympathies – she had inaugurated the Second World Youth Congress at Vassar College, near New York, to which young people from fifty-four countries journeyed to attend, to demonstrate their hatred of Fascism and war. This Congress followed upon the one held in Geneva in 1936, in which Kang Sheng had taken part. At Vassar College the Chinese were numerous and optimistic: many of the American youngsters voiced their hostility to American isolationism and, in particular, to Japanese expansionism. For this reason, and many others, American counter-intelligence, J. Edgar Hoover's famous FBI, kept a close watch on Eleanor. Her telephone was tapped. But did the FBI ever discover how the beautiful young Chinese girl sent back her reports to Yan'an?

8
Dai Li, Masterspy of the Guomindang

Meals with Kang Sheng, in the Fishermen's Garden, were always sumptuous affairs. There was no lack of festivities, celebrations, anniversaries. Kang kept an open house, on a magnificent scale, like some lord of bygone days. For all that he was as thin as a rake, Kang Sheng was nevertheless a big eater and a heavy drinker (although no one could recall ever having seen him drunk in public).

There would be sixty-course meals at big feasts, twelve on more modest occasions, washed down with large quantities of *huangjiu*, the yellow wine from Shaoxing, or spirits such as *baigan*: duck with scented mushrooms or chrysanthemums, meat with peppers, chives, ginger, broccoli or almonds; a thousand aromatic soups; chicken in sweet-and-sour sauce with bamboo shoots, one of the host's favourite dishes. Sometimes guests were served with game that had been bagged by the head of the *Tewu*, in which case Kang's plump little wife Cao Yi-ou would announce the fact very proudly: 'Zhao Rong himself shot the young tiger whose flesh you're eating . . .' (She still called him by the name he had used underground in Shanghai, when he was first courting her.)

But everyone wanted to congratulate the chef and wish him a thousand-year-long life. Where had Kang Sheng managed to find a cook as remarkable as this Gong Tao? Very few people, Li Kenong among them, knew: before working for Kang, Gong Tao had been the chef for the last Emperor of China, Pu Yi.

And behind Gong Tao's secret lay the tragic end of a long chapter in China's history. Pu Yi, the Son of Heaven, last Emperor of the Manchu dynasty (the Qing), had ruled in Beijing until the Revolution and the founding of the Republic – 'ruled' being a manner of speaking. He was barely six years old when his abdication was declared in February 1912. The republic was a loyal daughter: he was allowed to keep the honorary title of Emperor, granted an allowance of four million *yuan* a year and the right to keep all his servants, including his treasured cook. The Son of the Dragon remained dear to the hearts of many Chinese. Four years later Prince Su, known as 'the Mad', raised an army to fight the Republican troops in Manchuria and re-establish the Qing dynasty. This 'Mad' Manchu hoped that the young Pu Yi would regain his empire. The whole affair ended in fiasco. Then again, in 1917, a warlord entered Beijing at the head of his army and proclaimed the restoration of the dynasty. Pu Yi's reign lasted two weeks.

And in that time the child captured a glimpse of a divided China, torn apart by fighting between clans, lying outside the walls of the Forbidden City: neither empire nor republic, but chaos, a tragedy to which the Chinese had grown accustomed over the centuries.

His was a strange adolescence spent in the precincts of the age-old palace. Pu Yi fretted inside the Forbidden City, surrounded by his eunuchs and concubines. He allayed boredom by reading *Alice in Wonderland*, or applauding the pranks of Harold Lloyd in an old imperial theatre converted into a cinema. The Great Powers observed him, watched him stir in his jade cocoon, certain that they would one day be able to use him. Cossack chieftains, Japanese diplomats, English spies, Italian traffickers, French doctors urged themselves upon him. Enjoined to leave the palace, Pu Yi sought refuge with the diplomats for the Great Powers. Despite the strong representation made on his behalf by one of his English friends to the British legation, London considered Pu Yi a 'has-been'. The Japanese courted him frantically, and their legation in Peking offered him asylum for a while. Then Pu Yi went to Tientsin with his young wife, Wan Rong – meaning Beautiful Countenance – a child of sixteen, already doomed.

They moved into a palace in Tientsin, the 'Garden of the Zhang', under the kindly supervision of Captain Mino, head of the intelligence service in the Japanese Concession.

'Our special services will ensure the protection of Your Illustrious and Venerable Majesties,' the Japanese officer assured them, falling over himself in his obsequiousness, which was revealing of his real intentions. But Pu Yi had never reigned and knew little of human nature. By 'guarding' the deposed emperor the Japanese were drawing him ever deeper into their ambitious designs. As the months went by, he abandoned his glittering Manchu robes and took to wearing top-hat and tails and Harold Lloyd type spectacles, growing ever poorer and poorer.

One evening, his cook announced pitifully: 'I don't deserve to live. I'm no better than a worm . . .'

Pu Yi realised what his cook was trying to say: there was no food left . . .

The Japanese did not leave the imperial couple and their half-starved retinue to perish. They gave them provisions sparingly, in order to bring home to them their dependence. This was even more true of the delicate Wan Rong, who had 'special needs'. Regularly at nightfall she would go into the slums of Tientsin. The Japanese were able to keep track of her depravity: they had imported hundreds of Korean woman into Tientsin who worked as prostitutes in the brothels in Dublin Road and kept Captain Mino's intelligence service supplied with information: 'Wan Rong was in an opium den again last night!'

Year by year the little sheets of rice paper describing the empress's decline accumulated. In 1927 Japanese counter-intelligence tightened up its security. The communists were organising their riots, and the young emperor had only one obsession: that he would end up like the Russian imperial family, massacred by the Reds. Semenov took advantage of his contacts in the Zhang Garden to suggest to Pu Yi that he seal a pact with the White Russians, the Sino-Russian Anti-Bolshevik Accord.

The Japanese did not interfere. But they began to get worried when a young general with strong anti-Japanese feelings, Zhang Xueliang, started negotiating with Pu Yi in the secret hope of winning him over to the nationalist cause. Tokyo had quite a different plan in mind.

In the summer of 1931 a captain in the Japanese secret services, Nakamura, was assassinated by the nationalists. This provided the pretext the Japanese had been seeking for military intervention in China.

A potbellied little man, with a crewcut and a Charlie Chaplin moustache, conceived a whole series of operations of which he alone held the secret. Despite his unprepossessing physique, Colonel Doihara Kenzo, born in 1883, had earned the nickname of the 'Japanese Lawrence'. Extraordinary stories were told about him: he spoke an incredible number of languages and dialects, Asian and European; he could shed or gain twenty pounds in weight in no time in order to change his physical appearance; he was without equal in his ability to organise assassinations that no one could ever explain. In short, he was a Japanese masterspy. Doihara had an expert knowledge of China. Formerly military attaché in Beijing, he had set up a special service, the Tokumu, based in Mukden. He organised the famous '18 September Incident' (perfectly illustrated by Hergé in *Tintin and the Blue Lotus*), whereby Japanese agents caused an explosion on the express railway line to Mukden and then, in retaliation for this action that they themselves had carried out, the Japanese sent their troops into Manchuria.

In order to legitimise their occupation, they needed Chinese collaborators. Their choice naturally fell on Pu Yi. All smiles, Doihara went down to Tientsin to propose a pact with the Son of Heaven, now in Hell.

'We're offering you the opportunity to rule over the new kingdom of Manchukuo . . . You will receive 600,000 dollars a year . . . And naturally as soon as circumstances allow, the Japanese army will reinstate you on the imperial throne . . .'

Pu Yi was perplexed. A short time before, Chinese nationalists, convinced that he was part of a vast Japanese conspiracy, had thrown grenades into his garden. But on the other hand, Chiang Kai-shek's party had recently maintained excellent contacts with the deposed emperor. Doihara, who was acting independently of official Japanese diplomacy, considered it imperative to act quickly. On the evening of 10 November he organised the 'Tientsin Incident'. Some forty Chinese in the pay of the Japanese crossed the Japanese Concession to the Chinese quarter and fired shots at a police patrol. In the shooting that followed, numerous passers-by were killed.

It was a diversion. Doihara's car sped to the Quiet Garden, where he had arranged to meet Captain Mino. Then both men drove to Pu Yi's house. The poor dazed emperor allowed himself to be dressed in Japanese army uniform, and then found himself in the black car already racing through the English concession towards the Bund.

The next day Pu Yi became the official leader of Manchukuo, and on 1 March 1934 he was declared emperor.

But Pu Yi clamoured after his wife. The evening he was abducted, the young Wan Rong was lost in a haze of opium in a smoking den in the lower depths of Tientsin. 'The Manchu Mata-Hari is the person I need!' thought Doihara. She was his best agent. Hot-blooded and masculine, with short hair, thighs of bronze, and blazing eyes, Kawashima Yoshiko was one of the most amazing characters in the annals of secret warfare. Her real name was Jin Bin Hui. She was the daughter of Prince Su, the Manchu, who in 1916 had tried to restore Pu Yi to the throne. After her father's death, she was adopted by the Japanese Kawashima Naniwa, a samurai descendant, spy and guerrilla fighter in Manchuria, who was at one time a friend of Sun Yat-sen.

Kawashima Naniwa, who like Colonel Doihara belonged to the Black Dragon secret society, raised his adoptive daughter Yoshiko – meaning Jewel of the Orient – in Japan. The young adventuress married a Mongol prince, but never lived with him. In Shanghai in 1928 she became the mistress of the head of the Japanese secret service, Tanaka. Recruited by Doihara, she was sent to Tientsin. Her mission was to try to get Pu Yi and his people to embrace Japanese objectives.

She first tried to persuade Pu Yi to become Emperor of Manchukuo. But it was Wan Rong, the empress, with whom she was most successful. Yoshiko accompanied her on her numerous sorties. After Pu Yi had fled, Captain Mino tried to persuade her to join her husband in Manchukuo. In a state of hysteria, Wan Rong thought this was all part of a plot to kill her. Yoshiko was the only one who could talk to her.

'The house of Prince Su, my father, is at your disposal. I was raised there as a child. You will be very comfortable there, before you rejoin the emperor.'

Thin, with ravaged features, the empress's pallor stood out against the greyness of the real hovel her bedroom had become.

Yoshiko finally overcame her reservations: 'Naturally, you'll not go short of opium, we'll see to that . . .'

And so Pu Yi was reunited with his beloved wife, and became the puppet emperor of a rump state, Manchukuo. At that time, Kang Sheng, head of the communist services, was organising anti-Japanese resistance in Manchuria, before he went to Moscow. How did he recruit his chef Gong Tao from Pu Yi's entourage? He never revealed this. Before joining the communists, Gong became an intermediary between the emperor held hostage by the Japanese and the Red Army.

Then he went to Yan'an and became Kang Sheng's chef. He was able to give the communists some insight into the puppet emperor's psychology.

In 1945 the Soviets captured Pu Yi and deported him to Siberia. In 1950 Moscow handed him back to the Chinese. Public security, Kang Sheng's *Gonganbu*, kept him in the Fushun detention centre for war criminals, and in 1959 Mao pardoned him. Pu Yi, the little Manchu emperor, became a gardener and model citizen of the People's Republic, writing his memoirs to the greater glory of communism.

Gong Tao, the emperor's cook, was not the only one to change his allegiances. It is possible he played a part in recruiting Kawashima Yoshiko to Kang Sheng's service.

On 11 November 1945, a brief Guomindang communiqué announced: 'A beauty we have been pursuing for a long time was arrested in Peking today by Chinese counter-intelligence. She was executed for collaborating with the Japanese.'

A rumour went round that she had been working for Kang Sheng. 'Not at all, Jin Bin Hui was indeed a Japanese spy; that's why we shot her . . .' members of the Guomindang, now in Taiwan, told the authors.

Constantin Rissov, a White Russian now living in France who was imprisoned first by the Guomindang and then by the communists, knew the niece of Emperor Pu Yi very well – she was also the sister of Kawashima Yoshiko: 'As soon as the nationalist troops arrived in Beijing in 1945, she was arrested, tried and very soon hanged. She was said to have been working for the communists.'

At the same time, Yoshiko's devilish boss, Colonel Doihara, was hanged as a war criminal. But before meeting his fateful end, Doihara had become in the space of ten years the chief of Japanese intelligence in China. This meant that during the 1940s, three men waged a merciless war against each other: Kang Sheng the communist, Doihara the Japanese and Dai Li the nationalist.

'Kang Sheng is the man who knows most about what goes on in China,' Mao Zedong would readily admit.

'Yes, but there is an even more mysterious character, Dai Li. I've never met him, not even during the 1930s when he was hunting down us communists. He's a man who always keeps out of sight . . .'

On 14 August 1937, bombs exploded in the middle of Shanghai at the two busiest intersections of the French and International Concessions, causing dozens of deaths. This 'Bloody Saturday' followed upon the Marco Polo Bridge Incident, the confrontation between Japanese and Chinese troops that precipitated the outbreak of total war between the two nations. The Japanese army besieged the Chinese quarter of Shanghai. In the French Concession, which had so far remained untouched, a man who had taken refuge there observed the devastated town with rage in his heart. For Du Yuesheng, the godfather of the Green Gang, a whole world was collapsing . . .

Having put his affairs in order, left instructions to his lieutenants and drawn up an inventory – how many opium dens and brothels were likely to fall into the hands of the Japanese or their collaborators? – Du decided to leave.

In November, accompanied by his fourth wife, he boarded a French liner bound for Hong Kong. He wiped a tear from his eye as he leaned against the railings watching *his* city fade into the distance. Albeit a gangster, he was none the less Chinese, and therefore eternally in thrall to the call of the ancestral homeland.

Another secret world, where he had always had contacts and his own personal networks, was awaiting him in Hong Kong. But his worst fears were being realised in Shanghai: the Green Gang, left leaderless, lost its grip. The gambling dens where people staked fortunes on mahjong or the roulette wheel, the racing tracks, opium dens, Russian cabarets, Korean brothels became battlegrounds for bloody fighting between the Green Gang and its eternal enemy, the Red Gang.

The whole edifice was crumbling. Having settled in Hong Kong, in the majestic Peninsula Hotel, Du encountered a world as complex and as animated as Shanghai, where different secret societies held sway, the triads. An hour's sailing from Hong Kong was Macao, where the millionaire Stanley Ho, his *alter ego*, guided him through the casino jungle. At the Hotel Lisboa, people gambled feverishly all night long, playing *fan tan*, a Chinese game typical of Macao, with hundreds of pearls as stakes. 'These pearls come to us from Japan; according to an old tradition, the pearl divers who find them are naked women,' said Stanley Ho, smiling. Mr Du shuddered at the mere mention of Japan. The idea of the Japanese torturing his country was enough to make up his mind: it was impossible for him to remain here, courting the Macao and Hong Kong underworlds. He had to return to China and reconquer Shanghai.

In the face of the Japanese army Chiang Kai-shek had taken refuge in Wuhan. Du Yuesheng decided to travel there to meet him. He wanted to renew the old alliance to retake Shanghai, just as it had been snatched back once before from the Red hordes.

Dai Li, Chiang Kai-shek's masterspy, asked for a meeting with Du. With his squirrel-like head, his flat nose and malicious eyes, this young soldier was the rising star in the Guomindang. Because of the Japanese invasion, he made himself indispensable to Chiang Kai-shek. A graduate of the Huangpu military academy, where he had met Zhou Enlai as well as Chiang Kai-shek, Dai now controlled the all-powerful secret police, the Bureau of Investigation and Statistics. With Chiang's approval, he expanded the BIS, creating a vast worldwide intelligence network.

Dai Li's international network drew its resources from the old Huangpu academy, from which dozens of officers had been selected to become heads of intelligence units throughout the world. A former diplomat, born in 1890 and educated at the University of Michigan in the United States, was given the task of organising the international network under diplomatic cover. This Dang Yueliang, also a graduate of Huangpu, was Deputy Minister of Foreign Affairs in 1931 when Chiang decided to set up this ultra-secret agency. Dang was answerable only to Chiang and to Dai Li. A friend of Dai's, Deng Wenyi, was sent as military attaché to Moscow (and contacted by Kang Sheng in 1936 at the time of the Xi'an negotiations). In Paris, General Tang Zhi was responsible for liaising with Colonel Gauché's Deuxième Bureau, but, according to contemporary reports, French counter-intelligence distrusted this Chinese general who so readily exchanged information with the Japanese. However, in March 1938, Tang Zhi met General Dentz and asked for France's support against the Japanese. The Deuxième Bureau put the casualties suffered by the Japanese army by that time at 150,000 dead and injured; but their forces nevertheless remained superior to Chiang Kai-shek's troops. Tang asked for a French military mission to be sent to China, but nothing came of it. The French had difficulty in understanding the Chinese mentality, or at least Guomindang tactics.

No doubt they had learned that another leader of nationalist Chinese intelligence in Europe was pursuing a much more shady course of action. General Kwei Yung-chin, military attaché in Berlin, was trying to win the support of the Third Reich for the Guomindang. Contrary to the generally accepted view, the German–Japanese alliance was not a foregone conclusion. A German military mission had been sent to Chiang Kai-shek in China. Certain Guomindang leaders were open-mouthed with admiration for the German Nazi Party. The Blue Shirts had modelled themselves on their German counterparts. Hitler himself wavered . . .

In the Führer's entourage, the Minister of Foreign Affairs, Von Ribbentrop, and the head of the police, Himmler, were prime movers in the pro-Japanese lobby. But Air Marshal Goering, on the other hand, and the President of the Reichsbank, Schacht, hoped for an alliance with Chiang Kai-shek. The pro-Japanese lobby won.

Dai Li also wanted to acquire the services of special agents, adventurers, mercenaries who, whatever their own nationality, would agree to train Chinese agents. So it was that Commander Crabb, the founding father of naval frogmen, undertook to train Chinese for submarine sabotage missions.

In Washington, the deputy military attaché, Colonel Xiao Sinru, was not only one of Dai Li's masterspies but also a more astute, more effective diplomat than his own ambassador. With the backing of the large Chinese community, Colonel Xiao patiently forged the future Sino-American alliance that would come to fruition after the surprise attack launched by the Japanese on Pearl Harbor. But meanwhile he recruited for his bosses one of the world's best cryptologists, Herbert Yardley.

In Australia, another secret agent trained at Huangpu set in motion an affair that would only come to light forty years later. Li Hong, vice-consul in Sydney, recruited an Australian lawyer who later became a senior politician . . .

Dai Li had forged an intelligence agency, the BIS, equal to his ambitions and capable of holding its own against Kang Sheng's secret agents, or those of the Mikado. In the past he had concentrated his fire on the communists. Now the aim was to overthrow the giant Empire of the Rising Sun.

His meeting with that other colossus, Du Yuesheng, took place, as usual, in a shop selling coffins, a venue graphically emphasising the demise of Shanghai . . . for his casino the High Society had been attacked, and the Westerners, lodged in their Concessions, looked on as the Chinese quarter perished: on the top floor of the Cathay Hotel, the champagne had flowed, and people had danced and flirted, excited even more by the Dantesque spectacle of the Zhabei quarter in flames.

'This is my plan,' Dai Li explained to Du. 'We are going to organise a secret force, properly armed, units capable of guerrilla action, sabotage, and harassment of the Japanese in Shanghai . . .'

'Right, I understand,' said Du, smiling, 'I'll see to it.'

All he had to do was to select the best shots in the Green Gang to train a terrorist army. It was no small paradox to see this criminal syndicate transformed into a resistance movement. In the same way, Lucky Luciano and some of the Sicilian Mafia helped the American special services to organise the Sicily landings a few years later during the Second World War.

Within a short time Du Yuesheng had assembled a special force called the Jiangsu-Zhejiang Action Commission, 18,000 men strong, which he agreed to place under Dai Li's command. What pact had the two men signed? Was it a blood pact, such as was commonly made, in pure Taoist tradition, on entering the Green Gang? For Dai Li, the support of the leader of a secret society to which Chiang Kai-shek had belonged was a not inconsiderable factor in his rise to supreme control in the intelligence world. In exchange, the general facilitated the movement of Du's precious goods: drugs and currency. This was the birth of a real tradition of drug-trafficking directly promoted by the Guomindang special services, paralleling what the communist Li Kenong, Kang Sheng's deputy, was doing on his side. The people could obtain their opium: Red or White, communist or nationalist . . .

The capacity of Du's private army for resistance was limited. There were many in the criminal fraternity who would have preferred to adapt to circumstances and collaborate with the Japanese.

Meanwhile, the Japanese secret services had learned that the leader of the Green Gang sometimes stayed in rue Bourgeat, in the French Concession. Colonel Doihara, who had installed the former Emperor

Pu Yi on the phantom throne of Manchukuo, wanted to talk to him. Would he succeed this time in winning over the Green Gang to his Black Dragon Society? The emissaries that he sent to rue Bourgeat were quickly shown the door. Fearing that he might be assassinated, and seeing his resistance movement collapse, Du went into exile once more.

By way of consolation, Doihara managed to gain control of the Chinese police in Shanghai who for the most part decided to collaborate with the Japanese and the Chinese Laval, Wang Jingwei, betraying their former boss, Dai Li. The best policeman recruited by Doihara was incontestably Li Shiqun. Together with a couple of other renegades from Dai Li's camp, Zhou Fohai and Ding Mocun, he willingly agreed to set up a Chinese but pro-Japanese secret service at 76 Jessfield Road, simply referred to as Number 76. Li Shiqun excelled in the very Chinese art of betrayal. This former communist captured by the Guomindang had become one of the great headhunters working against the Reds in Shanghai; then, when he saw the Guomindang flee before the white flag bearing a scarlet sun, he sided with the Japanese. His death in the summer of 1943 was suitably sordid. While celebrating with his friends in the *Kempeitai*, the Japanese Gestapo, he died in agony. He had been poisoned. No doubt he was suspected of being a traitor once more . . .

Shortly after the surprise attack on Pearl Harbor, the Japanese took Hong Kong. Du Yuesheng had to flee once again, and he took refuge in the new Guomindang capital of Chongqing. He was to remain there until 1945. But his links with Shanghai and the rest of his organisation were severed. For at least a year, he led the life of a recluse, isolated and harried by fate. In the coolness of winter he was able to breathe, but the rest of the year the implacable heat brought on attacks of asthma. He played mahjong with his servants, indulged in more and more opium, and had someone read the newspaper and news of the war to him – for the dreaded Du was illiterate.

In 1942 he re-established contact with his empire, thanks to Dai Li, who repaid the debt he owed him. The head of the secret services was based some ten kilometres from Chongqing in 'Happy Valley', where he had built the most extensive intelligence and counter-intelligence complex there had ever been in China until then. It became the headquarters of the struggle against both the Japanese and the communists.

Xenophobia is second nature to the Chinese. Dai Li assiduously cultivated it. Only one man escaped his belligerence towards Caucasians and became almost a friend, able to stand up to him: this was the American Herbert O. Yardley, the cryptologist, recruited in 1938 by Colonel Xiao, the BIS man in Washington. The coding of messages and the decoding of intercepted signals posed some tricky problems in Asia.

Now, Dai Li asked two things of Yardley: that he should decode signals sent out by the Japanese army, and safeguard his own communications.

Herbert Yardley, born in Indiana in 1889, was a prime example of those badly treated geniuses born ahead of their time. Usually it is only after their deaths that it is appreciated what an enormous contribution to knowledge they have made, and it is difficult to imagine how much more they might have achieved had society not made life so difficult for them. Yardley's is an astounding case: he became a celebrity precisely because he was prevented from pursuing his career. When he graduated from Chicago University as a very young man, he had a keen interest in all kinds of secret writing, ancient codes and hieroglyphics. A humble telegrapher working for the railways, he made himself known to the State Department through his skill in the art of ciphering.

No code seemed unbreakable to him. When the First World War broke out, he ran the whole of the new section 8 of military intelligence, known as MI8, devoted to ciphering. He achieved miracles. Promoted to the rank of major, he was even seconded to the French. In 1918, Yardley was sent to Paris to assist the French intelligence service – one of the most successful in this area. (The other was the Polish service – in 1919, the Polish Captain Kowalewski went to Japan, where he helped the Japanese army develop eleven different codes.)

After being demobilised, Yardley was forgotten. The cipher war was no longer relevant. The 'war to end all wars' was followed by the Roaring Twenties. The United States did not yet have a large enough secret service to employ a genius like him. So it was as an amateur that he began to take an interest in Japanese codes, and even managed to decode the signals intercepted by the State Department.

The Japanese language had inherited the old Chinese ideograms – that is to say, a system whereby a concept, an idea, a word is translated by an image, or a collection of images – but pronounced them differently. For example, 'England' in both countries is translated as 'The Land of the Heroes', 英国 , but is pronounced *Ying Guo* in Chinese and *Eikoku* in Japanese. But the Japanese also use another simplified script called *kata-kana*, of which there are seventy-three, which corresponds to a phonetic transcription of words, a little like Arabic or shorthand. So, the word 'France' is *Fa Guo*, 法国 , (the Country of the Law) in Chinese, but has two ways of being written in Japanese: either with Chinese-looking character 仏国 or else with *kata-kana*, as *Furansu*, フランス .

Yardley realised that the Japanese army and diplomatic staff were using this system to encode their secret messages. But no one was interested in his discoveries any more. He scraped a living somehow or other, doing odd jobs. After the financial crash in 1929, he was left without a cent. But for the salary of his mistress Edna Ramsaier, who worked in diplomatic communications, he would probably have starved. It was then that he thought of writing a book on secret codes and about his experiences in the First World War, under the title of *The Black Chamber*. The American government did everything it could to prevent publication of this work which was considered to be against the nation's interests. In vain. Within a few weeks it had become a bestseller. People were tearing copies away from each other, as they might a new novel by Scott Fitzgerald. Yardley's fame crossed the oceans. And so it was that Colonel Xiao Sinru contacted him.

'We would very much like to make use of your knowledge. You can help us to win the war against the Japanese!'

'All right, but on two conditions: I want 10,000 dollars a year and I'm bringing Edna with me . . .'

In November 1938, under the name of Osborn (his second given name turned into a family name), Yardley arrived in Chongqing, on the banks of the Blue River, a mass of mud, bamboo huts and hastily constructed buildings.

After a month's waiting, spent working out the size of the rats, which he found extremely large in Sichuan, Yardley finally met Dai Li, who gave him the go-ahead to train signals specialists and to intercept and translate the Japanese codes. Over a period of time Dai Li endowed the BIS with the best cipher system in Asia. But would the communists not succeed in breaking Dai Li's codes? In order to protect Dai Li's codes, Yardley had to tackle the tricky problem of Chinese cipher. Without any equivalent of the *kata-kana*, it was impossible to get round the problem of ideograms that way. Some people envisaged the possibility of 'romanising' words, using the Roman alphabet. But Chinese has hundreds of phonemes pronounced in the same way. Only by the tone of voice (and the context) is it possible to deduce the sense. Not to mention the number of absolute homonyms, with the same sound and the same tone. A real headache! The solution turned out to be accessible to the public (the educated public, that is). Post and Telecommunications had produced a code book for sending telegrams. It consisted of a directory listing some ten thousand characters, with their pronunciation, like a dictionary, except that they were numbered, each with a four-digit number. The first character was 0000, the second 0001, and so on, up to 9999. So the character signifying 'the country', *guo*, was the number 0948. In transmissions only the numbers were used. By playing around with the numbers, substituting one for another or scrambling them by introducing series so that the character did not correspond with its original number, the character was rendered impossible to read. Only the transmitter and receiver of the message knew the grid by which the original number could be worked out. This was a long way from the famous *wan* of ancient times, the message that a warlord would write on paper or silk, and then roll up into a ball and seal with wax; the messenger would then carry it off on horseback, having swallowed it or concealed it in his rectum.

One day Chiang Kai-shek summoned Dai Li in a furious state. 'I entrusted you with the mission of infiltrating the communists whose public organisations are thriving here, instead of which it is they who are insinuating their moles into our organisations!'

Dai Li lowered his eyes. This was a serious loss of face. Since the Xi'an pact the communists had a liaison mission in Chongqing. A former member of the Communist Party's Central Committee, Zhang Guotao, who had gone over to the Guomindang, had become director of the BIS Research Bureau for special political affairs. As such, he spied on the liaison mission and his former comrades in their villa in the western suburb of Chongqing. Zhou Enlai was often there, along with Ye Jianying, Dong Bingwu and others. On the second floor was a secret transmitter-receiver, enabling the mission to remain in contact with Kang Sheng's radio service in Yan'an. And this is what had provoked Chiang Kai-shek's anger: the BIS listening service was supposed to intercept and decode communist transmissions. Instead of which, their listening station had been totally infiltrated by the communists, at the instigation of one of Kang Sheng's agents, Zhang Weilin.

The Yardley episode had led to further collaboration between Dai Li's services and foreign agencies of all kinds. In January 1942 a French officer came to Chongqing, sent by General De Gaulle. Representing the Central Bureau for Information and Military Action, the secret service of Free France, Lieutenant-Colonel Tutenges had just escaped from Singapore. The Japanese had captured him in the Malaysian capital, where he had until then been running the Asian networks. He hoped to gather intelligence on Vietnam, working with the French military mission. Dai Li dismissed him. He hated De Gaulle. Chiang Kai-shek, with his usual opportunism, did not recognise the leader of Free France; on the other hand, it was impossible to maintain relations with Vichy, which was on good terms with the Japanese.

There was a way round this. At the end of 1943 the same situation arose as in Algiers, where General Giraud, who had the backing of the Americans, had established his headquarters after escaping from Nazi captivity, and where friction between Gaullists and Giraudists in the special services was considerable; the two factions were happily united and a single command recognised. In Chongqing, Colonel Tutenges was replaced by Colonel Emblanc, whose boss was an exceptional character of Russian origin, General Zinodi Petchkov, the adoptive son of the communist writer Maxim Gorky. After they were joined by the best Sinologist in the army, Captain Guillermaz, this team won the confidence of Chiang Kai-shek. De Gaulle was no longer somebody to be avoided.

But Dai Li was not of the same mind as his leader. He was still playing the pro-American card. The head of the BIS installed Lieutenant-Commander Robert Meynier in 'Happy Valley'. This courageous seaman had been taken prisoner in 1940 and had escaped. Then he had commanded combat submarines, lending his support to General Giraud. Dai Li saw in him a formidable ally in Indochina for a very simple reason: Dai's fleshy wife, Katiou Do Hun Tinh, was related to the ruling family of Annam. With the help of her uncle, the former governor of Tonkin, Hoang Trong Phu, she hoped to set up a vast espionage network in Indochina in collaboration with the Guomindang and the Americans.

The day after Pearl Harbor, President Roosevelt decided to send a mission to Chongqing. Herbert Yardley, answering the call of patriotism, contacted the American military attaché, Colonel Barrett. On the one hand, he tried to influence his compatriots to collaborate with the Guomindang Chinese. On the other, he persuaded Dai Li to accept an alliance with the Americans. In Washington, his man Colonel Xiao had built up a Chinese lobby in favour of the Guomindang.

In the spring of 1942 Captain Milton Miles was sent to Chongqing to run a naval intelligence group under the command of the head of American forces in China, General Joseph Stilwell. Operation Dragon was under way. It consisted of creating a mixed Sino-American secret service. But in Washington, someone was ranting and raving: General Donovan did not appreciate his Office of Strategic Services being kept out of the affair. In every other corner of the globe the OSS was masterminding the war of partisans against German, Italian or Japanese occupying forces. But were OSS people not accused of being 'too left-wing' on the political spectrum, in other words democrats? Roosevelt had to give way to Donovan, in whom he had complete confidence. An OSS contingent left for China, but in exchange Captain Miles was co-opted to the OSS and given the prestigious post of head of the OSS for the Far East, while General Stilwell brought in a man more in tune with Chiang Kai-shek, General Claire Chennault, who had resigned from the American Air Force in order to become Chiang Kai-shek's air and sea adviser in 1937. Chennault and his famous Flying Tigers made life very difficult for Japanese pilots.

Meanwhile, Donovan, who considered Dai Li to be a 'Chinese Himmler', organised a second network without the Guomindang's knowledge. Since Dai Li detested the English, the OSS took over all the British Secret Intelligence Service networks, and set up units all over China; these were headed by Konrad Hsu. The operation, codenamed CLAM, received the unhoped-for assistance of the British insurance magnate C.V. Starr, whose commercial and financial presence throughout the whole of China and Taiwan offered excellent cover to OSS and SIS agents.

Dai Li was wary of the OSS. And he did not even know that one of its members, Diamond Kimm, who was of Korean origin, was in fact an agent working for Kang Sheng . . .

However, 15 April 1943 saw the birth of the Sino-American Co-operation Organisation (SACO), which embraced a vast conglomerate of secret services. It was headed by Dai Li, with Captain Miles as deputy, whose own second-in-command was a genuine OSS agent, formerly a correspondent for United Press in Shanghai, Alghan Lusey. Despite the deplorable image Dai Li enjoyed in the USA, the OSS had sent back a detailed report that was summed up in the following words: 'Dai Li is very competent and a nice guy.' In order to counter the reports filed by the State Department's adviser to Chiang Kai-shek, Owen Lattimore, who was rather sympathetic to the communists, a commission of enquiry even visited the prisons. They were clean, the prisoners were content with their lot and all swore by Dai Li . . . Of course the cells had been quickly whitewashed, the torture chambers had been cleared away, and thousands of prisoners removed from Happy Valley.

This valley soon became a kind of Disneyland of espionage. All the buildings bore American designations: Psychological Warfare Department, Special Operations, etc. SACO undertook numerous missions: the setting up of meteorological stations, the study of guerrilla techniques, the use of radio and Western methods of espionage. In the end, four hundred American officers and non-commissioned officers trained Dai Li's Chinese troops in guerrilla warfare not only against the Japanese but also against their 'communist allies'. Training for surveillance missions was acquired by spying on Zhou Enlai's villa or on the Soviet diplomatic mission run by Alexander Semionovitch Paniuchkin, an NKVD diplomat, and the military attaché, Colonel Chuikov.

In all two thousand Americans were deployed in this strange world of Chongqing. A mysterious Colonel Monroe ran the Psychological Warfare Department, assisted by Wu Li-chun, an advocate of black propaganda. In the laboratory at the school for sabotage, Dr Cecil Coggins designed gadgets worthy of James Bond. One day Dai Li came to see him: 'Doctor, we need a very special means of poisoning Japanese officers. I shan't attempt to conceal from you the fact that we employ a large number of women who are prepared, out of patriotism, to surrender their charms to the invaders, in Shanghai and elsewhere . . .'

Dr Coggins got the picture: what was needed was a weapon that would allow the young Chinese women, once they were naked in some brothel in Shanghai or Tientsin, to 'poison a Jap' while he was sleeping. The ingenious Dr Coggins came up with a tiny capsule of *bacillus botulinus*, a strong poison that leaves no trace, the effects of which can be taken for ordinary food poisoning. The capsule could be concealed in the women's hair.

Shortly afterwards, Dai Li returned to the special laboratory looking visibly pained: 'Your capsules have no effect, doctor.'

Dr Coggins scratched his head and decided to abandon his magnificent invention. But this result defied the laws of science. In fact, the Chinese, who were doubtful of the Americans' efficiency, had tried the poison out on donkeys. And by some mystery of nature, this is the only animal totally immune to the effects of *bacillus botulinus*.

Wariness was the key word in relations between the Americans and the SACO Chinese. In 1944, despite all the successes they had achieved together, Dai Li learned that the OSS were planning to send a team to Mao in Yan'an. In other words, his worst enemy, Kang Sheng, would also benefit from the advice of the American secret services. He later learned that the OSS had established more than cordial relations with the leader of the communist resistance in Indochina, Ho Chi Minh. And there was still more that he did not know. A much more mysterious operation was unfolding, without either his knowledge or that of the communists, with the end of the war in mind.

'Of what use would reason be to man if he can only be influenced by violence?' wrote Leo Tolstoy in his book *Human Thought* shortly before his death. First Maxim Gorky, adoptive father of the leader of the Free French movement in Chongqing; now we have Tolstoy, a formidable champion of humanism and non-violence. His grandson's name was Ilya, but since he had American nationality, he was generally known as Bill.

Bill Tolstoy, captain in the OSS, left New Delhi accompanied by a famous explorer, Brooke Dolan, in September 1942. His mission was to contact the young Dalai Lama, the Living God of the Tibetans, and assure him of the support of the United States of America. In the foothills of Tibet, the two Americans hired a sepoy guide, and all three, on wonderful ivory-coloured mounts, rode to the holy city of Lhasa. After three months' journey, they were finally able to prostrate themselves before the Living God in December. He was ten years old, but received these emissaries from the largest free country in the world in a fitting manner.

Unlike the Chinese, with their endless negotiations, the Tibetans were a straightforward people who rightly feared the Chinese. They needed arms and radio transmitters. When General Donovan heard this, he gave the go-ahead. His people had been Irish; he knew what the independence of a small subjugated nation cost. This did not go down very well with the State Department diplomats: 'This could prove to be very embarrassing and annoy the Chinese. Don't forget that they lay claim to Tibet. We might upset Chiang Kai-shek!' This was the drift of a memorandum addressed to the President of the United States. But meanwhile, in Lhasa, Bill Tolstoy and Brooke Dolan grasped the substance of Tibetan thinking: whatever happened, whether it was the communists or the Chinese nationalists who won the war, would the USA defend the integrity of Tibet? Would they once again stand by freedom and the independence of nations?

The first OSS radio arrived in November. Thrilled at the idea of holding a people's destiny in his hands, Tolstoy tapped out his message: 'We have been remarkably well treated here and I hope that we have laid the foundations for a fruitful future. The Tibetans have a better understanding now of what the United States of America stands for. We have friends here.'

Then the two OSS emissaries travelled on to Chongqing. The journey took them five months. Not a week went by but when Tolstoy did not hear talk of an impending invasion of Tibet by the Chinese. On their arrival in Chiang Kai-shek's capital, where they were coolly received by certain Americans, and particularly by Dai Li, who suspected something was afoot, they sent a final message to Washington: 'We underline this important point: the United States must support the Tibetans against the Chinese.'

Tolstoy's mission unwittingly contained the germ of the most incredible post-war epic in that region: Tibet's secret war for independence.

For in Yan'an, capital of the Revolution, a plan for a communist seizure of power had been developed. It involved the annexation of Tibet. In the interim, Mao Zedong and Kang Sheng had a great deal to do: organise the first purges, implement the first 'cultural revolution' in China's history.

9
The Invention of Maoism

'It is not absolutely necessary or reasonable to own clothes in three colours or to eat five different dishes. But if, on the one hand, sick comrades and young students only eat two meagre meals of boiled rice per day and, on the other, there are self-important 'bigwigs' in perfect health indulging in luxurious and extravagant pleasures to the point that their juniors come to believe that not only do they bear them no love but . . . well, just the thought of all this cannot help but make one feel depressed . . .'

This Wang Shiwei was an agent provocateur, or worse, a madman! How dare he, the head of the Party's Bureau of Literary and Artistic Research, say such iconoclastic things in public? Where did he get the audacity to pose as a righter of wrongs, denouncing without any restraint the existence of a privileged stratum within the Soviet Republic of Yan'an? He must be in the pay of Chiang Kai-shek's special services, for sure: only an agent who was being handsomely paid by the Guomindang reactionaries could have any interest in leading young people and students down the path of subversion and anti-communism in this way!

In March 1942 a wind of rage and liberty gusted over Yan'an. And the writer Wang Shiwei, a translator into Chinese of the sacred works of Marx and Lenin, but also of the 'bourgeois decadent' works of the French novelist Colette and the English poet Thomas Hardy, posed as the standard-bearer of an open rebellion that raised his young brother comrades against the dictatorship of the Party in the realm of arts and letters. It was the hour of revolt among the intellectuals of the Chinese Soviet Republic: an insurrection all the more unacceptable in that Chinese tradition, contrary to that in the West, makes its writers and artists zealous servants of the prevailing power, and not anti-establishment irritants.

Whilst Wang Shiwei was brandishing the flag for freedom of expression, Ding Ling played the part of La Pasionaria. This courageous and determined young woman was a diehard non-conformist. In Shanghai in 1933 the Blue Shirts abducted her from her apartment in Quisan Road. After three years' detention in Nanking, she was released on Chiang Kai-shek's orders. According to him, she had mended her ways in an honourable fashion. But Ding Ling had taken advantage of her newfound freedom to travel secretly to Yan'an.

Now, here, she was preaching revolt against the official Marxist-Leninist art – in other words, anarchy! The young writer was a veteran of the bold stand: she had caused her former lover, Comrade Mao, serious loss of face by ostentatiously refusing to attend his wedding to Jiang Qing, on the grounds that she was a free woman and not some vulgar concubine. She had just published 'Thoughts on 8 March', an essay that gave uncompromising expression to the disillusion and bitterness of militant communist women daily confronted with the male chauvinism of their Chinese comrades. Ding Ling was playing with fire: no one was safe from Party justice. So why did she support the disrespectful and malicious criticisms of those ungrateful children of the Revolution, Luo Feng, Xia Jun, Ai Qing, He Qifang?

Enough was enough. The proletarian forces had to react against this nihilistic tide. In Yan'an there was no question of letting irresponsible young people sap the authority of the Party under the wishy-washy pretext of creative freedom and the struggle against inequality. Mao, who for several months had been contemplating making a decisive intervention in the artistic domain, lost no time in sharing his thoughts with his private secretary, Chen Boda. Aged thirty-eight, Chen was a comrade of proven talent with a genius for political propaganda, for which he was responsible at the Party's Central School. He in turn discussed the Wang Shiwei case with Kang Sheng. The two men quickly agreed: as usual, Comrade Mao was right. These dissident writers must cease their foolishness at once.

It was at the instigation of these two accomplices, backed by a puppet 'philosopher', Ai Siqi, that the 'Campaign of Criticism Against Wang Shiwei' was launched on 27 May. His students from the Bureau of Literary and Artistic Research were summoned to mass meetings, where they were instantly requested to repudiate their teacher and friend.

'. . . Wang is a patent counter-revolutionary! He has proven links with Trotskyists in the service of the Japanese and the Guomindang . . .' This argument was all the stronger for containing an element of truth: Wang Shiwei was certainly no counter-revolutionary, or a secret agent, but it was true that he had kept company with Trotskyists in Shanghai and translated several of Trotsky's works for them.

The students were not very keen on this 'intellectual kill' to start with, but after being duly admonished by Chen Boda and Kang Sheng's men, who surrounded the hall, they gradually warmed to it. The less courageous resigned themselves to baying with the wolves from the Social Affairs Department.

'Wang must explain himself to the masses! Wang must make a statement of self-criticism! Wang must repudiate his mistakes!' But the wave of hysteria did not break the writer's courage. Wang stood up to the pack and would not recant. In the face of his unexpected resistance, the meeting ended with no decisive outcome.

Faithful to his line of conduct, Wang Shiwei decided to take the initiative himself: on 2 June he offered to leave the ranks of the Communist Party, affirming without any ambiguity: 'There is practically no way of resolving the conflict of interest between the individual and the Party.'

Two days later, at another accusation meeting, he turned his adversaries' arguments against them: it was not he who was Trotskyist. It was the Party that was using Trotskyist methods to bring him down. And the arrogant Chen Boda, chief prosecutor of the cultural tribunal, would do better to look to the mote in his own eye: he was 'a sectarian', 'an opportunist in the style of the Second International!' By attacking someone so close to Comrade Mao in this way, the reckless Wang Shiwei was setting the seal on his own destiny.

Enraged, Chen Boda and Kang Sheng prepared a detailed counter-offensive. They extended the permanent meeting of accusation against Wang for eight days. At the same time, they summoned Ding Ling to special 'criticism of her thought' meetings. A patient campaign to sap the morale of both of them had got underway. The two writers had to contend with gibes and insults every day, while Kang Sheng secretly subjected their friends to threats and blackmail, and Chen Boda played the part of master of ceremonies.

On 11 June Ding Ling finally succumbed. The meetings 'criticising her thought' were exhausting. She could not take any more. Abandoning her comrade, she agreed to make a public retraction and to condemn Wang Shiwei, in compliance with the Party's wish. Chen Boda was exultant. Kang Sheng rejoiced more discreetly. One by one, the young dissidents made their 'submissions' – all except the uncompromising Wang Shiwei. But isolated, he became easy prey. Kang Sheng had him arrested for having 'opposed the people, the nation, the Revolution and Marxism', and for the expression of 'Trotskyist thinking in the service of the bourgeoisie, Japanese imperialists and international fascism'.

Wang Shiwei was never freed. In March 1947, when Chiang Kai-shek's forces were threatening the Yan'an region, Kang Sheng had him assassinated before withdrawing. By that time, the head of the Social Affairs Department had set in motion the terrible mechanism that was to crush thousands of human beings under the almost anodyne name of 'Campaign of Rectification', and which marks the beginning of the Maoist era.

The system had been in operation long before Mao Zedong established the Chinese Soviet Republic in Yan'an at the end of the legendary Long March. It was in South China, the cradle of communism, that it first came into effect, when the Jiangxi rural bases were first set up. These still very weak, small groups of communists had to be protected against frontal attack from Chiang Kai-shek's soldiers, but also from the subtle workings of his secret services, which were expert in sophisticated methods of psychological manipulation.

Chen Lifu and his brother, ever full of twisted ideas, had immediately thought of a way of retaliating against the development of the Red bases in the countryside. Before they became too strong, they had to be infiltrated, and relations between the leaders undermined by introducing the poison of mistrust, the worm in the bud.

The instrument of this clever policy was the Anti-Bolshevik League, created as early as 1927 and known as the A-B League. The communists had an urgent need for new cadres. The A-B League undertook to provide as many as they needed, selecting them by preference from the Three Principles of the People Youth League, a mass organisation that ran a very secret service indeed: the Association for Strong Action.

The OGPU would have admired the neatness of the set-up. The three-pronged attack by the A-B League, the Three Principles of the People Youth League and the Association for Strong Action led to the rapid penetration of the enemy's defences. The Chen brothers managed to recruit several senior Communist Party members, who had grown weary of the constant factional infighting. Better still, by giving wide publicity to the success of the A-B League, the Chen brothers further undermined the Reds. For there is nothing more dangerous for a revolutionary movement, albeit a rural one, than the obsessive fear of treachery.

There were only a handful of communists who had been 'turned'. A carefully orchestrated propaganda campaign represented them as a veritable army, clandestine, deeply rooted and omnipresent. Suspicion in the Reds' closed world quickly degenerated into a rejection of any critical attitude, which was identified with secret allegiance to the A-B League. Comrades no longer trusted each other. On top of the difficult living conditions in the Red bases, the atmosphere became intolerable.

Mao Zedong cleverly decided to exploit this collective paranoia to his own advantage. In November 1930, he got Chen Yi, one of the historic leaders of the Red Army, to liquidate several hundred officers, non-commissioned officers and ordinary soldiers accused of being secretly sympathetic to the A-B League. The communist cadres opposed to the Maoist leadership conveniently disappeared in what is known as the Futian Incident. In this manner, the real but grossly exaggerated spectre of the Guomindang and its secret agents served as an alibi for a radical purge.

Though he was not afraid to spill the blood of his own comrades, Mao was no madman. After the Futian Incident, he decided that it was high time to counter the subversive machinations of the A-B League and the Chen brothers. The communist leadership set up a Bureau for Political Security, headed by three experienced militants: Deng Fa, Li Kenong and Li Yimeng, a failed writer. These three men, very different in character, had one thing in common: experience of the leaders of the Guomindang, whom they had encountered during the period of flirtation between nationalists and communists, from 1924 to 1926.

Under their leadership, the struggle against 'reactionary activity' within the Jiangxi Soviet Republic was vigorously pursued, that is to say, with singular brutality. Accused, sometimes rightly but often unjustly, of belonging to the A-B League, many cadres were ruthlessly purged, learning to their cost what Comrade Mao had been saying with his usual verve for the past three years: 'The Revolution is not a gala dinner . . .'

Determined to deal once and for all with the 'communist bandits', Chiang Kai-shek, aided by his German military advisers, launched one 'extermination campaign' after another. To win the Jiangxi zone from his enemies, he naturally used the same methods as their spectacular repression, terror, brainwashing, intimidation of the population. Sinicised Nazi methods versus sinicised Stalinist methods: Red totalitarianism fed off White totalitarianism and vice versa.

To spearhead this politico-military offensive, the Special Movement Force was set up. It was so forceful and so special that foreign observers, clear-sighted for once, gave it an appropriate name: 'the Generalissimo's OGPU'. Five auxiliary groups of four thousand men each and a main detachment twice that size were operative in sixty different regions of China, employing extreme measures to deal with the 'bandits'. These experts in intense psychological pressure 'cleaned up' suspect villages with ruthless efficiency, monitored supply and access routes, bought people off, infiltrated intelligence agents disguised as Red soldiers, tortured recalcitrant peasants. Gradually, drawing on inspiration and experience, they arrived at a process used by the British against the Irish and the Boers that was developed and generalised by Stalinist and Nazi alike. But of course they took great care to adapt it to the Chinese context. 'When the Reds are captured or surrender,' noted the French Deuxième Bureau in a report on the Generalissimo's OGPU in 1935, 'they are not executed any more but put into concentration camps called "repentance camps" where they are shown the error of their ways . . .'

'Turning' individuals, brainwashing – now, these were interesting ideas, thought the communist leaders. The antidote, no doubt, was brainwashing and 'turning' individuals . . .

Even today it is difficult to put a precise date on the beginning of the 'rectification of style campaign', there were so many events leading up to it: the 'study campaign' of 1939–40, Mao Zedong's speech delivered in May 1941 in which he called on communist cadres to 'reform' their style of study, a document published under Liu Shaoqi's name in July of the same year on the 'struggle within the Party', the temporary closure of the Central Marxist-Leninist School. But the campaign can be regarded as having kicked off on 8 February 1942, when Mao Zedong, the future Chinese Premier, delivered a key speech to the communist élite in Yan'an. Having vehemently denounced the 'petty bourgeois' influence within the Party itself, he made clear how the antidote should be administered: 'The action that needs to be taken consists first of all in giving the sick man a good shake and shouting at him, "You're ill!" so that he starts sweating with fear, and then in telling him kindly to follow some treatment.'

Persuasion, then terror, the carrot and the stick. All Mao needed now were the people to wield them and, above all, an experienced leader to co-ordinate their efforts.

Comrade Mao personally selected the team. There were six of them: Liu Shaoqi, an exceptionally brilliant student who remained in Central China, where he worked as Secretary of the Central Committee; Chen Yun, Kang Sheng's companion in Shanghai after the defection of Gu Shunzhang, and then in Moscow, before he became head of the Organisation Department: Gao Gang, Party Secretary for the border region and the North-West; Peng Zhen, director of the Party's Central School, reopened after a major shake-up; Li Fuchun, one of the evil geniuses of the leadership; Chen Boda, his lively personal secretary. And overseeing their activities was Kang Sheng himself.

On 12 February 1942, the conductor of the newborn rectification campaign had his aides at the Central Committee's Social Affairs Department summon some two thousand communist cadres to the Eighth Route Army barracks, in Yan'an. The aim of this meeting was simple: to explain to those attending it that they should give some thought to the speech given by Mao four days earlier.

'Those who cannot open their mouths without mentioning Ancient Greece and deliberately neglect the study of China, those who choose to ignore practical problems, will never be able to implement the Marxist-Leninist spirit even if they have read hundreds of Marxist-Leninist books. The real theoreticians are those who develop theories out of practice,' he declared before exhorting the men present to study carefully and respectfully the writings of Comrade Mao.

A few days later, for the benefit of those who might not have understood, he drove the point home in the columns of the newspaper *Jiefang ribao*: 'All organisations and all comrades must study in depth the last two speeches of Comrade Mao Zedong.'

This incipient 'Mao-olatry' did not meet with immediate universal approval. It frankly displeased Wang Ming, who thought that only Joseph Stalin was entitled to a personality cult of this kind or, just possibly, his best Chinese disciple.

Wang Ming had been very ill since October 1941, and his wife was terribly worried. The truth was that her poor husband was slowly dying, the victim of Mao's machinations. Every day, while pretending to cure him, a doctor called Jin Maoyao gave him a strong dose of mercury-based medication. Under orders issued by Li Fuchun, one of the six men appointed by Mao, Jin Maoyao was poisoning Stalin's loyal servant, the former leader of the 'twenty-eight returned Bolsheviks'. And had it not been for the vigilance of his wife, who had not lived for years in Moscow for nothing, it would not have been long before Wang Ming joined the Marxist-Leninist-Stalinist paradise.

However, he survived. Bedridden, weakened, but still alive, a considerable obstacle to the rectification of style campaign – for although in a political minority, Wang Ming was still a senior cadre within the Communist International. And as such, he was a nuisance.

The rectification campaign in progress was aimed not only at dissident artists. To impose the dogma of Maoist infallibility in the matter of revolutionary war, communist policy, culture and even private life, it was necessary to get rid of the pro-Soviet clan, those 'dogmatic' individuals too loyal to Moscow and too attached to the outdated concept of class warfare. The main thrust of the campaign was to forge, by forced marches, a specifically Chinese path towards communism, an autonomous and more radical path than that advocated by the Comintern. It meant casting all Chinese comrades in the same mould, and eliminating all form of opposition or even merely critical thinking. It meant building up a monolithic party, united in the cult of a single man: the brilliant Comrade Mao.

On 3 April 1942, the Central Committee of the rectification campaign's Propaganda Department, headed by Kang Sheng, solemnly issued a list of twenty-two basic texts to be studied forthwith. Two of them were penned by Kang Sheng himself.

At the same time, Kang persuaded Mao to get rid of Deng Fa. The former head of the Political Security Bureau, unwilling to turn his back on what had been the object of his adoration, clung to a position judged to be too neutral, halfway between the Maoist lobby and that of Wang Ming. As far as Kang was concerned, Deng Fa's fall from favour was entirely to his own advantage: it increased his authority as head of the Social Affairs Department in the field of counter-espionage, one branch of his activities that, as it happened, he intended to develop on a large scale, seeing it as the indispensable complement to the 'rectification of style': isolate the black sheep first, then accuse them of being involved in Japanese/Guomindang espionage.

Yan'an turned into a communist school of exceptional proportions. On pain of being denounced to the masses – what this really meant was being denounced to Kang Sheng's henchmen – everyone had to devote two hours a day to reading the twenty-two sacred texts, and, furthermore, make sure everyone else knew about it. Overzealousness was better than discretion. The best people were soon spending three hours a day studying.

To cap this 'spontaneous' initiative, a special committee was set up on 13 April to run the 'rectification campaign'. There were twenty-one members, including Comrade Mao himself, who was nominally chairman. But the day-to-day business was undertaken by a group of five militants, led by Kang Sheng and his aide Li Fuchun, responsible for the poisoning of Wang Ming.

Kang Sheng now harboured a strong hatred of Wang Ming. Forgotten were the years spent together in Moscow. The head of the Social Affairs Department remembered only the Kremlin man's intrigues within the underground Party in Shanghai, and Wang Ming's fearfulness, holed up with his wife in a suburban sanatorium after Gu Shunzhang's treachery. He felt nothing but a deep-seated hatred: hatred of the Muscovite arrogance of Wang Ming at the time of his Muscovite glory; hatred of the Russians, those impudent 'long-nosed devils' who had thought that he, Kang Sheng, would agree to be their lackey!

Fate often arranges things badly. It was just when the rectification campaign had finally got under way that Stalin remembered Mao. On 12 May 1942, a Soviet plane landed in Yan'an. The aircraft brought a Russian mission, led by a Comintern cadre called Piotr Vladimirov. Forewarned by radio of their arrival, Mao came to meet the Kremlin guests in person, at his side a morose-looking Kang Sheng, his lips clamped round a cigarette, who said with a chilling smile: 'We are brothers!'

Vladimirov remained inscrutable. 'Kang Sheng always smiles. You get the impression that his smile is stuck to his thin worried face. When he listens, he exhales noisily, like the Japanese, as a sign of the pleasure he takes in his interlocutor's voice. He hasn't changed in all these years. He's just as I've always known him, sullen, energetic but nervous. The impression he gives is of a puppet on a string,' he wrote in his personal notebook.

This was not very kind. But Vladimirov had no reason to be kind to Kang Sheng. As the days went by, he had less and less reason: agents from the Social Affairs Department stuck to their 'Soviet brothers' like limpets, scrupulously recording their every word and gesture. Like silent shadows, they were everywhere. In short, it was not long before Vladimirov and his companions felt as free to do as they wished as a Western diplomat or journalist in Moscow today. In other words, they were kept under very, very close surveillance.

Kang Sheng probably did little to ease the situation, except smile mysteriously behind his thin-rimmed glasses or smoke more than ever. His secretary, Xiao Li, went further in demonstrating his open hostility and one day made this astonishing declaration of faith to the alarmed Soviets: 'What were you white men doing thousands of years ago? You were using bows and arrows, while we had gunpowder. We knew how to build canals, dikes, fortresses, we were capable of making china, silk, paper, ink. And you white men were still eating raw meat. We had already evolved a philosophy as you were just beginning to learn the alphabet. Our culture nourished the whole of the East. It's the womb from which all other cultures derive . . .'

What price 'international proletarianism', wondered Vladimirov and his comrades. Day by day their displeasure increased. Not content with reducing the Russians' freedom of manoeuvre to practically nil, and making sure they knew it, Kang Sheng's men kept the pro-Soviet clan virtually locked up. Confined to his bed, Wang Ming was inaccessible. Bo Gu, one of the 'twenty-eight returned Bolsheviks', proved extremely difficult to meet without others present. Luo Fu, Kai Feng, Zhu Rui, Wang Ji xiang were in the stocks, or near enough.

'All these dogm. ists, all these sectarians! It's the Party's role to isolate them lest they harm the Chinese people's struggle against the Japanese imperialists and the Guomindang!' was the constant refrain of official texts and oral propaganda. It was not very subtle but it was perfectly clear: Mao and his comrades would not stand for Stalin supplying arms to their enemy of yesterday – and their enemy of tomorrow. Looking above all to the interests of the USSR, if not of her people, the Soviet dict.tor was fostering good relations with the Generalissimo's government in the name of solidarity against 'world fascism'.

This was extremely hard to swallow, for Mao and his companions considered the Guomindang as a form of Chinese fascism. So they did not intend to carry very far an alliance with such a dubious partner, with whom they would probably be doing battle sooner or later. Like Chiang Kai-shek himself, they preferred to settle for a smiling façade and stabs in the back. Only Wang Ming, unshakeable in his loyalty to Stalin, despite his ruined health, continued to affirm pro-Soviet sentiments in innumerable pompous poems.

This was a turning-point: for the first time in their history, the Chinese communist leaders became aware of the divide between their policies and those of the Kremlin. Yan'an really was the furnace in which the elements of Red China's future identity were already being forged – beginning with the cult of Mao's Thought, and with the embryo of an autonomous foreign policy of which Zhou Enlai was becoming the guiding light and the champion.

But the Maoist group had learnt a long time ago to come to terms with reality. If Vladimirov is to be believed, they gave further proof of this on the announcement of the Red Army's victory at Stalingrad. In the face of this demonstration of strength, their latent hostility towards the Soviet CP delegates suddenly evaporated.

Happy about their country's victory, Vladimirov and his friends invited the leaders of the Chinese Soviet Republic to a celebration party, at which Kang Sheng apparently did ample justice to the reserves of alcohol. Two days later – out of politeness maybe, out of a desire not to be beholden to the Soviets certainly – he invited them to a sumptuous banquet, attended by Mao. In an almost relaxed atmosphere, those present enjoyed all kinds of delicious dishes prepared by Kang's personal chef, Gong Tao. We do not know whether Wang Shiwei, the dissident who had violently denounced the rise of the privileged in Yan'an, was given special rations that day.

In any case, this honeymoon period lasted only a few days. Mao and his companions had a great many other concerns than pleasing Stalin's envoys. They had to carry through to the end the 'revolution of minds' they had embarked upon.

> The cadres are the most advanced elements of the masses and they have generally received more education; they need a more advanced literature and art, and it would be a mistake not to take account of this need. What you do for the cadres, you also do for the masses, for the masses can only be educated and guided through the intermediary of the cadres. If we turn away from this aim, if what we give the cadres cannot help them to educate and guide the masses, our efforts to raise literary and artistic standards will no longer have any point, and will deviate from our fundamental principle, which is to serve the popular masses. . . .

This was one of the key elements in Chinese communist thinking, as expressed by Comrade Mao himself on 23 May 1942, at the end of the forum on literature and art held in Yan'an: the privileged political role of cadres in the education of the masses, and the rigorous subordination of all forms of art to this fundamental principle.

Two men in particular contributed to this decisive clarification of the thinking of the future Premier of Red China: Chen Boda and Kang Sheng. Even if the country's official history prefers to forget the fact, at that time both men were close associates of Mao Zedong. They belonged to the very restricted circle of comrades authorised to meet their leader without any witnesses present. And the cave that served as a home to Jiang Qing and her husband was often the setting for strange philosophical evenings when the head of the Social Affairs Department and Mao's personal secretary argued with the man they were on the way to turning into a living god. It was not long before Wang Shiwei and Ding Ling suffered the consequences of these nocturnal meetings.

The rectification campaign spread its grey mantle over Yan'an. Everyone was obliged to read carefully the 'twenty-two documents' and show that they had properly taken them in. They had to criticise the mistakes of others and, above all, beat their own breasts, expose backsliding comrades and deviationist cadres, denounce the 'dogmatic' Wang Ming and company, and their underhand anti-Maoist intrigues. Only Mao the infallible, Mao the omnipresent, Mao the superlucid escaped criticism. And just for good measure, even Kang Sheng and Chen Boda publicly admitted to dogmatic and opportunistic tendencies.

On 8 June the Central Committee's Propaganda Department, spurred on by Chen Boda, officially announced that the rectification campaign would extend to all levels of the hierarchy, and all regions under Party control. To facilitate this widespread diffusion of

Marxist-Leninist thought, the number of sacred texts was reduced to twelve. In mid-October, the special committee presided over by Kang Sheng organised a 'seminar' for high-ranking cadres, held in Yan'an. For three long months, 280 Party officials attended this decisive meeting in turn. The seminar began with a detailed assessment of the rectification campaign, sector by sector and region by region. Then came the time for 'self-criticism'. Nearly seventy participants took the stand to vie with each other in self-flagellation: yes, they had been guilty of 'subjectivism', of a petty bourgeois attitude. Yes, they had been sectarian or dogmatic. Yes, they had played a part in 'leading the masses astray'. Yes, they were seriously guilty in respect of the Party and Comrade Mao.

The Party's leading lights who succeeded one another on the platform exhorted their comrades to mend their ways: Chen Yun, He Long, Zhu De, Ye Jianying, Lin Boqu, Ren Bishi, Liu Shaoqi and Kang Sheng all spoke. All insisted on the imperative necessity of extending the current campaign. Just as the spark ignites the whole plain, the whole people needed to be inflamed. Alongside the Leninist idea of an avant-garde party enlightening workers in order to lead them to victorious revolution, there was now the idea of a complete recasting of the individual under the exclusive control of the CP and its supreme leader.

To underline the importance of the seminar, Mao graced it with his presence. Exhorting Party cadres not to waste time on secondary issues, he insisted on this crucial point: it was the total reform of everyone's thinking that had to be aimed at, not purely formal changes.

On 17 November Gao Gang made a speech that drew a lot of attention. The Party leader in the border zones had the wind in his sails, his confidence boosted by several very favourable remarks Mao had made about him. To the great displeasure of Kang Sheng and Chen Boda, he happily posed as Mao's 'best disciple'. He gave the Yan'an cadres a real lesson in applied Maoism.

Kang Sheng decided to outmatch him. In the course of his various haranguing sessions, he insisted on a new concept that he had just formulated in his Zhaoyuan headquarters. 'This is the great revelation,' was the drift of what he said on 16 December; 'there is a close link between the two crimes of espionage and deviationism. A person is not deviationist, as we had believed until now, by chance or error. A person is inescapably, dialectically deviationist because he is a Japanese agent, a Guomindang spy, or even both at the same time. We must therefore embark on a merciless quest to extirpate these two scourges, for, in combating deviationism, we undermine the underground machinations of our enemies and vice versa.'

This astonishing realisation opened the most brutal period of the rectification campaign. With their boss's encouragement, the men from the Social Affairs Department, Marxist-Leninist bloodhounds of a new order, arrested people, beat them up, tortured them, drove them to self-criticism and mutual denunciation. Those beyond rehabilitation, they liquidated.

'Yan'an became a real concentration camp,' Wang Ming was to write later, and he should know, having spent many years in the USSR and sent many comrades to Siberia.

But it no longer mattered what Wang Ming thought. Only the attempts of the leaders of the rectification campaign to outdo each other were of any significance. To carry out this immense work of 'mass counter-espionage', Kang Sheng was released from the chairmanship of the Special Commission. Liu Shaoqui replaced him. Recklessly ambitious, Liu helped introduce, at the expense of others, the inquisition process to which he would himself fall victim a quarter of a century later, at the time of the Cultural Revolution. Kang Sheng pretended to accept the Party's decision gladly. Deep down inside, he nursed a grudge: Liu Shaoqi had made him lose face by supplanting him on the Special Commission; one day he would pay for it a hundred times over.

All forms of communist propaganda harbour a latent preoccupation. In stressing the vital necessity of long-term action to get the better of those Guomindang agents who had infiltrated the Party, Kang Sheng was not prompted by demagogy or a desire to defend his personal interests. The Party leadership was genuinely worried about the progress of their nationalist enemies in the matter of espionage. The person they feared the most was none other than Dai Li. Thanks to his privileged contact with the godfather Du Yuesheng and the OSS, his BIS was scoring new successes against the Chen brothers' clan. Dai Li admittedly chose his aides well: in Chongqing, his director of 'Special Political Affairs' was Zhang Guotao. Zhang was one of the founders of the Chinese CP, and later Mao Zedong's unfortunate rival whom Gu Shunzhang had escorted to the Red bases in April 1931, just before falling into the hands of the Guomindang. Having repudiated communism in 1938, he was now very actively engaged in infiltrating his agents among his former comrades in the border region of Shaanxi-Gansu-Ningxia.

There were even BIS military personnel, agents of Dai Li, in the very heart of the Red zone, in the communist capital. It was in Yan'an, for instance, that Shen Qiyue made his debut in the murky world of espionage and counter-espionage. He was then just a student, a member of a secret society controlled by Dai Li. Having penetrated the very heart of the communist apparatus for a period of months, he managed to escape Kang Sheng's nets and get back alive to the zone held by the Guomindang. This remarkable and extremely rare achievement made him a star of the Generalissimo's secret services. From 1964 to 1968 he ran the Ministry of Justice's Investigation Bureau (MJIB) in Taiwan.

Admittedly, there were not many who fared so well. Kang Sheng was ever vigilant. He relied on an important decision taken by the

Yan'an revolutionary seminar: the implementation of a 'screening of cadres campaign'. This new initiative meant that every Party official, every head of department, had to re-examine, under the eye of expert bodies, the 'biography' of every one of his subordinates. Those who did not undergo this examination successfully were downgraded, or else completely purged.

'Kang Sheng invited us to see three Guomindang spies – three wretched youths in a thoroughly emaciated state,' Vladimirov noted in his personal diary on 30 March 1943. 'Yuzhin says that such "exhibitions" have already taken place before now. The Chinese CP leaders use these methods with the aim of proving to us that their anti-Guomindang propaganda is justified. Yuzhin is certain that these three boys will be shot. Whether or not they are spies is of little interest to Kang Sheng. What counts is being able to exhibit them!'

Ten days after this display, which no doubt upset Stalin's envoy only because it was staged by the Chinese, Mao Zedong took a decisive step towards supreme power. He was appointed Chairman of the Politburo.

Within a year of intense activity, the rectification campaign had achieved its major aim: Comrade Mao was dead. Chairman Mao was born.

'If Chiang Kai-shek did not exist, I would have to invent him!' seemed to be Kang Sheng's new motto. Since 1 July, when he had inaugurated a 'campaign for the salvation *in extremis* of those who have fallen into error', the man seemed to be in the grip of a fever. At once the Fouquier-Tinville and the Beria of the Chinese Revolution, he had one overriding fear: that of being caught out by Mao failing in vigilance. Day and night, he saw his deputies, he wrote, he brought accusations, he built up files. Apart from the Chairman, no one, it seemed, could escape prosecution.

On 15 July, he put the final touches to an explosive report arguing that at all costs 'a climate of anti-subversive struggle must be instilled in the masses'. And to this end, a policy of mercy was to be developed, intended to allow sinners to repent. What this really meant was that only the fear of torture or death would force the individual to merge with the masses, as required of him. Pardon was therefore an incomparably powerful weapon in the leadership's arsenal.

According to Vladimirov, he then attended a huge meeting, with several hundred militant communists.

'The Special Affairs Department cannot catch all the spies swarming in Yan'an,' explained Peng Zhen, the first speaker. 'That is why the Department is asking all comrades to help!'

A very nervous Kang Sheng then took the stand.

'All of you, such as you are, are spying for the Guomindang!' he exploded. 'Why do you want our destruction? What harm have we done you? You have everything you need: a roof over your head, food

. . . why do you all want our death? Show that you have repented and
we will forgive, but always remember this: not every repentance is
sincere. Re-education is a long process . . .'

The audience was chilled. This man would have made anyone tremble. Perhaps because he himself was being called to account: the
special judicial enquiry into the Jin Maoyao affair would soon complete its investigations. Taking advantage of the relative improvement
in the climate of relations between the Russians and the Chinese leadership, Wang Ming and his wife had openly accused the doctor of
being a 'white-coated assassin' recruited by Li Fuchun, Kang's henchman. And Jin Maoyao seemed on the verge of breaking down, not
without reason in fact: already a medical commission had found him
guilty, despite the obstruction tactics of Ma Haide, the Lebanese
doctor who was a close ally of Kang. But a great deal depended on
Jin's discretion: if he lost his nerve in public, Li Fuchun would in turn
be discredited. So Kang had plenty to worry about.

Happily for him, Chairman Mao did not intend in any event to
abandon such an intelligent and effective servant. When the judicial
enquiry delivered its verdict in the Wang Ming poison case, Kang
Sheng was able to breathe more freely. The affair was completely
buried – although not Wang Ming. Condemned for form's sake to
five years' imprisonment, Jin Maoyao received authorisation not to
serve his sentence, in line with the policy of clemency. Kang and Li
were not even mentioned. The fact that they were on the committee of
enquiry and that this was chaired by Liu Shaoqi, their old accomplice,
was obviously not without some significance with regard to this
strange verdict.

Sick, bedridden, Wang Ming could only implore Comrade Stalin a
little more loudly to send a plane to fetch him lest he die in Yan'an.
The plane arrived but flew off again without its passenger. Mao and
Kang Sheng did not want a dangerous witness to their grand operations going back to the USSR at any price . . .

Once the Jin Maoyao episode was finally settled, the head of the
Social Affairs Department forged ahead with the campaign of salvation. It was in the border zones, where the Red bases were in contact
with the Guomindang, that it reached its height. After having extorted
confessions from several students at the teacher training college in
Suide, a town situated a hundred kilometres to the north-east of
Yan'an, Kang Sheng's men accused the whole student population of
being agents of the Guomindang. Between June and September 1943,
160 of these unfortunate people were brought to trial. They were
supposed to belong to a group controlled by Dai Li, the Springtide
Society.

'Sex is the favourite weapon of the Springtide Society!' proclaimed
the newspaper *Jiefang ribao* for the edification of the virtuous masses.
For page after page, the communist daily paper explained in what
shameful manner Dai Li's agents were ruining the reputation of hon-

est young girls, spreading slander, without any foundation, so that once compromised in this way they became easy prey for the Guomindang, who forced them to do what they were accused of, thereby making them whores of the counter-revolution. Using their charms for the reactionary cause, they would bewitch their male comrades on behalf of the Springtide Society.

'This is the favourite slogan of Chiang Kai-shek's masterspies: the number one battlefield of female secret agents is their bed!' the newspaper announced in all seriousness.

Workers and peasants could rest assured: such methods would never have occurred to Kang or any of his deputies! Maoist totalitarianism and age-old Chinese puritanism made good bedfellows. Between the two of them, they produced the strange equation: sexual liberty equals espionage equals anti-popular intrigue. In the communist republic of Yan'an, whilst it was perfectly commendable to denounce one's neighbours, to drive relatives and friends to humiliating self-criticisms, it was considered highly immoral to write what one wanted or live as one pleased.

Unless one was a Party leader, of course! It wasn't the same for them. Mao himself set an example of a fairly stormy love life, but it was entirely excusable in him because of his immense services to the Chinese people.

Of the Party leaders, only a few lived according to the family principles prescribed for the *hoi polloi*, among them Zhou Enlai, who remained faithful to his wife Deng Yingchao, and Kang Sheng.

As it turned out, this was to prove a great advantage. For, before long, Kang Sheng was appealing to all his friends, and to his own wife Cao Yi-ou, to help him face the consequences of his own excesses.

'Overconfidence is harmful: good horsemen are unseated, excellent swimmers drown,' according to an old Asian proverb. At the end of 1943 Kang Sheng suddenly had experience of this, when he unexpectedly found himself out of favour.

What had the head of the Social Affairs Department done to merit such ingratitude? Nothing, or virtually nothing. Nothing worse than before, in any event. Kang Sheng had not changed his behaviour one iota: it was Mao's behaviour that changed without warning. A good Marxist always takes account of the balance of power, and the leader of the Party, drawing his own conclusions from the Red Army's spectacular victories against the Wehrmacht, had taken this to heart. Now he wanted to re-establish contact with Moscow.

In the Chinese communist tradition, when the leadership makes a 180-degree turnaround in its policy, it is good to find a scapegoat for the 'errors' and 'excesses' of the past. Covertly attacked by Liu Shaoqi, incriminated by several members of the 'old guard' for his absence from China at the time of that great initiatory test, the Long

March, Kang Sheng sensed that he was the one likely to be cast in this unenviable role.

He could not afford to take any chances. Together with his loyal wife Cao Yi-ou, the head of the Social Affairs Department took stock of his remaining trump cards.

The couple decided they had three, all very important. Although challenged by his deputy Li Kenong, the pederast buddhist, who had decided to play his own game, Kang Sheng could rely on the power of his espionage apparatus headed by several trusted friends, including Xiao Li and Zhao Yaobin, his assistant since 1942. Nor should he neglect the political importance of the voluminous files he had been keeping since 1937 on the other Party leaders. Above all, he could count on the Chairman himself: Mao Zedong would suffer greatly from a public campaign against Kang Sheng. Mao certainly had the means to weaken the position of his accomplice and subordinate, but the wholesale calling into question of the rectification campaign would only have led to tarnishing his image as 'enlightened guide' of the people and the Party. Not to mention, of course, the active sympathy of Jiang Qing, who had more and more influence over her husband, for whom she arranged most of the meetings with the Soviet mission in Yan'an in the context of the new policy.

So, the situation was not all that bad. Putting on a brave face in these hostile circumstances, Kang Sheng carefully studied his plan of action. Like a reed, he had to yield, let the wind blow and admit to a few small 'errors' during the rectification campaign, which overall had been a positive venture. It was a small price to pay to safeguard what was essential.

On 20 March 1944, the head of the Social Affairs Department submitted a report entitled 'The Development of the Anti-Subversive Struggle' to a conference of leading cadres from the Party's North-West China Bureau.

'Most of the BIS agents in the border region betrayed themselves during the "confessions" campaign. The BIS envoys were all captured,' he said without batting an eyelid. 'Many of them had already made their submission. They now work for us. Twenty-two rifles, 10 pistols, 480 rounds of ammunition, 12 grenades and more than 100,000 Chinese dollars have been seized.'

In short, everything was progressing nicely. The 'Trotskyite-Guomindang' spies, such as Wang Shiwei, had been unmasked. It would not do the other deviationists any harm to wait.

This was of course just the first volley. No one could question the principle of the rectification campaign launched by Mao. It was the manner in which it had been conducted that could be disputed. Kang Sheng had primarily to deal with the increasingly less veiled insinuations of those who accused him of having developed an unprecedented system of repression defying all bounds and relying on confessions extracted under torture.

'The mistake in torturing people in order to extort confessions from them and accepting these as genuine is a subjectivist kind of mistake,' he said, taking the bull by the horns, and laying the blame for the countless incidents of violence during the rectification campaign on local agents with insufficient political training. They had not taken account of Mao's policy of clemency, a policy of which Kang himself had always been the most zealous servant.

He went on to define six major categories of people who had confessed: categories one and two, spies and communist renegades, the most dangerous; category three, all Party members who had not taken care to give a satisfactory account of their political past when they joined; category four, those who had indeed acted as spies but without their knowledge; category five, those militants, prompted by personal ambition, who had falsified their Party record; and finally, category six, the innocent. This category could be accounted a matter of 'technical' error. And if errors of this kind had occurred, then the victims should be 'rehabilitated', that was all there was to it.

Kang Sheng was not so candid as to admit the truth: according to his statistics, the proportion of unmasked spies and renegades dropped suddenly from ninety per cent to ten per cent. Leaving aside the human consequences, even as mere figures, there is a dramatic difference between the two.

With this speech, made on 20 March, Kang Sheng had played and won. By saving his own face, he could also impress upon Mao that he had also saved that of the whole Party and therefore of its leader. He had the intelligence, if not the generosity of spirit, not to do so.

The head of the Social Affairs Department slowly continued the backtracking process. Vladimirov and his companions were very surprised to find him being more and more friendly towards them. They concluded that the Chinese CP's policy towards the USSR had undergone a significant change.

At the end of August 1944, before the imminent arrival in Yan'an of an American military mission led by Colonel Barrett, the climate changed yet again. Mao began to cold-shoulder Kang Sheng and Cao Yi-ou. Chen Yi, the Red general who had been one of those spearheading the rectification campaign, kept a notable distance from the couple.

Why this renewed sullenness and mistrust on the part of the Chairman and those close to him? Basically, the reasons were very simple. Because no revolutionary leader, however Marxist-Leninist he might be, ever forgets the art of government bequeathed by his predecessors, whether emperors or ministers. Because Mao Zedong, the son of a Hunan landowner, had no intention of putting anyone, not even the son of a Shandong landowner, in the position of being able to call the Party to witness while throwing in his face these fateful words: 'Who made you king?' Skilful, admittedly, but too ambitious and too brutal, Kang Sheng did not have the extraordinary flexibility of a

Zhou Enlai, a much more brilliant man than the Party leader, but prepared always to play a secondary role, through Party discipline. At all costs he must not be allowed to let power go to his head. For several months, the head of the Social Affairs Department had in effect been the number three, if not the number two, in Yan'an. It was better that this state of affairs should not become permanent. It was better that he be restored forthwith to a more reasonable rank in the communist hierarchy.

In entrusting Kang Sheng with almost total responsibility for the intelligence services and for the secret police after Deng Fa's fall from power, Mao had let a mad horseman have his head. Heeding the example given by his arch-enemy, Generalissimo Chiang Kai-shek, the Chairman of the Politburo decided on a complete change of policy. From now on, no man, not even the most loyal, was to have sole control of the secret services. Li Kenong would share this task with the overly intelligent Kang Sheng, each of them keeping an eye on the other.

A fundamental principle of modern China's security and special services bodies was hereby established: the division of power.

10
The Japanese Network

On 26 January 1946, a large crowd, consisting of Japanese from all over the archipelago, assembled in Tokyo in Hibiya Park in front of the imperial palace: some fifty thousand men and women had come to welcome their hero, the leader of the Communist Party, Nozaka Sanzo, observed by alarmed GIs. He was returning from China. And he was being congratulated for his major contribution to the defeat of the Mikado's armed forces by taking part in secret missions never made known to the general public. There was no question in post-war Japan of advertising the fact that Nozaka was the friend and agent of Kang Sheng.

'We must create a democratic front in Japan! We must take away the imperial family's powers! Perhaps it should be done away with altogether? The people will decide!' This is what Nozaka Sanzo said.

This shopkeeper's son from Hagi had come far: having taken his mother's name when he was nine, he became an orphan at the age of fourteen, in 1906, and yet managed to pay for his own studies and his young brother's. One day, one of his teachers lent him a book in secret. It was no pillowbook, but Marx and Engels's *Communist Manifesto*, in English. The young Sanzo copied it out overnight. Shortly after, he made contact with *Yuakai*, the socialist party of that period.

England, the cradle of Marxism, fascinated him. In the early 1920s he wanted to settle there with his young wife, Kuzuno Ryo, but Scotland Yard noticed that he had joined the British Communist Party. The couple were immediately deported. He spent some time in France, Switzerland, and Germany before returning to Japan. In March 1924, after Lenin's death, Nozaka became head of what was ostensibly a university organisation, secretly connected with the Communist Party; this was the Institute for Investigation into Industrial Work, the *Sangyo rodo chosajo*, which published magazines and papers and gathered economic information. The same two characters are used in Japanese and in Chinese for the word 'investigation' (*chosa* in Japanese, *diaocha* in Chinese), but they are also used to denote the word 'intelligence' as used by spies. Comrade Nozaka's institute was simply the Japanese answer to other economic intelligence agencies set up by the Comintern in Germany, France and elsewhere.

In March 1928 there was a military crackdown, during which

General Giichi Tanaka's government had thousands of leftists arrested. Sixty thousand arrests were made between 1928 and 1936. A primary target, the Communist Party was completely wiped out by the police by 1931. The remnants of this group were ruthlessly hunted down. Wholesale torture followed, with the result that communist leaders agreed to turn against their own movement.

'We denounce the crimes of the Comintern, which drove us to organise subversion in Japan!' Sanu Gaku and Sadakichi Nabeyama chorused in 1929.

Hundreds of communists changed their allegiance. The *Tokko* secret police did not do things by halves.

Young Ryo feared the worst when her husband was taken into custody during the first wave of arrests. He escaped relatively unscathed: hospitalised for an eye operation, he gave his guards the slip while convalescing. Having escaped, he had to face the fact that the entire left had been completely destroyed, as though by an earthquake.

In March 1931 Nozaka and his wife arrived in the USSR via some tortuous route. The dismantling of the Japanese Communist Party meant that numerous intelligence sources had dried up. So General Berzin, head of the GRU, recalled his masterspy Richard Sorge from Shanghai and suggested that he set up a new network in Japan under his cover as a German journalist. Sorge was advised not to get involved with any Japanese communists who had escaped captivity. As always with Sorge, there was one exception to the rule. It proved fatal. A member of his network recruited one Ritsu Ito. However, the Japanese police had arrested this former communist in 1933, then again in 1939. Was he 'turned' on that occasion, as was alleged in 1953, when he was expelled from the JCP for 'betrayal'? Or did he talk under torture? In any case, Sorge's network was dismantled in 1942 – Ritsu had talked.

To return to Moscow: the Nozaka couple became friendly with Kang Sheng and Cao Yi-ou. The work of the two men was identical: political intelligence and representation of their Party within the Comintern. Nozaka went by the name of Okano Susumu. He had come to the attention of Stalin, who chose him as a replacement in Moscow for the patriarch of Asian communism, the Japanese Katayama Sen, who had just died.

Okano attended classes at the Leninist School. He went on several secret missions among the strong Japanese community in the United States. Then in 1935, like Kang Sheng, he was appointed a delegate to the Comintern's Seventh World Congress.

In April 1940, he made another trip, for two reasons: Stalin sent him to Yan'an to strengthen his own camp and to keep an eye on the Chinese; Kang Sheng also wanted him there, hoping to be able to extricate him from the Russian orbit. A man of at least this stature was needed in order to promote a vast movement of demoralisation, desertion and capitulation within the Japanese army. The head of Chinese espionage, who was inevitably concerned with problems of security, had already planted pro-communist Japanese agents within the enemy camp, outside the networks financed by the Russians. This was the case with Soejima Ryuki who, as early as 1931, had joined the dreaded military police, the *Kempeitai*, in order to obtain confidential information for the Chinese on this Japanese Gestapo-style outfit. Similarly, a celebrated writer, Nakanishi Ko, worked as a mole for Kang Sheng. But in 1942 he was arrested in Shanghai along with hundreds of others. This time, the Chinese had committed the same blunder as Sorge, but in reverse. Without knowing it, they had attached their network, somewhere along the Shanghai–Tokyo line, to that of Stalin's spy, Sorge. Nakanishi fell in the aftermath of the round-up in Tokyo and the arrest of Richard Sorge.

With the arrival of Nozaka, Kang hoped to draw up a new wide-ranging plan of action. Mao Zedong warmly welcomed his Japanese *alter ego*. Then Kang Sheng took him under his wing. Nozaka took a Chinese name and was given a job with the Eighth Route Army's Propaganda Unit. At the same time Kang put forward the idea of his setting up a purely Japanese section: the Japanese Affairs Research Centre. Naturally associated with the Social Affairs Department, Nozaka's Centre analysed information on the Japanese coming from the front; collated the information for the Chinese; provided cross-referencing facilities and a publicity department; wrote propaganda documents in Japanese and assisted in the interrogation of compatriots who had been taken prisoner.

There was no question of confining Nozaka to a purely technical role. He founded a political party which underwent several name-changes before joining up with several other groups in 1944 to form the Japanese People's Liberation League (*Nihon Jinmin kaiho renmei*). For whom was the exiled movement intended? A few old militants, of course, who had followed Nozaka on his Long March. But the majority, the ordinary rank and file, were soldiers in the Japanese army who had been taken prisoner and indoctrinated on the model of the rectification campaign currently raging in Yan'an. On Pagoda Hill, Nozaka had set himself a three-point programme: 'Indoctrination of Japanese prisoners or deserters who had fallen into the hands of soldiers of the Eighth Army; psychological warfare directed against the Japanese troops, conducted by radio, by distribution of pamphlets; and finally aid to Chinese guerrillas in their campaign of sabotage and resistance in Japanese-controlled areas.'

Obviously it was easier for Japanese to cross enemy lines for reconnaissance purposes. As the war drew to an end, the two hundred Red samurai working for Nozaka and Kang Sheng came up with a very daring plan, whereby an infiltration operation would be launched simultaneously in Manchuria, Korea and even Japan. The only drawback was that the communists did not have the means to transport troops, let alone provide for parachute landings. There was only one solution if seeking help from the 'Soviet comrades' was to be avoided: an appeal to the Americans.

The major part of the United States contribution to the war effort took the form of aid to Chiang Kai-shek. But the special services decided it was time to send a mission to Yan'an, if only to find out what the communists' intentions were. On 24 July 1944, a Douglas DC4 damaged its undercarriage on the small Yan'an runway. This was the first American plane to venture into the Red base, and the crowd that gathered to welcome the Dixie mission concluded that American planes were less solid than Soviet planes. Actually, no one had remembered to warn the pilot to avoid an old stone tomb.

Colonel David Barrett, a stocky, broad-shouldered man, straightened his tie, put on his officer's forage cap, and wiped the row of medals on his chest with the back of his hand – they were covered with that yellow dust which was all-pervasive in Yan'an. He gave a firm handshake to the two men waiting to greet him with triumphant, almost wolfish smiles on their lips: Chairman Mao and Marshal Zhu De. With the exception of the State Department's John Service, everyone on the Dixie mission belonged to the OSS, and was already a Far East veteran. Barrett met Zhou Enlai and greeted Jiang Qing, whom he found 'prettier and better dressed than the other women there' and able to express herself in better Chinese than the rest of the band: Colonel Barrett had been selected for the mission on account of his excellent knowledge of Mandarin Chinese, and was not expecting the leaders of the Revolution to speak with such horrible regional accents.

Kang Sheng put in only a furtive appearance at the festivities. He had recently been criticised for his very controversial role in the rectification campaign. Piotr Vladimirov, the Russian delegate of the now defunct Comintern, was delighted by Kang's fall from grace and told everyone how Mao had said to him one day: 'Kang abused his authority, he brought a valuable venture into disrepute, and made a mess of cadre policy.'

'Vlad', the Moscow observer, was very worried by the presence of the American delegation: for the past several months, Kang Sheng, Zhou Enlai and their secret services had been supplying the Anglo-Americans with a lot of information that they were not giving to the Russians. And now, horror of horrors, the Dixie mission was here in Yan'an to exchange intelligence about the Japanese.

'The communists are nice guys and totally open about exchanging information,' was one of the first dispatches sent by the OSS envoys to their headquarters. They were already falling under the spell. And Kang Sheng was keeping a low profile because he was already preparing the ground with the Americans for his infiltration operation . . .

Professor of Japanese Geography and Civilisation at the University of

Michigan during peacetime, Colonel Robert Burnett Hall had already served in military intelligence during the First World War, that heroic period of reconnaissance aeroplanes and carrier pigeons. In 1936, at the age of forty, he was teaching in Japan. So he was a first-class recruit to the OSS after the Japanese attack on Pearl Harbor. In 1942, he trained for his new employers small teams of Americans of Japanese origin (usually chosen from the left, for fear of Japanese fifth columnists). Having run the OSS bureau in San Francisco, Hall went to Kunming. It was there, in September 1944, that he received a top secret report, filed by the fiery Captain John Colling, born in China twenty-five years earlier, who was with the Dixie mission.

Nozaka Sanzo and Kang Sheng had shown him the two hundred Japanese ex-prisoners who had been converted to communism, superbly brought into line, fanaticised, as though galvanised by the idea of betraying their former leaders. They were ready for anything. Even to sacrifice their own lives, if necessary.

Colonel Hall could not contain a sigh of admiration: 'A wonderful idea, the best in all Cathay!' (This strange academic persisted in using this medieval term to denote China.)

Their mission was to infiltrate not only into Manchuria but also Korea and Japan, by whatever means possible, preferrably by parachute. The plan was promptly adopted. There remained the problem of transport.

From 1943, the Soviet NKVD had at its disposal a flight of Wellington bombers and Spitfire fighters from Great Britain, and Dakotas given to Beria by the Americans. If the Chinese communists had chosen to seek help from the Americans, it was of course in order to increase their independence vis-à-vis the Russians. But on the other hand, it was difficult if not unthinkable to use planes belonging to Chiang Kai-shek to parachute in communists. Especially as the American ambassador to Chiang Kai-shek created a furore when he found out that the Dixie mission had offered to supply Mao with arms.

In retaliation, the State Department's man, John Service, was recalled to Washington on Ambassador Hurley's insistence, accused of pro-communist sympathies. But Hurley had no control over the OSS, which was under the command of General Donovan, who had persuaded the President of the United States not to put all his eggs in one basket. The Americans still favoured Chiang Kai-shek, but all the same the door was half-opened to Mao. After all, one never knew, he might win in the end! And suddenly the American position became the same as that adopted by the Soviets . . .

In Europe the thousands of GIs hoping to be repatriated began to find they had a long wait: a number of C54s originally destined for Europe had been rerouted to Asia. An aerial bridge of C46s, codenamed HUMP, kept the India–China route open, achieving the extraordinary feat of flying over the Himalayas. But in December

1944 the Japanese lost North Burma, so it became possible to use C54s to fly from Calcutta to Kunming, avoiding the Himalayas. A few long-haul aircraft could be redeployed and assigned to the operation planned in Yan'an. But the file on the communist infiltration organised by Kang Sheng and the OSS would have to remain top secret even after the end of the war. What would the American public say, if by any chance they found out about the aid given to Kang Sheng's moles and his Japanese friends?

Since the war was about to end, Nozaka intensified his already feverish activity. Hiroshima. Nagasaki. After Japan's capitulation, he published a stirring 'Appeal to Japanese officers and men', which was displayed on placards all along the Eighth Route Army front lines, as well as those of the New Fourth Army, calling on the Japanese troops to surrender.

Nozaka did even more. He acted as an intermediary between Kang Sheng's Social Affairs Department and the Japanese intelligence services in the North. One of his Liberation League groups made contact with Kawagushi Tadanori, head of Japanese counter-intelligence in Tientsin.

'We offer to mediate on your behalf with the Chinese communists . . . It's all over for you now. You may as well surrender with dignity, and come out of this with honours of war . . .' Contrary to legend, all Japanese officers did not end up by committing hara-kiri, especially not in intelligence, where it is always possible to change sides! Nozaka had of course sinicised his communism over the past five years in Yan'an. But he still retained a code of honour common to all Japanese combatants, whether military or political. This proved generally effective – it certainly won Kawagushi's support. A clause in their agreement provided for the integration of several hundred technicians and engineers who were to work henceforth in the Red zones. In other words, under this gentlemen's agreement the communists were offered Japanese brains on a silver platter.

It went without saying that Nozaka was valued by Mao and his Party: already at the Seventh Chinese Communist Party Congress in May 1945, he had been the only foreign delegate allowed to speak. In September 1946 he travelled to Tokyo for the first time in fifteen years. The day before his departure he had a long discussion with Mao. Their conversation went on all night. It concerned the future. What would become of their two movements?

The 270 Japanese trained in Yan'an, indoctrinated and groomed by Kang Sheng's men, went back to Japan in small groups. They were not worried about the American occupation forces. The Cold War had not yet begun and the communists were considered the only Japanese to have fought on the right side. On the way back, Nozaka met a new star in the communist firmament: he stopped off in Pyongyang for a few weeks and spoke at length with the new communist leader, Kim Il-sung. He asked both Kim and Marshal Malinovksi, head of the

Soviet army occupying the north-east of China, to treat Japanese prisoners well.

Then came the triumphant return to Hibiya Park. Nozaka, having become leader of his country's Communist Party, opened a new chapter in Japanese politics, under the watchful eye of the 'Chinese comrades'.

Kang Sheng and his team had managed to reconcile two opposites, to confound light and dark, yin and yang; in other words, to turn to the communists' advantage missions undertaken by enemies of communism and to lay the foundations for relations with a new circle of communist movements, of which the Chinese constituted the centre of gravity. China: the Middle Kingdom. For their part, the Westerners agreed to support these Chinese communists in the overriding interests of defeating the common enemy: the Japanese – besides, they seemed fairly independent of Moscow, somehow 'a little less communist'.

An admirable chess-player, General Donovan, the head of the OSS, had the good taste to send left-wing Americans to help the communist resistance movements: the Yugoslavs, the Albanians, the Italians, the Chinese, the Vietnamese . . . A few years after the OSS was wound up, its successor, the CIA, would use some of these old contacts to exploit differences within the communist bloc.

In 1943 the Comintern was officially dissolved. This was Stalin's gift to his new friends Churchill and Roosevelt. At Ufa in the USSR, the delegates of the Western communist parties packed their bags and awaited the end of the war, often in order to take over power in the wake of the Soviet tanks. But in Yan'an it meant that the communists had even fewer scruples about forming a new brotherhood. Not only were some of the major leaders, such as Nozaka, part of it, but the Chinese CP had given a lead to some of the smaller parties in this war against Japan that had spread throughout the whole of Asia, with the result that a new communist circle was taking shape. Kang had already prepared the ground for it in Moscow, no doubt unconsciously, rather by intuition. But like Mao Zedong, Zhou Enlai and Chen Boda, he was already thinking of founding a new 'International'.

A puny figure, almost as thin as Kang, whom he had known in Moscow, painfully thin in fact, pushed his barrow. He wore canvas trousers and a threadbare peasant shirt, patched and dusty; his face was thin, emaciated, like old ivory, already wrinkled with worry – the worst kind of wrinkles, those of youth . . . His name was Ho Quang and he spoke in a dreadful Cantonese dialect. He finally reached Yan'an, where he was welcomed with open arms. What, this little fellow represented the Indochinese rebellion? The real Chinese sniggered. The pseudo-Chinese laughed with them and, since there was no opium, lit one of his Thuoc Lao cigarettes, made with that horrible black tobacco which inflames the lungs. He introduced himself: Nguyen Ai Quoc – 'He who loves his country' – soon to assume the name by which he would for ever after be known, Ho Chi Minh.

When the Popular Front in France collapsed, his Indochinese Communist Party was proscribed, a state of affairs he was used to. He was plunged back into illegality. Then professor at the Leninist School in Moscow under the name of Linov, Ho Chi Minh decided it was time to reorganise. However, Stalin suggested that he went to see Mao. Was this to help the Chinese or to strengthen Soviet influence? Probably both. Ho was already familiar with China. In the 1920s he had served as an instructor under the guise of a diplomat at the Russian consulate in Canton. The Chinese, like magnets, were already then attracting all the Asian revolutionaries. Since that time, they had built up a Red republic in a large part of China. And they had just sealed the grand alliance with the Guomindang nationalists. So the little Indochinese fellow made his way to Yan'an. The Chinese knew who he was: his life could be summed up in this quatrain that he had written one day in prison:

Dragged through thirteen *xian* in the land of Kuangxi
And incarcerated in eighteen wretched prisons
What crime have I committed, venerable mandarins?
The crime of loving one's people and devoting one's life to them!

Kang Sheng gave him a place to live in the Apple Orchard. There, Ho studied Chinese methods of combat, which differed little from his own. On 22 September 1940, the Japanese army invaded Indochina. That day France lost face, for the indigenous population saw the Vichy administration compromise itself with the Japanese. A power incapable of defending its colony is reduced to the level of its colonised possessions, who know that they will one day be able to free themselves of that power. On 23 November the Communist Party organised local insurrections. Ho Chi Minh was champing at the bit. He wanted to fly to the aid of his comrades, but the Chinese assigned him quite a different mission. Ho was attached to the Eighth Route Army and met the future Marshal Ye Jianying, a close friend of Kang Sheng.

'Comrade, we would like to send you as political administrator and technical officer on a mission to give guerrilla training to Chiang Kai-shek's élite troops!'

This was part of the Xi'an Accord, which was more or less observed. For Ho Chi Minh, nationalism and communism were not contradictory. So he headed south in order to train Dai Li's commandos. (Today, experts in Taiwan maintain that history has got it wrong: it was Dai Li who trained Ho Chi Minh's Vietnamese units in guerrilla warfare by mistake, taking them for authentic nationalists like himself. As though Ho Chi Minh or his friend Vo Nguyen Giap had much to learn about the art of guerrilla warfare . . .)

In southern China, Ho encountered his friends from the Politburo of the exiled Indochinese Party. He then brought together the team that was to foment revolution in Vietnam: Pham Van Dong and Vo Nguyen Giap. In February he set up his headquarters in the region of Cao Bang, to the north of Tonkin, close to the Chinese border, exchanging the caves of Yan'an for those of Coc Bo.

A little while later, just like the Chinese, he accepted the precious aid of the Americans in order to defeat the Japanese, and, some time afterwards, to drive the French out of Indochina.

Coded messages such as the following have finally come to light, taken from American archives: 'We hope to continue supplying arms to Ho Chi Minh,' said Major Austin Glass of the OSS in June 1945.

Or there is this other communication from an OSS officer who claims to have become a friend of Ho Chi Minh, and says: 'The Vietminh are supported by China. But this movement places all its trust in the United States. The Vietminh control a large part of the country. It has the support of the population.'

No doubt Ho proved too independent to let himself be made a client of the Chinese. Kang Sheng realised this and chose to back another revolutionary he had known in Moscow. This was Hoang Van Hoan alias Li Quang Hoa, who reorganised the clandestine Indochinese CP under cover of the Association for China against Japan. In Yan'an, until 1942, he built up the pro-Chinese faction, which naturally tried to exert its dominance within the Vietnamese movement. As ever, it was Kang Sheng who acted as intermediary between the Chinese leadership and Hoang, who proved to be one of Kang's most influential agents. Hoang became ambassador to Beijing in 1951 until the battle of Dien Bien Phu in 1954, when he flew to Geneva as one of the negotiators, together with big brothers Zhou Enlai and Li Kenong, to bring hostilities between the French and the Vietnamese to an end. Then he was given the ultra-sensitive post of head of international relations with the other communist parties. At that time, Kang Sheng had the same job with the Chinese. While Ho sought to strike a balance between Chinese and Soviets, Hoang's heart lay with the Chinese. He was not alone in this. There was also Tran Quoc Hoan of the Politburo, who since 1951 had been in charge of state security, the *Cong An Bo*, a secret police modelled on the Chinese *Gonganbu*; as head of this operation, Tran was Kang Sheng's Vietnamese opposite number. The Chinese agreed to exchange information with the Indochinese communists: this was effectively helping the Vietcong in their war against the USA.

In Yan'an, in addition to China's relations with the Japanese and Vietnamese communists, the crucial question of the political future of China's neighbour Korea had to be confronted. Mao needed the Koreans: a fighting force of three hundred Koreans was set up, headed by a friend of Marshal Zhu De, Mu Chong: this was the Korean Volunteer Corps, Chinese Red Army auxiliaries, later swelled by the Federation of Korean Youth of North China.

The Korean groups were divided, chaotic and swift to quarrel with each other. It was said that a guerrilla war was being waged in Korea but without the aid of the Russians it would have long since collapsed. Its impact was weak. The legend of Kim Il-sung, great leader of the Korean guerrilla war, as Mao was of the Chinese Revolution, was a complete invention. At first, it is true, Kim Song-ju joined a little group of left-wing guerrillas, in 1928. He was just eighteen at the time. The leader of the group, Yi Chong-nak, was captured in January 1931 by the Japanese. Having changed his name from Kim Song-ju, Kim Il-sung was in turn arrested. Because he was so young, the Japanese released him. He then joined the army of a Chinese warlord in Man-churia that became famous mainly for its depredations and extensive pillaging. Two years later, this horde of ruffians was wiped out by the Chinese communist army.

Kim made a cardinal virtue of being an opportunist: once again he changed allegiance. His only feat of arms, which alone fills volumes to the greater glory of the 'great leader of the people', was a raid on the town of Ponchonbo on the Manchurian border that took place on 4 June 1937, when Kim Il-sung did after all manage to set fire to a police station. Then he stayed on with his group in the Manchu hills. A wise revolutionary, he took the time to give his wife, Kim Chong-suk, three fine children, one of them the present heir-presumptive to North Korea, Kim Kong-il.

Finally, in 1941, the Japanese had so saturated the region with their troops, he took refuge in the USSR. The Russians did not find him so stupid; they made him a sergeant in military intelligence, the GRU. While training at the famous espionage school in Khabarovsk – which Kang Sheng had also passed through – he learnt to parachute. This training proved useful. Stalin already had it in mind to drop him into Korea as soon as the country was liberated.

The real Korean strength in China was not communist; there was a vast nationalist contingent attached to the Guomindang, and their leader, Kim Won-bong, had established a very active corps in Chongqing. These Koreans were as hostile to the Japanese, conquer-ors of their country, as they were to the communists. But, officially, Chinese Reds and nationalists were allies. So the intellectual Si Malu (who later took refuge in the USA during the 1950s), a communist with the cunning of a snake, and considered a great expert on the Korean problem, was sent to Chongqing to make contact with Kim Won-bong. Though Si Malu was not really a friend of Kang Sheng, he was wary of him, and for that reason, like many communists, fol-lowed Kang's orders all the more closely. He flattered the Korean, coaxed and cajoled him, almost converted him. A clever vixen, Im Ch'ol-ae, Kim Won-bong's wife, warned her husband against infiltration by the communists, or by Chiang Kai-shek's men – to no avail. One day, one of the *Tewu* ace operatives, Chen Jiakang, Zhou Enlai's secretary, who was being sent backwards and forwards between Yan'an and Chongqing, invited him to a lavish dinner, at which some sixty delicious dishes such as only the Chinese know how to prepare were served. The yellow wine of Shaoxing flowed freely. Zhou Enlai himself attended the dinner.

'The liberation of Korea, for which you yearn, as we do, will only be achieved with the liberation of China . . . You have seen the Guomindang's delinquent troops for yourself. They make a lot of noise, but the Japanese laugh at them! How frustrated your troops must be, not being able to fight alongside a great national army like ours . . .'

The communists then suggested that Kim sent his soldiers to Yan'an to join those of Mu Chong, a communist perhaps, but a fine fellow. Zhou's words had found their mark. Kim resented being treated as only an auxiliary of the Guomindang. He was invited to join the allied high command.

'But the real centre of command is here in Chongqing, since that is where both high commands are based.'

Kim naively accepted the invitation. He became a general without an army, while his guerrillas, after a few sessions of technical training, indoctrination and 'rectification', were integrated into the Korean army in Yan'an.

After the liberation of Korea in 1945, their leader Mu Chong, backed by the Chinese, became one of Kim Il-sung's ministers, Kim being the Soviets' candidate.

Kim turned out not to be a mere puppet of the Soviets, however. The nationalist within him began to get the better of his communism. He implemented purges against Soviet as well as Chinese agents. In 1950, in a remarkable bid by Kim Il-sung to secure his power base, Mu Chong was arrested as a 'foreign agent' and condemned to life imprisonment. No doubt Kim secretly held against him the fact that he was a genuine resistance fighter. Mu Chong, the Party's second secretary, was above all head of the Yan'an faction, Mao's protégé, the former general of an artillery division in the Chinese Eighth Route Army.

However, as soon as the Korean War broke out, relations between the Chinese and Korean security services, the Social Affairs Department and the Ministry of Social Security, were strengthened. But old rivalries died hard, for the Yan'an Koreans remained powerful. One starlit night in July 1951 eight men dressed in black, members of the Chinese *Tewu*'s Action Service, the future élite 8341 Detachment, stole into the heart of the North Korean capital. Mu Chong, a sick man, was under close guard in his own home. The Chinese commandos neutralised the Social Security agents, seized the Korean leader and disappeared into the night. Kang Sheng was not the kind of man to abandon his own. Kim Il-sung was doubtless enraged by this daring feat, but Chinese divisions had crossed the Yalu River in May, repulsing the United Nations forces and advancing deep into South Korea. It was impossible for Kim to level reproach at Mao under these circumstances. A rumour went round that Mu Chong had been assassinated by 'foreign agents'.

Another 'son of Yan'an' who came over from the Soviet camp into the Chinese orbit was the Indonesian Mas Prawirodirdjo Alimin, a character after Kang Sheng's own heart. He was an orphan, like Nozaka, but born into a poor family. Colonial paternalism meant something to him: a kindly Dutch official adopted him. This did not prevent him, though, from fighting Dutch control of the Indonesian archipelago alongside the Chinese, who were always trying to organise mutinies in the Dutch fleet. A very young member of the Partai Kommunis Indonesia (PKI), the Indonesian Communist Party, he went to China for the first time, according to the French Deuxième Bureau, in 1924, when he attended a huge union congress for the Pacific nations, organised by the Comintern, in Canton. The English, ever vigilant, arrested him in 1927 in Singapore, on his way back from Russia. Released the following year, he returned to Moscow, where he attended classes at the Leninist School. In 1933 he became an inseparable companion of Nozaka Sanzo and Kang Sheng.

'You must follow the OGPU training, you'll learn a lot!' Kang Sheng suggested to him.

Alimin ended up with a first-class knowledge of how to make bombs with alarm clocks, detect traitors within the Party, thwart enemy networks, encode a radio message. A diligent student, he was noticed. He took part in numerous operations all over the world: Paris, Brussels, London, Berlin, Smyrna in Turkey, the Middle East and Mongolia. In 1936, the British Special Branch discovered he was organising sabotage operations in Palestine. At that time, Jews and Arabs were working together, at least within the Comintern. But one fine day the members of the Palestine Party's Central Committee – both Jews and Arabs – were summoned to Moscow by Stalin. All of them ended up with a bullet in their necks in Lubyanka or some camp in the Siberian gulag. Alimin, who was known as Padi, found the atmosphere unhealthy. Then he was sent to Yan'an. In this factory for Asian communist cadres, he was told to follow the development of the situation in the Indonesian and Malaysian archipelagos.

In 1941, like Hong Kong, Singapore, that other jewel in the British Crown, was in danger of falling to the Japanese. Alimin was sent there. His mission: to organise the resistance. In Malaysia, the Chinese minority, who were hated by the Malays, provided most of the membership of the Malaysian Communist Party, which, since it was founded in the 1920s, had formed part of the Chinese Communist Party.

To prevent the fall of Singapore, the British hastily organised a guerrilla force. Lim Boh Seng, of Chinese origin, and a member of the

Communist Party, raised a militia of some ten thousand men for this purpose – though he did not prevent the Japanese from taking Singapore.

Lim continued the clandestine struggle and managed to take refuge in India. Alimin, meanwhile, returned to Yan'an to report to Kang Sheng.

From then on, he devoted himself to converting his own Indonesian Party to Maoism, while awaiting the defeat of the Japanese.

But the war was not over in Malaysia. The British had set up a special guerrilla training school called STS 101. Before the fall of Singapore, nearly two hundred communist cadres had been there. Some of them came straight out of British gaols, having previously been considered 'dangerous communist agents'. Thus was born the Malayan People's Anti-Japanese Army, the MPAJA, organised in accordance with their usual tactics as a united front. Some of the more conservative British, among them Louis Mountbatten, would have preferred to make an alliance with other Chinese forces in Malaya – the Guomindang and the secret societies, the Triads: 'Let us be clear about this, there is considerable political danger in using the MPAJA because of the importance this movement will have after the war, when it will no doubt insist on equal rights for the Chinese of Malaysia.'

In Colombo, on the island of Sri Lanka, Force 136 was training thousands of resistance fighters, guerrillas, saboteurs all prepared to jump into the Asian jungles, to lay ambush to Japanese units. 'Put Asia to fire and sword!' was the war cry of Force 136, the British equivalent in Asia of the Special Operations Executive (SOE) that was supporting partisans in Europe.

Graduates of the Malaysian STS 101 training school came to Colombo. Among them was John Davis, a former policeman in the Malaysian Federation, who had managed to escape from Singapore. Despite being a policeman, or perhaps for that reason, Davis knew Chin Peng, the main Communist Party leader. When he arrived in Colombo in April 1942, he was amazed to find that Malaysian Chinese belonging to the Guomindang were being trained in Force 136.

'I have no particular sympathy for the communists,' Davis told Colonel Basil Goodfellow, the head of the Malaysian section of Force 136, 'but it must be admitted that in Malaysia they represent by far and away the only force that can really worry the Japanese. We must be realistic . . .'

The British made realism their guiding principle throughout their dealings in the Far East, one that would lead them one day to abandoning Hong Kong to the communists on the worst possible conditions.

In any case, Operation Gustav was launched: on 11 May 1943, John Davis sailed to Malaysia with five Chinese radio operators; Gustav II took place on 15 June, Gustav III on 4 August, Gustav IV on 12

September. On each occasion, teams of secret agents on Dutch East Indies' submarines chartered by the British Intelligence Service landed on the Malaysian coast. Gustav V, on 25 November, brought the communist guerrilla Lim Boh Seng back to his native country to keep communication channels open.

After long negotiations that took place in the heart of the Malaysian jungle, Davis obtained Chin Peng's signature to an agreement that delighted senior British officials. Beside himself with joy, Davis asked one of his radio operators to send this coded message to Colombo: 'The guerrillas have agreed to co-operate with the Allied armies in their operations against the Japanese, but also to co-operate fully in the maintenance of law and order after the occupation.' In other words, there was to be no question of turning their weapons against their former British colonists after the liberation of Malaysia.

Everyone in this game thought they could get the better of each other, for all that they were allies, for as long as the war against the Japanese lasted. Chin Peng, acting on orders from Yan'an, hoped to organise an uprising, take over power and prevent the British from setting foot again in Singapore or on the peninsula. The British suspected there was a catch, the possibility of being double-crossed.

Then, on 1 September 1943, a drama erupted in the humid torpor of the jungle. Against all security rules, the biggest communist jamboree took place in the Batu caves of Selangor: members of the Malaysian Communist Party's Central Committee, senior officials of the MPAJA, guerrilla leaders, regional directors – in all some hundred Chinese converged on the meeting place, to discuss the people's new war strategy. Squeezed together on bamboo benches, the communist partisans were taking notes, religiously listening to their leaders, when suddenly a heavy silence fell on the jungle. Monkeys and birds made no sound, terrified by a hostile presence. Suddenly Japanese commandos appeared on all sides, surrounding the communists, and subjecting them to sustained fire. Nearly all of them were killed in the ambush.

For those who escaped the immediate question was who had betrayed them?

Suspicion fell on Lai Tek, a former underground militant in Shanghai and general secretary of the Communist Party. Especially as he was not present at the meeting . . . Until the end of the war, Lai Teck remained the titular head of a weakened Party, although the main cadres were replaced after the Batu caves treachery. In 1946, at the instigation of the Chinese, Chin Peng instituted a big commission of enquiry into the Lai Tek case. In March 1947, Lai Tek disappeared, 'absconding with Party funds', according to official sources. Did he seek refuge in the West, or was he assassinated by his 'communist comrades'? The mystery remains. The enquiry, which was made public, ruled that since 1930 Lai Tek had been working for Western secret services. During the 1950s, the head of the British secret police in

Malaysia, Alan Blades, revealed that Lai Tek had indeed been recruited by the British in the interwar period, and in September 1945, a 'penitent' member of the Malaysian Communist Party had denounced him as an agent working for the Japanese. In fact, Lai Tek, prompted by resentment, or by the lure of gain, had made his career in those secret services combating communism. During the 1930s, he worked for the French Sûreté in Indochina; then for the British Special Branch in Malaysia. In 1942, the Japanese *Kempeitai* had captured British archives. Some of the Crown's detectives had even collaborated with the invaders by drawing up lists of communists. Lai Tek had agreed to serve new masters. But he remained in contact with his English friends. They suggested that he betray the communist leadership to the Japanese, thereby politically weakening the force with which they would be negotiating a few months later.

After the anti-Japanese war was over, Chin Peng reorganised his forces. On the Chinese mainland, Mao's troops launched new offensives. Emissaries from Kang Sheng arrived in Malaysia in large numbers. A 'new people's war' began to develop.

The British also helped Maung Thein Pei, a communist of Chinese origin, in the war against the Japanese in Burma. When the Japanese invaded, he became the number one secret agent of the British, first taking refuge in India, then returning to his country, where he established numerous radio links with the operational centres of Calcutta and Colombo. He took part in the raising of an anti-Japanese army of fifty thousand men, in liaison with the Chinese in Yan'an.

In India, one of the future senior officials of the Chinese Communist Party, Chen Hansheng, worked throughout the war for the British propaganda department, the Political Warfare Executive (PWE), making programmes in Chinese in the psychological war against the Japanese. His employers in New Delhi were well aware that they were dealing with a communist who had been recruited as early as 1928, during a trip to Moscow. But again pragmatism prevailed, the British were investing for the future.

Yan'an also kept an attentive eye on the Philippines, where again a huge guerrilla movement was taking shape. Acting on the Comintern's orders, the *Partido Komunista ng Pilipinas* (PKP), like the Chinese, decided to form a united front. On 29 March 1942, the PKP decided to launch its armed force, which its military chief, Luis Taruc, suggested calling the People's Liberation Army. However, the Chinese adviser to the group proposed a name that reflected Mao's desire to ratify his policy of a broad alliance against the Japanese in all his spheres of influence; this army therefore took the name of *Hukbo ng Bayan Laban sa Hapon* (The People's Anti-Japanese Army) and a shortening of the first word became famous throughout the world: the Huks (or Hukbalahap).

The Philippine military intelligence archives are insistent on this point: 'The influence of the Chinese communists on the local communist movement weighed heavily throughout the war years. Aware of the theoretical and practical superiority of their Chinese comrades, the leaders of the Philippine Party agreed to the presence of the Chinese within their main organs of leadership. These Chinese advisers greatly influenced the formulation of the PKP's policy and plans.'

A group of three Chinese participated in the deliberations of the Central Committee. Their leader Co Keng Sheng also belonged to the supreme body, the Politburo. This trio was answerable only to Yan'an and put into effect methods of action Kang had learned from the Comintern in Moscow . . .

Consulted by the leader of the Eighth Army, his friend Ye Jianying, Kang Sheng agreed to the proposal of sending Colonel Ong Viet to the Philippines as military adviser. Under his aegis, in May 1942 the PKP set up a political and military training school in the mountains of Arayat, in the heart of the Pampanga region. Other Chinese experts arrived secretly to serve as guerrilla instructors. The military texts of Mao and Zhu De, as well as Edgar Snow's book *Red Star Over China*, in translation, were used as works of reference.

For a year the Hukbalahap harried the Japanese in small ambushes and skirmishes that led to reprisals being taken against villages, an old tactic aimed at winning popular support.

However, in March 1943, the Japanese launched a flushing-out operation in the Arayat Mountains. The PKP suffered a major internal crisis which culminated in the elimination of its leader, Vincente Lava, who was accused of being 'responsible for the defeat'. A mini-secretariat was appointed in his place, headed by the mysterious 'Comrade C', the Chinese adviser, Yan'an's observer. At the end of the war, after the American landings, the PKP was weak but strongly sinicised. It would not be long before it resumed the armed struggle.

Kang Sheng would soon reap the dividends of his policy of expansion, particularly as head of the Chinese Party's International Relations Department, a body directly modelled on the now defunct Comintern.

First of all, though, he had to devote his energies to the total defeat of the Guomindang.

11
Civil War in China

Having effectively begun in 1936–7 with the intervention of the German-Italian forces against the Spanish Republic and the Japanese attack on Chinese soil, the decade of the Second World War ended in a nuclear apocalypse. Nazi Germany had already surrendered. On 6 August 1945, a US Air Force plane dropped an atomic bomb on the Japanese city of Hiroshima, causing the deaths of one hundred thousand people. Forty-eight hours later a second nuclear missile was dropped on another Japanese city, Nagasaki, killing nearly eighty thousand people, and leading to the capitulation on 15 August of the Empire of the Rising Sun.

In the Soviet Republic of Yan'an, news of the Allied victory was not greeted with much emotion. Mao and his companions did not feel much sense of relief. For a long time the communist leaders had known that Japan was defeated. They were preparing themselves for another trial of strength: the second round of a civil war not yet settled against the Guomindang. Everyone knew that the end of the global conflict marked the beginning of a ruthless struggle for power, a decisive battle that could only end in total victory for one side or the other.

Chiang Kai-shek was equally aware of what was at stake. In eight years of fighting against the Japanese invader, the leader of the Guomindang had tried above all to conserve his forces, keeping them in reserve to crush the Reds the moment the Allies claimed victory. Of course the regular nationalist troops had fought against the Japanese courageously. Of course the guerrillas organised by Dai Li under the aegis of SACO had dealt some severe blows to the invading army. But this military activity had never reached a level of total engagement.

'The Generalissimo is an ace non-combatant!' the American officers assigned to work with the Chinese said with a touch of bitterness. 'He has always felt it was up to us, the "foreign devils", to fight the Japanese. He's only really interested in the fight against the Reds . . .'

The Reds in question were not far from sharing the same ideas as their mortal enemy. Led by a pleiad of militant generals – Chen Yi, Lin Biao, Peng Duhai, Zhu De and He Long – their troops had certainly demonstrated more spirit and aggressiveness than Chiang Kai-shek's. They had scored some fine partial successes that a well-conducted propaganda campaign, orchestrated by two past masters of the art, Lu Dingyi and Chen Boda, turned into decisive victories, increasing their real impact tenfold. Mao Zedong and his Party took advantage of these achievements to portray themselves as the only 'genuine patriots' compared with a Guomindang accused of spine-lessness, of having compromised with the enemy, indeed of rampant treachery. The communists were determined to tap national feeling, and even Chinese xenophobia, to their own advantage.

This was an astonishing game of bluff. A few cards had been placed on the table, but each of the two players kept his best up his sleeve. As soon as the Japanese surrender was announced, a fantastic race began as to which of the two, the Communist Party or the Guomindang, would be first to disarm the Japanese soldiers, thereby acquiring their equipment and taking control of the areas they had occupied. As befitted their official legitimacy, the nationalists emerged as convincing winners of this trial of strength. Only thirty thousand Japanese chose to surrender to the Reds, whereas Chiang Kai-shek's generals were able to equip forty entire divisions with their spoils.

Stalin tried to limit the damage. In flagrant violation of the treaties just signed, the Soviet troops in Manchuria handed over to the Red general Lin Biao's soldiers most of the arms they had recovered when the Japanese capitulated. This was not sufficient to restore a balance of power, but allowed the Chinese communists to escape disaster.

Torn between their political sympathy for the nationalists and their admiration for the efficiency and discipline of the Reds, the American liaison officers watched powerless as this merciless strug-gle for power took place. Those of them who liked the country and its people – and there were quite a number – did not hide their pessi-mism: it was heading straight for civil war, a war that the commu-nists, spared the terrible virus of corruption which blighted their adversaries, were very likely to win. (Numerous nationalist generals were selling case-loads of brand-new military equipment, supplied by the United States to its ally Chiang Kai-shek, on the black market.)

Compared with these corrupt and demoralised officers, Mao Zedong had at his disposal a matchless instrument: the Chinese Communist Party, steeled by years of underground struggle, com-pletely centralised round its leader, purged by the rectification cam-paign; a totally dedicated war machine, ready for any sacrifice.

Was this enough? Not quite. The Reds also had their weaknesses. When the essential factor was speed of communications, the two-headed *Tewu* – run by Kang Sheng and Li Kenong – did not stand up to comparison with Dai Li's beloved creation, SACO, equipped with ultra-modern radio equipment 'Made in the USA', long-distance telephone lines, a squadron of American C46 and C47 trans-port planes to shuttle his staff to and fro, and brand-new jeeps and gleaming Buicks.

Kang Sheng had been faced with worse challenges since Shanghai and was not afraid to meet this new challenge. If Dai Li was waging a war of the rich, then the communists would wage a war of the poor. The *Tewu*'s Indian network was given the job of buying up one by one in the shops of Calcutta all the essential spare parts for transmitter-receivers. Under the vague pretext of 'professional training', the agents obtained all available journals on radio techniques. Kang was very satisfied when he learned of their success: Dai Li was nothing without the help of his American protectors. The *Tewu* relied principally on their own efforts and managed very well without the Soviets.

However, it was Dai Li who, aware of the communist danger, resolutely took the first serious initiatives in the post-war conflict.

In the early days of September 1945, a few old Shanghai hands almost fell into a dead faint. They thought they had seen a ghost, dressed all in black. The incredible news was soon travelling from one end of the city to the other: Du Yuesheng was back in town.

After eight long years of exile in Hong Kong and Chongqing, he had returned to reconquer his kingdom. Accompanied by his two bodyguards, a doctor, a masseur and his personal secretary, this sixty-year-old man had just accomplished an exhausting journey, travelling to Hunan aboard a SACO C46, then continuing on foot to Dai Li's headquarters in Chun'an. In this discreet place, he had prepared the ground for his mission.

For Mr Du was not operating solely on his own account. On the contrary, he was acting in total accord with Dai Li, who had become both his friend and associate in opium-trafficking. Fearing that the Japanese troops would sack the town before leaving Shanghai, the head of the BIS and SACO had asked Du to prevent this disastrous eventuality from coming to pass. And Du, whose main concern was the survival of a city that had already given him so much, accepted the task with enthusiasm.

For the whole of July and August, he had been seeing his Green Gang deputies in Chun'an, and drawn up his battleplan with them and with Dai Li's men. The gangsters were first of all to mobilise transport workers and public service employees through the unions controlled by the Green Gang. A hundred and fifty of his henchmen would receive training in combating sabotage. Then they would be secretly introduced into the town with the task of occupying key positions, determined in advance, on D-Day.

Secret negotiations had been started with Ding Mocun. A former deputy of Kang Sheng in the *Tewu*, Ding Mocun had been captured and 'turned' by the Guomindang in 1934, and had since become one of the senior officials in the special services of Wang Jingwei's pro-Japanese collaborationist government. Now he was trying to change sides yet again in order to save his skin.

190 THE CHINESE SECRET SERVICE

'We can trust Ding! He is much too afraid that Dai Li will torture him to death if he proves to be a traitor once more!' thought Du Yuesheng, not unreasonably.

In fact, the ex-communist appeared very eager, supplying Du with a huge amount of convincing information about Japanese thinking. Contrary to fears voiced by Dai Li, they had no intention of destroying Shanghai before withdrawing.

Satisfied, Du boarded a tugboat on 29 August. After stopping over in Hangzhou, he took a train to Shanghai.

After years of war and political unrest, life seemed to resume its normal course in Shanghai. The Western Concessions no longer existed, having yielded to the Japanese. But the rest was not much changed. Prostitutes once again walked the streets, the cabarets were gradually opening their doors one by one, the opium dens were always full. Everyone looked forward impatiently to the arrival of the American Pacific fleet and meanwhile paid their dues to the Green Gang. As for the Reds, victims of Japanese repression, hunted down by their former comrade Ding Mocun, they lay low. This handful of ultra-clandestine militants dared not raise their heads.

In the communist republic of Yan'an, obviously things were different. The communist leaders had summoned nearly 750 delegates to their stronghold between April and June 1945. It was a sign of the times: the Seventh Congress of the Chinese CP was going to meet on home ground, whereas the previous congress had taken place on foreign soil, in Moscow. And Mao, who had not attended the discussions in July 1928, was today the undisputed leader of the Chinese revolutionaries.

As usual, the debates were confined from the outset to the framework set by the leadership. Party policy was explained to the delegates: it consisted of strengthening the Red Army, extending its area of influence, calling upon the people and Chinese intellectuals to set up a 'New Democracy', a concept particularly close to the heart of its inventor, Chairman Mao himself.

A 'New Democracy' meant firstly a sharing of power. The nationalists would have to accept the reality of the outcome of the Sino-Japanese war. They would have to allow the presence of the communists within a coalition government. On several occasions already, Zhou Enlai had tried to negotiate a formula of this kind with the Guomindang, without success. Chiang Kai-shek had no desire to give the Reds such legitimacy. It was essential they remained for ever in the eyes of the whole world 'communists bandits' – anything but 'politicians'.

Alas for the Generalissimo, he no longer had the means to refuse Mao Zedong's 'proffered hand', even though he knew Mao's words of reconciliation to be as disingenuous as his own. His adversaries had emerged from eight years of conflict with a steely morale and considerable prestige. They had been able to take advantage of his least mistakes, playing the role of liberators of China to perfection.

'The Reds must be taken into account, since they're there' was the line the American ambassador Patrick Hurley adopted. He ardently wished for a rapprochement with the communists and made this known: it was, in his view, the only way of avoiding a disastrous civil war.

Chiang Kai-shek would have been happy to tell this Texan oilman, as tall as he was naive, to go to hell, but he had too great a need of American aid. His wife, Song Meiling, had been brought up in the United States. She spoke impeccable English and tried successfully to create a Chinese lobby in Washington, with the support of ultra-conservative businessmen and political leaders. In these circumstances, the head of the Guomindang simply could not afford to give offence to his US protectors.

The Chinese Communist Party's Seventh Congress was, in addition to the political debates, the occasion for Kang Sheng to make a strong comeback. After the rectification campaign, his opponents believed him to be 'finished', reduced to playing secondary roles for many years to come. On the contrary, the head of the *Tewu* showed what influence he had. The Congress – in other words, the Party leadership – immediately appointed him a member of the Praesidium, with responsibility for organising its work.

After a long speech by Mao Zedong, who proudly estimated Red Army forces at 900,000 men and the population in the 'liberated zones' at ninety million, Kang Sheng took the platform on 2 May. Wisely, he confined himself to a purely formal speech. The essential thing, after all, was simply to take part.

At the close of the Congress, he was officially elected to the Politburo – not bad for a loser. His deputy and rival, Li Kenong, did not even figure among the seventy-six members of the Central Committee. Whereas Kang Sheng was considered above all to be a 'politician', Li remained a mere 'technician'. Other specialists in secret affairs also appeared on the Central Committee: Chen Yun, Luo Ruiqing, and even Liao Chengzhi, formerly the Comintern man in the ports and docks, who had been a prisoner of the Guomindang since 1943.

'Politicians', 'technicians' – the Party needed both. With the Americans on the one hand, naive but so powerful, and the Guomindang on the other, weakened but ready for anything, it was wise not to take any chances.

Boosted by the success of this 'Victory Congress', Mao Zedong decided that negotiations with Chiang Kai-shek should be speeded up. For months, Red soldiers and Guomindang troops had been engaged in sporadic fighting. The communist Chairman arrived in Chongqing on 28 August. An obvious sign of the American desire to

see discussions between the two Chinese camps brought to a successful conclusion was the fact that he travelled from Yan'an aboard a
US Air Force plane.

Mao met Chiang Kai-shek, for form's sake, but the meeting
between the two spiritual sons of Dr Sun Yat-sen is unlikely to have
been a very warm occasion. 'The water in the well does not mingle
with the water in the river!' The real business went on elsewhere, in
the almost daily meetings between Zhou Enlai and the nationalist
diplomats. If not openly friendly, they became more relaxed than
they had been at the outset. The personal charm of Zhou
Enlai – courteous, witty, attentive – worked on his counterparts, for
all their wariness. How could anyone quarrel with Zhou, who was
always ready to understand the arguments of the other side, even if
he never conceded an inch?

After much bargaining, as laborious as it was sordid, an agreement was reached, which the Chairman and the Generalissimo signed
on 11 October. The US ambassador Patrick Hurley could feel
satisfied. At last his policy was resulting in something concrete . . .
In Indochina, an agreement between Ho Chi Minh, now leader of
the Vietminh, and the French seemed imminent.

On 10 January 1946, a ceasefire between Red militants and
Guomindang troops came into effect almost everywhere. On 6
March, the Franco-Vietnamese discussions ended in compromise.
For ten months already the guns had been silent in Europe. Perhaps
now Asia could enjoy a state of grace. After the unprecedented cycle
of violence that had begun at the turn of the century, perhaps now
this vast country, China, would at last come to know peace and
gentleness. This was no doubt being too optimistic . . .

General Dai Li was an extraordinary man, prepared to make any
sacrifice for the Chinese nationalist cause. Any delay in the
accomplishing of his mission, however small, made him seethe
with impatience. It was this great haste of his that cost him his life!
The head of the BIS went to Beijing to check up on his agents. He
was eager to return to Nanking, the Guomindang capital, to
report back to the Generalissimo.

Despite warnings from the technicians, Dai Li categorically
refused to wait until the fog cleared. He ordered his pilot to take
off immediately. They had almost reached Nanking when the
plane crashed into a hillside, which it was unable to avoid due to
limited visibility. There were no survivors. His body damaged
beyond recognition, the General was identified by a gold tooth
and an American pistol Milton Miles, his SACO friend, had given
him as a present a few years earlier.

This is the Taiwanese version of the accident which robbed the

Generalissimo's special services of their chief. As one might expect, it is completely untrue.

Dai Li's great haste was not prompted by patriotism: he was not going to Nanking to meet the leader of nationalist China, but for personal, indeed private, motives. In Shanghai, his friend Du Yuesheng was about to bring to a successful conclusion tortuous negotiations he had been conducting with the husband of a very beautiful film actress, the celebrated Butterfly Wu. In exchange for a rather hefty sum, payable in cash, Du had managed to persuade the poor fellow to leave his wife. Having regained her freedom, Madame Butterfly was to spend the rest of her life – or a few years at least – in the arms of Dai Li, whose mistress she had become. Anxious about the result of this unedifying sentimental bargain, the head of SACO and the BIS had in his haste rejected the advice of the experts and categorically refused to brook any delay. Love will not wait, and Dai Li had total confidence in his good luck.

Unfortunately for him, he was wrong. His C47 left Beijing all right but, because of dreadful weather conditions, was forced for technical reasons to land at Qingdao for a short while, to refill its tanks and even take on additional fuel. So, by a stroke of irony, it was in Shandong, the home province of his sworn enemy Kang Sheng, that Dai Li spent his last moments of life on this earth.

Loaded with as much fuel as it could carry, the C47 took off again. But the pilot had been paid by *Tewu* agents to sacrifice his life on the altar of his family, which, in accordance with the old Chinese custom, the communist agents had promised to take care of after his death. He nose-dived straight for the ground and the plane crashed.

The death of Dai Li left his colleagues grief-stricken but also angry. At the SACO headquarters in Nanking they vowed to avenge him. Two commando units abducted the families of the pilot and the co-pilot and simply executed them. Dai Li's men knew precisely who was responsible for killing their boss. The press officer who was with the Chinese CP's military mission to the Guomindang, the very special 'diplomat' Huang Hua, virtually admitted to the murder, telling his Western contacts that Kang Sheng and the *Tewu* had shown themselves to be more cunning than their enemy.

The air crash was not universally greeted as a disaster within the Guomindang. The Chen brothers in Nanking were delighted: they had never made any secret of their hatred for their rival, too subtle and too much liked by his men, to whom they had gradually had to surrender command of the nationalist secret services, retaining only control of the overseas Chinese, whom they kept in thrall by means of threats, violence and the secret societies. As for Chiang Kai-shek himself, he felt suddenly relieved. Dai Li's intelligence and efficiency had eventually begun to frighten the nationalist leader. He had even started to wonder whether Dai Li did not intend to depose him and take over the leadership of the Guomindang. Chiang knew that this was an attractive prospect to several American officers who found the Generalissimo too dictatorial and too inept to be able to deal with the Reds.

The head of the BIS and of SACO, the victim of 'an unfortunate accident', was given a state funeral. But Dai Li was no sooner buried than the struggle resumed for control over his empire.

His former colleagues in SACO remained doggedly loyal to their deceased leader. They decided that taking vengeance on the families of the C47 crew was not enough. They had to hit back at Dai Li's real assassins: the communists.

Three weeks after the death of Dai Li, a second air 'disaster' took place in the west of Shaanxi province, on the road to the Soviet Republic of Yan'an. The aircraft that crashed on 8 April 1946 was carrying several senior CP officials: Wang Ruofei, formerly in charge of political work in the White zone; Ye Ting, a Red general and leader of the abortive insurrection in Canton in 1927, his wife and his daughter; and Bo Gu, one of the most eminent members of the group of 'Twenty-eight Bolsheviks'. Deng Fa also died in the accident, along with four American crew.

The former head of the Political Security Bureau, a position he held at the time of the Jiangxi communist maquis and the Long March, Deng Fa was returning from a trip abroad. He had attended the inaugural congress of the very progressive World Union Federation in Paris, where he had met Zhu Xuefan, a unionist once connected with Du Yuesheng but who was now moving closer to the Reds. In London he had visited the Chinese community in exile, preparing the ground while he was there for the setting up of secret networks. In Italy and Switzerland, he had met some European 'fellow unionists'. And now the vengeance of Dai Li's loyal servants had robbed China of this brilliant and highly dedicated politician.

The Communist Party leadership, with Zhou Enlai acting as their spokesman, paid tribute to the 'Martyrs of 8 April' but proved unforthcoming as to precise details of the circumstances of his death, adopting the same attitude as that of their nationalist enemy. The Reds were no more eager than the Whites to 'lose face' by admitting the superiority of the other side in back-stabbing.

On 17 March, the day of Dai Li's assassination, the communists went on to the offensive in Manchuria, imprisoning the local nationalist governor. Ten days later, they took by storm the great industrial centre of Changchun, less then a hundred kilometres from Mukden. Violent fighting ensued.

Equipped with more than enough American material, the Generalissimo's troops began to drive back their enemy. After three months' hostilities, Zhou Enlai, promoted to grandmaster in relations with the Guomindang, suddenly surrendered: the Reds were losing. He asked for a new ceasefire, which an angry Chiang Kai-shek had to concede under pressure from his American allies in June 1946.

*   *   *

Comrade Yang Zhihua was a legend within the Chinese Communist Party. This young militant woman, formerly a fellow student of Kang Sheng at Shangda University, married the eminent leader Qu Qiubai in 1924. Having taken part in three Chinese Party Congresses, including the one in Moscow in 1928, she encountered Kang Sheng once again in Shanghai. He was already with the *Tewu*, whilst she was involved in union affairs. After her husband was captured by the Guomindang and shot in 1935, she returned to Moscow, on Party orders. In the Soviet capital, she renewed her acquaintance with Kang Sheng.

In 1941 Yang Zhihua received orders to return to Yan'an. She did so immediately, but while crossing Xinjiang, the region bordering the Soviet Union, she fell into the hands of Sheng Shicai. The warlord had changed allegiance since 1937; he was no longer Red but White, now an ally of the Guomindang and an adversary of the communists, with whom he had only recently been flirting.

Not content with imprisoning Yang Zhihua, in September 1942 Sheng Shicai denounced a supposed conspiracy by the communists in Xinjiang, his 'kingdom'. More than a hundred Reds were thrown into prison. A few, like the communist Chairman's younger brother, Mao Zemin, were simply executed. At the same time, Sheng Shicai sent back to Stalin his Russian military advisers. He obviously believed that Hitler was going to get the better of the Soviet leader.

When the Soviet armoured divisions began to drive back the Nazi army, Sheng Shicai was seized with doubts: had it been wise to abandon the Soviet line? In 1946, he suddenly changed his mind. He had always been a convinced anti-Fascist. His opposition to the Reds stemmed from a misunderstanding. He wanted to become their friend again.

'Excellent intentions! But put them into effect . . .' the communist leaders told their new – and former – ally. They insisted on the release of Yang Zhihua and her companions in misfortune.

The Chinese communist universe is, by nature, one of mistrust. No sooner had they arrived in the Red Republic of Yan'an than the little band of a hundred militants fell under suspicion. In four years of captivity, it was impossible that they not made their submission to the Guomindang. One by one, they were interrogated by the Social Affairs Department counter-espionage service. Kang Sheng and Li Kenong were keen to identify some potential enemy secret agents within the ranks of those who had just returned.

The two spy-hunters soon had to acknowledge that they could not find any prey among the Xinjiang ex-prisoners. All were cleared. Yes, they had stood up well to Sheng Shicai and the Guomindang. No, they had not collaborated with the warlord. To demonstrate that all suspicions had been laid to rest, Kang Sheng publicly paid tribute to his lifelong comrade, Yang Zhihua.

Since one can never be too careful, the head of the Social Affairs Department decided to keep the transcripts of the young woman's interrogation and those of her fellow detainees. An old stager of the Stalino-Maoist inquisition, he knew that in this world everything is forgotten except the written word, and he knew by heart the proverb: 'What the mouth emits is wind; the pen leaves traces . . .'

The crisis with the Guomindang became more and more acute. In November 1946 the Communist Party announced that it categorically refused to take any seats in the National Assembly convened in Beijing by the Generalissimo. Not without reason, they considered it to be a puppet institution. In January 1947 the American general George C. Marshall returned to the United States, having explained to journalists that he no longer believed in the possibility of agreement between Mao and Chiang.

This was precisely the Generalissimo's opinion. Having decided to make the first move, he ordered his troops to attack communist positions. In Shandong, half a million nationalist soldiers broke through enemy lines, forcing the Reds to retreat. Led by a crack corps of 250 soldiers, the offensive spread out from Shanxi, where the communists had had their bases since the Long March. It seemed that nothing could stop the nationalists.

19 March 1947 was an historic day for the Chinese nationalists: Guomindang troops finally entered the 'tiger's den', the Red capital of Yan'an, after twelve years.

The tiger had fled. When the pressure from the Whites became intolerable, Mao and the communist leaders had resigned themselves to evacuating the big Red base.

> To keep Yan'an is to lose Yan'an!
> To lose Yan'an is to win Yan'an.

So said Chairman Mao, who had a real gift for coining historic phrases, even at the worst of times. What the communist leader meant by this was that in order to save the revolutionary gains – that is to say, the spirit of Yan'an – the head of the Party had to be saved at all costs, even if this entailed conceding territory to the nationalists.

So the communist exodus began, not before some final accounts had been settled, including that of the dissident writer Wang Shiwei, who was killed at the last minute on Kang Sheng's orders, by way of completing the work of the rectification campaign.

Wang Dongxing's hour of glory came with the falling back of the communists. This heavy-featured colossus, an orphan from his earliest years, had joined the ranks of children reared by the Chinese Red Army at the age of twelve. The son of poor peasants, he had boundless admiration for Mao, and was totally loyal to him, a feeling that was reciprocated: Mao had complete confidence in Wang Dongxing, his bodyguard during the hard days of the Long March.

Wang, having returned from a mission to the North-West, had just replaced Comrade Chen Changfeng at the head of the Central Committee's Security Department, an embryonic Praetorian Guard, devoted exclusively to the protection and service of Mao Zedong and those close to him. The Department already had its first martyr, the young soldier Zhang Sende, who died in 1944 cleaning the leader of the Chinese Revolution's chimney. Distressed by this terrible accident, Mao had written a poem, dedicating what became one of his most famous texts to the deceased soldier: 'To serve the people . . .'

Wang Dongxing called together the men in the Central Committee's Security Department and explained to them the importance of their new mission at a time when the Red Republic of Yan'an was succumbing to force of numbers: like the young but illustrious Zhang Sende, they should be prepared to make the supreme sacrifice to protect the Chairman and his wife.

Zhou Enlai also entrusted his life to Wang Dongxing, having decided to bind his destiny to those of Jiang Qing and Mao. All three would live or die together.

For eight nights, the high command of the Chinese communist movement marched in the direction of the Yellow River, sleeping during the day to avoid being spotted by Guomindang planes. Acting on the advice of Zhou Enlai himself, Wang Dongxing's soldiers built a bridge. It was raining. And so it was that the fugitives crossed the longest river in China, famous for its violent and extensive floodings.

'As long as one is not attending the funeral of a loved one, one does not weep. As long as one is not surrendering to the waters of the Yellow River, one does not lost courage . . .'

Mao did not lose courage, any more than Zhou Enlai. In that moment of crisis, as during the days of the Long March, the Chinese communist leaders achieved real grandeur in adversity, having plumbed the depths of ignominy and baseness during the rectification campaign.

Like his companions, Kang Sheng escaped the Guomindang soldiers. The leaders of Chiang Kai-shek's secret services had too many questions to ask him if he were captured. Far too many. Determined to commit suicide rather than fall into their hands alive, the head of the *Tewu* provided himself with a phial of poison. He was not obliged to use it.

It was in the district of Lin Xian, close to the Yellow River, that he resumed his activities. In the spring and summer of 1947, while the Guomindang tried in vain to finish off its enemy, Kang Sheng devoted his energies not only to reconstructing the *Tewu*, most of its apparatus having disintegrated, but also to promoting agrarian reform.

The Guomindang still held the towns. The Communist Party, now more than ever, had to cling to the land.

'It is true that we can also make mistakes. When the war with Japan ended, we invited our Chinese comrades to reach an accord whereby some kind of *modus vivendi* with Chiang Kai-shek could be found. They agreed with us verbally, but once they were back in China, they went their own way; they assembled their forces and they launched their attack. It turns out that they were right and we were wrong . . .'

Stalin made this amazing self-criticism to the Yugoslav communist leaders in February 1948. Comrade Tito could not get over it: they were not accustomed to such modesty from the Kremlin leader. They concluded, not without reason, that the cunning Georgian must have sound motives for talking in this way.

Stalin's motives were inscribed on the maps of Asia that he regularly consulted, aware of the USSR's key position between East and West. They were written in gold letters on the new page of world history that opened with the creation in October 1947 of Cominform, the Communist Parties' Bureau of Information: the Cold War era.

Mao and his comrades were returning to the fold in style. In the eyes of the Kremlin, they were no longer the 'soft communists' of the past but real Bolsheviks of iron, brilliant seconds to their big Russian brothers in confronting the capitalist world. The fight to the death against the Guomindang, once again regarded as a product of imperialism and no longer the faithful ally against Fascism, now took on a global dimension. Helping Red China to win became the duty of every communist. In Indochina, Ho Chi Minh's Vietminh had taken arms and risen up against French colonialism and its lackeys. In the Philippines, the rebel Huks were challenging the pro-American regime. In Malaysia, Comrade Chin Peng's communist guerrillas were preparing to fight a just war against the British. The whole of Asia was rising up under the scarlet banner of communism.

In March 1948, exactly one year after the humiliating defeat of Yan'an, a Red general, Chen Geng, redeemed communist honour. Chen was an old acquaintance of Kang Sheng, whom he had met during the 1930s in Shanghai. The future general was then assigned by the Communist Party to secret missions, and was partly responsible for liaison within the German GRU spy Richard Sorge's network. Kang sometimes accommodated him in one or other of his hideouts, but it was at the home of the great writer Lu Xun that Chen Geng was finally captured, having been wounded. As has already been mentioned, because he had saved the Generalissimo's life during the Northern Expedition, the Guomindang were unusually indulgent towards him. He took advantage of this to escape and resume the struggle and carry off the first genuine communist victory of the civil war at Luoyang.

In April, troops serving under Peng Dehuai, the son of humble farmers in Hunan province, forced the Whites out of Yan'an, thereby redeeming Communist Party honour. It was not Mao any more but Chiang who was seriously losing face! The revolutionary leader had been proved right, as usual: to lose Yan'an had indeed been to save Yan'an.

In June, the Battle of Kaifeng, an engagement involving several hundred thousand men on either side, ended in a draw. This was proof that the communists, now supported by the peasantry, could hold their own against the nationalists in the field of conventional war.

And in the field of secret intrigue as well. The *Tewu* was probably not unconnected with the sudden surrender of the 84th Division of Chiang Kai-shek's army, a reversal that decided the fate of the town of Jinan, taken on 24 September, and then of Weifang. Almost the whole of Kang Sheng's native province of Shandong was now in the hands of the communists. In Manchuria, General Lin Biao took the fortified camp of Mukden.

Chiang realised that he had overestimated his strength. Having failed to crush the head of the 'Red octopus', he was reduced to seeing its tentacles grow back one by one. He summoned his closest advisers and asked them what line of conduct he should follow:

'We must be prepared for anything, even a communist victory in Northern China,' was the reply. 'We must make Southern China an impregnable fortress. And meanwhile, safeguard the cultural treasures of our country against the Red bandits!'

Ships began to sail back and forth between the mainland and the island of Taiwan, which lay 160 kilometres to the south-west of the maritime province of Fujian, opposite Canton, the big port that Sun Yat-sen had made the headquarters of the young Guomindang, in the now far distant days of the alliance with Borodin. Modern Noah's Arks of Chinese nationalism, the Generalissimo's vessels carried off, carefully packed into cases, the statues, sculptures, vases, paintings, jewellery and countless works of art one can now admire in the National Museum of Taiwan, and of which the People's Republic of China is demanding the return to the mainland.

Kang Sheng had a connoisseur's appreciation of the operation. He realised that Chiang, in organising this huge maritime transfer, was not acting solely out of greed. The Generalissimo knew what he was doing: by depriving his enemy of the benefit of a prized part of the Chinese cultural heritage, he was seeking to rob them of a formidable psychological weapon – legitimacy.

Chiang was cunning. Kang Sheng, a lover of art and painting, was convinced of it; he knew full well that possession of the country's cultural treasures had always been linked in China with the possession of power.

This did not prevent military disasters from happening. Chiang Kai-shek's advisers were not mistaken: Northern China was already lost to the Guomindang. Only the nationalist commander-in-chief of that region, General Fu Zuozi, refused to accept this. In December, he decided to go for victory or death. Before being caught in a communist stranglehold, the army must attempt one last offensive. He regrouped his best troops for a desperate assault on Yan'an. If the Red capital were to fall into his hands once more, the psychological advantage would be enormous in a country where it was best to be blessed by the gods.

On the eve of the attack, the General did not know very much about the Reds' plan of action. He bitterly regretted the death of Dai Li. Without their leader, the nationalist secret services were worthless, whereas the communists had plenty to show for the activities of theirs. Under the division of labour, Li Kenong controlled the Red zone, while Kang Sheng, aided by his friend Zhao Yaobin, was in charge of infiltration operations in the White zone.

'I'm going to listen to the propaganda programmes. Perhaps I'll manage to glean some information about the communists' intentions from them,' Fu Zuozi said to himself.

Hardly had he switched on his field radio than he heard an enemy broadcaster commenting in considerable detail on his planned offensive. The communists knew everything: it was clearly a matter of betrayal. But the nationalist commander was hard pushed to name the source. He had more than twenty generals under his orders. All of them knew of his plans.

The traitor, he learned much later, was one of his lifelong companions, his own signals officer, General Deng Baochan, who held the secret code for communications with the nationalist capital of Nanking, and who, for a long time, had been a 'mole' for Kang Sheng. He had secretly joined the Communist Party well before entering the ranks of the Guomindang.

Despite hastily issued counter-orders, the nationalist offensive ended in disaster. Completely demoralised, the nationalist troops scattered at well-founded cries of 'Treason! Treason!' In desperation, General Fu Zuozi asked a Belgian missionary, Father Raymond de Jaegher, to negotiate on his behalf in favour of an American nuclear attack. The priest agreed to undertake this mission so little in keeping with his ecclesiastical status. He met the commander of the United States naval forces anchored off the big Shandong port of Qingdao. The response, of course, was negative. Fu Zuozi's confidence in the Guomindang's fortunes was severely shaken.

Lin Boju and Ren Bishi, who had warmly recommended Kang for this 'special' job in the White zone, could congratulate themselves on their choice.

The Red Army thrust and the *Tewu*'s infiltration and brainwashing ploys finished off the nationalist army of Northern China. Only Beijing remained Guomindang-controlled, defended by a contingent of half a million men. But completely demoralised by the betrayal he had suffered, and with a view to the future, Fu Zuozi began secret negotiations in the firm hope of being able to find an honourable way out. In the end, he surrendered without a fight, defeated psychologically as much as militarily.

On 23 January 1949, the world learnt, to its astonishment if not indifference, that communist troops held the northern capital and that they were preparing to sweep down on the big southern cities: Nanking, Canton and Shanghai.

Nanking was known as the City of Stone, the Heavenly Capital. Its inhabitants were proud of their ancient monuments – the Tower of Tambour, the Temple of Qingliangshansi, the Tomb of Hongwu and even the mausoleum of Dr Sun Yat-sen – but when the Red General Chen Yi's Third Campaign Army forced its way into the fortress of Kiangyin, betrayed by its leaders, they began to grow disillusioned: the communists were bound to make them pay dearly for the privilege of having been Chiang Kai-shek's capital for more than twenty years.

The nationalist army scattered after 20 March, with the leaders setting the example, fighting for a place on a boat or military aircraft bound for Taiwan, talking for hours on the phone for the sake of a few litres of petrol, hastily getting their family possessions, their jewellery and their money out of the country.

The civilians realised that the military were not going to fight. They waited, with bated breath, as the last miserable Guomindang cadres fled. A cold silence descended.

On the morning of 24 March, the Red Army entered an undefended city, carrying their own weapons slung over their shoulders. The inhabitants of the city were amazed by how disciplined Chen Yi's soldiers were. Unlike other Chinese armies, they did not pillage, they did not take houses by force, they did not rape the girls, they were as sober as judges. Even their language gave cause for surprise: being from the north, most of them did not speak Cantonese.

The Reds were already in Shanghai, or at least their fifth column was. The *Tewu* showed its face: in April agents shot Zhou Tianlu in his own apartment. Zhou was a former militant Trotskyist 'turned' by Dai Li after his capture and recruited to the anti-communist struggle.

On 2 May 1949, Du Yuesheng decided it was high time to leave. He did not want to see his kingdom engulfed by the huge Red tide. His ship was waiting for him close to the docks, flying the red, white and blue flag of Holland. A few of his henchmen came to see him off. They were staying behind to check the lie of the land.

A few days later, Du Yuesheng moved into a sumptuous apartment in Kennedy Road, Hong Kong. It was here, in the British colony, that he was to die in 1951, like some aged fish out of water.

His friend 'Pockmarked Huang', the former head of Chinese police in the French Concession, preferred to stay in Shanghai, come what may. He locked himself up in his house and awaited the arrival of the Reds. He was not afraid of them. Only death frightened him.

Shanghai seemed to be sleeping. Then the news began to travel by word of mouth: the nationalist army was already negotiating with Chen Yi the surrender of the city. The Reds would soon be there.

It was as though the place was seized with a fever. Suddenly panic set in and within a few hours it had overtaken all the well-to-do, or even simply modest, areas. The rich of Shanghai mobbed planes, trains and boats in their hundreds. The humblest sampan, the most third-rate junk, the most broken-down rickshaw became a real treasure for which people were prepared to negotiate, bargain, beg. Fortunes changed hands before the astonished gaze of the last remaining Westerners. Daughters of good families sold their bodies in exchange for a ticket to leave. It was like Saigon or Phnom Penh in 1975, on a smaller scale, without the newspaper photographers, without the American helicopters.

A few communist pamphlets circulating round the city said there would be no fighting, no reprisals, no penalties exacted.

'After all, we've already suffered the Green Gang, the Westerners, the Guomindang and the Japanese! This Chairman Mao can't be any worse . . .' the man in the street tried to reassure himself while waiting.

On 26 May Chen Yi's Red Army quietly entered Shanghai, although a few shots were fired for form's sake. There were no reprisals, any more than there had been in Nanking. The soldiers were like creatures from another planet; oddly, they even obeyed their officers. It was only later, much later, that the people of Shanghai would be led to the Canidrome, the stadium built by the Frenchman Louis Bouvier for dog racing. There, rather like the Red cadres in Yan'an, they would be 're-educated'.

China became entirely Red. While the Guomindang army imposed itself by fire and sword on the local population of Taiwan, who were anything but convinced, a new state came into being under a red flag spangled with yellow stars.

On 1 October 1949, from the Gate of Heavenly Peace, the entrance to the old imperial palace, a communist leader whose name, Mao Zedong, was known to only a few Westerners, officially proclaimed the birth of the new People's Republic of China.

That day the journalist Van Putten, of the United States Information Service in China, met several of his former Chinese employees. They were all wearing brand new Red Army uniforms. The newspaper man suddenly realised why his most zealous Chinese colleagues had reported sick when the Reds were taking Beijing. They were all working for the *Tewu*.

They soon made it clear to their former boss that, not being of any further use, he would soon be expelled. Kang Sheng and Li Kenong liked journalists as long as the news stories and scoops they filed were supplied by the *Tewu*. Besides, the communist leaders had only one concern: to bring down the bamboo curtain.

12
Laogai, the Chinese Gulag

The TT33 pistol, a semi-automatic weapon, worked on the principle of a short slide of the barrel. The Cossack Fiodor Vassilievich Tokarev had stolen the idea for the locking mechanism from the original Browning version, and had of course given his name to the Soviet model. The general design of the Tokarev was also copied from an American weapon, the Colt Government model 1911. But without the safety device . . .

Produced in the USSR from 1933, the Tokarev measured 190 millimetres, weighed 1 kilo, had a 7.62 calibre (although it could use ammunition for the Mauser, which was 7.63), and could fire eight shots. In the USSR it replaced the Nagan as standard issue for the Red Army. It began to be mass-produced in China as soon as the communists seized power. The Soviets, who considered it a rudimentary weapon, were about to stop using it, but must have persuaded the Chinese to buy up their surplus war stock. Of course, the black bakelite plaques on the butt, which bore the Soviet star and the Cyrillic letters CCCP (i.e. USSR), were left off the Chinese models. Beijing even changed the name of the gun, and the Tokarev TT33 became the Shike 51 (the date it was first issued).

The great novelty of this pistol was the removable platinum firing mechanism consisting of a hammer, trigger, separator and main spring, which was lodged in the back of the stock so that it could be easily taken out. During the 1930s the French had already come up with a similar system and again the idea was probably stolen from them by the OGPU.

If eight 'counter-revolutionaries' were lined up, on their knees, with their hands tied behind their backs, all eight could be shot with a bullet in the back of the neck, in twenty seconds.

On the night of 27–8 April 1951, the *Gonganbu* arrested more than three thousand people in Shanghai. The former Canidrome, the famous dog track, opened in 1928 by Louis Bouvier, with a capacity for fifty thousand spectators, served as an internment camp. A symbol of the wealth and splendour of the French Concession, situated at the intersection of avenue du Roi-Albert and route Hervé-de-Sieyès (renamed Shaanxi Street and Jongjia Street) was transformed into a death camp. Gone were the joyful cries of the gamblers when a hare crossed the line, the laughter of the women, the tinkle of crystal champagne glasses in the ballroom or the dining-rooms next to the betting cubicles and the training tracks. The banker Louis Bouvier, a friend of Du Yuesheng, was dead, so was not there to mourn the destruction of his work. His son George, a resistance fighter with the Free French movement during the war, had been placed under house arrest by the *Gonganbu*, accused of being 'a financial criminal', before being stripped of his assets and deported from China.

The Canidrome was now a camp where 'counter-revolutionary criminals' were tried and executed in public. These men and women executed in Shanghai in 1951 were basically killed in revenge for 1927, when the Guomindang and the Green Gang had wiped out the communists. It was in fact at that time, in 1927, that summary execution by pistol was first introduced.

It all came about because when a police superintendent from the French Concession emerged one day from his headquarters in rue Stanislas-Chevalier he witnessed a public execution. A row of Chinese, on their knees, were waiting with their heads on the block for the executioner to decapitate them with his enormous sabre. They watched, wild-eyed, as the heads of those next to them were cut off one by one and the highly sharpened blade approached them. The policeman felt that the civilising mission of the West ought to prevail once more over the barbarism of the East. He consulted the Catholic priest who had come, as usual, to convert the condemned men to Christianity before their execution, and both men suggested a new method of execution to the Chinese authorities – which was how firing a bullet in the neck was adopted. The public accusation meetings that followed the great tradition of the rectification campaign in Yan'an became all the rage. On 5 April, the *Gonganbu* distributed a practical manual on 'How to Hold an Accusation Meeting'. The first real trial had taken place a month earlier in Beijing. On 25 March, the *Renmin Ribao* published the proceedings of a huge psychodrama, in which hundreds, indeed thousands of people were indicted. After five hours, the mayor of Beijing, wiping his brow, addressed the crowd in a state of hysteria:

'Comrades, what should we do with all these criminals, these bandits, these secret agents, these bad landlords, these leaders and organisers of reactionary Taoist sects?'

'Shoot them!' shouted the frenzied crowd.

'Should we show them mercy?'

'No! No!'

The mayor brought the meeting to an end. The people's representatives had asked the people what they wanted. The people had replied that they wanted the death of the 'counter-revolutionaries'. This was democracy, a 'new democracy', since the people were dictating their orders to the rulers.

'Those who ought to be killed will be killed. In cases where we could kill or not, we will not kill. But when there is killing to be done, we will do it . . . Now you want them to be killed. Tomorrow the court will deliver its verdict and they will be killed.'

In all the big cities, the same Dantesque scene unfolded, with wall posters announcing the meetings, with loudspeakers in factories, parks and main thoroughfares. The meetings were organised by Communist Party committees in order to denounce counter-revolutionaries to the *Gonganbu*. In Shanghai, a city of five million inhabitants, one million of whom were blue-collar workers, the situation was all the more dreadful because more than half the Chinese had worked directly or indirectly for foreigners, made money out of industry or commerce, or from prostitution, gambling, opium trafficking – all the foul activities of the secret societies.

In Shanghai the sword of justice was wielded with an iron grip by a triumvirate installed shortly after Mao Zedong's speech to the Central Committee in July 1950 that had launched the 'mass campaign for the elimination of counter-revolutionary elements'.

Whilst the repression set in, Mao reiterated his orders in December 1950: 'In the repression of counter-revolutionaries, take care to strike with sureness, precision and severity.'

The deputy mayor of Shanghai, Pan Hannian, organised the repression, acting in concert with two *Gonganbu* officials, Li Shiying and Yang Fan. Pan was one of the famous 'group of five' who, under Kang Sheng's aegis, had reorganised the communist special services in Shanghai in 1931. Then he had been involved in the kidnapping of Chiang Kai-shek in 1936. Finally, based sometimes in Hong Kong but more often in Shanghai, he had been responsible for maintaining clandestine communications between the Comintern and the Party under the Japanese occupation and then during the civil war. Completely adapted to a life of secrecy, this inflexible supporter of the Comintern had suffered too greatly to show mercy to his former enemies. Under the political leadership of Chen Yi, the new mayor, he pursued a policy of ruthless repression. At the end of the summer a new *Gonganbu* official arrived, the 'Shanghai executioner' Xu Jianguo. Having formerly worked for Kang Sheng's Social Affairs Department, Xu Jianguo, a native of Hubei province, was to brand Shanghai with a red-hot iron, having had a remarkable career in foreign intelligence and diplomacy.

The Communist Party Central Committee had drawn up a hit list of counter-revolutionaries to be flushed out, divided into distinct categories.

First of all, there were the former Guomindang leaders, civilians and military personnel. Those who had not fled to Taiwan were mostly executed, to set an example. Contrary to the current propaganda, former nationalist supporters were lying low, hoping that it would all blow over. The organisation of a resistance movement was far from their thoughts. A tiny minority of Guomindang leaders made their submission to communism and were presented to the people like animals in cages. A relatively high proportion of Dai Li's BIS men were spared. There was a need for them in counter-espionage, if only to expose the vast infiltration operations that had poisoned the communist movement. Labelled 'Guomindang war criminals', they were imprisoned for some ten years, re-educated and later amnestied. The most famous case was that of Shen Zui, Dai Li's former deputy, who today holds several honorary posts and has written numerous works on the history of nationalist espionage, and apologises profusely for having served under Chiang Kai-shek.

'Traitors', 'Japanese collaborators', 'spies in the pay of foreign powers' abounded. The *Gonganbu* took advantage of their existence to eliminate political dissidents, including a Trotskyist organisation that had survived until 1952, the Chinese Communist League.

With his round smiling face, set off by his steel-rimmed glasses, Zheng Chaolin was a communist of long standing, born at the turn of the century. He had helped Zhou Enlai set up the Chinese Communist Party in Paris, before going to Moscow, where he attended the Workers University of the East. After the abortive uprising of 1927, in which he had played an active part, he blamed Stalin for its disastrous failure. Together with others, he then founded the Chinese Trotskyist movement, but ended up in the Guomindang gaols. Freed in 1937, while the war was raging, Zheng undertook an apparently innocent task: that of translating Trotsky's work into Chinese. Then he published his small journal, *The New Banner*, hoping, despite his criticisms of the Stalinist system, that the communist revolution would raise the red curtain on a new dawn. History sets little store by romanticism. The *Gonganbu* came and got Zheng Chaolin from his apartment in Shanghai at dawn. After seven years in prison under Chiang Kai-shek, Zheng the Trotskyist was to spend thirty-five years in Mao's gaols! Apparently, he was lucky: most of his comrades ended up with a bullet in the back of their necks.

Generally speaking, the *Gonganbu* mistrusted intellectuals. In 1951, in Shanghai as elsewhere, the campaign for 'thought reform' was organised in the universities. These techniques of indoctrination were related in varying degrees to the rectification campaign implemented by Kang Sheng and Chen Boda in Yan'an in 1942. These methods, called *xinia* in Chinese, used on Chinese political prisoners, as they were on those who fell into the hands of the Chinese and North Koreans during the Korean War, became known worldwide as brainwashing. The captives had to learn by heart the prison rules and the political statements published in the *Renmin Ribao*. Then in August 1951 a special section of the Central Committee began to publish the *Selected Works of Mao Zedong*, which, it was suggested, should be studied throughout China.

The repression rapidly gained ground: on 1 May – Labour Day, appropriately enough – 1951, the public execution of five hundred people was announced. In Shanghai, Pan Hannian and his friends turned their attentions to a third category of counter-revolutionaries:

members of the secret societies. The days of an alliance with the triads in the anti-Japanese war were far behind, although the Green Gang was still something of a legend.

But was it not a shadow of its former self? In their pursuit of the members of this secret society, were not the *Gonganbu* mostly dealing with all the small fry operating a black market? In Hong Kong that summer, Du Yuesheng, a sick man, considered the decline of his secret society with sadness. His links with Shanghai had been severed since the seizure of the city by Chen Yi in 1949. Despite everything, he had managed to re-establish communications, to follow the fate of the six hundred or so followers who remained loyal to him. The *Gonganbu* came down hard on them. On 1 May, one of his assistants, the former head of the Chinese Chamber of Commerce, was 'purged'. Then the communist security forces pulled off a master coup: another leader of the gang, Huang Jirong, Inspector 'Pockmarked Huang', was caught in the *Gonganbu* net. He had realised for a year, as he moved from one hideout to another, that his days were numbered. The crackling loudspeakers, the huge banners clattering in the wind – 'Eliminate all counter-revolutionaries!' 'Long live the Chinese Communist Party' – were so many nails in the coffin awaiting him. The winter of 1950 was particularly harsh in Shanghai. Holed up in his hideout, Huang realised that the end was near. When he was arrested, he almost sighed with relief. After several sleepless nights, seated on a stool, harassed by Li Shiying's agents, he confessed to everything: economic crimes, opium trafficking – he and his Gang were guilty of them. The massacre of communists in 1927? Yes, he was guilty of that, too.

His public condemnation of the Green Gang created a great stir. Then he was executed, along with five other leaders.

Another Green Gang veteran, Zhu Xuefan, head of the Guomindang unions, had already made contact with Pan Hannian in 1937, at the time of the holy alliance against Japan. And he had gradually been drawn into the CP: in 1945 he was in Paris for the Congress of the World Union Federation with the 'Red bandit' Deng Fa. And when the communists came to power four years later, Zhu offered them his unconditional support. Du did not live long enough to witness the outrage of this former post office worker unionist, a member of the Green Gang crime syndicate, becoming Minister of Post and Communications.

For Du was suffering from ever more frequent bouts of asthma in his Hong Kong retreat. He had been given the most modern type of oxygen mask. Chiang Kai-shek, who had heard that he was wrestling with death, sent his kind regards from Taiwan. On 16 August 1951, Du Yuesheng fell into a coma and died just one day before his sixty-third birthday. The Hotel Luk Kwok was then visited by all his friends who came to pay their last respects as he lay in his cedarwood coffin. While Taoist monks and nuns intoned prayers, and orchestras played funeral music, people came and went, meeting up afterwards in nearby restaurants to reminisce about the Du legend. His sons went their separate ways. One vowed to continue the great work of the dear departed – opium trafficking. Another went to Taipei to work as an adviser to the Minister of Defence, Yu Dawei, uncle of the communist Yu Qiwei, Jiang Qing's former lover. Chiang Kai-shek paid public homage to the deceased, a great man who had been 'so loyal to China and to himself'. It is traditional for the bodies of Chinese who have died overseas to be repatriated and their corpses flagellated during the voyage. Du's body could not be repatriated to Red China. On 22 October 1952 his remains were taken by ship to Taiwan.

The Green Gang was well and truly dead and buried.

The communists gradually dismantled the secret societies. However, some survived. The *Gonganbu* considered it more useful to infiltrate them in order to penetrate their branches in Hong Kong, Macao, Taiwan or San Francisco.

As far as religions were concerned, the *Gonganbu* designated Buddhism, Catholicism, Protestantism and Islam as 'patriotic associations', within the context of the famous United Front with the Communist Party. Basically, the aim was to dissociate them from their traditional clergies in order to absorb them. At that time the head of the United Front Work Department – which came under the Social Affairs Department, and therefore the secret services – was Li Weihan. This skilful negotiator with the Guomindang had started out as an underground communist working with Kang Sheng. He knew the art and subtlety of infiltrating 'allies'. In a confidential document for the attention of the International Liaison Department (that other *Tewu* cover), he laid down the tactics to be adopted in dealing with the Catholic Church during the 1950s:

The Catholic Church with its Pontiff in Rome is an organisation which is a source of counter-revolutionary activity within a people's democracy. It is impossible to attack it head on because we have not sufficiently prepared the masses, and we would only create martyrs. We cannot allow the Church to preserve its supranational character, which places it above the will of the people. We must establish a government department to deal with religious affairs and organisations. This department will organise national, regional and local associations that will gather the Catholics within patriotic bodies. Each association will have to declare its loyalty and submission to the laws of the nation . . . During this period the masses will suffer a psychological conflict because on the one hand they will feel they owe their loyalty to the Church and its clergy, while on the other their patriotism binds them to support the people's government.

Of course, in the long term, Li Weihan and his friends were planning the suppression of religions, in accordance with the canons of communism. For the aim of the mysterious Section 106, a very special secret service unit within the Religious Affairs Department, was to 'divide the Churches from within and set the various religious organisations against each other'.

But the *Gonganbu* had also violently attacked the foreign monks, nuns and missionaries, accusing them of being spies and 'agents of subversion'. It is perfectly true that some of the missionaries did devote some of their spare time to working for Western special services, but primarily as China-watchers. Father Jean-Elie Maillot, for instance, is still remembered as an SDECE informer who helped French agents to enter and leave Yunnan. Father Léon Trivière, who was expelled from China and settled in Hong Kong, annoyed the Chinese because for over thirty years this admirable analyst followed their every movement, information that found its way into hundreds of publications. In the mountains of the New Territories, his colleague the Hungarian Father La Dany, together with his Jesuit priests, was responsible until his retirement for organising a formidable network of listening stations tuned in to mainland China. But generally speaking, the communists martyred priests for what they were, that is to say, representatives of Churches that had to be destroyed. These foreigners were imprisoned, often tortured, and eventually expelled from the country. In 1949, when the communists came to power, there were some three thousand missionaries and nearly as many foreign nuns and monks. Ten years later, there were no more than twelve in the whole of China, and they were either in prison or under house arrest. Religious communities were broken up, and of course Chinese monks and nuns were persecuted. Of nearly three thousand priests, the *Gonganbu* shot 200 in the first few years, 500 were exiled, 500 were imprisoned, together with their nine bishops. The number of Christians who disappeared was soon put at 600,000. On 7 October 1954, Pope Pius XII addressed an encyclical letter 'To the Chinese Nation' – *Ad sinarum gentes* – in which he expressed his sorrow and anxiety.

It was in the context of the campaign against counter-revolutionaries that the Archbishop of Shanghai, Ignatius Gong Pinmei, was eventually arrested at the end of 1955. 'You have been running a counter-revolutionary group under the mask of religion,' was the main accusation against him when he was tried in 1960. 'You tried to sabotage the national patriotic Catholic movement, spread false rumours, obtain secret intelligence for imperialist spies . . .'

Detained in the Shanghai central prison, Bishop Gong was given a life sentence. At first, the communists so feared his influence that he was kept in solitary confinement. Then during the 1960s his conditions were relaxed a little, and he was given a few days' work outside, herding buffalo. But for thirty years Monseigneur Gong remained hostage to the communists in Shanghai.

By the summer of 1951 there had already been some 200,000 arrests and executions in Shanghai. As well as the Canidrome, the famous Bund – the promenade along the Huangpu River – had also been used as a place where prisoners were assembled, while a guard was kept on tall buildings in the area to prevent the roofs being used for suicide attempts, which at one point became so numerous in Shanghai that people avoided walking too close to buildings on account of falling bodies.

With regard to the big foreign companies, the Chinese CP advanced cautiously, as they had with the churches. Thanks to his friendship with Zhou Enlai and Great Britain's recognition of the People's Republic of China in 1950, the Englishman John Keswick, who had served in the secret services during the war, managed to obtained preferential treatment for his firm Jardine, Matheson. So did others. But in fact the Beijing authorities were fully determined to appropriate foreign interests.

In the summer of 1950 the French Communist Party sent Marius Magnien alias Rondet, a graduate of the Leninist School in Moscow who had studied the techniques used by the Comintern's Anti-Militarist Section and faithfully applied them in France, to conduct a survey on Mao's China (his journalistic activity also provided a cover for discussions with the special services and with Mao himself on how to undermine the French army in Indochina from within). As far as the economic battle was concerned, Pan Hannian put it straight:

All these foreign companies, like many banking and industrial firms, tried to fool us at first, thinking they could take advantage of their enormous experience of scheming, speculation and duplicity to outwit our young administrators who know little or nothing of the arcane mysteries of capitalism. But our just regulations, the vigilance of Chinese employees and workers, the firmness and speed with which our cadres, ex-combatants and students at the Party schools have been brought up to date, as well as the loyal collaboration of healthy and patriotic elements of the bourgeoisie, have enabled us to thwart the intrigues of capitalist imperialists and Chiang Kai-shek's agents . . .

These two euphemisms were used to refer to the victims of renewed purges and summary executions. In December 1951, the 'Three Antis Campaign' was launched (sanfan: anti-corruption, anti-waste and anti-overbureaucratisation). This was followed in January 1952 by the 'Five Antis Campaign' (wufan) against all kinds of tax evasion, theft of economic secrets, bribery – all crimes which served to purge those who were resistant to the new communist policy, within and without the Party.

This repression was not confined to Shanghai but was implemented all over China. The main activity fell to Luo Ruiqing, Minister of Security, who worked with Peng Zhen, the son of a poor peasant from

Shanxi, who became Mayor of Beijing in October 1951. Working within the Politburo and a body called the Committee of Political and Legal Affairs, Peng was responsible for designing the legal framework within which the merciless justice of the people was to be applied.

Widescale repression in the countryside in 1949, when agrarian reform was introduced, was followed by really savage repression. Today the number of 'local despots' and 'other counter-revolutionaries' executed is put at three million, less than one per cent of the rural population. But this does not take into account the executions in towns. The Minister of Finance Bo Yibo wrote in 1952 in a report on 'The Economic Achievements of the New China': 'In the past three years we have eliminated more than two million bandits. Counter-revolutionaries and secret agents have also been placed under close guard in a secure place.'

Mao delivered a report in February 1957, 'On the Correct Way of Treating the Contradictions within the People', in which he estimated that during the terror directed against counter-revolutionaries, the *Gonganbu* had sentenced 800,000 people to death. In the report as officially published, this reference did not appear . . .

On 30 May 1957, the novelist Lin Xiling made public a secret *Gonganbu* document in which Luo Ruiqing claimed responsibility for 770,000 deaths. All these figures are the lowest estimates; it is always difficult to be sure of the facts. American experts on the period of the Great Leap Forward (1958–61) put the number of dead at two million, and were accused of anti-Chinese propaganda – until the day when the Beijing Bureau of Statistics confirmed that between 1959 and 1961 ten million Chinese had perished as a direct result of bad economic management at the time. But in the early years, leaving aside the inevitable effect on the economy of all the revolutionary turmoil, there were at least five million executions.

At the same time, the *Laogai*, 'reform through labour', was instituted, in other words the Chinese gulag: fifteen million Chinese were soon interned in some two hundred camps and State farms. In June 1951, Luo Ruiqing defined the *Laogai* as, 'Reform through labour is both a kind of punishment and an education for offenders. Forcing these offenders to work and be productive can only prevent them from indulging in their counter-revolutionary activities.'

Four months later, the head of the *Gonganbu* was more specific: 'As well as those anti-revolutionaries who were executed in order to satisfy the just indignation of the people, a great many others were sentenced to prison and subjected to obligatory reform through labour.'

The little passage called Gongxian Hutong (Bowstring Alley) in Beijing was very quiet. But number 15 was a hive of activity. Inside these little old-style houses, under special guard, was the heart of the Chinese espionage service, the *Shehuibu*, the Central Committee's Department of Social Affairs.

There were not many cars in the imperial capital at that time, so the Russian Pobiedas, gleaming like lacquered cockroaches, attracted attention as they purred along the two parallel roads, Beiheyan Dajie and Nanheyan Dajie, that ran alongside the Forbidden City, before joining the Dong Chananjie. This thoroughfare separated Tian'anmen Square from the Great Gate of the Forbidden City. The big revolutionary buildings on Tian'anmen Square were then just being erected. The men in Social Affairs were in contact with every section of security, the army, the Party, the ministries. Sometimes a Pobieda stopped not far from the Temple of Confucius to deliver the latest intelligence reports on the Korean War or the war in Indochina to the Russian Embassy. Ivan Andreievich Raina, a colonel in the Soviet services, an expert on aeronautics, received them with an air of condescension befitting a special adviser posted to Mao's China. Shortly afterwards, a courier would set off with an important coded message in a sealed envelope which was to be sent to the leading embassies abroad by a radio officer trained at the special school in Nanyang. The car then had to go by the special services' publishing house, the *Renmin Chubanshi*, which was beginning to publish edifying works to the glory of the *Tewu* and its agents. Finally, it was to go to the *Gonganbu* to fetch an officer who was expected an hour later at the Politburo's Secretariat.

The Ministry of Public Security, the much dreaded *Gonganbu*, run by Luo Ruiqing, was situated on Dong Chanan Avenue, just as you came out of Tian'anmen Square, with some one hundred offices (*Gonganju*) in Beijing and large regional and local offices all over the country. In the 1950s there were three hundred thousand men working for the vast *Gonganbu* web, one for every two thousand of the country's inhabitants. In accordance with Mao's orders, this department relied heavily on the Communist Party committees present at every level of Chinese life, spreading such a fine-meshed net that no one could escape it. When the People's Republic of China was founded, Stalin had sent intelligence experts – no doubt Beria hoped that China, like the Eastern European countries, would become a USSR satellite, at least in the area of intelligence. The *Kitaiskii Otdyel*, or Chinese section of the Russian Ministry of State Security, would then have been in charge of its Chinese counterpart. Moscow was quickly disillusioned and had to be content with recruiting agents prepared to work for Russia within Mao's services.

In fact, considerable rivalry existed within the Chinese teams. Already Mao Zedong and Liu Shaoqi were both trying to control the enormous security and counter-espionage apparatus. Luo Ruiqing, who ran the *Gonganbu*, was closer to Liu and had laid claim to an empire consisting not only of the three hundred thousand members of the *Gonganbu* but also the armed police force, the *Gonganbu Dui*, whose headquarters were located in the old British barracks, not far from Tian'anmen Square, and which had its own tanks and aeroplanes. Better still, he had carved himself a little niche within another, more mysterious body, the *Gonganerju*, a second security service, answerable to a Party Central Committee body, the Political Defence Department (*Zhengzhi baoweiju*). One of the few heads of the Chinese secret police who had a reputation for integrity and for being a man without personal ambition on the political stage, the incorruptible Luo did of course allow many supporters of Mao to worm their way into his empire. It would have been impossible for him to do otherwise. The responsibility for managing the daily repression and deportation to the *Laogai* fell to the Minister's principal private secretary, Liu Fuzhi (who would himself become Minister of Security under Deng Xiaoping) and the *Gonganbu*'s Eighth Bureau, which dealt with deportation and guarding and economic management of the camps. Thanks to him, the *Gonganbu* met all its own costs: prisoners erected buildings and cultivated vegetables on State farms (as for instance at the Chinho farm, in the Tientsin region, which was totally dependent on the Beijing Central Bureau).

The head of the Eighth Bureau was an administrator who had been chosen more for his talents as a designer of a slow death and architect of the vast concentration-camp labyrinth than for his experience in the special services. His name was Liu Wei. But his deputy was actually the real brains of this gigantic section in the communist apparatus: Wang Dongxing.

This robust peasant from Jiangsi province was thirty-four when, in December 1950, he was made responsible for the great 'thought-reform' campaign, the brainwashing that went on in the camps. Legend has it that after he became Mao's bodyguard in 1935, Mao taught him to read and write. Mao Zedong would never venture outside of China – which he did only once in his life in 1950, at Stalin's invitation – without his chief bodyguard. The friendship between the two men never wavered. Those in the know in Beijing liked to say that Wang's daughter, Yanqun, was actually fathered by Mao Zedong. In 1947 Wang Dongxing, in command of his guard battalion, managed to lead to safety Mao, Jiang Qing and Zhou Enlai by taking them up Mount Ansai, to the north of Yan'an, while nationalist troops were threatening the area. Jiang Qing was in fact political adviser to this First Guard Battalion. After the 'Liberation', Wang was made head of the security department, and put in charge of the special guard, the famous 8341 Detachment, a division of 15,000 men whose job it was to protect the Central Committee. His men, dressed in green tunics and blue trousers, constituted a large presence in the western suburbs of Beijing, with four mysterious barracks in the heart of a pine forest, a staff headquarters and its own politico-military intelligence service.

But, in principle, the highest authority in the world of intelligence and counter-espionage remained the Social Affairs Department, based in Bowstring Alley. It was directly answerable to the Central

Committee and had overall responsibility for all the services, but also for offensive intelligence abroad. From 1949 this department comprised some ten or twelve sections and delegated powers of investigation, research and espionage to other ministries. This explains why some directors, like Li Kenong's son-in-law, Li Qiming, belonged to both the *Gonganbu* and its tutelary department, Social Affairs (*Shehuibu*). When Beijing was taken by the communists, Li Kenong became head of the section Kang Sheng had founded eleven years earlier. The whole team trained by Kang, which has ensured the success of the *Tewu* right up to the present day, was already in place: Luo Qingchang was the overall administrator; Ling Yun was in charge of the Chinese equivalent of M15 and of offensive intelligence; Liu Shaowen covered the whole military sector; and Zou Dapeng centralised information in the general secretariat. But Kang was not among them any more – and Li Kenong, his former deputy and rival, who had replaced him, rubbed his hands in satisfaction. What had happened?

As the victory to which he had so greatly contributed approached, Kang had been gradually displaced as head of the services. When victory came, he was appointed governor of his province, Shandong. In 1945, he had been criticised for his part in the rectification campaign. Zhou Enlai himself had criticised Comrade Kang. Things had really gone too far. Even Mao, to protect himself, had had to denounce to some extent the man who had assisted him in this insane campaign.

In April 1948, in a speech addressed to cadres, Mao had moderately criticised 'Old Kang' for shortcomings in the way things had been carried out in the Lin Xian region. Then something much more serious happened: while Kang Sheng devoted himself to clandestine work in the White zone, as the civil war drew to an end, his own principal private secretary Zhao Yaobin defected to Chiang Kai-shek. It was impossible to criticise Kang openly without revealing the nature of numerous special operations and the impact of Zhao's defection on the communist ranks. But all this aroused considerable hostility against the head of the secret services.

One other factor forced Kang Sheng to leave Beijing and take refuge, with all honour intact, in Qingdao with the ever-loyal Cao Yi-ou. Mao Zedong and Jiang Qing's relationship was foundering in 1949. Mao was eager for a new mistress and the faithful Wang Dongxing was eager to introduce new women to him. The Communist Party leader did not want the crisis he had known in 1937 to recur in his private life. As with his third wife, He Zizhen, Mao sent Jiang Qing for a rest cure in the USSR. Which meant, of course, that Kang had lost his greatest asset in Mao's entourage. Jiang was no longer there to intervene on his behalf with Mao in the face of criticism from Zhou Enlai (who was trying to advance his own men, Li Kenong and Liu Shaowen, in the Social Affairs Department) and Liu Shaoqi (who proposed Luo Ruiqing as head of the *Gonganbu*). And Wang the bodyguard remained impassive . . .

There is no doubt that Mao, without actually having drawn a line through Kang's name, preferred that there should not exist, within the People's Republic, a state within a state, a secret service run by a single man. Events in Russia in 1953, when Stalin died and the head of the secret police tried to take over power, retrospectively justified his fears.

Despite everything, Kang was to retain a moral influence over the men he had trained, and solid contacts within the *Gonganbu* and the Social Affairs Department. As governor of Shandong, he was responsible for repression in the province and for the activities of the local *Gonganbu*. He did not lose the upper hand. His worst enemies feared him. He had kept an enormous number of archive documents, of biographical statements concerning the members of the CCP. Furthermore, in March 1949, on the instructions of the Central Committee, he had taken possession of enemy archives, belonging to the Guomindang and its agents containing, perhaps, compromising details on certain cadres who had been imprudent in their youth, among them his friend Jiang Qing. In any case, these archives had not been placed in the central files. Had he destroyed them or kept them? Kang Sheng remained a kind of consultant adviser to the special services, even though he was no longer in charge of them. Officially, he no longer appeared at major celebrations alongside the leadership of the regime. However, in 1951, Kang took part in the Third Conference on State Security and the suppression of counter-revolutionaries in Beijing, and on that occasion he suggested the creation of a secret service modelled on that of the Soviets, and divided into two branches. In fact, Mao and Liu favoured this suggestion, which in a way gave them a service each. Kang saw in this the long-term possibility of regaining a say in political decisions concerning the world of intelligence. But he would have to play a waiting game . . .

This was confirmed on 30 March 1951 when, in a review of the repression campaign being conducted in every province, Mao criticised Kang Sheng in a scarcely veiled manner, reproaching him for not doing enough: 'In certain parts of Shandong we note a lack of vigour and in other parts some ill-considered action has been taken; these two tendencies are evident in all the provinces and municipalities of the country, care must be taken to rectify them.'

Was Kang succumbing to the particularism so frequent in his native province, and showing special consideration to his Shandong compatriots? Or was he deliberately not throwing himself into a new rectification campaign which would entail new setbacks for him within the Party? For the first time in his life, Kang Sheng devoted himself, in what was to become his bastion, to various pastimes that had nothing to do with politics or secret agents. Put out of commission by the People's Republic, he turned his attentions, deep in the seclusion of his retreat, to a few projects so secret that not even the Chinese leadership of the day knew anything of them.

While China remained isolated from the rest of the world, the worst fears of a small proud and peaceful people were realised: the military annexation of their territory, Tibet, by Chinese troops. The Dalai Lama had already envisaged this eventuality during the Second World War and had welcomed the American envoys with the Tolstoy mission. As soon as Mao moved into the Forbidden City in 1949, like all Chinese Emperors he cherished the dream of extending his dominion over Korea and Tibet. A year later, his expeditionary force was fighting alongside Kim Il-sung's troops. That left the little kingdom of the lamas, Tibet. His best military leader, Lin Biao, was given the task of working out a plan. *Tewu* agents began to swarm around this country, 1,200,000 kilometres square, with three million inhabitants, 180,000 of whom were lamas living in the monasteries dotted about the rugged hostile landscape. Neighbouring India grew anxious. Zhou Enlai sent his emissaries to reassure Nehru, with whom he was reckoning to launch the great Third World movement that would take shape at the Bandung Conference. The 'liberation of Tibet from the yoke of feudalism and imperialism' was to be achieved peacefully.

All through 1950 came a series of statements preparing the ground. On 1 January: 'The People's Liberation Army must liberate Tibet as a matter of urgency.' On 5 August, the Xinhua news agency quoted General Liu Bocheng, a leader of the Military Commission: 'Tibet must be brought back within the great family of the homeland!' On 30 September, the Prime Minister, Zhou Enlai, added his voice to the cause, on the occasion of the first anniversary of the People's Republic: 'It is high time Tibet was liberated!'

The Chinese were well aware of the differences between Lhasa, the sacred city, the seat of the Tibetan government, and Chamdo, six hundred kilometres away, the capital of Kham Province, Eastern Tibet. The proud horsemen of Kham had always despised the lamas of Lhasa. Beijing wasted no time in deciding to intervene, making diplomatic overtures directed in particular at the Dalai Lama's young brother, aged only fourteen, the Panchen Lama, in an attempt to win round the Tibetan government. By the end of 1949, Beijing agents had managed to get the young boy to appeal to Mao Zedong for the liberation of Tibet. At the same time, the Chinese army was to come down on Kham, without the people of Lhasa shedding a single tear over the fate of the eastern province.

In July, the Chinese sent a monk called Gerda to Chamdo to negotiate. He died a violent death in unexplained circumstances. Chinese radio let rip: 'Anglo-American imperialism is oppressing Tibet, which must be liberated.' No 'foreign interference in the affairs of Tibet would be tolerated'.

On 7 October 1950, Chinese forces invaded Tibet, beginning one of the longest secret wars of this century between a small freedom-loving country and the world's most densely populated communist power, although this war did not find the same favour with the media as the Afghanistan . . .

One man found the call to battle against Anglo-American imperialism somewhat startling: former RAF pilot Robert Webster Ford was employed by the Lhasa government and lived in Chamdo. He had been asked to set up the country's first radio and communications network and he was, in a way, London's diplomatic representative in Tibet. While tens of thousands of Chinese soldiers were making their way up the foothills of Kham, he said to himself with typically British humour: 'Anglo-American imperialism in Tibet! Who? Me?' Mr Ford was in fact the only Englishman living in the region. The Chinese perhaps did not need to send several divisions in to capture him . . .

On 19 October, Chamdo fell without offering any resistance, and Ford ended up in the *Laogai* for five years. He was accused of the assassination of Gerda, and like hundreds of Tibetans he was taken to special interrogation centres set up by the *Tewu* in Chengdu province. Then the Red Army advanced on Lhasa. The Dalai Lama took refuge in Yatung on the Indian border. Tibet lodged a protest with the United Nations, finding itself in the same superb isolation as the Emperor Haile Selassie when he protested to the pre-war League of Nations about the Italian invasion of Ethiopia. America was at war in Korea, and engaged in the Cold War in Europe. India was profuse in offering diplomatic warnings. Nationalist China was the only country that would have taken any action, but she had not recovered from the military defeat suffered in 1949. However, she did start training teams of special agents who were parachuted into Tibet some years later, to assist the anti-communist resistance, with CIA support.

In invading Kham, Beijing made a serious miscalculation. It was impossible to keep a permanent army in these distant lands. The Khamba horsemen were the most incredible guerrilla fighters imaginable. They harried the Chinese convoys – backed by 120,000 men – massacred them, and then took refuge in the mountains. Men and horses were used to high altitudes. After each attack they withdrew to the mountain summits while the Chinese soldiers who set off after them blacked out, one by one. Lin Biao realised that they would never crush these proud nomads. However, down in the valleys, the communists indulged in their favourite pastimes: agrarian reform, 'rectification', mass executions of recalcitrants, desecration of sanctuaries, reprisals and massacres. But in martyring Tibet, they certainly did not turn it into a Chinese-style communist paradise. In the years that followed, the American, Indian and Taiwanese secret services began to help the Tibetan resistance movement and the Dalai Lama's government in exile. Then, in 1959, there was a national uprising in Tibet and the Dalai Lama fled to India.

From his retreat in Shandong, the former head of the *Tewu* was champing at the bit, and doubtless felt that since his departure the special services were no longer what they had been. The Tibetan incident was not a success. It remained to be seen whether the big Red sun would disperse the clouds and shine brightly over the rest of Asia.

13
Red Flag over Asia

Charlie Song was the son of poor peasants from the island of Hainan, who after a truly fabulous career became the most powerful Chinese banker and Dr Sun Yat-sen's personal treasurer. In 1927, his beautiful third daughter, Song Meiling, married Chiang Kai-shek, thirteen years her senior. In doing this she opened to him the doors of one of the most astounding politico-financial groups in the whole of Chinese history: the Song clan.

Madame Chiang was very familiar with the United States. She had done all her studies in America and spoke impeccable English. From the mid-1930s she went out of her way to win transatlantic support for her husband, the Generalissimo. She did not lack resources: little by little, she built up the Chinese lobby – that is to say, the pro-Chiang lobby. Led by influential personalities such as the press baron Henry Luch, his wife Clara, and the industrial journalist Alfred Kohlberg, this pressure group achieved some notable success.

In 1945, when the *Amerasia* scandal broke, the group believed they had won. The occasion to open the eyes of American citizens to the subversive activities of the Reds in China had finally presented itself. Here, at last, was proof that all espionage routes led directly back to Moscow.

The *Amerasia* affair began on 11 March 1945, when the OSS conducted a search of the premises of the magazine of the same name, a progressive publication whose editor, Philip Jacob Jaffe, made no secret of his sympathies for the Chinese communists. He had met them in 1934, when reporting from the Red zones. Won over by the dynamism of Mao and his comrades, he had since been advocating a pro-Mao American policy, and therefore the breaking-off of relations with Chiang Kai-shek and his dictatorial regime.

In the *Amerasia* offices, the OSS discovered photocopies of confidential documents emanating not only from the British Secret Intelligence Service but also from the American Army Intelligence Service, G2, and the OSS. This was proof of the existence of leaks to *Amerasia*, an evidently well-informed magazine. Taking together the mysterious profusion of classified information and the pro-communist nature of Jaffe's magazine, the Chinese lobby, with an astonishing lack of discernment, detected a conspiracy of the Soviet espionage services.

The idea that ruled the thinking of Song Meiling's American

friends was Mao's total subordination to Stalin. For Henry Luch, as for Alfred Kohlberg, it was the 'hand of Moscow' that had just been caught delving into the pockets of *Amerasia*. The Chinese communists were no more than mere agents of Stalin, incapable of coping with any serious degree of independence of the USSR. Typically for the period, their analysis was not at all subtle: the fact that several of *Amerasia*'s contributors were obviously supplying information to Mao Zedong's comrades on American policy in Asia did not prove the existence of complicity with the Russian secret services; quite the contrary. The journal was a forerunner of forthcoming trends in the Third World, seduced by Beijing's 'communism of the poor', but no more than that.

For the leaders of the Chinese lobby, this made little difference. It was too good an occasion to denounce Soviet espionage, a very profitable propaganda theme in the USA at that time, when the country was justifiably worried about the advance of Stalin's acolytes in Central Europe. The *Amerasia* journalists were immediately dragged through the mud, their naivety transformed into shameful collaboration, or downright treachery. These people had the impudence to forecast a Maoist victory in China; they had to be discredited once and for all. In the wake of this, Owen Lattimore, John Service and other Americans were accused of being spies. Lattimore, an academic who was very well informed about Chinese affairs, was 'repatriated' to the United States at the instigation of the American ambassador Patrick Hurley, who could not tolerate his hostility towards the nationalists. Service, a former member of General 'Vinegar Joe' Stilwell's staff, was the man who had come up with a particularly offensive nickname for Chiang Kai-shek: 'the peanut general'. Both men were choice targets.

The *Amerasia* affair led mostly to verbal immoderation that was certainly unlikely to advance by one iota any understanding of the dramatic events taking place in China.

The Central Intelligence Agency, the famous CIA, was founded in 1947 to replace the OSS, but in a radically new context: that of the Cold War. The new American intelligence and operations agency without further ado simply adopted the same view of the communist world as its predecessor. The same was true of the External Survey Department 44, a service created by Dai Li's old friend General Milton Miles to keep a watch on Chinese affairs. Its headquarters were initially based in Qingdao, the US naval base in Shandong, then on the island of Taiwan, where Chiang Kai-shek's supporters, completely routed on the mainland, had withdrawn to 'prepare for the reconquest of China'.

Like their Guomindang friends – on whom they were largely dependent for sources of information – the ESD 44 men were constantly denouncing the perfidy of the Reds, recalling in particular how the *Tewu* infiltrated the American press agencies during the civil war through their Chinese employees.

'The dog benefits from his master's prestige. Li Kenong's *Tewu* is simply an appendage of Beria's NKVD!' ranted the nationalists, who had resorted to a few dreadful massacres on Taiwan in order to impose their presence while they waited for action. In fact, they were sufficiently well informed to realise that Mao Zedong was pretty much as nationalist as General Chiang Kai-shek. But they could not forgive the Reds for having caused them to lose face. They also wanted to please their American allies – the better to exploit them.

The nationalists' arguments and those of the Chinese lobby could not fail to appeal to the CIA, which was passionately committed to the struggle against communism. In the face of the Red peril in Asia, there was no salvation outside a close alliance between the American and Chinese nationalist secret services. Thanks to their frogmen operating from Taiwan, who were picked up by American warships, the Guomindang had already pulled off some promising commando raids on the mainland. In 1951, William Ray Peers, an expert in this type of action, was sent to Taipei as head of the 'Company's' station there. (Many years later, Peers, after handing over to a CIA big shot, Ray Cline, was to lead the commission of enquiry into the My Lai massacre that took place during the Vietnam War.)

Straight after the rout suffered by the Guomindang soldiers, the Civil Air Transport had established itself in Taiwan. The CAT was the jewel of the CIA air empire: a company founded in 1946 to support Chiang Kai-shek's army, it recruited its pilots among the legendary General Claire Chennault's Flying Tiger aces (Chennault was a personal friend of the Generalissimo). In 1950, the Civil Air Transport was reorganised in the form of a subsidiary of a holding company connected with the CIA. Under this shelter, CAT pilots took part in opium-trafficking.

When Red Army troops broke through nationalist lines in 1949, some ten thousand Guomindang soldiers fled across the border into Burma. Their leader, General Li Mi, hoped to be able to carry out anti-communist guerrilla attacks from his base there. But he encountered nothing but failure. As for his men, they developed a taste for the country and for its women and many of them married young Burmese girls. Suddenly they were no longer interested in fighting to the death for the nationalist cause, which seemed already lost.

Li Mi found the solution to his problem. His soldiers were settling down in Burma? They needed to eat? The general embarked on the cultivation of poppies, with the aid and blessing of a 'charitable organisation' presided over by the Generalissimo himself, and of course with the help of their American ally. CAT pirate aircraft transported arms and ammunition to Burma for Li Mi's men. They returned to Taiwan with their holds filled to bursting with top-quality opium which Guomindang agents distributed throughout Asia via what remained of the overseas networks of the Green Gang. This CIA–Guomindang joint venture was a very lucrative enterprise. As it expanded, a newcomer came into play: the navigation company Sea Supply Inc. A senior official in the American intelligence agency, Desmond Fitzgerald, personally supervised Li Mi's operation. At his request, the CIA sent several dozen experts in guerrilla warfare to Taiwan. They were to train Chiang Kai-shek's soldiers with a view to the reconquest of the Chinese mainland, which was thought by nationalist experts to be imminent.

But, showing great foresight, the *Tewu* had already infiltrated several agents on to the remote Pacific island that had become the Generalissimo's last refuge. In 1948 Fu Yei and his wife landed in Taiwan as refugees from the mainland. Both in fact belonged to the Social Affairs Department: Fu Yei, whose real name was Zhu Fangqun, came from Beijing. A secondary school teacher at the time of the civil war, he had belonged to a clandestine communist network and militated in 'cultural' circles. He had been a Party member for ten years already but had never publicly aired his opinions. His 'wife', Xia Minghua, was also a teacher. In June 1949 the couple had already achieved substantial results, setting up two clandestine movements called the Youth League for the Liberation of Taiwan and the New Organisation of Young Democrats. On the mainland, the civil war was going in their favour. They were discreetly recalled in July to receive new orders from Li Kenong himself. Li wanted them to devote themselves solely to espionage activities and to drop their political work.

After making a detour via Canton and then Hong Kong, the two *Tewu* agents returned to Taipei, capital of Taiwan. They were very active and set up a very effective intelligence network within the university, with some contacts in private industry and inside the Ministry of Defence, where their friend Si Yilin was a member of staff. The network was financed by a fourth *Tewu* agent, a rice factory owner, Song Yuling.

Gradually Fu Yei and Xia Minghua extended their secret organisation until they had agents in the Ministry of Agriculture, the Taipei Oxygen Factory, the police academy, the administration of the railways. The Social Affairs Department set them huge objectives: to become acquainted with the topology of the Taiwan coastline, and find out about the organisation of the nationalist forces, the communications system on the island, and relations between the Guomindang services and those of their American and British allies.

There were other *Tewu* networks in Taiwan, operating completely independently of this one, in accordance with the basic rules of clandestinity. One of the best was run by Hong Guoshi. A former mathematics student at the university of Chongqing, he was already a longtime member of the Communist Party who had been assigned to 'special tasks' from the moment he joined. In December 1949 he began to throw his nets in Taiwan and very quickly brought in a fine catch, recruiting Zhou Shu, a journalist who specialised in Sino-American relations; Hua Chen, a sociology researcher; his brother-in-law Liu Tianming, a company chairman and a former senior official in Manchukuo. Unfortunately for Li Kenong, who once again was supervising the operation, Chiang Kai-shek's counter-espionage service broke up this organisation as early as February 1950.

The *Tewu*, however, was not alone in its intelligence activities in Taiwan. Stalin's intelligence service, the NKVD, also wanted information about the alliance between the CIA and the Guomindang. It was significant that it had only limited confidence in its collaboration with the *Tewu* and had decided to set up its own network. The lynchpin of Russian intelligence in Taiwan was a Chinese, Li Peng. A former freelance journalist for *The New York Times*, Li Peng had worked in Chongqing, the nationalist capital during the war, for the Central News Agency. It was there that he had met Sinenakov, a 'reporter' for the Soviet Tass agency. Both men were fervent admirers of literature. They had got on well together. Then, in line with classic secret service techniques, Sinenakov had given his Chinese friend money. More and more money. In October 1949, Li Peng decided to leave the mainland and go to Taiwan. The NKVD agent Sinenakov persuaded him to enter the service of the Kremlin. Besieged by his creditors, Li Peng was all too ready to agree.

In Taipei Li Peng made contact with another Soviet agent. Like Kang Sheng a native of Shandong, Wang Sheng-hu was an engineer who specialised in radio communications. He had been working for the Russians since February 1942. In February 1949 the Soviet Military Attaché in Moscow, Kulunchi, had sent him on a reconnaissance mission to Taiwan, where the skilful Chinese engineer established clandestine radio contact with NKVD headquarters for the Far East, Vladivostok.

Li Peng was for a while employed at the British Consulate in Taipei, then he joined the British section in the Taiwan Ministry for Foreign Affairs, becoming a first-class source of information for Wang Sheng-hu. Unfortunately for the two of them, Taiwanese counter-espionage became aware of their activities when they discovered Wang Sheng-hu's clandestine radio station (a 25-watt transmitter and a receiver of Soviet manufacture installed in his apartment at 113 Amoy Street). On 13 February 1950 the network ceased operating. The NKVD was thereby deprived of the precious information it needed on the American–Taiwanese alliance.

The *Tewu*, meanwhile, methodically continued its infiltration work. The CIA, without opposing the arguments of the pro-Taiwanese lobby, arguments whose premises at least they subscribed to, had set up their own department specialising in the problems of communist China. Logically enough, they decided that the best possible analysts of the country ought to have an in-depth knowledge of the language, and of local customs and attitudes. In a word, they ought to be Chinese – like Larry Wu Tai Chin, for instance, an ideal candidate totally won over by the American Way of Thinking, who had begun working for 'the Company' in 1948, as a translator at the American consulate in Shanghai, then in Hong Kong. In 1952, the Year of the Dragon, 'Larry', as he was known to all his American colleagues, decided to betray them by returning to the Red China fold. Larry Wu Tai Chin became an agent, a *Tewu* 'mole' within the the CIA. He was recruited by the Chinese in Japan, where the CIA had set up its listening post trained on China. For thirty-four years he was to supply his Beijing masters with intelligence on the intentions of their Washington adversaries, applying to the letter the Chinese precept: 'Dripping water eventually pierces the stone.'

The twenty-ninth of November, in the Year of the Dragon, was a baleful day for the Company. The pilot of one of their spy planes on a photographic mission over North-East China was shot down by the DCA. Jack Downey alias Jack Donovan was the first pilot working for the Chiang–US espionage team to fall into the hands of the Chinese communists. However, his arrest and trial by the military tribunal of Beijing's Supreme Court did not put an end to the programme of flights over mainland China by American planes, which was thought to be more productive than the frogmen operations organised from Taiwan.

The Year of the Dragon was a decidedly bad year for American citizens. In 1952 a young Chinese woman from Chicago decided to retrace her roots and visit her native country. Unfortunately for Min Chiau-sen, the ship she was sailing on sank off the Chinese coast. She drowned and her body was found by communist coastguards. The Social Affairs Department and its director Li Kenong believed in neither God nor the devil. But they recognised this as a heaven-sent opportunity to introduce into the United States a female mole as valuable as Larry Wu Tai Chin. Anxious not to waste time, Li Kenong asked one of his assistants to select an agent of the same age as the unfortunate Min Chiau-sen.

The choice fell on 'Lily Petal'. Despite her poetic name, she was a *Tewu* expert on American affairs. She spoke passable English. Armed with the drowned woman's passport, she arrived in Hong Kong, claiming that after being shipwrecked she had been picked up by Chinese coastguards then released by the Beijing authorities.

'A very strange story indeed!' marvelled the British Special Branch officers who interrogated her. It was not customary for the People's Republic, so given to spy mania, to show such kindness. But gradually they succumbed to Lily Petal's ingénue charm, for she gave a moving account of 'her' shipwreck and 'her' stay among the terrible Reds – why should anyone suspect her?

One of the British sleuths eventually stamped her passport. She had pulled it off. The Special Branch men went off to have a cup of tea without realising that, her innocent smile notwithstanding, they had just let a wolf into their American ally's sheepfold. No sooner had she arrived in New York than Lily Petal opened a Chinese restaurant and set up a spy network for the *Tewu*. It was to continue functioning without a hitch for the next thirteen years.

'Life is just a passing visit, death a return to the homeland . . .'

Lee Meng calmly awaited the moment when the executioners would come and open the door of her hot humid cell. The court of appeal in Kuala Lumpur, in rejecting her appeal, seemed to have rung her death knell. And her lawyer had just informed her that an appeal to the British was legally impossible. Was there any hope left?

Lee Meng was a young Chinese communist woman who had been arrested by British soldiers in Ipoh, a town in the state of Perak, on the Malaysian mainland. For possession of military weapons – a hand grenade – a jury composed of an English judge and two local assessors had passed the death sentence on her. A member of the Malayan People's Liberation Army, Lee Meng, like many others, had taken to the bush to protest against 'British colonialism', which, not content with refusing to grant the country its independence, had in 1946 divided it into two: Malaysia on the one hand, and the island of Singapore, with its huge port, on the other.

Stirred by the fate of the young militant woman, fifty British MPs decided to intervene by signing a petition. The Sultan of the state of Perak was not about to refuse these honourable Members of Parliament their request. Lee Meng, having been spared at the eleventh hour, remained in prison for some time and was then sent back to the People's Republic in an exchange of prisoners. Five of her Malay comrades less fortunate than herself did not escape the death penalty. Neither the British democrats nor the Chinese communists tried to save them.

There were a great many Chinese in Malaysia, not least of whom was Chin Peng, founder of the Malayan People's Liberation Army, who succeeded the traitor Lai Tek as leader of the Communist Party. The Chinese in fact constituted a majority in the country, a situation that made their struggle doubly exemplary in the eyes of Beijing, directed as it was against British colonialism and conducted by fellow Chinese. For this reason the Soviet NKVD were obliged by 'circumstances beyond their control' to stand down in favour of the *Tewu*, who were much more at home in Malaysia, if only for ethnic reasons.

In the Chinese capital a trustworthy comrade was following

closely the development of the conflict which the proclamation of a state of emergency by the British High Commission had officially sparked off in June 1946. Head of the Chinese CP's International Liaison Department's Research Bureau, Ke Bonian was very familiar with the situation in the Malay peninsula, with good reason: after graduating from the Sun Yat-sen University in Moscow, he had continued his studies in the United States and then in Australia, before moving secretly to Singapore. There he was active as Chinese 'Big Brother' to his young Malay comrades. It was largely because of his resolute action that the Chinese communists were able to take over the former Communist International networks in the ports and docks. The Chinese jealously guarded their new hunting ground, unwilling to share it with the Soviets. As a top-ranking militant very close to Kang Sheng, Ke Bonian's new responsibilities within the Research Bureau involved his being ready at any moment to assess the progress of the Malayan People's Liberation Army. An expert in intelligence and clandestine struggle, he proved thoroughly equal to the task.

The rebellion gained ground in the jungle but also in the villages. In the face of the Chinese and their agents, the British had to strengthen their operation. In the spring of 1950 Maurice Oldfield arrived in Singapore. He was to prove a formidable opponent for the *Tewu*. Having joined the intelligence service in 1941, he was an experienced veteran of counter-espionage and its labyrinthine complexities, and, at forty-five, four years older than Ke Bonian. It was to be a long and cruel war.

The British special services had to deal with a real epidemic. Since 1948 the Red fever had been spreading throughout the European possessions in Asia and the pro-Western regimes. Two large semi-clandestine meetings held in Calcutta served to launch this general offensive: the Conference for the Youth and Students of South-East Asia, on 19–20 February, and the Second Indian Communist Party Conference, on 1–2 March. These gatherings provided a cover for secret meetings between Chinese, Malaysian, Indonesian, Philippine, Vietnamese, Burmese and Indian communists. The aim of these discreet talks: to co-ordinate guerrilla activities that differed greatly in style and in objective, and to turn them into an effective strike force.

Naturally, the Chinese did their utmost to take control of this strange constellation of clandestine movements. They wanted to act as the link between all the communists in Asia, and for this reason were strongly opposed to the leftist initiatives and proposals of the Indians, who were eager to break out of Mahatma Gandhi's non-violent movement. While at the same time respecting the Soviet leadership of Cominform, for Mao Zedong, Kang Sheng and their comrades, it was a question of investing the Chinese CP with the role of protector over all the Asian communist organisations, an idea born of the contacts made by the Shanghai underground communists with 'fellow parties', Japanese, Korean, Vietnamese, and developed in Yan'an, the great Red university of the peoples of Asia.

'A spark can set fire to the whole plain,' Mao Zedong was asserting as early as January 1930. While the USSR and the West were moving ever closer towards the Cold War, for the Chinese it was a question of setting the whole of Asia alight, and of tending the fires that had started spontaneously.

In the Philippines, war had broken out again. The Huks were no longer fighting the Japanese alongside the Americans. They were no longer even asking for independence: the country was given independence in July 1946, when the United States renounced official control. But Washington had no intention of carrying these concessions too far: it had already imposed a client politician on the Philippines, Manual Roxas. This proved to be the spark that started the fire: Roxas, who had been more or less a collaborator during the Japanese occupation, was not much liked in the country.

In 1948 the Huks returned to the resistance, having changed their official name to the *Hukbong Magapalaya ng Bayan*, or National Liberation Army. But they remained essentially the same people. And the Philippine Communist Party continued as undisputed leader of the struggle.

Having learned the techniques of Marxist-Leninist guerrilla warfare in the texts of Mao Zedong and Zhu De, the Huks had a great admiration for Red China. Mao's victory over Chiang Kai-shek served to strengthen this sentiment.

What the Chinese communists could not understand was why they appeared so ungrateful. After all, they were helping the rebels by every means possible. Beijing mobilised all its nationals in the Philippines, bringing them together in satellite organisations such as the Philippine Committee of Overseas Chinese or the Philippine Branch of the Chinese Communist Party. The Chinese CP's clandestine bureau in the archipelago operated within these two organisations. The bureau's general secretary, Chanh Shan, the head of the Organisation Department, Yang Li-chao, and the treasurer, Lin Ke, were of course of Chinese origin. All of them worked in close contact with the local communist leadership and with the Huks.

However, this was not all. Eager to prove effective, the *Tewu* did not content itself with acting through its 'natural constituents', the communist militants. In true secret service fashion, it recruited agents within the enemy camp. Two individuals of aristocratic descent were selected as targets. The Philippines were formerly a Spanish colony ceded to the United States in 1899 after the short Spanish–American War. The descendants of the former colonisers still held a key position in a society in which they constituted the ultra-conservative wing. What better specimen of the élite Hispano-Filipino than Pedro de la Peña? He was not prepared on any account to conceal his anti-communist feelings. Head of the country's Defence Ministry's intelligence service, he was seen as an inveterate anti-Red. And yet de la Peña was working for the *Tewu*. His friend Antonio Chua Cruz, a millionaire press baron, was also employed by the *Tewu*, despite the anti-Huks and anti-Soviet crusade permanently conducted by his newspaper, *Free Asia*.

These two Caucasian agents of the Chinese secret services hid their game well. They were not unmasked until 1952 when the police arrested William Pomeroy and Celia Mariano. Pomeroy, who was with the US Air Force during the war, had settled in the Philippines as a journalist and student at the state university. Celia, who became his wife, persuaded him to share her communist convictions. Discovered among the couple's belongings were documents and detailed notes on the recruitment of Pedro de la Peña and Antonio Chua Cruz. The downfall of William Pomeroy and Celia Mariano and the arrest of the two Hispano-Filipinos marked the collapse of one of the best Chinese espionage networks, one that for two years had supplied the *Tewu* and the Huks with first-rate intelligence on the military and on the business fraternity. This excellent work could not but increase the prestige of their 'Big Chinese Brother', so efficient, so invaluable, in the eyes of the Huks.

In Malaysia, the British not only brought their secret agents into play – men such as Maurice Oldfield, or the former Coldstream Guard John Halkett Badderley – but also experts in guerrilla tactics and psychological warfare. In itself, this was a kind of tribute to the Chinese. The Americans thought it an excellent idea and dispatched one of their best professionals to the Philippines, an expert in psychological techniques and a veteran of counter-guerrilla action: CIA officer Edward Landsdale.

Edward, known to his friends and everyone else as Ed, did not have the same social pedigree as some of his better-connected colleagues in the CIA. He was a former employee of a publicity agency who, thanks to the Second World War, became a secret service and special missions ace. Furthermore, he was familiar with the Chinese way of thinking, having served as military adviser to the Guomindang army. To get the better of the indomitable Huks, he combined traditional methods with techniques of his own devising. It was Ed who put Ramon Magasaysay in power, as a new puppet leader. A kind of Ferdinand Marcos of his times, he was a little more presentable than Roxas, one-time collaborator with the Japanese. But he also invented an original psychological warfare ploy: exploiting the fear of vampires. A captured rebel had only to have his neck pierced with two little holes and be bled white to look like a victim of the bloodsuckers and the terrified Filipino peasants evacuated en masse the zones held by the Huks deemed to be haunted by the creatures. It was a cruel exploitation of popular superstition, but this was Asia, where the communist propagandists, or even the nationalists, would often break an egg in order to demonstrate the truth of the maxim: 'The yellow stays, but the white runs away.'

(Edward Landsdale was, incidentally, the inspiration for Graham Greene's portrait of the Quiet American: naive and cunning at the same time, whose perverse actions, undertaken in the name of democracy and effectiveness, lead only to disaster. Greene himself was a former secret agent, expelled from Indochina at the time of the French war.)

Nevertheless, the Maoist conflagration encroached on the plains, forests and towns of Asia. In Burma, there were several uprisings: the Karens, a national minority, rebelled with secret backing from the Chinese; so too did the Red Flag faction of the Burmese Communist Party, which tended to be pro-Maoist, while the White Flag faction remained close to Moscow. This was actually unusual at the time; it was not the intention of the Beijing leadership to launch pro-Chinese parties anywhere.

In Indonesia, the situation, which was extremely complex, required the *Tewu* to show exceptional diplomacy. The fairly large Chinese community was divided between those who supported Red China and those who supported Taiwan. At the beginning of the 1950s, the balance was still in favour of the Guomindang, which gave Beijing's men less room for manoeuvre.

Fortunately, the Chinese had an excellent ally within the leadership of the Partai Kommunis Indonesia in Alimin. Remembering the lessons he had learned from his communist teachers during his stay in Yan'an, he was able to explain the failure of a premature uprising that started in 1948 at Madion. Mao had himself said in 1934: 'Revolutionary war is the war of the masses: it can only be waged by mobilising the masses, by relying on their support.' Two survivors of the Madion, Aidit and Lukman, took refuge in China. They returned convinced of the effectiveness of the methods used by their Chinese comrades, and suddenly the pro-Chinese camp was in a stronger position.

Indonesia became independent in 1950. Beijing sent a very special 'diplomat' to Djakarta, the capital of the new state: the energetic and cunning Wang Renshu, who, having been born there, was very familiar with Java, the most densely populated of the Indonesian islands. After active service in the guerrilla war against the former Dutch colonisers, he had spent some time in Moscow as a representative of the People's Republic of China, before returning to Djakarta. A little too obvious, his subversive activities against the young Indonesian regime quickly earned him the acerbic criticism of the Minister of Foreign Affairs. So Wang Renshu had to soft-pedal his agitation, propaganda and intelligence activities. For he was, of course, a *Tewu* agent.

The Chinese communists were gaining ground in Asia, step by step. But they could not forget two major confrontations with the

West: the war in Indochina and the Korean War, which were to give the *Tewu* the chance to really show its worth. As usual, it was chance that lit the powder keg. A warrant officer with the paratroopers, wanting to fill his water canteen in a stream, came face to face with a Vietminh soldier wearing the traditional latania head-dress. Each as surprised as the other, both men fired their weapons and fled.

'Captain, there are Viet around!' the warrant officer told his superior in the First Foreign Battalion of Paratroopers, Captain Garrigues. A few hours later the jungle woke up. The Viets attacked the paras with machine-guns and mortars. They had a steely morale and their conduct in action was exceptional, surprising even the veteran paratroopers.

What followed was hell. Operation *Phoque* (Seal), started on 29 September, was intended by the leaders of the French expeditionary force in Indochina as an evacuation exercise for Cao Bang and the posts situated along the Chinese border. It quickly turned into a disaster. The Viets were resentful. They were also numerous and well organised. Moroccan troops and Legionnaires fell back along Colonial Route 4, ceaselessly harried by troops fighting for Vo Nguyen Giap, a former teacher at the Lycée in Hanoi. On 18 October, the French, who were completely disoriented, hurriedly evacuated Langson fortress, abandoning tons of ammunition to the enemy.

The disastrous flight along Colonial Route 4 cost the expeditionary force 2,000 dead, 13 canons, 112 mortars, 160 machine-guns, 380 automatic rifles. Under the surveillance of the Vietnamese People's Army's 'Bo Doi', 3,000 prisoners began a forced march to the prison camps. There, officers and men were 're-educated' with the help of methods inspired by those developed by Kang Sheng during the re-education campaign in Yan'an.

The Chinese in fact had a lot to do with this resounding defeat, the first suffered by the French during the Indochinese conflict. Mao had even sent to the aid of his comrade Ho Chi Minh one of his best generals, Chen Geng. However, he was not the only officer sent to help co-ordinate the Sino-Vietnamese offensive against the French. At Ho Chi Minh's personal request, the Chinese CP had dispatched to Indochina a team of military advisers led by Wei Guoqing, an excellent Red soldier who had been initiated into the techniques of guerrilla warfare in the shortlived rural base of Guangxi where he had fought alongside Vietnamese exiles and the future leader of Red China, Deng Xiaoping.

The grand Chinese CP–Vietminh alliance was extremely effective, thereby, they hoped, delivering a decisive blow to French colonialism and demonstrating to the Asian revolutionary movement the superiority of communist solidarity. Other men, Europeans, had already given proof of their internationalist sentiments – men such as Ernst Frey, an Austrian communist deserter from the Foreign Legion who became one of the first of General Giap's military experts, going by the name of Colonel Nguyen Dan. In September 1950, while his former companions in the Legion were being beaten on Colonial Route 4, Ernst Frey went to China, the Vietnamese comrades large rear base. The *Tewu* and the Chinese CP's International Liaison Department looked after him until he reached Vienna, where he was 'demobilised' by his country's Communist Party.

The *Tewu* had good reason to take an interest in France and the conflict in which she was involved in Indochina. And it was not simply because they wanted to help Ho Chi Minh and his comrades. Another motive was piastres, the currency minted by the French colonisers. The *Tewu* needed money to finance its foreign networks in Asia, Europe and the United States, and also discreet channels along which to transfer capital from one country to another.

This is how one of these networks operated in 1950: the Bank of Communications, in Hong Kong, which had official links with communist China, was the first relay post; through the intermediary of another company, it transferred the money to its Saigon branch, run by Cheng Zoukang; the piastres were then transferred to Paris. There, Lucas Pun, a Chinese of Portuguese origin, took care of the money. Born in Macao in 1921, Pun had been in France since 1939. He travelled a great deal, particularly to Britain and Switzerland. In both countries he had excellent contacts with some rich Armenians. The money went to wherever it was needed via the Union of Swiss Banks in Geneva, or even the Commercial Bank of Northern Europe, in other words the Soviet bank in France.

The newly founded People's Republic of China was engaged on several fronts: Malaysia, Burma, Vietnam, Korea, the Philippines, Indonesia. It all cost a great deal of money. Smuggling piastres was not enough. Like their Taiwanese enemies, the Party leadership decided to resort to a weapon as old as time: opium. In 1950 the *Tewu* recruited some former members of the Green Gang and Chinese gangsters who had been 'taught' by the Yakusa, the Japanese mafiosi, while the Japanese were in Shanghai. In exchange for their lives, and a privileged existence, they had to impart to communist agents the secret of how to manufacture the drug. In the regions of Shanghai, Beijing and Tientsin, but also in Xinjiang, special kinds of farm were set up to experiment in what the communist leadership discreetly called 'special products'.

Since the days of the Red Republic of Yan'an, it had been agreed that poppy-growing and drug-trafficking were the province of the special services. Deng Fa, former head of the Department of Public Security, and Li Kenong were already responsible for this 'work'. The *Tewu* therefore controlled the distribution of the 'special products' that went mainly to Hong Kong, on board harmless-looking junks. An additional but by no means negligible advantage was that the opium trade opened the way to establishing contact with the secret societies, which were very powerful in the British colony. Perhaps the legendary triads, not in the least bit communist, could be persuaded to become so in exchange for more sizeable sums of money?

'No!' was the response of the leaders and members of 14K, the most influential of the triads. This secret society, which was very closely connected with Chiang Kai-shek's special services and had numerous branches among expatriate Chinese communities, definitely preferred a free enterprise system to a planned economy, which was much less lucrative. However, this did not discourage the *Tewu* or Hong Kong's clandestine communists, who had been galvanised by Liao Chengzhi's frequent visits between 1947 and 1949. Party Secretary for South China since his release by the Guomindang in 1946, Liao Chengzhi, the 'Red seaman', was fully aware of the importance of Hong Kong. Someone who shared the same name as him, Liao Mosha, who ran the Hong Kong *Chinese Journal of Commerce (Hua Shang Bao)*, helped him in his work.

If the war in Indochina had obliged the *Tewu* to set up an international network as a matter of urgency, another conflict had the same effect: the Korean War. After the Second World War, Korea was divided because of the failure of the Americans and the Soviets, who together ousted the Japanese, to come to an agreement on how the country should be run. The North remained under communist control, with its capital at Pyongyang, while the pro-American South made Seoul its capital.

The Soviets attached ever increasing importance to the Korean peninsula, situated just opposite Japan, and now occupied by General MacArthur's American soldiers – and just opposite the USSR. The Russians continued to support Kim Il-sung, promoted through their efforts to the position of 'great war leader', within a leadership that remained none the less collective.

But Kim had dreams of glory. In 1949 he was already planning a grand-style military offensive to 'liberate' the South from American tutelage. Stalin may have encouraged him in this bellicose project, but certainly not Mao, who advised the Korean communists to be cautious: China was just emerging from a terrible civil war, she did not need another conflict on her doorstep. Kim Il-sung and his friends deliberately paid no heed to Beijing.

Numerous, well trained and well supplied, their troops attacked in June 1950, overwhelming the unfortunate Southern army, which came close to total collapse in the face of the communist invasion.

Western leaders were completely taken by surprise, although they had been warned of an imminent communist attack. The British vice-consul in South Korea, George Blake, had repeatedly informed his government of the aggressive plans of Kim Il-sung and the *Puk Choson Rodong Tang*, the North Korean Communist Party. Blake was a strange character, the son of a Dutch mother and an Egyptian father. Although he always had excellent information on Korea, he was not listened to by the British Foreign Office. There was good reason for this. The 'expert' on Red China whose opinion was most valued by British diplomats at the time was none other than Guy Burgess, who had been fascinated by Chinese communism since his student days at Cambridge, and who, together with his friends Philby, Maclean and Blunt, had been working since then for Stalin's secret services. In the summer of 1949, the Foreign Office asked him to deliver a series of lectures on the Far East and China to university students, but also to agents working for the Secret Intelligence Service.

Ironically, George Blake, who was captured by Kim Il-sung's soldiers, was in turn recruited by the Russian communist special services, after being subjected to intensive brainwashing. For it was during the Korean conflict that the methods tried out in Yan'an and in the first Vietminh prison camps were systematised. Western prisoners, particularly Americans, in North Korean gaols, where *Tewu* advisers and a few Soviet specialists were in control, were subjected to total indoctrination, using the most advanced methods of psychological manipulation. Western communists were apparently mobilised for this rather 'special' task – according to certain witnesses, the Australian journalist Wilfred Burchett, for instance, was seen talking to American prisoners wearing a Chinese uniform.

On 15 October 1950, the first detachments of Chinese 'volunteers' – they were actually regular forces – entered Korea. Their enthusiasm sustained by political commissioners, they came to the aid of the *Puk Choson Rodong Tang* troops, who were being harried by the Americans.

So, scarcely a year after it was founded, the People's Republic of China found itself deeply involved in an international conflict. Astounded by such 'madness', Western observers deduced that Mao could only be acting on Stalin's orders, forgetting that, regardless of the nature of its own political regime, China had always considered itself Korea's natural protector. Rather than lose face, the Beijing leadership was prepared to undertake enormous risks.

Mao sent General Lin Biao's army to Korea under the command of another military leader, Peng Dehuai. This was one way of reminding the young People's Liberation Army that no officer could lay claim to his men. Alongside Peng Dehuai appeared the inevitable Chen Geng, the survivor of the Shanghai underground who had become military adviser to the Vietnamese. Under their orders, hundreds of thousands of Chinese soldiers courageously faced the American and United Nations troops, who, although numerically inferior, were incomparably better equipped and backed by the most powerful airforce in the world, the US Air Force.

Each Chinese 'volunteer', by contrast, was equipped with a warm jacket, a gun and a piece of advice from Chairman Mao: 'The

Chinese People's Volunteers must look after every hill, every river, every tree, every blade of grass in Korea.' They also had to take care not to be captured alive by the imperialist enemy, of course. Unfortunately, many of them were captured and the CIA 'turned' a great number of them in the prisoner-of-war camps. When the war was over, they were released and returned to China. There they were treated initially as genuine 'martyrs of imperialism', then they were allowed home. Six or eight months later, men from the *Gonganbu Dui*, the armed military police who formed part of Luo Ruiqing's department, summoned them one by one for interrogation. The poor wretches who had agreed to work for the US secret services were all executed. The others, those whose only fault had been to fall into enemy hands, suffered the same treatment as their Soviet counterparts after the Second World War: they were sent in droves to the Chinese gulag, the sinister *Laogai*.

What precipitated the end of the Korean War was not anything that happened within the country but far away: in the USSR. On 5 March 1953, Joseph Stalin died. Mao was extremely upset: the Chinese communist leader revered Stalin, even though the latter had made things difficult for him. But Stalin's death left Mao with more leeway to bring to an end an increasingly absurd conflict.

The negotiations took place at Panmunjom, close to the front line. Xinhua journalists (New China News Agency) were among the first to arrive. One of them, Zhu Jiping, was very closely associated with Burchett, but also with the Chinese secret services, whom he conscientiously provided with first-hand details on the international press journalists, their states of mind and their views of events. In this way, the *Tewu* learned a great many important facts about what was going on behind the scenes on the Western side during negotiations.

On the Chinese side, a close collaborator of Zhou Enlai, an ex-Xinhua correspondent in Hong Kong, Qiao Guanhua, played an extremely important role in secret. The armistice was finally signed on 27 July 1953, in Panmunjom, confirming the division of the country into two fiercely opposed states who have been negotiating a definitive peace for more than thirty years now. For form's sake . . .

Almost immediately, Kim Il-sung regained a position of power. Stalin's death left him too with more room for manoeuvre. Surprising all those who had seen him as a mere lackey of the Russians, Kim Il-sung proceeded to carry out a massive purge of pro-Soviet Koreans. Nine hard-line Stalinists were actually executed. Their leader, Ho Kai-ye, 'committed suicide'. Coincidence? He just happened to be the head of the regime's secret police, which he had modelled on the NKVD with the help of Russian experts.

In Beijing, *Tewu* leaders, headed by Li Kenong, rubbed their hands, even though they were well aware – being better informed than the West, and with good reason – of Kim Il-sung's aspirations towards independence. In removing the head of the special services, the North Korean leader was leaving the door open to closer co-operation with China in a very sensitive area.

Since 1950 and their resounding defeat on Colonial Route 4, the situation had deteriorated for the French in Indochina. Despite several serious setbacks, the Vietminh became ever stronger, ever more aggressive, ever better organised. While Chen Geng had gone to Korea to help Peng Dehuai command the 'Volunteers' and then returned to China, the chief military adviser, Wei Guoqing, had remained in Indochina. Alongside the Vietminh, he played an active role in battles at Trung Du, Cong Bac, Ninh Binh. On several occasions French military intelligence registered the presence on Vietnamese soil of Chinese units specialising in military intelligence, without being able to do anything about it. Sometimes it was a matter of whole battalions, several hundred men . . .

This is not the place to review the whole Indochinese conflict until 1954. Everyone knows how it ended: in the débâcle of Dien Bien Phu, where French crack troops, in accordance with a debatable strategy, were parachuted in only to find themselves surrounded by the Vietminh's best units.

After intense fighting, the French position fell on 7 May. It was the first time a Western power had suffered a major military defeat at the hands of a colonised Asian people. The event had an enormous impact throughout the world, while the Vietminh press agency put out humiliating photographs in which exhausted French soldiers were shown with their arms raised before Vietnamese soldiers who stood a good ten or fifteen centimetres shorter than them. The agency proved less forthcoming on the very important, indeed essential role of the Chinese at Dien Bien Phu: the personal participation of Wei Guoqing in the Vietminh command aside, they were responsible for setting up a huge supply network of guns, ammunition and equipment.

Their underestimation not only of the strength and determination of Ho Chi Minh's soldiers but also of the support provided by Red China cost the French very dear, as was acknowledged in a secret telegram sent four days after Dien Bien Phu by the commander of French troops in Indochina, General Henri Navarre, published here for the first time: 'We were informed in reasonable time but Chinese aid did not begin until after we were already at Dien Bien Phu. We did not know of it until after they crossed the border, because of lack of information on China itself.'

After the French defeat, it was time for negotiations to begin. And the fledgling Chinese diplomatic services, backed by the *Tewu*, were about to show their worth . . .

The Soviet Dakota from East Berlin landed at Geneva-Cointrin

Airport at three thirty p.m. on 24 April 1954. An impassive-looking man in a long black coat emerged from the aircraft to a warm welcome from the Chinese and General Nam Il's North Korean team. He was wearing a borsalino hat of the kind worn by gangsters in the 1920s, pulled down over his eyes, and bore little resemblance to the young underground communist whose picture had been posted on the walls of Shanghai a quarter of a century earlier over the legend 'Wanted for murder'. And yet they were one and the same person: Zhou Enlai, who had come to Switzerland to negotiate the end of the war in Indochina with American, Russian, French, English, Vietnamese, Laotian and Cambodian delegates.

The head of the Chinese diplomatic service made a striking entrance on to the international stage in the Swiss capital, astounding journalists and observers once again with his ease of manner, his courtesy and his intelligence. His assistants, cloistered in their villa Grand Mont Fleury in Versoix, were much more discreet. And yet what a remarkable team they were: Qiao Guanhua, the former journalist who had been so active behind the scenes at the Sino-American negotiations in Panmunjom; Huang Hua, the man who informed the Western press that the Reds had 'liquidated' Dai Li; Zhang Weitan, a veteran of the legendary Long March, who had been promoted to the position of deputy minister; Ke Bonian, attaché at the Chinese CP's International Liaison Department, previously the architect of the first underground networks in Singapore, but now secretary to an even more important individual – Li Kenong himself.

The international press focused its attentions on Zhou Enlai, training its telephoto lenses on the villa Grand Mont Fleury, its mysteries and its exoticism. Only one Westerner, an employee of the telephone company, had entered the premises. So, apart from a few experts in secret affairs, no one else had noticed that the Chinese had sent the head of their espionage service abroad to negotiate in the West. While Zhou Enlai remained slim with the passing years, Li Kenong had changed: a moustache now adorned his fleshy face, he wore thick round glasses and, with his short-cut hair and inevitable Mao suit, he looked like a slightly ridiculous fat puppet.

Whenever Zhou was absent, Li Kenong became the official head of the Chinese delegation. He made notable efforts, often very successfully, to charm other representatives, appearing affable, courteous, accommodating. Like all the Chinese diplomats, he carefully avoided adding fuel to the fire, trying above all to restrain the Vietminh delegates, who wanted to make the most of their victory and obtain the maximum concessions from the defeated French.

'Man's heart is insatiable, the snake would swallow the elephant: remember, one must exercise self-control!' Li Kenong kept telling the Vietnamese communists, only one of whom, the very pro-Chinese ambassador to Beijing, Hoang van Hoan, seemed to agree. The others could always make sarcastic remarks about Li Kenong's paunch, irrefutable proof that their Chinese comrades had eaten the elephant Chiang Kai-shek.

Western diplomats fully appreciated this unexpected Chinese restraint. 'After dinner, a conversation took place between myself and Mr Li Kenong in the presence of Mr Tchang' noted the head of the French delegation, Jean Chauvel, in a confidential telegram addressed to the French Prime Minister, Pierre Mendès France, on 9 July 1954. 'It concerned Laos and Cambodia,' he added. 'I told Li Kenong of the difficulties that had arisen in recent days in the course of discussions between military experts. He said that he had not been informed of them and described them as regrettable. He added that in his view the problem of Laos ought to be resolved by the Laotians themselves.

'We then spoke of Vietnam. I said that Mr Pham Van Dong [one of the Vietminh delegates] having given me the idea, I was studying a political guarantee formula that would enable the Vietminh to accept a demarcation line that the conference could adopt. He thanked me for this information, adding that he considered it very good news . . .'

Evidently, Li Kenong could not have been more reasonable, or more understanding. Nor could the Chinese position at the Geneva conference have been more moderate – so moderate was it that it contained the seeds of differences that would later turn into open conflict between Chinese interests and those of their Vietnamese 'brothers'.

On 21 July, the peace accords were signed. These diplomatic negotiations had whetted Red China's appetite and allowed the Republic to appear as a fifth great power and not as a brilliant second to the Soviets, paralysed since the death of Stalin by a ruthless internecine war.

Working alongside Zhou Enlai, the architect of this great political coup, was Liao Chengzhi. The former 'Red seaman' knew the world and spoke several languages fluently. Thanks to his past service as a loyal son of the Comintern, he had the Soviet leaders and their Eastern allies just where he wanted them. Through his family, he was associated with the great upheaval of the early days of the Chinese Revolution, since his father – who had been assassinated in Canton in 1925 – was respected both in Taiwan and in the People's Republic.

His extensive travels abroad had taught Liao Chengzhi the importance of the overseas Chinese and he suggested to Zhou Enlai and some of the other leaders that the Party should firmly establish itself among them: allowing the Taiwanese to take advantage of Chinese nationalism by abandoning to them body and soul the 'overseas compatriots' would be the worst possible policy. On the contrary, Mao Zedong's red flag should supplant the Guomindang tricolor everywhere.

In 1952, while his comrades were inaugurating a propaganda radio station directed at neighbouring Japan, Liao Chengzhi arrived in the country under the pretext of attending negotiations between the Japanese and Chinese Red Cross organisations. In his youth, Liao had been a student in Japan. He spoke the language very well. Was it by chance that his stay there coincided very closely with the date when Larry Wu Tai Chin, the *Tewu* mole in the CIA, was recruited? A clever diplomat, Liao Chengzhi did not forget his rigorous training in 'secret tasks' and 'special missions'.

Throughout the whole of Asia the 'hundred flowers' of friendship associations were blossoming, thereby opening the doors to ideological penetration: in India, Pakistan, and Ceylon (now Sri Lanka), and in Indonesia, Laos and Cambodia. Dedicated to 'bringing together nations', they, along with the Xinhua news agency, served as a cover for *Tewu* operations. Having initially firmly placed itself in the socialist camp, renouncing any middle way between capitalism and communism, following the lead given by Zhou Enlai and Liao Chengzhi, Red China now sought to free itself of this too restrictive image and to open up to the Third World. Meanwhile, in the rest of Asia many pro-communist insurrectional movements were marking time. When Nehru's India and Tito's Yugoslavia invited China to take part in a world conference of 'non-aligned countries', their invitation was enthusiastically welcomed. The proletarian peoples of Asia, Africa and South America arranged to meet in April 1955 at Bandung, a small Indonesian town on the island of Java.

Zhou Enlai almost failed to turn up at the conference. A member of the Hong Kong airport cleaning staff, Zhou Zeming, known as 'Cho Cho', had placed a bomb, supplied by Taiwanese secret agents, in the hold of an Indian aeroplane, the *Princess of Kashmir*, in exchange for six hundred thousand dollars. The Generalissimo's spies thought that the Chinese Minister for Foreign Affairs would be travelling aboard an Air India craft. The plane exploded in midflight and fell into the sea, killing eleven people, but Zhou Enlai was not among them. Tipped off by its informants in Hong Kong, the *Tewu* had asked Zhou Enlai to change planes. The Chinese secret service even took the precaution of informing their British Special Branch counterparts in Hong Kong, through the local Xinhua representative. The British, who thought it was a mere propaganda exercise, conducted a very superficial search. Nehru's counter-espionage service, the Intelligence Bureau, took the matter very seriously. Also alerted by the *Tewu*, they dispatched one of their best officers to Hong Kong; working hand in hand with the Chinese, he took part in the investigation that led to Cho Cho's undoing.

Having travelled via a different route to Bandung, Zhou Enlai, with his usual panache, caused considerable surprise among most observers by giving a very 'Third World' speech. With the assistance of such high-level colleagues as Liao Chengzhi and Huang Hua, the head of the Chinese diplomatic services was determined to play the card of 'openness' to the full.

Thanks to the work of this team, China gradually forced its way into the very select club of world powers. She lacked only the supreme symbol of military power: the atomic bomb. A terrifying weapon, the secret of which a man forgotten by everyone was trying to give to his country. His name was Kang Sheng.

14
Kang Sheng's A-Bomb

'The Chinese communists have stolen the plans of a Japanese missile. Their spies have also stolen numerous documents in France concerning the manufacture of nuclear weapons.'

So said the *Naicho* in May 1960. The *Naicho*, the abbreviated name for the *Naikaku chosa shitou*, the Cabinet Research Office in Japan, which acts as the Prime Minister's own security service, was already at that time the most discreet, the most effective, the best informed of the Asian secret services with regard to Red China. It was not, like its Taiwanese allies, drunk on ideology. And the Japanese interest in nuclear research in China was very understandable. Scarcely fifteen years had passed since the explosion of the first atomic bombs on Hiroshima and Nagasaki.

The CIA, whose U2 spy planes continued to fly over China, reached the same conclusion: it would not be long before the People's Republic had the bomb. However, they lagged behind the Japanese on information.

On 23 January 1963, the big Tokyo daily the *Yomiuri Shimbun* published a scoop: 'The *Naicho* has discovered that a member of the Japanese Communist Party's Central Committee, Riken Hakamada, has been told by his Chinese friends that they will soon be carrying out a nuclear test.'

To forestall these rumours, Marshal Chen Yi, Chinese Minister of Foreign Affairs, summoned the Japanese press in Beijing: 'We do not have any plans to carry out nuclear tests for a long time yet,' he assured them in his Sichuan accent. 'We have practically solved the problems of manufacturing the atomic weapon, but our industrial under-development constitutes a serious handicap for the present.'

The Marshal was lying, but some people were not taken in.

At about the same time, in Paris, a solidly built man with a chiselled face, a roguish look in his eye, his hair dyed black – more out of vanity than any taste for mystery – climbed the steps of the Elysée Palace. Thanks to his friend the head of the President's bodyguards, he could come and go as he pleased. Marc Bergé was trusted by De Gaulle. A former resistance fighter, now head of the police intelligence department Renseignements Généraux (General Intelligence), he had been responsible for bringing Nazi war criminals to trial. His sound international contacts, his taste for secret worlds, his common sense – all these things made him perfect to run his scarcely concealed little strategic intelligence unit at the Quai d'Orsay, the French Foreign Office. Reliable sources in Asia, contacts in the British Intelligence Service in Hong Kong, a host of missionaries, Jesuits and other China-watchers, old stagers in cassocks, had enabled him to penetrate the Chinese mystery.

General De Gaulle understood the first time he glanced through the file compiled by Bergé: his analysis, the most thorough yet compiled, contained disturbing news indeed. 'This time there's no room for any doubt,' the General must have thought, 'we must recognise China!'

The General was well informed on China. There was a flourishing literature on the subject, from Simone de Beauvoir to Etiemble, calling for its official recognition. André Malraux, who had a passionate interest in China and respect for the historic stature of people like Mao, was soon sent to the Far East as a kind of super-ambassador. And then of course there was Edgar Faure. At the end of 1957, the former Prime Minister had published a book on China, *Le Serpent et le Tortue* (*The Snake and the Tortoise*). By way of conclusion, he raised a question that could not fail to be of interest to De Gaulle: 'Should we not throw a bridge between East and West, as between the snake and the tortoise? So that one day men shall no longer have any memory that there used to be an impassable abyss between them.'

Edgar Faure was well informed: his source in China was a personal friend, Jacques Locquin, head of the Agence France-Presse in Beijing and political adviser to the SDECE, the French secret services. Six months later, having come to power, De Gaulle turned to Faure for advice. Malicious cartoonists depicted Faure with slit eyes, eating a bowl of rice; malicious tongues dubbed him the French government's *'éminence jaune'*.

General De Gaulle had a thousand reasons for recognising China, both strategic, and for internal policy. He would have liked to strike a blow against the Soviets, who were then urging the French Communist Party to form a Union of the Left with Guy Mollet's SFIO (the socialist Section Française de l'Internationale Ouvrière). The Chinese card was a trump. It would also allow the President to distance himself from the Americans.

The Bergé file gave De Gaulle all the information he needed. Never made public, this is what it said:

In just a few months from now, Popular China is going to explode its first atomic bomb. Kang Sheng, the head of Chinese espionage, has for a long time been in charge of the special services in this matter of nuclear armament. He has been able to make progress in this field thanks to his Swiss network in Berne, run by the Third Secretary at the Embassay, Lin Shuhua. It has to be noted that there are some one thousand Chinese agents operating throughout the whole of Europe, a good hundred of them in France. Kang Sheng has had missile launching pads set up in Tibet, and the main base for carrying out nuclear tests is on the border of Xinjiang with Lob Nor, where preparations for the first atomic explosion are being made.

Kang Sheng has done everything to get rid of the Soviet secret services. His counter-espionage department has eliminated all the KGB networks in the vicinity of these nuclear bases.

Having obtained the help of Russian scientists, including the father of the Russian A-bomb, Piotr Kapitza, he has now got rid of them too, relying solely on Chinese atomic scientists.

On 27 January 1964, France recognised Beijing as the sole representative of the Chinese people. At a single stroke of the pen, Chiang Kaishek's Nationalist China seemed to have been deleted from the diplomatic map. In April, Major-General Huang Zhen, who had met Kang Sheng in Shanghai during the 1930s, presented his letters of credit to the French President.

Then, on 16 October, Bergé's prediction came true: in the deserts of Xinjiang, China exploded its first A-bomb, a 20-kiloton device. On the same day, so propitious for China in that Year of the Dragon, Nikita Khrushchev fell from his pedestal like a rag doll. A double victory for Mao.

China had joined 'the club', as that select group of nuclear powers was referred to at the time. Thanks to its scientists, its strategists and its secret agents. And largely thanks to Kang Sheng, who, it was erroneously thought, had been removed from power, when in fact he had been operating in the shadow kingdom of which he was master.

As previously mentioned, in the summer of 1936, Kang Sheng had made a brief trip to Geneva as one of the hundreds of delegates attending the World Youth Congress. A summer marked by the outbreak of civil war in Spain, it had brought democrats, republicans, communists and anarchists from all over the world to form the International Brigades against Franco.

Another militant just as mysterious as Kang Sheng also came rushing to Geneva. The two men had met in Shanghai at the beginning of 1933, then again in Vladivostok, where they had both been involved in the setting-up of Red squadrons of Koreans, Manchus, Chinese. This man of tremendous drive called himself Kleber, after the revolutionary leader of the Army of the Rhine. As a senior officer in the Soviet Army of the Far East he had inflicted a resounding defeat on the Japanese at Lake Khasan. But he will always be remembered as the defender of Madrid. In Spain he was said to be Canadian, a soldier of fortune converted to communism. In fact he was an Austro-Hungarian whose real name was Manfred Stern.

A career officer, Stern had joined the Bolshevik cause in 1918. After having familiarised himself with all the intricacies of the art of insurrection at the famous Frunzé Military Academy in Moscow, he was sent to join the Red Army's secret services, run by Jan Berzin (whom he would meet again in Spain). With the Russian Revolution of 1917 as its model, the military section of the GRU, together with the Comintern's 'M Apparatus', taught local Communist Parties paramilitary techniques for seizing power by violence. Stern became the leader of this operation. Concealing his real identity and going by the name Stein, he was behind the disastrous Hamburg uprising at the end of 1923. In 1927 he had been involved in the setbacks suffered in Shanghai and Canton. Attached to the Army of the Far East, he basically felt more at ease with conventional war. The war in Spain drew him from his Siberian retreat.

But the stout fellow in the buff-coloured raincoat who slipped into Switzerland that summer of 1936 had also been charged with a mission as a secret agent. In addressing the small group of men and women, residents of the Eastern bloc and Swiss communists, he was as direct as usual: 'The Centre is planning a reorganisation. The war in Spain is just a prelude to an even greater conflagration. It has already begun in China . . . We must organise small cells in Lausanne, Berne, Geneva, Basle and Zürich . . .' That is, a support network for the Russian forces fighting in Spain, but also a clandestine nerve centre in anticipation of a general war.

His mission accomplished, Kleber went to Spain and officially took charge of the International Brigades in November. His network lay dormant, then, at the approach of the Second World War, it underwent a metamorphosis. Under the leadership of the Hungarian Sandor Rado, the GRU's *rezident direktor* in the Swiss Confederation, this group – soon linked up with the Red Orchestra – rendered the most useful service to the Centre, to Stalin and the Soviet Union.

Until the end of 1943, they sent thousands of radio messages giving information on the Nazi war machine to Stalin's office. At the beginning of 1944, the *Bundespolizei* (BUPO), the Swiss Federal Police, carried out an enormous raid which led to the dismantling of the network set up seven years earlier thanks to Stern. Rado and his deputy, the German Rachel Dübendorfer alias Sissy, were arrested, which made them famous overnight. Released in 1945, they returned to Russia. Stalin sent them straight to the Gulag, where they encountered their old friend Manfred Stern. Some members of the Stern network, however, escaped arrest in Switzerland and remained undetected. By the most extraordinary coincidence they were part of the team that enabled Kang Sheng, twenty years later, to give China the bomb, as the 'Sonia' File proves.

It was from the winter resort of Caux, overlooking Montreux, that Stern's network had been broadcasting since 1936. A pretty little chalet where 'Sonia' lived quietly, with two children and a housekeeper, who, like her, was German. According to her passport, 'Sonia's' real name was Ursula Hamburger, born in 1907. Under the name of Maria Schultz, wife of Alfred Schultz, she had become adept in the art of espionage first in Poland, then in China. The Schultzes had settled in

Shanghai in 1931, after 'Sonia' had trained as a radio operator at the Leninist Technical School. Their arrival coincided with that of Richard Sorge, the Russian espionage and Comintern superstar, who, from his small hotel in Hong Kong, established a vast Asian network. It was the journalist Agnes Smedley – one of Mao Zedong's American Egerias – who introduced Sorge to Sonia, and doubtless to their mutual friend, the secret agent Wang.

'I arrived in China accompanied by two foreign colleagues, who had been assigned to me by the Red Army's Fourth Bureau,' Sorge later recounted, when he fell into the hands of the Japanese counter-espionage service. 'I knew there was only one person in China I could count on, Agnes Smedley, who I heard of in Europe. I asked her to help me set up a network in Shanghai and in particular to select my Chinese collaborators. I worked mainly with Wang, my relations with the others being only incidental. Wang supplied me with intelligence from various sources.'

Wang was none other than the expert on military intelligence and infiltration of the Guomindang, Chen Geng. Whenever he passed through Shanghai, he usually stayed with Kang Sheng, in the peace and quiet of the French Concession.

When Richard Sorge went back to Moscow at the end of 1932, the Schultzes' mission assumed even greater importance, especially as Chinese radio communications were often interrupted on account of the repression. Moscow decided to reorganise its espionage operations in the West, beginning with that in Switzerland.

'Military Intelligence is bristling with Trotskyites!' the NKVD henchmen would readily say of their great rival the GRU, the head of which, Berzin, had just been sent to Spain. Thus it was that Maria Schultz became Ursula Hamburger and found herself in Switzerland organising a new network. Manfred Stern had chosen her because he liked her sangfroid, her initiative, her expertise as a radio technician in China.

Alfred Schultz remained in China. Disoriented, probably incapable of overcoming his loneliness, he made some security mistakes and ended up in one of Chiang Kai-shek's gaols. Sonia was badly hit by this, but continued none the less to operate with a rare energy. The misfortune stimulated her. She benefited from the support of the Swiss Communist Party's clandestine apparatus. Pierre Nicole, her boss, nicknamed her 'The Mouse' the first time he met her, because she was 'small, with a pointed face, and as though made restless by a feverish inquisitiveness'.

At that time they were operating from a chalet on the shores of Lake Gabiule, with a transmitter-receiver usually hidden with Nicole's parents-in-law. One evening Moscow Centre complained that the signals from Sonia's radio were too weak.

'Obviously, comrade! You set up the aerial between two trees!'

Nicole exploded: 'Do you want it to be visible from the road, which is regularly used by military patrols? It has worked all right until now, there must be some other reason . . . perhaps something to do with atmospheric conditions.'

'I suppose you know more about it than I do, although I'm the one who studied radio at special school.'

In a frenzy now, Sonia banged her equipment, trying to get it to work. There was a blue flash and the valve went dead. 'God, it needs a new valve. We must re-establish contact. I'm going to give you an address, of someone reliable who will give you a replacement,' murmured Sonia to Nicole, almost purring like a a cat.

'In the middle of the night, it's out of the question! Do you want to get us caught?'

Showering Pierre Nicole with abuse, Sonia turned on her heels and slammed the door behind her.

The very next day, Nicole had the radio repaired, but insisted to Rado that Sonia should be thrown out and replaced by a radio technician friend of his, who was a member of the Communist Party. Only Moscow Centre could take such a decision. And Sonia's group did not really depend on Rado, who was lying dormant, recruiting intelligence sources for the future. Sonia meanwhile recruited Alexander Foote, a British citizen who had fought with the International Brigade. She patiently introduced him to secret warfare so that one day he would be able to take her place. And that day was nearing.

Sonia had been shaken by the signing of the Nazi–Soviet pact on 23 August 1939. The very next day Moscow Centre announced that it would have to withdraw its agents from Germany and sever radio links with German nationals working for the Russian services within the Third Reich. In other words: we are not going to spy any more on our new Nazi friends. And she was unaware at the time that the Soviet NKVD was handing over to the Gestapo German communists who had taken refuge in the USSR . . .

In September something else cropped up. His name was Alex. A German – real name: Franz Ahlmann – he had also fought with the Brigade in Spain. The GRU sent him to Switzerland to set up a new radio station and Sonia undertook to find him a place to stay. But as soon as he arrived in Switzerland, he was caught by the Federal police and the network came within a hair's breadth of catastrophe.

Meanwhile Foote was happily tapping out messages and was able to take over from Sonia. She changed her name once again, by marriage this time: she married Leon Beurton, a British citizen who was a member of the network. This enabled her to travel to London in December 1940. (Her husband did not join her there until 1942.)

The main reason for Sonia's transfer did not become clear until a long time afterwards. Over and above the war between the Axis powers and the Allies, by 1942 another, secret battle was being waged, between the USA and the USSR: the battle over nuclear research.

In Russia, a team of atomic scientists had been assembled directly under the aegis of Beria, the Russian spy chief, who sorted through information received, checked it and evaluated it. They were Piotr Kapitza, Dimitri Ivanenko, Igor Tamm and Nobel Prize-winner Nikolai Semenov. However, another scientist in the West decided to help them. Not through any love of communism, nor admiration for the USSR at war, but prompted by a sense of balance. Klaus Fuchs, the son of a Lutheran pastor, had inherited some sound principles: peace, he believed, could not be guaranteed as long as any state had a monopoly of nuclear weapons. So this German émigré, a recently naturalised British citizen, decided to hand over the secret of nuclear arms to the Russians. He confided in Professor Jürgen Kuczynski, who, of Polish origin, had like him emigrated to England. In principle, Kuczynski was a man above all suspicion: his father, a professor at Oxford University, was renowned for his teaching of economics. He had himself worked for the American intelligence agency, the Office of Strategic Services (OSS), during the war. However, Jürgen Kuczynski had a sister, Ruth. In 1942 she was living in England under the name of Ursula Beurton.

After the war, Klaus Fuchs confessed all. Yes, he had informed the Russians about the Manhattan Project, about the nuclear tests, about their experimental centres in Birmingham, Canada, Los Alamos. Yes, since 1942, Ursula alias Sonia was not only his 'contact', but it was she who transmitted the precious secrets by radio, which meant that Fuchs did not have to make any contact with an embassy.

Fuchs, who was condemned to twelve years' imprisonment, gave the British and American counter-espionage people enough information to identify other atomic scientists guilty of treason. One of them, an Italian physicist who had fled Mussolini's regime, had worked with Fuchs in Canada; his name was Bruno Pontecorvo. He had emigrated first to the USA, and then to Canada and was connected with the Swiss network through one of his brothers. When the Western authorities began closing in on him, in 1950, he disappeared and went over to the East.

In fact, the Red Orchestra in Switzerland had a lot more surprises in store. One of its leaders was responsible for liaising with the French Communist Party's espionage network, the famous 'Service B'. Later, he worked with the French atomic scientist Frédéric Joliot-Curie. Another Swiss member of Service B recruited the film-maker Gillo Pontecorvo, the brother of the scientist who was a disciple of Joliot-Curie – the Bruno Pontecorvo who subsequently worked for the Chinese. The Chinese themselves were part of the set-up. In Berne, for instance, at the Nationalist Chinese Embassy, the press attaché, Pao Xienju, was in fact working for the communists. In the Red Orchestra he was known as Polo, as in Marco Polo.

At the heart of the secret battle that enabled China to manufacture the atom bomb, though, was a slender little man with penetrating eyes masked by large horn-rimmed glasses. Born in 1907 in the province of Zhejiang, he was the son of one of the leaders of the huge Fourth of May movement. At the university of Beijing, his physics professors had noted that Qian Sanqiang was several light years ahead of his fellow students. Having carried off numerous diplomas and obtained a grant from the nationalist government, he was eager to discover the world. In 1937, China rose up against the Japanese. Researchers of Qian's stature require the serene calm of laboratories, subdued debates in large amphitheatres, stimulating meetings with the greatest minds of the century. France, with its Popular Front government, seemed to him a haven of peace. At the end of 1937, no one would have thought that this Chinese youth timidly walking up and down rue du Cardinal-Lemoine was going to change the face of the world.

On Paul Langevin's recommendation, Qian Sanqiang was eventually admitted to the Collège de France. The man who admitted him had just founded a 'laboratory for atomic synthesis' at the Centre National de la Recherche Scientifique (National Centre for Scientific Research); before even proving himself, his name was known around the world, for he had married Irène, the daughter of Pierre and Marie Curie.

Within two years, Frédéric Joliot-Curie produced experimental proof of 'the explosive rupture of uranium and thorium nuclei under the action of neutrons', in other words one of the experiments that led to the discovery of artificial radioactivity. The two men got on wonderfully well together from the outset. The entire team worked hard at new discoveries: Qian Sanqiang, Frédéric and Irène Joliot-Curie, but also Lew Kowarski, Hans Halban, Francis Perrin and the inevitable Bruno Pontecorvo, one of Joliot's favourite students.

In politics, where scientific certainties do not apply, Joliot was a tormented man. A patriot in 1940 during the Phoney War, he managed, together with French Service de Renseignements (SR, Intelligence Service) agents, to help remove samples of heavy water from the Collège de France before the Germans moved in. Two years later (the Nazi–Soviet pact having collapsed), he told Pierre Villon he was prepared to join the Communist Party. Cleverly, Villon suggested he remained an 'unofficial member', not actually recorded on the Party roll.

Qian Sanqiang understood his 'boss'; his country too, despite the Japanese attack, was torn apart by the struggle between communists and nationalists. Then the Beijing scientist's whole world was turned upside down in June 1940. He Cehui, a beautiful female atomic scientist with degrees from Shanghai and Berlin universities, joined the team; Qian married her.

When German troops entered Paris that month, the Joliot-Curie team lost many of its members.

'And you, my friends,' Joliot-Curie asked the Chinese couple, 'do you not wish to leave, like Halban and Kowarski, to continue your research work in a safer place? Will you not regret staying on in Occupied France?'

'We're staying. We have a lot of work to do here. And besides, what do we risk? After all, China is not at war with Germany.'

(This was true. Hitler had hesitated for a long time deciding which was the Third Reich's best potential ally, Hirohito's Japan or Chiang Kai-shek's China. And, despite the Sino-Japanese War, Berlin continued to maintain diplomatic relations with both governments.)

Qian was awarded his doctorate under the Nazi Occupation. Joliot seemed to be in league with the devil, taking part in scientific conferences in front of audiences of Wehrmacht officers. Once the Gestapo arrested him, only to release him again. His wife, Irène, even got authorisation from the Germans to go to Switzerland for medical treatment. Qian Sanqiang, who had been awarded a chair under the Nazi Occupation, also established a link with Switzerland, making contact via Lyons with a member of the Red Orchestra.

This group of atomic scientists was heavily protected. Everyone was courting them, starting with the Nazis, but they took advantage of their situation to play a double game – in favour of the Resistance.

The Germans tried several times to seduce the Chinese couple: 'We will place at your disposal everything you need to work under the best possible conditions on the manufacture of the new weapon,' proposed Admiral Canaris, the head of the Abwehr, German military counter-intelligence, who in September 1940 paid them a personal visit. The British, slower off the mark, said more or less the same: 'You ought to rejoin your friends Kowarski and Halban in London, so that you can continue your work,' suggested Colonel John S. Wilson, an Intelligence Service emissary. Wilson knew what was at stake: he had recently been head of the Norwegian section of the Special Operations Executive, and the SOE in Norway was the prime mover in the 'heavy water battle' – heavy water, or deuterium oxide, $D_2 0$, being a liquid capable of curbing neutrons and therefore an ideal agent for the disintegration of the uranium chain. This heavy water – including the samples saved thanks to Joliot-Curie in 1940 – came from the Rjukan factory, in the mountains of Telemark in Norway. Colonel Wilson and his successors in SOE had organised an unremitting series of attacks and acts of sabotage on the factory, which was under German control.

Professor Qian turned down both offers. From the pretty Savoy chalet where these discussions had taken place, Qian could easily communicate with the people he considered worth talking to: the Russians. All he had to do was cross the border. One of the leaders of the local communist Resistance was a member of Red Orchestra, and also a close friend of Joliot-Curie . . .

Playing an active part in the liberation of Paris as President of the Front National (National Front), a cover organisation for the Communist Party, Joliot-Curie, a deputy in the Consultative Assembly, became High Commissioner for nuclear energy. His first initiatives were welcomed by everyone: the atomic reactor Zoe and the creation of the Centre for Atomic Studies in Saclay. That year, at Joliot's request, Qian Sanqiang received the prestigious Henri de Parville Prize from the Académie des Sciences de Paris. As an article in the Chinese press belatedly revealed, 'with his wife He Cehui, also a physicist, [Qian Sanqiang] discovered in 1946 and 1947 the principle on which the tripartition of uranium and its quaternary fission is based. His work led to a deeper understanding of the way nuclear fission works.'

Another of Mao Zedong's mistresses was the American journalist Anna-Louise Strong, so it was easy for her to obtain an 'exclusive' interview with the leader of the Revolution. The publication of her interview became a world scoop, of the kind every reporter dreams. Some time later, Kang Sheng and Chen Boda decided to include it in the *Selected Works of Chairman Mao*. In August 1946, when fortune seemed to favour Chiang Kai-shek, Anna-Louise Strong asked Mao what he thought about the atomic bomb.

'The atomic bomb,' replied the leader of the Chinese Revolution, stubbing out one of his Manchu cigarettes, 'is a paper tiger which American reactionaries use to frighten people. It looks terrible, but it isn't. Of course, the atomic bomb is a weapon that can cause huge massacres, but it is the people who decide the outcome of a war, not one or two new weapons.'

But Mao had vowed to tame this 'paper tiger'.

Two years later Qian Sanqiang returned to China and promised to work day and night on the creation of the Chinese bomb.

At the end of 1949, the People's Republic having only just been founded, a restricted, ultra-secret committee was set up, directly under Mao's supervision. The chairman of the Nuclear Council, as it was called, was the celebrated writer and President of the Academy of Sciences, Guo Moro.

At that time Kang Sheng was officially excluded from the highest offices, and even from the leadership of the special services. Seemingly, he devoted himself entirely to his role as governor of his native province, Shandong. In reality, he became responsible for the Nuclear Council's monitoring group. A past master in the field of disinformation, Kang Sheng knew how to make his opponent mistake the shadow for the prey itself.

In the 1950s, Qian Sanqiang was appointed deputy for Shandong. It would have seemed logical, therefore, that the two men should meet to discuss the running of their province. But Kang's conversations with a dozen or so scientists and with the security and Party leaders in the know were of quite a different nature: 'We must repatriate the maximum number of scientists who have studied in the West, such as Comrade Qian, as quickly as possible. We are going to ask the Soviets for practical help, without harbouring any illusions. We must determine which regions are the richest in the non-ferrous metals necessary to this project. I shall be responsible for the protection of the whole operation as regards the Americans and all those who might try to put a spoke in

our wheel . . .' There was no doubt to whom Kang Sheng was referring: in the long term the 'Soviet comrades' fell into the latter category.

The first strategic region was Xinjiang, Chinese Turkestan. For Kang
Sheng, a new battle was about to take place in Xinjiang, where he had
confronted the Soviets fifteen years earlier. But he was in a different
position now, representing the power of sovereign state, and not the
doubtful enthusiasm of a band of vagrants and starving revolutionaries.

In December 1949, Mao Zedong went to Moscow, the one and only
trip he ever made outside China. He was accompanied by Wang
Dongxing, his chief bodyguard but also the person who kept the Chinese Gulag supplied. Agreement was reached on the joint exploitation
of the Xinjiang uranium deposits. But the secret accord was not signed
until 27 March 1950. Russia also promised to withdraw its troops from
this vast desert region. In exchange, plans were made to set up a company run jointly by Moscow and Beijing to exploit the non-ferrous
metal resources of the province – in other words, all those necessary
for the nuclear programme.

The indefatigable Qian Sanqiang immediately went up there.
Already a caravan of rust- and sand-eaten old jeeps full of technicians were driving backwards and forwards across the province. Their
mission was to detect uranium or thorium deposits and identify the
most suitable sites for the establishment of nuclear bases. They settled on Alashan Kou, Dzungarian Gate, on the border with Soviet
Kazakhstan, whose bunkers are today full of nuclear reserves. Close to
the villages of Ürümqi and Yining loom the dismal blockhouses of the
Laogai labour camps. The 'living dead' incarcerated there laid the
foundations of the nuclear kingdom.

The triangular area between Lake Lop Nur, the town of Yuli and the
Turfan Depression soon became famous when nuclear tests began. It
was quite a venture at the time. Mongol bandits, Uygur pillagers, Red
Army deserters, desert brigands, stray Guomindang soldiers and the
famous Manchu tiger-hunters attacked Qian Sanqiang's flying col-
umns. When, one day, Qian was injured in an ambush, his wife He
Cehui was able to replace him at a moment's notice. The conquest of
Xinjiang continued.

Meanwhile, the Korean War was at its height. The Americans were
threatening to use the atomic bomb against the North Koreans and
therefore against the Chinese expeditionary force. Mao Zedong, who
had just lost one of his sons in Korea, berated the Nuclear Council:
'We must tackle our enemies quickly. We must have the bomb!'

The Russians, on the other hand, were no more anxious than the
Americans to see the Chinese in possession of atomic weapons.

Kang Sheng underlined this problem at one of his briefing sessions:
'The exploitation of the mineral wealth of these regions will no doubt
lead to major difficulties. For we must not forget the Soviets. In
Dzungaria, situated between Russian Kazakhstan and Xinjiang,
Soviet engineers are building a railway which will extend to Dubna in

the USSR. To guarantee the security of their technicians and workers against rebellious Uygur, Kazakh and Kirgiz tribes, the Russian troops have occupied this territory. Under one pretext or another, they do not allow anyone to enter the area, or travel in it, except those carrying a special pass.'

At first, the Chinese accepted Russian assistance in exploiting Xinjiang. But they had no choice. And they were not fooled. Kang Sheng set up parallel networks to manufacture the atomic weapon. Furthermore, he and his services pursued a kind of non-violent guerrilla war, constantly harrying the Russian border guards. A persistent story that went round at the time was that special teams of young Chinese women, would make surprise visits to the border posts. The Russian KGB guards would be invited to drink large quantities of Manchurian liquor and while they snored in a drunken stupor, the Chinese would move the frontier markers in order to gain ground. At the same time, Kang Sheng's men falsified maps with the purpose of claiming back territory from the Soviets that had been taken from the Chinese during the time of the tsars.

During the same period, Soviet scientists welcomed their Chinese counterparts in Moscow, starting with Qian Sanqiang and his assistant Wang Ganzhang. On their first trip, in February 1953, the Chinese team visited the biggest power station on the western shores of Lake Baikal, Atomgrad Number 2. The head of the *Gonganbu*, namely the incorruptible Luo Ruiqing, Minister of Security, was a member of the delegation. The secret services were involved in every stage of the manufacture of Beijing's atom bomb. In April 1955, Luo Ruiqing nominated his own administrative director within the *Gonganbu*, the Manchurian Zhou Xiong, to the post of Deputy Minister of Geology. He was in charge of prospecting in Xinjiang and other regions, with the aid of Soviet equipment for detecting radioactivity. His role in the operation was essential . . .

The *Gonganbu* was deeply involved in the nuclear programme for another reason: the manpower needed to build the atomic sites – exhausting work in the deserts of Xinjiang and Mongolia – was drawn from the Chinese labour camps. It was the *Gonganbu*'s Eighth Bureau that kept charge of the human masses in the camps. The head of that department, Liu Wei, also became Deputy Minister of Geology in 1955, whereupon his deputy, Wang Dongxing, took over the running of the infamous Eighth Bureau.

In Xinjiang, several thousand men were detained in Number 1 Prison near Ürümqi and in the labour camp of Tatamutu, near Yining Airport. In Mongolia, those held in Pashan Camp, near Hohhot, were also put to work. The 'Mining Department Area' of Baotou was a cover for another concentration camp, but a very special one this time, whose inmates built the atomic factory that began producing plutonium 239 in 1964, the Baotou mines being rich in the requisite deposits.

The year when the first Chinese A bomb exploded, a persistent rumour circulated, even reaching Hong Kong, which claimed that before the Lop Nur explosions, the *Gonganbu* had offered almost a hundred prisoners a strange deal. 'If you agree to build shelters in the area around the Turfan test site you will be given a remission of sentence, and you will be released.' These guinea-pigs would not have stood much chance of surviving the ordeal unharmed, and even if they had, it is highly unlikely that the *Gonganbu* would have let them live. No one knows if the *Laogai* prisoners agreed. Or even if it happened at all.

It is possible this was a story deliberately circulated by Red China's enemies, lurking in Moscow, Washington or Taipei. Maybe it was simply another instance of psychological warfare – like the rumour put about by the Chinese themselves during the Korean War in which the Americans were accused of resorting to germ weapons.

In March 1955, Guo Moro publicly applauded the Sino-Soviet Scientific Alliance. In April, the Chinese and the Russians signed a new agreement relating to the setting up of an experimental nuclear reactor and the sending of some one hundred Chinese technicians to the USSR. Everything seemed to be going well. But Chinese distrust of Moscow was beginning to strengthen.

Kang Sheng and Qian Sanqiang had settled upon a crucial objective right from the start: the building-up of a huge team drawn from Chinese citizens trained abroad returning to the mother country. Stalin, in his day, had acted similarly when he fixed the return of Piotr Kapitza to develop the Russian atomic weapon. Credit for the setting-up of a Chinese brains trust, though, must mostly fall to Kang Sheng, who enjoyed the support of two Central Committee bodies, the International Liaison Department headed by Wang Jiaxiang, and, in particular, the United Front Work Department, headed by Li Weihan. The Department of United Front Work, operating inside China and abroad, aimed to attract politically uncommitted men and women to Communist Party policy. Abroad, it played on the patriotism of the huge overseas Chinese communities: what Chinaman does not at least dream of being buried in the land of his forefathers?

There was, however, an external factor which played a significant role in the repatriation of Chinese brains: the Peace Movement. Frédéric Joliot-Curie was president of the movement. Scientists such as Pontecorvo, Fuchs and Bernal had decided to supply information to the communist states out of their concern for equity; to secure peace in the world, they thought, it was better that there should be a balance of nuclear power and at the same time a huge international movement for denuclearisation.

The writer Guo Moro was, from 1955 to 1963, Vice-President of the World Peace Congress chaired by Joliot-Curie. But at the same time, as President of the Academy of Sciences and a member of the Nuclear Council's secret triumvirate, along with his friends Kang Sheng and

Qian Sanqiang, he hoped to provide China with nuclear armaments as soon as possible. This was a classic technique of the communists, who talk all the more loudly of peace in order to drown the rumbling of their death-producing factories.

Dismissed from office after Stockholm's appeal in 1950, Frédéric Joliot-Curie never made the trip to China. But in Vienna, in 1952, at an executive conference of the World Peace Congress, he met his student prodigy, Qian Sanqiang.

The Chinese atomic scientists who had returned to the homeland were active in the World Peace Movement. Wang Ganshang, for instance, a graduate of Berlin University, had gone to the USA in 1943, where he had worked at the University of California. In 1948, the Chinese services organised for his return and he became deputy director of the Physics Institute of the Academy of Sciences. The mathematician Hua Luogeng, on the other hand, studied at Cambridge. He then spent time in the USSR before teaching at the University of Illinois in the USA. In February 1950 Hua returned to China to take charge of the Academy of Sciences' Institute of Mathematics.

The return of the physicist Zhao Zhongyao was extremely eventful. After completing his studies in England and Germany, he joined the Institute of Technology in California in 1934. For quarter of a century he specialised in research into gamma rays. This Chinese scientist was so trusted by the Americans that he was authorised to observe the first atomic tests at Los Alamos. Then suddenly, in September 1950, at the instigation of the United Front, he packed his bags for Beijing. But at Yokohama, in Japan, the American authorities grabbed him and castigated him for divulging nuclear secrets to the communists. At the height of the communist 'witch-hunts', the FBI could not be accused of being over-subtle: the following month they handed Zhao over to the Guomindang. By some strange convolution, though, he turned up in February 1951 among the communist delegation at a meeting of the World Peace Congress in East Berlin. Subsequently made deputy director of the Nuclear Physics Department, he spent long periods at the Russian nuclear research centre in Dubna.

Equally active at the same Californian Institute as Zhao was the atomic scientist Qian Weichang, who returned to China in 1946. Of all these scientists, he was without doubt the closest to the Communist Party, if not one of its secret members. His former head of research in the United States carried even more weight with Kang Sheng: Qian Xuesen was indisputably one of the world's greatest specialists in aerodynamics and aeronautical research. During the Second World War, he became head of the rocket section at the American Bureau of the Scientific Council for National Defense. His old professor, Theodor von Karman, insisted that the formula for supersonic propulsion, which he had discovered, should carry his name: the Qian Formula. After the fall of the Third Reich, Qian was one of the scientists sent to Peenemünde to interrogate Nazi scientists. But the Cold War set in immediately afterwards and the FBI decided to prevent him from leaving the USA.

Qian Xuesen even had a taste of prison, when American counter-intelligence services announced that they had seized eight big trunks in Honolulu, destined for China, stuffed full of documents, reports and scientific theses. But it was impossible to prosecute one of the greatest scientists of the age for espionage. On payment of a fine of $15,000, Qian was released and allowed to return to his Californian Institute of Technology where he was confined to working on preparations for the first lunar expeditions. Not until October 1955 was he allowed to return to China, in exchange for nine American citizens. Unlike ninety per cent of overseas Chinese who returned to the People's Republic, including some of his many scientist friends, Qian Xuesen suffered no persecution during the Cultural Revolution, and, thanks to him, Beijing fired its first nuclear warhead missile in 1966.

In August 1958, Qian Sanqiang became China's official Director of Atomic Energy. This was public acknowledgement of the existence of a vast atomic research programme and a barely concealed way of marking the beginning of a new era, of China dissociating itself from the Soviets.

In May, at a meeting of the Warsaw Pact countries of Moscow, Chen Yun had warned the Kremlin against an 'overestimation of imperialist forces'. The following month, in an article in the *People's Daily* that drew a lot of attention, Kang Sheng reproached Yugoslavia for 'playing into the hands of American imperialism'. Kang Sheng was making strikes against Khrushchev indirectly . . .

A secret document took account of this new situation. In 1958 the Central Committee's Military Commission issued an eight-point statement for limited distribution. The Military Commission is the highest military authority in China, since it determines the Party's national defence policy and also serves as a chamber of political control over the army. It was mainly addressed to the Technological and Scientific Defence Committee:

1. Whilst developing nuclear capability, our country does not intend to attack any adversary, but to dissuade an enemy from attacking us. This will prove an advantage in propagating the international proletarian revolution and colonial independence movements.

2. Our main objective can be summarised as developing nuclear weapons in order to safeguard peace, to prevent the disaster of a nuclear war overtaking the human race, and bringing about disarmament and the destruction of all nuclear weapons.

3. We must concentrate all our efforts in order to build thermal nuclear warheads capable of powerful explosions, and carriers capable of transporting these warheads over long distances. We do not at present envisage constructing tactical weapons.

4. While developing nuclear weapons, we ought to adopt a dual policy of 'pressing on in order to make big gains' and 'leading from the front' instead of following in the wake of others.

5. The nuclear armament programme must take priority over all other national projects.

6. Developing the nuclear weapon is a key policy of our Party, both at home and abroad; scientists must serve this policy, not the opposite.

7. We must quickly train young technicians and scientists drawn from the ranks of workers and peasants. The training of those who still continue this work is decisive.

8. We must create an independent security system to ensure absolute secrecy and protect our nuclear programmes.

On 20 June 1959, the rupture with the Soviets was brutal. Moscow, no doubt encouraged by the dismissal of the pro-Soviet Marshal Peng Dehuai, tore up the secret treaty uniting China and Russia in the field of nuclear development. Krushchev ordered the recall of the thousand technicians sent to assist China. China itself, meanwhile, maintained contacts with atomic scientists from the Eastern European countries. So it was that Klaus Fuchs met Qian Sanqiang in the German Democratic Republic and gave him numerous documents that helped to speed up Chinese research. He had just emerged from prison in England, after obtaining a remission of his sentence for reasons of health. He was a broken man. If he had in the past given help to the Soviets, it was with one idea in mind: that no state ought to have nuclear supremacy. Under these circumstances, it was logical that he should come to the aid of the Chinese, who were faced with a certain degree of nuclear supremacy within 'the socialist camp'. Bruno Pontecorvo had helped the Chinese for the same reason, working in Xinjiang with the American atomic scientist Joan Minton.

Xinjiang was in fact a hive of activity. All the nearby Soviet consulates were closed. Kang Sheng carried out raids and neutralised dozens of spies working for the KGB. Two armoured divisions moved into the area around Lop Nur. Dummy buildings were erected to dupe foreign reconnaissance flights (several American U2s were shot down over China during that period). The Chinese built numerous installations in the Alashan Plateau caves. According to the Taiwanese special services, in 1962, physicists from North and North-West China arrived *en masse* in Xinjiang, as well as large numbers of geological teams. Uranium 235 was produced in Lanzhou from 1963.

Mao's dream was about to come true. Within fifteen years, the Kang–Guo–Qian triumvirate had pulled it off: at 3 p.m. Beijing time, on 16 October 1964, a huge explosion shook the Turfan Depression. In the middle of the rocky desert steppe a big red mushroom suddenly appeared.

15
The Great Return

In the more distant past Kang Sheng's native province of Shandong had been called 'Lu', a handsome character which combines *yu*, meaning fish, with *ri*, meaning sun. But a fish which comes out of the water to bake in the sun is but a fool. So the character *lu* also means 'imbecile'. Kang Sheng therefore demonstrated indisputable humour in adopting as a new pseudonym the name of Lu Jushi, which means both 'the gentleman scholar who has retired to Shandong' and 'that old intellectual fool'.

In painting these three characters with his finest brush, the former head of the secret services not only gave an accurate description of his situation but was also indulging in his favourite pastime. From March 1949, when he was removed from office as supreme head of the *Tewu* and returned to live in Shandong, Kang Sheng devoted his time to a number of artistic activities: engraving in jade and agate, drawing on lacquer, rereading the great classic novels he was so fond of, or rare pornographic books officially banned by the censors. However, his passion was painting and calligraphy, and he signed his works, executed in the classical style, with his new name. He would often stay up late at night, as he had done in his early youth when he copied out whole passages of *The Dream of the Red Chamber*.

But how could a person as nervous as Kang, who chain-smoked and drank too much and who was, furthermore, shortsighted, produce such graceful works, full of freshness and attention to detail, in which one could almost sense the rustling of a leaf, the quivering of a butterfly, the rumbling of a mountain?

Lu Jushi had chosen to emulate a master who shared his temperament: Bada Shanren. In 1644 this painter-poet, related to the imperial Ming family under the name of Zhou Da, saw Beijing fall into the hands of the Manchu invaders. It was the end of a dynasty. A small Ming empire took refuge in the South. At the age of twenty, he gave up public life in order to become a monk, and for the next twenty years of his life he became a wanderer, roaming the monasteries along the Blue River. It was then that he began to paint, and his art was a rejection of the Manchu world rather than a renunciation of life. One day a Manchu gang tried to take him captive – perhaps they knew that Bada Shanren was related to the deposed Ming emperor? – but he got himself released by pretending to be mad. In depicting the simple joys of life, the quiver of happiness to the point of ecstacy, Bada launched the Chinese school of symbolism and allegory in painting that revealed a hatred of the Manchu invaders through the most innocent subjects. And the delicate vein of leaf, the velvet smoothness of a lotus flower, the airy softness of a feather in the wind, the lustre of a scarab could turn at any moment to rage.

In the shadow of the monasteries, Bada Shanren would give himself over to spiritual experiences in order to achieve harmony of body and soul, unifying chaos and ecstasy. He would attack the paper, stark naked, in a complete frenzy, having consumed large quantities of liquor, and transcribe on to the virgin sheets the total opposite of his state of near madness: joy in life and the sweetness of nature.

Bada Shanren belonged to the school of Xie Yi, painting with broad strokes, but he revolutionised his art. It is understandable why Kang Sheng should have subscribed to this tradition, through a kind of identification with Bada Shanren; some would even say it was a matter of reincarnation. (Only his closest friends knew that Kang Sheng concealed his identity behind the name of Lu Jushi, and they noted that his pseudonym had a religious meaning in the Buddhist world: 'the man bound by religious vows'. Kang Sheng never left anything to chance . . .)

In 1949 Zhou Enlai and the official poet Guo Moro protected Rongbaozhai, the Beijing art gallery founded in 1906 specialising in reproductions. In the 1960s, its director, Huang Mao, agreed to make prints of some of Lu Jushi's works. Some orginals found their way into art galleries in Hong Kong, London, New York and Tokyo. How many art lovers have a canvas by Lu Jushi in their private collections, unaware that he was for fifty years the head of Chinese espionage? Kang himself was a collector of old masters, but also of contemporary works. The Lu Xun Academy of Arts in Yan'an had a department of drawing and painting. Kang Sheng, who had overseen the Academy since the time when his mistress Jiang Qing was taking the drama department by storm, discovered some very talented artists there, among them the painters Li Shaoyen and Sheng Rojian. Another artist who rightly attracted his attention was the veteran of the Long March, Huang Zhen, future ambassador to France and then Minister of Culture.

Meanwhile, Guo Moro's Japanese wife Guo Anna had abandoned her kimono in favour of the sober suits worn by wives of Party officials. Her great pleasure in life was to go and have a giggle with the lively Cao Yi-ou, Kang Sheng's wife, who was for the first time enjoying the tranquillity of a 'bourgeois' existence. Anna and Yi-ou opened exhibitions and bought paintings. Their husbands, meanwhile, exchanged *chengyu* – four-character proverbs – and other magnificent calligraphic works that adorned Chinese reception rooms. Out of deference to that other great master Mao Zedong, people did not say that Kang Sheng had the finest brush stroke in China, but it was not far from the truth. When the great theoretical magazine *Hongqi* (*Red*

Flag) celebrated its twenty-fifth anniversary, it was Kang Sheng whom they invited to do the calligraphy for the editorial on the front page.

The poet Guo Moro and Kang Sheng were good friends. As though to console Kang for what seemed to all intents and purposes like a temporary fall from favour, Guo one day sent him a *chengyu* he had written, magnificently calligraphed. Its message was clear: 'The important thing is to remain on the left.'

Kang hung the silk scroll inscribed with four characters in the 'wild grass style' in the entrance hall of his house and kept it with him for the rest of his life.

Qingdao, 'green island' and beer capital!

Let us put ourselves in Kang Sheng's position. It was better for him to spend most of his time there than in Jinan, the administrative capital of Shandong. Admittedly, you could get a good pancake in Jinan, but it was no longer the chic dynamic place it had been in the 1920s. From 1949, Qingdao, under Kang's governorship, became a developing seaside resort as well as a big industrial town and military port. Situated less than a hundred kilometres from Zhucheng, where Kang had trained as a teacher, perched on the peninsula between the Yellow Sea and the magnificent Jiazhou Bay, Qingdao enjoys a very gentle climate all the year round. Originally a little fishing village, the town was born, like Kang Sheng, in 1898, with the German invasion, which explains the breweries and famous Qingdao beer that goes so well with a dish of prawns and sea cucumbers. This was the town – that today has a population of one million inhabitants – for which Kang Sheng, as a young man in 1919, had thrown himself into political battle against the Japanese who had taken over from the Germans. And it was on these fine sandy beaches that he one day persuaded his former pupil Cloud Crane to become his mistress – unbeknown to Comrade Yu Qiwei!

The lovelives of the communist leaders were never simple. As has been previously mentioned, Yu Qiwei had a sister, a superb actress called Yu Shan, who took against Jiang Qing the moment she set eyes on her, in Qingdao in 1931. Mao's future wife also wanted to be an actress: undeterred by Yu Shan's attempts to put her down, she flirted with all the men in the small world of theatre, wearing her tightly fitting green *qibao*, with a mandarin collar and a slit up the side of the dress, under which, in the Shanghai fashion, she wore nothing else. Yu Shan was afraid her rival would pounce on her husband, like an eagle on a hare, so she urged her young brother, Qiwei, a romantic revolutionary, into the arms of Jiang Qing.

All this was past history. Had much changed since? Thanks to Kang Sheng, Jiang Qing had now become Madame Mao. And everything was more or less fine during the Yan'an period. As the wife of a senior official, anxious to become China's First Lady and dreaming of former empresses, she did not want to squabble over Mao's philandering.

However, he continued to bed more than one comrade. The other Party leaders accepted his indiscretions without a word: 'To carry out the Revolution well, I need to be able to keep up my morale!'

In 1948 the People's Liberation Army was approaching Beijing. They bivouacked some three hundred kilometres from the city. The General Staff was preparing for the final offensive. Then a theatrical troupe turned up to entertain the men. Leading the troupe was the devilish Yu Shan, now divorced and living further north, in Zhangjiakou. The mayor of Zhangjiakou was a big bloated administrator who was calmly waiting for the end of the war and for the 'liberation' in order to take office as mayor of Tientsin. He was none other than Yu Qiwei, Yu Shan's brother and Jiang Qing's former lover.

Mao was bewitched by the charms of the spirited Yu Shan and had a passionate affair with her, to the point that she entered Beijing with him on the Day of Victory. Was Mao going to abandon Jiang Qing, as he had abandoned his previous wife, He Zizhen? Installed in the Palace of Zhongnanhai, Yu Shan became the leader of the Revolution's official concubine, and Jiang Qing simply a second wife. She grew fearful and turned to her friends. Kang Sheng was one thousand kilometres away, but Zhou Enlai lent her a sympathetic ear. A man who favoured stability, Zhou preferred Mao's legitimate wife to the new intruder – exactly as he had done in 1937, when, as far as Jiang Qing was concerned, the roles were reversed. However, in the autumn of 1949, the Communist party leadership, deeming Jiang Qing to be 'very tired', sent her for a rest cure in the USSR.

It is true that she was tired. It is true that she wanted to travel. But it is also true that she became the deserted wife of China's leader at the very moment when he came to power. Yu Shan's standing was so high that she accompanied Mao everywhere, even attending his official meetings. However, Mao eventually tired of her. At the beginning of 1950, Jiang Qing was back in Beijing and moved into Mao's sumptuous apartments. Jiang Qing had come a long way from the poverty, destitution, cold and hunger of her youth. But she and her husband now slept in separate bedrooms.

Jiang Qing's 'relapse' was not long in coming. In 1952 the Shanghai starlet was again deemed to be 'very tired' and again sent to Russia. On the way there, she stopped over to visit Kang Sheng in Shandong. While Cao Yi-ou served tea, the two former lovers readily agreed: 'Basically, we have fallen from favour, because of each other!'

Kang Sheng did not doubt that his dismissal had come as a result of political disagreements. Liu Shaoqi, Premier of the Republic, wanted to install his own men; and the former chief of the Social Affairs Department was Mao's most loyal supporter. His comrade from Shanghai days, Zhou Enlai, as usual favoured moderation: Kang Sheng's part in the appalling rectification campaign in Yan'an reflected badly on the whole Party nomenclature. The army, for its part, had not appreciated his attempt to take control of military intelligence and security. Finally, in the early 1950s, it was expedient to humour Stalin, and parodoxically Kang Sheng, once a Comintern delegate and one of Stalin's favourites, had already blotted his copybook by liquidating pro-Soviet elements. A technical detail had allowed the secret service chiefs Li Kenong and Luo Ruiqing to point to a grave error of judgement.

In March 1949, Kang Sheng was given the responsibility of organising the 'liberation' of his native province, Shandong. He had intended to capture the leaders of the Guomindang garrison in Qingdao, and in particular Wang Zhi, author of a famous manual on 'Mao Zedong Thought on Military Insurrection', and head of Chiang Kai-shek's military intelligence service, the *Qingbao*, during the civil war. Not only had Kang Sheng drawn a blank but, worse still, his own principal private secretary, Zhao Yaobin, had turned traitor and gone over to the Guomindang. Wang Zhi had taken him to Taiwan, where he concentrated on the anti-communist struggle, working for the new military intelligence service, the *Qingbao Ju*.

Jiang Qing's stay in Shandong was brief, but no doubt, even then, as they recalled the good old days in Yan'an, the former actress and the 'retired gentleman-scholar' thought that they should mount a come-back.

Kang Sheng had not been stripped of all power within the Communist Party. On the contrary, as governor of Shandong he was the most senior official in the province, conserving a place in central government (as well as in the crucial Sino-Soviet Friendship Association). His wife, Cao Yi-ou, also had a seat in the Shandong people's government, which was where she made her first major public appearance. She also acted as second-in-command in the running of the regional Communist Party.

Finally, in January 1950, Kang Sheng added to his panoply of titles that of Member of the Administrative and Military Committee of Eastern China, one of the five big geographical areas established after the communist takeover of power. Kang was well acquainted with the head of this important politico-military body. Born in 1905 in Nanchang – the cradle of the Red Army – Rao Shushi had been a student with Kang Sheng at Shangda, the famous revolutionary university of Shanghai. Before the 1927 uprisings, Rao, together with Liu Shaoqi, had organised the workers' movement in Shanghai. Then he had taken the same route as Kang Sheng: after receiving secret service training in the USSR, he had been sent to Europe and America to carry out clandestine missions on behalf of the Comintern. And like Kang Sheng, Rao returned to China in 1937. In Yan'an he ran the Social Affairs Department's radio section, and was chiefly responsible for communications with Moscow. Finally, as deputy to Liu Shaoqi, political commissioner to the new Fourth Army, he had ended up in the highest echelons of Eastern China. The two men, who both respected and feared each other, had therefore followed parallel careers.

Kang Sheng did not know it yet, but in joining this alliance forced upon him by destiny he was getting caught up in something that a few years later could well have cost him his life. Kang Sheng's efforts were obviously focused on building up a sound economy in a province bruised by war. Qingdao was a wonderful example of the way in which he had turned his native province into a political stronghold where he could enjoy a lot of support. After 1949 Qingdao became a major centre for the textile industry, but it also had a steelworks and tractor factories. The first totally Chinese-manufactured locomotive, the famous *Red Orient*, was made in Qingdao, with a 5,000 h.p. diesel engine. Major manufacturers of foodstuffs established themselves in the city and the distribution of Qingdao beer was expanded. A commercial port undergoing a rapid process of modernisation, Qingdao also became militarised, reusing some of the American wartime installations. After the first submarines arrived from the Soviet Union, Qingdao also became one of the Chinese navy's major strategic ports. All these achievements, obviously put in hand by a collective leadership, could not but enhance Kang Sheng's image as a clever administrator.

The development of tourism was another aspect of Kang's policy. Qingdao became a large seaside resort like Beidaihe, to the north of Beijing – that was very highly rated by senior Party cadres. But it also attracted ordinary tourists who liked the big sandy beaches, protected by nets – 'the sea's teeth' – put up to prevent naval frogmen spies landing from South Korea. Holiday camps, sanatoriums and oceanographical museums opened to complete the picture. Sometimes Qingdao was closed to foreigners, which meant that very senior officials were paying a visit. Kang Sheng was only too pleased to welcome them: for someone supposedly 'in retirement', he saw a great many people.

Of course, Shandong was no Garden of Eden. As in the rest of China, the rural areas were undergoing agrarian reform and 'counter-revolutionaries' were falling victim to repression. But Kang Sheng soft-pedalled the implementation of these policies – hence Mao's public criticism of the Shandong leadership at the conference on state security in 1951. The former head of the secret services was treating his citizens with kid gloves – and playing on the rivalry between Li Shiying, regional head of the *Gonganbu*, soon to become deputy governor of Shandong, and Wang Jinxiang, an administrator obviously keeping an eye on Kang Sheng. Wang was a personal friend of Luo Ruiqing, head of the *Gonganbu*, who soon summoned him to become vice-minister of security.

On 5 May 1952, Father Edouard Sauvage, a brave Breton missionary with a flowing white beard, was brought before the public prosecutor of Qingdao.

'You understand Chinese, Su Guanghu [Father Sauvage's Chinese name]?'

The priest nodded. He had begun working as a Franciscan missionary in Shandong in 1928.

'I have been officially assigned by the People's Government of China to inform you of its verdict on your case. It is as follows: you are first of all accused of having corresponded regularly with Corentin Legrand and of having supplied him with intelligence on China. You have furthermore been in regular contact with Fulgence Grosse, head of American espionage. In view of the enormity of your crimes, you are liable for the most severe punishment, but since you have shown good will in taking advantage of the efforts that have been made for your re-education, the People's Government of China, in its generosity, will not inflict any particular penalty on you but simply expels you from its national territory and forbids you ever to re-enter the country.'

The Chinese government may well have been indulgent, but Father Sauvage had nevertheless just spent two years in Qingdao prisons, accused of being a spy for the French Deuxième Bureau. The local *Gonganbu* were no jokers, whatever Mao might say. In his testimony, a further addition to the long list of Christian martyrology in China, the Franciscan would later give a detailed account of his imprisonment and describe his companions in misfortune: the mayor of a small town imprisoned for bad management, later transformed into a 'crime against state security'; a Jew from Chernigov in the Ukraine, former president of the Soviet Club of Qingdao; a German who was also accused of working for the US special services. (Three years earlier the Americans were sympathetic allies, but the *Gonganbu*'s new campaign gave free rein to traditional Chinese xenophobia.)

These prisoners, like Father Sauvage, had to learn two pages of characters, listed in vertical columns, from the moment they arrived in prison:

I On the manner in which the criminal should behave in his cell:
1. The criminal must confess to all his crimes, with total sincerity, before the People's Government of China.
2. He must denounce all the criminals of whom he has knowledge, whoever they may be.
3. He must study hard to rid his brain of anti-revolutionary thoughts and to acquire sound ideas.
4. He must set a good example and help other prisoners to trust in the People's Government.

II On the manner in which the criminal infringes the rules of the cells:
1. By obstinately refusing to confess his crimes.

2. By protecting criminals or refusing to denounce them to the People's Government.

3. By clinging to counter-revolutionary ways of thinking.

4. By displaying a lack of zeal in correcting the subversive thoughts of fellow prisoners.

5. By showing sympathy for any of his fellow inmates, which behaviour is directly opposed to the good of the People and liable for the most severe sanctions.

Father Sauvage had had a good taste of the *Laogai*, the Chinese Gulag. He therefore found it easy to understand how the Revolution could devour its children. On 15 September 1951, the chief warder had the priest brought from his cell. A cadre from the *Gonganbu*'s Qingdao office then asked the Frenchman all the same questions he had answered a dozen times already:

'Is the Church the only authority you recognise? Are you directly answerable to the Vatican? Can you give details of the forty crimes of which you have been found guilty? Do you belong to the espionage organisation called the Legion of Mary? Describe the other service in France to which you supplied information, the Deuxième Bureau.

'Write a potted biography of yourself – we will compare it with those you invented in the past! – describing your youth in Europe, your entry into theological college, and giving details of your activities in China since 1928 and the history of the apostolic curacy in Shandong to which you were responsible.'

The local *Gonganbu* – whose 'special section' was run by a woman – showed no mercy. What it wanted was a complete confession. Edouard Sauvage was prepared to admit to anything as long as he was not asked to renounce his faith. To his surprise, a few months later, he was joined in prison by his *Gonganbu* interrogator. In view of the criticisms made by Mao, who felt that repression was not being carried out with enough 'vigour' in Shandong, and in accordance with orders issued by Luo Ruiqing, he had been purged along with many of his comrades.

Kang Sheng had always laid great store by the solidarity between people from Shandong. Of course, his involvement with Jiang Qing, now no longer in Mao's favour, was the most striking example of this. In Russia, he had trained special agents such as Liu Changsheng, who was responsible for provoking the mutiny on the Dutch ship *De Zeven Provinciën*. And, going further back in time, he had also of course succeeded in penetrating the Green Gang in Shanghai, finding a job with Yu Qiaqing, opium-trafficker and President of the Chamber of Commerce. All because they had one thing in common – Shandong.

All this constituted the 'divine web', according to the theory of espionage elaborated a thousand years before by Sun Zi. Kang had his own theory of what he called 'invisible relations' (*touming guanxi*). It involved winning the allegiance of people who would help him to regain his lost power, sleeper agents, kept in reserve, who would be activated on a signal from him when the time came. Some of them remained so long crouched in the shadows that they did not become active for twenty years, until the time of the Cultural Revolution. Kang Sheng's critics found a name for it: the Shanghai Mafia.

Like any politician, he did people great favours, gaining the loyalty of civil servants promoted through his intercession, of soldiers, cadres, artists. His wife, Cao Yi-ou, canvassed the women's movements. The Guomindang archives that he had kept enabled him to blackmail comrades who were guilty of error. He continued to be thought of as a *Tewu* adviser, and it was easy for him, thanks to his contacts and his Beijing networks, to consult certain confidential archives belonging to the Social Affairs Department. There were many *Tewu* special agents, trained in the Kang Sheng school, who regretted the fact that the Old Man (*Kang Lao*) had been temporarily dismissed.

Four comrades in particular, all from Shandong, benefited from Kang Sheng's largesse. Frequent guests in his home, they formed a magic circle: Guan Feng, head of the Social Sciences Department at the Scientific Institute; Li Guangyen, of the Party's Upper School, to which Cao Yi-ou had free access; Zhou Jingfang, a woman who was on the new committee for the city of Beijing; and, above all, Wang Xiaoyu, who certainly deserved the label of 'Shandong mafioso'. A former commissioner in the Red Army, who had become deputy mayor of Qingdao, he was also known as the 'Drugs Baron' – for Wang was the drug-trafficking organiser for Kang Sheng's secret networks.

The Dixie mission was a rather quaint affair. The reader will remember Colonel Barrett who came to Yan'an in 1944 with the OSS mission and, speaking perfect Mandarin, could only make himself understood by Jiang Qing . . . At the time, Kang Sheng, like his comrades, could not but laugh at the sight of another cowboy, a robust 36-year-old graduate of the Wharton School of Finance, Lieutenant-Colonel Willis Bird. This friend of the 'Old Irishman' who headed the OSS, Bill Donovan, wandered all over China, a pair of revolvers inlaid with mother-of-pearl slapping at his thighs. In Chongqing, Dai Li, Chiang Kai-shek's masterspy, had been very much taken with Colonel Bird, who seemed to be reliving, here in China, the great exploits of his American ancestors during their conquest of the Wild West. The two men had become friends. Then, after the war, Dai Li was assassinated and Bird had joined the newly established Central Intelligence Agency. Under the aegis of Desmond Fitzgerald, head of CIA operations in the Far East, Bird went to Bangkok and founded a company, Sea Supply Incorporated (he had previously been a director of Sears Roebuck of Pennsylvania). It was via this company that the CIA supplied arms to the routed Guomindang troops from Yunnan, as well as to Phao Sriyanonda, leader of a Thai army consisting of 45,000 men that was in turn protecting the Guomindang.

In 1951 the CIA took a keen interest in the famous General Li Mi's stray soldiers, who were supplying the Agency with intelligence. But even more interesting was the fact that Li Mi and his army had made incursions into Popular China's territory on seven occasions. By 1952 it was all over. Li Mi settled in Burma with his 'Anti-communist Army of National Salvation' – and became involved in drug-trafficking. This was nothing new for the Guomindang: during the last part of the war against the Japanese, Dai Li had helped Du Yuesheng, the godfather of the Green Gang, to distribute the opium harvested from the huge fields in Yunnan, South China, which had been planted with poppies under the close guard of Dai Li's secret services. But the communists had gained possession of them and in their turn exploited them. It was then that a vast trafficking business was set up in the Golden Triangle, which was to flood the world with the drug right up to the present day. Incorporated within certain CIA paramilitary operations, this trafficking was mostly organised from Taiwan, where certain sectors of the Guomindang, in Chiang Kai-shek's son's entourage, were actively involved in it. Western Enterprise Ltd, the CIA's cover in Taipei, was also involved in an operation intended primarily to finance the anti-communist struggle, and which was run by a mysterious 'Mr Ku' who was in charge of the 'rescue' of Chinese citizens trying to get out of Red China. One of his agents, Chung Wing-fung, leader of the pro-Guomindang lobby in the United States and of the American People Against Communism League (APACL), found himself behind bars in San Francisco in 1958, having been caught by the Narcotics Bureau trying to import 130 kilos of pure heroin into the United States. The CIA's interests in Asia and the protection of the ordinary American citizen did not always coincide.

'It's not us, it's them!' the Guomindang nationalists reply whenever anyone mentions trafficking in opium and its derivatives, heroin and morphine. And they point an accusing finger in the direction of mainland China, alleging the communists of being behind a vast plot to 'turn the whole world into drug addicts'. However, the opium certainly exists and both Chinas are involved in it; and, as in the area of espionage, they are also engaged in destroying each other's networks.

In 1928 the communists had carried out an experiment that was to prove very successful: cultivating a field of poppies, making opium from them, and using it to debilitate the Guomindang army in the White zones. The future military leader of South Fujian, Tang Zhenlin, was put in charge of this secret mission and his men cultivated fields in the Jingganshan area in Jiangxi. Ten years later, trading in 'special products' was devolved upon the Social Affairs Department set up by Kang Sheng in Yan'an.

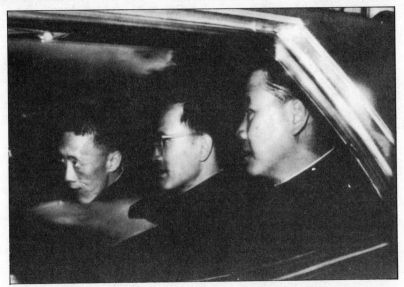

Gao Liang (*middle*), Chinese espionage chief in Africa (*A.F.P.*)

Behind Zhou Enlai and Norodom Sihanouk, Kang Sheng, the spiritual father of the secret police of the Khmer Rouge (*Keystone*)

Lin Bao and Zhou Enlai followed by the creators of the Little Red Book, Chen Boda and Kang Sheng (*Keystone*)

Madame Mao, Chen Boda and Kang Sheng lead the Cultural Revolution among the dancers of the Shanghai Ballet (*A.F.P.*)

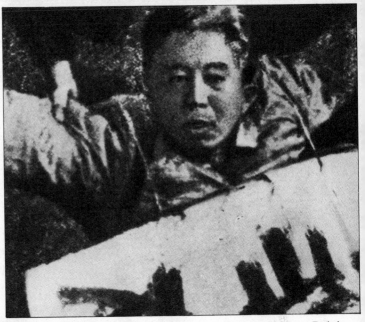

Head of the *Gonganbu*, Luo Ruiqing, humiliated by the Red Guards on Kang Sheng's instructions (*D.R.*)

Kang Sheng on parade between Liu Shaoqi (whom he would kill) and Deng Xiaoping (whom he would throw in prison) (*Archives Patrice Fava*)

The file of the Taiwan special services on Luo Qingchang, head of the Daochabu (*authors' collection*)

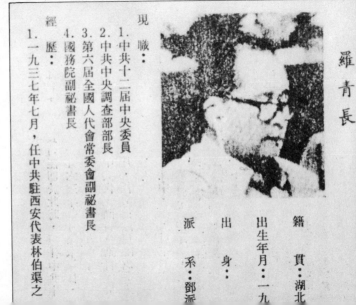

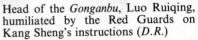

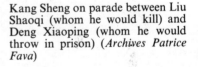

Facing Deng Xiaoping, Liu Shaoqi and Kang Sheng are the Belgian Marxist–Leninists Henri Glineur and Jacques Grippa (*Jacques Grippa*)

Jacques Jurquet, leader of French Maoists, being greeted by Kang Sheng in Beijing in 1967 (*Humanité Nouvelle*)

Deng Xiaoping greets Jacques Grippa, the 'father' of Maoism in Europe (*Jacques Grippa*)

Tirana, October 1966. Kang Sheng in the company of the Albanian leader, Mehmet Shehu (*Keystone*)

Rennes, 1979. Behind Hua Guofeng and Pierre Méhaignerie, founder of the new Chinese secret services Ling Yun (*in the centre*) (*A.F.P.*)

Bernard Boursicot and the Chinese opera–ballet dancer Shi Peipu (*Olivier Boitet Associated Press and Associated Press*)

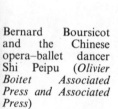

Larry Wu Tai Chin, the Chinese secret services' mole in the CIA (*Associated Press*)

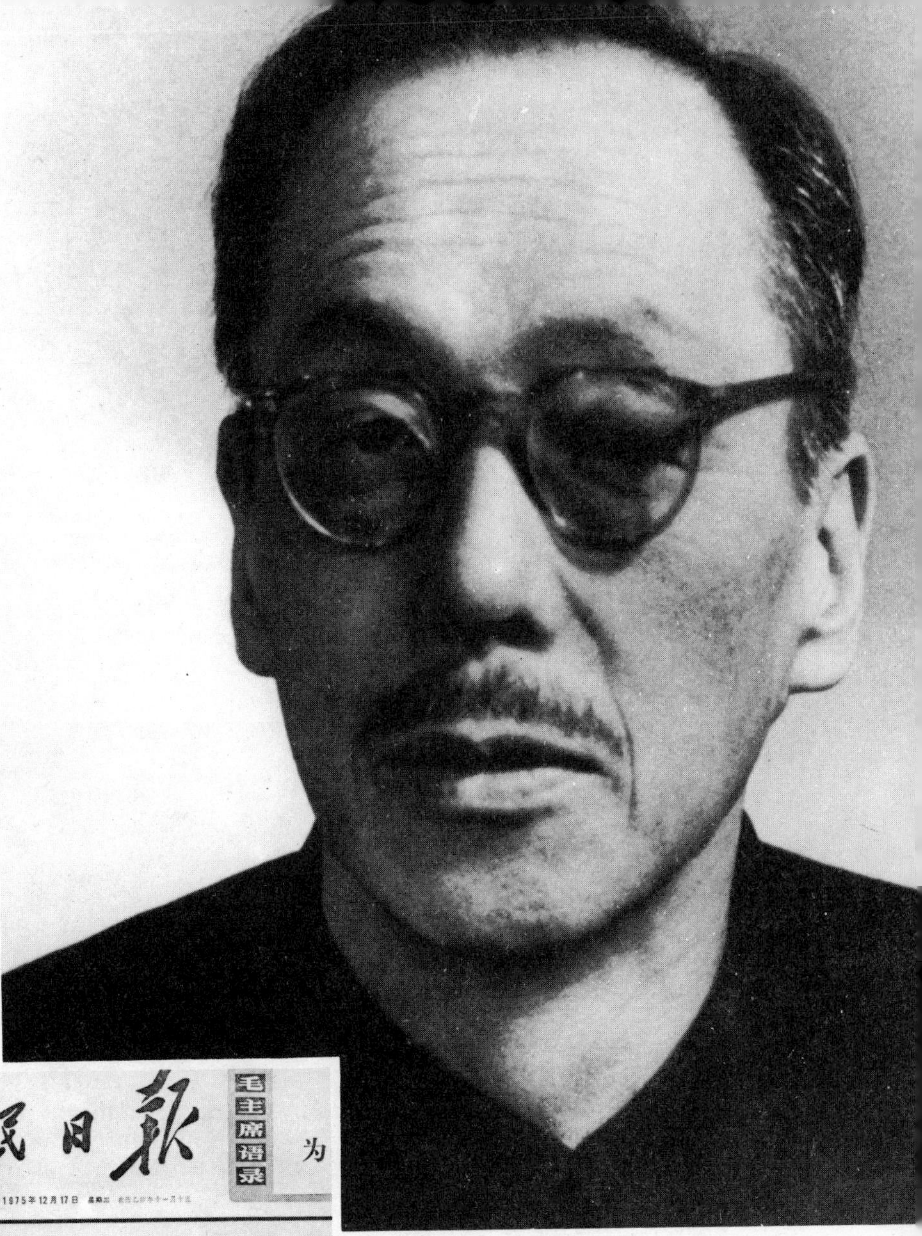

Kang Sheng: for half a century the head of the Chinese secret services (*Associated Press*)

人民日報

毛主席语录　为

1975年12月17日

中国人民的伟大的无产阶
光荣的反修战士康生同志

中共中央、人大常委会、国

康生同志

新华社一九七五年十二月十六日讯　中国共产党中央委员会、中华人民共和国

康生同志治丧

新华社一九七五年十二月十六日讯

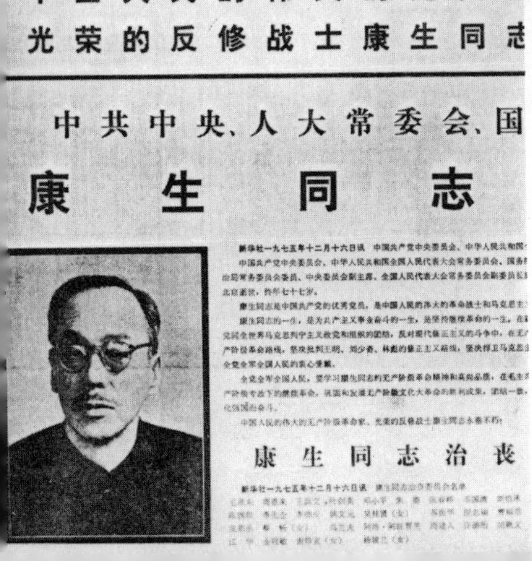

The *People's Daily* announces the death of Kang Sheng

Last official appearance of Kang Sheng, September 1973
(*Pékin Information*)

The funerary homage to Kang Sheng at the Palace of
Culture of the workers of Beijing (*A.F.P.*)

Kang Sheng's widow and son (*A.F.P.*)

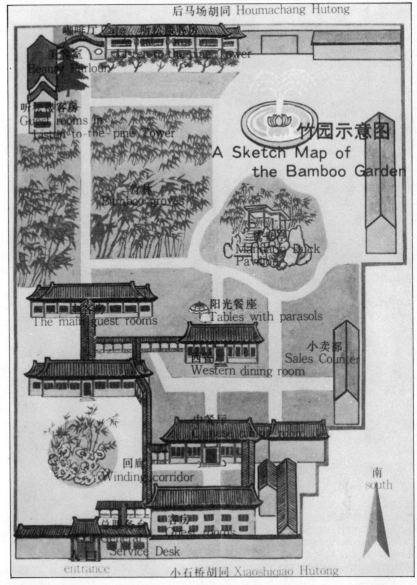

后马场胡同 Houmachang Hutong

咖啡厅 Cafe
Listen-to-the-pine Tower

美容室
Beauty Parlour

听松楼客房
Guest rooms in
Listen-to-the-pine Tower

竹园示意图
A Sketch Map of
the Bamboo Garden

竹林
Bamboo groves

鸳鸯亭
Mandarin Duck
Pavilion

The main guest rooms

阳光餐座
Tables with parasols

小卖部
Sales Counter

Western dining room

中餐厅

回廊
Winding corridor

南
south

总服务台
Service Desk

entrance

小石桥胡同 Xiaoshiqiao Hutong

The Bamboo Garden, residence and retreat of Kang Sheng in Beijing. Nowadays it is a hotel for tourists (D.R.)

Du Yueshing, the 'god-father' of the Shanghai secret services (*D.R.*)

The Great World in Shanghai, secret meeting place between Soviet and Chinese communists during the 1920s (*Pierre Verger/Black Star, New York*)

Borodine, Stalin's man in China (*Collection Roger-Viollet*)

1927: militant communists await the hour of execution (*Visnews*)

Yu Qiaqing (*to the right of the photograph*), associate of Du Yuesheng and Kang Sheng's protector, posing with his wife and children (*D.R.*)

Kang Sheng's and Wang Ming's manifesto, 1934 (*Archives S. Courtois*)

Kang Sheng, Chinese Communist Party representative to Stalin, 1933–7 (*authors' collection*)

Dai Li, Chiang Kai-shek's chief spy (D.R.)

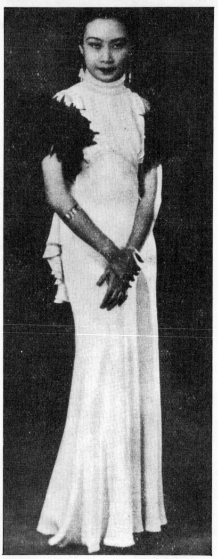

General Doihara, head of Japanese secret services in China (D.R.)

Butterfly Wu, Dai Li's mistress and the possible cause of his death (D.R.)

Kang Sheng in Yan'an: the grand inquisitor of the 'Correction Campaign' (*authors' collection and film* Life in Yan'an, *Collection C. H. Favrod*)

Mao Zedong and Jiang Qing in Yan'an: it was Kang Sheng who arranged their marriage (*Harrison Forman, Triangle*)

Moscow 1961, on the eve of the Sino-Soviet break. *From left to right:* Zhou
Enlai, Peng Zhen, Kang Sheng (*Keystone*)

Geneva, 1954. President of the Council, Pierre
Mendès France, shaking the hand of Zhou Enlai
under the watchful eye of Li Kenong (with dark
glasses), the secret services man in Beijing (*Keystone*)

Kang Sheng on his return from Moscow
after the break: the triumphant smile
(*authors' collection*)

LUO YINONG
(*D.R.*)

DENG FA
(*Collection Nym Wales*)

PAN HANNIAN
(*D.R.*)

LIAO CHENGZHI
(*A.F.P.*)

LUO RUIQING
(*Chine Nouvelle*)

LIU SHAOWEN
(*D.R.*)

XIE FUZHI
(*East Photography*)

WANG DONGXING
(*Keystone*)

CHEN YUN
(*Chine Nouvelle*)

LING YUN
(*Chine Nouvelle*)

ZHAO CANGBI
(*Inter Topics/Viva*)

LIU FUZHI
(*Inter Topics/Viva*)

RUAN CHONGWU
(*Chine Nouvelle*)

HEADS OF THE SPECIAL SECRET SERVICES AND CHINESE COMMUNIST SECRET POLICE SINCE 1927

←
QIAO SHI
(*Chine Nouvelle*)

周恩来、姫鹏飞

会见巴勒斯坦解放组织代表团

同阿布·尼达尔团长和团员阿布·达乌德

进行了亲切友好的谈话

新华社一九七二年三月三十一日讯 国务院总理周恩来、外交部长姫鹏飞，今天下午会见了巴勒斯坦解放组织代表团团长阿布·尼达尔和团员阿布·达乌德，同他们进行了亲切友好的谈话。

会见时，巴勒斯坦解放组织驻北京办事处主任哈穆德在座。

参加会见的我有关方面负责人和工作人员有：何英、柴成文、周觉、高建中、林倩丽、李留根、张真、胡凤仙、袁天伟等。

中共安庆市委

团结干部

据新华社合肥一九七二年三月三十一日电 在党的"九大"团结、胜利路线指引下，中共安庆市委认真落实党的干部政策，实行"惩前毖后，治病救人"的方针，团结了干部的大多数，使他们在各条战线发挥了骨干作用，促进了革命和生产沿着毛主席革命路线胜利前进。

安庆市委成立后，反复学习了毛主席关于"团结起来，争取更大的胜

这是会见时合影。　　　　　新华社记者摄

Next to Zhou Enlai, the two Palestinian leaders Abou Nidal (*left*) and Abou Daoud (*right*) visiting Beijing (People's Daily, *March 1972, authors' collection*)

Chan Tak Fei, Kang Sheng's eye in the 'Great English Ears' of Hong Kong (*New Statesman*)

Gong Pusheng, very special Beijing ambassador to Ireland (*Irish Times*)

His deputy, Li Kenong, maintained contact with certain triads and more generally with the criminal fraternity in towns controlled by the Japanese and the nationalists. He inherited a new realm of responsibility, for opium. Again, enemy soldiers were the target consumers, and the Social Affairs Department accumulated considerable funds through selling the drug. After the 'Liberation', the drug-trafficking continued. Having become the big boss of espionage headquarters in Bowstring Alley, Li extended his operations, particularly after 1951, during the Korean War, to the Pyongyang soldiers and the American expeditionary corps. He even acquired 'technicians', former gangsters in the Japanese laboratories, who were only too happy to escape the vengeful hand of the People's justice in this manner. It was estimated at the time that production of opium in China increased within five years from 2,000 tonnes to 10,000. In Hong Kong and on other underground markets, consignments appeared that did not carry the stamp of the usual sources: Du Yuesheng's network, that of Liu Zhouzhui in Bangkok, or simply the Taiwanese.

'The Two Tigers', 'The Strong Lion', 'The Single Dragon', 'The Golden Deer' and 'The Double Dragon' became very highly valued brands. It does not take much to work out who was responsible for them.

In Yunnan, on the border with Indochina, the army chief was none other than Chen Geng, the former head of the OGPU's bureau in Shanghai during the 1930s. While giving logistical backing to Ho Chi Minh, which became evident at the battle of Dien Bien Phu, he also kept an eye on the poppy fields that had been taken from the Guomindang army. In the province of Guangdong, which lies opposite Hong Kong, the head of the trafficking operation was Vice-Admiral Zeng Sheng. In the 1930s, Zeng had been responsible for the Comintern's clandestine relations within the British colony. Twenty years later, the military commander of the Pearl River region (Zhujiang) was using the same networks: the famous Hong Kong Seamen's union. The International Seamen's Club of Qingdao was a favourite meeting place for the Shandong sailors who had to smuggle the drug into countries at their various ports of call. Japan was one of the major targets. In 1951, the commander-in-chief of American forces in Japan published a report giving an account of the spread of drug-trafficking from Red China. Several communists in Tokyo and a senior official of the Party in Kyushu were arrested. Some of the money acquired by the *'Tewu* seamen' went into the coffers of the *Nihon Kyosanto* . . . Kang Sheng had not forgotten his old comrade from Moscow days and Yan'an, the Chairman of the Japanese Communist Party, Nozaka Sanzo.

It was during this period that Harry J. Ansliger, Narcotics Commissioner in the USA, submitted a strong report to the Drugs Commission, giving details of Beijing's tactics:

Thorough investigations into several seizures of heroin amounting to a total of 3,413 grams of narcotics had all proved that the goods came from Red China, in particular from Horai, between Qingdao and Tientsin. The communists use as agents, to smuggle the drugs into Japan, sailors or ships' passengers, airmen, and of course their secret political agents . . . Moreover, large quantities of heroin from Red China have entered the United States. Secret agents have been sent to America to step up the drugs trade. One of these agents, caught red-handed with a large consignment of heroin, has just been sentenced to ten years' imprisonment.

The Qingdao network, run by Wang Xiaoyu, the 'Drugs Baron', did not escape the prying eyes of Li Kenong or Luo Ruiqing, the two *Tewu* bosses at the beginning of the 1950s. Wang was involved in Red China's opium trade, acting with a certain degree of autonomy. If the evidence is to be believed, a kind of tacit agreement allowed the man behind Wang, Kang Sheng, to take advantage in a marginal way of the whole operation. Fifteen years later, Wang Xiaoyu was to enjoy a spectacular rise, during the Cultural Revolution, to become President of the Shandong Revolutionary Committee, still under the protective wing of Kang Sheng – while Kang himself was to return to centre stage in the most sensational manner, in 1954.

Officially cured, Jiang Qing joyfully returned to Beijing – and Mao's open arms. The leader of the Chinese Revolution, having grown weary of passing mistresses, once again placed his trust in the woman who had been his companion during the difficult Yan'an years, a wise and discreet woman to whom he could open his heart about all his problems. And, in October 1954, his problems were legion, since many people within the Party had unashamedly started criticising Mao. He needed Jiang Qing as his confidante. She thought this return to favour gave her an unhoped-for opportunity to plead Kang Sheng's cause with her husband. A man such as he could not be left to vegetate in Shandong in this perilous hour . . .

But what exactly was going on in Shandong? Strange signals were coming from the province. A local magazine published an article by a certain Yu Bingbo entitled 'A Short Discourse on *The Dream of the Red Chamber*'. Jiang Qing immediately took a keen interest in the matter. *The Dream of the Red Chamber* was part of her youth. Kang Sheng himself was a fervent admirer of this great Chinese classic. Many were the times that he had told Mao's future wife how much he enjoyed this magnificent portrait of the decadence of feudal life. And here was Yu Bingbo pillorying this wonderful masterpiece, arguing that it did not express any serious criticism of feudalism. 'And by not taking a stand on the future collapse of the family of feudal land-owners,' he wrote, 'the author remains relatively objective and is able to hold the same opinion on the two categories of characters, those who are in favour of safeguarding feudal domination and those who are opposed to it: he supports them without praising them and criticises them without unmasking them, his praises often serving as simple compliments and his criticism never revealing the substance of things, the thesis and antithesis both making a point.'

Jiang Qing was seized with a frenzy: this novel was nothing but a 'poisonous weed', as the accepted expression put it. Yu Bingbo should never have been able to publish a revolutionary exegesis without the imprimatur of the political leaders of Shandong, in other words Kang Sheng himself. So what was the meaning of all this? Had Kang, alone in Shandong, radically revised his past views on *The Dream*? No, it was not possible. Kang Sheng must have had other, pressing, reasons for behaving in this way. The article by Yu Bingbo was a veiled attack against Party writers steeped in idealism and subjectivism. This was a revolutionary offensive along the lines of 'Talks on Art and Literature in Yan'an' and the rectification campaign. Were there not artists who had in the past been purged by Kang Sheng and his accomplice Chen Boda who now had the upper hand? Those such as that 'scheming counter-revolutionary' Ding Ling, now very much in favour with a public perverted by a lack of radical criticism? Ding Ling, who could claim with impunity to having been Mao's mistress in Yan'an, who could say that the Chairman was in fact just like any other man . . .

An ideal opportunity for breaking on to the political stage presented itself through this cultural controversy. Jiang Qing got hold of a copy of *The Dream* and read it avidly, underlining all the passages that might be considered obscene. (This was all the more comical in that Madame Mao secretly adored the *Jin Ping Mei*, Plum Blossom in a Gold Vase, translated in English as *The Golden Lotus*, an erotic story about the depraved life of a Shandong merchant.)

In the days that followed, she showed the article to her husband, suggesting that it should be published in Beijing and a big political debate be opened on the matter. Like Kang, Mao Zedong adored the novel. But being an astute tactician, he immediately realised what advantage could be drawn from a cultural offensive when he was being harried in the economic and political domains. Mao was not a guerrilla theoretician for nothing. He gave her the go-ahead and Jiang Qing went from one editorial office to another in order to get it published, organise its distribution, set up discussion groups, canvas those writers who might rally to her cause. As for Mao, he kept her at his side, taking her with him everywhere, as in the good old days. She was with him at the big celebrations for Khrushchev's visit. The debate on *The Dream of the Red Chamber* had begun. Jiang Qing had just launched her first big political campaign. In Qingdao, Kang Sheng rubbed his hands.

In December 1954 Kang Sheng went up a step in the Party hierarchy. In the course of a Central Committee meeting, Kang was elected to the Executive Committee.

*　　*　　*

Gao Gang was a great war leader. Born in Shenxi in 1902, he established a soviet base there in 1935 with survivors of the Long March who had found refuge there. Mao naturally made him one of his senior officials. During the conquest of the North-East, in 1945, he sent Gao to Manchuria, together with Chen Yun, Peng Zhen and Lin Biao. This trio later joined the offensive in the South, but Gao Gang remained in the big industrial bases of Manchuria, where he became the 'lord of Mukden'. And it was then that suspicion arose within the Party that, like some warlord, he wanted to create an independent state, after the fashion of Manchukuo, a bogusly autonomous state controlled by the Japanese. But it was no longer Tokyo that was interfering; rather it was towards Moscow that all eyes were turned.

Manchuria, like Xiangjiang, had always been a subject of Russian strategy. At the very least, Stalin wanted to turn the two into pro-Soviet buffer states. Gao Gang had made several long trips to the USSR and Stalin held him in high esteem. Lavrenti Beria, head of Stalin's secret services, encouraged his fanciful ambitions, and also sent him good advisers. In his *Memoirs*, Nikita Khrushchev was later to state that not only did Gao Gang have excellent relations with Moscow but he supplied Beria with information about the anti-Soviet sentiments of the leaders of the Chinese Revolution.

Gao Gang a Russian agent? They thought so in Beijing. But he was too eminent a person to be easily dismissed. At the end of 1952, Gao was appointed head of the State Planning Committee, backed by Rao Shushi, Kang Sheng's colleague in the North-Eastern leadership. An epic debate followed. Gao and Rao defended the idea that economic planning should primarily support the richest industrial regions, which were their own. Deng Xiaoping, on the other hand, defended Mao's arguments: the most underdeveloped regions of China should be given economic aid. In 1953 Stalin, Gao Gang's protector, died. Beria followed him to the grave soon afterwards.

It was time to sound the mort and get rid of Moscow agents. The Chinese Communist Party held a National Conference from 21 to 31 March 1955. On the agenda of its secret sessions was the condemnation of the 'Gao–Rao faction'. And who better than Kang Sheng to deliver the deathblow? He had been Beria's pupil in the 1930s. He knew the workings of the Russian secret services. Better still, Kang knew exactly what to use against Rao Shushi, formerly responsible for radio links in the Red Republic of Yan'an.

Kang delivered a speech in pure 'rectification' style, denouncing deviationists and their partners outside China. In fact, Gao Gang and Rao Shushi had been disposed of the year before. After the fourth plenary session of the Central Committee, set up by the party's Seventh Congress, called to liquidate the Gao–Rao clique, Gao Gang had 'committed suicide'. Rao Shushi and his family had disappeared. And Lin Biao, who had made the mistake of fighting alongside them during the civil war, was relieved of all responsibilities for a whole year.

Pan Hannian, the deputy mayor of Shanghai, Kang's former companion, and head of the Asian Section in the Social Affairs Department, was also purged . . .

The main aim of the 1955 meeting, though, was to warn the new Soviet administration, led by Khrushchev, against any interference in China. To have the Soviet services denounced by a man who knew what he was talking about, who had indeed been trained in Moscow. To put Kang Sheng back in a position of authority.

A subscriber to the *Great Soviet Encyclopedia* of 1954 would have been sent a separate sheet in the post and asked to remove the page containing Beria's biography and to insert the more anodyne entry he had graciously been offered in its place. Two years later, he would be asked to remove page 213 of volume X and to replace it with a page about a pretty little Tibetan town; page 213 previously contained biographical details and a photograph of Gao Gang. The Soviets had taken Kang Sheng's warning to heart.

In 1955, Kang moved to Beijing for the first time, together with his wife, Cao Yi-ou, and their two sons. They took up residence in a huge house built during the Qing period, not far from the Russian embassy. Honours were showered upon him. His first appointment, in February 1956, was Vice-President of the Committee for the Vernacularisation of the Spoken Language. The President was Marshal Chen Yi, Mayor of Shanghai.

The Chinese language is not simple. In the 1950s the vast majority of Chinese could not write it. So the Beijing leadership decided to simplify the characters. But at the same time, China is made up of several population groups that speak Chinese with different accents and in different dialects. And when Chinese from different regions meet, the character becomes the only means of communication. It is written in the same way throughout the country. For this reason, it is common to see a Chinese person drawing a character in the air or in the hand of the person he is addressing.

The communist government decided that it had to deal with two major problems: it had to simplify the characters in order to speed up the literacy programme and forge a spoken language that would be pronounced in the same way throughout the whole of China, based on *putonghua*, Mandarin, the Chinese spoken in Beijing. However, some communist linguists had been dreaming since 1946 of dispensing with characters completely and using a Roman transcription of words; in this case, it was even more important that there should be a single spoken language, that of Beijing. Chinese characters had been dropped in Vietnam since the beginning of the century, and only the Roman alphabet was used. Was it possible to do the same in China, where multiple tones were so important to the spoken language?

At the beginning of the 1930s, following the lead given by Qiu Qiubai, former director of Shanghai University, whose pupil Kang

Sheng had been, an attempt had been made to Romanise the Chinese language for the Chinese communists in Vladivostok. Russian scholars and linguists were, for obvious reasons, keen for the experiment to succeed. (Kang Sheng's aide Liu Changsheng took part.) A group in favour of adopting the Roman script left Moscow for Vladivostok. A conference on the subject set up a committee to implement the new alphabet. Chinese newspapers in Vladivostok and some fifty books were published in *latinghua*, as it was called. This initiative was greeted as a great success in the Kremlin, but the Chinese in Vladivostok could not make head or tail of it. It was a complete fiasco.

Twenty years later, the communists, by then in power, did not want to repeat this lamentable failure (even if certain Western intellectuals, such as Simone de Beauvoir, thought it was all right!). It was necessary to advance in stages, they felt: simplify the characters; at the same time, oblige the Chinese to speak one language only; then suppress the characters, which were a relic of feudal China. Meanwhile, a whole vocabulary of Chinese newspeak, a shortened vocabulary directly related to communist jargon, was introduced.

In December 1954 a Committee for the Reform of the Written Word was formed, led by Wu Yuchang, who had studied alongside Deng Xiaoping in Lyons. A 'scientific' conference ratified his committee's decisions in January 1956. 1,055 characters with multiple written forms were suppressed; 515 characters had the privilege of being in standard usage; 56 radicals – the key component of a character – were simplified and another 196 simplified characters added. Furthermore, the committee adopted the practice of reading from left to right, as in the West, instead of from top to bottom and right to left. A great of advantage of this was that young people could no longer read the few novels of the past which had escaped being pulped.

In 1955, the committee (*Wenzi gaige weiyuanhui*) published a list of 1,000 characters deemed to be incorrect. Of course these changes carried very carefully considered implications. The word *Gonganbu*, meaning 'Department of Public Security', was given a positive connotation, whereas the word for 'party', *dang*, which appeared in the word *Gongchandang*, meaning 'Communist Party', was simplified; it had a pejorative meaning in old Chinese: 'a group of men plotting in the dark corner of a hearth'. The simplification gave it a more neutral signification.

Kang Sheng oversaw this whole process. While he became involved in the secret services once more, he controlled the transformation of the language. Deep down inside, he no doubt regretted the disappearance of calligraphy, and the fact that young people would no longer have access to *The Dream of the Red Chamber* in the original. But the intoxication of power, the chance to control even the language of his fellow citizens got the better of his romantic tendencies.

His Committee for the Reform of the Spoken Language made *putonghua*, the main dialect of the Beijing region, the compulsory vehicle for all communications within state services – in another step towards the centralisation of power. The ridiculous thing was that the official head of this committee, Chen Yi, was almost unintelligible on account of his Sichuan accent.

The great offensive for the transformation of Chinese and the introduction of a Maoist newspeak was going to have an uphill struggle.

Yet Kang Sheng's prestige rose because of it. Though anyone who had been able to sound out his true feelings on the subject would have known that he detested this woeful destruction of the ancestral language, an initiative based on absurd Stalinist theories . . .

16
The Break with Moscow

Like all the leaders of the People's Liberation Army, the Red Marshal Peng Dehuai, formerly commander-in-chief of the Chinese forces in Korea, prided himself on being a son of the people. But, unlike the majority of his colleagues, he actually tried to remain one. This was enough to make this rather exceptional Minister of Defence a very popular personality in the country. Not at all a person to stand on his dignity, Peng liked to go back to his native province of Hunan whenever he got the chance. There – another fundamental difference between him and his colleagues in the higher echelons of the Party and the army – he would spend hours conversing with the peasants; captivated by his willingness to talk to them, they would tell the Marshal of their everyday problems, their misfortunes, their fears. And rather than crush them with a senior official's haughtiness, Peng felt that he could learn from them. In short, he was the ideal Maoist: patient and willing to serve the people, humble and attentive – more Maoist than Mao himself in fact, who was becoming a little more puffed up with power every day.

An unruly boy who had taken to the road at the age of eleven, an ordinary soldier and then an officer in the nationalist army, a key figure behind the most daring communist uprisings, Peng Dehuai was adored by his men. He had also taken part in thousands of skirmishes and battles before becoming one of the leaders of the revolutionary army during the Yan'an years. In the Red Republic, however, he had lost most of his political innocence. He held no illusions about the personality of Mao, with whom he had had many confrontations regarding military matters.

'Mao is above all an old-style lord. You made him lose face in public: you can rest assured he will never forgive you for that,' he told his friend Ding Ling, the non-conformist writer who was later subjected to 'rectification' by Kang Sheng's henchmen. That day, she had just caused something of a sensation by refusing to attend the marriage of her former lover, Mao Zedong, to Jiang Qing, saying that she was a free Chinese women and not a slave who had to obey the orders of a mandarin!

However, although a realist about Mao and his entourage, Peng Dehuai remained incurably naive about the country's 'Soviet comrades'. A student in 1957 at their military academies, he returned to China a sincere advocate of their strategic ideas which coincided with his own on more than one point: the need for modernisation, professionalisation, and for excellent training.

This sympathy extended to the economic domain. As a result of his conversations with his peasant friends in Hunan and elsewhere, the Red Marshal knew what suffering was caused by the policies enshrined in the Great Leap Forward, which was a product of Mao's self-willed theories. In setting up 'popular communes', the Chinese communist leader considerably worsened the people's living conditions, under the pretext of taking a gigantic step forward towards socialism. And 'the real China', in which Peng Dehuai believed, basically rejected this new initiative. Instead, Peng turned to the Soviets for a more sensible and less brutal economic theory.

Peng was sympathetic towards the new leader in the Kremlin, Nikita Khrushchev, indisputable winner of the race to succeed Stalin – moreover, his keen sympathy was initially shared by Chairman Mao himself and by his heir apparent and future successor, Liu Shaoqi; both men had been sensitive to the show of friendship Khrushchev had lavished on them on first coming to power. They responded less well – although they perfectly understood his reasons to advances the Soviet leader made to Tito, who had been abhorred under Stalin as a dangerous 'counter-revolutionary'. They finally turned against him when they realised that Khrushchev was behaving on the international level much more like the leader of the USSR defending the interests of his country as a world power than as the world revolutionary leader they had hoped for. Once again, the Soviets had deceived the Chinese leadership.

In a curious reversal of policy, very much in the Maoist style, the Chinese diplomatic corps began to attack Tito and the Yugoslavs. For the hardliners in the Maoist group, this was obviously a way of shooting Khrushchev in the back, having deemed him incapable of replacing Stalin.

Kang Sheng embraced this new programme with enthusiasm. On 14 June 1958, he took up his pen to heap insults on Tito – that is to say, on the Russians. In the *Renmin Ribao* (*The People's Daily*) he declared unequivocally that Belgrade was 'playing into the hands of American imperialism'. The rest of the article was in keeping with this statement: it was brutal and menacing.

For the outside world, the 'big socialist family' carefully maintained a show of unity. But inside, tension was rising. At the end of January 1959, Kang Sheng and his friend Liu Xiao, together with Zhou Enlai, flew to Moscow to attend the Twenty-first Congress of the Soviet Communist Party. Discussion between the two parties remained polite but increasingly bitter. It quickly turned to military problems. Like all Soviet leaders, like Stalin himself in the past, Khrushchev was wary of the Chinese. While they argued that the socialist camp ought to have common military strategy, including a joint atomic programme, the Kremlin leader brazenly proposed a merger plan that practically put the Chinese army under the direct control of the Soviet high command.

'To accept this plan would be to renounce our independence! Khrushchev overestimates imperialist strength, of which he is afraid, and underplays the possibilities for popular guerrilla war, of which we have set an example!' cried the horrified leaders of the Chinese People's Liberation Army, Lin Biao leading the chorus. All except Peng Dehuai, whose pro-Russian sympathies became more marked. In the summer, he went on a trip to Eastern Europe. Here, he had a discreet meeting with Khrushchev in Tirana, the capital of Albania, on 25 May 1959. The Red Marshal unwisely unburdened himself to the Soviet leader, explaining what he thought of the Great Leap Forward and of the guerrilla-inspired ideas of Lin Biao and company on the 'people's invincible war'.

Did he go so far as to promise Khrushchev he would build up a pro-Russian faction within the Chinese Communist Party? Enver Hoxha's Albanians assumed so, and immediately notified their Chinese friends, in particular Kang Sheng, whose anti-Yugoslav sentiments they relished. If the hardliners in the Chinese Communist Party were trying to get at the USSR through their attacks against Tito, the Albanians were doing exactly the opposite: they were trying to get at their longstanding enemies Tito and the Yugoslavs through the Russians. It was because of the rapprochement between Tito and Khrushchev that they had taken such a dislike to the Soviet leader. It was because Mao and Liu Shaoqi apparently wanted to denounce the Yugoslavs that the Albanians sided with Beijing.

Poor Peng Dehuai bore the brunt of this muddle – 'contradictions among the people', according to Maoist doctrine. He had no sooner opened fire by addressing a virulent ultimatum to Mao, and even more to Liu Shaoqi – who had become President of the People's Republic of China, thanks to a weakening of the 'Old Man's' political position – than he was accused by the hardliners, of which Kang Sheng was of course one: the Red Marshal, yesterday's hero, was today's traitor, who had conspired with Khrushchev against Chinese sovereignty; he was a potential counter-revolutionary, a defeatist element, who should be purged as soon as possible. Already supplanted at the Ministry of Defence by a hardline Maoist, Lin Biao, Peng Dehuai was ousted once and for all, like the unfortunate Gao Gang before him.

A prelude to the rupture between Beijing and Moscow, the Peng Dehuai affair contained all its elements in miniature: personal hatred of Khrushchev, thought to be unequal to his task; the strange alliance between Enver Hoxha's tiny country, Albania, and mighty China; mutual denunciations and actions against intent; the predominant role of the hardliners; and Kang Sheng sent into a whirl of activity at the idea of settling scores with Moscow that dated back more than thirty years.

*   *   *

There was a general outcry when Peng Zhen leapt on to his seat and accused Khrushchev of behind-the-scenes intriguing to influence the fraternal parties. Having successively accused the Chinese communists of being 'raving mad', 'Trotskyites', 'warmongers' and 'nationalists', the Soviet leader at the last minute, as if by chance, circulated a document refuting Maoist arguments from A to Z. All was all right in the best possible of post-Stalinist worlds. And now the accused had the temerity to defend themselves, and even to counter-attack without any inhibition. Never within communist memory had such a scandal been witnessed before: the supreme leader of the 'workers' homeland' being carpeted by those who only yesterday had been loyal supporters and had now suddenly become enraged protesters!

Kang Sheng, who recalled without nostalgia the weighty ceremonial of Comintern Congresses, smiled, revealing his tobacco-stained teeth. His response and the attack from Peng Zhen, mayor of Beijing and one of Mao's trusted aides in the area of foreign policy, were obvious signs that times had changed, as had the balance of power within the communist world: the Moscow era was over . . .

In June 1960, the big socialist family selected Bucharest as the place to wash its dirty linen. Everything lent itself to a discreet settling of scores: the holding of the Rumanian workers' Third Party Congress and the almost simultaneous meeting of twelve Communist Parties summoned by their Russian Big Brother to take stock of the deterioration in Sino-Soviet relations and the 'attempts to divide the socialist camp' by the Chinese.

Since Marshal Peng Dehuai's dismissal, there had been a running battle between the two powers. In September 1959, Mao and Khrushchev had parted on very bad terms after a stormy meeting in Beijing, their last meeting in fact. In February 1960, Kang Sheng, now responsible for relations with the other Communist Parties, took pleasure in adding fuel to the flames. The Chinese representative at the Political Conference of the Warsaw Pact countries, he set the official seal on the Sino-Soviet quarrel by criticising the USSR in no uncertain terms for its overly conciliatory attitude towards the 'imperialists', and proclaiming that any disarmament agreement signed by Moscow and Washington would not be binding on Beijing.

'The present situation is extremely favourable towards us. Let us firmly carry the banner of peace, the banner of socialism and of communism, and let us march victoriously towards our great objective,' he concluded, deliberately inflaming the situation while his inseparable ally, Liu Xiao, vice-minister of Foreign Affairs, looked on. Too violently anti-American for the Russians, the plan of action put forward in Kang Sheng's speech was roundly censured in *Pravda* and in the rest of the Soviet press, whereas the Chinese took pleasure in publishing the full text.

The quarrel was resumed at the beginning of June in Beijing. At the regional council of the World Union Federation, Liu Changsheng, the vice-president of the organisation, launched a frontal attack on the Soviets and the Chinese *bête noire*: Khrushchev's policy of disarmament and conciliation with the United States, which the Chinese considered 'unrealistic'. Liu Changsheng was a close ally of Kang Sheng and, like Kang, familiar with secret operations: before joining Kang in Russia, Liu, as we have already seen, had devoted his energies to organising the mutiny on the Dutch war vessel *De Zeven Provinciën*. In 1942, he became political head of the Chinese CP's intelligence operation in Eastern China. If he was now turning against yesterday's ally, doubtless it was no accident . . .

In Bucharest, relations grew even more acrimonious. Kang Sheng was very active among the Albanian delegates to the congress, who subscribed wholeheartedly to the ideas of their Chinese friends. But he also took advantage of the opportunity to renew his friendship with his old Rumanian contacts, Emil Bodnaras, a friend from Moscow days, and Ion Maurer.

These two men, both extremely tough, had, in August 1944, disguised themselves as SS officers and freed the communist leader Georgiou-Dej from the prison where he had been languishing for seven years. But Kang and his Rumanian friends did not dwell on the past; they also talked politics. For the Chinese communists hoped to win over the Rumanians, whom they knew to be harbouring a desire for independence which the Chinese took every opportunity to encourage. In Bucharest the person assigned to this important task was none other than Ambassador Xu Jianguo, an expert in relations with the Rumanian *Securitate* and a former vice-minister of the *Gonganbu*.

The Bulgarians were still split on whether they should throw in their lot with Moscow or with Beijing. There was no agreement. Nevertheless, the majority tended to back a Chinese success in the struggle for control of the world communist movement.

This is bound to have greatly annoyed the Soviet cadres responsible for relations with the fraternal Parties. Boris Ponomarev, head of the Russian CP's International Liaison Department, was not at all keen on these Sino-Rumanian and Sino-Bulgarian secret meetings. And his right-hand man, in charge of relations with the Communist Parties of the Eastern countries, did not appreciate them either . . .

This Yuri Vladimirovich Andropov, cold-eyed behind his horn-rimmed spectacles, with an impassive but intelligent face, had a certain style, for someone accustomed to carrying out discreet tasks. He had shown his mettle during the Soviet invasion of Hungary in 1956. As USSR ambassador there, he had cynically duped the Hungarian leaders into believing that the Red Army would never invade; meanwhile the tanks' engines were already running!

Kang didn't like Andropov when he met him before at a kind of pre-negotiation meeting in Beijing in September 1959. As far as Andropov was concerned, the enemy was inside the walls, within the

Eastern bloc countries. Nothing daunted, this senior Soviet official also 'overran' the offices and alleyways, the corridors and hotel bedrooms of Bucharest, a city that was beginning to take on an increasingly surrealist aspect: it is not easy to serve as a combat area for a major conflict and not very pleasant to watch 'friends' tearing each other apart.

Kang Sheng versus Andropov, the founding father of the *Tewu* versus the future head of the KGB – it had the makings of a spy-film poster. The confrontation was silent but ruthless. Yet, when it was over, nothing had really been settled between the Soviets and the Chinese.

'With its back to the wall, the rat bites the cat,' says the proverb. Convinced that a demonstration of force would bring the Maoists to their knees, Khrushchev did not take account of this folk wisdom. The Bucharest Congress was no sooner over than he suddenly withdrew all Russian specialists and technicians who were helping the Chinese 'comrades' to develop their economy. Sickened by this display of pettiness – everything that did not emanate from them was by definition petty – the Beijing leadership adopted an even tougher line. They found their first opportunity to demonstrate this in developing closer ties with Albania. Enver Hoxha and Kang Sheng exchanged numerous messages and winks throughout the whole of that summer.

In November 1960, on the forty-third anniversary of the 1917 Revolution, delegates from Communist Parties from all over the world converged on Moscow, undisputed capital of the revolutionary Marxist movement for the last time. Despite their wrath, the Chinese did not prove an exception to the rule and sent a delegation led by Liu Shaoqi, Head of State since April 1959. As usual, Liu Xiao and his inseparable companion Kang Sheng also attended.

Kang was in better form than ever, smiling ironically, confident of his position and grating more and more on the Russians every day, as he had in Yan'an with Piotr Vladimirov when Maoism was still in its infancy. He was certain his country would triumph.

Like all the Chinese delegates, he was surprised by the vehemence of Khrushchev, who, *à propos* of Stalin whose name the Chinese had raised yet again, threw back these words in Liu Shaoqi's face:

'If you have such need of Stalin, you can have him! I'll give him you, the body, the coffin and everything . . .'

Taking advantage of the ceremonies for the forty-third anniversary, the Soviet leader brought together in Moscow a conference of eighty-one communist and worker parties which more than one observer saw as a kind of 'conclave' with a religious aspect. This was a last attempt to avert a schism. But from the outset, the two sides clashed head on.

The number one ideologue of the Soviet regime, Mikhail Suslov, failed to get adopted the text of the 'unanimous' resolution which he was expecting to have passed in preliminary meetings. The Chinese were bitterly opposed to it. They were not willing to allow disagreement about the future of the world soviet camp to be buried. Nor did they want the forthcoming conference to rule out a full-length discussion on the nature of that dreadful evil which they denounced at length, 'modern revisionism'. Taken aback, although he gave no sign of it, Suslov resigned himself to deferring a discussion on his resolution until the plenary session. He certainly regarded this enforced delay as a victory for the Maoists, their Albanian acolytes buzzing around them self-importantly.

At the opening of the plenary session, Suslov soon realised that his fears were well founded. A newcomer, the then leader of Red China, Deng Xiaoping, attacked the Soviets for being guilty in his eyes of having betrayed the spirit and even the letter of the 'resolutions jointly passed in 1957' and of shamelessly leading 'the socialist camp to capitulate in the face of imperialism'.

It was unmistakably clear: whilst the Soviets were still hoping to save an illusion of unity, if not the real thing, the Chinese were pressing for a rupture. The Albanian president, Enver Hoxha, drove the point home, affirming in his own dull, unsubtle way that the Russians were subjecting his small country to economic blackmail and that 'the Soviet rats had plenty to eat while the Albanian people were dying of hunger'. In order to show just how angry they were, the Albanian delegation, led by Hoxha, left the USSR before the end of the conference.

Kang Sheng, a smoother customer altogether, was delighted to note the soundness of the spider's web that he had had the patience and foresight to cultivate in Yan'an: the Asian network. The North Koreans and the Indonesians had already voted with the Chinese at the preliminary sessions. The Burmese, Malaysians and Thais were inflamed by the straight hard talking of the small but pugnacious Deng Xiaoping. With the exception of the Vietnamese, who were very much in favour of unity despite their pro-Chinese sympathies (encouraged by the head of their party's International Liaison Department, Hoang Van Hoan), Asian Marxism – representing a collection of political convictions and temperaments, cultures, interests and experiences totally different from those of the Russians – went against Moscow.

Deng Xiaoping and the Chinese iconoclastically smashed to pieces everything Khrushchev was proud of: the Soviet CP's Twentieth Congress, at which the Russian leader had denounced the cult of Stalin's personality and his crimes; the policy of peaceful co-existence with the United States; the *rapprochement* with Tito and the Yugoslavs, 'the damned of the earth' in the Stalinist world; the very notion of introducing socialism by peaceful means in the economically developed countries. They put forward their own ideas without any inhibition: the cult of the 'genius Stalin'; confrontation with American imperialism, if need be at the expense of an atomic war; and the conquest of power through 'long people's wars' on the Chinese model.

But either because they were simply horrified by the Maoist arguments, or because they considered it of primary importance to preserve unity, the great majority of the Communist Parties finally accepted the compromise put forward by the Russians: a declaration that was neither one thing nor the other, and settled nothing, but which saved appearances.

The delegates parted, none too pleased. Everyone felt that the issue had just been temporarily shelved. The Russian Revolution had just celebrated its forty-third anniversary; the Chinese Revolution was barely eleven years old, but like some unruly child, the Chinese already wanted to run the affairs of the whole socialist family. This situation could only worsen as time went by.

On 12 January 1961, several officers of the CS, the *Controspionnagio dell'Arma dei Carabinieri*, arrested the infantry Captain Luigi Spada on the Piazza Istria in Rome, just as he was handing over to the Albanian 'diplomat' Kallco Koko a detailed map of the Puglia NATO base. Koko in fact worked for President Enver Hoxha's secret service, the *Sigurimi*, which was run by the highly mysterious Colonel Mawsi.

This sadly banal incident would have been of only relative importance had it occurred within a different context. But in the light of the conflict between the USSR and Albania, it took on an unusual dimension. For the *Sigurimi*, which was half a secret political police organisation, and half an intelligence service, had just changed its allegiance: it was still anti-NATO, but now sided with the *Tewu* and no longer with the KGB.

In the domain of the secret war, this was one of the consequences of the Conference of Eighty-one Communist Parties: a kind of realignment. In future, the heads of the Chinese and Albanian intelligence services would work hand in hand with each other, exchanging their most precious information, on the Russians and their plans in particular.

At the same time, in keeping with the Marxist-Leninist dialectic, the Soviet CP's Central Committee instructed the KGB's Far Eastern Bureau based in Vladivostok to undertake as a matter of urgency an intensive intelligence-gathering operation with regard to Popular China. Comrade Nikolai Georgievich Soudarikov, ambassador to Beijing since 1956, but also an unofficial member of the Soviet special services since the Second World War, started carrying out this confidential work.

In the East, espionage is the continuation of politics by other means. The febrile activity of their intelligence services was a clear indication of the temperature within government circles in Beijing, Tirana and Moscow. Outwardly, of course, care was taken to present a façade of marbled serenity.

On 17 October 1961, Zhou Enlai returned to Moscow for the Soviet

CP's Twenty-second Congress. He was accompanied into this now uncertain territory by the architect of the rupture, Kang Sheng, and also by Peng Zhen and Tao Zhu. As soon as the Congress opened, Khrushchev publicly attacked the Albanians – those ingrates, those irresponsible extremists. The temperature immediately rose by at least fifteen degrees in the hall in the Kremlin Palace where everyone was gathered. The Soviet leader was, however, lambasting people who were not there. Incensed by the latest internal confrontations, Enver Hoxha and his companions had decided not to make the trip to Moscow.

Khrushchev was none the less virulent, and aware of the step he was taking: moving to the public stage the controversy raging within the socialist camp. 'The line worked out by our Party's Twentieth Congress,' he rapped out, underlining each word with an energetic gesture, 'is a Leninist line. We cannot give way on this matter of principle whether to the Albanian leadership or to anyone else . . .'

Everyone realised immediately that 'anyone else' was a reference to the Chinese who, not content with urging the communists to revolt, were now presenting themselves as the only true heirs of Marxist-Leninist thinking, which, according to them, had been perverted by the 'opportunist' leadership in Moscow.

To make things even clearer, Khrushchev singled out Stalin for condemnation throughout his long speech. This attitude did not please the Chinese. Zhou Enlai and Kang Sheng had known the Soviet dictator. Both had regarded him with wariness, admiration, hatred, respect – but never with contempt. And yet, here was his impious successor once again publicly repudiating 'the People's Little Father'. Here he was attacking their loyal Albanian ally.

They had to retaliate. On 20 October, Zhou Enlai mounted the rostrum for the traditional message of friendship from one Communist Party to another. True to form, he did not resort to verbal excess in his condemnation of the Khrushchev manner of conducting debate within the revolutionary movement or his defence of the Albanians who had been so unjustly attacked. However, at the end of his speech, he conspicuously avoided shaking hands with Khrushchev, which was tantamount to a new challenge.

More uncompromising than their comrade, Kang Sheng and several other Chinese delegates considered Zhou's performance skilful but too moderate. As for the refusal to shake hands, this seemed to them an insufficiently dramatic gesture. They felt, and Zhou Enlai quickly took the same view, that Chinese disapproval should be marked by some striking gesture that was so unambiguous that no one could ever accuse it of being 'divisive'.

'In order to unmask Khrushchev's opportunist and counter-revolutionary tendencies, what better than a public tribute to Comrade Stalin?' Kang Sheng and Zhou Enlai suggested.

The idea was greeted with enthusiasm.

The next day, the entire Chinese delegation, led by Kang Sheng and Zhou Enlai, turned up with great pomp at the mausoleum in Red Square that for a few weeks longer was still to bear the name 'the Lenin–Stalin Mausoleum'. After a couple of moments' respectful silence, a wreath of flowers was laid on each of the tombs of the two dead communist leaders. The second needed no commentary, since it bore an enormous inscription in gold letters: TO JOSEPH VISSARIONOVICH STALIN, THE GREAT MARXIST-LENINIST.

Two days later, a plane took the Chinese delegates to the Twenty-second Party Congress back to Beijing. As though unburdened by his gesture of two days before, Zhou Enlai seemed to be on particularly good form, teaching his travelling companions several traditional songs from his native province of Jiangsu. In an attempt to drown the throbbing of the engines, the group sang at the tops of their voices. Less expansive than the others, Kang Sheng nevertheless shared their exultation: there was no going back, a split was inevitable.

After so much excitement, 1962 began on a quiet note. In the name of his Vietnamese comrades, Ho Chi Minh was behind a new initiative for conciliation between the fraternal Parties. 'Uncle Ho' was torn between two contradictory loyalties: the loyalty of an old revolutionary cast in the Comintern mould towards the Russians, and the loyalty of a Yan'an veteran towards these friendly Chinese who had offered him unfailing support during the difficult days of the Second World War and again during the long struggle against the French colonialists. He did not like the climate of ideological war between the Chinese and the Russian CPs. Furthermore, he did not like Khrushchev's aggressive stance towards Albania, in which some of his comrades, the very pro-Chinese Hoang Van Hoan in particular, detected a latent contempt for the peoples of the Third World, the smaller nations and their difficult fight for 'national liberation'. Without going quite so far, Ho Chi Minh decided that he would be the instrument of reconciliation between his Chinese and Russian comrades.

'When brothers are at one with each other, clay turns to gold!' he reminded the Maoists, who no longer believed in the brotherhood he was referring to. The days when they considered the Soviets as their intellectual guides and comrades in battle were long past. To please 'Uncle Ho', whom they hoped to swing over to their side, they took a few purely formal steps, without conviction: they no more intended to give way than did the Russians.

Besides, a new area of discord appeared in Xinjiang, where Kang Sheng and the printer Chen Yun, a former employee of the Commercial Press, had met at the home of the warlord Sheng Shicai. Trouble broke out in this border region between China and the USSR. 'Provocation by Russian agents who want to annex the region!' claimed the

Beijing leadership. The People's Liberation Army and the armed police intervened in force, not hesitating to pursue those Chinese nationals who fled into the USSR. Inevitably this led to several incidents with the KGB border guards.

'The Russians are protecting subversives!' the Chinese then proclaimed, increasingly incensed. Khrushchev and his comrades replied that in taking in persecuted Chinese they were simply observing the traditional right of asylum.

As these signs showed, the situation was deteriorating. Kang Sheng redoubled his activities. He sent message upon message to his Rumanian comrades Bodnaras and Maurer, inviting them to defy the Russians. Moscow was then urging Bucharest to accept its plan for integrating all the Eastern bloc countries within COMECON, a common market for the socialist countries.

The Rumanian leadership did not want to go any further down the road of economic co-operation with the USSR: a member of COMECON, yes; but a satellite state, never. Heeding the warnings coming from Beijing, they were responsible for the failure of the great COMECON reform project as devised by Khrushchev. The Soviet leader was thrown into a great rage: just who did these Rumanians think they were? The Bulgarians had chosen the sensible course in rallying to the Kremlin's banner . . .

Kang Sheng was triumphant! At the tenth plenum of the Central Committee in September, he was appointed to the CC's secretariat, run by Deng Xiaoping. There he once again encountered his old rival Luo Ruiqing, former grand master of the sinister *Gonganbu*, who had become military chief of staff. There was no love lost between the two men and the meetings of the secretariat, under the chairmanship of the cunning Deng Xiaoping, could not have been very friendly occasions.

Deng, the future leader of post-Maoist China, had immediately grasped the implications of Kang Sheng's new promotion: a secret agreement with Mao Zedong to remove Liu Shaoqi from power. The future 'Chinese Khrushchev' of the Cultural Revolution was no Khrushchev, as we have seen. He was as eager as his comrades, if not more so, in pressing for a split with the USSR. But he was irksome to Mao, who had been obliged to step down as Head of State in Liu's favour. The 'enlightened guide' of Red China had decided to launch a second Long March in order to reconquer his throne. As during the period of the 'rectification campaigns' in Yan'an, he was counting on the help of Kang Sheng.

October 1962 saw a war of nerves between Kennedy and Khrushchev: the Cuba crisis brought the world to the verge of a nuclear apocalypse, which the Russians feared, whilst the Chinese maintained that the Americans were no more than 'paper tigers'. Khrushchev wanted to base nuclear missiles in Cuba, the Caribbean island where his ally Fidel Castro had been ruling since 1957. Kennedy was categorically opposed to this, and ordered American vessels to intercept the Russian cargo ships transporting the rockets. It was the Russian leader who backed down, 'losing face' in the eyes of the Third World, according to the Chinese.

'You see: the Russians are afraid of the imperialists! They are afraid of war. Under these circumstances, the oppressed peoples cannot count on them,' the Maoists exulted. For them, the Cuba crisis was a godsend, a means of demonstrating the inanity of Khrushchev's arguments for peaceful co-existence.

They were not afraid of war. After repeated border incidents, war was declared between China and India. Nehru had unwisely attacked first but the People's Liberation Army, duly alerted by the military intelligence service, the *Qingbao*, was ready for the Indian troops, who fell into a massive ambush. Having been hacked to pieces, the Indian army withdrew, abandoning to the Chinese an appreciable portion of their national territory.

The next question was whether the People's Liberation Army would follow up this victory and pursue the offensive. On the astute advice of Zhou Enlai, the Chinese leadership adopted a very conciliatory position. The psychological impact of such moderation was doubly effective: Maoist China had first of all shown its strength, and then its 'desire for peace and harmony between nations'. It emerged from the Sino-Indian war with its prestige considerably augmented – which was yet another thorn in Khrushchev's much abused side.

The final round had yet to be played.

'It is in the vast regions of Asia, Africa and Latin America that the different contradictions of the contemporary world converge. These areas today constitute the main zone in which the storms of the world Revolution rage.'

It was in these terms that the Chinese communist leadership responded to their Russian counterparts in a document submitted to Mikhail Suslov, the Kremlin's chief ideologue, on 15 January 1963, by the Chinese ambassador in Moscow. This was taking the opposite view of what communist tradition decreed: that the touchstone of proletarian internationalism was loyalty to the Soviet Union.

On 24 January, a Chinese delegation left Beijing on a special flight for a final bilateral meeting between the Chinese CP and the Soviet CP. It was led by the 'holy trinity' who had masterminded the split: Deng Xiaoping, Kang Sheng and Peng Zhen, a shock commando that Suslov welcomed at the airport with more than his usual frostiness: a monk of the Inquisition without any real powers over the 'heretics'.

The three Chinese once more put their views to their ex-comrade: the centre of gravity in the revolutionary struggle had shifted to the Third World. The workers in capitalist countries had become bourgeois and were no longer ideal revolutionary material. On the other hand, the avenue that should be explored was that of an anti-imperialist alliance of non-aligned forces or forces hostile to the

Americans, even if they were governed by a 'feudal' leader such as the Cambodian Prince Norodom Sihanouk, or a 'bourgeois' head of state such as General De Gaulle.

In order to disseminate Chinese thinking, students and diplomats posted to Moscow distributed pamphlets. This unexpected initiative deeply shocked the Soviet leadership, who prized order above everything. On pain of losing face yet again, they had to take up the challenge. Which was exactly what the Chinese had hoped to achieve: the 'troublemakers' were arrested by the KGB, and sent under military escort back to their country.

It is easy to imagine the climate that prevailed at the talks between Deng Xiaoping, Kang Sheng, Peng Zhen and their Soviet interlocutors in such circumstances. The talks begun on 6 July were adjourned indefinitely on 20 July. The 'holy trinity', emboldened by the Soviet tendency to play for time, had taken the liberty of going so far as to demand the head of Khrushchev himself as the price of reconciliation. In so doing, they made a clash inevitable, no doubt willingly. So, on 20 July, Kang Sheng and his companions took the flight home to Beijing.

Vice-Minister Liu Xiao, Kang Sheng's longtime friend, welcomed them as veritable martyrs of the revolutionary cause. 'Honest Soviet citizens cannot be in agreement with their government,' he declared at a public meeting, an obvious instance of interference intended once again to get a rise out of the Russians.

Kang Sheng and his companions had been the architects of one of the most important events of the century, so important – and so incredible – that many in the West could not credit it.

'It is a ploy to deceive the free world! The communists are old hands at this kind of wiliness. They want us to take this split for the real thing, while the Russians and Chinese launch a surprise attack on us,' proclaimed several theoretically well-informed individuals, among them the CIA's director of counter-espionage, James Jesus Angleton himself, who was completely intoxicated by the 'revelations' of a very strange Polish defector, Anatoli Golytsin, and crammed full of Taiwanese propaganda on the 'fundamental duplicity of the Reds' by Ray Cline, the CIA's station chief on the island where the Guomindang had taken refuge.

'A narrow-minded man creates problems for himself. The stupidity of our enemies adds to our strength,' thought Kang Sheng, delighted by this lack of discernment, which was catastrophic for the CIA, and which would considerably facilitate the work of the Chinese special services.

But Kang had too much at stake to content himself with smiling. In December, he welcomed with great ceremony Dipa Nusantara Aidit, the General Secretary of the Indonesian CP, the most powerful of the world's Communist Parties not in power, with 500,000 members.

'The friendship and unity between the Indonesian and Chinese

Communist Parties are deep and indestructible. They are based on Marxism-Leninism and proletarian internationalism, on the defence of Marxism-Leninism and opposition to revisionism and dogmatism,' he declared by way of welcome, at the reception for Aidit held at the Chinese CP's Central Committee High School.

Yet it was in Africa that the great Chinese offensive on the Third World, after the split with the USSR, was to begin.

17
Africa: Ripe for Revolution

Abu Nidal, a small, nearly bald Palestinian, had not yet bathed all the capital cities of the globe in blood. He was completely unknown to the general public. He was already waging a secret war against Israel, but the Palestinian cause was still respectable. It was 30 March 1972 when he came down the gangway at Beijing airport, where flags fluttered in the breeze.

'Greetings to the heroic Palestine people! Long live military solidarity between the Chinese and Palestinian peoples!'

The Chinese capital was in mourning. It had just buried the head of counter-espionage, the *Gonganbu*, with great pomp. By a strange coincidence, the deceased minister, Xie Fuzhi, Kang Sheng's deputy, had played an important role seven years earlier in meetings with the Egyptian President Gamal Abdel Nasser, which led to the recognition of the Palestine Liberation Organisation by Red China.

An old friend of Kang Sheng, the Foreign Affairs Minister, Ji Pengfei, welcomed the Palestinians. Accompanying Abu Nidal, the head of the delegation, was his deputy, Abu Daoud, a giant of a man with Italian-style moustaches, wearing dark glasses. This courtesy visit concealed a highly technical meeting, for the two men belonged to the PLO's special services.

That evening there was a lavish Chinese meal. At the end of the banquet, Minister Ji, who had just returned from Paris where he had led the Chinese delegation at the Conference on Vietnam, paid rousing tribute to his guests: 'The liberation of the Palestinian people is a just cause. You have widespread support for your just cause; all the revolutionary peoples of the world stand beside you. I would like to reaffirm that, as in the past, the Chinese government and people will resolutely support your just struggle against American–Israeli aggression and your fight to return to your homes.'

Abu Nidal replied: 'The Palestinian people is convinced that armed struggle is the only means of liberating the whole of Palestine, which extends from the Jordan to the Mediterranean. Whatever the obstacles and pitfalls on the road to revolution, we are determined to bear aloft the battle flag without any slackening or hesitation.'

The next day, the PLO people had numerous political and technical discussions with Ji, but also with Zhou Enlai, with whom they had their photograph taken for posterity. The picture appeared in the

Renmin Ribao (*The People's Daily*), after the delegation had flown to Kim Il-sung's Korea.

Within a year, the two leaders of special operations were going to become famous, and bring dishonour upon the Palestinian cause.

On 6 September 1972, a Black September commando unit assassinated eleven members of the Israel Olympic team in Munich, in front of the whole world's cameras. The brain behind the operation was Abu Daoud, backed by Abu Jihad (whose real name was Khalil al-Wazir), who had also made numerous visits to China on various military training courses there.

Abu Nidal was condemned to death by the PLO in 1974 as 'a dissident who had provoked serious conflict within the ranks of the Palestinians'. Moving first to Damascus and then to Baghdad (as it happened, two centres of Chinese espionage in the region), Abu Nidal set up his own organisation. Within a few years, his terrorist activities stained the world's capitals with blood, striking in particular at moderate Palestinian elements prepared to recognise Israel. It was Abu Nidal who was behind the assassination of the Israeli ambassador to London, providing the Tel-Aviv army with a pretext to invade Lebanon in 1982.

The Chinese, who had nurtured these vipers in their bosom, dissociated themselves from the consequences. However, it remains the case that since the 1960s they have played an important role as regards the Palestinians, partly for reasons of political principle, but also motivated by their usual concern – to put one across the Soviets.

It had all begun in 1964, after the Chinese supported the Algerian revolution. Beijing recognised the first Palestinian nationalist movement, Fatah, whose leader, Yasser Arafat, visited the new communist Mecca. At the same time, at the Arab summit presided over by Nasser, the Palestinian Liberation Organisation was founded; it was based in Cairo. The Chinese ambassador, Chen Jiakang, the leader of Zhou Enlai's special services during the Yan'an days, and a master of intrigue, sensed that Ahmed as-Choukeiri, the PLO's general secretary, wanted to obtain the support of China. In March 1965, Ahmed as-Choukeiri was welcomed to Beijing with open arms. From that time, the diplomatic corps and the special services built up contacts with the dozen or so Palestinian organisations that in the course of time came to make up the PLO, or broke away from it. Leaders of the Palestinian resistance went to China to consolidate relations with diplomats, the Red Army, or Kang Sheng's services. This was true of the leader of the pro-Syrian movement Saika, Zuheir Mohsen, a friend of Rifaat el-Assad, head of the secret services, who died in Nice in 1979, probably killed by the Israeli intelligence service, Mossad.

Beijing's sympathies went out particularly to those who paid explicit homage to Marxism-Leninism: George Habbache, the leader of the Popular Front for the Liberation of Palestine, and Nayef Hawatmeh, leader of the Popular Democratic Front for the Liberation of Palestine. Dr Habbache went to Beijing in 1970, while his PLFP were hijacking planes, with the technical assistance of North Korea. But Fatah was the largest of the groupings within the PLO, hence its numerous representations to China.

Yasser Arafat went to Beijing in 1964 and 1966. However, according to Abu Iyad, the head of the PLO's secret services, it was not until after the Six Day War that the Chinese offered the Palestinians the opportunity of military training in China. In February 1970, Abu Iyad and Arafat travelled discreetly to Beijing via Pakistan. They were worried by the ferment of the Cultural Revolution and especially by the violent attacks directed against the USSR. In the course of lengthy discussion with Zhou Enlai, the two Palestinians explained that it was impossible for them to break with Moscow.

'I understand your worries very well,' replied Zhou. 'You represent a national liberation movement. It is therefore natural that you should try and obtain support wherever you can.'

During Arafat's visit, the *People's Daily* declared its position: 'For Palestine, as for all nations, national independence cannot be achieved except by trusting in the gun.'

And indeed hundreds of Palestinian guerrillas received military training in China. At the Military Academy of Nanking, General Wang Ping, a veteran of the Long March and a former adjutant to Lin Biao, taught them how to wage a 'people's war', the techniques of guerrilla warfare, the use of Kalashnikovs – the Chinese bayonet model or with PGR 7 rocket-launchers. Other Palestinians trained at the Huangpu Academy, in Canton or Beijing. Kang Sheng's Investigation Bureau (the *Diaochabu*) had its own school in Nanyuan, south of Beijing, for the training of intelligence cadres. The *Tewu* and the PLO's security services worked out a programme for exchanging intelligence. In October 1971, it was the turn of Abu Jihad – one of the chief organisers of the Munich assassinations one year later – to visit China, along with many other less notorious Palestinians. Colonel Gan Mai, an expert on Africa and the Arab countries, strengthened ties with their special services. Then a year later came the visit of Abu Nidal and Abu Daoud. In fact, Chinese strategy changed rapidly over the following decade, because of the country's *rapprochement* with the Americans, developments in the Arab world, and a pragmatic attitude towards Israel. In this respect, Kang Sheng's special services anticipated official diplomatic policy. As early as 1970, the *Tewu* was working with the French SDECE and Israel's Mossad against the Russians, at the time of the Sudan crisis.

The aid initially given to the terrorist extremists in the Palestinian movement was just a phase in Beijing's secret – and even official – policy in the region. It can be said in their defence that the period of the Cultural Revolution was favourable to great revolutionary aspirations, and that the Palestinian movement seemed more coherent and less split than today.

As early as 1965, Zhou Enlai's friend, diplomatic supremo Chen Jiakang, had developed this Arab strategy in his luxurious embassy in Cairo as accredited ambassador to Egypt since 1956, on the eve of the Suez crisis. We have already encountered Chen Jiakang in Yan'an, where Zhou Enlai noticed this talented youngster, who studied languages at the university in Wuhan, and who had been initiated into secret work in the United Front Work Department. Zhou had appointed him his personal secretary, a role that was not confined to paperwork. On the contrary, Chen set up the diplomatic intelligence network that Zhou needed, his contact in the Social Affairs Department being Li Kenong and in Military Intelligence, Liu Shaowen.

There were other delicate missions: Chen controlled the activities of the Korean communists in Chongqing and – together with the Gong sisters – had special contact with the American OSS mission. Then, after 1945, he became a kind of roving ambassador for the communists. He was seen at all the big international conferences: in New York, for the founding of the United Nations in Paris, at the International Labour Conference, where the Chinese delegation was headed by the former head of secret services and veteran of the Long March, Deng Fa. He also attended all the conclaves held in the communist world. Chen Jiakang, Zhou Enlai's man, imposed the idea on both East and West that China was awaking.

In 1954 he was again in the company of Zhou Enlai and Li Kenong, attending the Geneva Conference, sealing the destiny of Indochina. A year later, the Zhou lobby took part in the Bandung Conference . . .

Such a record of achievement and faultless progress automatically marked Chen out for one of the new China's most ambitious enterprises: that of rallying Arabs and Africans to the Beijing banner. In May 1956, Egypt and the People's Republic established diplomatic relations. In July, Chen presented his credentials to Nasser. He was to serve as ambassador in the same post for ten years – a record – before his posting ended in drama . . .

Chen Jiakang was one of the most prominent diplomats but he was also one of a remarkable team of special ambassadors – including journalists Huang Hua and Zeng Tao, and the enigmatic Bai Ren – who for more than ten years made these the glorious days of the Chinese presence in the world.

Zeng Tao became the first Chinese ambassador to Algeria, Huang Hua to Ghana before he replaced Chen Jiakang in Egypt, and Bai Ren, after serving in the Yemen, became Beijing's representative in Morocco. A strange plan of action was going to be based round these men, a curious ballet in the shadows.

Theoretically, in 1956, the ambassador to Cairo, Chen Jiakang, also acted as China's representative to the Yemen (as he did, from 1958, to the whole of the United Arab Republic, thanks to an alliance between Egypt and Syria). However, Bai Ren went to Rabat as ambassador, and left behind him several hundred technical advisers. He next exercised the consummate art of making inroads without any ideological demands in Sekou Touré's Guinea, where the *Tewu* was also having to deal with the advances made by the KGB ambassador, Daniel Semenovich Solod.

The war in Algeria was raging at that time. Chen Jiakang forged an alliance with the Algerian National Liberation Front, through representatives of its provisional government in Cairo.

In 1959 Major Azzedin was a member of an NLF military delegation to Beijing. He later noted: 'Our trip constituted a new step for the NLF, firmly committing us to the two big people's democracies in Asia: China and North Vietnam. Our liberation movement thus took a clear turn to the left, in accordance with the internal logic of all revolutionary struggle that emanates from the people . . . In China, we had found effective military and material aid.'

Indeed, in November 1959 the Algerian units stationed in Tunisia received a large sum of money from China. The most important thing, though, was China's diplomatic recognition of the NLF in 1958.

Then, again from Cairo, the Chinese established links with the main African guerrilla movements, starting with that of the Congo.

Nasser, for his part, let them get on with it. It was important for him to maintain an equal distance from the two communist brother enemies. However, in September 1959, there occurred a regrettable incident for the Chinese.

Khalid Baghdache, a Comintern veteran, head of the Syrian Communist Party, took advantage of a visit to Beijing to criticise Nasser. 'He has set up a terrorist dictator regime which uses the worst fascist methods against all democratic and nationalist forces.' In short, he reproached the Egyptian government for siding diplomatically with the Russians and the Chinese, while at the same time suppressing communists within the United Arab Republic. The controversy caused a stir in China, with Beijing comparing Nasser in its propaganda with Chiang Kai-shek.

In Cairo, Chen Jiakang managed to calm things down, at the cost of a lot of bowing and scraping. But Nasser's supporters were wary of the Chinese, more tortuous and less oafish than the Russians. At the same time, a Xinhua press agency journalist in Cairo took refuge in the West. Young Jiang Guiling explained in detail to his CIA interrogators how Xinhua, which had been operating in Cairo since 1956, acted as a cover for the special services, in particular for Kang Sheng's Social Affairs Department. Close observers of the African continent knew that the Xinhua's military section constituted the spearhead from Chinese penetration of Africa. In countries where there was no official Chinese representation, the press agency frequently served as a substitute. An agency boss or a mere correspondent could serve as ambassador, commercial adviser, military official, secret agent and even press attaché. This was not the case in Cairo, where Chen Jiakang had an embassy with 150 diplomats and secret agents working for him and the Xinhua press agency engaged in some surprising activities. It was thanks to the agency that in 1965 ten years of painstaking work was swept away like some shack caught up in a typhoon . . .

Colonel Essam ed-din Mahmud Khalil, Nasser's trusted aide, was in overall charge of special service operations. But the information that Colonel Salah Nasr, head of general intelligence (the *Mabahes el-Asma*), brought him at the beginning of the summer of 1964 defied understanding.

'Are you sure of what you're saying – that the Chinese are in on it too?' repeated Khalil. The son of an extremely wealthy surgeon, he had a moustache like an English Guards officer. 'They plan to assassinate Nasser with a telescopic rifle. They must have got the idea from what happened in Dallas last year . . .'

Unlike his huge boss Khalil, Salah Nasr was rather bloated, and wore black bakelite glasses and a little black moustache. As straightforward as a Nile crocodile, Salah Nasr always seemed to be involved in some dubious deal or other. In 1953, he was accused of having established contact with the committee of former Nazis who had sought asylum in Egypt: aeronautic scientists, atomic scientists, survivors of the Gestapo who provided Egyptian intelligence with 'useful' advice on how to deal with the Jews.

It had not escaped Khalil's notice that the head of Egyptian counter-intelligence detested the communists. So it was important to verify the quality of his information before disturbing Nasser and advising him to take action that would lead to an eventual diplomatic rupture with Beijing.

In July, Salah Nasr was given the go-head. Huge raids took place throughout the country. The number one target was the Arab Communist Party, the underground organisation in direct contact with Beijing. Its leader and founder, the lawyer Mustafa Aga, had laid its foundations after his expulsion from the Egyptian Communist Party, which was loyal to Moscow. As soon as that happened, members of the Muslim Brotherhood, a fundamentalist organisation, contacted him: they were conspiring to assassinate Nasser and overthrow the regime. Before it could happen, seven hundred people were arrested, half of whom faced trial. The pro-Chinese elements had entertained the dream of a People's Republic of Egypt which was totally incompatible with the Islamic rule envisaged by their fellow conspirators. Both sides, however, had received encouragement from the dynamic Xinhua press agency. Egyptian justice dealt with them severely: some were condemned to death, others to life imprisonment. Mustafa Aga happened to fall into the second category. His trial in February 1966 was surrounded with mystery, although it emerged from discussions held *in camera* that China was at the centre of accusations.

Retaliation came swiftly. Ambassador Chen Jiakang and the senior officials in the press agency were expelled. In the process, Beijing's largest intelligence and diplomatic base in the Arab world and in

Africa disappeared, which came as a very heavy blow for Kang Sheng.

Despite all this, relations were later resumed and Huang Hua, expelled from Ghana in 1966, went to Cairo as ambassador. But it was not the same any more. The golden age of Chinese diplomacy in Cairo was over.

The only consolation the Chinese had was learning of the arrest of Salah Nasr, the head of the secret police, after the Six Day War in 1967. He was held responsible for Egypt's defeat. It is possible that he had knowingly falsified intelligence reports. He admitted to belonging to a CIA network, to having misappropriated State funds, and torturing people innocent of any wrongdoing.

Nevertheless, Damascus and then Baghdad became the new centres for Chinese operations. The embassy in Damascus, a hive of activity, with a hundred agents who flew all over the Middle East, specialised in intelligence-gathering, while weapons destined for the Palestinians passed via Baghdad.

But at the time of the Cairo affair, and at the beginning of the 1960s, everyone – Mao and Liu Shaoqi, Chen Yi and Zhou Enlai who travelled the length and breadth of Africa, Deng Xiaoping who replaced Zhou during his African trip, and finally Kang Sheng – was agreed: it was in the African continent that they would take on the Russians.

In June 1965, at the Second Congress of the Afro-Asian Conference held in Algiers, Zhou Enlai uttered his famous cry: 'Africa is ripe for revolution!'

This was the official rallying cry for Chinese subversion on the continent – although in fact subversion had already been going on in secret for several years. One had only to look at the composition of Zhou's delegation to realise that he was not joking: apart from the two Gong sisters (Peng and Pusheng), it included Liao Chengzhi, the former Red seaman who was in charge of numerous 'Sino-African friendship' organisations, Luo Qingchang, head of the 'offensive intelligence' section of the Social Affairs Department, Zeng Tao, formerly with the Xinhua press agency and now ambassador to Algeria, and Chen Jiakang, his equivalent in Cairo. In March, Zhou, backed by the head of counter-intelligence in the *Gonganbu*, Kang Sheng's immediate deputy, Xie Fuzhi, had paid a visit to Ben Bella and Nasser to sound them out. Whatever their feelings, one thing was clear at the beginning of the 1960s: the Chinese had certainly decided to do everything possible to win Africa to their cause.

Beijing organised a galaxy of organisations dependent on the Ministries of Defence, Foreign Trade, Foreign Affairs or on the Chinese Communist Party's Central Committee, operating in association with the International Liaison Department. Seventeen friendship associations – this was an old communist ploy – made it possible for the Chinese either to extend invitations to visit China to nationals of the target country, or to be constantly sending delegations there. The

Chinese, probably more than any other nation in the world, were always sending abroad theatrical troupes, acrobats, orchestras, sporting teams. Take, for instance, the Chinese circus: it promoted a dazzling, entertaining, dynamic image of a travelling China, while allowing dozens of spies to travel incognito.

On 12 April 1960, the Friendship Association of the Peoples of Africa and China was founded in Beijing. Its director was a very well-known personality, formerly an intelligence expert trained in the USSR and a representative of the union movement: Kang Sheng's friend from Shandong, Liu Changsheng.

Liu was also one of those in charge of the People's Association for Cultural Relations with Foreign Countries, another *Tewu* front organisation intended to establish relations in the 'cultural domain' with target countries. This alibi did not fool expert China-watchers: an old acquaintance, the Manchurian Zou Dapeng, was deputy director. He was also head of the Central Committee's Investigation Bureau (the *Diaochabu*, the body which after the death of Li Kenong in 1961 replaced the famous Social Affairs Department). Zou was therefore Kang Sheng's right-hand man.

Liu Changsheng took part in numerous union assignments that were totally honourable, to the point where sinologists generally thought of him only as a great professional trade unionist, failing to take into account his work for the *Tewu*. However, in the impenetrable world of communism, the two go hand in hand. The Chinese were keen to get the better of the Soviets in the world of international trade unionism. Nor were they unsuccessful . . .

In 1961, Liu and his men were in Guinea, Ghana and Mali. According to Western counter-intelligence, it was at that time that, together with Marshal Chen Yi, Liu began to promote the organisation of military training facilities for the African guerrilla movements, in particular at the Nanking Military Academy. Guerrilla fighters from Cameroon, the Congo, Portuguese Guinea and many other countries became familiar with the art of *The People's War*, according to the famous title of the work by Marshal Lin Biao published at that time.

From June to August 1960, young cadres from the Cameroon Union of Populations went on courses in Beijing. The courses were held in French. *Tewu* senior officials taught propaganda methods, sabotage techniques, the use of explosives, training in guerrilla weapons. The historic Marxist texts were read assiduously, with the works of Mao Zedong serving as bedside reading.

The guerrilla movement in Cameroon assumed such proportions that it began to worry the protecting country, France. At the beginning of autumn 1960, the French Prime Minister summoned the head of the SDECE, General Paul Grossin, to the Matignon: 'What's going on in Cameroon? Something must be done.'

The reply was laconic: 'Because of their tribal organisation, with them you simply have to get their chief and there's an end to it.'

The chief's name was Felix Moumie, and he happened to be coming to Europe. Under the supervision of the Prime Minister's technical adviser, his murder was arranged. On 2 October 1960, the SDECE (the forerunner of the DGSE) poisoned Felix Moumie in Geneva. This was the period when the Cameroon chief was developing a close relationship with the Chinese. He had met Mao Zedong on a visit to Beijing in 1959 with his trusty aide, Ernest Ouandie, who was to die ten years later. By way of paying posthumous homage to this black revolutionary, the Chinese services kept Moumie's daughter in Beijing until 1967, as a kind of frivolous ambassadress of an illusory Africa who had a great deal of difficulty in leaving China.

The assassination effectively robbed the CUP of its leadership and took Kang Sheng's men by surprise: Moumie had been in contact with the head of the *Tewu*'s Africa section, Liu Yufeng, who was also one of the Chinese representatives on the Committee for the Support of Afro-Asian Emancipation. This body, founded in 1957 after the Bandung Conference, was based in Cairo. The Committee was made up of representatives of the United Arab Republic, Nehru's India, Sukarno's Indonesia and China. A forum for the exchange of information between the Egyptians and the Chinese, the committee initially had an Egyptian secretary. Naturally, the Chinese appointed as its representatives experienced agents such as Major Pan Zhenwu, previously the military attaché in Moscow, whose role within the committee as far as Beijing was concerned was to extend the anti-Soviet struggle. Then, in June 1965, there was a change of secretary. On to the scene appeared a 40-year-old whose bony face was accentuated by the intellectual-looking pince-nez he wore, a syndicalist who had proved his mettle in Shanghai in the forties. Qiao Shi, whom Kang Sheng had singled out as a rising star, was quickly making his way through the hierarchy of the International Liaison Department. Eventually Qiao's brilliant career would see him in 1986, under the aegis of his friend Deng Xiaoping, become co-ordinator of the Chinese Security Services. In other words, he would take Kang Sheng's place.

It was like a set of Chinese dolls: the friendship and solidarity associations were manipulated by the International Liaison Department, which was itself run by the Central Committee's Bureau of Investigation (the *Diaochabu*), run by the Manchurian Zou Dapeng and his deputy Luo Qingchang, and controlled from the top by Kang Sheng – judging by the fact that he saw very few African delegations, a Kang Sheng, it is true, who was temperamentally more accomplished in operations in the rest of the world.

Leading members of the Sino-African friendship associations were not necessarily members of the secret services. One of the most outstanding diplomats of the period, Wu Xueqian, a member of the Sino-African Friendship Association Committee, attended the Second and Third Congresses of Afro-Asian Solidarity in Conakry (in 1960) and then in Accra in 1965 – also the year when he became Qiao

Shi's deputy at the head of the Solidarity Committee. The dividing line between the special services and the diplomatic corps had always been a very fine one in the Chinese world . . .

Queen Theresa Kanyongau, sovereign of Burundi, returned from China absolutely bowled over. It was March 1963. As her trusty adviser Nyamoya had told her before she left Bujumbura: 'Basically, the Tutsi and the Chinese are brothers.'

The expression pleased her. She repeated it in Beijing and her hosts applauded her perceptiveness. Burundi, like neighbouring Rwanda now independent of Belgium, was a small country 28,000 kilometres square the size of four French *départements*, situated in Central Africa. The Hutu, small people distantly related to the Pygmies, and the giant Tutsi were traditional enemies. 'We want equality with the Tutsi, we must cut their legs off at the knee!' said the Hutu, who had hoped at independence to see the birth of a fraternal democratic state. The Tutsi, on the contrary, wanted to preserve a feudal archaic state, but they hated the Belgians and by extension all Westerners. It was they who had assumed power. The Chinese communists decided to go along with them.

The amazing Gao Liang had organised the Queen's trip. With his froglike head, his mouth twisted in a rictus of perpetual bitterness, his ebony hair parted straight down the middle and plastered down on to his temples, and his large-frame glasses that made his domed forehead seemed even longer, Gao was a *Tewu* legend. A Shanghai militant, he was a great correspondent with the Xinhua press agency, based in Dar es Salaam in Tanzania. It was noticed in every capital in Africa that he lived in grand style, for a Red Chinese: he drove fast cars, ate gargantuan meals, and always tipped generously in the hotels where he booked his princely suites. Kang Sheng's spy came and went freely in all the palaces and in all the ministries.

The CIA and the KGB, which were very active in the region, noted Gao's arrival immediately. Expelled from India for spying, based in Tanzania since 1961, Gao Liang was unquestionably one of the leading members of the *Tewu* in Black Africa. Shortly afterwards, another of Kang Sheng's foremost agents, Liu Yufeng, turned up. In December 1963, he became accredited ambassador to Burundi. Bujumbura rapidly became a Chinese hive of activity, with dozens of secret war specialists buzzing around, headed by the chargé d'affaires, Jiang Yen, who built up relations with the Congolese refugees who were masterminding the guerrilla war in their homeland and whose Liberation Committee was based in Burundi. Meanwhile, Gao Liang maintained relations with the exiled Tutsi who came from Rwanda, Uganda and the Congo.

During 1964, the local CIA chief, Laurence Devlin, future personal adviser to the President of Zaire, Joseph Mobutu, became convinced that the secret aim of the *Tewu* was essentially to gain a foothold in

Katanga and Kasai, through the intermediary of guerrilla fighters. With their uranium mines, these Congo provinces were the object of desire of all the powers – the USA, the USSR, France and Belgium – which at the time were promoting different factions in the civil war.

In 1964, China had nearly completed the development of their atomic bomb. Their great asset in the Congo was Pierre Mulele. After Independence in 1960, the Chinese, like the USSR, had backed the nationalist government headed by Patrice Lumumba. When he was assassinated at the instigation of the West, two and a half million Chinese demonstrated in ten cities in China. Mulele was then Minister of Education and he rallied to Antoine Gizenga, the man who took the torch from Lumumba in 1961; Mulele believed in the birth of a beacon state in Africa along with that other great man of pan-African nation-alism, the Ghanaian chief, Kwame Nkrumah. In July 1961, Colonel Zhang Tong, formerly military attaché in Idian, was sent to Gizenga to strengthen the alliance between Stanleyville and Beijing. Mean-while, Gizenga had sent Mulele as ambassador to Cairo. The Egyptian special services introduced him to Chen Jiakang, and the two ambassadors agreed on diplomatic recognition.

In March, Mulele sent his friend Felix Mukulubundu to China as military attaché. He was to supervise the hundreds of men who had been sent to China to learn the techniques of guerrilla warfare at the Nanking Military Academy. Mulele was clear to Mukulubundu what his mission was: 'Take advantage of your stay in China to get some military training, learn the techniques of guerrilla warfare, familiarise yourself with the handling of the weapons that China is going to supply to the Congolese nationalists.' The Congolese 'ambassador' was assigned to the 129th Division of the People's Liberation Army, based some one hundred kilometres outside Beijing. He also acquired an intensive political education, and was fascinated by the veterans of the Long March, who told him how their revolution had succeeded.

Back in Cairo, Mukulubundu enthusiastically told Mulele about his trip: 'I would have liked to continue my training in Beijing. There, they teach really good methods for liberating our country. When I saw China, I realised that we have a long way to go yet.'

Mulele frowned and scratched his moustache: 'Now, careful, Felix, they are communists! You aren't going to bring back a communist influence to our country?'

Seized with dismay, Felix recounted at great length all the merits of Popular China, a communist country perhaps, but communist in a class of its own.

'Stop, stop. I simply wanted to test you. I have a plan. We are going to liberate our country.'

Mulele did indeed have a plan. But in the Congo, Lumumba, his brother in arms, was dead and Mobutu was, with American aid, on the point of seizing power. They should now start fighting a guerrilla war from the border countries, with Chinese backing.

'I hoped you learned in China how we can create an army that will be truly dedicated to our liberation struggle.'

Mulele went to Beijing with his deputy Theodore Bengila in May 1962, as Chen Jiakang announced publicly. There, he was given advanced military training at the Beijing Military Academy. Then Mulele began to organise the armed struggle from Burundi and Congo-Brazzaville. In January 1964, the insurrection became so widespread that Larry Devlin, the CIA one-man band, organised a counter-attack with the aid of the former head of the Belgian Sûreté, Colonel Frédéric Vandewalle. Under cover of an airline company based in Liechtenstein, Western International Ground Maintenance Operations, mercenaries were recruited who were trained near Albertville. At the same time, WIGMO hired anti-Castro Cuban pilots to bomb rebel positions. Following the example of Che Guevara, whom he did not meet until 1966, Pierre Mulele became a living legend. But hunted down like the Argentinian revolutionary, Mulele was assassinated a year after Guevara, in 1968. In the meantime, the Chinese had abandoned him to his fate.

Besides, the CIA had set a trap for them in Burundi, where Martin J. Bergin Jr, a former captain with American counter-intelligence during the Second World War, had been running the local US secret service station since June 1963. To halt the development of the rebellion in the Congo, Chinese aid had to be cut off at the source, in Bujumbura and in Brazzaville, the other bridgehead of Mulele's liberation movement.

Fate favoured Bergin. A very young Chinese diplomat, Dong Jiping, had decided to defect to the West. Born in Shanghai in 1940, he was a student at the Institute for Foreign Languages there. In 1963, he was appointed to the post of deputy cultural attaché in Burundi. But he had been shocked by the way black Africans were treated in Beijing, and the way students who naively went along with the wishes of the Chinese and became their agents were trapped. Like the Russians, the Chinese took a long-term view of things. It was not simply a question of raising revolutionary ferment; Kang Sheng's men intended to recruit men who would remain sleepers for years.

Dong Jiping asked for CIA protection in May 1964. He handed over full details of the Chinese special services' order of battle and revealed the true activities of his ambassador Liu Yufeng. Martin Bergin, the CIA man, took to King Mwami Mwambutsa IV documents proving that the Chinese wanted to assassinate him, and that they were directly financing the guerrilla movements led by Pierre Mulele and Gaston Soumialot.

The Chinese embassy protested virulently: 'The abduction on 26 May by the United States Embassy of Dong Jiping, a member of the Chinese Embassy staff in Burundi, is one of the latest in a series of hostile actions carried out by American imperialism against the Chinese people. Despite repeated demands from the government of Burundi, the United States Embassy has refused to release the kidnapped Chinese diplomat.'

Martin Bergin had won the first round.

As soon as he arrived in the USA, Dong met two other Chinese defectors who were now working for the CIA: Robert Loh, who had defected in 1957, and Zhao Fu, formerly head of security at the Chinese embassy in Stockholm, who had gone over to the CIA in 1962. These two persuaded the young man to go public with his revelations. After all, there was a price to be paid for freedom. Later, they promised, he would be employed by the CIA as a translator. Plastic surgery would enable him to be given a new identity and sink into anonymity. The young diplomat was won over, and agreed.

On 31 October 1964, Dong Jiping publicly denounced in great detail the subversive activities of the Chinese secret services in Africa, without however giving away certain information considered 'top secret' by the CIA, which wanted to protect its own operations. Could a mere cultural attaché have known as much as he claimed to, or had the CIA debriefings helped to bulk out his testimony? In any event, he was a perfect illustration of the warning given by the former head of the CIA, Allen Dulles, who a year earlier had declared: 'We have not yet begun to consider Chinese espionage as a serious threat to our own security in the United States; and yet, in the years to come, it could well become a formidable instrument of intelligence and subversion in the West, as it is already throughout Asia and the Pacific.'

Meanwhile, Gao Liang in Burundi had not thrown in the towel. He was even determined to win the second round of the contest! As though by magic, disturbances broke out between the ethnic Hutu and Tutsi. The King, alerted by American warnings, sacked his Prime Minister, Prime Niyongabo, deemed to be too greatly influenced by the Chinese siren. He was replaced by the man who had been dismissed from the post a few months earlier, Pierre Ngendandumwe, a member of the Hutu tribe. He was a moderate reformer and, like most Hutu, pro-Western.

However, Gao Liang had been very clever. While the CIA had managed to infiltrate the Chinese embassy and recruit one of its members, the Americans were unaware that their own embassy had been infiltrated. Gonsalve Muyenzi, a Rwanda refugee of the Tutsi tribe, was employed by the American embassy, but he was also working for the *Tewu*. On 15 January 1965, Muyenzi assassinated the Prime Minister Ngendandumwe. This was supposed to be the signal for a coup d'état, masterminded by the Chinese and led by Niyongabo, the ousted Prime Minister. Thanks to Gao Liang, Niyongabo's followers, largely from the Rwagasore Nationalist Youth Movement (Rwanda exiles), received automatic weapons that would normally have gone to Mulele and Soumialot's guerrillas. Acting on CIA advice, the King of

Burundi reacted promptly. The same day, the rebels were arrested, the youth movement and the Federation of Burundi Workers were disbanded.

Martin Bergin had won the contest of wits and wills. The Chinese 'diplomats' were expelled and diplomatic relations broken off. On his return to Beijing on 8 February Liu Yufeng, the ambassador spy, was warmly greeted by Marshal Chen Yi. The Foreign Affairs Minister did not mince his words: 'The American and Belgian imperialists are responsible for the assassination of the former Prime Minister of Burundi, Ngendandumwe, but they have conspired to throw the blame on others. Everyone knows that the author of the ex-Prime Minister of Burundi's assassination is American and Belgian imperialism.'

But his denials did not fool anyone.

In his delightful home, the Bamboo Garden, Kang Sheng had every reason to grind his teeth. China's image in Africa was seriously tarnished. And the *Tewu* had just lost its biggest espionage base in the region.

Gao Liang was not, however, a man to be easily daunted. While co-ordinating activities relating to Burundi, he was sent, still under cover of the Xinhua press agency, to the islands in the Indian Ocean. The object of the exercise: to concentrate the energies of the Chinese networks on provoking a revolutionary situation there, from which would emerge the creation of a socialist federation grouping together Madagascar, the island of Réunion, Mauritius and the Seychelles. There were more than 50,000 Chinese living in these islands, eighty per cent of the size of the Chinese community in Africa.

Gao Liang's first stop was Réunion, where he tried to persuade the Communist Party of Réunion, run by Paul Vergès, of the justice of Chinese arguments. Paul's twin brother, the lawyer Jacques Vergès, was after all publishing an international pro-Maoist magazine at the time. But the CPR remained intractable. In the Sino-Soviet quarrel, it had already opted for Moscow. The head of French counter-intelligence, Major Boulle, warned his British counterparts in Mauritius of Gao Liang's imminent arrival there.

This paradise island, which was soon to gain its independence, was multi-racial, with an Indian majority but with large Creole and Chinese minority populations. The latter were the target of the *Tewu* agent.

Pierre Perrier, a Creole, was then in charge of the local Special Branch, the British counter-intelligence organisation. He recalls those troubled times with amusement: 'John Morton, one of the chiefs of MI5, came to Mauritius to reorganise the Special Branch department there. In 1963, a co-ordination meeting was held in Nairobi, in Kenya, of all the counter-intelligence chiefs in the region, MI5 and the Special Branch units in Kenya, Tanzania, the Seychelles and Mauritius. The first item on the agenda was Chinese communist subversion. This meeting ended in a comic fashion: we had reached the point where we were enjoying excellent Havana cigars and sipping brandy, when suddenly the doors were flung open. A huge demonstration of Kenyans, led by Jomo Kenyatta, the great nationalist leader himself, burst in on us . . . The revolution was at our gate!'

Back in the Mauritian capital of Port-Louis, Pierre Perrier, a methodical man, organised the surveillance of the Chinese Sing Sung Bookshop, the Overseas Sino-Mauritian Association and the Mauritius–China Association. For months, his agents watched the comings and goings of the cardiologist Ng Yin Kin, considered to be the number one Chinese agent on the island. Perrier's department even carried out an inspection of a Chinese boat: it was at the height of the Cultural Revolution and the vessel was loaded with copies of Chairman Mao's famous little red book, destined for the Chinese on the island.

Gao Liang did not have time to see his mission through, though. He had no sooner arrived on the island than he was arrested and expelled for spying in August 1964. An indefatigable traveller, he returned to Burundi to organise the assassination of the Prime Minister and the abortive coup d'état. This further setback prompted him once again to go to a different country, where he could create the spark that would ignite the whole area.

One fine day in February 1965, Gao Liang arrived in Brazzaville, capital of the former French Congo. Less than two years earlier, the French-backed Fulbert Yulu was overthrown and replaced by Massemba-Debat, who was very open to communist influence. This marked the beginning of a ruthless war between the Russians and Chinese, with Sergei Nemchina's KGB trying to wrest the National Revolution Movement, the party in power, from Beijing's orbit. But the *Tewu* retaliated in force. In April 1964, Colonel Gan Mai arrived in Brazzaville. (He was the officer who, in the 1970s, would be responsible for relations with the PLO.) One day 'chargé d'affaires', the next 'military adviser', he changed his hat according to his mood. Under his orders, three hundred Chinese advisers (a hundred of whom were based in the embassy) trained guerrillas in both Gabon, in the Franceville region, and in the Congolese National Liberation Committee in exile, run by two of their agents, Christopher Gbenye and Egide Bochelez Davidson.

These experienced war veterans also trained the official People's Liberation Army of Congo-Brazzaville, which was renamed the People's Republic of the Congo. Gan Mai had assigned twenty military officers to liaise with each commander of the PLA. Furthermore, the colonel set up training camps in Gamboma and Imfono for Mulele's guerrilla fighters, who launched another offensive in the other, ex-Belgian Congo. Xinhua journalists, from Algiers and Cairo, saw to co-ordination between various guerrilla factions. When Gao Liang arrived at the beginning of 1965 to back up Gan Mai, he was put in charge of the political training of Congolese cadres at the Ideology School at Djoué. There was no shortage of propaganda: the Chinese set up a 74-kilowatt transmitter at Pointe-Noire to spread the good Maoist word in the direction of eastern Congo. During the same period, Gbenye instructed Gaston Soumialot to organise a Lumumbist government in the province of Kivu, in Burundi. This was before the crisis and the Congolese leader was staying in the same hotel as the Chinese mission ruled by Liu Yufeng, who was again providing financial back-up and advisers: three Chinese lost their lives in the fighting.

But the great design cherished by Kang Sheng's men faded like a mirage. The Congolese rebels were gradually crushed by government forces, and Mobutu, with US aid, consolidated his power. The influence of the Chinese was reduced in Brazzaville in favour of the Soviets. However, in August 1968, a coup d'état overthrew Massemba-Debat, who was replaced by Captain N'Gouabi. Western counter-intelligence thought at the time that Beijing was behind this, acting through the local Xinhua press agency correspondent, Mao Ling. Turning its back on the rest of the world, China closed in on itself during the Cultural Revolution, and furthermore its ambassador to Congo-Brazzaville was recalled to Beijing, where he disappeared in the great settling of scores that was raging at the time.

In 1964 Gao Liang also took part in the pro-Chinese coup d'état in Zanzibar, which brought to power Sheik Abdul Rahman Muhamed Chick Babou, a one-time correspondent for the Xinhua press agency . . .

'This is the first African revolution that has a class basis. Zanzibar proves that in Africa there are not the Arabs on one side and the blacks on the other, but only Africans united in the same common anti-imperialist struggle.' So wrote the lawyer Jacques Vergès in his pro-Chinese magazine, *Révolution*. Babou, it is true, was his friend and figured in the 'boomerang-magazine' published in Geneva and soon banned by the Federal authorities. Half French, half Chinese, educated in the political seraglio of the Colonial Section of the French Communist Party – just like his brother Paul – Jacques Vergès had attracted strong animus by defending the Algerians of the NLF.

His prestige then stood very high in the Third World. At the end of 1962, with the independence of Algeria, he had become principal private secretary to Ben Bella's Foreign Affairs Minister, Mohamed Khemisti. As general secretary of the General Union of Muslim Students of Algeria, Khemisti had travelled to Beijing in 1957. In March 1963, having received an invitation through the intermediary of Ambassador Zeng Tao – previously head of the Xinhua bureau in Havana – Jacques Vergès also went to China, met Mao Zedong and came away delighted with his visit. 'Like most politically committed people in the 1960s, I was inclined to favour Chinese theories,' he says. 'Because it was there that we were best understood, and because Beijing supplied most of the military aid.'

In any event, the coup in Zanzibar had unexpected repercussions on the Chinese presence in neighbouring Kenya. One of the participants in the Zanzibar revolution, John Okello, nicknamed 'the Marshal' because of his imposing physique, planned to export the revolution to Kenya. The Xinhua correspondent, Wang Deming, was given the task of channelling funds to him. A former officer in the Chinese Red Army in Korea, then the Xinhua correspondent in Burma, Wang Deming was obviously a *Tewu* specialist. He attempted to split the Kenyan nationalist party, the Kenyan African Nation Union (KANU), by backing the leader of the leftist faction, Oginga Odinga, who was also deputy minister. When Kenya became independent in 1964, the charismatic leader Jomo Kenyatta seemed too close for Westerners to the communist bloc. The Chinese, still more fervent than their Soviet brothers, tried to move faster. A coup d'état was planned for July but it was foiled. On 22 July, Wang Deming was expelled from Nairobi, declared *persona non grata* because of his 'activities against the interests of national security'. For the Chinese, this was the beginning of series of disasters in Kenya. In 1967, the Chinese ambassador Wang Yutian publicly denounced the Economy Minister Tom M'boya as 'an agent of American imperialism'. M'boya in fact represented the African Bureau of Free Unions, which was financed by the big American union AFL/CIO, which was generally known to be funded by the CIA. Ambassador Wang was in turn expelled. The situation degenerated into a real vendetta.

CIA agent Robert Leroy, an occasional collaborator with the Portuguese PIDE, managed to infiltrate the pro-Chinese Communist Party in Switzerland. He was presented as a serious 'comrade' to the Chinese embassy in Berne, which then recommended him as a 'progressive journalist' to the Frelimo rebel fighters in Mozambique. Leroy interviewed the leader of the guerrilla movement, Edouardo Mondlane, for *L'Etincelle* (*The Spark*), the Swiss Maoist journal. But in fact he compiled a detailed dossier on Frelimo logistics, crossing points and tactics. Mondlane, who had trained in China, was considered one of China's great assets in Portuguese Africa. But their hopes were dashed on the day in February 1969 when Mondlane received a parcel bomb that exploded in his hands . . . He died instantly.

The *Tewu* reacted swiftly. In Nairobi, M'boya, 'the CIA's man', was assassinated in turn by an agent working for the Chinese, one Njoroge, who had been given training in Bulgaria, Albania and China. Understandably enough, diplomatic relations between Kenya and China were completely suspended.

The list of *Tewu* misadventures in Africa during the 1960s would fill volumes. In Tanzania, after the honeymoon period with President Nyerere, Ambassador He Ying was suspected of trying to organise a coup. In Guinea, the battle between the Chinese and the KGB, headed by Ambassador Daniel Solod, 'the Soviet Lawrence', was bloody. In

1960, Solod was expelled. All President Sekou Touré's sympathies were with the Chinese, who organised his secret services, and he vowed eternal gratitude to Kang Sheng. Not that this prevented him from renewing relations with the Russians when the time came . . .

The strangest battle the *Tewu* fought, however, took place in southern Africa, where one would least expect the Chinese to have been operative: in South Africa, where 8,000 Chinese were classed as 'non-whites'. The *Tewu* resident in Pretoria, Guo Qiangqi, who played an important role in the research carried out for the manufacture of the Chinese atom bomb, was an extraordinary character. A Chinese born in Mexico, he had left that country in 1940 after becoming involved in the assassination of Trotsky.

From 1958, the *Tewu* in South Africa recruited a number of Indians, especially in Durban, to set up pro-Chinese intelligence networks. At the time, just after the Bandung Conference, China's prestige stood very high with the Indians. This state of affairs ended abruptly with the Sino-Indian War in 1962. In August 1966, the head of BOSS, the South African counter-intelligence organisation, Hendrik van den Bergh, summoned all his officers: 'The illegal immigration of Chinese into this country is becoming alarming. These illegal immigrants claim to be fleeing Red China. In fact, many of them are communist spies. Act promptly.'

The round-up began in a restaurant in Johannesburg, the Chong Hing. A waiter, Ho Chee Kai, confessed under torture that hundreds of 'refugees' were coming from Red China via Hong Kong. 382 Chinese were arrested, three waiters 'committed suicide' in prison. Van den Bergh's paranoid madness did not distinguish between genuine refugees and communist agents.

Determined to follow their work through, BOSS arrested the twelve members of an illegal pro-Chinese society, the Yu Chi Chan Club, run by a black pastor, the Reverend Don Davis. The eleven Chinese were sentenced to ten years' imprisonment, the priest was severely castigated.

By 1966 it was clear that the strategy of the Chinese secret service in Africa had misfired. There remained only one large base, Kwame Nkrumah's Ghana.

'It's extremely simple, we clean up the "Chicom" embassy,' said Howard Bane with Virginian common sense. 'We attack the embassy with rocket launchers, we spray it with machine-gun fire, and sprinkle it with grenades! Once the "Chicoms" have been liquidated, we take all their archives and blow the whole lot up with dynamite. In the coming chaos, no one will ever know that it was us!'

Howard Bane, as CIA station chief in Accra, capital of Ghana, had several reasons for wanting to do battle with the 'Chicoms', CIA jargon for Chinese communists. Ten years earlier, he had fought against them in Thailand. Then, having been posted to New Delhi as 'political officer', another transparent cover, he had taken great pleasure in helping the Indians to expel Gao Liang for espionage.

But the decision of Admiral Raborn, head of the CIA, supported by the director of operations Desmond Fitzgerald, came down like the blade on a guillotine: 'Bombing the Chinese is out of the question. Just overthrow Nkrumah!'

There was no arguing with that kind of order.

The CIA agent, by cleverly manipulating a part of the army, overthrew Kwame Nkrumah, the champion of pan-African nationalism. Bane pursued a brilliant career in the CIA: in the 1970s he was very appropriately appointed head of the anti-terrorist division.

Kwame Nkrumah was overthrown on 24 February 1966, while on a visit to China. For Beijing, this was the ultimate African reversal, for the charismatic leader of Ghana was moving closer to Mao Zedong day by day. Of course, the Soviets were a strong presence, but the usual rivalry between the two this time favoured the Chinese. Marshal Ankrah, who expelled Nkrumah's foreign advisers, noted that there were some hundred Russians, but three hundred Chinese backed up by several dozen North Koreans.

Being the pragmatist he was, Zhou Enlai in Beijing no doubt came to the conclusion that Africa was simply not ripe for revolution.

But Kang Sheng seemed much more pessimistic. Already, at the end of 1965, the crushing of the huge Communist Party in Indonesia had been a severe blow to Chinese policy. In the autumn of 1966, Kang wrote in a letter to one of his friends: 'Very few people are not afraid of being isolated, myself included . . . And I have to admit that our Party has just suffered a great loss of international sympathy and support. As one can well imagine, it will be very difficult to break out of this isolation.'

And the head of *Tewu* did not even mention the great saga of Chinese involvement in Latin America . . .

18
The *Tewu* in Latin America

The Chinese prefer blondes. The comings and goings of Zeng Tao in the colourful streets of Havana provided ample proof of this. With his exotic charm and his nicely cut pearl-grey flannel suits, Zeng was an attractive man. A former municipal councillor in Shanghai, he was approaching fifty.

He performed his journalistic tasks with a great deal of energy: since May 1960, Zeng had been running the Havana bureau of the Xinhua press agency. But revolutionary Cuba did not yet have diplomatic relations with Beijing, and, as always in such cases, the press agency served as the Chinese representation – and as a cover for its secret services.

In March, before leaving Shanghai, Zeng Tao had been appointed to the committee of the recently created China–Latin America Friendship Association. In Cuba it could draw on the support of one of the largest Chinese communities in Latin America. Its chairman was Chu Tunan, but the real force behind it was Yu Sang, one of Kang Sheng's closest collaborators in the area of counter-intelligence.

Zeng Tao was involved in diplomacy. We have seen how he organised the mutual recognition of China and Algeria and sent the lawyer Jacques Vergès to visit Mao. In 1962, he actually became the first Chinese ambassador to Algiers. But two years earlier, in September 1960, Zeng was in Cuba. Recognition of Cuba by China was imminent and obsessed him as much as a blonde enchantress with a long nose.

Marjorie Lennox was a 26-year-old divorcee, with a body to rival that of Jane Mansfield, and she worked as a secretary at the United States embassy . . .

In a magnificent house on Fifth Avenue, on the corner of 14th Street in Havana, Ramiro Valdès, head of State Security, the organisation known as G2, summoned his assistant: 'That Chinese guy has got himself in a fine mess, according to reports that I've been receiving. We must get him out without delay!'

'We'll take action, there's no need to worry,' replied Osvaldo Sanchez, one of Fidel Castro's original companions in arms.

On 15 September, at one o'clock in the morning, G2 moved in on the residential area of Vedado beach. On the twenty-third floor of the Seguro del Medico Building, the door of the apartment swung open, thanks to the use of a pass key, creaking a little. The buxom Majorie lit the bedside lamp only to find two automatic pistols trained on her. The G2 captain noticed that she did not turn a hair. No doubt she had received excellent training. She had time only to put on a dress before being taken down to the offices of Cuban counter-intelligence. On 17 September, she was expelled under military escort, as an American spy. The same day, G2 arrested six Americans, three of them 'electrical engineers'; the eldest, the leader of the team, was Daniel L. Carswell. At CIA headquarters at Langley, the news was greeted with shock. When Stanley Archenhold, head of clandestine operations against Cuba, told Allen Dulles, the Director, what had happened, his pipe fell out of his mouth.

'Carswell is our best "plumber" . . . He has operated all over the world . . . laid miles of cable, planted thousands of microphones, telephone taps, electronic bugging devices, and he's never been caught before . . . He mustn't talk . . . We must get him out of that hornet's nest . . .'

Meanwhile, in Havana, Ramiro Valdès, all smiles, visited the Xinhua offices with Zeng Tao, who had seriously lost face. The place was riddled with countless bugging devices and a few other gadgets 'Made in the USA'. Out of courtesy, because Zeng Tao's wife Zhu Liqing was on the guided tour, Valdès did not dwell on the role played by the voluptuous Marjorie Lennox. Zeng Tao needed no explanations.

A week later, according to plan, the first Chinese ambassador arrived in Havana. Younger than Zeng Tao, a graduate in English, and of course a member of the China–Latin America Friendship Association and of the International Liaison Department, Shen Jian had been weaned in the *Tewu*. He remained in his post as ambassador until 1964, then in the years that followed, close observers noted that he went round Latin America and other continents, as supervisor of the famous troupe of acrobats from Wuhan.

The American spies adopted a remarkable line of defence before the military tribunal at the end of the year: 'Mr Robert Neet, an embassy employee, simply asked us to carry out some small electrical repairs in his apartment,' Carswell calmly explained.

'And his apartment just happened to be located above the offices of the Xinhua press agency?' slyly asked the state prosecutor, Fernando Flores.

The 'engineers' agreed, and were sentenced to ten years' imprisonment.

The CIA did not leave its 'boys' to languish in the sinister Cuban gaols. The lamentable Bay of Pigs fiasco in April 1961 (when the CIA landed anti-Castroist Cubans on the island to overthrow Castro) did not make it any easier to obtain their release, but two years later, Carswell and his friends were eventually exchanged for Cuban prisoners in the USA. The Xinhua incident was closed.

*   *   *

Relations between the Cubans and the Chinese were exceptional within a socialist bloc on the point of imploding. The hearts of the Cubans tended to favour Beijing. However, the Chinese remained very dogmatic and it was not until 1962 that they recognised Castro's island as a socialist state. In December 1960, while the CIA spies were being tried, Ernesto Che Guevara visited Beijing. Guevara did not hide his admiration for Mao Zedong's military achievement. The situation was ambiguous: the Maoists believed in the virtues of armed struggle based in the countryside, as did Guevara, who had just published *The Guerrilla War*, drawing a considerable amount of his inspiration from Mao and Lin Bao. But the Chinese continued to insist that only a communist party could run a guerrilla war successfully. This was a secondary point, according to Guevara. There was a small Cuban Communist Party, whose views the leader Blàs Roca had aired in Beijing a year earlier. Roca shared with his Beijing hosts the idea that only a communist party could be in charge of a revolutionary situation, as in Cuba, but he was pro-Soviet and did not have the same prestige as someone like Castro or Guevara, not having participated in the guerrilla war against the ousted dictator Batista.

'We Cubans understand the Chinese people very well, because we have both been victims of the American imperialist blockade, of humiliation and aggression,' declared Guevara, while stressing that 'the liberation struggle in Latin America is an armed struggle of the people'.

The Chinese are practical people. Cuba was the throbbing heart of the revolution in South America, and they saw an opportunity for getting one over Khrushchev, whose advisers were beginning to invade the Caribbean island. So Beijing decided to lend economic aid to Cuba and at the same time to favour the alliance between Maoist and Castrist movements in the Latin American continent. Zeng Tao and Shen Jian's mission seemed simple. At the Tricontinental Conference – the alliance of revolutionary movements on the three continents Africa, Asia and Latin America – the Chinese backed the Cubans. In return, in January 1963, Cuba refused to condemn China's ally Albania in the ideological conflict in which China stood opposed to 'Soviet revisionism'.

Born at the turn of the century, General Alberto Bayo, who took a keen interest in voodoo, was a revolutionary veteran. In mid-July 1936, when the war in Spain had just got under way, the then air force Captain Bayo was in command of anarchists and Trotskyists, and Catalan communists, who wrested from the Falangists the Balearic islands of Ibiza, Majorca and Minorca (finding Raoul Villain, the man who had assassinated Jean Jaurès, on the island, he had him shot). Having retired to Mexico during the 1950s, the one-armed general agreed to become Fidel Castro's military adviser. At Castro's request, he founded the first big guerrilla training camp in Latin

America and trained eighty guerrilla fighters at a ranch in Santa Rosa, not far from Mexico.

Bayo's lectures, later published in a pamphlet, resembled the advice issued by Mao: 'We are superior in brain power and in technique. We are disciplined and we are driven by a spirit of camaraderie. The enemy, with all its equipment and its thirty thousand men, does not have any of this. We are going to learn how to worry them and then disappear after every action. We already know how to instil panic and uncertainty within their ranks. We do more than attack. We avoid their fire. We return to the attack. We demoralise the enemy by our initiatives and our skill.'

Bayo's technique achieved wonders. Castro came to power shortly afterwards, overthrowing the Batista regime.

Promoted to the rank of general in October 1962, Bayo was chosen to set up a new school for secret warfare. Its purpose – to set alight the pampas and sierras of Latin America. The Russians, already firmly installed on the island, imposed Colonel-General Afanasi Pavlantevich, 'a hero of the Soviet Union', at the head of it. He had commanded the Manchurian garrison, the Port Arthur special forces, and in 1945 he had encircled five German divisions with his troops. In this special Cuban school, those attending would learn rural guerrilla warfare, sabotage, urban terrorism. Bayo taught students who spoke Spanish, including those from Spain. It was in this way that the anti-Franco anarchist militants of the Revolutionary Directory of Iberian Liberation, which came to the world's notice in 1961 when they seized the Portuguese transatlantic liner the *Santa Maria*, came about.

The Haitian poet René Depestre, who in November 1960 had had meetings with Mao and Zhou in Beijing, was also at the school, where, it was said, he gave lessons to the African students. In any event, he wore the uniform of a political representative of the Cuban army. It was the period when he was writing his 'Ode to a Militiawoman of the Revolution':

> While we make love
> Our two Colt 45 pistols keep watch
> On the same marvellous night-chair.

A Pole of a kind, Welinsky, taught subversion to the other Europeans. Then there was a Chinese. Luo Ruiqing 'the Incorruptible' had sent an instructor, Lin Xiaoyen, to train agents recruited from among the 160,000 overseas Chinese living in Latin America. But the Sino-Cuban honeymoon did not last. In January 1964, Fidel Castro went to Moscow, after which, relations between Beijing and Havana deteriorated extremely quickly. In the rift between Khrushchev and Mao, Castro sided with the Russians. At the beginning of 1965, Che Guevara once again flew to Beijing; he wanted good relations with the Chinese. But he now represented no one but himself. After a final trip to Africa, where he fought alongside the pro-Chinese, he decided to return to the guerrilla war on *his* continent and died fighting in Bolivia in 1967.

In September 1965, G2 discovered that the Chinese were disseminating their own propaganda in the Cuban army. Castro's government lodged an official protest.

'China does not keep its commercial pledges!' declared Castro, drawing on his cigar, in January 1966.

'China is betraying the good faith of the Cuban people!' he stormed on 6 February of the following year.

The next day the Chinese commercial mission left Cuba.

'We must go it alone from now on,' became Beijing's watchword.

In fact, for some years already, the Chinese had been trying to provoke divisions within the pro-Soviet Communist Parties in Latin America and set up its own movements. Their objective was the same as in Africa: to launch a guerrilla war and create 'the spark that would set the whole plain alight'.

Carlos Luis Prestes, the most eminent of Latin American communist leaders, became a living legend during the 1930s when he conspired on behalf of the Comintern, a scarlet galaxy that oppressed peoples then looked up to with stars in their eyes. To achieve celebrity at the Seventh World Congress – which saw the consecration of Kang Sheng – Prestes travelled fifteen thousand kilometres through the Brazilian jungle with the police hot on his heels. He arrived in Moscow in 1934, a year too early – for Stalin had decided to postpone the famous congress. A disciplined man, this former regular officer, now a guerrilla fighter, killed the intervening time at the Hotel Lux, the Comintern's 'Tower of Babel'. Kang Sheng met him there.

Born in the same year, 1898, these two communists found much they could agree on. They both represented the largest country in their respective continents, where they had built up clandestine combat apparatuses that were the jewels in the Comintern crown. The two men also had a mutual friend, Otto Braun, the famous German adviser and Mao Zedong's rival during the Long March. In fact, Prestes stole Braun's mistress, Olga Benario, from him. This gorgeous brunette, a German Jewess and a shock militant, organised Braun's escape from the Berlin prison of Moabit in 1926. But she fell hopelessly in love with the Brazilian adventurer . . .

However, Kang Sheng felt that Prestes had one great fault: he was blindly obedient to Moscow's instructions, the same instructions that had almost destroyed the Chinese Communist Party. He was to pay dearly for it.

After returning to Brazil, Prestes formed the National Liberation Alliance, in accordance with the new popular front policy adopted by the Congress. But Moscow instructed him to organise an uprising in December 1935. It was a disaster. Carlos and Olga ended up in prison, with dreadful consequences: in 1940, the Brazilian police dragged Olga from her cell and handed her over to Gestapo agents. She was already pregnant, and gave birth off the German coast, on the ship she was sailing on. Olga Benario died in a concentration camp.

Prestes was released in 1945 and met with the double joy of being united with his daughter and then of being elected senator. The Communist Party won ten per cent of the votes. But he lived through other dramas, and had to plunge back into secrecy.

In Beijing in the 1950s, Kang Sheng was organising his International Liaison Department with Wang Jiaxiang, and was beginning to sound out the fraternal parties of Latin America. In 1959, Prestes travelled to China. The head of Mao's secret services was delighted to meet his old friend once again, but noted that he still remained deeply pro-Soviet.

So in Brazil, as elsewhere, it was necessary to break up the parties and organise their infiltration. *Tewu* agents from Macao, where the people spoke Portuguese as well as Chinese, arrived in Rio de Janeiro, Brasilia and São Paolo, integrating into the Chinese community, of which there were about three thousand in Brazil. One of the great achievements of Kang Sheng's agents was the recruitment of the governor of São Paolo, Lionel Brizzoeo, a member of the same family as the democratic President Goulart, who spoke out strongly against 'yankee imperialism' in Latin America, to the extent that the CIA helped in his downfall in 1964 and the military takeover of power.

The previous year, Kang Sheng had organised the visit to Beijing of two leaders of the Brazilian Communist Party, Jaime Mihanda and Manuel Jover Telles. On 13 March, Kang, Peng Zhen (the mayor of Beijing) and senior International Liaison officials feasted with the delighted Brazilians.

'It is time to break away from the pro-Soviet revisionists' was the watchword of the day. They would be given the technical means, in collaboration with Kang Sheng's men in their country, in particular those at the Xinhua press agency (as ever, the number one cover organisation in those places where China did not have an embassy). The Chinese objective was to identify those favourable to armed struggle.

Jover Telles, acting on the impetus given by the Chinese, gathered together in Guanabara, near Rio, the pride of the Brazilian Communist Party – Mario Alves, Jacob Gorenber and Apolonio de Carvalho – while the celebrated author of *The Mini-Manual to Urban Guerrilla Warfare*, Carlos Marighela, won support in the São Paolo region.

Of this whole generation of Brazilian communists wooed and fascinated by Beijing, Apolonio de Carvalho was indisputably the most remarkable. Even Carlos Prestes paled in comparison. Apart from his good looks and Latin charm, Carvalho emanated a warmth unusual in men of his calibre. In 1936, at the age of twenty-three, as a young officer in the Brazilian army, he had crossed the Atlantic to fight in Spain in the International Brigade. Having fled to France after the fall of the Republic, Apolonio very soon joined the clandestine communist organisation there. According to his companion in arms in Spain, André Breton, he was even given the task of setting up the very first intelligence service of the special communist organisation, Service B.

As soon as the Franc-Tireurs et Partisans (Irregulars and Partisans) was created after the Nazi invasion of Russia, the Brazilian masterminded a whole programme of activity in the southern zone carried out by the foreigners' resistance group, the FTP-MOI. Here, he gathered intelligence on the Wehrmacht and organised desertions and the infiltration of the German armed forces. In Villefranche-de-Rouergue, he organised the revolt of Yugoslavs in the Wehrmacht. No doubt his friendship, since Spain, with the military leader of MOI, General Lioubomir Ilic, helped him a lot. Then there were the attacks against the Baumettes prison in Marseilles, for instance, leading to uprisings in Toulouse, Carmaus and Albi.

Meanwhile, in Toulouse, Carvalho had taken over the leadership of the MOI, after the arrest of his superior, Marcel Langer, who was beheaded on 23 October 1943. On 15 October, Maurice Schumann, speaking on the radio from London, had called on Resistance fighters to strike against those who were collaborating with Vichy justice. The Brazilian did not delay in responding to the call: on 24 October, the day after the death of his comrade, the leader of the 35th Brigade, Carvalho organised the commando unit that shot dead the assistant public prosecutor in Toulouse, Lespinasse.

It might be said that Apolonio de Carvalho was a born terrorist. But in 1945, he was a hero: a lieutenant-colonel on demobilisation, decorated for his contribution to the Resistance, awarded the Croix de Guerre and the Légion d'Honneur.

Was this his farewell to arms? Having returned to Brazil Carvalho devoted himself to organising the Communist Youth Movement, and even published a book in Rio in 1947 entitled *Os Problemas da Juventude Brasilieira*.

The Chinese revolution, the Cuban revolution – all encouraged the belief in the 1950s that 'power was at the end of a gun' in South America, too. The old guerrilla fighter could not resist taking down his gun from its rack in response to the call of a new adventure.

Argument was raging within the Communist Party. In 1956, the Brazilian militants had rebelled against Khrushchev's attacks on Stalin – just like the Chinese. In 1962, for the first time, a pro-Beijing party was founded in South America, in Brazil. The following year came Jover Telles' visit to China. So an external group already existed, while inside the Communist Party another faction was also establishing relations with the Chinese.

In April 1964, encouraged by the CIA and the US military attaché

Vernon Walters, the Brazilian military overthrew the liberal government of João Goulart.

On the morning of 3 April, police from Guanabara's State Security burst into the offices of the Xinhua press agency in Rio de Janeiro. They arrested the correspondents Wang Weichen, Jiu Qingdong, Ma Yaozeng and Su Zeping. Colonel Gustavo Borgès, head of the security police, then produced evidence that the Xinhua men and those at the Chinese commercial mission in Brazil were engaging in espionage activities. Furthermore, they were directly funding local communist groups. Wang Yaoting, who specialised in the import and export of textiles, and was head in Rio of the Council for the Promotion of International Trade, came under particular fire: the police had found at his home 53,000 dollars, 3,000 pounds sterling, in addition to various sums in other currencies. Shortly afterwards, the police discovered large supplies of weapons and unsophisticated bombs of the same manufacture as those that had been used to set fire to sugar plantations in the Recife region.

Until just before then, Wang had been directly answerable to an astonishing character, the representative of the Committee for the Promotion of Trade for Latin America, Ji Chaoding. An economist by training, he had studied in the USA, at Harvard, where, with the agreement of the communist leader Earl Browder, he had set up the Chinese Section of the American Communist Party. In this capacity, he played an important role in the pro Red China lobby in the USA, notably in contributing to that controversial journal *Amerasia*.

Ji travelled freely from one continent to the other, ostensibly for trade, but Western counter-intelligence had no doubt that his comings and goings concealed other kinds of business. The CIA at Langley, their headquarters, got to the bottom of it when he died in 1963. The funeral oration on the day of his obsequies, delivered in the presence of Zhou Enlai, paid homage to the 'clandestine activities' of the commercial traveller Ji Chaodin.

However, in Beijing, the authorities raged against the 'anti-Chinese acts' that had taken place in Brazil. On 16 April the *People's Daily* denounced an operation that had been organised from start to finish by the cruel state police, the DOPS, the CIA and, inevitably, Chiang Kai-shek's special services: 'It is increasingly obvious that the operation organised by the Brazilian authorities against Chinese personnel was inspired by American imperialism with the aim of damaging the friendship between the Chinese and Brazilian peoples and of provoking anti-Chinese hysteria in Brazil and other parts of Latin America.'

The usual complaint of the Chinese when caught red-handed.

The CIA undoubtedly added fuel to the flames. This happened to suit the Soviets, who were worried by what the Chinese were up to in Brazil as elsewhere, and by defections from the Soviet camp. Wang

Yaoting was the ideal target because of the great amount of travelling he did, supposedly to buy cotton.

On 8 May, the DOPS issued to the press a strange document found in a torch, an ultra-secret message signed by one 'Comrade Cheng' in Berne on 20 March 1963, and addressed to a 'Comrade Wang' – this was evidently Wang Yaoting, who had in fact been to Europe the previous year, which at that time meant going through Switzerland. So Berne, the capital of Chinese espionage in Europe, had given directives to the itinerant agent.

'I'm giving you the names in Portuguese of the main people you can contact and who are in a position there to help you, as comrades, accomplish important tasks in our common struggle, and your clandestine work, as well as the maintaining of contacts with the real leaders of the Brazilian Communist Party. We have a close and personal friendship and a very satisfactory working relationship in Brazil with the following orthodox Brazilian communists: João Amazonas, Lincoln Oest and Mauricio Grabois.'

In fact, these individuals had been expelled from the pro-Soviet Party in 1961 and had set up the more 'Chinese' group, the Communist Party of Brazil, or *PC do B*. This incredible missive went on to cite a whole series of members of the administration or the army who were in contact with the Chinese. It is quite possible this was part of a disinformation campaign. In any case, on 24 December 1964, the nine Chinese appeared before a military tribunal that sentenced them to ten years' imprisonment. However, six months later, the Brazilian dictatorship sent them home. They were met with a triumphal welcome in Beijing, presided over by none other than Liu Shaoqi.

In Brazil, the pro-Chinese within the CP left the Party in 1967. But their Maoism was crossed with 'Castroism' after the big Tricontinental Conference that took place in Cuba, which gave a filip to the guerrilla movements. Marighela founded a National Liberation Army. Carvalho, Alves and Telles – Kang Sheng's friend – created another guerrilla group, the Revolutionary Brazilian Communist Party. At the instigation of Beijing, Telles rejoined the more orthodox *PC do B* the following year. These groups and others formed the guerrilla front. Raids, assassination attempts, abductions of foreign diplomats came thick and fast. A state of siege was decreed. The repression was brutal, as always in such countries. In 1970 this alliance of disparate groups was severely weakened. Marighela was shot dead in an ambush. Alves and Carvalho were captured and imprisoned on the Island of Flowers, a penitentiary off the coast of Rio de Janeiro. Alves died under torture, and Carvalho's friends feared the worst for him too.

But in France, for all his pro-Chinese convictions, Carvalho's former comrades in the Resistance had not forgotten the proud guerrilla fighter (whose wife, a Frenchwoman, had taken refuge in the French embassy). Maurice Schumann, then Foreign Affairs Minister, remembered that the Brazilian had answered his appeal from London and organised the uprising in Toulouse. He intervened with the Brazilian military junta.

In June, a commando unit managed to obtain his release, together with that of other guerrilla fighters, in exchange for the German Ambassador (and former Nazi) Werner Holleben. Carvalho took refuge in Algeria, then in Salvador Allende's Chile. When the coup d'état came in 1973, he became active in the underground movement training guerrillas in the Third World run by Henri Curiel. The aim of Operation Jack, as it was called, was to enable all those revolutionaries being hounded by Pinochet's police to escape to Europe. A beautiful woman named Celia, daughter of one of Apolonio's former companions in arms in the Resistance, and a Breton woman who became a Maoist at the time of the war in Algeria were responsible for providing contacts, supplying false passports, establishing escape routes and hideouts in Europe.

At the end of 1973, Carvalho managed to organise the escape of Jacques Chonchol, leader of the Christian Left party, the Movement for Unified Popular Action, and former Minister of Agriculture in Allende's government. (His party was the only Latin American party to be represented at Kang Sheng's funeral in December 1975.)

During this time, the first and last Maoist communist party in Brazil, the *PC do B*, was taking a beating from the DOPS. On 15 December 1977, the police captured the Party leadership in a number of raids. A military justice report established that the accused had undergone training in the USSR and in China, and that they had set up a guerrilla base in Upper Araguaria. Jover Telles, the friend of Kang Sheng and of Apolonio de Carvalho, was among them; he was 'reported missing', which in Latin America was an invitation to fear the worst. When democracy was restored to Brazil in 1979, Carlos Prestes, who had taken refuge in Moscow, and Carvalho in Paris, returned to their country.

The Nueva Cultura Bookshop looked like any other little militant enclave in the Third World, piled high with copies of the works of Carlos Marx, revolutionary newspapers, pamphlets printed on yellow paper with the distinctive smell of publications printed in Moscow or Beijing, and a few thousand leaflets calling on the people to follow the glorious Ecuadorean Communist Party down the saving path of Revolution.

Quito, the old Spanish capital of Ecuador, a country nestling between Peru and Colombia on the shores of the Pacific Ocean, lies imposingly at an altitude of nearly 3,000 metres. Warren LaForest Dean, former insurance broker, former rubber planter, former FBI G-man, could not adapt to the altitude. His wife Robbie and his assistant Gil Medeiros Saudade found it difficult to understand: a huge chap like Dean – over six foot tall – should have been used to high altitudes, having just arrived from Mexico. But, made listless by the weather and weighed down by a feeling of sluggishness, he had not stopped groaning since he arrived. The CIA station he had just taken over was busy that early spring.

The CIA had mounted two operations to deal with the Ecuadorean communists: one to infiltrate the leadership, *Ecsigil*, the other aimed at gauging the tensions that existed within the leadership between those who favoured acting within the law and those who wanted to take up armed struggle. The operation was called *Echinocarus*.

It was at this time that two CIA technicians mounted an 'audio' operation in the little bookshop in Quito. This involved planting microphones in an apartment just above it, the tenant of which had a grudge against the communists. Thanks to these electronic bugging devices, the CIA in Quito were able to keep track of the activities of Jose Maria Roura, the bookseller, who was known to be a hardliner.

On 12 April, an early warning, as they say in the Company, started flashing. Mario Cardenas, an agent who infiltrated the CP, alerted his case officer: 'Roura is going to Beijing to seek funds. On his return, he will start a guerrilla war. Rafael Echeverria Florès, the Central Committee man, is the person sending him but without real authorisation from the leadership. They are acting on the quiet. They know that the pro-Soviets won't go along with them.'

A month later, Roura was arrested at the airport with 25,000 dollars in his pockets. On 23 May, in Guayaquil, the senior correspondent of the Xinhua agency, Alejandro Roman, was taken into custody. He too had just returned from Europe. Notes found in Roura's possession had led to his arrest. It was decided to release him. But the Xinhua agency found itself more than ever in the dock.

At his rather expeditious trial, Roura denied any evil intent in his trip: 'It's very simple. I was invited to London by the Chinese publishing house Guozi Shudian. I'm running a business, after all! The 25,000 dollars were to buy a printing works and publish here books written by Chinese authors. It's legal . . . Yes, it's true, I went to Beijing, I met Mr Chan Gongwen there, but our discussions were about literature. Why did I receive the money on my return to Berne? The Chinese considered that more practical. It was Comrade Bo Yibo who took care of it . . .'

The prisoner's denials did not deceive anybody – neither the Communist Party, which expelled Roura, Echeverria and the others, furious at having being made a fool of, nor the CIA, who checked and found that the names given by the accused were bogus. But the Chinese set-up – its press agencies, its international bookshops and the far-reaching tentacles of the Berne embassy – were now much better known.

In July, another Ecuadorean Xinhua correspondent was arrested, and the agency was closed down. As for Echeverria, he set up his own Marxist-Leninist Communist Party in the sierra.

The CIA had managed its operation *Echinocarus* perfectly. The pro-Soviet CP was weakened by the schism, which the Americans had brought to a head; the pro-Chinese were lost in the wilderness and Beijing's image tarnished for some time to come.

A few months later, Roura benefited from an amnesty, offered on the initiative of his worst enemy, Warren Dean. The CIA were hoping to recruit a disillusioned man, abandoned by everyone, while he wanted to go to Chile . . .

Overall, the CIA – and the KGB – had some reason to rejoice during the 1960s.

In most of the South American countries, the Chinese attempt at infiltration had backfired. After the reversals suffered in Cuba, Brazil and Ecuador, the Xinhua press agency continued to be the number one target of local police, at the Americans' request. In Chile, the Xinhua chief and head of the Chinese trade bureau, Li Yannian (who also operated in Uruguay), was constantly harassed. In Mexico, in February 1965, the Xinhua correspondent, Wu Chu, fled shortly before the police would have arrested him for spying.

Mexico, with its 10,000-strong Chinese community, was also a solid base for revolutionary intervention. In relations with the Mexican communists, Kang Sheng optimistically thought he could appeal to feelings of solidarity between former pupils of the Stalinist OGPU. He placed some hope in a rather unusual character, David Alfaro Siqueiros. This arch-Stalinist had been around for some time: as far back as 1940 he was, with the extremely active complicity of the French communist Georges Fournial, organising in Mexico a first assassination attempt on Trotsky, then in exile in Mexico City. An advocate of 'socialist realism' in the matter of art, Siqueiros on that occasion earned the sobriquet 'painter with a gun'.

In 1956 Siqueiros was invited with great ceremony to Beijing. If Kang intended to recruit this killer-artist on the basis of their shared admiration for Stalinism, he was surely disappointed. For Siqueiros, the mother country for communists remained without any doubt Russia. Kang Sheng consoled himself by setting up a Sino-Marxist-Leninist Party in Mexico and inviting the former President Cardenas, Trotsky's host in 1940, to meet Mao in person.

In Peru a strange development took place. The Taiwanese special services had anticipated that it would be impossible for a pro-Beijing movement ever to take root there. Once again they were proved wrong. There is today in Peru the largest Maoist guerrilla movement in the whole continent.

It is true that the largest Chinese community in South America lived here – nearly 30,000 residents in all, whose allegiance was hotly disputed by the Taiwanese and the communists. Kang Sheng's agents, working under cover of the Xinhua press agency, astutely established links with the traditional secret society called Hongmen. In January 1964, the official Communist party broke up, torn apart by the Sino-Soviet quarrel, and gave birth to the pro-Chinese group, *Bandera roja*.

The following year saw the creation of the Communist Party of Peru. Its leader, Saturnino Paredes Macedo, visited China. However, with the eternal debate of the 1960s – over the correct use of armed struggle – the CPP imploded.

A university teacher in Ayacucho in the Andes, who was also a Party leader, followed these developments. His name was Abimael Guzman, and he and his comrades had great influence on the local trade union movement – the mine workers, the students' and teachers' federations. In 1970, he set up the Mariategui's Shining Path. This underground movement took its name from the Jean Jaurès of Peru, whose socialist party became the Communist Party after his death. In the decade after it was founded, the Shining Path became the most effective guerrilla movement in the Andes, controlling entire zones and villages. Guzman – Comrade Gonzalo was his underground name – paid tribute to the Maoist tradition by defining their strategy as 'a peasant war run by the Party making the countryside the bastion of the army of the Revolution'. But in 1976, with Kang Sheng, Zhou Enlai and Mao dead and the Gang of Four overthrown, 'Gonzalo' took against the new political line adopted by China and blew up the Chinese embassy in Lima.

In 1982 the Shining Path organised 750 attacks, an average of two a day. The counter-guerrilla offensive was brutal, in accordance with the old tactic that consists of massacring whole villages deemed to be guerrilla supporters. By mid 1983, as ever, the repression had led to increasing paranoia. Those within the Maoist guerrilla movement who were in favour of a truce were branded traitors, 'supporters of the restoration of the Deng Xiaoping bourgeois line', and were therefore executed.

On Monday, 26 September 1983, the Chinese ambassador in Lima, Xu Huang, sent a coded message to Beijing: 'The Shining Path, supporters of the the restoration of the counter-revolutionary policy of the Gang of Four and Kang Sheng, has just blown up our embassy.'

Nearly twenty years after it had passed through communist China, Peruvian guerrillas loyal to the memory of Mao Zedong and Deng Xiaoping's Chinese diplomats were re-enacting the Cultural Revolution.

19
The Cultural Revolution

The East blazes beneath the rising sun
And Mao Zedong is on China's soil
He has brought happiness to the people
He is their saviour . . .

Tens of thousands, hundreds of thousands of people crowded into the legendary Tian'anmen Square on 15 September 1966 to the sound of drums and the rhythm of revolutionary anthems and slogans. Schoolchildren, students and teachers stood beneath a near cloudless sky. Surfeited on songs, intoxicated with incantations repeated a thousand times over, lost in a sea of red flags fluttering in the gentle breeze, they waited, their eyes fixed on the platform where, soon, their idol, the living god of Red China, would appear. Chairman Mao himself.

Towards five o'clock in the afternoon, a quiver ran through the huge square: 'Here they come! Here they come!'

'They' were the supreme leaders of the Revolution: Zhou Enlai, Chen Boda, Liu Shaoqi, Deng Xiaoping, Li Fuchun, Chen Yun, Xie Fuzhi, He Long and Chen Ye – legendary characters who one by one climbed up and took their places on the platform. And Mao! Mao who suddenly appeared, squeezed into his 'proletarian' uniform, his gestures slow, his face almost buddha-like, devoid of expression. Few, if any, in the crowd could see what was staring them in the face: that the great leader was also a sick man, power mad, a ruler who had long since suppressed any trace of spontaneity in himself. Then came the explosion: arms, hundreds of thousands of arms reaching out towards him, brandishing the sacred text of the new religion of the 'masses', the little red book: 'Long live Chairman Mao! May he live for a long, long time!'

Students and Red Guards jumped up and down on the spot, shouting. They were in a state of near hysteria, carefully stage-managed by experts in manipulating the masses. There was cheering as three hundred hand-picked students and teachers went up and joined the supreme being on the platform. Everyone was fascinated, with eyes only for Mao, who very slowly, very majestically descended and immersed himself in the ten thousand-strong crowd of excited Red Guards awaiting him.

All this was just a preliminary. Soon it was time for speeches and exhortations. Then the Master of Ceremonies, Comrade Kang Sheng, advanced towards his microphone and in a quiet but compelling voice declared the meeting open: 'In the name of the group in charge of the Cultural Revolution and acting for the Party's Central Committee, I welcome you and salute you: to you and, through you, to the teachers, students and revolutionary personnel of schools throughout the country, I address the militant greetings of the proletarian Cultural Revolution! Our great leader Mao is here to meet us. Let us proclaim together: long live the invincible thought of Mao Zedong! Long live Chairman Mao!'

Once again, there were choruses, anthems, slogans. These ceased only when Lin Biao began to speak in a hesitant voice. Despite his undistinguished delivery, the Defence Minister, who 'brought down' the Red Marshal Peng Dehuai in 1959, attempted to work up the crowd, calling on 'revolutionary combatants' to radicalise themselves. The next speaker, the Prime Minister Zhou Enlai, tried above all to calm things down. Though his tone was ardent, this was the better to put across a speech that was basically rather moderate. Cautious by nature, he had became increasingly worried by the excesses of the Red Guards, who a month earlier had sown panic in the streets of Beijing under the pretext of 'unmasking the counter-revolution and the accomplices of revisionism'.

And now here were the Red Guards. They followed one another on to the platform, each in a greater hurry than the next to welcome the comrades who had come from the provinces or to thank the Beijing militants for their welcome. But for the climate of intense excitement and latent aggression, this display of Asian politeness, these naive proclamations would have rendered the scene laughable.

'Our long-cherished desire to see our great leader Chairman Mao has finally been realised today. This is our greatest joy . . .'

'Our People, with all its nationalities, will always love Chairman Mao, will always remain true to his teachings . . .'

'We raise high the great red banner of Mao Zedong's thought . . .'

These short speeches over, the living god came momentarily to life. He saluted the huge crowd on several occasions, then, as though in a ballet choreographed by specialists in 'revolutionary protocol', he spent several minutes with a few of the three hundred happy elect, surrounded by flashing cameras.

That evening, giant projectors illuminated the platform and the whole of Tian'anmen Square. At ten thirty p.m., to crown the crowd's joy, Chairman Mao and Marshal Lin Biao made another appearance.

In the days that followed, hundreds of thousands of Red Guards, the amazing performance in Beijing fresh in their minds, returned to spread the word throughout the four corners of China. With Maoism in their hearts and the little red book in their hands, they carried the Cultural Revolution everywhere.

Before the Cultural Revolution, that radical upheaval in the second half of the 1960s which was to leave China almost drained of blood, there was a period when Kang Sheng, true to his education as a gentleman-scholar, appreciated Chinese classical drama without the slightest problem. Respectful of good manners and tradition, he would sometimes take out his best calligraphy brush to correspond with playwrights and directors, courteously informing them of his comments, and even his criticisms. Meiqian, for instance, received just such a letter from Kang Sheng: 'As you know, I am from Shandong. I very much liked your play *The Peachtree Fan* and its hero Kong Shangren . . .'

Nor was that all. Kang was also a patron of the arts. One New Year's evening, he invited another renowned artist, Zhao Yanzia, to his house, and entertained him lavishly. In exchange, he simply asked Zhao to play for him a few select pieces from traditional erotic drama on one of those Hu violins, the bow of which passes between two strings.

These were only rare moments of relaxation for Kang Sheng. Politics, as always, claimed most of his attention. Mao Zedong, furious at having been supplanted as head of state by his heir apparent, the dull grey Liu Shaoqi, was contemplating a counter-attack in the grand style, inspired by those high points of the Red Republic of Yan'an, talks on art and literature and the rectification campaign. He was counting on his old accomplices from that period to lead the counter-attack: his personal secretary, Chen Boda, and the indispensable Kang Sheng.

Jiang Qing, in particular, favoured the idea of a joint offensive with Kang and Chen in the fields of arts and letters. Ever since her much censured marriage to Mao, she had dreamt of eventually playing a prominent public role. She felt that the socialist education movement envisaged by her husband would provide her with a golden opportunity to make her re-entrance on to the political stage, while at the same time settling several scores with those who, during her time in Shanghai, had come between the young actress and the success she so greatly deserved.

'Chinese art must be purged of reactionary elements that denature it and want to turn it into a counter-revolutionary art!' she proclaimed.

Matching words with action, Jiang Qing took it into her head to reform Shanghai's artistic circles. For this urgent and salutary task, she needed the help of the mayor of the city, Ke Qingshi. That was no problem – Ke was an old companion of Kang Sheng, a survivor of the group of five appointed by Zhou Enlai in 1931 to rebuild the *Tewu* after it had been betrayed by Gu Shunzhang. With his support, Madame Mao could at last tackle the 'revolutionisation' of the theatre and opera of Shanghai, which, since 1949, had been the largest Chinese city.

Of course, Kang Sheng did his best to help her. Thanks to Ke Qingshi, he made the acquaintance of radical elements in Shanghai, including the real hardliners: Zhang Chunqiao, one-time writer and now head of propaganda for the city; and Yao Wenyuan, a 'literary critic' who specialised in making littérateurs with 'bourgeois' tendencies toe the line. These two future members of the Cultural Revolution's Gang of Four hit it off immediately with Jiang Qing.

In exchange for his good and loyal services, Jiang Qing helped Kang Sheng gain access to Mao, as she had during the Yan'an period. Thus it was that in 1965 numerous 'philosophical' discussions took place between Mao, his secretary Chen Boda and Kang Sheng, in an atmosphere strangely reminiscent of that leading up to the rectification campaign.

'The economic ideas of Bogdanov are better than those of contemporary revisionism,' affirmed Kang Sheng. 'Kautsky is preferable to Khrushchev. Djilas grovels before Stalin, but Stalin was wrong about the Chinese question. He opposed our takeover of power, explaining that *The Theory of the New Democracy* was a programme in itself . . .'

'Marx said: "Man is a social animal",' Mao replied learnedly. 'In the evolution of Man, the animal must develop. I believe that it is only Man who can evolve. In order to study the history of natural sciences, one must study natural sciences.'

Karl Kautsky, a German theoretician of social democracy; Alexander Bogdanov, a non-conformist Bolshevik; Milovan Djilas, a Yugoslav thinker whose texts on self-management Kang had had translated the better to combat his heretical ideas; Karl Marx – the discussions ranged far and wide! But none the less they did not neglect to work out the details of day-to-day tactics. Mao, Jiang Qing, Chen Boda and Kang Sheng decided to focus their immediate attack on Peng Zhen, the mayor of Beijing, who had stood up so well to Khrushchev at the meetings in Bucharest in 1960.

In November, one of his protégés, the playwright Wu Han, was carpeted by the zealous 'literary critic' Yao Wenyuan with regard to a play in which some people thought they discerned allusions to the disgraced Red Marshal Peng Dehuai. Nevertheless, Mao magnanimously proposed to Peng Zhen, via intermediaries, that he headed a Group of Five trusted militants charged with the task of preparing the programme for the necessary Cultural Revolution. The mayor of Beijing accepted, and either through naivety or ineptitude, seemed to pay no attention to the comrade imposed upon him: Kang Sheng himself. There was an interloper in the Group of Five, but this did not worry either Peng or Liu Shaoqi: Mao, it seemed, was ill. He was no longer seen in public. Only the faithful had the privilege of meeting the man who had led the Long March: Chen Boda, Kang Sheng, and also Wang Dongxing, his longtime bodyguard, head of Detachment 8341, (which was responsible for the protection of senior Party officials) and deputy head of the sinister *Gonganbu*.

Peng Zhen and Liu Shaoqi were mistaken in not taking the Maoist plans more seriously: gradually the group was taking shape that was going to lead the Cultural Revolution and cause Peng and Liu, and many others, to tremble.

Kang's first victim was the former head of the *Gonganbu*, Luo Ruiqing, who had become chief-of-staff of the army. A great admirer of Felix Dzerzhinsky, the Polish founder of Lenin's secret police, Luo annoyed Kang because of his still very considerable influence with the Public Security police, and he annoyed Lin Biao on account of his popularity in military circles. In short, he was a spanner in the works and a man to be got rid of before he teamed up with Peng Zhen.

Taking advantage of his new position within the Group of Five in charge of planning the Cultural Revolution, Kang Sheng ordered Wang Dongxing, Mao's bodyguard, to put Luo Ruiqing behind bars. Luo was accused of subscribing to the military theories of the dismissed Red Marshal Peng Dehuai, and was interrogated with scant ceremony. He eventually cracked and tried to commit suicide on 18 March by throwing himself out of a window. He was picked up, with both his legs broken. The incorruptible head of the *Gonganbu*, the clean tough general, was thus the first highly placed victim of the Cultural Revolution.

Mao now wanted to 'overthrow the king of hell and free the little demons', an image drawn from the legend of Yen Wang, who ruled over the kingdom of evil, and his eighteen servants. But it was no longer a matter of Buddhist tradition. What the enlightened guide of the Chinese people meant by his poetic image was: show no pity in bringing down those communist leaders who have taken the 'bourgeois path', namely Peng Zhen, and force their comrades to return to the correct proletarian line.

The key weapon in this task of revolutionary purification was to be the little red book, a small selection of texts by Mao, which was to become, along with the Bible and the Koran, one of the all-time worldwide bestsellers.

What crimes were committed in the name of the little red book. The Chinese version measured 10 centimetres long, by 7 wide, and weighed 70 grams. A 'pocket book' in the strictest sense, to be placed in all the calloused hands in the universe, it was filled with 270 pages of the Chairman's maxims and illustrated with a signed photograph of the leader, wart on his chin and all. It was published in April 1966, just in time for the great family dirty washing session with Peng Zhen.

A compilation of old texts and articles, the little red book was indeed Mao's masterpiece. It was, above all, the result of the cogitations of two past masters of propaganda and manipulation, Chen Boda and Kang Sheng. It was they who conceived of this collection of quotations as a decisive weapon in the conflicts to come, they who selected the extracts, they who supervised its production under the aegis of the Central Committee's General Office, Mao's preserve. Used to operating in the shadows, they did not claim responsibility for it, allowing Marshal Lin Biao, a brutal but shallow careerist, to claim credit for the invention of the sacred book. Lin, under whose auspices later editions of the anthology-programme would be graced with a preface and a sample of calligraphy, nevertheless had one great 'merit': he started the fashion for always having a finger marking the page in the little red book, in order to show that one had just broken off reading it . . .

Revolution and tradition gone haywire were the two underlying themes of the book. Previously, in the Red Republic of Yan'an, it had been necessary, in order to demonstrate one's militant enthusiasm, to recite for several hours a day the twenty-two campaign rectification documents. In the same way, the anthology of Mao's thoughts became the catechism of the Cultural Revolution, much to the great surprise of Western observers. However, this method of learning was rooted in Chinese tradition: in the olden days, young scholars were educated by repeating by rote the philosophical maxims of Confucius or Lao Tsu. This practice did not of course turn them into robots, but on the contrary contributed to increasing their knowledge of the characters of the Chinese language. Hence the ambiguity of the new system of indoctrination, which, by adopting certain features of traditional thinking, was that much more easily accepted.

The same was true of the famous *dazibao*, the 'big-character post-ers' which attracted so much attention from the outside world. The custom of informing the people 'on top' of the discontent of those 'at the bottom' went back a long way, to the times of the mandarins and emperors. The propagandists of the Cultural Revolution just turned it into a formidable weapon in the hands of the Maoists.

The first big-character poster appeared on 25 May 1966, put up, very appositely, on the walls of Beijing University by a young ultra-leftist assistant lecturer in philosophy, Nieh Yuanzi.

'Let us put paid to all controls and all the evil plots of the revi-sionists, resolutely, radically, totally, completely! Let us destroy the monsters, all the revisionist elements in the Khrushchev mould! Let us carry through the socialist revolution . . .'

Admittedly, the young assistant philosophy lecturer's spontaneity was only relative. It owed a great deal to a visit from Cao Yi-ou, Kang Sheng's wife, who went to Beijing University on 18 May. In any case, Mao liked it, and telephoned Kang Sheng as soon as he heard about it.

'Could you arrange for similar posters to be put up all over the country?'

Yes, indeed he could. Before throwing himself into it, the wily Kang had assured himself of the loyalty of the *Diaochabu*, the Central Committee's Bureau of Investigation, and of a consider-able number of *Gonganbu* personnel. He could also count on the 'Shandong mafia' and the support of the 'Shanghai group' – Zhang Chunqiao and the 'literary critic' Yao Wenyuan were becoming increasingly important in that city. Getting its own back on Beijing,

Shanghai was in fact the place from which the greatest thrust of the Cultural Revolution came.

Solidly realist, Kang Sheng had drawn his own conclusions from forty years of varied experience in the international communist movement: without an autonomous apparatus, there is no personal power that can last. For this reason, he selected his collaborators with care and never neglected an opportunity to extend the arms of his own network throughout China. Chen Boda, that bald wily intellectual, had no comparable support system in the country at his disposal. He was a head without a body. The very beautiful Madame Mao, despite her age, had a great influence over her husband. She was a body without arms. Zhang Chunqiao and Yao Wenhuan were masters in their Shanghai stronghold but nowhere else: they were arms without a body. Only Kang Sheng had everything: a head, a body, arms. More discreet than the others, he was also the most powerful of the initiators of the Cultural Revolution.

Thanks to him, it was not long before the thundering *dazibao* at Peking University was known to everyone. It was even published, again under pressure from Kang, in the *People's Daily*.

'The first canon shot of the Cultural Revolution has just been fired!' proclaimed Mao Zedong with obvious satisfaction. Thus was the power of his lieutenant proven.

Kang Sheng had already committed a few indispensably dastardly deeds. Sabotaged from within by him, the Group of Five gave up the ghost on 16 May 1966, when it was dissolved by the Central Committee. The Mayor of Beijing, Peng Zhen, Kang stabbed in the back: he was purged. So the trap had worked magnificently. It soon closed on other high-level cadres, such as Zhou Yang, formerly 'public prosecutor' at the trial of Wang Shiwei, the non-conformist writer from Yan'an who was assassinated in 1947 on Kang Sheng's orders. In the Cultural Revolution, as in all revolutions, the inquisitors themselves ended up victims, as others were to learn to their cost before very long.

Faith, like love, is blind. Neither Régis Bergeron, former duty editor of the communist weekly, *France Nouvelle* (*New France*), nor his comrades Francis Campestre, Raymond Casas, Jean Martin and Marc Tibérat knew exactly who Kang Sheng was – this great Chinese communist leader who did the tiny Communist Movement of France the remarkable honour of receiving it in person.

In their eyes, Kang was just the head of the Chinese CP's International Liaison Department. In fact it was with secretaries in this department, who had proved so fraternal towards the French revolutionaries, that the initial contacts had been made in Beijing a few days earlier.

As soon as they arrived at the People's National Assembly, the five men had to submit to the traditional 'family photograph'. Then it was time for the usual courtesies. They sat round a table in a little reception room, drinking tea and eating cakes, talking about nothing. Protocol demanded that only after a certain time had passed could the serious questions, political questions, be addressed. In order to mark the change of ambiance, everyone usually moved to another room more suitable for discussions.

On 23 August 1966, time seemed to stand still for the five French Maoists. However, in the schools, the universities and even several factories, the Cultural Revolution was at its height. Three days previously, thousands of Red Guards had invaded Beijing, each one more fanatical than the other, drunk on propaganda, frothing with vengeful slogans against the abominable 'counter-revolutionaries' who supported the 'black line'. Violence was the inevitable result.

The man who had masterminded this orchestrated invasion was sitting before Bergeron and his comrades, talking with concern about the ruthless factional struggles taking place and the need to pursue to the end the revolutionary process. To his visitors, Kang Sheng appeared above all to be a thin but very erect, almost stiff, man.

'I only sleep four hours a night!' he told them. He seemed tired, speaking in a very low voice and weighing up his every gesture to avoid any unnecessary effort. Each time they began to discuss a new problem, the secretary drew from Kang Sheng's small briefcase sheets of paper covered with Chinese characters and deferentially handed them to his boss.

Kang Sheng gave his French visitors a complete detailed exposé on the development of the Cultural Revolution as 'planned' by the leadership to which he had been 'adviser' since July. In the view of the Maoist leader and his companions, the unrest would last for another three years and then calm down. On this point Kang Sheng was categorical: once the inevitable disturbances were over, a new order would appear, sanctioned by a new social organisation.

Then they talked about France. Present at the meeting, French Maoist leader Raymond Casas recalled later for the authors that Kang Sheng explained how he had been in Paris in 1925, forming together with Zhou Enlai and French communist comrades the Chinese Party, and again in 1936 when he arrived on a Comintern assignment on May Day among a forest of red flags after the Popular Front had won the election. They talked at length about General De Gaulle, whose memoirs the Chinese leader had read.

At the height of the Cultural Revolution, Kang Sheng was one of the few senior officials in Red China to take an interest in the outside world, together with the Prime Minister Zhou Enlai and the Vice-Minister for Foreign Affairs, Chen Yi, already under fire from the Red Guards. Neither Madame Mao nor her friends in the Shanghai Group, nor even Chairman Mao himself really cared about the outside world. China once again closed in on itself, on its internal struggles, on its 'class' conflicts. And throughout the summer of 1966 these worsened daily.

* * *

Jiang Qing swam like a fish in the turbulent bloody waters of the Cultural Revolution, that gigantic witchhunt directed against revisionists that grew daily more dramatic, turning into a veritable spree of violence, collective incrimination and brain-washing. Swimming in the red shadow of her legendary husband, Madame Mao ceaselessly exhorted young 'revolutionary rebels' to destroy the work teams that had been set up in the university by supporters of Liu Shaoqi to channel the movement to their own advantage, on the typically Chinese pretext of giving it greater depth. She and Kang Sheng were in agreement on one fundamental point: these front organisations of the Chinese Khrushchevists had to be eliminated before they became dangerously entrenched.

Once again, the two ex-lovers advanced hand in hand towards the summits of power. More experienced, Kang Sheng worked out the tactics: Liu Shaoqi, although suspected of incubating the revisionist leprosy, was still the official head of state of Popular China. This institutional legitimacy had to be replaced by a higher, quasi-transcendental legitimacy, that of Mao, the Great Helmsman of the Revolution, infallible guide of the Chinese people. The only true head of state.

'We are all honoured: I bring you Chairman Mao's personal greetings!' Jiang Qing told the Red Guards at countless mass meetings held at the university. The crowd would go wild: Mao, the living god of Red China, was addressing them personally. And Comrade Jiang, his revolutionary companion, was speaking on his behalf, a part of him, as it were, exhorting them to pursue the struggle, to 'bomb the headquarters', shouting: 'To rebel is justified!'

The inspired director of this pseudo youth protest, Kang Sheng, accompanied his lifelong accomplice on these exhausting university visits. And Chairman Mao's wife never forgot to pay him public tribute in front of the 'revolutionary masses'.

'Comrade Kang Sheng does not belong to the Central Committee's Cultural Revolution Group, but he is our principal adviser. Comrade Chen Boda and I never decide or undertake anything without having first sought his advice. To tell the truth, Comrade Kang Sheng has very valuable experience of the class struggle.'

This was undeniable: no one survives unscathed the pitfalls of living underground in Shanghai, intrigues with the Guomindang, the grey Comintern years, the quarrels in Yan'an, the civil war and a period of semi-disgrace without drawing numerous lessons from the experience. During the period of the Cultural Revolution Kang showed that he had forgotten nothing of his turbulent past. Moreover, he demonstrated a talent for conditioning the 'masses', the highest form of expression in totalitarian regimes:

'Do you want to study the Communiqué and the Sixteen-Point Directive?' he would shout in a piercing voice.

'Yes,' the students replied, enthralled by his incantations.

'Do you want to study them again and again?'
'Yes!'
'Do you want to become really familiar with them?'
'Yes!'
'And use them for the great cultural revolution of your school?'
'Yes! Yes!'

Jiang Qing could not but admire the master demonstrating his art: how to manipulate a room full of people, how to 'work up' an audience, how to steer the 'spontaneity' of the masses in the desired direction, how to provoke hysteria, induce a collective orgasm by proxy. Much later, seized with an inexplicable fit of candour, Mao's wife woul: ir.genuously admit to an audience of Red Guards: 'I came here in great haste, but I have no idea what is going on. It was Kang Sheng who dragged me here.'

It is not too dramatic to say that the head of the secret services was also the secret master of the Cultural Revolution. *Diaochabu* couriers went all over the country delivering instructions and directives to cadres who already supported the Maoist faction. If the need arose, Kang Sheng's men would change their appearance, borrowing Red Guard blue overalls, or the khaki uniform worn by soldiers in the People's Army. They infiltrated Liu Shaoqi's supporters and the friends of Peng Zhen. They would put up inflammatory *dazibao* in strategic places, and when necessary do their best to avoid useless excesses.

It was with the agreement of Wang Dongxing, the Chairman's bodyguard, that Kang Sheng had the following directive of the Central Committee, dated 8 September 1966, posted on the walls of government buildings, factories and schools:

> Codes, telegrams, confidential documents, files and secret archives are essential secrets of the Party and the State; and their protection is the responsibility of all cadres, of the revolutionary masses, and revolutionary students and teachers. The Red Guards and the People's Liberation Army reservists must co-operate with government and Party bodies and with the People's Liberation Army in assuming the glorious responsibility for the protection of the secrets of the Party and the State.

This pointed to the limits of the 'revolutionisation' in progress. Neither Kang Sheng nor Wang Dongxing wanted the Red Guards to go too far. In the midst of the worst upheavals, these two Party apparatus men did not lose their appreciation of reality. Their destinies were linked since the Central Committee's quasi-clandestine session of August 1966, which confirmed Kang Sheng as a permanent member of the Politburo, of which he had previously been only a temporary member, and promoted the Chairman's bodyguard to the head of the Party's General Office.

Head of the International Liaison Department, head of the *Diaochabu*, the Central Committee's Investigations Department, adviser to the Cultural Revolution Group, theoretically number seven in the Party hierarchy, Kang Sheng saw his invisible power reduced. As for Wang Dongxing, he was not unaware of how wideranging were the prerogatives of the General Office, a veritable state within a state, at the virtually exclusive service of Mao. It was there that the distribution of the little red book had been co-ordinated and put into practice, after the purge of the person previously in charge, Yang Shangkun, accused of actively sympathising with the 'Soviet revisionists' and even of complicity with the KGB. Yang was in fact one of Kang Sheng's *bêtes noires*: a former student at the Sun Yat-sen University, he had been one of the key figures in the group of 'Twenty-eight Bolsheviks' and a personal friend of the last great Comintern representative in China, the Ukrainian Pavel Mif – and anything that reminded Kang of his former Comintern comrade Wang Ming, who had ages ago taken refuge in Moscow, made him see red. Even though Wang Ming was no longer of any consequence in China, Kang Sheng still persisted in indulging in violent diatribes against him.

With these promotions in the summer of 1966, the leadership team for the 'great clean-up' was now almost complete: an almost inaccessible living buddha, Mao Zedong, ideologues such as Chen Boda or Jiang Qing, men of real power such as Kang Sheng, Wang Dongxing and Lin Biao, head of the army, without which the Red Guards would never have been able to make their demands. And Zhou Enlai, of course, who tried from the outset to contain the damage, to protect his own. This solid realist, though he did not oppose the Cultural Revolution – he had lost the desire for a direct confrontation with Mao as early as the 1930s – intended to look after himself and save the most important thing: Chinese diplomacy. Applying the traditional principle 'the valorous man knows how to yield and recover', he put a kind of non-committal pact with the movement underway.

After the gathering of 'the one million Red Guards' in mid-September, the scales tipped decisively in the Maoists' favour, despite desperate counter-attacks from Liu Shaoqi. The Cultural Revolution spread through the provinces. Kang Sheng decided that it would do no harm if he were now to absent himself. The Albanian communist leader Enver Hoxha had invited the head of the International Liaison Department to attend the Fifth Congress of the Working Party.

On 26 October, the aircraft carrying Kang Sheng and his friend Liu Xiao, still Vice-Minister of Foreign Affairs, landed in Albania, the last stronghold of extreme Stalinism in Europe. But it was not until 5 November that Kang Sheng delivered his first big speech to the congress delegates and their guests:

The great proletarian Cultural Revolution in our country marks a new, deeper and more wide-ranging stage in the development of the socialist revolution in China. This movement focuses its attack on the handful of elements who hold positions of leadership but, although members of the Party, take the capitalist road. The large masses of revolutionary workers, peasants, soldiers, students and intellectuals, as well as the revolutionary cadres, constitute the main force of this great Cultural Revolution. The large masses of revolutionary youths and adolescents, and the Red Guard they have organised, have become courageous pioneers!

A hardened Stalinist, Enver Hoxha thought his Chinese comrade's stereotyped speech rather short and not clear enough: was it really 'correct' to say that Mao Zedong was 'the greatest Marxist-Leninist of our age', thereby consigning to the dustbin of history the founding fathers Lenin and Stalin? Above all, was it reasonable to incite fanaticised children to attack the leading cadres of the sacrosanct Marxist-Leninist Party? In order to discuss the issue, he invited Kang Sheng to visit him on Thursday, 10 November.

The meeting was very warm: Enver Hoxha liked Kang Sheng, appreciating especially the virulence of his anti-Yugoslav attacks. Besides, the head of the International Liaison Department was quite used to making himself sound reasonable and charming and at once explained: 'Chairman Mao said to me before my departure: "Bring our Albanian comrades up to date, for they must be very concerned about our problems, they are our closest comrades".'

This is a well-known technique: it is always the Red Guards from university W, the soldiers of unit X, the agents of department Y and the comrades of country Z who are the best Marxist-Leninists. Kang knew that his words would go straight to Enver Hoxha's heart, although they would not allay his mistrust. So Kang launched into a detailed exposé of the causes of the current conflict. According to him, the Peng Zhen affair had been settled a long time ago, the ex-Mayor of Beijing having betrayed the Chinese CP since 1925. His accomplice, Luo Ruiqing – former head of communist Public Security – was no better. They were thorough-going revisionists and bourgeois capitalists. Now that their group had been eliminated, there remained only two: that of the Maoists – the goodies – and that of the Liu Shaoqiists, who were crooks and villains. Naturally, Deng Xiaoping was tarred with the same brush as the wicked 'Chinese Khrushchev'.

Surprisingly, the Albanian leader was reassured by this 'analysis' and concluded that Mao had saved socialism in China.

Indefatigable as ever, Kang Sheng returned to Beijing, not without having extolled on several occasions the 'militant friendship between the two parties and the two peoples of China and Albania'. As soon as he reached the capital, he went back to work. This was reflected in results. At the end of the month came the appearance of the first posters accusing Liu Shaoqi and Deng Xiaoping by name of the ultimate sin: revisionism. Until then, they had not been challenged except in subtle circumlocutions . . .

On 4 December, Peng Zhen and several of his supporters were finally arrested by Kang Sheng's men, on Jiang Qing's orders, and were publicly humiliated, according to the latest fashion. It was not enough to throw opponents into prison, they had to be broken morally as well, monstrous 'confessions' had to be dragged out of them, and their families made to pay. The same Chinese torture was applied two weeks later to the Red Marshal Peng Dehuai, to Luo Ruiqing, whose daughter courageously refused to deny him even when he defied Lin Biao, and the former head of the General Affairs Bureau, the unfortunate Yang Shangkun. The bloodthirsty gods of the Cultural Revolution had to be assuaged.

'Imprison Zhou Enlai!' proclaimed the fifteen-foot-long banner put up in Tian'anmen Square by ultra-radical Red Guards, the May the Sixteenth Group. These super-revolutionaries hoped on 6 January 1967 to set in motion a process similar to that which had already led to the public denunciation of Liu Shaoqi and Deng Xiaoping.

This was rather jumping the gun. Unlike Jiang Qing, who was adulated by young people and students, but detested everywhere else, or Kang Sheng, who was universally feared, the Prime Minister enjoyed a genuine popularity throughout the country, which very quickly became evident. Other 'revolutionary rebels' appeared in the square and added their own words to the accusatory banner: 'To discredit Zhou Enlai is to discredit the proletariat's headquarters!'

In the Chinese jargon of the day, this meant something along the lines of 'Hands off Zhou Enlai!' Seeking to discredit Zhou also meant seeking the downfall of one of the oldest companions in arms of Kang Sheng himself, an inconceivable provocation without the tacit support, indeed complicity of the adviser to the Cultural Revolution Group. Immediately, all eyes turned in his direction in silent query: did Kang Sheng really want to have the Prime Minister 'criticised'? Was Mao prepared to let the faithful Zhou Enlai go?

Kang Sheng, like the Emperor's wife, had to remain above suspicion. Almost at once he called a retaliatory meeting.

'There are Red Guards,' he cried, 'who have put up wall posters criticising the Prime Minister Zhou Enlai in Tian'anmen Square. What is the meaning of this?'

Like a music hall artist, he gesticulated in order to encourage the crowd to respond.

'It's a counter-revolutionary act!' a well-prepared Red Guard – or one of Kang Sheng's men disguised as a Red Guard – hastened to shout back.

'So,' said Kang Sheng triumphantly, 'what are you going to do about it?'

'Catch them!' answered the crowd, who were perfectly well-acquainted with the rules of the game.

Kang Sheng of course endorsed their verdict. But this episode gave cause for reflection. A few days later new posters appeared on the walls of Beijing.

'To criticise Kang Sheng is a counter-revolutionary act!'

To criticise Jiang Qing too, and this dated back much longer. Since her marriage to Mao, Jiang Qing had been pursuing her obsession: to ensure the disappearance of all traces of her past and all irksome witnesses to it. The continual upheavals of the Cultural Revolution, and the arbitrariness and disorder attendant upon them, gave her the opportunity to do so. But she would not have been able to see this task through without the support, the help, the ingenuity of her old friend and ex-lover, Kang Sheng. In Kang's most secret offices, trusted agents busied themselves like the 'little demons' close to Mao's heart. They located all those whose paths had crossed that of Jiang Qing, if only momentarily. Actors or cinema directors, Party militants, mere witnesses of the past, sooner or later received a visit from a fairly special type of Red Guard who showed little interest in ideology and a great deal of interest in old documents: letters, photographs. Many of those visited were arrested on more or less spurious pretexts, then sent to rectification camps. Others simply disappeared.

Kang Sheng alone was no longer equal to this base work. Anguished by the idea of anything being overlooked, of a chink in the armour, Jiang Qing sought the help of the Chinese air force chief, General Wu Faxian, a friend of the Defence Minister, Lin Biao; and of Luo Ruiqing's successor in the Department of Public Security, Xie Fuzhi. To tell the truth, Xie did not have much room for manoeuvre in this matter. Handicapped by having been slow to rally to the Maoist cause, he only reigned over part of his shadowy *Gonganbu* empire, cornered between the powerful personalities of Kang Sheng and the Chairman's bodyguard, Wang Dongxing. Kang, for instance, had agents in every important section of the Public Security Department, a ministry that was practically under 'dual control'.

Xie Fuzhi, nevertheless, had certain major qualities: zeal, servility, obedience. He was also a realist. This cunning agent proved very efficient in tracking down witnesses, especially in Shanghai, the scene of Jiang Qing's past 'exploits'. The transcripts of her interrogation in 1934 by the Guomindang police, which were seized when the communists came to power in 1949, were burned in his presence and that of Jiang Qing herself. Thus, the material evidence of Madame Mao's weakness when confronted with the Chen brothers' men went up in smoke.

On 29 January, not long after Marshal Lin Biao's People's Liberation Army had received the official order to intervene in the revolutionary process in favour of the Maoists, Kang Sheng, cheered up by this succession of good news, violently attacked Deng Xiaoping, who was still a member of the Politburo, despite being the object of accusation. This was part of the duel being fought with buttoned foil between

Kang Sheng and the Prime Minister Zhou Enlai. The two men still got on well on the personal level, sharing Jiang Qing's friendship. But Kang Sheng did not like the protection that Zhou was extending to 'reactionary elements' such as that little ferret Deng, who was always ready to conceal his anti-Maoist opinions behind a superficial Marxism.

With the aid of Lin Biao and the army, revolutionary committees began to be set up. True to his usual line of conduct, Kang Sheng filled them with his own men or with sympathisers: was not the fortress already besieged from within easier to storm?

In Shandong, his native province, it was easy. On 3 February, the first provincial revolutionary committee of real importance was born, under the leadership of one of his own, Wang Xiaoyu. Two days later, the Shanghai allies Yao Wenyuan and Zhang Chunqiao created a similar structure. The apotheosis, the crowning of this new phase of the great proletarian Cultural Revolution, took place in Beijing on 20 April. In front of 100,000 Red Guards, Zhou Enlai, Kang Sheng, Jiang Qing and Chen Boda solemnly appointed Xie Fuzhi as head of the revolutionary committee of Beijing.

20
The Grand Inquisitor

'The monstrous crimes of the British authorities have provoked the keen indignation of Chinese patriots. Impressive big-character posters criticising the violence committed by the British have appeared all over the island, in Kowloon and in the New Territories; furthermore, balloons bearing inscriptions have been released into the skies over Hong Kong: "Down with British imperialism!" "We will triumph and the British authorities in Hong Kong will be defeated!" Wooden lifebuoys carrying the same slogans floated in the sea off Kowloon. Fearing neither the curfew, nor British troops armed to the teeth, nor the anti-riot police, people use all kinds of means to strike against and repel the fascist British brutes in Hong Kong . . .'

In that torrid month of July 1967, the official Chinese press surpassed itself in describing, with rampant dishonesty, the riots taking place in the British Far Eastern colony, shamelessly passing them off as a 'patriotic' popular uprising. The Maoist journalists conveniently forgot an elementary truth: the people of Hong Kong, most of whom were refugees from the mainland, were not at all anxious to become part of the mother country, especially not in order to be 're-educated' by Red Guards.

What actually happened had nothing to do with the people's war: demonstrations by young secondary school pupils who had fallen under the spell of the Cultural Revolution, or by the traditionally pro-communist dock workers, violent scuffles, cars and motorbikes set alight, a police van attacked with harpoons, the intervention of soldiers from the British Army's Welsh regiment, reporter-demonstrator-rioters from the Xinhua press agency put behind bars, English raids on the Chinese Goods Store, a mainland China shop, and on the Kowloon Dockers' Union – all in all, a rather shocking shambles for Her Britannic Majesty's loyal subjects.

The events were the main topic of conversation at the Royal Hong Kong Jockey Club, the usual rendezvous for the British secret services.

'It's been organised by our friends across the border!' claimed some.

'Not at all! It's an attempt by the Cultural Revolutionary extremists to revive the disturbances and cause problems for Zhou Enlai and the moderates,' replied others.

In truth, the two versions were not incompatible, since Kang

Sheng's influence reached everywhere. In any case, the Maoist disturbances set Hong Kong's little secret world in turmoil.

The Crown Colony, with an area of 1,031 square kilometres and a
population of four and a half million, had in fact one of the highest
densities of spies in the world.

The Chinese were particularly active, China's different governments, whether communist or Guomindang, having always demanded
the return of the colony. One of their principal targets, ever since its
creation, was the electronic interception base at Little Sai Wan, used
jointly by the British Government Communications Headquarters
(GCHQ) and the Australian Defence Signals Division. A listening
station trained on Asia, Little Sai Wan 'broke' the transmission codes
used by People's Liberation Army units, and intercepted radio communications. But there was already a worm inside the fruit: his name
was John Tsang. Recruited by the *Tewu* when he was a student at
Cambridge University, this young Hong Kong police officer was given
the task of setting up a network within Little Sai Wan. He acquitted
himself so well that a radio operator and two other employees at the
base agreed to supply him with classified information. Before his
exposure in 1961, the *Tewu* agent sent a daily report to his bosses for a
period of two years.

Another Chinese spy, one of much greater importance, also worked
for the police. In fact, he taught at the Hong Kong police training
academy. Zeng Zhaoke made life very difficult for British Special
Branch before being expelled to Popular China, shortly before the
rioting broke out, in the summer of 1967. There, he calmly resumed
his activities within the special services, which he performed in con-
junction with his duties as professor at the Jinan University in
Shandong. Now a deputy for the province of Canton to the Sixth
People's Congress, the ex-police officer had lost none of his passion
for Hong Kong, which lies so close to the big southern Chinese
metropolis. Zeng Zhaoke is a member of Deng Xiaoping's secret
service think-tank, which is now working hand in hand with the former British enemy to prepare for 1997 when the last Asian colony of
the British Crown will be returned to the bosom of Popular China.

Was it agents working for Chiang Kai-shek's special services who
betrayed him to the Special Branch? Some say that it was. The
Taiwanese agents were powerful in the Hong Kong underworld. They
used as cover the legendary 14K triad: 14 because that was the number
of its old headquarters in Canton, during the period of the Nationalist
regime; and K for carat. This secret society, which was very well
rooted in Kowloon, the Chinese part of the city, was involved in the
usual 'traditional arts': drug-trafficking, prostitution, racketeering,
illegal gaming, kidnappings and assassinations of every kind. Since
the beginning of the 1930s, it had worked hand in glove with the
Guomindang intelligence agencies, on the basis of a permanent
exchange of 'mutual services'.

For the Europeans, there was no question of benefiting directly from this kind of network. However, Hong Kong remained an important base for observing Red China. The French SDECE, who had hardly any presence in Asia since their defeat in Indochina, tried to glean precious information here. MI5 and MI6 would interrogate refugees from the mainland, day in day out, and obtain the first revelations of Red Guards disillusioned with Maoism who had defected to the West. The German Bundesnachrichtendienst, the Federal Intelligence Service (BND), deployed their greatest experts on Asian problems, Major Alfred Sagner and his friend Suzanne Sievers, in the colony, although Taiwan still remained their main Far Eastern base.

KGB agents eyed their French, German and English colleagues with jealousy, for Hong Kong was no espionage paradise as far as they were concerned. On the contrary, always anxious to remain in the good graces of the Chinese authorities, no matter how odiously communist, British officials gave the Russians a hard time, forbidding them access to the colony: they had no diplomatic representation, no overstaffed trade mission, no Tass agency branch stuffed full of excessively snooping 'journalists'. In short, none of the usual covers for Moscow's special services.

This was all the more serious in that in June 1967 the KGB had just acquired a particularly demanding chairman, Comrade Yuri Andropov. Formerly in charge of relations with the Eastern bloc Communist Parties, Kang Sheng's rival at the Bucharest Conference in 1960 was determined to watch Red China very closely. In Beijing, his appointment was greeted with considerable sneers: 'He zealously participated in international conspiratorial activities!' proclaimed the Chinese press, an accusation it would not have dared to have made ten years earlier, during the 'great alliance' with the USSR.

The new head of the KGB quickly realised that his agents' task was impossible during the Cultural Revolution. Beijing expelled them one by one, as Yuri Kusiukov, Andrei Kruchinsky, Nikolai Natachin and Valentin Passentchuk had already learned to their cost. So they would have to fall back on Comrade Igor Rogachev, a great specialist in Chinese problems who was obliged to operate from Washington, where he was first secretary at the embassy. It must have been a blow to Andropov's self-esteem that the route to Beijing had to pass through the United States capital.

For the Americans, then in the middle of the war in Vietnam, even more was at stake. The CIA had lost several U2 photographic reconnaissance planes in China. Worse still, in 1968 the North Koreans captured the *Pueblo*, a spy ship crammed full of ultra-modern electronic interception equipment. The 'Company' had to keep a low profile. Its Chinese specialists in Hong Kong nevertheless came up with several propaganda operations of great style. Already in 1964 and 1965, the CIA had given a task force responsibility for perfecting new techniques for radio propaganda to be broadcast in Red China. The personalities involved would in the future be famous worldwide: Professor William Griffith, President Carter's future adviser, Zbigniew Brzezinski, the diplomat McGeorge Bundy. On the basis of the conclusions reached by this trio, two radio stations were set up in Taiwan as soon as the Cultural Revolution got underway. Their broadcasts were partly relayed via the Guomindang army's underground installations on the islands of Quemoy and Matsu.

By supplying the Chinese with a carefully concocted cocktail of accurate information and alarmist news about Red Guard activities and the current factional fighting, the Americans hoped to worsen the situation and cause problems in the Maoist clan. Information gathered in Taiwan and Hong Kong by CIA agents very quickly confirmed the success of the enterprise. Further refinements were added to the operation, inspired largely by techniques of psychological warfare used by the Taiwanese: the publication of thousands of copies of a fake *Thoughts of Liu Shaoqi*, propaganda leaflets and tracts sent to the mainland by means of balloons by the CIA's Far Eastern Bureau.

The Hungarian Jesuit priest La Dany's listening post in the New Territories, in the British Crown Colony, was improved by the results of the Americans' campaign: genuine news and bogus information were frequently taken up by Chinese radio, if only in order to deny it, over and over again – which was tantamount to an admission that it was true, as far as most people were concerned. In the zones controlled by the anti-Maoists, the impact was even greater.

This form of psychological guerrilla warfare proved terribly effective in a country surfeited on slogans, lies, ideology, a country where even the opponents of the 'Great Helmsman' Mao Zedong used his own concepts and vocabulary to challenge him. In order to counter the Americans, the communists would have had to have had at their disposal their usual flawless counter-intelligence service and implacable political police. But the *Gonganbu* itself had been half swallowed up by the Cultural Revolution. And Kang Sheng had a lot to do with the wave of purges that swept through Chinese Public Security.

With his little pointed beard and his tousled moustache, Felix Dzerzhinsky bore a slight resemblance to Trotsky. As a young student, this son of semi-ruined Polish aristocrats initially devoted himself to poetry, writing lyrical texts against oppression and dictatorship. Quite naturally, he became an active militant, joining the Social Democratic Party of Lithuania. Thrown into prison on several occasions by the authorities in his country, he was forced to emigrate to Russia, where he joined the underground Bolsheviks. Lenin's new companion had a taste of the Tsar's prisons, then the October Revolution released him from his cell and restored his freedom. Thus it was that Felix Dzerzhinsky, the apprentice Polish poet, became the founder of the Soviet secret police, the redoubtable Cheka, forerunner of the OGPU and the KGB.

Lenin personally chose him for this difficult task. He thought that Dzerzhinsky, because of his temperament, because of his experience of life in prison, would not turn into a feudal satrap, abusing his power at the first opportunity. Hard but upright, severe but not too bloodthirsty, the Pole would be a new kind of policeman, the Saint-Just of the socialist revolution. Dzerzhinsky performed Soviet Russia's dirty work zealously but honestly until his death, following a heart attack in 1926, after a stormy session at the Party Congress.

The 'incorruptible' Luo Ruiqing could not remain indifferent to such a character. When he founded the *Gonganbu* in 1949, Luo Ruiqing took Felix Dzerzhinsky as his model. They were very alike: disinterested, without feelings but without personal ambition; servants of the Revolution, implacable, inflexible, convinced that repression was only the first stage towards a better society, hence the exceptional vigour with which they implemented it; torturers, too, but without any personal sadism. In fact, very dangerous men.

During the 1950s, at the time when 'landowners' and 'counter-revolutionaries' were being wiped out, Dzerzhinsky's portrait adorned the walls of Public Security offices. *Gonganbu* officers did not hesitate to tell their prisoners of their strong admiration for the Polish Chekist and of how they hero-worshipped their boss, Luo Ruiqing. Was not the *Gonganbu* the arm and sword of the Chinese Revolution, just as the Cheka, the OGPU and the NKVD had been successively the best defenders of the purity of the Russian Revolution?

One can imagine the astonishment, the indignation of these operatives, convinced of the importance of their task, when Luo Ruiqing was thrown into prison on Kang Sheng's orders at the beginning of 1966, tortured and then, despite his two broken legs, handed over to the Red Guards. He was paraded in public with a self-accusatory placard round his neck, abused, humiliated, and called a 'revisionist', 'bourgeois', 'traitor' by hysterical adolescents. The world had been turned upside down.

Kang Sheng's ferocity can be explained by his political ambitions. Confident of the support of a body of cadres in Public Security, which he had been conscientiously infiltrating for years, Kang wanted to use the Red Guards for his own purposes. These naive iconoclasts would unwittingly help him to destroy Luo Ruiqing's former kingdom. Weakened, the *Gonganbu* would fall into his hands, thereby extending his domain. In order to achieve this, Kang was prepared to go to any lengths – even to having Red Guards within the *Gonganbu*. Thus, in March 1967, a curious publication entitled *Hongse Gongan* (*Red Public Security*) appeared in Nanking. Directed against Liu Shaoqi, Luo Ruiqing's 'boss', this was the organ of the revolutionary rebels in the local police force; such a thing was unheard of.

Public Security veterans loyal to Luo Ruiqing's memory found all this increasingly hard to stomach. Like their USSR counterparts, they were completely set on the maintenance of order. They hated the continual disruption, the street demonstrations, the confrontations, in short everything in which Kang Sheng was revelling. What had to happen happened in Chang Avenue, at *Gonganbu* headquarters in Beijing: the rival factions within the political police resorted to guns to settle their differences. Several high-ranking officials died in these ruthless internecine struggles.

However, as an essential instrument of state power in China, Public Security was not going to simply cease functioning. Maoists and supporters of Liu Shaoqi agreed that the day-to-day work must go on, despite everything. Division 5, in charge of the surveillance of foreigners resident in the capital, did not halt its activities. It just carried on . . .

For Western or Soviet diplomats, the surveillance measures applied by Division 5 were not out of the ordinary in their scope. It was a question of preventing any interference by foreigners in the revolutionary process. But the small foreign colony in Beijing was not made only up of official representatives; there were also several hundred others: Maoist militants attending training, employees of Chinese administration departments. The police kept tabs on them thanks to the zeal of 'revolutionaries' from the Third World or Western countries who agreed to act as both judges and police over their comrades.

This was the case with Sidney Rittenberg, an American who had been a naturalised Chinese citizen for twenty years. Another Yan'an veteran, he was involved in Radio-Beijing's foreign language broadcasts. He was also behind a Yan'an-Bethune Regiment appointed to see to it that Western comrades' revolutionary spirit remained in good condition. The group took its name from Norman Bethune, the pro-Chinese Canadian who had died some years before, upon whom Mao had bestowed the remarkable honour of dedicating a posthumous eulogy. Rittenberg was less fortunate than his predecessor. Denounced by Arab Maoists – he was Jewish – as a 'Zionist spy' and 'CIA agent', he was thrown in prison and stayed there until the end of the Cultural Revolution.

While he was behind bars, the unfortunate Rittenberg encountered dozens of imprisoned Public Security employees who had acted on orders from Kang Sheng, who had acted on orders from Wang Dongxing, the Chairman's bodyguard, who had acted on orders from Minister Xie Fuzhi . . . This zealous triumvirate hid behind the sacred orders from Chairman Mao, who wanted the security bodies to be 'a knife in the hands of the proletariat'.

A number of the imprisoned *Gonganbu* officers felt that the implementation of the Chairman's ideas was, in their particular case, totally mistaken. Had they not worked wholeheartedly for the construction of socialism, in its purest form? These Chinese were the twin brothers of their Soviet counterparts in Stalin's NKVD, who were swallowed up one after the other by the death machine for which they had never ceased working. Let the individual perish if it furthers the march of socialism!

The imprisoned security police could appreciate as experts themselves at this type of work the style of the colleagues who interrogated them. The important thing was to get them to confess – to plots, crimes, dealings with the revisionist clique of the traitor Liu Shaoqi, espionage activities on behalf of American imperialists, or the Guomindang in Taiwan, or the socio-fascists in Moscow, it didn't really matter what! Very few did. They knew from experience the irremediable consequences of a confession extracted in order to 'render a last service to socialism'. So they used cunning. Some began to lose their reason, or simply their memories. Others suddenly became deaf, or mute, or both.

By an ironic twist of fate, or rather the perversion of the system, some of these unfortunate torturers-turned-victims were given a taste of the 'scrapheap', Zhazidong, a concentration camp opened during the SACO period near Chongqing by Dai Li. Hope kept them alive. Sooner or later their revolutionary purity would be recognised, the madness would cease, the world would return to normal, with themselves back in the *Gonganbu* and their opponents in the *Laogai*, the Chinese gulag.

But this was not what Kang Sheng wanted at any price, or at least not yet. With Comrade Minister Xie Fuzhi's help in carrying out the most squalid tasks, he accelerated the purge of counter-revolutionary elements in the *Gonganbu*. Nor was Xie Fuzhi short of ideas. One of the senior officials in Public Security, Zhao Dengcheng, was ordered to fabricate false documents intended to 'prove' that the Red Marshals Chen Yi and Zhu De had set up a clandestine Chinese opposition Marxist-Leninist party. It is true that Chen Yi was a particular thorn in Kang Sheng's side. This old soldier, Zhou Enlai's deputy at the Foreign Affairs Ministry, was vigorously opposed to Kang's attempts to gain control of Chinese foreign policy.

For Kang was indeed infiltrating the most sensitive preserves. To the great despair of the 'Red seaman' Liao Chengzhi, he ordered the *Gonganbu* to interrogate in depth those Chinese returning from overseas to visit the motherland. Many ended up in dungeons, which wrecked the policy Liao was attempting to pursue, of winning the support of Chinese emigrants for the regime. Since he protested, Liao fell victim to the purge. But his status as the son of a leftist Guomindang hero assassinated by reactionaries once again saved his life, especially as Zhou Enlai intervened very firmly on his behalf.

Zhou, without opposing Kang Sheng head on, tried to restrain his purificatory zeal and his growing ambition. Whilst he was unable to save the Manchu Zou Dapeng, head of the *Diaochabu*, the Central Committee's Investigation Bureau, he managed effectively to protect his deputy, Luo Qingchang, who was purged but not liquidated; the same was true of Ling Yun, a senior cadre in the *Gonganbu*, and two men in 1987 numbered among the heads of China's special services and secret police.

Liu Changsheng was not so lucky. This Chinese militant who, thirty years earlier, had organised the mutiny on the Dutch war vessel *De Zeven Provinciën* on behalf of the Comintern was assassinated by Red Guards. He had been Vice-President of the Council for the Syndicates of Red China.

Despite the obstructions raised by Zhou Enlai, Kang pursued his work of infiltrating the *Gonganbu*, which was indispensable to the success of his plans and those of his ally Jiang Qing. He tried to lay hands on all compromising documents in order to strengthen his blackmail operations. He had destroyed any that would have been a hindrance to him and of course those that might have incriminated Mao's wife. Accused by his liege man Xie Fuzhi of spying for the 'Americans and Chiang Kai-shekists', Feng Jiping and Xing Xiangsheng, the heads of Beijing's Public Security, were arrested. Then it was the turn of their colleagues in Shanghai – Liang Guobin, Huang Chibo and Wang Jian.

Kang Sheng was settling old scores more than ever before.

'Zhao Jianmin, you are secretary of the Party Committee in Yunnan, and yet you support the Pao Party! You have committed many harmful deeds, have you not?'

On 21 January 1968, in the assembly room in the Hotel Jingxi in Beijing, Kang felt full of cruel eloquence. This manhunt was reminiscent of his past flushing-out activities in Yan'an, but even more exciting. In the jargon of the Cultural Revolution, this ruthless persecution was called 'chasing the tiger', which meant hounding the bureaucrat or the revisionist into a corner. But Zhao Jianmin was not going to give in so easily. He was all too familiar with the rules of the game. Conceding the truth of even the slightest part of the accusation would mean capitulating right down the line. It would mean putting oneself in the same camp as the 'Black Inn' conspirators, who were set on Mao's removal from power. In short: it meant signing one's own death warrant.

'I have never supported the reprehensible activities of the Pao Party!' he protested energetically.

But Kang had got his prey. He had no time for petty bourgeois scruples.

'Don't lie to me!' he yelled. 'Liu Shaoqi lied to us. The rebel spies lied to me. When were you arrested during the period you were working in the white zones?'

'In 1936,' conceded Zhao Jianmin.

'In what manner did you voluntarily give yourself up to Guomindang justice?'

'I never gave myself up to the Guomindang!'

'You're lying, you're a rebel.'

'No, I'm not!'

'I repeat, Zhao Jianmin, that you are a rebel.'

'No, Kang Sheng! I am not a rebel. I stand by everything I've said . . .'

What a nuisance this 'Black Inn' conspirator was, with his refusal to make a just self-criticism! Sure of himself, Kang Sheng insisted. 'Stand by what you say if you like. You will write a note. Your activities have not just been occasional. You are a rebel, a rebel who has infiltrated our Party and plans to take advantage of the Cultural Revolution to sow disorder on our frontiers. I've seen the plans of the Guomindang group of spies in Yunnan. You were acting on those plans. Believe me, I'm relying on more than forty years' revolutionary experience: you retained a deep class contempt for us . . .'

Zhao Jianmin drew himself up. 'The Party can carry out an investigation.'

Kang Sheng sneered, once again baring his tobacco-stained teeth. 'Of course the Party will carry out an investigation! You are crazier than I thought to launch an attack against the proletarian classes' executive. And you still want the Party to carry out an investigation?'

'Yes, that's exactly what I want!'

'Suit yourself! Write down what you want then . . .'

Zhao Jianmin sat down at a table to write his plea. While he was struggling away, Kang telephoned the Minister of Public Security, the ever-devoted Xie Fuzhi, and asked him to send over some *Gonganbu* men to the Hotel Jingxi. When Zhao emerged, almost reassured, the police arrested him. He was to remain in prison until 1976. Kang Sheng always got his way.

The downfall of Zhao Jianmin gave the signal for a radical purge of communist cadres and militants in his region, Yunnan. Apparently, it caused nearly 14,000 deaths. The Cultural Revolution, to reiterate the famous words of Mao Zedong, the man who inspired it, was no 'dinner party'.

Already in April 1967, Kang Sheng and Xie Fuzhi, on the pretext of the clandestine activities of the *Nei Rendang*, the People's Revolutionary Party of Inner Mongolia, had dragged its local communist leader Wang Yilun through the mud. 34,000 cadres were incarcerated and 1,500 summarily executed. Reverting to the practices of the Yan'an Rectification Campaign, a model for the Cultural Revolution, Kang Sheng turned himself into a grand inquisitor. It was from his offices that emerged a tide of calumnies, or carefully rewritten truths, the files destined to discredit political opponents.

In January 1968, while wrapping up the Zhao Jianmin affair, Kang Sheng was planning the liquidation of Liu Ren. The second secretary of Beijing's Communist Party Municipal Committee, Liu was an old comrade of Kang Sheng. The two men met in Moscow during the

1930s, then again in Yan'an, when Liu Ren was sent as an active militant into the white zones. This did not, however, prevent Kang Sheng from condemning his former friend: 'The counter-revolutionary clique composed of Liu Ren, Gui Yueli, Feng Jiping and Xu Zirong is a collection of enemy elements opposed to the Revolution. They have sold secrets of the Party, of the State, of the government and the army. They are rebels against the motherland. Their offences must be crushed ten thousand times over. They must be bound hand and foot, and a thorough investigation of their activities carried out . . .'

There's no smoke without fire, or rather no fire without smoke, for Kang Sheng was adopting the tried and tested method of first proclaiming his victims' guilt and then doing the investigation work to establish it. Meanwhile, they languished in prison: Liu and his friends were in chains for five years. Xu Zirong died in his cell. Liu was to die four years later in 1973.

Kang Sheng's 'justice' wrought havoc. According to the present Chinese leadership, no less than 940,000 individuals, communist or otherwise, were affected. Why did the former Shanghai underground communist behave in such a cruelly systematic way? No doubt he was prompted by ultra-leftism. In Moscow, as in the Red Republic of Yan'an, Kang Sheng had always been considered exceptionally hard-line, always prepared to dirty his hands for the triumph of the Revolution. But at a time when the 'Great Helmsman' was visibly ageing and increasingly under the influence of Jiang Qing, there were plenty of additional reasons for acting in a radical fashion, for liquidating all opposition. Behind Kang Sheng's apparent 'murderous madness' lay his inordinate ambition. The man had for too long been pulling strings in the wings. From now on he wanted to do it openly.

Who could stand in his way? Zhou Enlai wanted above all to contain the damage; having identified himself for so many years with his party, he had renounced any personal ambitions. Jiang Qing, Kang's former mistress, his lifelong accomplice, could not but go along with him. The other senior officials were gradually knocked off their pedestals through his endeavours. Only Lin Biao remained.

Lavrenti Beria, Comrade Stalin's purger-in-chief, waited until his 'boss' was dead and buried before dreaming of taking his place. With Mao still alive, the question was whether Kang Sheng would go that far. In any event, he behaved like a man in a dreadful hurry.

In May 1968, while French Maoist students saw the approach of a hypothetical revolution, Kang Sheng committed a new outrage. His old comrade Liu Xiao, Vice-Minister of Foreign Affairs, was an obstruction in his race for power. Since it was in his interest to do so, Kang deliberately forgot the courage Liu had shown in saving his life by remaining silent when tortured by the British police in Shanghai in 1928. He fabricated an espionage charge against his old companion.

This rather unsavoury task accomplished, he invited Liu to dine with him at the Beijing Hotel.

That evening he was in a very good mood, and the hotel's banqueting room rang with his jokes. Suddenly Kang leant towards his friend: 'Tell me, Xiao, imagine there's a double agent, working both as an agent for the Guomindang and the Russians, what should be done about it?'

Liu Xiao, who was rather taken aback, decided to put Kang Sheng's strange attitude down to too much alcohol. He did not reply.

'He must be caught, of course! Caught immediately!' exclaimed Kang with laughter.

He insidiously steered the conversation to the subject of Pan Hannian, one of the *Tewu* Group of Five in Shanghai who had been imprisoned since the 1950s on grounds of his 'counter-revolutionary crimes'. Liu Xiao felt his stomach turn over: what did Kang Sheng mean by referring to their comrade-in-arms of long ago? However, his host's relaxed attitude encouraged him to remain calm. After that, the rest of the evening was very jovial. The two men parted, resolving to have dinner together again soon.

Just as Liu Xiao was going back to his car, he was unceremoniously hailed by police. He understood at once: Kang Sheng had invited him out in order to relish the spectacle of his future victim.

Jiang Qing and Kang Sheng allowed themselves to be consumed by the ambition they shared. They dreamed of transforming the whole apparatus of the Communist Party into the tame instrument of their ascendance. They already had control over the Red Guards, over a very large part of the special services and the secret police. Still they were not satisfied. In July 1968, Kang wrote a letter to his former mistress, which he sent under the 'highly confidential' seal. It gave all the explanations necessary for the changes in the list of Central Committee members that Kang Sheng advocated. According to Kang Sheng, 'three-quarters of the communist senior authorities were spies', 'rebels', dangerous individuals who had had 'secret dealings with the enemy', or who had 'flaws in their political history'.

Cao Yi-ou was just as zealous as her husband in promoting purges. As the Cultural Revolution gained ground, so Kang Sheng's wife gained in confidence, contributing to the most important decisions. In August 1968, as the Russian tanks were entering Czechoslovakia, the couple entrusted Guo Yufeng, head of the Chinese CP's Organisation Department with a task that they considered to be of paramount importance: Guo was to draw up the indispensable files bringing accusations against the 'rebel' elements that constituted three-quarters of the Central Committee. This meant that 800 senior CP cadres, 33 of them national leaders and 120 members or future members of the Central Committee, were called into question. Stalin himself could not have done better.

21
Western Intelligence against Kang Sheng

The Chinese student had taken a room in the little hotel right at the top of rue Monsieur-le-Prince, at number 65, in the heart of the Latin Quarter, next to the Luxembourg Gardens. This was not a coincidence. Numerous Chinese restaurants had just opened in the streets off the boulevard Saint-Germain and French counter-intelligence suspected several of them of serving as 'dead letter drops'.

The Service de Documentation Extérieure et de Contre-Espionage, the SDECE, France's intelligence-gathering service under its former name, had 'identified' the student, shortly after he arrived in France, in 1963; he was indeed a representative of Kang Sheng's secret service in Paris. The SDECE counter-intelligence people were beginning to get a fairly clear idea of the *Tewu*'s battle order. The head of the service, Colonel René Delseny, a veteran of the Colonial Infantry and of the war in Indochina, was beginning to achieve results. Thanks to the SDECE station in Hong Kong which was working away furiously, the British, Americans and French were exchanging lists of Chinese suppliers of dubious information, all too often designed simply to mislead the Westerners on behalf of Kang Sheng's secret services.

The Totem system, an 'intelligence exchange', operated regularly with the Japanese *Naicho* agents, or with General Yeh Hsiang-tse's Taiwanese people. But Colonel Delseny felt that the Japanese were in a hurry to do only one thing when they came to SDECE headquarters: to get down to Pigalle and have a night on the town. In fact, the Japanese intelligence agency *Naicho* remained one of the best informed on China, along with the Australian ASIS and the Indian RAW. But, like all Asians, the Japanese were extremely meticulous about exchanging information with the West. Moreover, they preferred to hand over their 'material' to the head of the SDECE station in Tokyo, a fine connoisseur of the Far East, Commander Robert Cantais. Already by the end of the Second World War, he had set up, on the borders of Indochina and the Yunnan frontier, a very active intelligence-gathering network run by missionaries, including the legendary figure Father Jean-Elie Maillot.

As for the Taiwanese, they had a mine of information, partly thanks to the ex-communist defectors: the former communist leader Zhang Guotao, the writer and historian Warren Kuo, or Kang Sheng's former secretary, Zhao Yaobin. But, it was said at the SDECE, they tended to lay the ideology on a bit thick, which became something of a delicate issue when General De Gaulle decided to recognise Popular China in 1964. Intelligence of equal quality to that supplied by the Taiwanese came to the SDECE via the CIA.

But this time there was a possibility of seizing 'raw material' right in the middle of Paris. A matter like this was the province of the SDECE's special operations department, Section 7. Colonel Morvan, a former member of the Resistance in Burgundy whose sympathies lay with the Socialist Party, and a freemason, was entirely responsible for putting together this unique team whose purpose it was to undertake impossible missions. The opening of an embassy safe, the spiriting away of a diplomatic suitcase in order to photograph the contents, the procurement of a copy of a foreign politician's speech before an important international conference, the theft of the patent for a jet – Section 7 specialised in the near-impossible.

Morvan chose his best agent to watch the Chinese student in rue Monsieur-le-Prince. Hotels were familiar territory to 'Monsieur Paul'. Of average height, with a sharp eye, nervous and lithe as a panther, this former Resistance fighter was the pride of the section. No safe had ever resisted him – he had accomplished hundreds of such missions all over the globe. Wresting documents from unwitting owners was nothing to him.

Once on the other side of the door to the small bedroom, 'Paul' had no difficulty in locating the briefcase on the table. Not aware that he was being watched by the French, the *Tewu* man had not taken the usual precautions. The SDECE agent began to examine the hundred or so pages covered with characters written in black ink. He smiled at the thought of Michel Couvert, the head of the Far Eastern Department of Section 7, grappling with the translation. Fortunately, 'Paul's' mission was only to photograph the documents.

Suddenly he started. He heard footsteps in the corridor, a key in the lock – the Chinese student was returning unexpectedly. The only thing to do was to hide in the bathroom. It took nerves of steel not to panic at a moment like that. As luck would have it, the Chinese spy immediately stretched out on his bed. A few moments later, he was snoring away. 'Paul' had no choice: he seized the briefcase and hurriedly left the hotel. The next day the student could not but notice the disappearance of his documents. If Beijing had only known how he had allowed himself to fall into the trap, Luo Qingchang, the head of the external intelligence service, would have given him a pretty hard time.

Shortly afterwards, he rented a studio flat on boulevard Raspail. 'Right, we'll have another go!' suggested Colonel Morvan. The SDECE rented the studio next door. This time, it was a question of introducing a microphone. A routine job. All that was needed was to bore a hole and thread a lead through it a few millimetres. Suddenly the line jumped and began to slip through the hands of the Section 7 expert. On the other side of the wall, the Chinese was pulling on the lead with all his might. This time, 'Paul's' secret mission had failed.

The Chinese student disappeared. But the SDECE had no difficulty in finding him again. In the spring of 1964, after De Gaulle's recognition of China, Ambassador Huang Zhen presented his letters of credit to the General. As they went through the list of Red China's diplomatic mission in Paris, the French counter-intelligence service noted that the young 'student' in rue Monsieur-le-Prince had become 'Second Secretary'. The SDECE wrote another report for 'the exclusive use of the French services'.

'The real head of the *Tewu* in Paris is the embassy adviser Song Zhiguang. He was born in 1916 in the Canton region. Studied in Japan. In the early 1950s he was Popular China's Embassy Secretary in East Germany, where he was in charge of relations with Walter Ulbricht's counter-intelligence outfit. His wife's name is Zhang Ru.' Song Zhiguang, one of Kang Sheng's aces in France, was later to become an ambassador in East Germany, Great Britain and Japan in the 1980s. Such is the life of the secret services.

Another Chinese who became the constant object of surveillance was the head of the Xinhua press agency for France and Switzerland, Yang Xiaonong. For all the foreign secret services operating out of France, whether KGB or CIA, Paris is also a vantage point for French-speaking Africa. So no one was surprised to see Comrade Yang making frequent visits to the African continent, nurturing contacts between certain African guerrilla groups and their immigrant cells in Europe. But for the most part, Yang Xiaonong travelled back and forth between the *Tewu* station in Paris and the headquarters of Kang Sheng's services for the whole of Western Europe, which was then located in Berne, in Switzerland.

At the same period, SDECE and DST (*Direction de la Surveillance du Territoire*, France's internal counter-intelligence service) experts noted the increasing activity of the *Sigurimi*, Colonel Mawsi's Albanian intelligence service. Under Chinese supervision, the Albanians' main activity centred round the groups of immigrant African students in France. However, while the Sino-Soviet conflict was reaching its height, Albania itself became a object of interest to observers. 'We are the Chinese of Europe!' said the Albanians. This was partly true: the Chinese used this little Balkan country as a relay station in the psychological war conducted by Radio Beijing. As well as the transmitters in Stalin Avenue in Tirana, there was talk of Chinese troops being based there, of rocket launching pads and submarine bases.

'We must get to the bottom of this,' Colonel Morvan told 'Monsieur Paul'. Alas, the SDECE had no one *in situ*. When 'Paul' arrived in Tirana, he received the unhoped-for assistance of the French ambassador Pierre Gorce, who for once was not one of those diplomats from the Quai d'Orsay who detest the secret agents from the *'Piscine'* (a colloquial, slightly pejorative name for the SDECE, derived from the location of its headquarters near a municipal swimming baths). Driving a decrepit old banger, the ambassador took 'Monsieur Paul' to all the sensitive areas that he was supposed to photograph from every angle with his Minox. The most tricky was the famous submarine base at Vlorë, tucked away in a gulf just to the north of the island of Corfu. In October 1961, after the rift between the USSR and Albania, Enver Hoxha's government seized the Russian-built base and simply took three Soviet submarines hostage. By March 1965, Zhou Enlai and Xie Fuzhi (the Vice-Minister of the *Gonganbu* and a friend of Kang Sheng) had concluded agreements between diplomats and secret agents of the two countries.

At the same time, 'Monsieur Paul' delivered his pictures to the SDECE. It was the first time a Western intelligence service had succeeded in confirming the Chinese presence in Albania.

Later, 'Paul', the service's ace agent, went to China, on four occasions. He always used the passport of an old Resistance comrade long since dead, but whose date of birth, in the summer of 1915, was near enough the same as his – only a day out. 'Paul' had changed his 'profession'. After having spent twenty years opening the safes of foreign missions, he was now entrusted, by the new head of the SDECE, Alexandre de Marenches, with the task of ensuring the security of the French embassies. He could not help chuckling to himself when he entered the French embassy in Litundongsi Street in Beijing and the militia guards greeted him with a magnificent: *'Ni hao, Tongzhi*!' 'Greetings, comrade!'

Whilst China became a major focus of interest for French intelligence, the SDECE were not the only people to follow closely the dreadful events that were taking place in the People's Republic. A host of officers, most of them sinologists, were put to analysing the Chinese phenomenon. Attached to the Deuxième Bureau, or later to the Intelligence Division of the General Secretariat for National Defence, they included: Colonel Garder, author of a book on Mao Zedong; Colonel Guillermaz, who was to write a very thorough *History of the Chinese Communist Party*; Colonel Bourgeois (whose Chinese wife, Penelope, taught her mother tongue in Saint-Germain-en-Laye) and Colonel Eyraud (military attaché in Beijing).

Normally, it was not the SDECE but the DST that was responsible for counter-intelligence within French territory. But the birth of a Chinese section was laborious.

Of average height, with grey hair and a slight stammer brought on by shyness, Inspector 'Michel' was an incredibly hardworking man. In the evenings, he would read dozens of pamphlets, tracts, works on China. He literally devoured them. This young man with no money, who seemed rather out of place in the world of counter-intelligence, had served as a non-commissioned officer in the war in Indochina, and he was fascinated by Asia. The decision was taken at rue des Saussaies to assign him to the DST's research unit on China.

One day in 1963 he picked up the phone to call his wife, Monique, a doctor in the Latin Quarter: 'Hello, darling, they've finally agreed, I'm finally going to be able to learn Chinese, isn't that wonderful?'

The director of the DST, François Beyze, had actually agreed to pay for him to attend classes at the Sorbonne. But they were very meticulous at the DST about false papers. For security reasons, it was decided that it would be best if he registered under a false name. He was therefore given a fake identity card. Alas, the day classes started, the professor wanted to identify his students and began to read the list on which the inspector's real name figured. The DST man was taken by surprise; according to his false papers, his name was Martin. Rue des Saussies had made a gaffe. His registration papers had been sent in under his real name, together with a photograph.

'But who are you then?' asked the astounded professor.

The poor inspector blushed, stammered out a few words: 'There must be some mistake . . .' and made for the door, his head lowered.

Inspector 'Michel' did not place much confidence in the Central Index, on the top floor. With all those Chinese names, documents were bound to be misfiled and in a state of chaos. Furthermore, the head of the Central Index, Commissioner Péjou, was a real tyrant. It was virtually impossible to get to consult his index; it has to be said that the DST had fought tooth and nail, during the time of its founder Roger Wybot, to prevent its being transferred to the Central Archives of the Sûreté Nationale. Commissioner Péjou therefore guarded it jealously.

Wanting to keep the Chinese index in his own possession, Inspector 'Michel' was confronted with the problem of where to put it. Especially as the big section on international communism had fallen into neglect at the time of the Sino-Soviet schism. From that point, the Chinese sector included the French Maoists. New card indexes had to be drawn up: BERGERON, Régis, JURQUET, Jacques, MARTY, François, etc. 'Michel' kept the whole lot in a grey metal filing cabinet beside his desk in a particularly cramped office on the third floor.

One morning, the deputy director, Auguste Sauzon, burst into the 'Chinese section'.

'Show me your classification system!'

The inspector hesitantly complied, and opened up his cabinet: out tumbled piles of papers, coloured pencils, spy novels by Jean Bruce *OSS 117*, sandwiches, bottles of Perrier water . . .

'I see, I see!' said Sauzon, slamming the door.

In 1964 a new director had been appointed to the DST who wanted to inspect the premises at rue des Saussaies. Entering Inspector

'Michel's' office, accompanied by Sauzon, he straightaway asked: 'I would like to see the file on the head of the Chinese intelligence services . . .'

Stammering, 'Michel' nodded, all smiles nevertheless, opened the door of his cabinet, blindly thrust his arm inside, rummaged through the hundreds of files and trimphantly withdrew a sheet: 'Kang Sheng, born 1898 or '99, or 1903. Friend of Zhou Enlai. Set up the CCP's secret services in Shanghai during the thirties. Then disappeared. Resurfaced. Runs the so-called *Tewu* secret service. Takes a keen interest in atomic affairs. A key figure in the conflict with the Soviets. In July last year was a member of the delegation to Moscow headed by Deng Xiaoping.'

Inspector 'Michel' had proved that, despite everything, his unsophisticated methods worked. He was unquestionably one of the best experts on Chinese espionage. Under the aegis of Commissioner Duranton, head of the CARU, the DST's Russian section, Inspector Thomas was put in charge of the DST's active service for Chinese and Vietnamese matters. It was he who, on the basis of information compiled by 'Michel' and supplied by the SDECE or the American FBI, had to recruit agents, and keep the Chinese community in Paris and elsewhere under surveillance. Born of a Breton father and a Vietnamese mother, he had married a very beautiful Vietnamese girl whose father was also Breton. Asia was not, therefore, unfamiliar territory to him.

The recruitment and surveillance of the Chinese, however, was no small enterprise. 'Michel' had supplied the *Tewu*'s battle order, under diplomatic cover. But these 'diplomats' who had come to France with neither wife nor children shared the same accommodation and lived the lives of reclusive monks. The use of listening devices – codenamed Orion – was tricky because of all the different Chinese dialects. Naturally, details of the Franco-Chinese Friendship Associations had been obtained. But the most interesting was basically the nationalist community. Section 5 of General Intelligence had supplied a dossier on the Guomindang in France: 'Headquarters: 6, rue Aumaire in the 3rd *arrondissement*, run by Messrs Hsia Ting Yao, Teng Yung Kong and King Sui Sin. 240 members in France (out of 300 in the whole of Western Europe); immensely active.' However, the DST had learned that this community had been infiltrated by Kang Sheng's *Tewu*. The great achievement of Inspector Thomas was to recruit a Chinese, who was officially a member of the Guomindang, but whose restaurant, near the Cluny Abbey in the Latin Quarter, also served as a meeting place for agents of Red China.

In the years that followed, the Chinese section of the DST matured, under the direction of a commissioner who had organised an excellent network in Hong Kong. But Police Superintendent Maurice Colomb of the DST found himself at the centre of a particularly strange incident.

On 28 April 1971, a rather unusual scene unfolded in the transit area of Orly Airport. The health authorities were worried to see a group of eight Chinese, in Sun Yat-sen suits, dragging along one of their compatriots, who looked decidedly groggy. This was a group of 'diplomats' from Popular China's embassy in Algiers. The DST knew that Zhang Shirong, the man they were hoping to get on board a Pakistan International Airways flight to Shanghai, was not a mere 'technical adviser' to Ambassador Yang Qiliang in Algiers but a cipher expert and an important member of the *Tewu* in North Africa.

For at the beginning of February, Zhang had surreptitiously approached the French embassy in Algiers. 'I want to change sides, I've opted for freedom,' he told the French.

The ambassador, who at that time was in line for a high-level promotion to the Quai d'Orsay, was worried. What should be done? His senior adviser, Jacques Dupuy, a veteran of the Free French movement, had been consul general in Hong Kong before being posted to Algiers, so he had some knowledge of Red China and its complexities. He suggested that they help the poor fellow who was risking his life.

By contrast, the SDECE representative was more wary. 'And what if this Chinese chap was a bogus defector, an agent detailed to infiltrate our organisation?'

The eternal dilemma. So the matter dragged on. Alerted by some indiscretion, the *Tewu* in Algeria kidnapped Zhang Shirong in April, intending to send him back to China via Paris to await his fate.

He had therefore been drugged for the journey. The DST men at Orly, who were hoping to short-circuit the operation, were convinced of it when they rushed at the group and seized the prisoner. A skirmish ensued, with punches being thrown right, left and centre. One of the Chinese ran to a telephone kiosk to contact his embassy in Paris.

In avenue George-V, action stations were sounded. Kang Sheng's representative in Paris – formerly a 'journalist' with the Xinhua press agency in Hanoi in 1954 – Cao Guisheng, raced to Orly with several cars crammed full of *Tewu* henchmen.

Meanwhile, the police had called in a CRS (Compagnies Républicaines de Sécurité – riot police) squadron. When Cao and his men arrived at the airport, a cordon of armed men prevented them from approaching the team of medical staff who could be seen carrying Zhang Shirong away on a stretcher.

Then came the protests and attempts to exert the sort of pressure to which China usually resorts when one of its nationals wants to defect to the West. In Beijing, the French ambassador, Étienne Manac'h, was summoned by the Foreign Affairs Ministry to explain his government's actions. On 1 May, International Labour Day, there was a big event in Tian'anmen Square and the ambassador expected to be challenged by the leadership. But he noted that day: 'I'm still awaiting the repercussions that the incident at Orly will lead to here. No doubt the crisis (if there is one) will only be triggered off if the party concerned seeks the right of asylum. On 1 May, Mr Zhou Enlai, when he came up to me on the platform, was just as smiling as ever.'

The French ambassador also noticed something strange: Kang Sheng was conspicuous by his absence, as was his deputy, the head of the *Gonganbu*, Xie Fuzhi, who was reportedly ill. The Xinhua press agency published a laconic statement: 'Certain members of the Politburo were unable to attend the First of May celebrations on account of work or illness.'

Was Kang Sheng so taken up with the Zhang Shirong incident that he wanted to follow its progress round the clock from his headquarters in Bowstring Alley? Or did he want to make a public demonstration of his ill humour towards the French representative, whose country had dared to thwart the *Tewu*'s plans?

Four days later, the French diplomat received an unexpected communication. Zhang Shirong, who was still in hospital in France, was asking to be repatriated. Or at least to be put in contact with representatives of his embassy. Things always look different from a distance.

Étienne Manac'h sent a note to Paris: 'I don't see why the presence of French witnesses should be necessary at this meeting (with a member of the embassy) since the party concerned is proposing to return to China. This presence and that of a Chinese witness would only seem indispensable to me if Mr Zhang Shirong was proposing to seek the right of asylum . . . Once he has freely expressed the wish, in the presence of the appropriate French officials, to return to his country, it seems to me that his embassy ought to be able simply to take him into their care.'

And indeed, Zhang Shirong, the man who had opted for freedom, was returned by French counter-intelligence to their *Tewu* counterparts. What awaited him once he returned to his country was, if not a cruel death, then at least twenty years in the *Laogai*, the Chinese gulag. But what had happened? Can one reasonably believe that Zhang had deliberately chosen to return to hell? No, there must have been good reasons for this apparently senseless behaviour. Was he afraid that his family, who remained at the mercy of the Chinese authorities, would be made to pay an exorbitant price for his actions? Did he succumb to pressure, and if so, what pressure? Was he simply sacrificed on the altar of reason of State, at a time when the prospect of the first visit to China of a president of the French Republic was imminent? For Georges Pompidou, together with Jean de Lipowski and Edouard Balladur, was indeed preparing to pay a visit to Chairman Mao.

The Zhang Shirong incident was not the only one to worry Western special services. The great centre for Chinese intelligence in Europe was Switzerland. As we have seen, its ramifications sometimes extended as far as Latin America and Africa.

Jose Maria Roura in Ecuador and Wang Yaoting in Brazil, at the time of their arrest, and later when tried for 'espionage and subversion', had revealed how Berne operated as a *Tewu* centre. As for Africa, the correspondent for the Xinhua press agency, Yang Xiaonong, who appeared on DST files as early as 1957, described as 'key agent for the *Tewu*', based successfully in Berne and Paris, was also active there. During the Congo crisis, the Belgian Sûreté identified him with Patrice Lumumba. When he went to organise the Xinhua agency in Paris, he was replaced in Berne by another very special correspondent, Peng Di. In January 1961 the Italian *Controspionaggio dell'Arma dei Carabinieri* arrested the Albanian agent Kallco Koko in Rome, and also Chinese agents at the Centro Cina, in Via del Corso. Six of them were expelled under military escort for spying on NATO installations. Among them was the reporter Peng Di, who took refuge in Switzerland.

It was from the embassy at 10 Kalchegwegstrasse that Colonel Ding Shan organised the gathering of intelligence with a master's hand. From 1964 onwards he had the help of Colonel Fang Wen in Paris. All these military intelligence networks (*Qingbao*) came under the authority of a Yan'an veteran working in the immediate entourage of Kang Sheng and Zhou Enlai, Liu Shaowen. Their number one target was for a long time Western countries' nuclear armaments, and the ambassador in Switzerland himself, Li Jingquan, co-ordinated operations as a whole. But the police, exasperated by Chinese scheming, quickly put an end to it.

During the period of the Cultural Revolution, the headquarters of Chinese espionage activities in Europe moved to Holland. The man in charge, Li Enqiu, was appointed chargé d'affaires to The Hague in July 1963, after several postings of a more diplomatic nature in Poland and Rumania. He was a man of iron. In Holland, a peaceful hospitable country, known for its great tolerance, Li could exert his influence over the whole of northern Europe. Moreover, the huge Chinese and Indonesian communities provided an excellent pool of talent for the *Tewu*. But woe betide anyone who caused a scandal.

On 16 July 1966, the Dutch police came across a Chinese tramp in a heap on the road not far from a house used by Chinese diplomatic staff in The Hague.

'Serious lesions to the vertebral column and a double fracture of the skull,' was the doctor's diagnosis. The police identified the injured man, one Xu Zicai, an engineer from Popular China who had come to Holland for a big international conference. The *Binnenlandse Veiligheids Dienst* (BVD), the Dutch counter-intelligence service, immediately directed its suspicions against the Chinese embassy. Together with the Belgian Sûreté, the BVD kept a close watch on Li Enqiu, because of the links he maintained with Maoist groups in the Benelux countries. But while an investigation was still being conducted, the engineer Xu Zicai disappeared. A Chinese commando unit had kidnapped him in broad daylight from the hospital. As in the

Zhang Shirong incident in Paris, the *Tewu* wanted to send him home. Kang Sheng's agents in fact thought he was an agent for the CIA. The atmosphere of hysteria that marked the Cultural Revolution lent itself totally to this kind of witchhunt. In 1966 special security agents were sent by the Central Committee's Investigation Bureau (*Diaochabu*) to China's embassies all over the world to root out 'traitors, revisionists, CIA agents'. Xu Zicai died shortly afterwards inside the embassy. On 19 July, a hearse tried to leave unobserved, but BVD inspectors had the place under surveillance and intercepted the vehicle. The autopsy revealed that Xu Zicai had died as a result of beatings. A few days later, Queen Juliana signed her government's order for the expulsion of Comrade Li Enqiu, a very serious measure indeed.

One man played a key role in the abduction of Xu Zicai from the hospital in The Hague, distracting doctors' attention while his commando unit kidnapped the poor engineer. With his bared brow, his bushy eyebrows and thick bifocal glasses, Liao Heshu loved to visit the expensive part of Amsterdam, accompanied by his wife and his two charming little girls, with two BVD tails close on their heels. But Dutch counter-intelligence already realised that the person who had replaced the killer Li Enqiu was also running the new *Tewu* station.

They could not have been more surprised when, on 27 January 1969, Liao Heshu, wearing pyjamas under his overcoat, went to the police: 'I want to defect to the West, put me in contact with the local CIA!'

On 4 February, Robert McCloskey, a spokesman for the State Department, confirmed to journalists the defection of the most important *Tewu* agent ever to have gone over to the West, 'Mao's masterspy'. 'We have taken Mr Liao to a secret place where he is under close protection. He has asked the USA for political asylum!'

Liao Heshu was in fact at Ashford Farm, 'the farm' where the CIA debriefed defectors from communist countries. There, he was given a lie-detector test. China experts interrogated him without respite.

'They wanted to assassinate me. Kang Sheng is ruthless. As soon as they suspected that I wanted to go to you, they kept me under constant surveillance. And I didn't want to go back to China, because there are terrible things happening there!'

Liao drew organisation charts of the Chinese special services, but CIA experts observed that all the names he gave were already known to them. The defector certainly gave a few new details about the Xu Zicai incident. All the same, this did not constitute a mine of information.

'Who is this guy really working for?' wondered the CIA's counter-intelligence chief, James Jesus Angleton.

Having got his fingers burned a few years earlier when some bogus defectors kindly supplied by the KGB had completely taken him in, Angleton was always wary.

'He's a poisoned present from Comrade Kang Sheng, a false defector,' concluded his colleagues.

Liao was therefore relegated to a harmless job in the Translations Department. Care was taken to keep him at a distance from all important projects. For a mole, this was the worst possible fate.

Liao Heshu was vegetating. He discreetly made this known to the Chinese embassy, which immediately began to reiterate its demand for the return to China of this 'victim of imperialism'. The CIA got the message immediately. This renewed interest in Liao was tantamount to an admission: the Chinese were implicitly acknowledging the failure of their attempt to infiltrate the CIA. They wanted to recover their agent.

'OK, but fair's fair . . .' was the reply. The 'Company' happened to have two officers it wanted to get back: Richard Fecteau and John Downey, captured by the Chinese on a photographic reconnaissance mission in the 1950s. After protracted negotiations, the two Americans were finally released. In exchange, Liao Heshu was returned to Kang Sheng.

There is an epilogue to this affair: in 1982, the People's Republic of China invited John Downey to visit the country to see for himself the 'reality of socialism under construction'. Which at least shows that the Chinese did not harbour any ill feelings about the Liao Heshu affair.

'The greatest threat to world security stems from Beijing's form of militarised communism, its armed aggression and its subversive activities in South-East Asia.' This was the conclusion of the plenary meeting of the ANZUS Council in 1967. ANZUS was the pact signed by Australia, New Zealand and the United States (with the tacit support of Great Britain, still very active in the Pacific Ocean). It was a military pact, but also an 'intelligence exchange' organised by the various secret services in the region. The most effective intelligence organisation with regard to China is undoubtedly the Australian (in association with the very efficient Japanese *Naicho*). But in 1967 Australia was rocked by a drama from which she has yet to recover.

In August, an extraordinary working party met in Beijing. Present were Marshal Chen Yi, Foreign Affairs Minister, Kang Sheng (who was preparing an offensive to bring down Chen Yi), two senior officials of the military intelligence service, Li Tao and Liu Shaowen (who had for a long time been in charge of the Australian section), and two Chinese naval chiefs.

'Our Australian agent is in a difficult position, we're going to have to intervene before long,' announced Chen Yi, looking visibly anxious.

'Will the navy be able to act when the time comes?' asked Kang Sheng, all smiles, as though there were nothing wrong between him and his old friend Chen Yi.

The two admirals nodded knowingly.

On 17 December 1967, Harold Holt, the Australian Prime Minister, was holding a small outdoor party at his cottage at Portsea, in Victoria. The weather was magnificent. There was not a ripple on the water. The crystal-clear sound of laughter hung in the air, along with the aroma of grilled meat being barbecued on the beach. Harold Holt, in an athletic mood, said he was going to take a dip in order to work up an appetite. What could be more natural? His friends watched the Prime Minister swimming towards the horizon. But suddenly he disappeared. There was panic: and yet he was such a good swimmer!

In the ensuing hours, neither the maritime police, nor naval divers, nor the helicopters that joined the search were able to find Harold Holt, Conservative Prime Minister of Australia.

In May 1983, Anthony Grey, in his retreat in the south of England, received a mysterious telephone call. Grey was a very well-known Reuters journalist who, for two years during the Cultural Revolution, had been imprisoned by the *Gonganbu*. That was the time when any English citizen was suspected by Kang Sheng and his men of working for the intelligence service. Anthony Grey was an expert on China, and perhaps a little too curious for the liking of the Maoist authorities.

'Do you remember the disappearance of the Australian Prime Minister Harold Holt?'

'Of course I do, he was never found!'

'Well, I can prove to you that he did not drown that day. An unidentified submarine was sailing in our waters. It was in fact a Chinese submarine. Chinese naval frogmen grabbed him by the feet, gave him an oxygen mask and took him to the submarine. Holt is today living in China.'

The person who spoke to Grey was formerly with Australian naval intelligence. His curiosity aroused, Grey began his own investigation, and gradually, thanks to numerous testimonies, he was able to piece together the astonishing career of Harold Holt and came to this astounding conclusion: Holt was one of the great successes of Chinese espionage. A mole in the same league as Kim Philby.

According to Grey, Holt became convinced during the 1930s that it was important for Australia to link its destiny with that of China, at least on an economic level. Thus it was that he became an agent of 'Mr Wong', one of Dai Li's spies in Australia. The Guomindang seemed to Holt, as a Conservative politician, a totally suitable ally. But in 1946 Dai Li was assassinated on Kang Sheng's initiative. The communists came to power. Holt became Minister of Immigration and Labour in Robert Menzies' government. And 'Mr Wong' changed sides, preferring to continue his work as a secret agent acting on behalf of the communists.

Harold Holt's case officer was now a Red. But he continued to regard him as a friend, the man whom he trusted to bring about a rapprochement between Australia and China. In 1954, when Kang Sheng returned to the foreground of Chinese politics, with the support of Liu Shaowen and Liao Chengzhi, the Comintern's Red seamen, who had met Holt on several occasions, he apparently decided to tell the Australian agent the truth. 'We want you to continue working for China, as you have done in the past. The country simply has a new master.'

If Harold Holt had refused, he would have found himself in a difficult position. How could he explain that he had been acting as a secret agent since the 1930s, and an agent for the Chinese, what's more? Whether it was Chiang Kai-shek or Mao Zedong in power made no difference under Australian law: either way, he was a mole working for a foreign state. Anthony Grey became convinced that, for fear of wrecking his political career, Holt succumbed to the Chinese blackmail. He, like 'Mr Wong', changed sides and joined the Reds.

In January 1966, Holt became Prime Minister of Australia. But his counter-intelligence service, the Australian Security and Intelligence Organisation, was beginning to have doubts. Cross-checking certain information gave rise to suspicion. It was then that Holt sent the signal to Kang Sheng: 'You promised that when the time came you would pull me out.'

For Kang it was important that his agents should not think that the *Tewu* would abandon them when things went wrong. On 17 December 1967, Harold Holt disappeared.

When Anthony Grey's revelations were published, they caused a sensation. An enquiry was launched. One thing remained unclear: why had the extremely efficient Australian counter-intelligence service not uncovered the betrayal of this exceptional mole sooner? There are a few new elements that explain this unusual blindness.

In 1949, while the communists were coming to power in Beijing, the British counter-intelligence service, MI5, was sending two men to Australia to set up a similar organisation in that distant part of the Commonwealth. The first, Courtney Young, was the only MI5 man who spoke Chinese fluently. During the war he had run Combined Intelligence Far East from Ceylon. Then he had been Security Liaison Officer (SLO) in Singapore, that is to say the MI5 person in charge of liaison with the other intelligence service agencies in Hong Kong, opposite the Chinese mainland. In 1949 he was made SLO in Australia. Because of his knowledge of Chinese, he helped set up the Defence Signals Directorate (DSD), a special agency to intercept communications in China, based in Darwin and Melbourne.

The second man sent to Australia by London was Roger Hollis. He was the deputy director of MI5 and his job was to advise Sir Charles Spry, the head of the Australian counter-intelligence service, ASIO. Courtney was naturally supposed to work with Hollis.

In 1949, a strange book appeared in London entitled *Manual for Spies*. It was signed by an ex-militant communist, Alexander Foote. As mysterious a character as his book, Foote had worked during the

Second World War for the Swiss branch of Red Orchestra, the famous Soviet intelligence network in Europe. He became disillusioned and 'defected' to the West. *Manual for Spies* told his story . . . In truth, Foote was not the author of this work, which was ghostwritten by Courtney Young himself, who in the course of countless interviews with Foote had reconstituted a major part of the story of the Red Orchestra network in Switzerland.

The world of espionage is a very small world indeed. The head of Foote's network at the time of his Swiss exploits was Ursula Hamburger: a character we have already come across under the name 'Sonia', but whom the facetious Swiss communist Pierre Nicole preferred to call 'the Mouse'. Courtney Young remembered this from his talks with Foote: while 'Sonia' was radioing intelligence to Moscow from the peaceful town of Montreux, his MI5 colleague, Roger Hollis, adviser to Australian counter-intelligence, was staying in a sanitorium in the same place.

Coincidence, perhaps. Another coincidence: in 1931, while Roger Hollis was working in Shanghai for the British American Tobacco Company, 'Sonia' was also in Shanghai, operating as a very special agent for Richard Sorge's Soviet network. On the basis of these two coincidences, Courtney Young conceived a mistrust of Hollis. The possibility of a relationship between Hollis and 'Sonia' would not have worried him had they been ordinary citizens. But what was one to make of this: a young Englishman sows his wild oats in Asia, his path crosses that of a Red Army secret agent; he returns to Europe, and again meets the Kremlin's femme fatale – and subsequently becomes deputy director of MI5, the high temple of the fight against Russian penetration.

Young's deductions were accurate. He was of course unaware of the precise manner in which Roger Hollis had been recruited in Shanghai by the Soviets, a manner that can be revealed today: through the intermediary of the two 'twin sisters' of the communist secret services in Asia, Agnes Smedley and Ursula Hamburger. Ursula-Sonia worked exclusively for Moscow. Her friend Smedley, a member of Sorge's network, also had a great many contacts with the *Tewu*. This very eclectic woman served as a 'bridge' between the two intelligence networks. It was for this reason that Roger Hollis 'benefited' right from the start from dual patronage. In 1956, Hollis was appointed director-general of MI5. He was to retire in 1965, with no other worries then his conjugal problems.

It was only at the end of the 1970s that the scandal broke, retrospectively justifying Courtney Young's concern. At the same time as Anthony Blunt was publicly exposed as having been a Soviet agent, the British press asked the question: was the head of British counter-intelligence at the end of the 1950s yet another Soviet mole within the British special services?

'No,' replied Mrs Thatcher virtuously, stating that an enquiry conducted by MI5 into the past activities of its former boss had not reached any conclusive result.

Few people were convinced, the facts being more stubborn than the Iron Lady herself. Roger Hollis had indeed worked within the British intelligence services on behalf of the Russians, but also the Chinese. His efforts to sow confusion reinforced those of that 'ungodly trinity', the most famous traitors in the history of espionage, Philby, Burgess and Maclean.

The trio's Soviet controllers were Colonels Ivan Andreyevich Raina and Filip Vassilyevich Kislytsin. Raina, we have already seen, became Soviet adviser to the special services of Mao's secret police in 1949. Kislytsin continued his career under diplomatic cover in England, and then in Australia at the same time – yet another coincidence? – as Roger Hollis was advising the new Australian secret service, ASIO, on counter-intelligence.

There are so many coincidences in the life of this very strange 'spycatcher' that one is entitled to ask the question: did Roger Hollis, by directing Australia's newly formed secret services on to the wrong track, cover up the recruitment by the Chinese communists of the future Prime Minister Harold Holt?

One learns by experience. ASIO subsequently took a much closer interest in the activities of Australian communist militants, one of whose leaders, a lawyer and member of the Central Committee, in charge of the Victoria area – where Harold Holt mysteriously disappeared – also became an agent for Kang Sheng. But Edward F. Hill was thrown out of the pro-Soviet party in June 1963. In 1964 he founded a pro-Chinese Communist Party and struck up a close relationship with Kang Sheng. Maybe, though, Kang Sheng, in the midst of the Cultural Revolution, was using Maoist parties all over the world for entirely other purposes than espionage.

22

The Secret of Maoists in Europe

At the end of 1967, at Puyricard, in the Bouches-du-Rhône, several dozen hardline Maoist militants, taking advantage of the traditional holiday period, held the founding congress of the Party which was intended to revolutionise the world of labour and destroy the exploitative bourgeoisie: the Marxist-Leninist Communist Party of France (PCMLF–Parti Communiste Marxiste-Léniniste de France).

Like their leader Jacques Jurquet ('Jacquin' in underground militant circles), many of the delegates attending the Puyricard congress were former members of the French Communist Party, which they reproached for its scandalous disloyalty to Stalin's great heritage, for the compromise deals it had made with François Mitterrand; in short, they accused the mainstream Communist Party of being bourgeois in outlook, opportunist and revisionist.

For the Marseilles leadership of the FCP this was too much. They were certainly not going to take lessons in Stalinism from these Maoist yobs.

In the early afternoon of 31 December, a young militant steward at the congress was taken by surprise by two men armed with large-bore pistols. Confident that they would not dare fire, he ran to warn his comrades.

'It's a fascist attack!' he yelled, convinced that these were members of an extreme-right commando unit. In fact, they were card-carrying members of the official Communist Party from Marseilles.

Six strapping fellows ran after the aggressors, who tried to beat a hasty retreat. When the Maoists caught up with them, a fight began. One of the official communists, seized with panic, fired his pistol and Christian Maillet, an artist and Maoist leader from the Marseille-Provence region, was shot in the foot with an 11/43 bullet. Raymond Cazas, a steel worker from the Loir-et-Cher, narrowly escaped being hit by two bullets fired at virtually point-blank range. 'Are you crazy!' he shouted at their assailants, who ran off without waiting to hear more.

A few days later, a vitriolic article in the communist daily newspaper, *L'Humanité*, suggested that the FCP had followed the Puyricard congress closely. 'There were thirty of them, with nine cars,' the paper said, adding, 'They dare to complain about the repressive apparatus of the State, while the regime guards their lives and protects their insidious work; their "great congress" took place under police protection: that of the CRS [Compagnies Républicaines de Sécurité – riot police], plainclothes policemen and Republican Guards. The bourgeois State obviously has unsuspected attractions.'

If the communist leadership was so concerned about the activities of tiny 'Marxist-Leninist' groups, it was because it was well informed. Since 1963, the French Communist Party's internal policing section, run by the die-hard pro-Soviet Gaston Plissonnier, had been following the activities of the 'secessionists' very closely.

A few days before the opening of the pro-Chinese group's congress, Plissonnier, secretary of the Party's Central Committee, signed an optimistic top secret note, delivered by hand to the Central Committee's secretariat on 28 November 1967.

The small pro-Chinese groups – which have practically no influence – are increasingly losing ground. The circulation of their newspaper has fallen to less than 3,000 copies. The fight for office, in order to benefit from funds provided by the Chinese, has led them to split up.

This situation results from the vigorous campaign led by the Party against these small groups during a period when the political line followed by the Mao Zedong group is increasingly unpopular.

However, we have not heard the last of these small groups. The Chinese leadership is insisting that they should turn themselves into a so-called 'Communist Party'. The French bourgeoisie supports this idea at a time when it is fostering anti-communism.

Moreover, there still exist within certain federations some small groups – two or three units, generally – who continue to issue leftist propaganda, especially in the universities.

We must intensify the ideological work within the Party and among the masses to combat leftism. We must cast discredit on the small pro-Chinese groups and others by demonstrating that they are financed by the 'Maoists' and the bourgeoisie to combat the French Communist Party and divide the working class and the democratic movement . . .

There followed upon this fairly contradictory statement an appendix several dozen pages long detailing, department by department, the establishment of pro-Chinese groups. The FCP had obviously mobilised all its local officials to carry out what was tantamount to a policing operation. The last time it had acted similarly was in 1961, when the attacks carried out by the OAS, the extremist organisation for a French Algeria, were bringing the country under threat of a military takeover. Six years later, did the Maoist peril demand the same kind of action? For 'small groups without influence', these pro-Chinese bodies were a cause of concern not only to the communist leaders but also, contrary to Plissonnier's simplistic declarations, to the corridors of power.

The 'holy alliance' between the Maoists and the bourgeoisie was nothing but a figment of the imagination of the French communist leaders. Western security services actually feared that the pro-Chinese young were being manipulated by Beijing.

Very few people, however, knew that the person behind relations between the Chinese CP and the European Maoist parties was also the most senior official of Red China's secret services, Kang Sheng.

The Chinese CP's International Liaison Department was an instrument of combat in the political and ideological struggle, as was evident at the time of the Sino-Soviet rift, when Kang Sheng confronted his Russian enemy Yuri Andropov. It was also evident during the 1960s when China believed it was about to take the world by storm.

At the heart of this offensive strategy were the *Thoughts of Mao Zedong*.

According to speeches addressed to the Red Guards, and the picturesque elegies of Guo Moro, official 'poet' and personal friend of Kang Sheng, it was these that were supposed to illuminate the world. Foreign-language Chinese periodicals printed page after page of edifying photographs of African guerrilla fighters, Indian peasants, European students rapt in contemplation of the little red book. This may have seemed ridiculous to some free spirits. But during twenty years of latent, if not open, civil war, during their thirty years of totalitarian power, the Beijing leadership had learned that political propaganda administered in large doses is a very efficient weapon. Kang did not intend to forget a lesson learned at such a high cost.

If he was determined to find ways of penetrating privileged circles in Western countries, it was because Kang had no great hopes of the European working class. He considered it to be bourgeois in outlook, rotten with revisionism, incapable of any revolutionary action. Salvation would come from elsewhere, from an encirclement of the West by the peoples of the Third World under the banner of Maoist China. With a little help from some clever sabotage . . .

Kang Sheng hated white people. In Shanghai, his self-esteem as a Chinese national had suffered under Western domination. He had taken his revenge, like so many of his compatriots, by assisting in driving the Europeans out of China, by fighting against 'American imperialism'. But this was not enough. For in the meantime, in Moscow, he had been inwardly sickened by the Russian dominance over the Comintern, by their arrogant behaviour and contempt for peoples of a different colour. And over the years all this had turned into a total disgust for the white world, a world to which Kang Sheng saw the Soviets as belonging. Because they claimed to be revolutionaries, they were even worse than the others. They would be spared no dirty trick.

To dynamite the United States from within, one could count on the revolts of the blacks in the ghettos. Did not the leader of the Black

Panthers, Eldridge Cleaver, advocate the creation of a united front composed of minorities of every kind: marginal whites, Puerto Ricans, blacks and of course Chinese? Did he not claim, like his companions, to draw inspiration from the little red book? In Europe, it was judicious to rely on other minorities, disillusioned communist militants, students enamoured of the Revolution, intellectuals fascinated by the Third World. To those, another myth was offered: that of the new China, capable of regenerating the old world. One need only look at Simone de Beauvoir, author of *La Longue Marche (The Long March)*, written as early as 1957, a very eulogistic work about the achievements of Chinese communism, to see that independent critical minds could also succumb to the delights of ideology. Others would follow, shock troops of Beijing snobbism: the film-maker Jean-Luc Godard, making the Maoist model an obsession for Western youth in his film-manifesto *La Chinoise (The Chinese Woman)*; Michelangelo Antonioni, projecting his cultivated Italian fantasies on Mao's China; the anti-establishment communist intellectual Maria-Antonietta Macciocchi, moved to tears by the 'spontaneous testimony' of a female factory worker fervently recounting to her the philosophy lessons given in all simplicity by those two great revolutionaries, Kang Sheng and his wife Cao Yi-ou; Philippe Sollers discovering one day in 1971 that the Cultural Revolution was 'the decisive event of the second half of the twentieth century'.

China was highly effective in cultivating its good image. On the one hand, Western intellectuals could admire the grandeur of ancient Chinese civilisation but also the power of Mao's thought, this 'spiritual atomic bomb' concentrated in the little red book. On the other, one could weep over this unfortunate people saved from misery by the sole genius of their leader who had been able to provide them with their daily bowl of rice. In fostering a Chinese lobby in the United States on behalf of her husband, Mrs Chiang Kai-shek had not done any different. And later, Deng Xiaoping and the leaders of the post-Maoist regime would do the same to promote in the West the idea of a China miraculously opened up to the outside world, democratised at the wave of a wand, almost innocent of all totalitarianism.

But no communist party, not even a minority communist party, is made up entirely of eminent intellectuals. In the framework of China's new foreign policy, aimed at detaching Europe from the two superpowers, it was incumbent on Kang Sheng, head of the Chinese CP's International Liaison Department, to help build up on the old continent Marxist-Leninist parties with as large a membership as possible. A difficult task to which he had already begun to devote himself long before the upheavals of the Cultural Revolution.

In his fifties, Jacques Grippa could well have rested peacefully on his militant laurels. This confirmed communist was in fact a legend within his own party. In October 1930, at the age of seventeen, he joined the

Belgian Communist Party, and immediately became regional director at Liège. In January 1943, under the Occupation, he became a cadre of the communist Resistance, the Armed Partisans. In July, he fell into the hands of the Gestapo, but refused to 'lie down' in front of the Nazis like several of his comrades from the Central Committee. As a result, he was tortured, held in Breenonk camp, and then deported to Buchenwald in May 1944. From the hell of the concentration camp, Grippa returned more communist than ever, resumed his post on the Central Committee and entered into the Cold War with a vengeance, becoming the *bête noire* of the royalists and the conservatives, together with his friend Henri Glineur. He was accused of being the Party's liaison officer with the Russians – it was not him. He was suspected of being behind conspiracies against the Belgian Royal Family, planned bomb attacks, strikes of all sorts. In short, to an extent, Grippa became the classic Red under the bed.

At the beginning of the 1960s, when the Congo dramatically attained independence, Grippa began to have doubts, not about communism, but about the revolutionary character of the leaders of his party. He had good reason to ask himself questions: one senior official of the Belgian CP's Colonial Section, Jacques Nemery, was in fact working as informer for the Sûreté.

In 1963, Grippa decided to make the break. Although still a member of the Central Committee, he was expelled from the CP. Henri Glineur – a communist since 1929 – left the Party in solidarity, as did several others. These eminent militants of the Belgian left set up an organisation even more revolutionary than the official communist movement. They were harsh critics of the Khrushchev line in the USSR, without being pro-Chinese. But as the arguments within the 'socialist camp' became more heated, they moved closer to Beijing.

Grippa was not just anybody in the small world of European Communist Parties. Kang Sheng and the International Liaison Department decided that he was a promising element, a leader to be won over at all costs to the Chinese way of thinking and its strategies. So he was invited to Beijing in June 1956, together with his wife, Madeleine, and Henri Glineur, in order to meet the élite among the communist leaders: Liu Shaoqi and Peng Zhen, still powerful at that time, Deng Xiaoping, who had not yet been discredited, and Liu Ningyi, a foremost syndicalist cadre.

The Belgian communist also met Kang Sheng, whom he found to be rather odd. Kang remained silent at discussion meetings, contenting himself with taking down endless notes, which surprised Grippa. 'He's certainly not taking any chances – after all, there are secretarial staff taking down our discussions in shorthand.'

A few days later, on 10 June, after a meeting at the Central Committee's Academy, Kang Sheng accompanied the old Belgian communist back to his room. A cautious private conversation took place.

'I'm not in total agreement with you,' Kang Sheng said to Grippa via an interpreter. 'In particular, when you say that the rank and file militants of the revisionist parties remain potential revolutionaries, and when you defend a policy of unity within the world communist movement.'

Of course, Grippa wanted to know why Kang Sheng did not agree with him. To his great surprise, Kang remained silent, smiling broadly but without explaining himself further. When Grippa met Chairman Mao the following day, he was still thinking about this strange conversation. He dined with Liu Shaoqi, whom he found very likeable and perfectly 'Marxist-Leninist' in his thinking, and also – a supreme honour – with Mao himself.

Other considerable surprises lay in store for the visitor to Beijing. During the course of the banquet, attended by the country's most senior officials, he found himself at a loss for words when asked by Mao Zedong whether railways already existed at the time of the Paris Commune in 1871. There was more to follow. A little later, the communist leader asked Grippa a kind of trick question: 'We have been accused of warmongering. What is your view of this?'

The accusers were of course the Russians. Thinking it was the right thing to say, the Belgian protested that this was a slander.

Mao nodded his head when this was translated, then replied: 'It is a slander and it is not a slander. There is some truth in it . . .'

This was enough to nonplus anybody. Grippa nevertheless did not lose heart. He had an excellent opinion of Liu Shaoqi, and rated Deng Xiaoping almost equally highly. Mao, after all, was not the only man in power in China. The real leaders seemed more serious, and that was the main thing. As for Kang Sheng, the militant Belgian did not spontaneously warm to him, and, being aware of only some of his powers, saw him as only one senior official among many.

On his return to Belgium, Grippa pursued his plan of forming a big Marxist-Leninist party. He very quickly brought together several hundred militants, some of them young, others more experienced, such as Sam Herssens or Hertz Jospa, both of whom were former Resistance fighters. Concerned to promote internationalism, he established links with the pro-Chinese French communists, who were divided into two violently opposed groupings, one of which, the Mouvement Communiste Français (French Communist Movement), or 'the Marseilles Group', gave him a rather cool reception, whilst the other, the Centre Marxiste-Léniniste de France (Marxist-Leninist Centre of France), or 'the Clichy Group', welcomed his overtures with enthusiasm. Of course, each of the two small groups denounced the others as 'provocative' and 'irresponsible'.

After his trip to Beijing, Jacques Grippa was a branded man. The Belgian Sûreté took a very close interest in his activities and started watching his party's premises, at 65 rue des Palais, in Brussels. But putting a tail on the former Resistance man proved difficult: he had experience of working underground. This did not prevent the Sûreté, though, from noticing his meetings with the Chinese chargé d'affaires at The Hague, Xie Li.

Under the supervision of a member of the Sûreté, Henri Delmarcelle, microphones were discreetly installed in the premises of the Sino-Belgian Friendship Association by another policeman, Joseph Szultos. The investigators were delighted with what they heard. As a result of the bugging, they became aware of the internal conflicts among the Marxist-Leninists. Even more interesting: the police discovered that Beijing was not financing Grippa as had been previously thought.

So what were the Chinese hoping for in Belgium? They knew perfectly well that the country was neither the most powerful nor the most populous in Europe. At the beginning of the 1920s, during their European wanderings, Zhou Enlai and Kang Sheng had been able to see that for themselves. But, rather as with that tiny country Albania, run by the perpetual Stalinist Enver Hoxha, they might hope, by using prestigious people like Grippa, Glineur and their friends, to set up a kind of Maoist pied-à-terre in Europe, a showcase on the continent. It fitted in well with their attempt at a similar operation on the other side of the world, in which they accorded a great deal of importance to the New Zealand and Australian Marxist-Leninist parties of comrades Wilcox and Hill.

In the summer of 1966, Jacques Grippa returned to Popular China. In Beijing, he saw Kang Sheng again, who was even more Red and aggressive than usual. The adviser to the group in charge of the Cultural Revolution, who was then extremely active, did not take kindly to this over-independent Belgian who seemed to think he was talking as one equal to another, 'between comrades'. How could Grippa compare the huge Chinese revolution and its leader, a Marxist-Leninist beacon for the whole world, with the tiny Communist Party of Belgium, useful no doubt but with little power. Kang Sheng only liked Western revolutionaries who prostrated themselves before the thoughts of Mao Zedong and their materialisation in the little red book.

The two meetings in August 1966 were therefore rather tense. Nevertheless, the artful Kang Sheng managed to captivate his visitor by showering him with praise before any discussions took place: 'We fully appreciate the achievements, the success of the Communist Party of Belgium. We believe that the ideas advocated by the Communist Party of Belgium are right for the tasks facing its country . . . Likewise, we set a high store by the CPB for its policy and its activities on the international level. The CPB carries aloft the flag of defiance against American imperialism, against revisionism, and of support for national liberation movements . . .'

After this totally hypocritical opening, Kang Sheng launched into one of those attacks he was so good at, against Wang Ming, Mao's former rival, and against the Communist International of the 1930s, of which he had been delegate. This was particularly shocking to Grippa, a pupil of the Stalinist school from his earliest years! He none the less remained silent, out of either politeness or diplomacy. His graciousness did not return, though, since Kang Sheng would not allow Grippa to visit Yan'an – because of bad weather – or attend a meeting with the PKI, the Indonesian Communist Party.

'They are in China but very far from Beijing!' the Chinese leader peremptorily told the Belgian visitor. In fact, the Indonesians were in Beijing, as Grippa saw for himself when he visited the Museum of the Revolution! There were at least twenty Indonesian delegates. But on Kang Sheng's orders, the interpreter categorically refused to organise a discussion between them and Grippa.

The final meeting between the two 'comrades' took place on 1 September. After a fairly animated discussion about the leader of the Maoist Australian Communist Party, Hill, Kang's personal envoy to the small world of Marxist-Leninist parties, their talks ended in virtual rift. Dismissing Grippa without any display of courtesy, Kang made it clear that he could not waste any more time with him.

For the Belgian communist, there was no question but he had been snubbed. He left Beijing in September, in a rage, not without having first had a foretaste of the joys of the Cultural Revolution and the prevailing cult of Mao: in Tian'anmen Square, he saw the 'Chinese Khrushchev' Liu Shaoqi, whom he so much liked, forced to elbow his way on to the platform.

Where could Grippa turn next? The answer was the Albanians, with whom his relations had always been excellent. But during a stay in Tirana, Grippa realised that his arguments were falling on deaf ears there too: the local petty tyrant, Enver Hoxha, summarily dismissed him, refusing to meet such a bad disciple of the Albanians' 'Chinese comrades'. His 'dissident' conversations with another senior official, the present-day leader of Albania, Ramiz Alia, had apparently been listened in on.

After a few final attempts at conciliation, Jacques Grippa broke first with the Chinese and then with the Albanians. The former left his party with the debts of the Xinhua press agency's bulletin as a parting gift. Then Sidney Rittenberg, the Sino-American responsible for Radio Beijing's foreign language broadcasts – in association with the *Gonganbu*, China's Public Security service – had some success in inciting several Belgian Maoists staying in the capital to 'criticise' their former leader in handwritten wallposters.

In Belgium itself two pro-Chinese parties emerged from the 'Grippist' movement, one in Brussels, the other at Charleroi. They failed to achieve any stability and both disintegrated into several very divided sub-groups.

Kang Sheng's first European initiative had ended in resounding failure.

*   *   *

There are days when one can hardly believe what is happening – take 14 December 1966, for instance, when the French CP newspaper, *L'Humanité*, carried an extraordinary front-page scoop exposing communist industrial espionage. What the paper was attacking was not the famous networks supplying economic intelligence to the USSR, which it had itself supported during the 1930s and then during the Cold War, but the Chinese 'false brothers', in the form of an open letter addressed to the French Communist Party's Central Committee by Louis Faradoux, from the Pierre-Courtade cell.

Faradoux was a worker at the Berliet factories in Vénissieux, in the Rhône. Following the signature of a trade agreement, his company was entertaining a delegation of some sixty Chinese who had come to see how the famous Berliet heavy goods vehicles were constructed. The leader of the delegation was a military man, Colonel Zheng Zhenglu. Faradoux did not have anything in particular against him, but accused Zhou Siangqi, a member of the Beijing CP leadership 'in close association with China's ambassador to Paris', and the treasurer of the delegation's Red Guards, Li Zhongshi, of having tried to extort information from him in return for the promise of a large payment. Worse still: the men from Beijing had tried to corrupt this loyal militant, openly inciting him to rally the pro-Chinese Marxist-Leninist groups.

Louis Faradoux's indignation in the face of this attempt at politico-economic manipulation was doubtless spontaneous, but that of *L'Humanité* was much less so: under no circumstances is this kind of text ever published in a communist newspaper without the support of the management, indeed without 'advice' from the top. As it was, this was a new initiative on the part of the Party's internal police section which, in its flushing-out of pro-Chinese dissidents, had taken a close interest in the Vénissieux affair.

Did the French CP feel so threatened by the activities of the Maoists in France? It would seem so. Having infiltrated the small pro-Chinese groups, the Party was fully aware that several of their leaders had already made the pilgrimage to Beijing. Jacques Jurquet was there in July 1964, then again in August 1965, together with Régis Bergeron, former deputy editor of the communist weekly *France Nouvelle* (*New France*), Paul Coste, a teacher, and François Marty, a former militant with the French CP in Perpignan, known as 'Commander Bourgat' in the communist Resistance. So the first contacts had been made.

In the summer of 1966, the reader will recall, Régis Bergeron and four other militants had met Kang Sheng in person in the Chinese capital. Although very tired by the factional struggles in progress, Kang nevertheless found the energy to talk to them about France and General De Gaulle, approving their decision to call for a vote against him in the elections of the previous year. But more importantly, he gave his guests a veritable lecture on the subject of the Chinese Communist Party and the Cultural Revolution.

For the former underground militant who had sought refuge in the French Concession in Shanghai, the spurious rickshaw runner, the ostensible tram conductor, the personal secretary to the wealthy Mr Yu Qiaqing, the informer who supplied information to the Corsican Commissioner Fiori's men, there was something intoxicating about seeing these Frenchmen paying allegiance, as it were, to Mao's all-powerful thoughts in this way. It was revenge on the past, but also a confirmation of the soundness of his political discrimination. By rallying to the Maoist cause in 1937, Kang had opted for the right side: the side that had made his country the rival of the Soviet Union in the hearts of revolutionaries throughout the world; the side that had put the new China in its rightful place: at the centre of the world.

The old rulers of China had wanted the country to remain the Middle Kingdom for ever. But they had failed and turned this vast nation into a semi-colony. Sun Yat-sen had tried to school Chinese nationalism in order to achieve liberation and modernisation. But he had died too soon. Mao Zedong dominated the whole world with his thought. The wind from the east – the wind of Revolution – was raging, forcing back the west wind. And old Kang could take pride in being one of the architects of this prodigious reversal.

Without detecting the incredible chauvinism that lay behind a superficial courtesy, many foreign Marxist-Leninists returned starry-eyed from these meetings in China. In Beijing they had seen a new, dynamic, colossal force emerge, a force that was going to regenerate the world. Received with a great deal of revolutionary decorum, they had visited factories where the workers acclaimed them as 'representatives of the glorious people of Karl Marx and Engels' or as 'the heirs of the Paris Commune'. It was enough to turn the heads of many of them.

In August 1967, Jacques Jurquet and Régis Bergeron went to China again. Now a permanent member of the CP's Politburo and secretary to the Central Committee, Kang Sheng received them also in his capacity as head of the International Liaison Department. Of course, the one thing he did not do was tell them about his role at the head of his country's special services, no more than he had told the Belgian communist Jacques Grippa.

Certainly, there were rumours about the mysterious Kang Sheng. But nothing serious in the eyes of committed – and, therefore, rather blind – militants. Can one blame them? Red China was so impenetrable that no one really knew about Kang Sheng's activities. The world had eyes only for the public stars of the Cultural Revolution: Chairman Mao, Zhou Enlai, Jiang Qing, 'the Chinese Khrushchev' Liu Shaoqi, Lin Biao. The secretive activities of an *éminence grise* such as Kang Sheng completely escaped its attention.

Jacques Jurquet was struck by Kang Sheng's insistence on hailing Mao's genius, the matchless power of his thought. It was almost an act of faith. In all things, inspiration was to be drawn from the Chairman's texts, they had to be studied as though they were Holy Writ, absorbed like the words of the gospel. Jurquet was much less happy about the attitude of the Chinese leaders who, wanting to keep two 'revolutionary brands' in the fire, had invited a delegation of young Maoists belonging to a rival organisation, the Union des Jeunesses Communistes (marxistes-léniniste) (Union of Communist Youth (Marxist-Leninist)).

But for the fact that they both subscribed to the thoughts of Mao Zedong, there was hardly any common ground between the PCMLF militants, who were generally older, and those of the UJC(ml), young intellectuals still influenced by the arguments of their original mentor, Louis Althusser, the fringe communist philosopher and semi-dissident.

The UJC(ml) had made their first public appearance in December 1966. The movement's journal was called *Garde Rouge (Red Guard)* and its leaders – Robert Linhardt, Olivier de Sardon, Christian Riss, Franços Leibovitz, Jacques and Claudie Broyelle, Roland Castro and Jacques Grumbach – saw the Cultural Revolution primarily as an iconoclastic liberation movement.

While Kang Sheng may have preferred the PCMLF of Jurquet, Bergeron and Marty, which was more straightforward, more proletarian, he felt that he must not break off communications with the UJC(ml), promising because it was composed of students who at some later date were bound to hold important positions in French society. He proceeded in the same fashion in Italy, encouraging all pro-Chinese groups via diplomats posted there, but nevertheless granting his favours to the Italian Marxist-Leninist Communist Party. It was in fact the leader of this organisation, Vincenzo Calvino, whom he first welcomed to Beijing.

The possibility of being able to rely on a nucleus of experienced ex-communists, like Jurquet, the existence of young intellectuals prepared to be fired with enthusiasm for the Maoist model, to become sinicised if need be, the rise of an undeniable anti-establishment movement among students – this time things were much more favourable to Kang Sheng and the Chinese CP's International Liaison Department. They could at last hope to make a breakthrough in France.

This was a rather less attractive prospect to the French Communist Party, which was becoming increasingly worried by pro-Chinese activism, even though it never ceased proclaiming the imminent demise of its rivals. The privilege of announcing the 'pro-Chinese débâcle in France' fell to the Party's deputy general secretary, Georges Marchais himself, in an article published in *L'Humanité* on 5 January 1968, which deserves to be extensively quoted, if only for its display of insincerity.

Considerable means have been put at their disposal by the Mao Zedong group. Hundreds of millions have been paid to them for their propaganda and in order to attempt to corrupt honest militant workers. Journals and brochures have been sent to them directly from Beijing. The Chinese embassies in Berne and in Paris have constantly supported their activities. Members of the Chinese Communist Party and the Albanian Communist Party have come to France in order to assist them in their enterprise. They have travelled incessantly to Beijing to receive advice and instructions from their masters.

The French bourgeoisie, for its part, has actively supported the pro-Chinese groups in France . . .

. . . This is why the Gaullist government has spared no effort to give them support, as, for instance, the activities of certain prefects and subprefects have demonstrated in their time.

It can be said that no opportunity has been lost to help the pro-Chinese in France in their nefarious enterprise . . .

Once again, the communist daily was giving its readers their money's worth: a virulent denunciation of those wicked Marxist-Leninists, financed and advised by a foreign power (which was not the USSR) and, for good measure, supported by the bourgeoisie via 'certain prefects' whose identity was unfortunately not revealed in Georges Marchais' perky piece.

With good reason. These senior officials with Maoist sympathies existed only in the fertile imagination of the deputy general secretary, whose star was increasingly in the ascendant within the FCP since the semi-squeezing out of the official leader, Waldeck Rochet, whose path once crossed that of Kang Sheng in Moscow during the time of the Comintern.

The police, if not the bourgeoisie, were watching the French Maoists very closely, contrary to Marchais' propagandist fantasies. Very aware of the endless comings and goings between Paris and Beijing, the DST (Direction de la Surveillance du Territoire), not very effective so far with regard to Chinese problems, tried to redress the balance. It used Orion telephone taps. One of its experts did some exhaustive research into the Franco-Chinese Friendship Associations, set up in 1956 by orthodox communists but controlled since 1963 by Marxist-Leninists such as Régis Bergeron. Gilbert Mury, Marcel Coste (PCMLF) and François Leibovitz (UJC(ml)). For French counter-intelligence had a suspicion that these friendship associations were instruments of the Chinese secret services, perhaps even a cover for them. Although, they did not find anything really suspect within them, one may wonder about the exact meaning of those 'reports' certain grass-roots workers' cells were asked to make by the leadership of the PCMLF on the position of the companies by which they were employed, and on their companies' production. Were they prompted by mere curiosity – scarcely in keeping with the rigid mentality of the Marxist-Leninist leaders – or was this the embryo of a network of 'worker informants' similar to those which the FCP had organised for the benefit of the Soviets during the 1930s and during the Cold War? In any case, the deputy director at the DST, Auguste Sauzon – the master researcher – protested against his service being used for political espionage, deviating from its original mission. He was expelled from the DST in July 1968.

Meanwhile, the Renseignements Généraux (RG), the French secret police, were not idle. This police service whose job it is to keep the government informed of trends of opinion but also of subversive activities was run by a seasoned officer, Henri Boucoiran. He kept a detailed index on militant revolutionaries. The Reds were at the top of this black list, and the Blacks at the bottom, since there were files on the leaders of the PCMLF François Marty and Jacques Jurquet long before those indefinable anarchists such as Daniel Cohn-Bendit, who was to play an important role in the events of May 1968, appeared on the scene.

The RG police feared above all the activities of structured groups with a clandestine wing, bound together by a rigid ideology, like that of the Maoists. They were not the only ones. Their strange 'colleagues' in the Communist Party's internal policing section analysed things in a similar manner. So it was that on 14 March 1968, their leader, Gaston Plissonnier sent to the Central Committee's secretariat a document revealing the 'secret list' of the thirty members of the Marxist-Leninist Central Committee of the PCMLF, and the fourteen members of the organisation's Politburo. Drawn from eighteen different *départements*, twenty-two of them were ex-members of the FCP. The list had been compiled thanks to indiscretions picked up by a communist mole within the pro-Chinese movement.

More systematic, but also more serious, the RG police paid close attention to contacts between Chinese diplomats and Maoist militants. Three commissioners assisted by several young police officers were detailed to keep an eye on the activities of the French pro-Chinese groups.

As well as political contacts with the Beijing diplomats, some militants, though not very many of them, had made financial contacts. Certainly, the Chinese were sufficiently shrewd – and most of the young Maoists sufficiently high-minded – to avoid any obvious transfer of funds. But they had recourse to a method as old as international relations, indirect financing. Rather than handing over sums of money, the embassies' contacts were given piles of propaganda leaflets which they could dispose of, making money from selling them. Later, when certain Maoists carried their fascination with China to the point of learning the language, they were commissioned to do translations, purportedly for Chinese magazines (in Beijing, several dozen foreigners from all countries worked for Chinese publishing), work which was totally useless but very highly paid.

'All this is not very commendable but on balance not very serious.

Nothing to do with espionage,' concluded the R G police, sensibly. In fact, the events of May 1968, which they had not foreseen, were the product of something quite other than the activities of Beijing's secret services.

'In all the countries of Europe, or nearly all of them, there is a Maoist party, there are Marxist-Leninist parties . . . It is reasonable to say – and the information that I have allows me to say it – that the leaders meet. It is easy to imagine who might be the leader of Maoism and of Marxist-Leninism . . .'

The French Interior Minister was not mincing his words on that day in May 1968. Yet his declaration was greeted with considerable scepticism, and with good reason: when something goes wrong within a country, it is customary for governments to see the hand of a foreign power behind the troubles. It is easier than trying to see what is really going on . . .

In fact, Raymond Marcellin was grossly exaggerating the role of Beijing in the wave of protest that was engulfing Europe. Kang Sheng had indeed tried to join forces with the Marxist-Leninists, but without any really significant results. Quite the contrary: May 1968 tolled the knell of Maoist hopes in France. The movement was too characterised by libertarian sentiments to willingly submit to the burdensome Marxist-Leninist orthodoxy. And the huge demonstrations of 'support for the students and workers of France' organised in Tian'anmen Square, in Beijing, did not alter anything. The hardliners in Jurquet's and Marty's PCMLF, trapped in their ultra-Stalinist oversimplifications, missed the bus right from the start. The U J C(ml) militants too. Their organisation broke up completely. A very small minority, frightened by such ideological chaos, joined the PCMLF. A far smaller number teamed up with some militants from the famous Twenty-second of March Movement to create the Gauche Prolétarienne (GP), the Proletarian Left, which incidentally acquired the newspaper *La Cause du Peuple (The People's Cause)*. A third small group, Ligne Rouge (Red Line) also appeared.

The *Cause du Peuple* certainly carried a picture of Mao, a proletarian cap on his head, but the GP drifted into various ventures that had little to do with Chinese Marxism-Leninism. Its militants took an almost libertarian view of the Cultural Revolution. They had less and less contact with the Chinese and after 1970–1 none at all. However, they represented by far the most dynamic faction in the former Marxist-Leninist movement. The rest broke up into ever more ludicrous small groups.

In 1969, it is true, this process – which was in any case not very reassuring to Raymond Marcellin, whom the GP caused some sleepless nights – was not yet complete. In April 1969 the GP was still sending a message of support to the Ninth Congress of the Chinese CP.

The Ninth Congress marked both a personal triumph for Mao, incontestably Red China's 'Great Helmsman', and the rise – a cause of concern to Kang and his friends – of the Red Marshal, Lin Biao. Lin was becoming, as it were, the number one heir in China. But Kang Sheng managed to come out remarkably well. Re-elected to the Politburo, he saw his official power increase when the Politburo reduced its numbers from seven to five: Mao Zedong, Lin Biao, Zhou Enlai, Kang Sheng and his old accomplice Chen Boda. As for his unofficial power, his role with the secret services, it had never been so great.

The first congress since the start of the Cultural Revolution seemed to mark a period of stabilisation in China. But it added grist to the mill of those who argued that there was 'an international Maoist conspiracy'. Seventy-three political organisations or militant newspapers sent messages of support to the Chinese. Some actually represented Communist Parties in power: Enver Hoxha's Working Party of Albania; the Rumanian Communist Party, for which Kang Sheng had a soft spot on account of his good relations with Emil Bodnaras and Ion Maurer, and because it was independent of the USSR; the Workers Party of Vietnam, already the ruling power in Hanoi. Others were serious opposition parties: the South Vietnamese National Liberation Front and the Burmese, Thai, Malaysian and Indonesian Communist Parties. Others still – the Marxist-Leninist Movement of Saint-Marin and the Polish, Yugoslav and Hungarian Marxist-Leninists – represented either very small countries or very small forces, if not imaginary forces, within their countries.

Organised by Zhou Enlai and Kang Sheng, the Maoist International was only a pale imitation of the defunct Comintern, and even of its postwar successor, the Cominform. It was only in Asia that it carried any real weight. Elsewhere, the support was from rump parties. The 'Marxist-Leninist leader' denounced by Raymond Marcellin certainly existed – he was none other than Kang Sheng in his capacity as head of the International Liaison Department – but, in Europe at least, his influence was pretty limited.

Limited in France by the rather crazy but completely independent path followed by the Gauche Prolétarienne. Limited in Italy by the violent internal quarrels among the Marxist-Leninists who did not accept – far from it – the leadership of the two militants solemnly welcomed by Kang Sheng in August 1968, Osvaldo Pesce and Dino Dini. Limited in Belgium by the defection of Grippa and his friends. Limited in the northern countries where Maoism simply did not catch on. Limited in Switzerland, where, to the great humiliation of the head of the Chinese secret services, a KGB agent, Marcel Buttex, an employee at the Lausanne municipal abattoirs, had infiltrated the Marxist-Leninist movements on behalf of Moscow. Limited in Austria, the home of Comrade Frantz Stobl's less than influential Marxist-Leninist Party. Limited in Germany, when the attempt to set up a Maoist group in East Berlin failed . . .

It is a paradox of history that while the mere mention of Kang Sheng's name made the blood of hundreds of millions of Chinese run cold with fear, his vast European projects failed one after the other with the ebbing of the Maoist tide. It is true that it was not very judicious to try to transform the Marxist-Leninists, convinced of the imminence of a 'proletarian revolution', into mere propagandists for the necessary expansion of the Common Market and European Union in order to confront the American and Soviet superpowers. What was annoying about Zhou Enlai's clever foreign policy was that it put Kang Sheng, head of the International Liaison Department, in an impossible situation.

Apart from espionage in its strict sense, which had always been his domain, what was left? Kang had entertained great hopes of Spain, where there was no lack of militant energy, on account of the continuance of the Franco regime. But after the rupture in 1966, he was severely criticised by Jacques Grippa, who accused him of having stirred up trouble within the small local Marxist-Leninist party. Grippa was particularly critical of his having spoken out against a Spanish leader who was then in prison.

The problem was that the clandestine movement most interested in contacts with the Chinese was the Patriotic and Anti-Fascist Revolutionary Front, an organisation for armed struggle against the Franco regime. Basically, they wanted material aid from Beijing, without being dictated to in terms of their political position. This was all the more problematic since Kang had no intention of allowing Beijing to get involved in a European urban guerrilla movement. He preferred to seek a rapprochement with Santiago Carrillo's clandestine Spanish Communist Party, already tempted by the Eurocommunist demon, or with the organisations that had sprung up among the Christian left.

Nevertheless, a member of the Central Committee of the Patriotic Anti-Fascist Revolutionary Front, the Colombian 'Frederico', went to Beijing, where he was employed as a proof-reader by the People's Publishing House. At the same time, the Front, which was completely obsessed with procuring arms for its anti-Franco guerrilla activities, was ordering thousands of copies of the Spanish version of *Beijing Information* and various Chinese propaganda magazines. No sooner were they received in Paris, or by those in charge of the guerrilla group's 'emigration' section, than these texts were put in a boiler and burnt. The Front, with scarcely two thousand supporters, did not want to risk their freedom by transporting the Marxist-Leninist propaganda from Beijing across the Pyrenees. They hoped, instead, that their large orders would convince the Chinese leadership of their numerical strength.

This did not resolve the thorny problem of arms. Seeing that they would get nothing but speeches and propaganda out of the Chinese, the Front went knocking at the door of the Albanians, and in 1973 a leader of the clandestine anti-Franco organisation went to Tirana. He met Mehmet Shehu, the right-hand man of Comrade-Dictator Enver Hoxha. Shehu had fought with the International Brigade in Spain, in 1936-7, so he was particularly well placed to understand the motivations of the anti-Franco Front. Especially as the main founder of the Front was none other than that former Republican minister and academic Alvarez del Vayo, a superb orator, an admirer first of Moscow and then of Beijing. However, these contacts did not lead to very much. The clandestine movement's envoy was employed to work on the Spanish-language broadcasts of Radio Tirana, while the Albanian leaders paid him 2,000 pesetas per month in the name of the People's Republic of China. Though limited, the aid given to the Spanish guerrillas by the Algerian National Liberation Front was less derisory. The Patriotic Anti-Fascist Revolutionary Front disappeared with the death of Franco, who in 1975 had two of its cadres executed. But the prestige attached to this drama scarcely concealed the fact that the movement had been infiltrated; in Switzerland, its main leader, Helena, was accused of working for the CIA.

Other clandestine groups in Europe also fell for the bellicose proclamations of the Albanians. In 1973, Director of Operations of the official IRA also went to Tirana. He was treated to a few fine words as a reward for this compromising visit, but nothing else. On his return home, he explained to his friends: 'Those blokes want to recruit us to their ideological cause, but we will never get a single gun out of them for our struggle . . .'

This remark was quite true. It also applied to the Chinese. Kang Sheng had tried to manipulate the European militants of the extreme left to the exclusive benefit of China. But Maoism had never attracted much support on the Old Continent. And revelations about the fierce factional fighting that marked the Cultural Revolution was to lose it what little support it had.

23

'Death to Lin Biao, Long Live Richard Nixon!'

Beidaihe, a magnificent seaside resort on the Yellow Sea, four hundred kilometres from Beijing, was developed at the beginning of the century, thanks to missionaries and foreign residents. It was there that the international expeditionary corps, which had come to assist the 'foreign devils' besieged by the Boxers in the Beijing legations, landed in 1900.

Ten kilometres of fine sand, today divided into sections: to the east are holiday camps for military personnel and the worker élite. To the west lies a tourist ghetto, and in the centre, a holiday fortress for senior Party officials.

On 11 September 1971, a bald, thin little man, with a bony face and bushy eyebrows was sitting there very pensive. Earlier that day he had learned that the former master of the Kremlin, deposed six years earlier, Nikita Sergeyevich Khrushchev, had just died. The anguished holidaymaker was none other than Marshal Lin Biao. Would he be deposed like the Russian, his former enemy, or would he succeed Mao, as Khrushchev had succeeded Stalin? Thanks to his considerable power, drawn from the People's Liberation Army and his contacts within the Party under reconstruction, he could hope for the latter.

Only a year ago Marshal Lin Biao was still 'Chairman Mao's closest companion in arms', and his declared heir at the Ninth Party Congress in 1969. Since then, he had become a focus for the hatred of those whom he had helped to destroy the Party, to overthrow the 'revisionists', to bring about the downfall of Liu Shaoqi, Luo Ruiqing, Deng Xiaoping and all the others. He had offered Mao's group the support of the army, to protect it against the excesses of the Red Guards who had grown uncontrollable. But Mao and his group had been caught out like sorcerers' apprentices. And now China was weak and drained. Those who wanted to put the economy to rights and rebuild the Party, now shattered into a thousand pieces, rallied round Zhou Enlai. Zhou had managed to protect numerous cadres – starting with Deng Xiaoping – and snatch them from the murderous frenzy of the Red Guards. But he was just as suspicious of the ambitions of the army and of its leaders . . .

There were also Jiang Qing and her fan-club, the famous Gang of Four, who were eagerly eyeing the post of Mao's successor. At the intersection of all these interests, a thin little man observed the strange contest with relish: Kang Sheng.

For him, there was no question of committing the same irretrievable blunder as Chen Boda: during the Ninth Party Congress, Chen had allied himself with Lin Biao, putting forward arguments that – the supreme disgrace – were rejected by Mao. Chen then became a target for Maoist attacks. Finally, he lost his preserve – the Central Group of the Cultural Revolution – which was abolished at the end of 1969. His 'friends' Jiang Qing, Zhang Chunqiao and Kang Sheng dropped him. Called all kinds of names, Chen Boda disappeared as he had caused so many others to disappear before him. Lin Biao sensed that, through Chen Boda, he himself was being targeted. When the second session of the Ninth Congress was held in Lushan in August 1970, a new clash took place, this time on who was to succeed as head of state.

The army and the Party were then very wary of each other. Lin Biao knew that he was being closely watched by Kang Sheng's men. The Chairman's bodyguard, Wang Dongxing, acted as Mao's observer at the Party's very important Military Commission in Jingshang Avenue. Previously Kang Sheng's deputy, Wang was a rising star. Vice-minister of the *Gonganbu*, head of Department 5, in charge of the *Laogai*, he was also responsible for Qingcheng, Beijing's number one prison, which was crammed with deposed cadres. Wang had supervised numerous arrests: that of Luo Ruiqing, who had in the past been his *Gonganbu* superior, and that of Liu Shaoqi, who was left to die in prison. As commander of the formidable élite Detachment 8341 (*Basansiyi*), he disposed of a small army of twelve thousand men, divided into eighteen battalions, whose task was to protect the Party leaders in Zhongnanhai, the new Forbidden City.

The men in Detachment 8341 shared one characteristic: they came from remote provinces of China, and felt no affinity with the Beijing population. Nor did they speak their language. They had no scruples. Wang also controlled Military Security, responsible for ascertaining the loyalty to Chairman Mao of officers close to Lin Biao. Lin's unquestioning supporters – Huang Yongsheng, the chief of staff, Wu Faxian, commander-in-chief of the air force, Qui Huizuo, the head of the Logistics Department, Li Zuopeng, political commissioner of the navy – knew that like their own boss they were being watched. And Wang Dongxing did not fail to observe the actions of a woman who also sat on the Military Affairs Commission, Lin Biao's wife, Ye Qun.

In addition to serious disagreements over internal policy, world strategy became another bone of contention between Lin Biao and Zhou Enlai. Should they negotiate with the Americans an honourable end to the conflict in Indochina? Resume relations with the United States, still an ally of Taiwan? Unite with 'imperialism' against 'Soviet social-imperialism', which at that time was actually threatening China militarily?

Lin Biao realised that negotiation was necessary. But in 1969, Ho Chi Minh died. Zhou Enlai, Kang Sheng and Chen Boda paid him tribute in the name of the Chinese government. Lin saw an opportunity to join up with the National Liberation Front in South Vietnam, without having to deal with Hanoi, which was thought to be too pro-Soviet; an opportunity to form a pro-Chinese party in Vietnam . . .

But in July 1971, when Henry Kissinger visited China, Lin Biao was absent. He appeared for the last time in public on 3 June, at Kang Sheng's side, when the Rumanian leader Ceaucescu came to China, accompanied by an old acquaintance of Kang from Moscow days, Ion Maurer. The embittered Marshal was taking his summer vacation at Beidaihe with his wife Ye Qun. The battlelines were drawn. Lin Biao, it was believed, wanted to set himself up as head of state and establish an alternative government in Canton. The question was, though, was Jiang Qing, with whom he had always got on very well, also involved?

Officially, Lin Biao and Ye Qun were preparing for the engagement of their daughter Lin Liheng. Meanwhile, Mao was travelling around the south of the country by special train in an attempt to rally his supporters and rebuild the Party. His 'moral support' was a beautiful young woman, Chang Yüfeng – 'Jade Phoenix' – whose job title said it all: 'Secretary Responsible for Daily Life'.

Mao met the beautiful Chang Yufeng through Wang Dongxing. Supplying the still very lively old man with fresh supplies of young flesh was in fact a sacred task of the Chairman's bodyguard, as it was for Kang Sheng. They had never failed in this special mission, especially since the Chairman and his wife now lived separately – there was only a tactical alliance between them. For Lin Biao, the question that arose was therefore the following: was it possible, playing on the jealousy of Jiang Qing towards her husband's new mistress, to turn her against Wang Dongxing, the overly clever procurer? By appealing to her political instincts, could she be persuaded to conspire against her own husband, Chairman Mao?

On returning from the beach in the afternoon of 8 September, Ye Qun telephoned Jiang Qing and spoke to her about her daughter's engagement, before adding: 'Comrade Lin Biao sends his greetings and asks me to tell you to take care of your health.'

Then, still on a friendly basis, Lin and Ye sent Jiang Qing four magnificent red-fleshed sweet-tasting water melons, which she relished, sharing them with her servants, to whom she said: 'Our deputy chairman Lin is always thinking of us.'

On Sunday 12 September, Lin and his wife and their secretaries returned to Beijing, no doubt in the hope of talking to Jiang Qing. At least, this was supposed to be their intention.

In the evening the Lin clan met up with a number of those who had remained loyal to them, at a restaurant in the *Taoranting gongyuan*, the park of the Pavilion of Joy. The meal that evening was a good-humoured family affair, although Lin Biao's air of gloominess contrasted with the radiant smile of Ye Qun.

Suddenly the waiters, dressed in white, the colour of death, burst in with *shike* submachine-guns. They released one, two bursts of gunfire . . . There were screams and bodies crumpled. They were men from Section 37 of Detachment 8341, who had been placed at the disposition of Kang Sheng. Now he bent over the bleeding corpses. Lin Biao and Ye Qun were dead all right.

Legend has it that Kang Sheng appeared from behind a screen, and, in that reptilian manner of his, slowly entered the dining-room in order to observe the scene.

Marshal Lin Biao had been Defence Minister since 1959, and already at that time it was Kang Sheng who had brought about the downfall of his predecessor, Marshal Peng Dehuai. Dissident officers certainly did not have much luck with the head of the secret services.

During the early morning of 13 September, some rather unusual scenes took place. Military lorries were positioned all round Beijing. In Tian'anmen Square, rehearsals for the First of October national holiday celebrations were cancelled – and shortly after, so were the celebrations themselves. Zhou Enlai cancelled a meeting with Japanese politicians, then announced a ban on all flights to China for a period of three days. There was great agitation in diplomatic circles, still awaiting some clue as to what was going on: it was murmured that Mao himself was dying. Gradually news of the Defence Minister's death became known. Along with the arrest of his supporters Huang Yongsheng, Wu Faxian and Li Zuopeng.

Classified *Mi mi* – top secret – one version of the Lins' deaths circulated then became quasi official: Lin Biao, his son Lin Liguo, Ye Qun and a few others had tried to organise a coup d'état, to assassinate Mao. But, faced with the failure of this enterprise, they had tried to flee to the USSR. Their Trident plane, having run short of fuel, had crashed in the Ondörhaan Desert close to Ulaanbaator in Outer Mongolia. Later, there were even photographs published of unrecognisable bodies, supposedly taken by Chinese diplomats in Mongolia. For its part, the KGB, which was able to recover the bodies thanks to its ally, Mongolian Security, found nothing which conclusively identified any of the dead as Lin Biao, who had on several occasions received medical treatment in the USSR.

In Beijing, the 'official' version of the Marshal's death was supported by the circulation of a file published in *Zhongfa* (internal document) number 4, dated 13 January 1972, for limited distribution within the Central Committee.

It was called 'Project 571' and its author was Lin Liguo. Written six months before the murder of Lin Biao, by his son, this battle plan explained how to get rid of 'B 52', a codename given to Mao:

'B 52' has constantly had recourse to that coup d'état technique that favours those who fight with the pen rather than those who fight with the gun. For this reason, we must put an end to this slow and peaceful evolution with a violent and radical revolution . . . A new confrontation is inevitable. If we do not seize control of the leadership of the revolution, the leadership will escape us . . . The problem-free days of 'B 52' are numbered. We worry him. It is preferable to be in a state of preparedness for action rather than wait to be caught and bound hand and foot; thus will we forestall the enemy, at first militarily, and then politically . . . The clique in power is extremely unstable and subject to the constant repercussions of the struggle for power; the conflicts between individual members have reached their height . . . The Red Guards, deluded and manipulated, served as cannon fodder during the first part of the Cultural Revolution and as scapegoats during the second . . . It is a merciless battle. If they succeed, we will be imprisoned or thrown inside a fortress. Either we win or they win . . .

This document smacked of forgery. And the Soviets made no bones about accusing Kang Sheng of being the person behind it . . .

After Lin's demise, the Central Committee set up a commission of enquiry into the affair (*Lin Biao zhuan'anzu baomizu*), which had a double objective: to piece together the details of the conspiracy and to hunt down the supporters of the deceased leader. Kang Sheng chaired the commission but was not the kingpin of it. This privilege fell to Wang Dongxing, at whose side appeared, like a jack-in-the-box, a little-known figure, Su Zhu, a regional cadre from Hunan, Mao's native province. He was as remarkable for his mediocrity as for his unconditional support for the beloved Chairman. In periods of unrest, bureaucratic mediocrity is a reliable asset. Su Zhu had earned the sobriquet of 'China's avant-garde' during the anti-Japanese war – in Chinese, Hua Guofeng. Mao and Kang had summoned him to Beijing in May 1971, where he had dealt with security problems. During the fateful summer that proved tragic for Lin Biao and his wife, Hua had travelled the length and breadth of China with Wang Dongxing, rallying Mao's supporters and organising Mao's own travels.

Two other men on the commission of enquiry were Wang's agents, Wang Liangen and Zhang Yaoci. The number one investigator was Li Zhen, Vice-Minister of the *Gonganbu*, which was in the process of complete restructuring. Also a member of the commission was his deputy Yu Sang, another vice-minister since 1964, who had escaped the purges thanks to the protection of Kang Sheng.

Yu had personally carried out the arrest of his former boss, the 'incorruptible' Luo Ruiqing. Lin Zhen was a more individual man. Some people thought him close to Zhou Enlai; others believed him to be an intimate of Lin Biao.

Li actually had a military background. Born in 1905 in Hunan into a rich peasant family, he had taken part in the Long March and had climbed the ranks to general. And now he was being asked to flush out Lin Biao partisans hiding in the shadows! A dramatic event occurred that led him to believe there were a lot of them. On 26 March 1972, in Beijing, his immediate superior in the *Gonganbu*, Xie Fuzhi, suddenly died.

At the funeral, attended by Cao Yi-ou but not Kang Sheng, Zhou Enlai delivered an oration and gave the official version of his death: 'Comrade Xie Fuzhi contracted a cancer of the stomach two years ago . . . He put up a valiant fight against his illness, undergoing lengthy treatment until his heart stopped beating on 26 March 1972 at 13.37 hours, following extensive metastasis. Comrade Xie Fuzhi was sixty-three.'

The head of the *Gonganbu*'s illness had worsened considerably after stopping a hail of 9mm bullets while walking in the Zhongnanhai maze with Jiang Qing. Was Jiang the intended victim? And was the assassin acting on behalf of Lin Biao's supporters?

Some time after, Li Zhen became minister in charge of the *Gonganbu*. This immediately gave him access to numerous archives and a much more panoramic view of counter-intelligence and the secret police. Curious, he tried to elucidate the mystery of Xie Fuzhi. He was reminded of what the priority was: the Lin Biao affair.

In October 1972, he came upon the interrogation report on one of the conspirators, Huang Yongsheng, a member of the Politburo and chief-of-staff of the People's Liberation Army. Huang alluded to a conversation that had taken place between him and Lin Biao and Qiu Huizuo, head of the PLA's General Logistics Department, as far back as the summer of 1971.

Lin asked Qiu: 'What do you think of Kang Sheng?'

'If we let him live, we don't know when he's going to stab us in the back.'

Lin became philosophical: 'Lenin had need of a Felix Dzerzhinsky for his secret police; Stalin of a Lavrenti Beria; Gomulka of a Moczár. We also have need of a man like Kang Sheng in order to wield a sabre and behead our adversaries.'

Then Lin Biao turned to Huang Yongsheng: 'You must know that the person we can most rely on in the 'B 52' affair is Kang Sheng. But the person we have to be most wary of is also Kang Sheng. He enjoys the complete trust of Mao, but Mao is also wary of him. That was why Xie Fuzhi and Wang Dongxing were promoted – in order to counterbalance the power of Kang Sheng and to keep an eye on him if need be . . . And he knows it, that's why we cannot consider him as one of them . . .'

The explosive file that Li Zhen scanned contained other surprising information: in August and September 1971, Mao was travelling round China on his special train in order to rally his supporters; Kang Sheng was then supplying Lin Biao with details about the Chairman's movements – Cao Yi-ou, Kang Sheng's wife, was conveying the information to Lin's wife, Ye Qun. It was thanks to this information that Lin Biao was able to construct his plan and give his colleagues the order to organise the murder of Mao . . . But the dates of Mao's movements were inaccurate. Did Mao return to Beijing earlier, having been tipped off in advance? Or had Kang deliberately lured the tiger out of his den?

As ever with Kang Sheng, the mystery remained. Throughout his career, the masterspy was caught in ambiguous situations. Had he flirted with the 'Lin Biao Gang', so that he could switch to their side in the event of a successful bid for power? Or, as was more probable, had he maintained good relations with Lin the better to catch him out, leading him to believe that when the time came the special services, even Jiang Qing herself, would side with the rebel army?

The ultimate paradox was that Kang Sheng had been playing a double game that would allow him to win, whatever happened. As he had in Shanghai in 1931, and Moscow in 1936, when he had masterminded the elimination of Li Lisan and Wang Ming. As when he took part in the Gao Gang affair, and the scuppering of the first group in charge of the Cultural Revolution, thereby precipitating the downfall of Peng Zhen, and the liquidation of his worst enemy Liu Shaoqi, whose perspicacity he had praised only five years earlier.

The fact that he presided over Lin Biao's assassination did not prove that he had not thought of conspiring with him. As he must often have been able to get rid of an inconvenient witness to dirty deeds. This is what the 'detective' Li Zhen began to think, as he feverishly examined the files concerning matters dealt with by Kang Sheng. Many of them gave rise to confusion. A lot of documents had disappeared in the vortex of the Revolution; others could not be obtained from the *Diaochabu* central files.

The Li Zongren affair seemed very odd. This Chiang Kai-shek collaborator, born in 1890 in Guangxi, had valiantly fought against communist forces, which was rare. Shortly before Mao came to power in 1949, General Li became interim president of the Guomindang. Chiang had fled to Taiwan. When the nationalist defeat was confirmed, instead of joining Chiang, Li and his wife took refuge in the USA. But, as he told President Truman, as a nationalist Chinese in the full sense of the word, he was opposed to the 'separatism' of Chiang entrenched on his island. Perhaps it was possible to form a 'third force', above and beyond the Guomindang and the Communist Party. Li Zongren immediately became a pawn and a symbol. Everyone wanted him on their side. American senators 'adopted' him as a preferable replacement for Chiang. In Beijing, there was an acute awareness of what publicity could be gained if he were to join the communists. The CIA, during the 1950s, thought of organising a coup d'état to overthrow the Generalissimo's dictatorship and replace him with his former deputy. Li sent a note to Beijing denouncing the CIA's planned coup as 'unrealistic'.

It was then that Zhou Enlai decided that the time was ripe. Kang Sheng was given the task of making contact with General Li, and trying to 'repatriate' him within the framework of 'a united front effort', as he had brilliantly managed to pull off ten years earlier with the Chinese atomic scientists. Speed was of the essence. On several occasions already, Chiang Kai-shek had tried to have his rival assassinated. In the summer of 1965, two of Kang's men travelled to the USA: Liu Shouzhou had just been named deputy director of the United Front Work Department, the special services' showcase, used both to rally stray sheep and to recruit agents among the overseas Chinese; he was accompanied by Luo Qingchang, the man who was then Kang Sheng's deputy and is today the head of the *Diaochabu*. His special area was the battle against Taiwan. Persuaded by their arguments, Li Zongren agreed to return to Beijing. Taking a thousand precautions, he embarked on what proved to be an incredible adventure and set off back to China with his wife, via Switzerland. Zhou Enlai and Mao Zedong gave him a triumphant welcome. But one man was beginning to kick himself for his own success: Kang Sheng. For no sooner had he arrived in Beijing than General Li made a serious revelation: 'You have been infiltrated by a great many Guomindang agents.'

According to the newcomer, some of these agents were still operative within the communist apparatus. Certainly Li was confusing spies who were genuine infiltrators, traitors who had changed sides, and those who at some point in their lives had been captured by the Guomindang, made their submission, thereby compromising themselves, but who had immediately reverted to the communist camp in all sincerity. But his declarations were none the less worrying. The traitors who had gone over to the enemy were known, at least in principle. They were Gu Shunzhang, the first head of the communist secret services in 1931; Zhang Guotao, the Central Committee member who became an anti-communist counter-intelligence ace; Zhao Yaobin, Kang Sheng's own secretary, who became an expert after his defection with Military Intelligence in Taiwan; or worse still, Mao's own secretary, Chen Zhiyue, with whom he had been supplied by Kang Sheng. Chen had fled to Europe and then to Taiwan, where he had become a deputy to the head of the secret services, Zheng Jiemin.

But how was any distinction to be made between real spies and sincere communists among the militants arrested by the Guomindang who had returned to the Chinese CP? Malicious tongues started to wag. People started talking about the arrest of the young Kang Sheng in Shanghai in 1930. And about his providential release, thanks to a senior official in the Guomindang. Had not Jiang Qing, whose marriage to Mao Kang Sheng had arranged, found herself in an identical situation? Why had Kang Sheng, in March 1949, seen to it that the files seized from the routed Guomindang disappeared?

Li Zongren, who had 'put his foot in it' by referring to 'Guomindang spies who had infiltrated the communists', had no opportunity to say more. He died, of poisoning, at the beginning of the Cultural Revolution. But Liu Shaoqi had taken the opportunity of raising the subject with Mao in 1966: 'We have already criticised Kang Sheng in the past, we have even removed him from the head of the special services for a while. However, there is still some explaining to be done about his role vis-à-vis the Guomindang . . . And remember what Li Lisan said at the Seventh Congress about Kang's relations with the Trotskyists in the 1930s . . .'

Bearing this in mind, it is easier to understand why Kang Sheng so relentlessly persecuted the 'Chinese Lenin', Li Lisan, who was beaten to death by Red Guards in 1967, and Liu Shaoqi, who died of ill-treatment in prison in 1969.

In 1972, Li Zhen, the new head of the *Gonganbu*, was raking over these past events, nervously examining files yellowed with age. Was there a 'Kang Sheng affair'? What was the connection with the 'Lin Biao affair'? These serious questions obsessed him. He confided his worries to his deputies, among them Yu Sang – Kang Sheng's friend. In January 1973, Li Zhen died suddenly, just like his predecessor, Xie Fuzhi. Wang Dongxing, who happened to be passing by, found his body, his face bruised and distorted, in a cellar adjoining his apartment. Li Zhen 'the detective' had been strangled. Later, the story went round that it was Li himself who had had the Guomindang defector Li Zongren poisoned.

The Kang Sheng file was closed. Under Kang's patronage, and with Mao's connivance, Hua Guofeng became head of the *Gonganbu*, the Public Security Ministry.

At the beginning of the 1970s, Kang Sheng's realm seemed to know no bounds. Technical adviser for the Cultural Revolution, he had what was on paper a harmless job in charge of 'Central Committee personnel'. But at the stroke of a pen, he could promote or dismiss a cadre. He had control not only over the Investigation Bureau, the *Diaochabu*, but also over the Organisation Department, the International Liaison Department and the United Front Work Department. However, as age encroached, he thought of relinquishing several of his preserves. So, at the end of 1971, the International Liaison Department fell to the former ambassador to Tirana, Geng Biao. Meanwhile, Wang Dongxing was carving himself an empire out of the Central Committee's General Office. From 1973, the special services came under joint command; having been his deputy, Wang took over Kang's job, while the latter continued to act as adviser to the services. It was a gradual process.

Officially, the Chinese CP's Tenth Congress, which was held at the end of August 1973, saw the political consecration of Kang. Hua Guofeng and Wang Dongxing – who together with Zhou Enlai had concocted the report on the Lin Biao affair – were appointed to the Politburo. Kang Sheng was already a member, but became, like Zhou, Vice-President of the Central Committee.

'Pu pa Yenwang, Zhi pa Kang Lao ban!' 'Old Kang's Bureau inspires more terror than the Realm of the King of Shadows!' was a view frequently expressed in Beijing and throughout China.

Three thousand men were employed in his *Diaochabu*, run by Luo Qingchang, who was also a friend of Zhou Enlai. These men kept him informed, day and night, by radio contact, of the doings of Party cadres, people in the *Gonganbu*, the army, in artistic circles. Abroad, the Party official in charge of intelligence and security was a *Diaochabu* man, officially Counsellor or Second Secretary at the embassy – sometimes even the chauffeur of the ambassador's assistant.

After the Lin Biao affair, Kang had even taken over the doomed Marshal's intelligence networks. They had no choice. Secret agent reinforcements from Shanghai, Hainan, Beidaihe, Wuhan and elsewhere bolstered the new 'Special Section', made up of five hundred men covering the fifty-four major towns of China. Kang Sheng, who slept only three or four hours a night, spent much of his time at meetings. He wanted to know everything. Yet he would set aside several hours in order to calligraph a poem or paint a picture.

Kang's territory in Beijing was like a Monopoly board. To appreciate the extent of it, one has only to unfold a map of the city and plant flags in it. In Diaoyutai, used to house guests of the government, Kang occupied a whole building. There he received his foreign agents, including the most famous, Edward Hill, leader of the Australian Maoist party. Kang frequently booked a special banqueting hall in the Beijing Hotel where he would entertain the heads of the provincial service stations; they were always astounded by the splendour and lavishness with which they were received. Was it not a sign that their master was all powerful, whatever certain rumours might say?

In Wangfujing, the big commercial district, were the offices of the Central Committee's Organisation Department. Kang had run this department in Shanghai, in the early thirties, then again from 1946 to 1949. He liked to use certain fittings and furnishings, concealed behind the tall crimson-lacquered doors, that had been left to him. One could work, dine and sleep here. One of the senior officials, a military man by the name of Guo Yufeng, had been promoted to this department thanks to Kang. Here, Kang maintained his contacts with agents who had discreetly infiltrated the highest echelons of the Party. Guo was so efficient that Kang had him transferred to his own office, which had several secretaries. Working with Cao Yi-ou, Kang's wife, Guo excelled in the fabrication of false documents.

Kang's most secret lairs were numerous: to the north-west of the Imperial Palace lay the most northerly of the Imperial City's three lakes, and all around it was the Northern Lake Park (*Beihai Gongyuan*). In the middle of the lake rose the island of Qiong Hua, where in the thirteenth century the founder of the Yuan dynasty, Kublai Khan the Mongol, grandson of Genghis Khan, had established himself. The Mongols had created the first global secret service, setting up an intelligence exchange with the Venetians through the mediation of Marco Polo. Six centuries later, Kang Sheng established one of his top-secret centres there. A little distance away, the people of Beijing would quicken their pace, shivering with terror as they passed by the 'Kang *Gongfu*', 'Kang's Retreat', in Dashizuo Alley, parallel to the Northern Lake Park. There was a whole array of ultra-modern equipment, bought abroad at fantastically high cost, for wire-tapping and intercepting communications. In December 1972, it was murmured, Mao himself had discovered bugging devices in his office, placed there by agents of Kang Sheng, whom he had taken to task in no uncertain terms.

The nerve centre of his personal empire was Kang Sheng's own home. It is now open to visitors: one can hear the squealing of children in the adjoining playground. The *Zhuyuan*, the Bamboo Garden, in Xiao-Qichiao Alley has become a hotel for foreign tourists. Located in the north-east of Beijing, it is very near the Tower of the Drum, not far from the Soviet embassy. In 1980, Cao Yi-ou was still living there, and today the *Gonganbu* continues to check visitors there. Even the servants are the same ones who worked for Kang – with the exception of the old cook, Gong Tao, who was assassinated by Deng Xiaoping's security services.

Kang Sheng chose to move into the Bamboo Garden at the beginning of the 1960s, because he wanted to get away from the Zhongnanhai Imperial residences, where Mao Zedong, Liu Shaoqi, and Wang Dongxing lived. Symbolically, the Bamboo Garden was, during the Qing dynasty, the residence of the Emperor's cousin, the Minister of Communications. It consists of a group of five large wooden pavilions, embellished with red lacquer, linked together by a series of wooded passageways in the midst of a garden with, of course, bamboo growing everywhere, but also dotted with rocks, fountains and the rarest of plants and flowers. It was to the two small pavilions, the Duck Pavilion and the Pavilion of the Young Drunken Beauty, that Kang liked to retire in order to paint or re-read the great classics.

The head of Chinese intelligence had installed the heart of his services here. In the main building, which had a first floor on the street (a very rare feature and a sign of imperial kinship), the *Diaochabu* engineers had dug out a veritable underground bunker. It was said that it was even connected by a gallery to the vast labyrinth dug out by Wang Dongxing's special troops, which allowed the leadership to leave Zhongnanhai, the new Forbidden City, in secret. In this bunker were kept part of the Central Index, transmitter-receivers that enabled direct contact to be maintained with the service's fifty-four stations throughout China. It was from this vantage point under his house that Kang Sheng had followed, hour by hour, the developments of the Cultural Revolution, sending out orders to the four corners of the country. Thanks to his Northern Lake base, he was able to establish contact with his agents in the embassies. Moreover, there was an alarm system connecting him with his Action Service, the former Section 7 of the Social Affairs Department, whose men were taught the use of firearms, martial arts, techniques of sabotage and offensive counter-intelligence in the Nanyan training camp, south of Beijing.

One of the most secret activities of the *Diaochabu's* special section had little to do with espionage. At the height of the Cultural Revolution of which he was one of the instigators, Kang Sheng realised that the destruction of an irreplaceable patrimony had begun. The auto-da-fés were in full swing, just as during the grim period when the Emperor Qin Shihuan simply banned books. People hid censored works in the walls of their houses. Anything that was not Maoist was considered a 'pornographic work'. The Red Guards destroyed the Old World with pickaxes: Ming vases, jewellery, thousand-year-old cultural treasures. It sickened Kang Sheng, the man who painted water-colours after Bada Shanren; who engraved jade and wrote elegant poems, and whose youth had been brightened by the splendour of the *Red Chamber*; who adored the ancient operas, even though under the requirements of activism he was supposed to approve the absurdities of the new style advocated by Jiang Qing; who sought out old editions of the *Jin Ping Mei* or had sent from Sichuan the work of the last great imitator, in the Shanghai tradition, of the erotic 'bed game'.

One day in 1966, Kang Sheng received a distress call from his old friend Wu Zhongchao, the curator of the Imperial Museum: 'They are beginning to loot the museums . . . Come and take away the archives I have in my cellars . . .'

The masterspy had in fact deposited several hundred kilos of secret archive duplicates in the museum. It was then that he had the idea of sending *Diaochabu* men disguised as Red Guards to remove, with Wu's complicity, thousands of museum objects: imperial inkwells, perfume clocks, mechanical toys, cloisonné enamels from the Ming period, carved inkpots, paintings, calligraphic works, piles of old books. Thirty times at least, the special commandos removed hundreds of cases from the administration of Beijing's cultural heritage, Kang Sheng having told them: 'Make an inventory of everything that is to go to the cultural heritage and confiscate it. We're taking charge of it . . .'

In addition, Kang took it upon himself to seize works of art discovered in the possession of Party cadres and other better-off people – all for the Cultural Revolution. A few years after Kang Sheng's death, huge warehouses full of all these riches were discovered in some of his 'retreats': nearly sixty thousand works of art and forty thousand books. Today, the official version is unforgiving: 'Kang Sheng tried to appropriate a great part of our heritage.'

Another way of looking at it would be to say that Kang tried to save from the collective madness of the Cultural Revolution the riches of ancient China and preserve them for future generations. After all, he knew he was going to die shortly. The question at least deserves to be raised . . .

If Kang Sheng's power was then at its peak, this was not only because he had the secret police firmly under control, but also because he agreed with Zhou Enlai on the need for a complete change in Beijing's foreign policy. For the time, the two men were in total accord, forgetting their past quarrels. In the greatest secrecy, they were going to mount an operation that changed the face of the world in strategical terms: an alliance with the United States. Quite the opposite of what they were saying in public.

Let us return for a moment to three years before, in 1970.

At the beginning of June 1970, Kang Sheng was delighted to meet his old Rumanian comrade Emil Bodnaras again. Bodnaras was in China on a 'short friendly visit'. In Bucharest, no doubt, Ceaucescu was worried about the upheavals of the Cultural Revolution and had sent the old Comintern veteran to find out what was happening.

On the evening of 9 June, a sumptuous banquet, presided over by Zhou Enlai, was held in honour of the Rumanian guests. There was a very large Cambodian delegation, led by Penn Bouth. Kang Sheng had been chosen to make the usual short speech. He paid heartfelt tribute to Rumania, and to 'Comrade Bodnaras, an old friend of ours'. But suddenly his voice rose, and became more penetrating, as he vigorously emphasised his words.

'Distinguished guests from Rumania, you have come to the East, you have seen with your own eyes the revolutionary situation, which is ever improving, of the fight against American imperialism. Unable to extricate itself from a difficult position in its war of aggression in South Vietnam, the Nixon administration shamelessly sent its troops into Cambodia and resumed the bombing of North Vietnam, in the hope of finding a way out by extending its war of aggression.'

Kang then hammered home his point: 'But contrary to Nixon's desire, the extension of its aggression by American imperialism has roused the indignant resistance of the three Indochinese peoples and has been firmly combated and condemned by the revolutionary peoples of the whole world . . .'

Kang Sheng's appearance created a sensation. It had been observed at the beginning of the 1970s that old Kang was appearing at events less often, completely taken up as he was by his intrigues and the running of his services. Since the end of 1969, however, his wife,

Cao Yi-ou – now a member of the Central Committee, to which she was elected at the Ninth Congress – made frequent appearances at official receptions, representing her husband.

But the impact of this speech on 9 June derived from the fact that by attacking Nixon and the Americans with such virulence Kang was aiming at those in Beijing who imagined that a rapprochement with the USA – the ultimate abomination – was possible. However, the head of the *Tewu* did not speak the truth as he saw it . . .

At the end of June, Kang Sheng, Zhou Enlai and Li Zhen and Yu Sang of the *Gonganbu* played host to Kadri Hazbiu, member of the Politburo of the Working Party of Albania in charge of the Interior Ministry and of the country's secret service, the *Sigurimi*. Various general topics were discussed, in addition to the technical problems relating to the close collaboration between the two secret services.

After Kadri's return, on 22 June, Enver Hoxha in Tirana noted in his diary how vague Zhou and Kang had been in conversations with his emissary. In the first place, the Albanian leader was worried by the fact that the Chinese had said nothing to him about the Rumanian Bodnaras's trip, whose plan for a Balkan federation they supported. However, Hoxha really could not see his country joining with Yugoslavia and Rumania. He therefore asked himself a burning question: were the Chinese not planning to collaborate with Washington?

In fact, a strange behind-the-scenes drama was already unfolding. On 27 April 1970, the Chinese military attaché in Paris, Fang Wen, received an unusual visit. His American opposite number, the huge General Vernon Walters, turned up on his doorstep: 'I'm General Walters, the American military attaché, and I have a message from my President for your government.'

The exchange took place in French, the only language in which the two men could communicate with each other. So, the terrible enemy of communism, Richard Nixon, wanted to open a dialogue with Red China!

Shortly afterwards, without the knowledge of the CIA, Vernon Walters began the first discussions that were to lead to a meeting between Henry Kissinger, the Machiavelli of American diplomacy, and the Chinese.

The *Diaochabu* representative in Paris, Counsellor Cao Guisheng – who spoke English – finally met Walters. The ball was now rolling . . .

Zhou Enlai and Kang Sheng followed these meetings from the ringside, kept informed by the head of the *Diaochabu*, Luo Qingchang. Despite their disagreements, Kang and Zhou now found themselves working alongside each other, just as in the good old days in Paris and Shanghai. Zhou organised all the diplomatic side of things, while Kang was responsible for security, thanks to his services. In Beijing, the green light was given for a first meeting at the end of June between Kissinger and the Chinese ambassador Huang Zhen, a former general in the

People's Liberation Army, who was also experienced in clandestine activity.

Meanwhile, poor Vernon Walters sweated blood getting Nixon's envoy on to French soil under conditions of the utmost secrecy. He decided to act without the knowledge of the head of the CIA station in Paris, David Murphy (formerly head of the Agency's Soviet division). Walters, as military attaché, was answerable to the rival organisation, the Defense Intelligence Agency, the DIA. He no doubt feared that the CIA, run by Richard Helms, might tip off its natural ally, Chiang Kai-shek's nationalist China. Worse still, David Murphy was considered by James Angleton, head of CIA counter-intelligence, to be a Russian mole. (In 1973, at the request of Alexandre de Marenches, the head of SDECE, Murphy was recalled to the USA. De Marenches must have confided in his old friend Walters, with whom he had fought during the Second World War in the Allied Expeditionary Corps in Italy.)

On 25 July 1970, Kissinger met China's ambassador. The main object of their meeting was the war in Indochina and the Sino-American rapprochement. From the moment he arrived in Huang Zhen's home, Chinese music playing quietly in the background, clouds of incense scenting the air, they were served with apricots, jasmine tea and golden Shaoxing wine. The ice was broken . . .

In subsequent meetings, preparations were made for Kissinger's visit to China, a prelude to a visit by Nixon.

In 1971, the Russians got wind of the negotiations. Ivan Agayants, head of the KGB's Disinformation Section, organised a special operation. It was aimed at discrediting Kissinger, and involved circulating the rumour, via the appropriate channels, that Nixon's adviser was in fact a Soviet agent.

The SDECE and the *Tewu* nipped this intrigue in the bud. But the Taiwanese were on the alert. They learned that Zhou Enlai was to go to Paris in 1971. With the consent of the CIA, they planned an extraordinary assassination attempt. It was not the first time they had tried to assassinate Zhou, public enemy number one in nationalist China. A 'kamikaze' dog, loaded with explosives, was supposed to rush at Zhou. The bomb would be detonated from a distance. For which task the Taiwanese had recruited some Italian neo-fascists. The secret war knows no frontiers . . .

But Luo Qingchang, head of the *Diaochabu* and an expert on Taiwanese affairs, had infiltrated Chiang Kai-shek's teams of killers. He warned Zhou, who in any case had decided to cancel his trip, because of the worrying internal situation in China. This was just as well.

When Kissinger went to China, extraordinary security measures were organised by the *Gonganbu* men Li Zhen, Yu Sang and Zhou's personal secretary, Yang Dezhong, leader of the guards. They were not going to be at the mercy of a second operation carried out by Taiwanese agents.

After the famous ping-pong tournament, preparations were made for the President's visit in 1972. Nixon the anti-communist had surrounded himself with such unusual advisers as those old American friends of Mao, Harold Isaacs and Edgar Snow. In fact, the difficulties came from his own counter-intelligence services.

The CIA found it hard to understand how they could be 'dropping' Chiang Kai-shek. As for the famous FBI, it had embarked on an anti-Chinese crusade only a few days before Nixon's trip was announced. In the summer of 1971, the old boss of the FBI, J. Edgar Hoover, actually launched a big national campaign against Chinese communism! In San Francisco's Chinatown and in all the Chinese communities in the USA, Hoover had posters in Chinese put up, asking the population to inform the authorities of any suspicious activities on the part of Maoist agitators in disguise: 'We must expand the programme to combat intelligence operations and attempts to foment revolution!' Hoover 'the incorruptible' had committed a terrible blunder. And the White House had to rap the knuckles of the only man in the world who had had a career in counter-intelligence almost as long as that of Kang Sheng.

Old Kang knew that, as in the Yan'an days of 1944, he now had to collaborate with the American special services. In fact, the head of the liaison mission that was set up in Beijing was David Bruce, formerly with the OSS. Another American, James Lilley, established the first CIA station in Beijing. The common enemy was marked out: the Russian KGB.

On his visit to Beijing in 1971, Kissinger had begun the meeting with a surprising declaration: 'You have recently tried to infiltrate the CIA using one of your agents in Europe who defected to us. We immediately saw through it. We are going to return him to you. And you have men whom we would like to recover. Let us hope that such incidents are not repeated in the future.' Kissinger was referring to Liao Heshu, the defector from The Hague who had 'given himself up' to the CIA in 1966. Liao was sent back to China in exchange for the CIA spies Fecteau and Downey.

Thereafter, the Chinese collaborated with the Western secret services. Luo Qingchang organised meetings with the SDECE, which had just set up a Chinese section. But there was at that point no SDECE station in Beijing. Alexandre de Marenches decided to send a representative as counsellor to the San Li Tun embassy, imposing his choice in the face of reservations from the Quai d'Orsay. Married to a woman who had worked at the Wagon-Lits Hotel in Beijing and knew the language, and equipped with a car and chauffeur (unlike genuine counsellors), Roger Aimé led a busy social life, in so far as the situation in Red China at the time allowed him to do so! He had ready access to senior Party officials and especially to Kang Sheng's men. His work consisted of preparing Georges Pompidou's 1973 trip.

The SDECE had the solid support of its key station in Hong Kong.

The representative of Kang Sheng's service in the British colony was the deputy director of the Xinhua press agency, Li Jusheng. He circumspectly entered upon an exchange of information with John Longrigg, head of the British Secret Intelligence Service there. Already in 1972, the Anglo-Chinese *entente cordiale* had come into play, allowing the dismantling of a vast KGB network run by Stepan Tsoumayev. But all the same, Kang Sheng did not cease to double-cross the British, who the following year suffered a major setback: the Government Communications Headquarters listening station at Little Sai Wan experienced an unprecedented betrayal. With the help of the Australians, the station had set up Project Kittiwake, a programme for intercepting and decoding Chinese army and diplomatic communications. Chinese analysts and translators from Hong Kong and Taiwan worked round the clock. However, in 1973, two of Kang Sheng's moles, both of them Taiwanese who had been won over to communism, made off to Red China taking with them piles of archives, documents, codes, etc.

In Africa, the Sino-American alliance gradually had its effect. On 23 January 1973, an Agence France Presse wire came through on the teleprinters of the world's newspapers: 'Chairman Mao Zedong has reportedly admitted that he has wasted a lot of time and money attempting to overthrow President Mobutu of Zaire.'

Indeed, Red China established cordial relations with Zaire. Mobutu even made the pilgrimage to Beijing, just as his worst enemy, Pierre Mulele, had ten years earlier. The wheel had turned. Kang Sheng organised a substantial intelligence station in Kinshasa. Two *Tewu* veterans of African affairs, Gao Liang and Liu Yufeng (soon to become ambassador to Gabon), organised China's new alliances in Africa.

In Angola, the CIA, SDECE and *Tewu* worked hand in hand together. The object was to bring down the new pro-Soviet government of Agostino Neto, which was backed by the Cuban expeditionary force. Tang Mingzhao, a representative of the International Liaison Department, was sent in 1973 to bring Chinese support to Holden Roberto's NLFA, and to the UNITA movement of Jonas Savimbi and Tony Fernandez, who had been trained in Beijing during the 1960s.

The Sino-American alliance also came into effect in the Far East, creating complex situations. Apart from the Japanese *Naicho*, the secret service best informed on China, in the East, was India's. The Sino-Indian war in the 1960s had left an indelible mark on relations between the two countries. In the residential quarter of Vasant Vihar in New Delhi, a huge four-storey building housed Indira Gandhi's new intelligence agency, called the Research and Analysis Wing (RAW), which came into existence on 21 September 1968. Seven thousand men belonged to it. Department 1 worked on the border countries; department 2 dealt with 'the analysis of communism'; 3 studied the armament of Pakistan and 4 organised intelligence networks among the Indian populations scattered throughout the world. A Bureau for Special Operations (BSO) was divided into another four sections responsible for action: Pakistan; China and South-East Asia; the Middle East and Africa; the rest of the world.

Future secret agents came to the RAW headquarters, 'the House of Spies', as it was called in the Indian press, in order to learn the basics of spying.

One day, the director, Rameshwar Nath Kao, welcomed the students: 'We are going to study the methods of the CIA, the KGB and the Chinese *Tewu* . . .'

A pupil raised his hand. 'Why are we not studying the history of intelligence in India, sir?'

'Good question. That's just the problem. Before us, there was nothing. Apart from the Intelligence Bureau, of course, which was set up by the British all those years ago . . .'

Yet within three years the RAW became an unrivalled service. One of its special sections, the Special Service Bureau (SSB), sealed the borders in an attempt to put an end to Chinese and Pakistani infiltration (especially during the war of independence in Bangladesh in 1971).

During the Cultural Revolution in China, Maoist groups abounded in India, organising a guerrilla campaign. The Indian Communist Party (Marxist-Leninist) had a huge guerrilla base in West Bengal. They called themselves 'Naxalites' after Naxalbari, where the rebellion had started. A ruthless civil war ensued. At the beginning of 1970, the director of the RAW received a report that left him perplexed. Charu Mazumbar, the historic Maoist leader, had gone to Beijing, where he was actually received by Zhou Enlai and Kang Sheng. Thanks to the fact that his movement had been infiltrated, the RAW was able to obtain a detailed account of these meetings. Zhou Enlai had criticised the 'Indian comrades' and their slogans 'Mao is our President' and 'China's Path is Ours'.

'The world is divided into classes and nations,' explained Zhou. 'The proletariat of each territory is the main representative of its own country. So we cannot but take into account national borders. To regard the leader of our country as that of another goes against national sentiments. Even the working class cannot accept it. To respect a great Marxist-Leninist is one thing, but to declare him the leader of another party is quite another thing.'

Kang Sheng was more explicit. 'We cannot agree to say that our party is in charge of you. Similarly, we cannot agree to your saying that our president is your president. It goes against Mao Zedong's thought. Our relations must be based on equality and fraternity.'

It was obvious from this lesson in Marxism that the Chinese were gradually going to abandon the Maoist guerrillas in India, as they did in Ceylon or Burma. Charu Mazumbar continued the fight alone. In

July 1972 the RAW captured him and he died in prison.

The Chinese had not, however, ceased their intrigues against India. The RAW had a shock when it learned in 1974 that the CIA and the Chinese *Tewu* were carrying out operations in the north-east of the country.

In February, under the aegis of the RAW, Skato Swu, a former leader of the Naga insurgents in the jungles, and Zuheto, ex-commander-in-chief of the Naga, held a press conference in New Delhi: 'Special camps were set up by the Americans and Chinese during the Bangladesh war of independence. Today, the *Tewu* is running camps in Yunnan to train the rebels, who are also supported by the CIA. These secret services are intensifying the struggle in order to create in the northern regions of India and Bangladesh a border state between the People's Republic of China, India, Burma, Nagaland. The CIA and the *Tewu* are co-ordinating the training of guerrillas among the Karen, Naga and Mizos tribes . . .'

The Chinese objective was clear: To gain control of the 'Seven Sisters', the north-eastern states Assam, Meghalaya, Tripura, Manipur, Nagaland and the allied territories Mizoram and Arunachal Pradesh.

But if China and the United States were jointly conducting this secret war, there was a much simpler reason for it: Indira Gandhi's India was increasingly becoming the ally of the USSR. And for Kang Sheng, as for the CIA, the Soviet Union was the number one enemy.

24
The Shadows Claim Their Master

It was so cold that night of 15 January 1974 that the streets of Beijing were deserted. Suddenly a light grey Volga shot out of the Russian embassy, heading straight for the north-eastern suburb of the capital. When it came to a little bridge, it stopped to let out two men dressed as Chinese. The smaller of the two, the military interpreter Kolossov, wore the padded overalls of an ordinary worker and a hat with ear muffs. His companion, the third secretary at the embassy, Semionov, had on a standard blue quilt coat. They were obviously trying to pass unnoticed.

After a half-hour wait, two more men appeared at the other end of the bridge and shouted out a password. These men were real Chinese: Li Hongzhou and his friend were both working for the army's secret service, the GRU. Li had been trained as a spy in Moscow in 1970. Then he was sent back to his own country in June 1972, armed with a transmitter-receiver and with precise instructions: he was to recruit new agents in order to create a network.

At the given signal, Semionov cautiously emerged from where he was hiding, and, coming up to Li Hongzhou, hugged him and repeated the password that had been agreed upon in advance: 'Good evening, my dear Alen!'

The Chinese handed the Russian a white canvas mask in which was concealed a hermetically sealed plastic pocket containing coded information, as well as the instruments for writing in invisible ink that Li had been told to return. For his part, Semionov handed him a heavy travelling bag in which was a high-frequency transmitter-receiver, a diagram showing how to set it up, a timetable for radio-communications with the frequencies fixed by the GRU for its Chinese agent and methods of establishing contact, instructions written in invisible ink, eight packets of drying powder to protect his equipment from humidity, forged passes and the sum of 5,000 yuans. In short, everything a secret agent would need . . .

But the *Gonganbu*, tipped off about the operation in advance, had them under surveillance. Suddenly a red rocket illuminated the sky, throwing the four conspirators into panic. Semionov threw what he was carrying into the river, but it was already too late: two Soviet 'diplomats' had just fallen into the net of the Chinese special services.

It was then that the light grey Volga returned to the scene: the Soviet embassy's first secretary, Martchenko, accompanied by his wife, had come to collect the spoils, and Mrs Semionov her husband. A fatal mistake, of course. The trio fell into the trap laid by the men from Public Security.

At his Bamboo Garden headquarters, Kang Sheng once again savoured the incomparable pleasure of the hunter when he finally gets his prey after hours of waiting. But he found this victory had a bitter taste: having reached the peak of his power, Kang was now a man threatened by illness.

'The ceremony and the meal were brief. Shortly before we rose from the table, two wheelchairs passed before us, carefully pushed one behind the other. These officials were being taken out first to avoid being jostled when everyone went out. The first man, who stopped for a moment at our table to shake hands with Ji Pengfei, was Kang Sheng, a sagging body, an emaciated face and dull eyes sunken in their sockets. The other, the person sitting next to me said, was the head of the revenue court. Madame Song Qinling also went out by the same side door: she walks slowly, leaning on the arms of two assistants.'

On the evening of 30 September 1974, the French ambassador to Beijing, Étienne Manac'h, wrote these few lines in his personal diary. He had been attending the celebrations to commemorate the twenty-fifth anniversary of the People's Republic of China. A doubly historic reception, since this was also the occasion of the last public speech made by the Prime Minister Zhou Enlai, who came out of the hospital where he was being treated for cancer specially. It also marked one of Kang Sheng's final appearances. Nearly half a century after the Shanghai uprising and the crushing of the Reds by Chiang Kai-shek, the two accomplices of years gone by found themselves side by side for the last time. Admittedly, there was no warmth in their meeting. The fratricidal struggle for power, the ruthless confrontations of the Cultural Revolution, old age and illness had long since killed any feeling of camaraderie between them. Hatred was taking hold. By supporting the Party 'innovators' led by Deng Xiaoping, Zhou came into direct confrontation with Kang, primarily concerned with safeguarding his creation – an omnipresent apparatus of repression, a civilian society totally gagged by 'revolutionary forces'.

Outside, the imposing Tian'anmen Square was lit by powerful spotlights. Red flags fluttered in the breeze. The banqueting hall in the People's Palace of Assembly was presided over by a huge portrait of Chairman Mao, his eyes resting on the guests at this strange meal: the Gang of Four in its entirety, Jiang Qing at their head, but also her worst adversary, Deng Xiaoping, who returned to the highest echelons of power in April 1973 after his relegation to a 'Seventh of May School'; the writer Guo Moro, a personal friend of Kang and of Hua Guofeng, Xie Fuzhi's successor at the head of the *Gonganbu* and a newly appointed member of the Politburo. There were also delegates of the 'brother parties': the Indonesian Jusuf Adjitorop and the very pro-Chinese Hoang Van Hoan, head of the Vietnamese CP's International Liaison Department. And finally, there were the 'distinguished foreign guests'.

Chief among these 'indestructible friends' of the People's Republic of China was none other than Prince Norodom Sihanouk. The Cambodian sovereign, driven out in March 1970 by a pro-American coup, no doubt looked back to those happy days in 1958 when an unusual alliance between the French SDECE and the Chinese *Tewu* had saved his country from a plot organised by the CIA. But that was past history now, and the former head of his secret service, General Sosthene Fernandez, was now making common cause with General Lon Nol's government.

Once the meal was over, Kang Sheng was almost immediately taken back to the Bamboo Garden. These festivities exhausted him. Eaten up by the most implacable of cancers, caused by smoking, Kang Sheng knew that his days were numbered. He read his death sentence in the sycophantic looks of the doctors who for some months yet continued to present him with reassuring reports on his state of health. He sensed his imminent demise in the ever renewed attentions of the faithful Cao Yi-ou.

The nights were terrible. Kang Sheng hardly slept at all any more. He would wake suddenly, his body bathed in a cold sweat. He was assailed by terrible nightmares. Then he would thrash about, crying out. His servants would come running, and whisper: 'He's going mad!'

And indeed he was. Cao Yi-ou tried to calm her husband. But what could be done to stave off the obsessive memories, the remorse? In an attempt to forget, Kang Sheng watched American crime films, screened one after the other, peopling his sleepless nights with imaginary characters. Then, it was said, he would sometimes fall asleep. At dawn . . .

The Bamboo Garden, a marvellous place, became for Kang a house of horror, haunted by the spectres of former comrades-in-arms, assassinated, betrayed, militants sacrificed to the expeditious justice of the Party, subjected to public trials, to humiliation and torture. What was the reason for the communists killed by the Green Gang, the clandestine militants shot by the Guomindang, the Red soldiers who fell in combat? Why the Trotskyists, the 'liquidated' dissidents? Why the mass executions carried out by the *Gonganbu* men, why the persecution of landowners, religious orders, opponents? Why the slow painful deaths of Liu Changsheng, Xu Zirong, Liu Ren? Why the public beating of Li Lisan, 'the Chinese Lenin' of the 1920s, by Red Guards, children drunk on violence? And what the reason for the Red Marshal Peng Dehuai dying behind bars?

There was no answer to these questions. None, in any case, which could satisfy Kang Sheng and allow him to sleep soundly again. He was being eaten up inside by his merciless disease. Death, he knew, would not spare for much longer the Grand Inquisitor of the Rectification Campaign, of the Cultural Revolution. For years, he had deified death, dressing conspicuously in white, the colour of mourning in China. But death was stronger than him, her most faithful lover, her indefatigable supplier.

At daybreak, the struggle for power would resume. With enormous effort, Kang Sheng sought to protect his shadowy realms, threatened by the expansionist ambitions of Wang Dongxing. Eighteen years his junior, Mao's former bodyguard was in peak form. He had ceaselessly gone about enlarging his domain, striving to gain control of all the Chinese secret services, military and civilian, with the help of his 'associate' Hua Guofeng.

The second war in Indochina, it is true, was claiming most of Wang Dongxing's attention. Like all the Chinese leaders, he met with mixed feelings the announcements of the continual progress being made by the Vietnamese CP and the National Liberation Front in their struggle against the Saigon government: they were too wary to place themselves willingly in Beijing's orbit, and no one was unaware of their plan for an Indochinese federation, drawn from Ho Chi Minh's spiritual heritage – a particularly dangerous plan since this alliance of states under Vietnamese rule would create a potential rival to China in South-East Asia.

Not least the Khmer Rouge. The Cambodian guerrillas, who became stronger day by day, consisted of three groups who had come to some provisional agreement with each other: the pro-Vietnamese supporters of Heng Samrin or Pen Sovan; Phouk Chhay or Hu Nim's pro-Chinese group, whose political consciousness had been awakened by the example of the Cultural Revolution; and that of Pol Pot, ultra-nationalists who entertained a deep-rooted hostility towards their Vietnamese Big Brother, considered the Cambodians' hereditary enemy.

The Chinese were well acquainted with Pol Pot, a former French Communist Party student in whom they alone had detected the makings of a political leader. On two occasions, the communist Khmer leader had secretly visited Beijing, in 1965 and then again in 1969. Both times, he had stayed several months in China, following training courses with Kang Sheng's special services. As for Wang Dongxing, he had been taking a very close interest in the Khmer question since 1964, the year of one of his rare trips abroad. Anxious for the success of Pol Pot and his comrades in their struggle against the pro-American regime of General Lon Nol, Wang had sent several élite cadres from his Detachment 8341 to fight in Cambodia. These Chinese from the Action Service also gave military instruction to the Khmer Rouge fighters.

In Vietnam, the Chinese still had a number of allies in the communist leadership of the North. Apart from Hoang Van Hoan, one of the most active was none other than Comrade Tran Quoc Hoan, who had been in charge since 1951 of the Vietnamese equivalent of the *Gonganbu*, the *Cong An Bo*. He was yet another 'son' of the Republic of Yan'an.

In the spring of 1975, the Vietnamese CP and the National Liberation Front, once very large but which as a result of the fighting and the purges had dwindled in size, launched a strong military operation called the Ho Chi Minh Offensive. The name itself indicated the objective better than any long speech: the founding father of Vietnamese communism and a convinced nationalist, Ho had never made a secret of his desire to reunite Vietnam, partitioned in 1954–5 after the Geneva Agreement. His heirs intended to implement this programme in full. Their troops very quickly achieved decisive victories, wiping out the élite of the South Vietnamese government forces on the high plateaux. A veritable panic ensued, while in Cambodia the Khmer Rouge were encircling Phnom Penh.

April was a blessed month for Kang Sheng, who immediately forgot the ghosts that were haunting him at night. On the island of Taiwan, Generalissimo Chiang Kai-shek, the communists' lifelong enemy, died. He left the presidency of nationalist China to his own son, Chiang Ching-kuo. In Cambodia, Pol Pot and his friends were victorious, seizing the capital. They were preparing to turn their whole country into a vast *Laogai*. On 30 April, the North Vietnamese army's tanks rammed the railings of the presidential palace in Saigon, watched by journalists. This in fact upset the Chinese: their honeymoon with Washington taking precedence, had not Beijing's diplomats and special agents tried at the last moment to bring about final negotiations to limit the Vietcong victory?

The enthusiasm with which Kang Sheng was fired by the death of Chiang Kai-shek and the victory of their Khmer Rouge allies quickly waned. His illness was constantly gaining ground. The doctors admitted to being unable to halt its progress. Kang Sheng was now confined to his Bamboo Garden, among the artistic treasures he hardly had the strength to admire. One is not a Marxist-Leninist 'exterminating angel' with impunity. Now himself on the threshold of death, Kang Sheng had no friends left. He had betrayed most of them and the others, such as Jiang Qing, paid him much less attention, for he was no longer anything but a weak and ailing man. Only Cao Yi-ou still stood by him.

The approach of death – and perhaps the influence of his wife – made another man of him. Almost imperceptibly, Kang Sheng returned to the philosophical teachings of his intellectual youth in Shandong. Increasingly detached from material things, through the intermediary of Cao Yi-ou, he established contacts with the Buddhist spiritual authorities, in particular with the venerable Zhao Puzhu. And the man who participated in the great anti-Confucius campaign directed against Zhou Enlai by the Gang of Four, the man who had even been the instigator of that campaign, again questioned the value of his own heritage.

How would he be remembered in the history of China. As a tor-turer, an *éminence grise*. As the life ebbed from his already skeletal body, this question came to obsess him. Suddenly he made up his mind – perhaps on the advice of Cao Yi-ou – to act. The man for the job seemed to him to be Deng Xiaoping, the man he once hated, whose downfall and death he had once wanted; who, each time rising from the ashes like the phoenix, was now, in the summer of 1975, gradually rehabilitating the victims of the Cultural Revolution. Already, in November 1973, Luo Ruiqing had been freed. The former head of the *Gonganbu*, Kang Sheng's rival in the past, was now reappearing in public. Despite his poor state of health, ruined by the torture he suffered during the Cultural Revolution, Luo was working for Deng Xiaoping. Head of a small team who all had experience of working for the *Gonganbu*, he was busy restoring from memory certain delicate files destroyed by Kang Sheng in his days of glory. Perhaps this was an omen?

'I want to re-establish the truth, to make certain revelations,' the dying man discreetly made it known to his former victim.

What revelations? Then in the middle of a covert struggle against the Gang of Four and the Wang Dongxing–Hua Guofeng clan, the newly appointed 'Senior Vice-Premier' Deng Xiaoping could not let slip an opportunity to strike against his enemies.

Kang Sheng was then in hospital in Beijing. One evening in August 1975, two of Deng's trusted aides appeared at Kang Sheng's bedside. One of them was a woman: Tang Wengsheng, director of American affairs at the Foreign Affairs Ministry. The other, Wang Hairong, her boss, was Vice-Minister of the Chinese Diplomatic Corps. Kang Sheng was still lucid when they visited him, and according to the 'para-official' version, said to them right out of the blue: 'I want to salve my conscience before the Party!'

A laudable intention for a communist, thought the two visitors, none the less perplexed.

They were completely dumbfounded when Kang went on to tell them: 'Zhang Chunqiao, Jiang Qing's accomplice, is a long-standing renegade, a traitor to the Party. Jiang Qing showed me a file one day that established his treachery beyond question.'

Zhang Chunqiao, a pillar of the all-powerful Gang of Four! Wang Hairong and Tang Wensheng looked at each other in increasing dis-belief. Coughing, Kang Sheng told them to contact Wang Guanlan and Wu Zhongchao to obtain details about Jiang Qing's past. Wang Guanlan was the husband of Xu Yiyong, a friend of Jiang Qing in Shanghai, then in Yan'an. Wu Zhongchao, an employee in Beijing Museum, was an underground communist during the 1930s.

Should an investigation be launched into the past of two members – and not the least important – of the Gang of Four? Tang Wengsheng and Wang Hairong met with a negative reply from their superior in the hierarchy, Foreign Affairs Minister Qiao Guanhua. His wife, it is true, was teaching English to Madame Mao, which prompted her husband to caution. More determined, Deng Xiaoping's friends tried to confirm Kang Sheng's declarations in order to build up files against the 'Four' and their supporters.

This 'good deed' towards Deng Xiaoping was probably insufficient to restore Kang Sheng's peace of mind. After four months' terrible suffering, he died of cancer on 16 December 1975, at dawn. Only the day before, an official Chinese communiqué virulently denounced the increase in Soviet 'revisionist espionage' activities throughout the world.

His funeral, as we have seen, was that of a senior official, of a communist leader worthy of praise for his revolutionary qualities and his 'anti-revisionist' militancy. It was attended by a majority of cadres in the secret police, the *Gonganbu* and in the secret services. And also by those bitterly opposed enemies, Deng Xiaoping and the Gang of Four.

His death came as no surprise to Cao Yi-ou, but it was certainly an enormous blow. Once he had gone, no one would come to her aid, nor that of their son, vice-mayor of Hangzhou since the Cultural Revolution. The Gang of Four had only to lose out to its redoubtable enemies and they would be done for.

Cao Yi-ou made herself very active, on behalf of her deceased husband – in fact, in the interests of herself and her son. She even tried, on the grounds of Kang Sheng's eleventh-hour conversion to the ancestral principles of Buddhism, to persuade the venerable religious leader Zhao Puzhu to help her protect the memory of the deceased. Zhao Puzhu took three days to consider her request then said no: a sincere Buddhist could not countenance the past actions of a man hated by an entire nation for whom his name was synonomous with adversity.

Cao Yi-ou almost sank into despair, especially when 'friends' hastened to report back to her Zhou Enlai's cruel words: 'I'm soon going to die. But on no account do I want to be buried, like Kang Sheng, in the cemetery of the Eight Precious Hills. Babaoshan is the resting-place of the heroes of the Revolution, Kang Sheng does not deserve to lie there, since he has been a disgrace to the Revolution.'

This was a sad funeral oration from an old Party comrade, a twin star of Chinese communism born, like Kang Sheng, in 1898. Kang, the intellectual from Shandong, would no doubt have preferred these words taken from the preface of the great Chinese erotic masterpiece *Jin Ping Mei*, of which he was so fond in his glory days:

> What is man? What is power?
> Comes the day when all is over.
> The flutes, the harps fall silent.
> The singing stops, the songs half-sung.
> It is the end.

What is man, what is power? In Red China at the end of 1975, these were pertinent questions.

The Public Security agents had never seen anything like it. On Tian'anmen Square, in the heart of Beijing, a 'calm disorder' reigned, with no regard to propriety. With a great many *dazibao* and multi-coloured wreaths of flowers, thousands and thousands of peaceable Chinese citizens were demonstrating that they had had enough of the Gang of Four, weakened by the death of Kang. The pretext for these demonstrations in April 1976 was a popular homage to Zhou Enlai, who died on 8 January, twenty-two days after Kang Sheng. But no one close to the seat of power was fooled: the demonstrators were in fact calling for a change of policy, if not of regime. They wanted an end once and for all to the Cultural Revolution.

At lunchtime on 5 April, acting on orders from the new Prime Minister Hua Guofeng and Wang Dongxing, the Public Security agents went on to the offensive. In the evening, some hundred demonstrators were killed and three or four thousand thrown into prison, according to the declarations of the deputy Public Security Minister Yang Gui.

Should Deng Xiaoping, considered by his opponents to be the main beneficiary of the scandalous Tian'anmen demonstrations, be arrested? Already ousted as Prime Minister by Hua Guofeng in February, the leader of the 'reformist' faction of the Chinese CP was dismissed from office, on Mao's orders, on 7 April. Sensing that the wind was turning, Deng had fled to Canton. General Xu Shiyou, commander of the Military Region of this great southern city, was one of his friends. Neither the Gang of Four nor Public Security specialists Hua Guofeng and Wang Dongxing would dare attack the army head on. They were too afraid of it. A quarter of a century after Mao's takeover of power, China had made an incredible leap backwards, returning to the golden age of warlords. These warlords simply wore a Red star on their brows. Deng Xiaoping's warlord was Xu Shiyou.

On 9 September 1976, Red China momentarily held its breath: Chairman Mao was dead. Expected and dreaded at the same time, the death of the man whom the whole world celebrated as a giant of twentieth-century history plunged his compatriots into anguish. With Mao gone, they suddenly felt orphaned, as is the case in all totalitarian regimes when the founding father dies. Worse: the death of the Chairman left the way open to the now inevitable factional fighting. And the burning question remained: who would win?

The race for the leadership began almost immediately, umpired by the elderly Defence Minister Ye Jianying, a supporter of Zhou Enlai but also a former friend of Kang Sheng, whose funeral oration he had in fact delivered. A determined man despite his advanced years, Ye Jianying urged Hua Guofeng to get rid of the Gang of Four before they made a bid for power. 'She's a schemer who has never taken part in the revolutionary fighting. Have her thrown in prison along with her three accomplices . . .'

The Prime Minister continued to waver. His position, he knew, depended primarily on a subtle balance between the Gang of Four and Deng Xiaoping and his supporters. Should he suddenly disturb such a delicate situation, and confront Jiang Qing head on in the name of 'Maoist legitimacy'? Naturally, this was tempting for the former head of the *Gonganbu*, who could wave in the air, like some talisman, a sheet of paper on which the dying leader of China had written a few words: 'With you in charge, my mind's at rest . . .' But his experience as a 'Marxist-Leninist policeman' prompted him to caution.

In fact, Madame Mao's arrogance led to her own downfall. Even those most reluctant to make the bid for power advocated by Marshal Ye Jianying felt threatened by the increasing ambition of Kang Sheng's former mistress. And fear, as is well known, lends wings to the least courageous.

The determined Ye Jianying finally carried the day. Accompanied by Hua Guofeng, he went to call on Wang Dongxing, who was unaware of the planned attack on Jiang Qing and her three allies. A lot depended on his support, for, apart from Detachment 8341, Wang had theoretical control of the *Gonganbu*. If he were to go against them, a veritable civil war would break out.

'You are either with us or against us: there is no other solution!' Ye Jianying made clear to him. What this really meant was: you go along with us or you are a dead man. Wang Dongxing grasped the hidden meaning of this message without any difficulty and agreed to prove his loyalty by personally putting his friend Jiang Qing behind bars.

Elite troops and armoured divisions were mobilised in every region of China. In Beijing, precautions had to be taken against a dangerous reaction from the tank unit under the command of Mao's nephew, Mao Yuanxin, who was completely devoted to the Chairman's widow. In Shanghai, the Gang of Four's stronghold, Deng Xiaoping's friend General Xu Shiyou would have the difficult task of dealing with any retaliation.

6 October 1976, was a day of anguish and hope for the Chinese. That day, the élite guards of Detachment 8341, commanded by Wang Dongxing, carried out the arrest of Jiang Qing and her Gang of Four allies. Xu Shiyou paratroopers from the Canton Military Region were deployed in the suburbs of Shanghai, while armoured troops surrounded the city where, half a century earlier, communist workers confronted the warlord Sun Chuanfan's soldiers in desperate combat.

As everyone knows, the Gang of Four was finally defeated by its combined opponents, and this defeat was primarily the product of what amounted to a military *putsch* that had little to do with the socialist principles cited by those behind it.

With the Gang of Four imprisoned, their supporters rendered harmless, the leadership question remained open. Taking advantage of his success, Hua Guofeng had himself named 'Chairman of the Central Committee' on 22 October. The former policeman was determined to oppose Deng Xiaoping's supporters, who were now more exacting than ever. He wanted, in a way, to implement a 'Maoism without Mao' and without the Gang of Four, whereas Deng and his friends wanted radical reform of the very workings of the regime. So the Indian wrestling went on, reaching a temporary conclusion in March 1977 with a compromise: Hua remained in power but accepted the gradual return of Deng Xiaoping and his management team.

In China one always fights with buttoned foil, under various pretexts that have nothing to do with the real issue. To launch the Cultural Revolution, Kang Sheng and Jiang Qing had taken refuge behind 'cultural' motives. To undermine Zhou Enlai, they had decided on the 'anti-Confucius campaign'. While the denunciation of the 'four dogs' was in full swing, *dazibao* appeared in Beijing in April 1978, on the second anniversary of the 1976 disturbances, denouncing the 'reappearance of a Chinese-style KGB exceeding the law of the State and the interests of the proletariat'. Ostensibly critical of Kang Sheng, they were directed against Hua Guofeng and Wang Dongxing. The people of Beijing – and Deng Xiaoping's friends – had not forgotten the major role played by these two 'associates' in the repression against the April 1976 demonstrators.

Wang Dongxing was then at the height of his power. He controlled a whole range of essential bodies. The Central Committee's General Office, for a start, which embraced the Central Committee's Security Office and the Special Investigations Department, was totally devoted to him. There was also the *Gonganbu*'s research department, with its thousands of card indexes and files on individuals; Detachment 8341, the Military Security élite force in charge of the personal protection of senior Party cadres, a veritable 'army within the State'; and last but not least, the Political Security General Department, a body for the protection of the Party's Military Affairs Commission, which provided an indispensable link with the People's Liberation Army general staff.

For Wang Dongxing, this burden of related offices was a guarantee of survival. Being well informed – with good reason – he knew that yet another day of reckoning was at hand.

The month of November 1978 was decisive in the race for power. Yet it began thousands of kilometres from Beijing with a trip by Wang Dongxing to Cambodia. He arrived in Phnom Penh on 5 November accompanied by two experts in secret relations with the 'Khmer Rouge comrades'. One of the two was the head of the *Gonganbu*, Luo Qingchang; a former colleague of Kang Sheng and Zhou Enlai's protégé, he had long ago established excellent relations with the secret police of Pol Pot and his friends, the sinister *Nokorbal* (State Security), or SO-21. He knew the head of it, 'Comrade Deuch' – probably

Kaing Shek Ieu, a former schoolteacher of Sino-Khmer origin; and he had a liking for Deuch's superior, the person in charge of internal security in the Khmer CP's Politburo, Nguon Kang alias Ta Mok: two fanatical militants whose zeal for purging did not spare their closest friends!

Travelling with Wang Dongxing and Luo Qingchang was the former very special ambassador to Cuba, Shen Jian, now a roving ambassador for the special services under cover of being leader of the Wuhan acrobatic troupe. He was another expert on Cambodia . . .

In China itself, the 'reforming' faction was making great strides towards a takeover of power. On 9 November, Hu Yaobang delivered a very important speech to the cadres at the Party's central school, of which he was deputy director. Hu was a pure product of the Deng Xiaoping system: aged sixty-three, he was an ex-political commissar with a background in dealing with problems of scientific development, and determined to go very far down the road of modernisation, while maintaining the communist character of the regime. Sacked twice on the personal instructions of Madame Mao, in 1966 and again in 1975, the future General Secretary of the Chinese CP had a few scores to settle with the Gang of Four.

It was with brutal frankness combined with subtle, completely unverifiable, propaganda arguments that, taking many by surprise, he launched an attack on Kang Sheng. His thundering speech was most like a summing-up speech delivered by a prosecuting lawyer.

'Kang Sheng passed himself off as an old Party member and a genuine Bolshevik, but he was in fact an opportunist and a Trotskyist in disguise . . .' he began telling his dumbfounded 'students'.

Pursuing this implacable posthumous indictment, he accused Kang Sheng of having committed 'all kinds of evil' since his entry into the communist ranks, and cited all sorts of evidence to support his case.

For good measure, Hu Yaobang admitted implicitly – but with a great deal of prudence – that the Party itself had some responsibility for the rise of this 'demon'. In Yan'an, in particular: 'He was given the chance to transform the Party's security bodies into an impervious, impenetrable, totally independent realm . . .'

Kang Sheng had committed countless crimes. He had completely trumped up 'espionage incidents' like that of the Clique of 61 Renegades; established links as early as the 1930s with counter-revolutionary and Trotskyite organisations; liquidated good comrades during the rectification campaign in Yan'an; placed the Party's security bodies in the hands of the Guomindang and the Japanese, his real masters; he had introduced the dubious Jiang Qing into the Party; created the Shandong Clique at the time of the Soviet Republic of Yan'an; destroyed secret documents revealing his arrest by the Guomindang in 1930; maintained a secret correspondence with Lavrenti Beria, Stalin's 'cop'; acted during the Cultural Revolution as a 'black counsellor' to the advantage of the Gang of Four; he had set up a clandestine political police force in violation of socialist law; spied on Chairman Mao himself, by placing microphones in his personal library; schemed to bring down Peng Zhen, Luo Ruiqing and numerous other good leaders; conspired with Lin Biao, and then against him; he had fabricated false directives from the Central Committee, indeed from Chairman Mao; persecuted innocent writers and artists; shamelessly seduced and even raped the wives of senior comrades. In short, he was 'a tyrant worse than Satan', 'not a man, but a monster'.

In conclusion, Hu Yaobang declared, there should be a serious posthumous investigation into the Kang Sheng case. The names of those close to him who had refused to take part in his machinations should be cleared, but no weakness should be shown towards the others who, like Cao Yi-ou and her son, obstinately refused to recant.

The Chinese Communist Party's future General Secretary already had a lot of powers, including, it seemed, the power to predict. While demonstrators kept putting up ever bolder wallposters on the 'Democracy Wall' at Xintan Lu, in the heart of Beijing, the very decisive Third Plenum of the Eleventh Central Committee was held from 18 to 22 December 1978. Hua Guofeng and Wang Dongxing were forced by the Deng Xiaoping faction to make a humiliating self-criticism. At the same time, the Central Committee adopted a 'new economic policy', and decided to open an investigation into Kang Sheng and his accomplice Xie Fuzhi, the former *Gonganbu* minister who died in 1973.

One of those most bent on this display of dirty linen was none other than Chen Yun, the former printer at the Commercial Press, a *Tewu* colleague of Kang Sheng in Shanghai during the 1930s. Chen took every opportunity to remind people that in Yan'an he had opposed the admission of Jiang Qing into the Communist Party, and then her marriage to Mao.

The day after the Plenum, on 23 December, the *People's Daily* launched a virulent attack, without actually naming him by name, against Kang Sheng. From then on, there was a flourishing of the most diverse epithets for this 'thug without equal' who had for years betrayed the Party and Chairman Mao. Many wallposters put up on the Democracy Wall denounced this monster until March 1979, when the *Gonganbu* threw into prison Wei Jingsheng and the main people behind the 'Chinese democracy movement'. Deng Xiaoping and his friends, now at the head of state, did not intend to let the protests get out of hand. The regime, it had to be emphasised, remained above all unflinchingly communist.

On 31 October 1980, the Chinese Communist Party's Central Committee announced the posthumous expulsion from its ranks of Kang Sheng and Xie Fuzhi. 'The funeral orations of the two expelled members,' it was made known, 'have been burned. Their counter-revolutionary crimes are now known to all Party members.'

Even the memory of the 'monster' had to be expunged. Fearing that

Kang Sheng's ashes would be exhumed, his family went at night to the cemetery to remove them. They did not want his remains to be scattered so that, according to the ancestral tradition of Bian Shi, the deceased should never find rest.

After his physical death, the time had come for the political death of the former head of Red China's special services. The hour of reckoning for Jiang Qing and the Gang of Four came in January, when they were tried by a tribunal, before the eyes of the international press. Violently attacked by Chen Yun and by Liu Shaoqi's widow, Madame Mao stood up to her judges with a great deal of courage, leading some Western feminists to defend her, alleging that she had been persecuted as a woman, through sheer male chauvinism, as it were. Her three acolytes more cautiously preferred to adopt a repentant attitude. They were sentenced to prison and Jiang Qing to death – her sentence being deferred for a few years to give her time to repent.

Mao's widow made dolls during the two thousand days or so she spent in her prison cell. In December 1986, she was admitted to a military hospital, suffering from cancer of the larynx, and she died. That at least is the story that filtered out through the Chinese press in Hong Kong and then in the West. The *Gonganbu* emerged from its splendid isolation and declared that the story was false and that this was an attempt to spread disinformation.

Better off than her past rival for Kang Sheng's affections, Cao Yi-ou escaped imprisonment as she did the death penalty. Having sat on the Chinese CP's Central Committee, Kang's widow today lives in an apartment in Beijing, a stone's throw from the Gate of Refound Happiness.

As for Red China's special services, they fell into the hands of new men who replaced the 'monster' Kang Sheng, father to them all, and divided between them the empire of his shortlived successor Wang Dongxing, who was kept under very close watch by Deng Xiaoping's friends.

25
The Deng Xiaoping Era

Monday, 15 October 1979: it was with clockwork precision that the B 2046 jet bearing the insignia of the People's Republic of China came to a halt at the stroke of 11.30 in front of the ceremonial flags at Paris-Orly International Airport. Dressed in a dark grey suit with a Sun Yat-sen collar, a 60-year-old man came slowly down the steps, a fixed smile on his face, followed by about fifteen others. At the foot of the gangway, Valéry Giscard d'Estaing, President of the French Republic, stood waiting to greet him. The two men shook hands warmly.

Hua Guofeng, the former head of the *Gonganbu*, had, after Zhou Enlai's death, become Prime Minister of the Council of Affairs of State of the People's Republic of China. Now he had come to France on a state visit.

The following day he would lunch with the French Prime Minister, Raymond Barre. In the company of the President of the Republic, the Foreign Affairs Minister, Jean-François Poncet and the Mayor of Paris, Jacques Chirac, he would unveil a commemorative plaque at 19 rue Godefroy, dedicated to Zhou Enlai, founder of the French Section of the Chinese CP in 1922. On Thursday, he would fly to Brittany accompanied by the Agriculture Minister, Pierre Méhaignerie, and the Post and Telecommunications Minister, Norbert Ségard. In Rennes, he would visit the Centre Commun d'Études et de Télécommunications (Joint Centre for Studies and Telecommunications); in Brest, the CSF-Thomson centre, where an ultra-modern radar station was being built for his country. Mr Hua certainly appreciated modern Western technology.

He was not the only one. Two much more discreet men in his retinue had eyes only for the most up-to-date equipment being shown to the Chinese visitors. One was called Ling Yun. Now sixty-six, he had been head of a reconnaissance section, then in charge of the Deuxième Bureau of the famous Social Affairs Department, which served as a cover for China's spies. In February 1964 he had become Vice-Minister of the *Gonganbu*, then, in September, deputy for the Shandong province in the People's National Assembly. The 'elected' representative of this maritime region dear to the heart of Kang Sheng, he thus followed in the footsteps of the founder of the Chinese secret services. For this reason, no doubt, the fury of the Cultural Revolution had spared him. In January 1965, he had taken part in discussions with the Indonesian Foreign Affairs Minister, Dr Subandrio. Then he disappeared for a decade, re-emerging in September 1975 to resume his functions as Vice-Minister of Public Security, as though nothing had happened. And to attend that December the funeral of Kang Sheng, along with the élite of the Chinese secret services. Since then, he had been ever more active, in China and abroad – in July 1979, as one of the members of a Chinese delegation, he was received in Britain by Queen Elizabeth II.

If a furtive smile sometimes animated his austere features, it was because Ling Yun had just learned the good news: France had agreed to deliver to Beijing twelve Control Data France computers, invaluable for anyone who wanted to strengthen their control over the Chinese population. At the end of September 1979, the German super-police of the BKA (*Bundeskrimalamt*) had received with great ceremony a delegation of Chinese 'colleagues' from the *Gonganbu*. It was led by Zhou Canbi, a Public Security specialist, with heavy features, rotten teeth and a crewcut. In the BKA headquarters in Wiesbaden he had tested the efficiency of the German computers which reputedly had led to the capture of the Baader-Meinhof gang. In other words, co-operation was the order of the day.

The German police and French industrialists did not share the reservations of the average Chinese for the attractions of the 'socialist order'. At the beginning of the 1980s, the West, in need of new markets, suddenly became interested in China. Under these circumstances, how could a regime that was daringly opening up to international trade be described as 'totalitarian'? How could they fall out with the new authorities for moral reasons? Better to give oneself a clear conscience and reckon on a liberalisation of the system. Whilst maintaining law and order, of course. Anarchy would not suit anyone. Thus, within scarcely five years, Comrade Li Guangxiang would learn from the West German BKA the most up-to-date surveillance techniques. No one in the West worried about how they were to be applied. Yet they were to serve the police of Section 2 of the Beijing's Public Security Bureau, who were thereby able to intensify their control over Western diplomats and journalists posted to the Chinese capital. Within seven years, Zhu Entao, the deputy director of the *Gonganbu*'s Co-operation Office, would be sitting on the executive board of Interpol. French experts would train Chinese police instructors in modern techniques of automated fingerprint files; others would train them in the fight against drug-traffickers. No one would express surprise at this sudden adoption of an anti-drug stance on the part of the Chinese leadership. It was as though communist police now fell into two distinct categories: the 'bad' – the Soviet KGB; and the 'good' – the Chinese *Gonganbu*.

This was not yet the case in 1979, the beginning of the big thaw. Behind the red shadow cast by Hua Guofeng stood that of a second head of the communist special services, Yang Dezhong, one of the old brigade, a protégé of Wang Dongxing. Already director of one of the *Gonganbu* departments in 1964, unlike Ling Yun, he had played an active part in the Cultural Revolution in his capacity as chairman of the Revolutionary Committee of Beijing University. In 1979, this strange visitor was in fact in command of the regime's Praetorian militia, the *Gonganbu* Guards Office. He built up this totally loyal élite corps out of the most reliable elements of the former Detachment 8341. The other 'doubtful elements' died in combat on the Sino-Vietnamese front where they were entrusted with suicide missions, in line with an old technique inherited from the Soviets. After all, let the regime's henchmen die if that is the price of its survival.

Those members of the Chinese delegation in Europe who, like Ling Yun or Yang Dezhong, had been able to learn from their Western 'colleagues' the most advanced techniques were extremely happy.

As for those techniques that the Western authorities were less keen to impart, why not steal them as their fraternal enemies in the KGB did?

It was visiting day at the Institut National de Recherche Agronomique (National Institute for Agricultural Research), one of French science's brightest jewels. A day for the exotic too: a delegation of Chinese colleagues had come to see for themselves what the West had achieved with fertilisers.

After the usual greetings and speeches, they got down to business. But the French researchers were amazed: their Far Eastern colleagues behaved more like a swarm of Colorado beetles than scientists at work. Some surreptitiously tore labels off bags that gave the composition of the products used, stuffing them in their pockets. Others insisted, to the astonishment of their guides, on having cupboards opened. No one dared refuse them for fear of creating a scandal. Then they brought out mini cameras – Japanese, of course – and started 'shooting' the shelves with the frenzy of Italian *paparazzi*.

'But why don't you just ask us what you want to know?' an exasperated French scientist exploded.

Why? Because the Chinese only really trust information they have stolen. Any information willingly given seems to them suspect. Each participant in a delegation of this type has to prove, by his 'illegal' actions, his zeal to his country's authorities. To settle for 'open' information would be a sign of weakness, laziness. Hence a rather peculiar result: the socialist emulation of theft. Everyone has to try to prove himself a better scientific pickpocket than the rest. Everyone has to bring home some spoils. The leaders will sort the wheat from the chaff.

Chinese delegates quickly acquire an unequalled aptitude for this game. They have a consummate ability to exploit the force of numbers. While some of them distract the attention of their guides, others dextrously rummage, snatch, spirit away, pocket, photograph, copy.

To prevent them from doing this would require the skills of a wrestler and a good dose of sangfroid. Besides, how can one react adequately after all one has read in books about Chinese politeness? So one lowers one's arms and gives up. And one says to oneself that their lack of technical expertise limits the consequences of this 'spying by theft' – which is true, but becoming less and less so.

'It is because for a long time they have had a high level of technical expertise that the Japanese are so effective in economic intelligence. With them, it's a real industry,' the experts say.

The Chinese leadership is well aware of their inferiority in this essential area. In order to rectify this, in 1984 they opened a 'technical college' – in actual fact, a school for industrial espionage. Specially selected students, recruited from universities throughout the country, receive a very advanced scientific and technical training there. Referred to, according to need, as 'representatives of Chinese industrial and commercial firms', or 'embassy attachés', or even 'students on courses', they home in on their objectives: American, Japanese, West German, French or British industry and research. The results obtained by these super-professionals are apparently most encouraging.

Since Deng Xiaoping's victory over the old Maoist guard and the advent of the 'four modernisations' in 1978, it has been open season for hunting Western manufacturing secrets. Any means will do: if the ground seems favourable, it is done in the name of the 'poor and starving people of China who have such great need of aid'. Because it appeals to finer feelings, the argument very often works. If it proves inadequate, a traditional but no less effective weapon may be resorted to: the lure, even the illusion, of gain.

There are a few French examples which illustrate the point. Despite their anecdotal nature, they are significant. The students and teachers at the Parisian university of Jussieu are amazed by the enthusiasm for work of their Asian colleagues: the Chinese on geology courses are always the last to leave in the evenings. Comes the day when an administrative stock control reveals that there are whole reams of photocopying paper missing. The zealous Chinese 'students' have spent evening upon evening photocopying thousands of maps in secret. A coincidence? The Chinese ministry that deals with geological works just happens to be crammed full of *Gonganbu* leaders.

At the Centre d'Exploitation des Océans (Centre for the Exploitation of the Seas) near the large Breton port of Brest access is limited and foreign delegations are not allowed to spend the night there. But the Chinese manage to get a dispensation. They sleep there. The next morning, awake before everyone else, they 'shoot' the premises, using their Japanese cameras. It is difficult to know how to stop them. No one wants to use force, so they are left to get on with it.

A Chinese specialist in forest entomology asks to be posted to a tiny surveillance station in the depths of Provence. The place is without great interest but situated right next to the Albion plateau, where the land-based missiles of the French atomic strike force are sited. On his return to Paris, he joins a Chinese delegation and it becomes obvious that this 'humble scientist' is in fact a high-ranking official.

This kind of spying may be relatively low-level, but it is none the less harmful. In the 1970s, French Military Security investigators laughed when they discovered how the Chinese 'visitors' took a close interest in the photographic processes of the German firm AGFA: delegates wearing very fine ties would dip them nonchalantly into the developing bath. Naturally, these ties were as special as their owners, who cut the ends off them as soon as the visit was over and then dispatched them to Beijing for analysis.

'It is entirely possible that Chinese intelligence operations have not been informed that we have so liberalised our trade policy with China that they probably could have obtained what they wanted through a formal, legal transaction. I favour this liberalisation with respect to the Republic of China, because it seems to me they do not, for the foreseeable future, pose a threat the way the Soviets do to the United States and our principal allies and some strengthening of the Chinese ability to defend themselves on the Eurasian land mass is probably in our interest. . . .'

When he explained this to the American senators on the Committee on Government Affairs in December 1985, Richard Perle, Secretary of State for Defense, was no doubt summing up US doctrine as regards commercial relations with Popular China. If Western leaders were pursuing commercial and technological exchanges with China, it was partly to put one over on the Russians, partly to make viable investments on the economic level. Thanks to the West's well-disposed attitude, Deng Xiaoping's China had made a great leap forward – in terms of the law. After its founding in 1949, the People's Republic of China was classified by the Americans as category 'Y' for export purposes. This meant that transatlantic industrialists could not export their products to this new state, which was placed on an equal footing with the USSR. At the time of the Korean War, the situation became even worse since, unlike the Soviets, General Peng Dehuai's Red soldiers actually took up arms against MacArthur's GIs. China was therefore put in category Z by the American Trade Department. In other words: it was under total embargo.

Not until 1972, after Richard Nixon's famous trip to Beijing, did the thaw set in. As a sign of good will, Popular China was again placed in category Y. Then, after the invasion of Afghanistan by Soviet troops, Jimmy Carter authorised the creation of a new category for China alone. So in 1980, China was reclassified in 'Country Group P', which meant much less rigid controls as far as technology was concerned. Certain US equipment with potential military use could now be sold to the Western world's newest partners.

In June 1981, Ronald Reagan further relaxed controls, by authorising the American Trade Department to place China in category P, which amongst other things meant that Deng Xiaoping's compatriots could buy Electronic Associates' Hybrid 700 computer, which was used at that time by the American military to calculate the trajectories of nuclear missiles. Finally, China's 'Long March' towards regular economic standing with Western states reached an end in May 1983 when Ronald Reagan agreed to put her in category V – Western powers and countries friendly to the United States.

It seems, however, that these very liberal measures are not enough to curb the development of Chinese scientific and industrial espionage, as the Americans learned from bitter experience in February 1984, when the FBI, in the course of Operation Exodus, put an end to an economic intelligence network run by Kuang Shin Lin, a naturalised American Chinese born in Taiwan. This Lincroft computer expert worked for the famous American Telephone and Telegraph Company (AT & T).

Kuang Shin Lin was working for Red China's special services, on research into advance radar and electronic surveillance technology, when he was trapped by a G-Man in a restaurant in New Jersey. His 'associate', Da Chuan Zheng, was also arrested. A respectable businessman from Hong Kong, Da was only acting as a commercial go-between for Red China. He had a pretty large budget with which to acquire the most sophisticated American technology in the military domain: no less than one million dollars. For the high command of the People's Liberation Army, who paid particularly close attention to the Falklands War in 1982, had managed to persuade Deng Xiaoping to invest huge sums in the modernisation of Chinese military equipment. And this counted more, apparently, than concern for honest dealings with the USA.

'They had virtually covered the whole country,' declared Andrew K. Ruotolo Jr, the Federal attorney dealing with the case, speaking of Kuang Shin Lin, Da Chuan Zheng and their accomplices, all of them Chinese.

The FBI, not to be outdone, made it known through their spokesman that 'if the transaction had actually gone through, the Chinese would be behind the United States in terms of sophisticated military equipment'.

US counter-intelligence came out on top. It had succeeded in trapping Chinese agents – always a very difficult task, for it is not easy to police representatives of friendly countries, still less allies. The French DST, for instance, is particularly set on surveillance of foreign scientific delegations. It enjoys the privilege of being able to look through in advance the lists of their members and frequently uses this to challenge such-and-such a Russian or Czech 'researcher' whose connections with his country's intelligence services are known to the DST. But, owing to the demands of political necessity, it is much more easy-going about authorisations to visit accorded to the Chinese, who are able to come and go virtually anywhere.

Keeping Chinese nationals in France under surveillance is not easy, it is true. They have at their disposal meeting places that are practically beyond control: Asian restaurants. Some of them provide cover for Taiwanese agents, others – an increasing number, as the Chinese communist emigrés consolidate their position – pay allegiance to Beijing. There are legion Chinese restaurants in France. The first opened in 1910 in rue des Carmes, Paris, equipped with a hospitable back room where diplomats posted to Paris came to smoke their opium pipes in peace. In 1969, Military Security estimated there were three hundred, some fifty of which were in direct contact with Red China.

'Because of the importance of the information that can be gathered in these establishments, frequented by all levels of society, the embassy has managed to introduce into nearly all of them one or several informers posing as chefs, cashiers or waiters,' said a Military Security report at the time, adding: 'Furthermore, the staff of certain Chinese restaurants go through the pockets of clothes left in the cloakroom. The location of the cloakroom out of sight of the customers facilitates this practice.

'Finally, the presence of tape-recorders has been noted in several sculleries, although it has not been possible officially to establish their use.

'It is certain that diplomats from Popular China posted to France manage in this way to tap a huge amount of intelligence of every nature, economic, administrative, political.'

Nowadays, there are about four thousand Chinese restaurants in France. Taking into account the activity of the United Front Work Department, in charge of recruitment and of propaganda directed at the Chinese abroad, the communist influence in their midst is ever on the increase at the expense of the Taiwanese. The Chinese restaurant scene remains a parallel world, very difficult to penetrate, where certain members of visiting scientific missions 'quite naturally' go. They sometimes bring ready cash for propaganda or espionage purposes. They collect information verbally. Not being able to speak Chinese, agents from Military Security or the DST following them can only kick their heels outside.

Even if they did, it would not do them much good, as DST telephone-tapping experts know well: every day they run into the insurmountable problem of dialects. Even an experienced interpreter, capable of grasping nuances of Cantonese or Mandarin, cannot capture those of such-and-such province or local dialect. There is little point, under the circumstances, in wasting valuable tape-recording equipment. Once again, the regional dimension, which Kang Sheng exploited so masterfully at the time of the 'Shandong Mafia', plays into the hands of Chinese espionage.

The same is true in Paris when the Chinese special services form an alliance of convenience with the Chaozhou gang. In this town and region situated slightly below Canton, a particular dialect is spoken that serves as a means of identification among the Parisian members of the gang. Expert in the art of producing false Cambodian identity papers, which have been completely unverifiable since the events of 1975, the Chaozhou mafia have contacts even in the Civil Service: one of their suppliers of residence permits in the Paris Prefecture has in fact recently been exposed. In exchange for a reciprocal arrangement in China for their associates, they agree to take responsibility for certain Chinese agents, finding them a suitable 'cover'. These agents are sometimes flown directly into the country by the *Luxingshe*, Red China's travel agency, on board charter flights, some of whose passengers, on the organisers' initiative, 'spontaneously' opt for freedom.

A well-tried system, and practically undetectable, unless every Chinese is to be considered a potential spy. However, one is entitled to wonder about certain Chinese nationals, such as Miss Zhao, who had a good introduction to circles close to UNESCO and was generously supplied with air tickets by the Chinese airline. This woman, who is much more 'sociable' than most of her compatriots, frequently travels back and forth between France and Popular China, via Hong Kong, where she is met by official Chinese cars . . .

Hong Kong is full of Chinese agents, but this does not really worry the British authorities and its Governor, the eminent Sinologist David Wilson. The Sino-British declaration of 26 September 1984 stipulates that the Chinese government will regain its sovereignty over Hong Kong in the year 1997, and has no plans for a referendum on self-determination for the inhabitants, who are known to have great reservations about communism and its benefits. It ratifies British withdrawal, the extreme rapidity of which surprised most observers. One practical consequence of this good relationship between the Chinese and British governments is the co-operation between the police and secret services of the two countries. The British Special Branch has given up chasing communist agents. Instead, it has turned against the Taiwanese networks: in January 1986 a Hong Kong Chinese connected with the nationalists was sentenced to eight months' imprisonment.

'The Public Security Bureau for the Canton province has maintained relations with the Hong Kong police for several years. The two parties often meet at the border to exchange information on offenders. They have already obtained satisfactory results. This year they have also exchanged visits,' admitted the new head of the *Gonganbu*, Ruan Chongwu, in December 1985.

He certainly was not lying. The previous month, Special Branch had organised a raid in the Chinese town of Kowloon and in the New

Territories. Several Chinese had thus found themselves in solitary confinement. Gradually, the information filtered out: British counter-intelligence had just dismantled an intelligence network run by a Taiwanese, Mui Yi-chung. Immediately afterwards, a persistent rumour began to circulate that Special Branch had been tipped off by Beijing secret agents about the activities of Mui Yi-chung's network.

There is no doubt that, as the day of reckoning for Hong Kong approaches, Taiwan is trying to infiltrate the maximum number of agents into the British colony: 'sleepers', who in principle will not be activated before the end of the century, but also experts in infiltration and sabotage whose task it is to create the maximum disturbance at the time when Hong Kong returns to the Chinese communist fold.

Several key men supervise the work of Beijing's special services in Hong Kong. The head of the Xinhua news agency, Xu Jiatun, was the Chinese representative on the 'Hong Kong and Macao Workers Committee' in 1985. In charge of the Party's internal police in Hong Kong, this body has extensive powers which include dealing with military intelligence in the British colony, the sale of arms and the work of infiltrating enemy circles: pro-Taiwan networks or Trotskyite groups.

A former member of the Shanghai Municipal Office's Foreign Affairs Department, Li Chuwen succeeded Li Jusheng in 1983 to the post of deputy director of the Xinhua agency, the traditional cover of the head of the Chinese secret services in Hong Kong. Nicknamed 'the Zhou Enlai of Hong Kong', Li Chuwen is an interesting character. This former clergyman in his sixties speaks Cantonese with a strong Shanghai accent, expresses himself extremely well in English and even better in French. In 1983, he was already developing a friendly relationship with the American consul John Gilhooley, head of the CIA station there. Since then, Li Chuwen has proved himself to be more attentive than ever to the wishes of the Western journalists whom he shows round Hong Kong and the Chinese town of Kowloon. This Operation Charm is very understandable at the time of this Sino-British courtship, but does not prevent Zeng Zhaoke, the former Hong Kong police officer expelled by Special Branch shortly before the Maoist riots in the summer of 1967, from supervising from Canton 'the return of the former British colony to the mother country'. For this special task, he works in close liaison with the Cantonese head of the *Gonganbu*, Wen Guangzhi, and with his 'fraternal enemy' of the *Guojia anquanbu*, Zhang Youheng.

The *Guojia anquanbu*, or Ministry of State Security, deserves a special mention: the most recent of the Chinese special services, it is also the most notable product of the Deng Xiaoping era in terms of espionage.

'With a view to guaranteeing the security of the State and strengthening counter-intelligence, the Council for State Affairs submits for the approval of the present session a plan to establish a Ministry of State Security to deal with these tasks.'

On 6 June 1983, before the first session of the Sixth National People's Assembly, the Chinese Prime Minister Zhao Ziyang officially announced that Popular China would now have a new secret service.

'Over the next five years,' he added, 'it is necessary to speed up drastically the setting-up of a strong contingent of lawyers and public security agents and to improve, on every level, the political and professional training of cadres and all personnel. We must also improve their social standing, renew their technical equipment and strengthen their fighting spirit, so that the Public Security contingent really becomes a well-trained force, liked by the people, and fulfilling the function of a pillar of public security . . .'

In the days that followed, Deng Xiaoping, Zhao Ziyang, General Secretary of the Party Hu Yaobang and the rest of the Chinese leadership began to implement this speech – certainly a very full programme. On 20 June, control of the Ministry of Public Security, the terrible *Gonganbu*, fell to Liu Fuzhi, a man in his sixties from Canton, with a long thin neck, a thin face and grey slicked-back hair. He inherited a service that had been entirely rebuilt since the troubled days of the Cultural Revolution, by two experts with experience of political police and of espionage: the vice-minister Ling Yun, who accompanied Hua Guofeng on his European tour, and Yu Sang, Kang Sheng's former deputy.

'Renew their technical equipment,' Zhao Ziyang had said, referring to the *Gonganbu* agents. Thanks to contacts with the French and German police, this had largely been achieved. The Public Security agents now used high-fidelity tape-recorders for their work, bought from the Swiss firm Nagra-Koudelski. The scramblers they used for telephone communications also came from Switzerland. Evidently, the 'four modernisations' also concerned the political police.

In October, a senior *Gonganbu* official, Tao Suji, travelled to the Federal Republic of Germany, to Great Britain, and then to France to meet Western 'colleagues' there. In the Yugoslav capital of Belgrade, he had lengthy discussions with an old acquaintance, the Federal Secretary for Interior Affairs, Stane Dolanc. Deng Xiaoping and the new leaders of Popular China liked this discreet militant, the official co-ordinator of his country's special services. They knew they were doubly indebted to Dolanc: first of all, in 1977, he had accompanied Marshal Tito to Beijing, thereby enabling the General Secretary Hu Yaobang to complete the indictment against Kang Sheng under preparation by adding the crime of 'Trotskyism'; then, in 1978, at the time of the sudden rupture between the Chinese and the irascible Enver Hoxha's Albanians, when Stane Dolanc closed his eyes to the massive withdrawal of Chinese special agents operating under diplomatic cover and allowing Belgrade at a moment's notice to replace Tirana as

Beijing's observation post in Eastern Europe. This kind of favour is not forgotten . . .

While Liu Fuzhi settled into his position of command over the *Gonganbu*, Ling Yun gave up his position as Vice-Minister of Public Security in order to climb another rung up the hierarchical ladder. The Sixth People's National Assembly in fact entrusted him with a task of paramount importance: that of setting up Red China's new secret service, the *Guojia anquanbu*, and to use it to 'judge' Kang Sheng's supporters, still too active for the liking of the new leadership. According to Deng Xiaoping's supporters, this brand-new Ministry of State Security was to find the right balance between intelligence-gathering outside the country and internal repression.

'The intelligence agencies and secret services of certain foreign countries have increased their spying activities as regards China's state secrets and have sent special agents into our country for the purposes of subversion and destruction,' Ling Yun declared categorically, adding that effective measures would be taken to oppose 'counter-revolutionary intrigues that undermine the socialist system'. The head of the *Guojia anquanbu* and his right-hand man, the Vice-Minister Hui Ping, announced without ambiguity their intention to vigorously pursue Chinese dissidents, elements causing 'destabilisation' of Deng Xiaoping's regime. They thus followed in the footsteps of Wang Renzhong, then the Central Committee's head of propaganda, who declared on 1 March 1982: 'There will always be espionage intrigues directed against us!'

By espionage Wang Renzhong meant basically the support of certain Westerners posted to Beijing for the semi-clandestine leaders of the Chinese democratic movement. He was thinking of the brutal response of the *Gonganbu* to the idyllic love affair between the young and very pretty Li Shuang, a non-conformist artist, and the French diplomat Emmanuel Bellefroid, an ex-militant Maoist. Faced with Li Shuang's determination to marry 'her' Frenchman, the Chinese police arrested her on 9 September 1981. After close interrogation in the *Gonganbu*'s sorting office, the young woman was sentenced on 5 November to two years in a re-education camp. Despite an appeal from the French Minister for Overseas Trade, Michel Jobert, Deng Xiaoping refused to give way: there could be no question of letting foreigners move about freely in China and meet people at will. In June 1982, the young American Lisa Wichser had to bear the brunt of this chauvinistic obstinancy: she was expelled on the pretext of spying.

A year later, Ling Yun was confronted with a cruel dilemma: incautiously using repression against Westerners was to turn outside public opinion, outraged by such inhuman behaviour, against China. It was in fact to compromise the policy of opening up to the West. But to cease 'to constrain' the Chinese population would be even more dangerous for the regime. So a middle way had to be found. Especially as the West was obviously not going let them get away with anything.

Thirteen days after Ling Yun's appointment as head of the *Guojia anquanbu*, on 30 June 1983, the DST summoned an employee of the French Foreign Affairs Ministry, Bernard Boursicot, to Paris. On 3 July, it was the turn of his Chinese 'case officer', Shi Peipu (like Kang Sheng, a native of Shandong). Very well known in trendy Parisian circles, Shi was a traditional opera dancer, a pupil of the great master Mei Lanfang, who, before his death in 1961, had been ambassador for his art in the West. Shi Peipu and Boursicot got to know each other in Beijing in December 1964, when France opened its first embassy in Popular China. Boursicot was a nice guy but unstable. His French diplomatic colleagues, aware of his homosexual proclivities, considered them incompatible with a society as closed as that of Maoist China. In short, he first succumbed to the charms of Shi Peipu, and then to the blackmail of Public Security when the opera dancer introduced him to an intelligence officer named 'Kang', no doubt a reference to the boss at that time, Kang Sheng. In the course of a fairly incredible relationship, Shi managed to convince his French friend that they 'had a child' and turned him into an agent.

In 1983, the French press lighted upon this mysterious and rather disturbing love story. Was Shi Peipu a man or a woman? People became fascinated, questions and speculations were rife.

Less susceptible to romance, the Chinese leadership none the less appreciated the significance of the two arrests in Paris. There was of course no question of exchanging Shi Peipu for Li Shuang, the young fiancée of the ex-Maoist Emmanuel Bellefroid. On the other hand, the DST's reaction indicated the French authorities' determination to achieve some positive result. Their firmness paid off, for in November 1983 Li Shuang was finally released. She went to live in France. As for Bernard Boursicot and Shi Peipu, the unfortunate heroes of a peculiar spy affair, they were both sentenced to six years' imprisonment.

In the meantime, Ling Yun and Hui Ping made the *Guojia anquanbu* an efficient service, in the oriental sense of the word: very sophisticated intellectually if not in its equipment. This is what *Naicho* (Japanese Prime Minister Nakasone's intelligence service) experts say about it today: 'The *Guojia anquanbu* uses the latest data-processing techniques only to a very limited extent. But it devotes a lot of attention to training new cadres, all of whom have to know at least two languages and have what their bosses call a very active attitude towards pursuit of intelligence. The *Guojia anquanbu* is particularly entrenched in three Asian bases: Hong Kong, Singapore, and of course Tokyo . . .'

These statements can be relied upon as the Japanese intelligence services are among the best experts on their Chinese counterparts – with good reason. They meet each other, they even socialise together, although the distrust between them never entirely disappears: it is a situation of 'armed peace'.

The head of the *Guojia anquanbu* in the Japanese archipelago is none other than the Counsellor at the Chinese embassy in Tokyo, Xu Dunxin. He operates with the help of only carefully selected collaborators: three or four close at hand in the capital, a little group at the consulate in Kobe, another larger group, consisting of eight to ten people, in Osaka, where they liaise with the North Korean special services. The North Koreans are understandably active in Japan, given its importance: 700,000 Korean nationals live in Japan, half from the North, half from the South – fertile ground, whose potential Liao Chengzhi, the 'Red seaman' of the 1930s and post-war representative of the Chinese Red Cross in Japan, had perfectly divined.

There is also a very high proportion of intelligence experts among the Chinese diplomats on postings to Japan. The first communist ambassador, Chen Chu, worked underground in Shanghai during the 1930s. His successor, Fu Hao, was secretary with the *Shihuibu*, the Chinese secret service created in 1938 by Kang Sheng in the Red Maoist base of Yan'an after the Long March. Today, he is in charge of Sino-Japanese friendship associations. The military attaché in 1983, Ding Shang, exercised his talents as an expert in secret affairs in Berne, headquarters of Maoist espionage in Europe during the 1960s. He then played a key role in Tokyo for the *Qingbao*, Chinese military intelligence. Now a Major-General, he is the number two at Red China's Institute for Strategic Affairs.

As for Ambassador Song Zhiguang, special services ace and former Chinese Counsellor in Paris, he cultivated relations with his South Korean counterpart, Huang Teng, local head of the KCIA, Seoul's secret service. These 'unnatural' contacts between die-hard communists and fierce anti-communists led to an exchange of information about the USSR – they were, at least, united in their hatred of the common enemy.

'Obtaining valuable information about the USSR is a real obsession with the Chinese agents,' Japanese experts explain. 'They spend all their time on the phone to the *Naicho* trying to get some gen on them . . .'

In order to get into the good graces of the Nakasone government, Beijing's representatives make numerous concessions, being careful to keep away from Japanese CP militants. This does not prevent Japanese counter-intelligence from keeping an eye on the Xinhua news agency, run in Tokyo by Liu Wenyu, which is a little overstaffed for the Japanese liking: 38 reporters and some 50 other employees. The Japanese are all too aware that the Xinhua agency provides Beijing's special services with one of its most common covers. But they also know that it does not come directly under the control of the *Guojia anquanbu* or the *Gonganbu*'s section for external operations. The Chinese news agency in fact comes under a third intelligence body, the

Diaochabu, the Central Committee's Bureau of Investigation, whose director in Tokyo is Guan Zhong Zhou.

Deng Xiaoping has no desire whatsoever to rebuild an intelligence empire of the kind Kang Sheng established; he is also keen to maintain a balance between the various factions in the communist leadership. As a consequence, the world of Beijing's secret services is actually rather complex.

There is no mistaking some signs: a few months after its creation, the *Guojia anquanbu* was already being referred to by the Chinese man in the street as the *Gonganbu*. The Ministry of State Security had spared no effort to stake its claim to a place in the sun. In accordance with the decisions of the People's National Assembly, it had taken control of the border guards on the frontier with Russia to the north, and with the Vietnamese and the Indians to the south. This control over militarised bodies made it akin to the Soviet KGB, as several observers began to note.

Paradoxically, one of the first tasks of Ling Yun's subordinates was to make a tour of the embassies to keep an eye on Chinese diplomats posted abroad. Some of them, whose conduct left something to be desired, were recalled to Beijing to be interrogated in great depth by *Guojia anquanbu* experts. This 'tightening-up', which passed unnoticed at the time, was significant. It showed that the Chinese leadership had a thorough appreciation of the pitfalls of the open-door policy they were resolutely preaching. The facts were undeniable: the same crusading spirit could not be expected of Chinese representatives abroad as during the period of frenzied Maoism and the Cultural Revolution. On the contrary, the Operation Charm launched by Popular China exposed them to the 'temptation of the West'. Intensified surveillance was necessary to prevent them from succumbing to it.

The same argument applied to Communist Party cadres in general. Over the thirty years of austere socialism, the regime had managed – at what cost! – to curb that traditional tare in China: corruption. This had been very widespread in the higher echelons of power, but much rarer among middle-ranking cadres. However, the opening up to the West, to private capital, led very quickly to a return in strength of this corruption. By the end of 1982, several ministries were already affected by financial scandals, in particular the Coal and Geology Ministry, where it was noticed that cadres had embezzled sums of money. A 'railway gang', which had been misappropriating wagonloads of raw materials in the town of Zhengzhou, was arrested. And there was further consternation at the end of 1985 when, after two years' existence, the Chinese Revenue Court registered 8.9 thousand million yuan's worth of fiscal fraud and waste.

'We cannot attack the flies first and forget the tigers. Senior cadres and Party members who are engaged in illegal activities must be punished, however highly placed they are within the Party and however longstanding their membership,' wrote Bo Yibo, the Vice-President of the CP's Consolidation Commission.

More recently, *Beijing Information*, the propaganda organ abroad, tells us – in August 1986 – that 'the crimes perpetrated by private entrepreneurs have increased over the last two years' and that an investigation carried out in the town of Wuhan reveals 'the high level of divorce among private entrepreneurs'. In short, the socialist ethic is beating a retreat. This at least is the opinion of the *Gonganbu* 'old guard', who hope for a toughening-up of repression. They still owe their allegiance to Luo Ruiqing. Paradoxically, some of them are turning against the regime and have started dreaming of the USSR, where KGB agents can play their part as the 'sword of the Revolution' effectively whilst here the relative liberalism of Deng Xiaoping prevents them from striking openly. The student demonstrations in Shanghai and then in Beijing in December 1986 only served to add grist to the mill of these hard-liners, at the same time as they brought into conflict 'conservative' believers in strong measures and 'liberals', among the leadership.

Of course, the differences at the top have repercussions on the 'special' bodies. A modern-day intelligence agency, according to its promoters, the *Guojia anquanbu* could count on the understanding and support of the Party's General Secretary Hu Yaobang until January 1987, when his period of office expired. Falling as it did within the ambit of the CP's Central Committee and not that of the government bodies, the Ministry of State Security was, in effect, under the indirect control of this 'liberal'. But it was also exposed to the latent hostility of conservative leaders who preferred the old *Gonganbu* with which they were familiar. Although the men from the two services generally worked on the same premises and on good terms with each other, a latent guerrilla war divided them. The *Guojia anquanbu* cadres complained of a lack of funds: they did not have an air force and the number of vehicles they had on the road was notoriously inadequate. In short, their brand-new service was already the poor relation in the family of Chinese bodies of repression and espionage.

This did not displease two representatives of the conservative lobby, Peng Zhen and Chen Yun. Peng Zhen was seen in the West as a victim of the Cultural Revolution. But he readily took part in the terrible campaign of repression carried out in 1951 by the *Gonganbu*. Thirty years later, in 1980, he was head of the new 'People's Armed Police Force'. Despite his seventy-nine years, he then tried to extend his influence within the Chinese special services. In 1983, at the age of eighty-one, he joined the secretariat of the CP Politburo's Committee of Political and Legal Affairs. In 1987 he acted as arbiter in the renewed factional struggles within the leadership, and suggested launching a 'new rectification campaign', as in the good old days of 1942.

Chen Yun, for his part, was a secret service veteran turned economist. As the reader will recall, during the 1930s in Shanghai he ran the *Tewu*, the CP's special apparatus, along with Kang Sheng and Zhou Enlai. Exorcising the memory of Kang, Chen Yun discreetly intensified a press campaign to rewrite the history of the 1930s in his favour. According to this version, Zhou Enlai always regarded Kang Sheng as a potential traitor; he was wary of him to the point that he concealed from his comrade the fact that communist cadres such as Li Kenong and Qian Zhuangfei had infiltrated the Guomindang secret services, vital information of which only Chen Yun, apart from Zhou himself, was in possession. In 1931, when the head of the special apparatus, Gu Shunzhang, went over to the nationalist side, it was supposedly Chen Yun and not Kang Sheng who told Zhou Enlai, thereby saving his life. The communist leadership always kept Kang Sheng out of important decisions and away from confidential information.

Some of the declarations are plausible, others not at all. It is ridiculous to present Zhou Enlai as 'the Good' and Kang Sheng as 'the Bad and the Ugly' of some communist Chinese western. Quite the contrary, relations between them, in a climate of permanent factional fighting, were reasonable. It was only during the dark days of the Cultural Revolution that they turned sour. And even then, at the beginning of the 1970s, Zhou Enlai and Kang Sheng together planned the great turnaround in Chinese strategy, the agreement with the United States. It was only when they reached death's door that they developed a real hatred for each other.

It is absurd to claim that Kang Sheng never enjoyed the confidence of the communist leaders, his peers. It does not make sense to let an acknowledged 'Guomindang spy' build up a veritable empire within the Chinese CP. In its more extreme statements, the mini anti-Kang Sheng press campaign was intended primarily to establish Chen Yun as a brilliant special affairs man, even at the age of over eighty-five and confined to bed by illness.

Thus, 'liberals' and 'conservatives' confronted each other through the intermediary of the secret services. However, the importance of this conflict should not be exaggerated. There again, the Cultural Revolution served as a lesson: everyone knew that factional fighting cannot be taken too far without risking the survival of the regime itself. The Central Committee's Investigation Department, for instance, managed to remain untrammelled by the most violent polemics. Luo Qingchang, head of the *Diaochabu* since 1978, was in himself a model of Chinese-style 'co-habitation': a protégé of Zhou Enlai who had risen through the special services apparatus in the shadow of Kang Sheng with Deng Xiaoping's approval.

Within the Chinese intelligence community, the *Diaochabu* occupies a place apart. Although it has agents in Chinese embassies abroad, it is above all a body devoted to co-ordination and synthesis.

As during the time when Kang Sheng was in charge, its staff is limited: 3,000 hand-picked experts. They work in close contact with the *Guojia anquanbu* cadres, for whom they organise, to some extent, the search for intelligence abroad. But the *Diaochabu* also controls an essential part of the apparatus: the Central Archives, which comes under its management. It has contacts within the United Front Work Department (which deals with propaganda and organisation within the overseas Chinese communities), run since 1982 by Yang Jinren, and within the International Liaison Department. In abeyance since the death of its former boss Kang Sheng, this department is gradually regaining strength as Chinese external policy develops, under Qian Liren. Like the *Guojia anquanbu*, the United Front Work and International Liaison Departments come under the CP's Central Committee. They are therefore in constant contact with the Ministry of State Security.

In December 1982, a new special service was set up especially for Gao Liang. Red China's former masterspy in Africa, the travelling salesman of the revolutionary wave promised in 1964 by Zhou Enlai, runs the Propaganda Department's Overseas Information Office. This new body deals with the perfecting of techniques of psychological warfare.

However, it is another kind of warfare that the Soviet leadership fears. For years, they have been setting up *spetsnaz*, special units intended, when the moment arrives, to take by surprise an enemy's key positions, industrial complexes, vital administrative centres. Suddenly they noticed that the Chinese had created their own *spetsnaz*. The KGB estimates at two to three million men the number of Chinese commandos who could, in the event of war, attack Soviet installations in Siberia, in groups of six. The latest of Deng Xiaoping's precious *spetnatz* was created in 1985: Detachment 8189, an airborne commando group run by Zhang Shihai. Being even more specialised, it supplants Detachment 57003, heir of Wang Dongxing's now-defunct Detachment 8341.

Shortly before Zhang Shihai's appointment as head of 8189, a change took place at the top of China's secret services. In September 1985, two young leaders assumed the highest offices. When Ling Yun went into semi-retirement (while retaining the privileged status of 'consultant' and becoming temporary tutor to his replacement), Jia Chunwang became head of the *Guojia anquanbu*. National head of the Communist Youth League in 1982, deputy secretary of the Beijing Party Committee in August 1984, he ran the district of Haidian. Hui Ping, Ling Yun's right-hand man during the setting up of the *Guojia anquanbu*, kept his post as vice-minister for the time being. He bridged the gap, as it were, between Ling and Jia.

Also in September 1985, Ruan Chongwu succeeded Liu Fuzhi at the head of Public Security. Born in 1933, the year when Kang Sheng left Shanghai to represent the Chinese CP in Moscow, Ruan left Moscow's Institute of Mechanical Engineering in 1957. On his return to China, he worked for the first Ministry of Mechanical Engineering Industries' Research Institute into Casting, in Shenyang, in northeastern China. In 1962, he became deputy director of Shanghai's Research Institute into Materials before assuming in 1971 the post of deputy secretary of the city's Associations of Scientific Workers. Then he became scientific and technical attaché to the Chinese embassy in Bonn, in West Germany. In 1983, he was appointed deputy mayor of Shanghai.

'This forward-looking security chief, who enjoyed playing tennis, reading and music, did not remain long as head of *Gonganbu*. In April 1987, with his tutor, Secretary General Hu Yaobang, he fell victim to the conservatives' offensive. A 66-year-old security professional from Zhejiang, Wang Fang took over the Ministry of Public Security. Unlike his *Gonganbu* colleagues, the head of Party intelligence, *Diaochabu*, remained in firm control of department which, contrary to speculations, was not dismantled. Luo Qingchang had for a long time already been an active Party militant, personal secretary to Lin Boqu, the communist leader in Xian, before taking charge of Section 1 of Kang Sheng's secret service, the Social Affairs Department. At sixty-five, when he took office, he belonged already, despite his acknowledged capabilities, to-the old guard as far as intelligence was concerned.

A logical consequence of the 'four modernisations' and of Deng Xiaoping's policies was the rise within the secret services of experts in economics, new technology, geopolitics. Universities were even called upon to help train future cadres. Thus, Chen Zhongjing has been running Beijing's Institute of Contemporary International Relations since January 1980, assisted by Zhou Zhixian and Wu Xuewen. However, Chen has been a *Guojia anquanbu* adviser since 1984, whilst Wu Xuewen is a distinguished secret agent who, as a Xinhua news agency correspondent, was expelled from Japan for spying in 1964.

This is no accident. The Institute in fact houses the ultra-secret centre where the *Diaochabu* runs a training school for intelligence agents about to go abroad: *Guojia anquanbu* agents, agents working on *Gonganbu* external operations, for the Foreign Affairs Ministry's Intelligence Department, or the Defence Ministry's External Relations Bureau. Thus, this alliance between the world of intelligence and university circles is rigorously copied from the system set up by the neighbouring Japanese n the 1950s.

There is a man who is following in Kang Sheng's footsteps: Qiao Shi, the rising star of Chinese communism, provides the link between two generations of special services cadres. Within the Party, Qiao likes to calm things down in the battle that frequently brings the old guard, led by Peng Zheng, into conflict with the young reformers who flit around Deng Xiaoping.

In Hong Kong and Tokyo, experts began predicting a fine future for him – to the point of seeing him one day becoming number one in the

Party. In April 1986, Qiao became simultaneously Vice-Prime Minister, Zhao Ziyang's right-hand man, Deng Xiaoping's preferred colleague and the supreme co-ordinator of the Chinese security services.

Qiao Shi was born in 1924, not far from Dinghai, in Zhejiang, and his first name was Jiang Zhaoming. His political awakening took place in Shanghai, and he joined the underground Communist Party at the age of sixteen. In 1947, he was already in the envied position of deputy secretary of the local Party Committee. At that time, as head of Party secret communications, he carried out key intelligence work together with Wang Yuwen. At the 'Liberation', in 1949, the CP noticed his talents as an organiser. He was therefore sent to Hangzhou, to take charge of the youth movements.

The career of the young communist leader then branched off into another area and progressed in tandem. As deputy chief of the United Front Work Department of the East China Bureau's Youth Committee, he came into contact with the security services. The United Front Work Department, as we know, is part of counter-intelligence, for which it acts as a showcase both within and outside China. But above all, Qiao Shi took on important economic and technical functions: as senior official in a steel-making company in Anshan, and as President of the Research Institute of the Steel-Making Company of Jiuquan. This company worked in a sensitive field, under Ministry of Defence supervision, producing weapons for the People's Liberation Army.

In 1964, this multi-talented man entered the world of the external secret services. He joined the Central Committee's International Liaison Department and rose through its ranks. As we have already seen, just before the Cultural Revolution, Qiao Shi, as secretary of the Afro-Asian Solidarity Committee, was behind certain special operations on the African continent. He disappeared during the turmoil of the Cultural Revolution, without actually being liquidated, and then re-emerged as deputy director of the International Liaison Department. His career then took off. On two occasions in 1978 he went to Rumania and Yugoslavia, the second time at the end of August, in the wake of Hua Guofeng. Hua was obviously trying to strengthen alliances on the Soviet empire's doorstep. At a time when Albania and China were falling out with each other, Qiao Shi had other ambitions: to rebuild large intelligence bases in the Balkans, a nerve centre for intelligence-gathering both in the Eastern bloc and in the West. And indeed, shortly afterwards, the Chinese embassies in Bucharest and Belgrade received cohorts of very special diplomats.

On the way back, at the beginning of September, Hua Guofeng made a stopover in Iran that attracted attention. The Chinese leader suggested to the Shah that they enter a grand alliance in order to thwart the Russians, and, more precisely, made proposals for operations that would prevent the consolidation of the pro-communist regime in Afghanistan. Mossad, the Israeli secret service, had already brought the Chinese and Iranians into contact. General Nasser Moghadam, the new head of Savak, the Shah's dreaded police, met Qiao Shi. The secret war was to be launched jointly in Afghanistan. Chinese agents flocked to Pakistan; the Iranian ambassador, General Nematollah Nassiri, the former head of Savak, was already there. But at the beginning of 1979, the Shah's regime was overthrown and at the end of the same year Soviet tanks invaded Afghanistan.

The Chinese diplomatic and special services did not really lose out, however. Qiao Shi and Luo Qingchang, head of the *Diaochabu*, felt they had more room for manoeuvre: the Russian enemy was clearly identified in Kabul, whilst in Teheran the new government of the mullahs seemed more honourable, initially, than the fallen empire. At the beginning of 1980, the Vice-President of the Chinese Islamic Association, Muhammad Al Zhang Jie, arrived in Iran to negotiate with the Islamic Republic. The China–Iran–Pakistan axis was strengthened. Deng Xiaoping would not hesitate in future to supply arms to Teheran in its war against Baghdad.

The aid lent to the Afghan resistance began with a misunderstanding: American narcotics agents based in Pakistan mistook the first Chinese instructors for drug-traffickers from Hong Kong and had them arrested by the local authorities. But soon the alliance between the CIA and the *Tewu* was complete. The Karakoram Road, the 700-kilometre pass linking China with Afghanistan, allowed the Chinese services to transport arms for the anti-Soviet resistance. Some Maoist groups, such as *Sholee Javid* ('Eternal Flame'), were particularly adept at guerrilla warfare. In 1981, the Russians even accused the Chinese of having masterminded attacks in the centre of Kabul. In Peshawar and on the Pakistani border, training camps for mujahideen Afghans were set up under the joint tutelage of the *Tewu* and the CIA. Several thousand Mujahideen received military training in Xinjiang, and China supplied machine-guns, rocket-launchers and anti-air missiles.

As in Cambodia, Beijing sustained the guerrilla war against the pro-Soviet authorities, whilst at the same time opening negotiations with a view to normalising relations with Moscow. At the beginning of 1982, Qiao Shi began as head of the International Liaison Department. The following year, in the shadow of Hu Yaobang, the Party's First Secretary, he again inspected the Rumanian and Yugoslav bases. But he became increasingly involved in internal politics. Appointed vice-minister and head of the security services, Qiao was well aware of the rift between conservatives and reformists.

The huge student demonstrations that took place in the winter of 1986–7 gave the old guard the opportunity to make clear its opposition to the policy of relaxation in politics and economics advocated by Deng Xiaoping and his entourage. The Prime Minister, Hu Yaobang, had to bear the brunt of this. There was anxiety within the security services. On 12 January 1987, Peng Zhen, who had always had an influential role within the organs of repression – except in relation to his disappearance during the Cultural Revolution – presided over a meeting at the headquarters of the People's Armed Police Forces in Beijing.

'Supporting the Four Modernisations is one thing. But that goes hand in hand with an opposition to bourgeois liberalisation and spiritual pollution,' he stormed.

Qiao Shi, who was in the hall, smiled amiably. He is said to be a moderate, the man of compromise between the different factions. But that is to forget that a year earlier he had been given the task of setting up a new body, the Group in Charge of the Rectification of the Work Style. 'Rectification'? Self-criticisms, purges, expulsions, liquidations . . . This has an ominous and all too familiar ring to it.

26

The 'Son of Kang Sheng' Defects to the West

Hong Kong, November 1985: the teeming crowds of Asia and the modernity of the West in the shadow of the skyscrapers, of the imposing façades of 450 banking establishments; construction frenzy – the life of a building is five or six years; the mad pursuit of money; traffic jams stretching all the way from the Chinese town of Kowloon to Causeway Bay, via the road tunnel under the harbour: a noise level of 80 decibels. On the trams, a proliferation of multicoloured advertisements; in the underground Mass Transit Railway, automatic ticket machines. And an omnipresent youth, dressed like Westerners, walking the streets hand in hand beneath a forest of neon signs . . .

Could this be the same town that sixty years ago launched a boycott on British and Japanese goods under the aegis of the Comintern delegate in China, Mikhail Borodin? A lot of salt water has flowed between the Kowloon Peninsula and Hong Kong island since then.

Chiang Kai-shek's Nationalist Party, the Guomindang, failed in its attempted unification of China. It now occupies no more than the 36,000 square kilometres of the island of Taiwan. As for Mao's communist revolution, it has led to the creation of a totalitarian state in Popular China. In the end, the British presence has brought its colony one positive advantage: a legal system. Rule by law. Hong Kong capitalists like money, of course. But they respect the Anglo-Saxon conciliation procedures. They understand that their employees are also consumers, therefore clients. Consequently, there is a very mobile labour force, but an extremely low rate of unemployment. And an annual income of nearly 6,000 dollars per head, an excellent achievement in Asia.

Of the 500,000 union members in Hong Kong, three-quarters are in organisations controlled by the communists. The authorities are engaged in a relentless battle against secret societies such as the famous K14 triad. The police, the law and the administration operate autonomously, except at the highest level, without the intervention of British civil servants and magistrates. In short, it is a mini state that works well.

But Great Britain has decided to leave the colony as quickly as possible, handing over control to communist China. Special Branch, as we have seen, is working hand in hand with Deng Xiaoping's special services, the most colourful of whose representatives is the former clergyman Li Chuwen, 'the Zhou Enlai of Hong Kong'. This is a new-style *entente cordiale*.

Economically, the Reds already control the most dynamic sectors: a large part of trade, small shipbuilding companies, insurance. Banking is the only thing they have not mastered: they still lack the expertise.

'Even if Deng Xiaoping wanted to keep Hong Kong going, the economic machine is too fragile for communist management. The narrow-minded cadres from communist China will soon destroy it!' protest the most worried, who are trying to emigrate to England (which is difficult), to the United States, Canada, Taiwan and even France. And the local press asks why there is such a very high suicide rate among young people in Hong Kong . . .

The man in his forties, in grey-coloured clothes, who is hiding in an apartment in Hong Kong has no intention of resorting to suicide. No more than he intends to wait and see what will happen when the British colony returns to the communist fold. Yu Qiangsheng, alias Yu Zhensan, is a 'deserter' from the *Guojia anquanbu*, the Ministry of State Security. He wants to defect to the West.

A defector from the Chinese secret services is a sufficiently rare phenomenon to claim attention. Especially when this defector is none other than the great-great-nephew of Chiang Kai-shek, the son of the first husband of Mao's wife, Jiang Qing, and the adoptive son of Kang Sheng.

It was in 1931, the reader will recall, that Mao's future wife met Yu Qiwei in Qingdao, in her native province of Shandong. Jiang Qing was then still called Yunhe, 'Cloud Crane'. The friend and then the mistress of Kang Sheng, she was introduced to Qiwei by his sister, Yu Shan. A very beautiful woman, Yu Shan was a celebrated opera singer and actress, her brother, Yu Qiwei, an attractive communist cadre, head of the clandestine CP's Propaganda Department in Qingdao. The two young people were attracted to each other. They lived together. They were married after the fashion of militants of the period: without any ceremony or official certificate.

But Yu Qiwei fell into the hands of the Guomindang secret police, leaving 'Cloud Crane' in a state of utter confusion. Would he die under the most dreadful torture, like most of his communist comrades? This was to discount Uncle Yu Dawei, an important Guomindang cadre, future nationalist liaison officer in Berlin, who was married to the sister of Chiang Ching-kuo, Generalissimo Chiang Kai-shek's son and in more recent years President of Taiwan. An influential man, who did not let politics stand in the way of his family duty, he managed to obtain his nephew's release, despite his communist activities.

'Cloud Crane' and Yu Qiwei could at last savour happiness. But then the voice of the Party made itself heard, issuing instructions: Qiwei was transferred to Beijing. Alarmed that he should have accepted this distant posting out of a spirit of discipline, the young woman decided to leap into the void: she went to Shanghai to see Kang Sheng, her faithful friend and ardent lover, and to make a career for herself in the cinema, putting her past behind her. But she would always remember with nostalgia those happy days in Qingdao with her beloved.

She encountered Qiwei again in Yan'an, the Soviet Republic of China founded by Mao after the Long March, in 1935. Kang Sheng was there too, urging her into the arms of the communist leader. Party discipline prevailed once more: Qiwei stepped aside in favour of Mao, future President of China. He married an intelligent spirited militant, Fan Jin, and Jiang Qing eventually became Mao's wife.

His wife, but not always his mistress. We know that he often discarded her – in December 1949, for instance, when he made his victorious entry into Beijing on the arm of Yu Shan, the very seductive sister of Yu Qiwei. This amorous intrigue worthy of vaudeville had consequences which were to prove genuinely dramatic. In China as elsewhere, whom the gods wish to punish they first make mad.

In the summer of 1958, Yu Qiwei died of a heart attack at the age of forty-seven, having held important positions in the People's Republic of China. His uncle Yu Dawei was at that time Defence Minister for the nationalist government of Taiwan, whose troops were then confronting those of the People's Liberation Army on the islands of Quemoy and Matsu. Chiang Ching-kuo, his uncle by marriage and the son of Generalissimo Chiang Kai-shek, was running the VACRS, the association of former combatants, one of the essential wheels of the Taiwanese administration. Secretly, he was also head of the Guomindang's paramilitary operations in mainland China and the co-ordinator of his father's secret services. Chiang Ching-kuo's daughter, Jiang Xiazhang, known as Amy, married her cousin Yu Yanghe, the son of Yu Dawei.

An unusual family saga, and at least as complex as that of the Ewings in *Dallas*. The young Yu Zhensan is then on the one hand related to Mao Zedong, the onetime lover of his aunt Yu Shan and husband of his father's first wife, Jiang Qing. On the other, he is related to the Chiang Kai-shek dynasty, which has ruled the destinies of the Guomindang and the island of Taiwan.

This is not the first time in recent Chinese history, it is true, that families have played a key role between the communists and nationalists. Liao Chengzhi, the 'Red seaman', was captured by Chiang Kai-shek's men in March 1933, in Shanghai, and then in May 1943, in the north of Guangdong, and freed on both occasions on the Generalissimo's orders, in memory of his father Liao Zhongkai, a Guomindang leader assassinated in 1925 by secret society assassins. There is also the Song dynasty: the father, Charlie, main financier of the nationalist movement, his eldest daughter, Qingling, wife of Dr Sun Yat-sen and later Vice-President of the People's Republic of

China, her younger sister Eiling, wife of the nationalist government's Finance Minister, and the youngest daughter, Meiling, Chiang Kai-shek's wife: three sisters, of whom 'one loved Chiang, the second money and the third power'.

Not that this mattered to Yu Zhensan, who was mourning the loss of his father. His mother, Fan Jin, played an important role in the personal intelligence networks of the Prime Minister Zhou Enlai, along with her friend Gong Peng. But it was another professional of the secret services and covert action who was going to lend the orphan a helping hand – and what a professional. None other than Kang Sheng himself.

With the agreement of Fan Jin, whose main concern was for her son's future, Kang became, as it were, the adoptive father of Yu Zhensan. In memory of Yu Qiwei, his onetime friend and comrade-in-arms. And also out of friendship for Madame Mao: Jiang Qing bore a fierce hatred towards Fan Jin for having married her former husband. On the other hand, she took an interest in Yu Zhensan, in whom she recognised Yu Qiwei, the man who for a few months had made her happy.

In China, where the sense of family is very strong, there was nothing extraordinary about Kang Sheng becoming an adoptive father. It is how special relationships of trust and collaboration are formed. Chiang Kai-shek, for example, adopted the nephews of his mentor and friend Chen Qimei, who was assassinated in 1916. As we have seen, he made them the first heads of his secret police, in 1923. Thirty years later, Kang Sheng opted for a very similar line of conduct. Under his protective wing, Yu Zhensan was soon admitted to the *Gonganbu* training school, instead of attending university courses like most of the children of the nomenclature in communist China, and rapidly became an expert in secret warfare.

Then came the turmoil of the Cultural Revolution. It nearly carried off Yu Zhensan's mother, victim of Madame Mao's deep-rooted hatred. Because of her relations with the 'Three Family Village', a circle of intellectuals belonging to the Beijing branch of the Party, Fan Jin was arrested. Pleased to weaken Zhou Enlai's rival networks as embodied by her, and also to satisfy a personal vengeance, Jiang Qing and Kang Sheng went out of their way to condemn her. Abused and beaten, Yu Qiwei's unfortunate widow was dragged out in public by Red Guards with a humiliating placard round her neck. She also suffered physical torture. Kang Sheng still did not protest but, true to his role as adoptive father, he protected Yu Zhensan.

While a murderous frenzy once again seized China, Yu Zhensan made his way up the secret service apparatus, eventually being transferred to the *Waishiju*, the *Gonganbu* section that deals with the surveillance of foreign nationals inside Red China.

In Chinese communist thinking, there is no distinction between this 'surveillance' and the recruitment by persuasion or blackmail of secret agents. In the spring of 1970 it was perhaps Yu Zhensan himself whom the Chinese opera dancer Shi Peipu introduced under the pseudonym of 'Kang' – a private joke – to the French diplomat Bernard Boursicot. In any case, it is certain that Kang Sheng's adoptive son played an important role in the recruitment of Boursicot by the Chinese. Having been caught in a well-laid 'honey trap', Boursicot succumbed to blackmail and agreed to hand over to 'Kang' confidential French embassy documents: for he was set upon continuing his relationship with Shi Peipu. From 1970 to 1972, Boursicot was to hand over to his case officer more than 150 of these documents, at the same time pursuing his love affair with Shi Peipu.

Transferred in 1979 to Outer Mongolia after an interval of five years spent outside China, Boursicot continued his spying activities, transmitting to the Chinese the texts of numerous dispatches. To such an extent, moreover, that Deng Xiaoping's secret services agreed in 1982 to Shi Peipu's going to France to pursue his romance with their informer, who had returned to his country a year earlier. As we have seen, the DST put a sudden end to this situation in July 1983, in retaliation against the internment of the young artist Li Shuang, who was also in love with a French diplomat, the former Maoist militant Emmanuel Bellefroid. Shi Peipu and Bernard Boursicot were arrested and sentenced to six years' imprisonment, while Li Shuang regained her freedom and now lives in France.

In Beijing, the authorities managed to break up her little group of dissident painters. The Chinese communists never have any qualms about persecuting independent writers and artists, or even ordinary citizens who keep dubious company, as Jiang Youlu, a trainee engineer studying in Paris, learned from bitter experience in January 1981. Like Shi Peipu, a Chinese opera dancer, and like Mei Lanfang, master to them both, a specialist in female roles, Youlu shared his apartment with a student from Hong Kong. But in the eyes of Popular China's embassy, Jiang had a serious flaw: he liked not just human contact but free discussion with French and even Taiwanese friends.

Summoned on 16 January to the embassy's cultural section in Paris, he was taken into custody in order to be interrogated about his relationships, all under the pretext of the fight against espionage. And on Wednesday 21 January, some ten Chinese diplomats were ready to throw him on to a flight to Beijing. His destination: the *Laogai*.

Alerted by friends of the engineer, the French DST police were at hand. They successfully prevented the enforced departure of Jiang Youlu to his country. More fortunate than his predecessor, former agent of the Maoist secret services Zhang Shirong who defected to the French in April 1971, Jiang Youlu was not subsequently handed over to the Chinese authorities. But then it emerged that he was in fact working for Taiwan, where he finally fled to.

Whilst they strike against dissident writers and artists, Beijing's special services have no scruples in manipulating the rest to act as intelligence agents. We have just seen how the opera dancer Shi Peipu played the rather unenviable role of recruitment bait. And the reader will recall Shen Jian, very special ambassador to Cuba, who became a roving representative of the secret services under the convenient cover of 'leader of the Wuhan troupe of acrobats'; Shen Jian, who in November 1978 paid the Khmer Rouge a 'friendship visit'.

Others lend themselves willingly to this game. In December 1985, a very beautiful young dancer called Lee Wai Ying had her Philippines tour suddenly cut short. After being closely interrogated, she was expelled on 1 January by the local authorities for spying. Yet President Marcos was known for his excellent relations with Red China.

So the Shi Peipu affair is not a unique, isolated case of artists of renown being used by Beijing's secret services. Bernard Boursicot's recruitment – a masterstroke – marked a new development in Yu Zhensan's career. In a strong position because of the public and not so public influence of Kang Sheng, Yu Zhensan survived without mishap the difficult period of the Cultural Revolution when so many communists, including his own mother, stumbled. In January 1973, the young *Gonganbu* cadre once again demonstrated his flair and discretion, apparently playing a very active role in the 'mysterious death' of the over-curious Minister of Public Security, Li Zhen, who was found strangled in a cellar.

In 1974, following Deng Xiaoping, who was rapidly fighting his way back up again, Yu Zhensan was promoted to bureau chief within the *Gonganbu*. His superior was none other than Yu Sang, who, though not related to him at all, took him under his wing. Yu Sang was, of course, Kang Sheng's right-hand man, whom Kang was relying on to counterbalance the increasing influence of Wang Dongxing in the Party. In December 1975 came a new drama: the death of Kang Sheng. By 1978 Kang Sheng's memory was no longer sacred and he was virulently criticised at the Party's cadre school by Hu Yaobang, then head of the Central Committee Department. In 1980, he was posthumously expelled from the communist ranks and officially became a 'demon'.

Yu Zhensan could have foundered with his adoptive father. However, he survived the event. He even had the joy of being reunited with his mother. Having been rehabilitated, Fan Jin returned to the foreground, like many of those who had worked with Zhou Enlai.

In 1985, Fan Jin had a seat on Beijing's Municipal Committee. Yu Zhensan became one of the senior officials at the head of the secret service set up in 1983 by Deng Xiaoping and his supporters, the *Guojia anquanbu*. Still in charge of the surveillance and infiltration of foreigners, he was responsible for liaising with *Gonganbu* colleagues, and with the Central Committee's Investigations Department, the *Diaochabu*. A delicate task, in fact, for the rivalry – if not the war – between Popular China's various special services was at its height.

Yu Zhensan worked closely with the head of the Beijing *Guojia anquanbu* Bureau, Min Buying. But he had to pay heed to those in charge of the Beijing's Public Security Bureau's Section 2, which also dealt with the surveillance and repression, if need be, of foreign nationals.

The capital's Public Security Bureau was located at 83 Beichizidajie Street, a road parallel to the Forbidden City that ran directly into the street where the national cadres of the *Gonganbu* and the *Guojia anqanbu* 'cohabited'. The rivalry between the 'security organs' gave rise in 1984 to the 'Terziani Affair'. An Italian journalist, Terziani was a recognised expert on the Far East and the correspondent in China for the German magazine *Der Spiegel*. He was arrested by the *Guojia anquanbu*. Yu Zhensan and Min Buying intended to make a scapegoat of him, and brand him as a 'spy'.

'My only crime is to have got off the treadmill, travelled on uncomfortable seats, cycled across the country, worn Chinese clothes, tried to build up normal relationships with normal Chinese [this was considered to be 'illegal' although no one seemed able to recall the law that forbade it], tried to understand what the Chinese dream of and what they fear . . .'wrote Terziani on his release.

In fact, it was these contacts between foreign journalists and Chinese citizens that the *Gonganbu* and the *Guojia anquanbu* were trying to prevent. This was because of traditional chauvinism, heightened by more than thirty-five years' isolation, as well as an ancestral liking for secrecy. It was also because of a very simple fact: the Chinese communists, who daily use their Xinhua news agency as a cover for their special services, are incapable of imagining what the freedom of the press means in the West. So the foreign journalist who goes off the beaten track and is not happy to settle for official information is considered a spy.

So too are the native population who have dealings with him. In Deng Xiaoping's China, as previously in Mao's, there is a 'crime' that is dealt with very severely: *Li tongwaiguo* – communicating with the outside world, which, according to the logic of the regime, means communicating with the enemy.

Arrested in 1973 for having, among other charges, transmitted to foreign journalists information on the course of the Sino-Vietnamese war, and then sentenced to fifteen years' imprisonment, the dissident Wei Jingsheng learned this to his cost. The young student Lin Jie, too: at the end of January 1987, he was arrested for 'colluding' with the American correspondent of Agence France-Press in Beijing, Lawrence MacDonald. While on a trip to Hong Kong, MacDonald was informed by the *Guojia anquanbu* that he could no longer work in China. Then he was unceremoniously expelled on 30 January.

Six months earlier, in June 1986, his compatriot on *The New York Times*, John Burns, had had the same misfortune . . . with an additional six days' imprisonment. In the name of the *Guojia anquanbu*,

General Zhang accused him, without the slightest evidence, of course, of spying. Clearly, the opening up of China to the outside world does not extend beyond the limited domain of industrial and commercial exchanges.

What was Yu Zhensan's view of this climate? It is difficult to say. In September 1985, the former second-in-command of the Chinese troops from Shenjiang, on the northern border, Gao Ke, assumed control of the Beijing bureau of the *Gonganbu* and became to some extent Yu Zhensan's *alter ego* but also his rival.

In November 1985, the *Guojia anquanbu* was rocked to its foundations by its first major setback: the son of Madame Mao's first husband, Kang Sheng's protégé, went in secret to Hong Kong. He hid for some time in the British colony before going over to the West, probably to the United States.

What was the reason for this defection that deprived the *Guojia anquanbu* of one of its bosses and provided the West with its first defector of real standing within Red China's special services?

'It was love. Yu Zhensan fell for a beautiful young Chinese-American woman!' say some.

'Out of hatred for the regime that brought nothing but misfortune to his family,' say others.

Perhaps it was simply because Yu, as a senior official in close contact with the *Gonganbu*, was well placed to appreciate the limitations of the liberalisation conducted in China by the Deng Xiaoping team: 950,000 arrests from the beginning of August to November 1983, nearly 10,000 summary executions . . .

Whatever the answer, this defection had a shocking effect within the closed world of Popular China's special services. It was in the medium term one of the reasons for the promotion of the very skilful and very diplomatic Qiao Shi to the post of 'co-ordinator' of Deng Xiaoping's intelligence agencies, with a view to preventing any further defections from the *Guojia anquanbu*, the *Diaochabu* or the *Gonganbu*.

The 'Yu Zhensan Affair' was a severe blow. When questioned by a foreign journalist with particularly good contacts in Chinese upper echelons, the head of the *Guojia anquanbu*, who had plenty to say when it came to accusing the American journalist John Burns without any proof, suddenly immured himself in silence.

Jia Chunwang evidently did not like any reference in his presence to this 'betrayal'. Yet, as a former colleague of Fan Jin, Yu Zhensan's mother, on the Communist Party's Beijing Municipal Committee, he had the reputation of being an affable and very open man. This young dynamic leader, who made no secret of his bad memories of being a prisoner during the Cultural Revolution, nor of his hatred of the KGB, nor of his admiration for the American CIA or the French DGSE, finally said in English: 'It's very regrettable.'

All the more regrettable since on 22 November 1985, the FBI

arrested in Alexandria, Virginia, one of the Chinese secret services' most distinguished moles. Jin Wudai, alias Larry Wu Tai Chin, had infiltrated the CIA thirty-four years earlier. The investigators who interrogated him were sent reeling. Larry Wu Tai Chin had been recruited in Japan in 1952. In Okinawa, to be precise, where 'the Company' was then setting up its electronic listening post trained on Red China. His recruitment was carried out under the aegis of the 'Red seaman' Liao Chengzhi, that legendary character in communist Special Affairs, future Vice-President of the Chinese National People's Assembly.

A translator at the American consulate in Shanghai, Larry Wu Tai Chin had joined the CIA in 1948. For the Chinese, he was a top-class recruit. An interrogator of communist prisoners on the Korean front, he began to inform his new masters and compatriots on the results of these interrogations. As time went on, he became one of their best informers on American plans in South-East Asia, particularly during the Vietnam War.

An officer in the CIA's Radiodiffusion Department at Langley, in Virginia, then still very active after his retirement, Larry Wu Tai Chin confessed to the investigators that he had received since 1952 the handsome sum of $140,000 for his good and loyal services. The most 'fair-minded' of the CIA men readily admitted that he did not 'steal' this money (paid in small amounts in Hong Kong), considering the quality of the information of all kinds that he shamelessly gleaned over thirty-four years' covert and solitary work to the advantage of Red China.

Why was he caught? Although US counter-intelligence refuse to admit it, it was doubtless because of information supplied by the recent defector Yu Zhensan. Kang Sheng's adoptive son completely disappeared from view after going over to the West, which was only reported in September 1986. He is believed to be living under a false identity in the USA. But the American authorities are being extremely discreet about his case. This is because it is difficult to acknowledge publicly that the CIA has taken in this very high-ranking *Gonganbu* officer without causing a rift with the representatives of Red China, a country with which Washington is on excellent terms. One must never make one's opponent lose face, especially as the Taiwanese, by virtue of family ties, no doubt played a significant role in the defection of Kang Sheng's adoptive son. After all, Yu Zhensan is the cousin of Yu Zusheng, the grandson of Chiang Ching-kuo and great-grandson of Chiang Kai-shek. Moreover, secret negotiations immediately began between US emissaries and Taiwan government envoys, anxious to welcome back the prodigal son.

Yu Zhensan's defection to the West did, in fact, put everyone in a difficult position. For diplomatic reasons, the USA could not officially acknowledge it. The leadership in Beijing or Taipei even less so: it would mean bringing to light the indirect family ties linking Mao

Zedong and Chiang Kai-shek. In sum, it would mean confessing that there were links between the caste in power in communist China and the Taiwanese élite. This was virtually throwing in the people's faces the fact that while they fought each other to the death, their leaders always landed on their feet.

So silence prevailed. Yet Yu Zhensan gained something of a following as a defector: in September 1986, a Chinese special services official known by the pseudonym of 'Fu Manchu' defected to the French; in November 1986 it was the turn of Du Bingru, in West Germany. This commercial attaché at the embassy in Bonn threw himself into the arms of the Germans. Deng Xiaoping's team came under sustained fire from the most conservative elements of the Chinese CP who, concerned, blamed their open-door policy with the West for this series of defections. And, of course, the student demonstrations of December 1986 did not help.

As for the men in the PRC's special services, they learned to excise the name of Yu Zhensan from their vocabulary. The adoptive son of Kang Sheng thus joined the founder of the communist special services in the great cemetery of oblivion.

Thus ends – very provisionally – a story that began in the mid 1920s in Shanghai, continued in Moscow, in Yan'an and then in Beijing . . .

Epilogue

THE SECURITY LOBBY AFTER TIAN AN MEN

What a surprise to see, among the Tian An Men protesters during spring 1989, students of the Public Security University or else demonstrators holding the banners of the International Relations College (國際關係學院), that is to say, where the future intelligence operatives learn strategy and politics for the other large agency, the Ministry for State Security (國安部).

China watchers of all sorts wondered whether, as was the case during the Great Proletarian Cultural Revolution, violent confrontations were going to occur, including the purge and assassinations of several secret service heads. Indeed, the head of the Public Security, Wang Fang (王芳), a career officer, sided with the conservatives in the CP leadership. In 1980 he was given the job of prosecutor in the trial of the Gang of Four. He had taken over as head of Public Security from Ruan Chongwu (阮崇武) in April 1987 when the latter's friend, prime minister Hu Yaobang, was overthrown.

Meanwhile another of Hu's friends, often described as liberal, Jia Chunwang (賈春旺), remained in firm control of the Ministry of State Security. Thus both trends, modern and conservative, were represented in the intelligence community: on the one hand, the traditional iron fist on the Chinese population, on the other, open-mindedness and flexible attitudes as regards methods of intelligence-gathering abroad. At the top level, the overall coordinator of intelligence and security, Qiao Shi (喬石), demonstrated in turn both tendencies.

This is why on 6 June 1989 Radio Beijing announced that Qiao Shi had taken over leadership of the party from reformist general-secretary Zhao Ziyang, who was purged. The same day the Supreme People's Court sent a telegram to 'comrade Qiao Shi and the standing committee of the Politburo to express support for actions to suppress counter-revolutionary riots.'

Whether he declined to take on the job of general-secretary, or whether he was not allowed to reach that position by leaders anxious not to see the intelligence supremo acquire the highest political position is a matter of interpretation. Whatever the case, Qiao Shi, always close to ageing Deng Xiaoping, remained in control of the security apparatus whilst another Shanghai man, Jiang Zemin, became general-secretary.

Yet, as the Japanese edition of this book is in press, Qiao Shi has grown more powerful than his mentor Kang Sheng had been during the Mao Zedong era. His irresistible rise, we have seen, started in 1982, when he had become head of the International Liaison Department of the Communist Party.

In June 1983, Zhao Ziyang had announced the creation of the Ministry of State Security (國安部) modelled on the Soviet KGB, whereas the old-style Public Security (公安部) remained as an internal repressive force seconded by the newly-born People's Armed Police.

Year after year Qiao Shi had broadened his field of operations, thus lining up with the security preoccupations of the old veterans, men like Peng Zhen or Chen Yun, Kang Sheng's comrade in the Shanghai underground of the thirties. Simultaneously, Qiao Shi was on good terms with reformists such as Hu Yaobang and Zhao Ziyang. In 1987 and 1989, he abandoned them only when their protector in Zhongnanhai, Deng Xiaoping, was pressurised into dropping them.

In October 1987, becoming No. 3 of the Party in the aftermath of its Thirteenth Congress, Qiao Shi led the battle against corruption, heading the Commission for Discipline Inspection. Then the old Peng Zhen handed over the leadership of the Political-Legal Leading Group supervising the security galaxy: three ministries—public security, state security and justice as well as the national minorities section.

In 1988, major international operations were thus carried out under Qiao Shi's personal intervention. In January, the American Federal Bureau of Investigation (FBI) had two Chinese diplomats expelled from the USA. Assistant military attaché Hou Desheng and the Chinese consul in Chicago, Zhang Weichu, according to the State Department, 'were engaged in activities incompatible with their diplomatic status.' According to off-the-record FBI sources, the two Chinese operatives had recruited an agent inside the National Security Agency (NSA) which deals with Signals Intelligence.

This unfortunate breach in the Sino-American cooperation as regards SIGINT operations directed towards the Soviet Union probably prompted the demotion, later in December, of the director of Military Intelligence (總參謀部情報部), Wu Jinfa, replaced by his right-hand man, a former military attaché in West Germany, Xiong Guangkai.

Around the same time in China a special State Secret Bureau was set up bearing the hallmarks of Qiao Shi. It replaced the Central Secrets Commission which established procedures for classifying secrets, including those concerning economic, social and scientific information.

Qiao Shi was also involved in key ventures such as the sale of Silkworm missiles and other weapons to Iran, a country where he had arranged intelligence services cooperation back under the reign of the Shah. Likewise the comeback of the dreaded Khmers Rouges in Kampuchea could not have occurred without a firm and constant financial, diplomatic and military support.

During autumn 1988, faithful to his tactics, Qiao Shi supervised the repression in Lhasa, but a moment after, extended an offer of dialogue with the future Nobel Peace Prize–winning Dalai Lama. . . . Indeed, in the meantime, the Guoanbu had launched a huge-scale psychological operation stating that the Japanese intelligence agency, Naicho (內調), was secretly training Tibetan suicide commandos!

A Chinese National Security Council.

As the student protests started in February 1989, the sudden death of top diplomat Huan Xiang (宦鄉) was barely noticed. The eighty year-old diplomat had studied in Shanghai and Japan's Waseda University before he joined Zhou Enlai's expert diplomatic team, enjoying in the post-1949 era a wide international experience especially in Europe. Emerging from the purge during the Cultural Revolution, Huan Xiang had led a new intelligence coordinating body — modelled after the US National Security Council: the International Research and Studies Center (國際問題研究中心).

In this body about forty analysts daily summed up key information for the inner circle of power in the State Council who decide foreign policy. At the time of Huan Xiang's death, besides himself they included prime minister Li Peng, CP general-secretary Zhao Ziyang, foreign affairs minister Wu Xueqian, the late Kang Sheng's friend and foreign affairs specialist Ji Pengfei and, of course, Qiao Shi. The latter benefited from Huan Xiang's death insofar as his specific weight increased within that body. But it was already very strong since the Research Center receives data from another information-gathering agency known as the Contemporary International Relations Institute (現代國際關係).

This Institute is partly staffed and subsidised by the intelligence outfit Guoanbu (係研究所). And many of its four hundred analysts, divided in seven geographical departments plus one global strategy section, are members of the secret services. A leading figure in the Institute is the notorious Wu Xuewen (國安部), who was expelled from Japan in 1964 for spying activities.

The Institute provides short-term analysis springing from all sources abroad and produces a well-researched magazine, called Contemporary International Relations (現代國際關係), dealing with world international relations and profiles of prominent heads of state.

No doubt during the Tian An Men protests the hesitations of the top leadership, especially of Deng Xiaoping, were reinforced by the influx of intelligence summaries reporting that the USA, Japan and Europe would condemn harsh repression against the students. There again, Qiao Shi was influential. Besides he had personal knowledge through his children abroad: his son Jiang Xiaoming was studying in Cambridge (Great Britain), his daughter-in-law was working for the BBC in London, whilst his daughter Qiao Xiaoxi was a student at Texas College in the USA. These family connections probably helped him to understand the students' profound grievances. On 19 May 1989, he was thus with general-secretary Zhao Ziyang in the discussions with the students on Tian An Men. The day after, he abstained during the vote imposing Martial Law. Thus repression was given a green light but Qiao Shi was not its prime mover. All his security system was used, however, in the following repression —the hunt for dissidents within China and outside and the purge of hundreds of thousands of cadres, not less than 80,000 arrests from June to December 1989.

But this did not prevent Qiao Shi from exerting a moderating influence. So in the *People's Daily* on 18 June, he was quoted as saying: "Dialogue will carry on as soon as the situation is stabilised!"

No doubt with Deng Xiaoping's disappearance, factional fights will resume in Zhongnanhai. Qiao Shi will not necessarily make a bid for total leadership of the People's Republic of China but at any rate, he and his powerful intelligence and security community will play a decisive role in the power struggle.

Biographical Notes

THE FIVE MUSKETEERS

AFTER Gu Shunzang's betrayal, the leader of the *Tewu* set up a special committee made up of five men, in April 1931, under the aegis of Zhou Enlai, whose task it was to reorganise the secret services.

Given the importance of this committee, the biographies of its members are at the head of the alphabetical list below.

KANG Sheng is the leader, he needs no introduction . . . On the other hand:

GUANG Huian 廣惠安
Deputy member of the leadership of the Communist Party in Shanghai in 1931. With GU Shunzhang's betrayal, he becomes the leader of the Stormtroopers, the Red Guard (*Hong-dui* 紅隊) in charge of executions. Arrested by the Guomindang on 27 September 1934.

KE Qingshi 柯慶施, real name: KE Gaijun (The Eccentric), (1900–1965)
Born in the Anhui province. In the 20s carries out clandestine work in Shanghai with Kang Sheng and LI Kenong. 1960: mayor of Shanghai, Mao relies on his support to prepare the launching of the Cultural Revolution against the Beijing revisionists. He dies suddenly in Chengdu, on his way to meet Mao.

PAN Hannian 潘漢年
Born in the Jiangsu province. Trained in intelligence in the USSR. 1931: reorganises the CCP networks orienting them towards Asia, from Shanghai and Hong Kong. 1933: sent to the First and Third sections of the Red Army as a liaison agent. 1936: Comintern representative in Shanghai, organises negotiations with the Guomindang. Early 50s: head of the Asian Bureau of the *Shehuibu*, director of the same secret service in Shanghai as well as deputy mayor of the town. Excluded from the CCP together with Fang Yan, assistant director of the *Gonganbu*, in July 1955, for 'counter-revolutionary activities'. Persecuted by Kang Sheng. Imprisoned for twenty-five years, released in 1979.

CHEN Yun 陳雲, real name LIAO Chenyun
The last of the 'five musketeers'. Born in Shanghai in 1905. Composi-

tor in the publishing house The Commercial Press. In the mid-20s: organises the local trade union movement together with Liu Shaoqi. Takes part in the uprisings of 1927. 1931: reorganises the secret services with Kang Sheng (his speciality: infiltration of the enemy). Joins Mao Zedong, becomes a member of the Central Committee and of the military revolutionary council. 1935: joins Kang Sheng in Moscow, attends the Seventh Congress of the Comintern. Leaves for Xinjiang on a mission. Joined by Kang and Wang Ming, returns to Yan'an. Becomes leader of the Organisation Department of the Party. Specialises in the economy. Publishes a document on 'The Treatment of Managers' in 1942 in the Rectification Campaign which he fully supports. 1945: sent to Manchuria with Peng Zhen, Gao Gang, Lin Biao. 1949: becomes Deputy Prime Minister and head of heavy industry and financial and economic affairs. Advocate of a relaxation of the planning of the economy, opposes Mao during the period of the Great Leap Forward (1957). Criticised during the Cultural Revolution, he remains on the Central Committee. But his career reaches its height in 1978 when he is propelled, thanks to DENG Xiaoping, to the fifth rank of the regime.

OTHERS

BADDERLEY, John Halkett (1920–1972)
Senior civil servant in the Secret Intelligence Service (M16). Coldstream Guards (1940–5), one of the organisers of special operations against Enver Hoxha in Albania (1949). 1952: controls SIS operations on China from Singapore and Hong Kong. 1970–2: counsellor at the Washington embassy: head of SIS station, liaison with CIA. Dies of a heart attack.

BAI Ren 白認
Veteran of the Long March, *Tewu* agent specialising in the Arab countries (Yemen, 1956; Morocco, 1959) and Black Africa.

BAI Shangwu 白尚武
1983: director of the *Gonganbu* in Sichuan. Political superintendent of the provincial armed police corps.

CAI Cheng 蔡誠
In 1984, Vice-minister of Justice, president of the University of Public Security (*Zhonggua Renmin Gongan Daxue*). 中国人民公安大学

CAI Yunling 蔡云岑
Head of the political department of the *Gonganbu*, 1973.

CAO Guisheng 曹桂生
1954: Xinhua correspondent in Hanoi; member of the delegation at the Geneva Conference. 1970: counsellor at the Paris embassy (organises together with Vernon Walters the Kissinger/Zhou Enlai meetings). In 1976: counsellor at Phnom Penh. 1985: ambassador in Vienna.

CAO Yi-ou 曹軼歐
Wife of Kang Sheng. Real name, Cao Shuying 曹淑英, alias Cao Ying.

CARREL, Ian
'Mole hunter' for MI5, the British counter-espionage organisation. Security Liaison Officer in Hong Kong. 1965: head of the central intelligence office in Curzon Street, London. Leader of Section K7, which specialises in the fight against Soviet infiltration into M15, until 1978.

CHAN, Tak Fei
Kang Sheng's spy who infiltrated the listening station of the Government Communications Headquarters (GCHQ) in Little Sai Wan (Hong Kong), arrested in 1961.

CHEN Changfeng 陳昌奉
Born in 1915 in Jiangxi. 1936: Red Army Academy. Mao's bodyguard. North-west Security Bureau: instructor. 18 May 1946: sent to Shandong, carries out clandestine work there in the 'white zone'. 1959: author of *With Chairman Mao*.

CHEN Chu 陳楚
Born in Shandong, 1917. *Tewu* chief under diplomatic cover. 1971: director of the Department of Information of Foreign Affairs. 1972: at the UN with Gao Liang. 1973-6: first ambassador of the People's Republic of China to Japan. 1977: permanent representative at the UN Security Council. 1984: member of the legislative commission concerning Hong Kong. 1986: director at the Ministry for Light Industry, in Shanghai.

CHEN Dayu 陳达昱
Senior officer in military intelligence (*Qingbao*) in charge of the USSR, 1971.

CHEN Geng (1940-1961) 陳賡
Alias 'Mr Wang', alias Chen Guang. One of the best generals of the PLA. Intelligence specialist in Shanghai and Hong Kong (1931-3). Arrested, he escapes and takes part in the Long March. In 1951: assistant to Peng Dehuai in Korea; in 1954: one of the mentors of Van Giap in Dien Bien Phu. Supervises the opium traffic of the Yunnan.

CHEN Hansheng 陳翰笙
Born in 1897 in the Jiangsu province. 1928: member of the CCP in Moscow. During Second World War, he works in India for the British Secret Service (Political Warfare Executive). 1949: returns to China. 1986: honorary president of the Institute of World History at the Academy of Science.

CHEN Huiqing 陳慧清
Wife of DENG Fa.

CHEN Jiakang 陳家康
Born in 1912, Hubei. In 1936: student agent, works at the United Work Front Department in Yan'an, then secretary to Zhou Enlai and member of his intelligence service with LIU Shaowen. Diplomatic career in the 1950s (accompanies Zhou to Bandung). Ambassador in Egypt from June 1956 to December 1965. Disappears during the Cultural Revolution.

CHEN Lifu 陳立夫
Born in 1899. Head of the intelligence section of the Department of Central Organisation of the Guomindang, and member of the central executive committee of the Guomindang (1929–51). Author of a number of works on Confucius, in Taiwan, where he still lived in 1986.

CHEN Ping 陳平
A Malayan of Chinese origin born in 1922. Head of the Malaysian Communist Party, during Second World War organises the Malayan People's Anti-Japanese Army (MPAJA) and later the anti-British uprising (1948–60) backed by the Chinese in Beijing.

CHEN Qihan 陳奇涵
Born in 1898. 1935: official in the Revolutionary Council and intelligence department of the CC and the CCP in Yan'an. September 1964: assistant to the head of the Public Security Force at the Third National People's Congress, with the rank of colonel-general.

CHEN Yang Shan 陳養山
November 1949: head of the *Gonganbu*, Xi'an, then in 1951 of Nanking and in January 1953 head of Public Security for North China. 1962: vice-president of the Institute of Foreign Affairs.

CHEN Zhongjing 陳忠經
January 1980: president of the Institute of Contemporary International Relations in Beijing. February 1984: adviser to the *Guoanbu* (Ministry of State Security).

CHI Yutang 池玉堂
Official in Detachment 8341, 1971.

CHOI Yong Kun (1900–1976) 崔庸健
Vice-President of North Korea. 1926: joins the Chinese Communist Party, and as a member of it fights the Japanese. Chief of the North Korean secret police, Minister of Defence in 1948. Central Committee of the Workers' Party in North Korea. Head of State 1957–72.

CLIFT, Richard Dennis
Born in 1933. Specialist on China for the Secret Intelligence Service (MI6) in Britain. Studied at Oxford and Cambridge. Opens the SIS office in Beijing in 1958. Posts under diplomatic cover in Berne, Paris, Kuala Lumpur (Malaysia). Head of the Beijing SIS (as 'commercial adviser' at the embassy) on the death of Kang Sheng; then in Northern Ireland. 1984: high commissioner in Freetown, Sierra Leone.

CUI Yi 崔毅
Head of 'a department of the Bureau of Foreign Affairs' in Shanghai. Sent to the *Fête de l'Humanité*, the French Communist Party annual event in September 1984.

DAI Li (1895–1946) 戴笠
Former pupil of the Military Academy of Huangpu, head of Chiang Kai-shek's special services (Bureau of Investigation and Statistics/ BIS), 1932–46. April 1943: head of the intelligence agency, Sino-American Cooperative Organisation (SACO). Dies in a plane crash due to sabotage on 16 March 1946.

DENG Fa (1906–1946) 鄧發
Born in Guangdong province. Takes part in the great Hong Kong sailors' strike in 1925. Director of the Bureau of State Political Security of the central government of the Republic of Soviets of China. 1930: member of the CC of the CCP. 1937: head of the Liaison Bureau of the Eighth Road Army in Xinjiang. 1945: in Paris, takes part in the World Trades Unions Federation Congress. Dies in April 1946 in a 'plane crash'.

DING Shan, Colonel 丁山
1960: military attaché in Switzerland, head of the military intelligence service (*Qingbao*) for Western Europe. 1983: military attaché in Tokyo. 1986: director in Institute for Strategic Studies in Beijing.

DOIHARA Kenzo (1883–1943) 土肥原賢二
Head of the Japanese military intelligence service in China. Nicknamed the 'Nippon Lawrence'. Ex-military attaché in Beijing, sets up the *Tokumu Kikau* (Mukden Secret Service). Member of the Black Dragon secret society. Engineers the incident of 18 September 1931.

Manipulates the former emperor Pu Yi after he becomes the head of Manchukuo. Until 1940, organises the special services in Shanghai against the CCP and the Guomindang. 1944: goes to Malaysia. 1945: in Japan, where he is arrested, sentenced as a 'war criminal' and hanged on 23 December 1948.

DOLANC, Stane
Born in 1925. Yugoslav Federal Secretary for Internal Affairs. In August 1977: visits China with Tito who brings up with Hua Guofeng 'the Kang Sheng case'. Autumn 1983: goes to China again, to boost the links between the security services of the two countries.

DU Changtian 杜長天
December, 1979: Vice-President of the Guangdong Regional Assembly. February, 1984: *Guoanbu* adviser.

DU Dianwu 杜殿武
Since July 1983, director of the *Gonganju* and political commissar of the People's Armed Police Corps for the province of Heilongjiang.

DU Yuesheng (1884?-1951) 杜月笙
Born in Shanghai, manager of a number of banks and member of the Control Commission of the Chinese Chamber of Commerce in Shanghai. Owner of a number of newspapers, including the *China Press* and the *China Times*. Grand Master of the secret society the Green Gang (*Qingbang*), he controls opium-trafficking and prostitution. A friend of Chiang Kai-shek and DAI Li. Dies in exile in Hong Kong.

FANG Wen 方文
1966-73: military attaché in Paris (organises together with Vernon Walters the secret Huang Zhen-Kissinger meetings). 1978: military attaché in London.

FANG Zhida 方知达
Africa specialist in the *Tewu* in the 60s. 1979: assistant director of the United Work Front Department of the Central Committee.

FENG Jiping 馮基平
Member of the *Gonganbu*, attacked together with Xing Xiangsheng by Kang Sheng in May 1968. 1980: assistant general secretary for the Council of State. 1982: Member of the CC of the CCP.

FENG Xuan 馮鉉
1946-7: head of the CCP/Guomindang liaison secretariat in Beijing. 1950-9: envoy, then ambassador in Switzerland. Vice-president of the China-Latin America Friendship Association (1961). An official, then assistant director of the International Liaison Department (ILD)

(*Duiwai Lianluobu*) in 1972. December 1973: together with Jiang Qing and GENG Biao, meets a French delegation led by J. Jurquet. From April 1982: adviser to the ILD.

FITZGERALD, Desmond
In the 50s, head of the *China Command*, the large superstructure in Japan in charge of organising secret American operations in China. 1958: becomes head of the Far East department of the CIA (Far Eastern Desk). 1965–7: assistant director of CIA Plans.

FU Daqing 傅大慶
Founder of the CCP. 1925: representative of the Comintern in Singapore. Arrested by the Guomindang in April 1931, following the capture of the Comintern agent, Noulens.

FU Hao 符浩
Before 1949: political head of a unit of the PLA and secretary of the *Shehuibu* (Department of Social Affairs of the Central Committee). Specialist in intelligence on Japan. 1977: ambassador in Tokyo. Since 1985: head of various Sino-Japanese friendship organisations.

GAN Mai 甘邁
Colonel in the PLA. Clandestine operations in Tibet and Nepal in the 60s. Expelled from New Delhi where he was military attaché at the beginning of 1964. April 1964: chargé d'affaires at the embassy in Brazzaville, Congo. Organises the guerrilla movement in Black Africa. July 1971: Assistant Director of Foreign Affairs at the Ministry of Defence (in charge of liaison with guerrilla movements, including the PLO).

GAO Ke 高克
1974: Deputy Chief-of-Staff of the Shenyang Units. September 1985: head of the *Gonganbu* in Beijing.

GAO Liang 高梁
Tewu specialist on Africa. Expelled from New Delhi in 1960. 1961: head of the Xinhua agency in Dar es Salaam (attends the Geneva Conference on Laos). 1964: expelled from Mauritius for espionage. Assists the coup d'état in Zanzibar. Organises aid for the African guerrillas. 1971: secretary of the Chinese delegation to the UN (present during the Indochina negotiations in Paris). 1983: becomes head of a new special service, dependent on the CC of the CCP, the Bureau of Overseas Informations in the Propaganda Department.

GAO Wenli 高文礼
1979: deputy for Shandong. 1978–84: Vice-Minister of Public Security (*Gonganbu*).

GENG Biao 耿飈

Born in 1909 in Hunan. Stands out for his military achievements, from the Long March to the taking of Beijing. Becomes a diplomat and ambassador to a number of countries including Albania. A protégé of Zhou Enlai, he escapes the turmoil of the Cultural Revolution. End 1971: replaces Kang Sheng at the head of the I L D. Vice-Prime Minister and Minister of Defence on the return in strength of Deng Xiaoping (1978–82). Enver Hoxha called him an 'anti-Marxist secret agent'. His daughter Geng Yan has a high-up position in the Xinhua press agency.

GREY, Anthony

Born in 1938, a British journalist, Reuters correspondent in Beijing. Arrested in July 1967 by the *Gonganbu* as an 'English imperialist spy journalist' (in return for the arrest of a member of the Xinhua agency in Hong Kong). Released in 1969, published *Hostage in Peking*, the account of his misadventure, *The Chinese Assassin*, on the death of Lin Biao, and in 1983 *The Prime Minister Was a Spy*, an investigation into the *Tewu*'s recruitment of the Australian prime minister, Harold Holt.

GRIPPA, Jacques

Born in 1913. Joins the Belgian C P in 1930. Head of the Liège region in particular of immigrant labour (*Main d'Oeuvre Immigré*), then from 1933, in Brussels. January–July 1943: an official of Armed Partisans against the Nazi Occupation. Arrested, tortured and deported to the camps of Breendonk and Buchenwald for twenty-two months. Member of the Central Committee of the B C P until 1963, where he organises a C P 'reconstituted on the basis of Marxist-Leninism' which brings it closer to the Chinese. But after a few trips to China (when he meets Kang Sheng in particular), in disagreement with the policies of the Cultural Revolution in 1966, he breaks with Beijing. Author of *Marxisme-léninisme ou révisionnisme* (1963) and *Chronique récue d'une époque, 1930–47* (1988). For his actions in the Resistance no chief-of-staff of the Armed Partisans, awarded the Officier de l'Ordre de la Couronne avec palme (Officer of the Order of the Crown with a bar), Croix de Guerre 1940 avec palme (Military Cross 1940 with a bar) and the Medal of the Resistance.

GROOT, Paul de, (1899–1986)

Born in Amsterdam, diamond cutter in Antwerp, member of the Belgian C P in 1921. Appointed by the Comintern to the secretariat of the Dutch C P, in 1930 is head of the daily newspaper *Volksdagblad* but also of the clandestine Comintern apparatus (*M-Apparat*). Together with the Chinese sent by Kang Sheng, organiser of mutinies. Delegate to the Seventh Comintern Congress in 1935. Active in the anti-Nazi Resistance. A deputy in 1945, President of the Dutch Party, represents it at all the ceremonies in the U S S R until his retirement in 1967.

GU Shunzhang 顧順章
Born ?1902. A worker from Shanghai and a member of the Green Band. Member of the CCP in 1924, goes on a course in Russia in 1926. After April 1927, head of secret services, under the auspices of Zhou Enlai. Arrested in April 1931, offers his 'submission' to the Guomindang and betrays hundreds of comrades. In August 1931, on the Executive Committee of the Guomindang, then privy councillor to Chiang Kai-shek. In spring 1932, head of the terrorist department of the 'Blue Shirts'. According to some people, shot in 1935 by the nationalists during internal fights. According to others, this execution was a masquerade: Gu is said to have secretly led anti-communist work on Chinese soil, then in Taiwan, where he would have been living till recently.

GUO Longzhen, (1893–1930) 郭隆真
Alias Guo Linyi. Joins the CCP in 1922. Born in Shandong, works with the young Kang Sheng. 1930: arrested by the Guomindang in Qingdao and shot in Jinan.

GUO Yufeng 郭玉峰
1958: Assistant Director, Political Department, Sixty-fourth Army Corps. 1968: director of a sub-department of the military administration, in the United Front Work Department of the Central Committee (*Tongyi Zhanxian Gongzuobo*). 1969: assistant member CC, Ninth Congress of the CCP. Secretary to the Organisation Department and member of the CC in 1973. Friend and secretary to Kang Sheng, specialises in the falsification of documents along with Cao Yi-ou. Disappears at the end of 1977.

HALL, Professor Robert Burnett
Born in 1896 in Spain. Geographer. 1916–18: officer in the Military Intelligence Service (MIS) of the American Army. 1935: studies in Japan. Colonel of the Office of Strategic Services (OSS), head of the San Francisco Bureau. 1943: based in Kunming, organises together with Kang Sheng and Nosaka Sanzo the parachuting of Japanese communists behind the lines of the Nippon army. 1947: director of the Centre for Japanese Studies at the University of Michigan.

HAN Suyin 韩素音
Born in 1917, doctor and writer. Marries General Tang in 1938 and in 1952 the British Colonel L. F. Comber. Friend of various communist leaders, including Zhou Enlai about whom she will be publishing a 3-volume biography in the 1990s. Author of *Destination Chongqing, Many Splendoured Thing, And the Rain My Drink, The Mountain is Young, The Morning Deluge*.

HAO Zhiping 郝治平
Widow of Luo Ruiqing. Fell victim to the Cultural Revolution. Witness at the trial of the Gang of Four.

HATEM, George, alias Ma Haide 馬海德
American doctor, born in Lebanon, 1910. 1932: goes to China, works in Yan'an. He and his wife, the actress Su Fei, are part of Kang Sheng's network. 1960: acquires Chinese nationality. Member of the CC of the CCP and adviser to the Minister of Health. Died 1988.

HE Ying 何英
Specialist in American affairs at the Ministry of Foreign Affairs. Ambassador to Dar es Salaam in 1964, then to Uganda and Tanzania. Member of the leadership of the Association for Sino-African friendship. 1972: Vice-Minister for Foreign Affairs. 1983: Vice-President of the Committee for Chinese Overseas and member of the CC of the CCP.

HILL, Edward F.
Born 1905. Member of the Australian Communist Party in 1936. 1948: member of the CC of the ACP and secretary of the committee for the province of Victoria. 1951: member of the Politburo. 1955: secretary of the CC. June 1963: expelled from the ACP. In 1964 set up the Australian Communist Party (Marxist-Leninist) on his return from a trip to China. Kang Sheng gives him the task of watching the other Maoist groups.

HOANG Van Hoan 黄文欢
Alias Li Quang Hoa. Born in 1905. From 1935 to 1942, this Vietnamese organises the clandestine Indochinese Communist Party with the help of the Chinese as the 'Association for Supporting China against Japan'. 1935–42: in China. 1951–4: ambassador to Beijing; takes part in the Geneva Conference. Head of the International Liaison Department of the Vietnamese Labour Party. Takes refuge in Beijing in 1979 during the Sino-Vietnamese war.

HSIAO Hsin-ju, Colonel
Representative of Dai Li's secret services in Washington in the 1930s and during the Second World War.

HU Zhiguang 胡之光
Vice-Minister of the *Gonganbu*, 1985.

HUANG Chibo 黄赤波
1950: director of the *Gonganbu* for south of the Jiangxi. 1979: Shanghai municipal committee.

HUANG Chongwu 黃崇五
Communist from Shandong. In the mid-twenties, Kang Sheng's teacher. Eventually joins the Guomindang. In Taiwan, from 1949 on, head of an anti-communist section of the secret services (Bureau of Investigation of the Ministry of Justice/*Fawubu Diaochabu*). Died in Taipei, in the early 1980s.

HUANG Hua 黃華
Born 1913 in the Hebei region. 1936: Edgar Snow's secretary, trained by the Department of Social Affairs in Yan'an. 1940: correspondent of the Xinhua agency in Chongqing. Various diplomatic posts after 1949. Ambassador to Ghana (1960–5), to Egypt (1966–9), to Canada and permanent representative to the UN from 1971. 1982: Minister of Foreign Affairs. Married to a diplomat, He Liliang.

HUANG Huoqing 黃火青
1926: section leader of the *Shehuibu*. 1979: public prosecutor and deputy for Liaoning province.

HUANG Jingxi 黃京熙
Vice-Minister of the *Gonganbu*, 1973–80.

HUANG Zhengui 黃政基
Assistant Director of Military Intelligence (*Qingbao*), 1980.

HUI Ping 惠平
1982: Vice-Minister of the *Gonganbu*, moves to the *Guoanbu*. Leading member of the CC in favour of the socialist ethic.

JI Pengfei 姬鵬飛
Born in 1909 in the Shanxi region, medical training, head of the medical department of the military committee of the CCP, then political head of the various PLA units. 1950–5: ambassador to East Germany. Diplomatic career and various postings within Eastern Europe, North Korea and Africa. 1972–4: Minister of Foreign Affairs and head of the Chinese delegation at the Paris negotiations on Vietnam. 1979–83: Director of the ILD. Friend of Kang Sheng.

JIA Chunwang 賈春旺
Born, 1938. June 1982: Secretary of the Committee of the League of Communist Youth; in December: Director of the LCY. 1984: Assistant Secretary of the Beijing Municipal Council. 6 September 1985: Minister for State Security (*Guoanbu*), taking over from Ling Yun.

JIANG Feng 江楓
Director of the Tientsin (Tianjin) *Gonganbu*, 1967.

JIANG Wen 江文
Born 1914. Specialist in communications. 1933: studies at the School of Telephone Communications in Ruijin. 1961: head of Signals at PLA headquarters; hands Lin Biao a bulky report on the 'coding of correspondence'. 1981: assistant public prosecutor and adviser to the general chief-of-staff of the PLA.

JIANG Youlu 姜友陆
Born 1936, Beijing. Former female role singer at the Peking Opera. Weights and measures engineer. Requests political asylum in France on 23 January 1981.

JIN Cheng 金城
Born in the Hebei region. 1939: director of the public relations department of the Shanxi–Gansu–Ningxia border government. 1952: director of the United Front Work Department's 'Deuxième Bureau'. 1956: Vice-Minister to the Minister of Aquatic Products. 1963: Vice-Director of the United Front Work Department. Disappears during the Cultural Revolution. Since 1980: adviser at the UFWD.

JIN Shusheng 金樹生
Director of the Jiangxi *Gonganbu* and political commissar of the Armed Popular Police, September 1983.

JIN Wudai (Larry Wu Tai Chin) 金無怠
Born 1920. Chinese of American nationality. 1948: US consulate in Shanghai. 1950: in Hong Kong. 1952: enters the Foreign Broadcast Information Service in Okinawa, then in Santa Rosa, California, as a CIA analyst. Arrested end of 1985 as a *Tewu* spy, commits suicide in prison beginning of 1986.

KANG Hyon Su
Member of the CC of the Korean Labour Party. Director of the Politburo of Korean Public Security. Frequently travels to China (1973, 1975). In charge of liaison with the Chinese special services.

KANG Keqing 康克清
Wife of Zhu De, Red Army officer. Under various identities, *Shehuibu* posts and President of the Union of Women.

KANG Sheng 康生
'Kang Sheng' is a *nom de guerre* and means, paradoxically, 'peaceful birth'. Shandong's most infamous son called himself in turn ZHANG Shaoqing, 張紹卿 (Zang is his surname), then ZHANG Shuping 張叔平. He arrives in Shanghai under the name of ZHANG Zhen. Still in Shanghai, but living clandestinely, he calls himself ZHAO Rong 趙爨趙蓉. KANG Sheng becomes his best known

name, at least after 1933, in the USSR. His painter's pseudonym is LU Jushi 魯居士.

KANG Ze 康澤
Head of one of the Guomindang's secret police forces, rival of that run by Dai Li. Captured by the communists in 1949.

KAO, Rameshwar Nath
Specialist in Indian Intelligence. Member of the Intelligence Bureau (IB), sent to Ghana in 1960 to organise Kwame Nkrumah's secret services. 21 September 1968: founds the new intelligence services, the Research and Analysis Wing (RAW) of which he is the first director. 1974: becomes Indira Gandhi's 'Security Adviser'. 1984: hands in his resignation the day after Indira Gandhi's assassination and is replaced by another former director of the RAW, G. C. Saxena.

KAWASHIMA Yoshiko 川島芳子 (金碧慧, Jin Bihui, in Chinese)
The Chinese 'Mata Hari'. Born in Manchuria, raised by a Japanese prince. Works for Colonel Doihara's intelligence service. Persuades the last emperor of China to become, under the aegis of the Japanese, the sovereign of Manchuko. Takes part in a number of secret activities, is said to have worked for Kang Sheng's people. Captured by the Guomindang, shot in Beijing in 1945 (or in Nanking – according to some rumours, is still alive today in Beijing).

KE Bonian 柯柏年
Born 1907. Studied in Australia. Representative of the CCP in the Malay CP in Singapore in 1933. Author of a work on the American economy. 1948: Head of ILD Research Bureau. In the 50s, secretary to Li Kenong. 1959–60: ambassador to Rumania. Member of the Sino-African Friendship Association. In the 70s, head of the Institute for Foreign Affairs. Died in 1985.

KIRSANOVA, Klaudiya Ivanova, (1887–1947)
Joins the Bolshevik Party in 1904. Deported by the authorities, marries Emilien Iaroslavski (1878–1943). Vice-rector of the Sverdlov communist university then the Comintern's Leninist school, from its inception. Replaced in 1936 by her assistant, Vulko Chervenkov, ('Vladimirov'). The *Great Soviet Encyclopaedia* curiously makes no mention of these ten years of her life (1926–36). She was, in fact, victim of a purge instigated by Wang Ming and Kang Sheng, who complained to Stalin. According to them, the school had become a hotbed of Trotskyism.

KOLESNIKOV, Vladimir S.
China specialist at the KGB. Second secretary at the Washington

embassy in 1972. March 1978: sent to Beijing with the adviser Viktor Kracheninnikov to organise the *Rezidentoura* of the KGB.

KUO, Warren (Chinese name: GUO Hualun 郭華倫 alias Chen Ran 陳然.)
Communist official who changed sides, becoming head of the China sector of the Taiwan Investigation Bureau at the Ministry of Justice (*Fawubu Diaochaju*). Vice-director of the Institute of International Research (IIR) of the national university of Zhengzhi. Author of a number of articles and an 'Analytical History of the Chinese Communist Party' (*Zhong gong lilun*). Died in 1983(?).

LI Chuwen 李儲文
The 'Zhou Enlai' of Hong Kong. Assistant director of the Xinhua agency in the English colony since 1983. Head of communist secret services; former Shanghai clergyman. 1977: under-director of the Bureau of Foreign Affairs in Shanghai. 1981: director of the same bureau as well as of the Bureau of Chinese Affairs Overseas.

LI Dongye 李東冶
Born in Shanxi. 1949: director of the *Shehuibu* for Rehe province. 1950: director of the *Gonganbu* Department, Rehe People's Government.

LI Enqiu 李恩求
Official diplomatic career: in Poland (1952), in Rumania (1954). July 1963: chargé d'affaires in The Hague (considered responsible for the reorganisation of the special services in Europe). In July 1966, expelled from Holland for his role in the assassination of the engineer Xu Zicai. 1975–8: ambassador to Czechoslovakia.

LI Guangxiang 李廣祥
Head of the Canton *Gonganju*. May 1980: vice-minister of the *Gonganbu*. April 1983: goes to West Germany to study electronic surveillance techniques with the Bundeskriminalamt.

LI Guangyen 李廣文
Friend of Kang Sheng. In the 50s head of the Shandong CP university.

LI Jinde 李金德
In 1949: assistant director of 'Confidential Material' at the CC Bureau of General Affairs. 1965: leading official in the UFWD. Disappears during the Cultural Revolution. Resurfaces in 1972, in the same post.

LI Jusheng 李菊生
Chargé d'affaires in Indonesia in the 60s. 1973–8: assistant director of the Xinhua press agency in Hong Kong, and head of local secret services. 1973: delegate at the Tenth CCP Congress.

LI Kenong (1898–1962) 李克農
In the 30s in Shanghai, member of a special section of the *Tewu*; infiltrates the Guomindang secret service. 1938–46: Kang Sheng's assistant in the *Shehuibu*, then director of the *Shehuibu* from 1946 until his death. In 1954, under cover as 'assistant minister for foreign affairs', is head of the Chinese delegation at the Geneva Conference on Indochina.

LI Qiang 李強
Born 1905. Telecommunications specialist in the 20s. Part of a group studying the special techniques of secret communication in the French concession of Shanghai. Head of communications in Yan'an in the service of Kang Sheng. 1948–9: goes on a course in Moscow. After 1949: Minister of Telecommunications then, in 1970, Minister of Foreign Trade. 1986: member of the Consultative Commission of the CC of the CCP and president of the Sino-Rumanian Friendship Association.

LI Qiming 李啟明
Born 1908 in the Shaanxi province. 1944: assistant director of the *Gonganbu* for the Shaanxi–Gansu–Ningxia frontier government. 1947: assistant director of the *Shehuibu*, for the North-east China Bureau. 1950: director of the *Gonganbu* department for the North-west. 1977: member of the CC of the CCP. 1980: president of the administrative committee for the Centre of Children's Activities. 1983: vice-president of the Yunnan provincial committee of the CCP. Son-in-law of LI Kenong.

LI Qingquan 李清泉
First ambassador in Switzerland from July 1959 to 1966, during the Cultural Revolution. Head of the first large Chinese communist espionage network in Europe at that time.

LI Shiying 李士英
1949–1952: director of the Shanghai *Gonganju*.

LI Tao 李濤
1936: organises the kidnapping of Chiang Kai-shek. In the 50s: head of military intelligence (*Qingbao*). 1972: same post. 1984: head of the Inspection and Discipline Commission, director of the Bureau of Foreign Affairs, first secretary of the Shenyang (Liaoning) Party Committee.

LI Weihan 李維漢 alias LUO Mai 羅邁 (1896–1984)
Born in the Hunan province. Co-founder of the CCP in France in 1922. Joined Mao Zedong during the Long March, having carried out clandestine work in Shanghai alongside Kang Sheng. 1948–64: direc-

tor of the UFWD. Disappears during the Cultural Revolution. Late 70s, adviser at the UFWD.

LI Woru 李握如
1979: head of the Yunnan CCP provincial committee. *Gonganbu* adviser. Dies in 1981.

LI Xiaohang 李曉航
1986: head of the *Gonganju* in Shanghai.

LI Xin 李新
Kang Sheng's secretary. 1982: director of the Party's Centre for Historic Research, a subsidiary of the Academy of Science.

LI Yimeng 李一泯
In the 30s: member of the Political Security Bureau (*Zhengzhi Baohuju*). In the 50s: leader of the World Peace Council. 1975: assistant director of the ILD. 1982 (?): ILD adviser.

LI Yunchuan 李雲川
Born 1919 in Shandong. Director of the unions' ILD. 1965–6: ambassador to Holland. 1970–6: to North Korea. 1976–81: to Switzerland. 1986: Vice-Minister of Labour and Personnel.

LI Zhen (1912–73) 李震
1947: political commissar of the brigade led by Deng Xiaopong. 1956: member of the CC of the CCP. Vice-Minister of the *Gonganbu*, replaces Xie Fuzhi at the head of this ministry in 1972. Assassinated the following year.

LI Zhongshi 李鍾奇
1964 until at least 1986: political commissioner of the PLA garrison in Beijing. 1966: involved in the Faradoux affair over recruitment of members of the French CP.

LIANG Guobin 梁国斌
Leading member of the Shanghai *Gonganju*, arrested in 1968 on the orders of Kang Sheng, together with HUANG Chibo and WANG Jian.

LIAO Chengyun – CHEN Yun's pseudonym.

LIAO Chengzhi (1908–1983) 廖承志
Born in Tokyo. Student leader in Canton, takes refuge in Japan in 1925, after the assassination of his father, Liao Zhongkai. End of 1920s: travels to Europe as a member of the Comintern; takes part in a mutiny. Arrested in Shanghai then released. Joins Mao's forces in 1934. 1938: director of the Xinhua press agency. Organises guerrilla

operations in the Guangdong, from Hong Kong, until 1942. Again imprisoned by the Guomindang. After 1949: distinguishes himself for his many activities in the international peace movement, the work of the 'united front' with regard to the Chinese overseas and Taiwan, as well as intelligence operations in Japan under cover of the Chinese Red Cross. 1958: president of the Afro-Asian Solidarity Committee. Supervises a number of propaganda and open intelligence operations for Kang Sheng, with whom he had worked in the Shanghai underground. Died in 1983, when he was about to become Vice-President of the Republic.

LIAO Heshu
1966: Chargé d'affaires at the Chinese embassy at The Hague. Official of the *Diorchabu*. 1969: goes over to the CIA who discover he is a false defector. Handed back to China in 1972(?).

LILLEY, James R.
Born 1928, in China, of American parents. Yale University. 1958: CIA officer in Manila. 1961: Phnom Penh. 1963: Bangkok. 1965: Vientiane. Hong Kong. 1969: 1973: first head of the CIA station in Beijing. President Reagan's adviser on China. 1986: ambassador to South Korea.

LING Yun 凌雲
Born 1917. 1949: head of the Second *Shehuibu* Bureau. In the 50s: director of the *Gonganju*, Canton 1964: Vice-Minister of the *Gonganbu*, and elected deputy of Shandong at the Third Congress of the People's National Congress. 1978: elected deputy for the municipality of Shanghai. 1979: member of the delegation led by Hua Guofeng in Europe. 1983: minister of the new *Guojia anquanbu*, of which he becomes the consultant on his retirement in September 1985.

LIU Changsheng (1904–1967) 劉長勝
Comintern sailor, takes part in a naval mutiny, specialises in trade union work. Early 1930s: works with Kang Sheng underground in Shanghai. 1942: head of the Bureau of Political Research (intelligence) of the CCP of East China. After 1949: member of the World Trades Unions Federation. 1960: president of the Sino-African Friendship Association. Assassinated in 1967 by the Red Guards.

LIU Fuzhi 劉復之
Born 1917. 1949: assistant director of the General Affairs Bureau of the *Gonganbu* at the same time as being director of the First section of the *Shehuibu*. 1964: vice-minister of the *Gonganbu*. 1982: various posts at the Ministry of Justice. 1983–5: minister of the *Gonganbu*.

LIU Minghui 劉明輝
1951: head of the *Gonganbu* in Chongqing.

LIU Ren 劉仁
Born 1905 in the Hebei province. 1958–66: head of the Chinese Trade Unions. Head of international relations, in particular with Kang Sheng with foreign trade unions and Marxist-Leninist organisations. Disappears during the Cultural Revolution; rehabilitated in 1979.

LIU Renjing 劉仁靜
Born 1902 in the Hubei province. Member of the CCP then leader of the Trotskyist group with Chen Duxiu, after studying in Moscow. Head of the intelligence service of the left-wing opposition. In 1929, in Turkey, visits Trotsky. On his return to China, goes over to the Guomindang, then back again to the CCP. 1986: works at the People's Publishing House (*Renmin Chubanshi*) which is directly dependent on the *Gonganbu*.

LIU Shaowen 劉少文
Born 1905 in Henan province. Studied in Moscow. In the First Army Front during the Long March. Political commissioner of various units, including the Country Army of North China. Responsible for the military section of the *Shehuibu*. On returning from the Korean War, head of the Pacific section of military intelligence (*Qingbao*). 1955: director of the *Qingbao*. Political commissioner of the Beijing garrison in the 1960s. 1978: Beijing deputy. 1981: adviser at GHQ of the PLA.

LIU Shouzhou 劉述周
Member of the UFWD, Shanghai, then assistant director of the same service from July 1955.

LIU Wei 劉偉
1949: vice-minister of the *Gonganbu*, head of the Eighth Department in charge of *Laogai*. In May 1955: Vice-Minister of Geology.

LIU Xiao 劉曉
Born 1907 in the Hunan province. 1927: clandestine trade unions work with Kang Sheng in Shanghai. 1934: cadre of the Long March. 1950: member of the Political and Military Council of East China. 1955–62: ambassador to Moscow. 1967: ambassador to Albania (purged in May 1968 by Kang Sheng). 1978: resurfaces.

LIU Youfa 劉友法
1973–77: head of the UFWD.

LIU Yufeng 劉雨峰
1959–63: embassy adviser in Indonesia. 1963–5: ambassador to

Burundi. 1980–5: ambassador to Gabon. 1986: vice-president of the Chinese Association for the Promotion of International Friendship.

LU Jianguang 呂 劍 光
1978: vice-minister of the *Gonganbu*. 1979: head of the *Gonganbu* delegation in Thailand.

LUO Qingchang 羅 青 長
Born 1920 in the Hubei province. 1937: Lin Boqu's secretary, CCP representative in Xi'an. 1947: head of the First Section of the *Shehuibu*. 1954: assistant head of the Prime Minister's bureau. In 1961: on the death of LI Kenong, the *Shehuibu* becomes the Investigation Bureau of the CC, *Diaochabu*. Luo becomes assistant director, from 1966 until the present day. 1982: deputy for Sichuan. (In November 1978: is part of the delegation led by WANG Dongxing in Cambodia.) Considered as one of the most important heads of the secret services and is an expert on the struggle against Taiwan.

LUO Ruiqing (1906–1978) 罗 瑞卿
Born in the Sichuan province, political commissioner of the Red Army during the Long March. 1949–59: *Gonganbu* minister. Chief-of-staff from 1959, under the command of LIN Bao, until his dismissal in 1966. Rehabilitated in 1975.

LUO Yinong 羅 亦 農
1921: student communist sympathiser. In Moscow, University of the Peoples of the Orient (KUTVA). 1926–7: regional secretary of the CCP for Shanghai. Head of the counter-espionage section, liaising with Achinin, the Russian head of the OGPU. Captured and executed by the Guomindang in April 1928.

MA Jiajun 馬 家 俊
1960: first secretary in Rangoon, then Yang Xiaonong's assistant at the Xinhua press agency in Paris. Consul until the establishment of official Franco-Chinese diplomatic relations. 1965–70: counsellor at the London embassy. Since September 1981: assistant commander of the PLA in Ningxia.

MAGNIEN, Marius, alias 'Rondet' (1903–1962)
Student at the Leninist School in Moscow (1927), works for the anti-militarist section of the Comintern. In France, one of the representatives along with Jacques Duclos of the special services in the CP apparatus (notably at the newspaper *L'Humanité*). During the Moscow trials, publishes *Trotskyism, Terrorism at the Service of the Fascists*. During the war, organises Russian eavesdropping facilities for the clandestine leadership of the CP, liaising with their Service B. 1950: goes to China and meets a number of leaders including Mao. Author

of two works on China: *La Guerre en Manchourie et le rôle de l'imperialisme français* (*War in Manchuria and the Role of French Imperialism*) published by CDLP, Paris, 1932; *Au pays de Mao Tsé-Toung* (*In the Land of Mao Zedong*), Editions Sociales, 1952.

MARTCHENKO, Vladimir Ivanovitch
First secretary of the Soviet embassy in Beijing, head of the KGB expelled for espionage in 1974.

MENG Zhaoliang (1916–1980) 孟 昭 亮
Born in the Hubei province, *Gonganbu* adviser.

MEYNIER, Commander Robert (Henri Auguste)
Born 1906. 1916: joins the Navy. Giraud supporter, former submarine commander at the beginning of Second World War; organises an intelligence network in China with DAI Li under the aegis of SACO, together with his wife, the Vietnamese princess Katiou Do Hun Tinh. 1947: forms a Vietnamese social democrat party in Saigon. Promoted to vice-admiral in 1960.

MIN Buying 閔 步 瀛
Director of the *Guoanbu* bureau in Beijing since December 1983.

NGUYEN Thi Minh Khai (1910–1941)
Leader of the Vietnamese schoolchildren's movement. 1930: liaison agent between the Indochinese CP and the CCP in Hong Kong. 1935: delegate at the Seventh Comintern Congress. 1937: member of the Party committee in Saigon. 1941: leads the Nam Bô uprising, arrested by the French criminal investigation department, dies under torture.

OU Tangliang 區 棠 亮
Assistant director of the ILD in 1978. 1986: ILD adviser, member of the Committee for Foreign Affairs, vice-president of the People's Association for Peace and Disarmament.

PAN Zhenwu 潘 振 武
Born 1908. 1938: head of a sub-department for clandestine work in the enemy zone. Member of the political department of the Eighth Route Army. 1959–63: military attaché in Moscow. 1965: leading member of the committee for Afro-Asian solidarity. 1970: member of the Hubei provincial committee.

PEERS, William Raymond
Born 1914. Commander of Detachment 101 in China, with the Guomindang. 1949: head of training at the CIA. 1951: head of the CIA station in Taiwan (with particular responsibility for training the

special Taiwanese commandos operating on the mainland). In the 1970s: lieutenant-general, head of the commission investigating the My Lai massacre in Vietnam.

PENG Di 彭迪
Correspondent for the Xinhua press agency in Berne, expelled from Italy for espionage in 1960. 1973–7: assistant director of the Xinhua editorial office. 1980: opens the agency's offices in New York and Washington.

PENG Mingzhi 彭明治
1950–2: ambassador to Poland. 1969: military chief in Beijing. 1974: head of military intelligence (*Qingbao*); PLA chief-of-staff. 1978: elected to the Fifth National Congress.

QIAN Liren 钱李仁
1983: director of the ILD. Previously, permanent delegate at UNESCO.

QIAN Zhuangfei 錢壯飛
Member of a special section with LI Kenong, end of the 1920s, in Shanghai, responsible for infiltrating the Guomindang's special services.

QIAO Shi 喬石 (Real name: Jiang Zhaoming)
Born 1924. In the 1960s: secretary of the Afro-Asian Solidarity Committee before the Cultural Revolution. 1978: assistant director of the ILD, then director of the same service in 1982 (during this period, pays several visits to Rumania and Yugoslavia). 1985: member of the CCP Politburo and of the CC secretariat. 1986: head of the group for the Rectification of Workstyle in the Party and director of the Commission of Laws and Political Science. April 1986: Vice-Prime Minister and coordinator of the security services.

RUAN Chongwu 阮崇武
Born 1933. End of the 1970s: deputy mayor of Shanghai; scientific attaché at the Bonn embassy in West Germany, then head of the Institute of Research in Shanghai. September 1985: replaces LIU Fuzhi at the head of the *Gonganbu* until April 1987. Replaced by WANG Fang.

SHEN Jian 申健
Born 1923. 1950: embassy adviser in India. 1960: member of the Council of the China-Latin America Friendship Association. 1971: ILD official. 1973: assistant director of the ILD. Head of the Wuhan (Hubei) company of acrobats, goes on a number of trips to South America and elsewhere. 1978: member of the delegation in Cambodia led by WANG Dongxing.

SHEN Zhiyue 沈之岳
Nationalist secret agent. Born 1918 in the Zhejiang province. Studies at the Guomindang central police academy. Sent with several others as a pro-communist student to Yan'an to infiltrate the communist base. Retreats to Taiwan. 1958–60: assistant director of the Investigation Bureau of the Ministry of Justice (*Fawubu Diaochaju*). 1960–3: director of intelligence at the Ministry of Defence (*Qingbao Ju*), member of the Guomindang Central Committee. 1964–8: director of the Investigation Bureau of the Ministry of Justice. 1978–9: director of the Department for Social Affairs.

SHEN Zu 沈醉
Former assistant to DAI Li in the secret services of the Guomindang. Prisoner of the communists 1949–60, publishes a number of works on the Guomindang special services: *Wo suo zhidao de Dai Li* (1964), *Juntong neimu* (1980); in English: *A KMT War Criminal in New China* (1986).

SHI Jinqian 史进前
1980: director of the Department of Security of the Political Department of PLA staff headquarters.

SHI Peipu 时佩璞
Singer at the Peking Opera, arrested in France for espionage for the *Tewu* in July 1983 with the diplomat Bernard Boursicot.

SHI Yizhi 施义之
1973–6: vice-minister of the *Gonganbu*.

SMEDLEY Agnes (1894–1950)
Born in Colorado, USA. 1925: marries the communist Wu Shaogua, in Germany. Mistress of the Indian communist Virendranath Chattopadhyaya. Goes to Moscow as correspondent for the *Frankfurterzeitung*. 1929: liaison agent for the Richard Sorge network (under the name of Madame Petroikos). In Xi'an in 1936, then the following year in Yan'an. On her death, her possessions and her ashes are given to Marshal Zhu De who buries them at Banaoshan, the cemetery for CCP dignitaries. Author of a number of works: *Red China on the March*, Hyperion, Conn. (1934).

SONG Enfan 宋恩繁
1970: counsellor at the Vienna embassy. Assistant director of the Bureau of General Affairs, Minister of Foreign Affairs (1980).

SONG Wenzhong 宋文中
1975: military attaché in Sweden. 1986: military attaché, Tokyo.

SONG: Zhiguang 宋之光
Born 1916 in the Guangdong. 1949: Tsinghua University. A year studying in Japan. 1950-4 : Embassy secretary in East Germany. 1964-70: counsellor in Paris (head of the *Diaochabu*), ambassador to East Germany (1970-2), Great Britain (1972-7), Japan (1982-5).

SONG Zhiying 宋志英
Director of the *Gonganting* in Canton (Guangdong), 1983-6. Replaced by WEN Guangzhi.

SOUDARIKOV, Nikolai Georgeyevich
Born 1913. Enters the NKVD in 1939, major in General Serov's special NKVD troops in 1943. 1956: becomes a diplomat (cover for the KGB): adviser in Beijing until 1962. Becomes a specialist on the Far East: ambassador to North Korea (1967-74), to Australia (1979).

STEPTOE, Harry Nathaniel (1892-1949)
Set up the Secret Intelligence Service (M16) networks in China (Chengdu, Xinjiang, Beijing and Shanghai). Arrested by the Japanese who believe he is a mere 'consul in Shanghai' in 1941. Exchanged in 1942, pursues his career in East Africa, then in Section XI (anti-communist) of the SIS under Kim Philby.

STRONG, Anna-Louise (1885-1970)
Born in Nebraska. Journalist. In the 1950s, founds the *Moscow Daily News*, then settles in Beijing in 1958. Arrested on a trip to the USSR as a spy.

SU Quande 苏荃德
Leading official of Detachment 8341.

SU Yiran 蘇毅然
1952: director of the *Gonganbu* for the administrative region of South Anhui. 1977: secretary of the CCP in Shandong. Elected member of the Eleventh CCP Congress.

TA Mok alias NGUON Kang
One of the three main Khmer Rouge leaders. Surfaces in 1978, at the time of the visit of the Chinese delegation led by WANG Dongxing. Head of the Khmer Rouge secret service SO-21 or *Nokorbal* together with Kaing Khek ('Deuch'). Organiser of purges and massacres in Democratic Kampuchea. Promoted to third highest position in the hierarchy of the Khmer Communist Party after the invasion of Cambodia by the Vietnamese in 1979. Military second-in-command of the Khmer Rouge guerrilla troops.

TAN Shu 潭述
Leading official of Detachment 8341 in 1971.

TANG Mingzhao 唐明照
Assistant secretary of the Chinese delegation at the UN in the 1970s. In charge of liaising with the FNLA in Angola in 1973. ILD adviser in 1981. Vice-president of the Association for International Understanding, 1983.

TANG Yueliang alias Y. L. Tong. 唐悦良
Born 1888 in Shanghai. 1928: deputy minister of Foreign Affairs, after training in the USA and having been secretary of the legation in Cuba. Becomes head of the Guomindang external intelligence service, answerable to DAI Li, from 1932.

TAO Siju 陶駟駒
Vice-minister of the *Gonganbu*, 1984.

TAO Zhu 陶鑄
Born 1906, Hunan. 1927: organises the communist uprising in Canton. 1933: arrested by the Guomindang in Shanghai, makes his submission, released in 1938. 1942: member of the CCP military commission in Yan'an. 1945: with Lin Niao in Manchuria. Leader of the South, and in the Propaganda Department before the Cultural Revolution, persecuted by Kang Sheng, killed by the Red Guards in 1969.

TOLSTOY, Ilya, known as 'Bill'
Grandson of the writer Tolstoy, American citizen. Autumn 1942: sent by the OSS to Tibet on a mission concerning the Dalai Lama. After the War, film producer and sponge fisherman in the Bahamas.

TRAN Quôc Hoan 陳国环
Born 1910. Member of the Politburo of the Vietnamese Communist Party. 1951–75: Minister for Public Security (*Cong An Bô*). Dismissed from all his duties in 1979, at the time of the Sino-Vietnamese war.

WANG Deming 王德明
1950: major in the Korean War, then correspondent for the Xinhua press agency in Burma. Correspondent in Kenya, expelled for espionage in 1965. 1983: head of the international news desk of the daily newspaper, *Guangming*.

WANG Dong 王棟
1954: First embassy secretary in Tirana. 1964: chargé d'affaires in Rumania. July 1969: ambassador to Sweden. 1976: ambassador to Canada.

WANG Dongning 王東寧
1951–61: assistant director of the *Gonganbu* department in Hebei. 1962–8: director of the *Gonganbu* of that region.

WANG Dongxing 汪東興
Born 1916 in the Jiangxi region. From 1933, Mao's bodyguard. 1937: instructor for the Central Regiment of Guards. 1949: director of the Security Department of the CC of the CCP and assistant director of the *Gonganbu*'s Eighth Bureau (in charge of *Laogai*). From 1959: vice-minister of the *Gonganbu*. 1967: director of the General Affairs Bureau of the CC, head of Detachment 8341. 1969: elected to the CC. 1973: promoted to the Politburo. 1976: organises the arrest of the Gang of Four. 1978: deputy for Beijing. Head of a delegation to Cambodia. 1980: loses his positions on the CC and in the government. 1982: is no more than a deputy member of the CC (after 1973, he succeeded Kang Sheng).

WANG Fang 王芳
Born 1921. 1949: political commissar 94th Division, 32nd Army, 3rd Field Army. Career in Public Security Department (*Gonganbu*) in Zhejiang, of which he becomes director in 1955. 1964: vice-governor of Zhejiang, purged as 'counter-revolutionary' during the Culture Revolution. Resurfaces in 1977. From 1979, vice-chairman of the People's Congress in Zhejiang province as well as deputy secretary of the CP. Married to LIU Xin. As of 11 April 1987 (the fall of HU Yaobang), becomes Minister for Public Security, replacing RUAN Chongwu.

WANG Jian 王鑒
Gonganbu official for Shanghai in 1968, arrested with LIANG Guobin and Huang Chibo, at Kang Sheng's instigation. 1977: vice-president of the Revolutionary Committee of Shanghai; member of the executive committee of the municipality of Shanghai. End 1979: deputy mayor of Shanghai.

WANG Jingrong
Spokesman for the *Gonganbu* in 1984.

WANG Jinxiang 汪金样
Born 1908 in Jiangxi. Director of the *Gonganbu* department for the Administrative Council for North-east China. 1954: vice-minister of the *Gonganbu* until the Cultural Revolution. Very close to LUO Ruiqing. 1975: resurfaces in the same post. 1982: vice-minister of the *Gonganbu*. Dies in 1983.

WANG Jun 王珺
Vice-minister of the *Gonganbu*.

WANG Li 王力
Head of the *Diaochabu*'s Department Nine, in 1970 attacks the Bureau of State Secrets with his Detachment 516. 1978: member of the Sixth National Congress, registered as 'non-Party'.

WANG Liangen 王良恩
1970s: Assistant director to WANG Dongxing at the General Affairs Bureau of the CC of the CCP.

WANG Lubin 王路賓
1950: assistant director of the *Gonganbu* department of Pingyuan.

WANG Ning 王宁
1964: director of the *Gonganting* in Canton. 1977: vice-president of the Revolutionary Committee of Canton. 1979: deputy governor of Canton. 1983: deputy secretary of the Fifth Guandong Provincial Committee.

WANG Rongyuan 王榮元
1970s: senior official in Detachment 8341.

WANG Shide alias WANG Zhuyu 王世德
Section leader of the stormtroopers of the clandestine CCP in Shanghai, the Red Guard. Goes over to the Guomindang after his arrest in August 1931.

WANG Shu 王殊
Correspondent for the Xinhua press agency in Ghana (1959), in the Congo (1961) and in Cuba (1962). Ambassador to West Germany then to Austria. 1977: editor of the theoretical review *Red Flag* (*Hongqi*).

WANG Wentong 王文同
1982: vice-minister of the *Gonganbu* and (1983) member of the ruling group for the rehabilitation of retired officials and soldiers.

WANG Xiaoyu 王效禹
'The Hemp Master of Shandong'. Friend of Kang Sheng. Political commissioner for a unit of the PLA in 1942. 1946: assistant prosecutor for Shandong. At the beginning of the 1960s: deputy mayor of Qingdao. Organises the struggle against Liu Shaoqi–Deng Xiaoping in Shandong. 1967: president of the Shandong provincial revolutionary committee and regional military leader. 1969: at the Ninth Congress of the CCP, elected to the CC. Organises the opium trade for the special services.

WANG Zhi 王之
Born 1906. 1946–7: director of the Guomindang Military Intelligence (*Qingbao*). 1949: assistant commander of the *Qingbao* garrison. Author of *Mao Zedong's Thought on Military Insurrection*.

WANG Zigang 汪子剛
1970s: senior official of Detachment 8341.

WEI Dong 韋東
1970: assistant to Ambassador Huang Zhen in Paris. Organises Kissinger's visit to China. 1985: ambassador to Morocco. 1987: ambassador to Madagascar.

WEI Guoqing 韋國清
Born 1906. Leader of the PLA. 1951: senior official with the Public Security forces of Fujian (opposite Taiwan). Together with CHEN Geng, masterminds the strategy trust which enables Van Giap to win the battle of Dien Bien Phu. 1982: political commissioner of the air force. Purged.

WEN Guangzhi 文廣智
1986: director of the Canton *Gonganbu* and political commissar of the Provincial People's Armed Police Corps.

WEN Minsheng 文敏生
Career in Security. 1953: assistant director of the *Gonganbu* of the administrative and military council of Central and Southern China. 1955: director of the *Shehuibu* for South China. 1984: adviser to the Minister for Post and Telecommunications.

WU Defeng 吳德峰 alias WU Chongshi 吳崇實 (1895–1976)
Takes part in the 1927 uprising in the Jubei, his native province. During the Long March, member of political security body (*Zhengzhi baohuju*) of the Fourth Army. 1936: head of the special services of Xi'an, then in charge of the intelligence school. Works for Kang Sheng in the northern provinces. Leading a political career in his native province, he pursues special activities under the supervision of LUO Ruiqing, XIE Fuzhi and Kang Sheng.

WU Li-chun, General 吳利君
1943: assistant to the head of the psychological warfare section of the joint Sino-American Intelligence organisation in Chongqing. Collaborator with the head of the CIA station in Taiwan, Ray S. Cline. Professor at the University of Tamking. Adviser to the Chinese section of the World Anti-communist League (WACL).

WU Xuewen 吳學文
Journalist with the Xinhua press agency, expelled from Japan in 1964 for espionage. May 1985: becomes adviser at the Institute of Contemporary International Relations, a subsidiary body of the Academy of Science (actually a *Guoanbu* institute).

XI Guogang 席國光
1978: vice-minister of the *Gonganbu*. 1982: adviser to the same ministry.

XIE Fuzhi (1897–1972) 謝富治

Trained as a soldier. 1959–72: minister of Public Security (*Gonganbu*), and in this capacity Kang Sheng's assistant. Also head of the People's Liberation Army Security Forces. Trips to the Balkans (Albania, Rumania), organises liaison between the special services; in the Arab countries talks with Ben Bella and Nasser. Kidnapped in July 1967 by Detachment 8201 at the time of the 'Wuhan incident'. End of 1967: president of the Beijing Revolutionary Committee. Expelled posthumously in 1980 from the CCP together with Kang Sheng. His wife, LIU Xiangping, was deputy for the Yunnan.

XIE Li 謝黎

1960s: chargé d'affaires in The Hague, maintains relations with the Belgian pro-Chinese. November 1963: disappears during the entire Cultural Revolution. 1978: general secretary of the Institute of Foreign Affairs. 1983: ambassador to Yugoslavia.

XU Jinaguo 徐建國

Born in the Hubei. 1938: director of the *Shehuibu* on the Shaanxi-Qahar–Hebei border. 1949: director of the *Gonganbu* in Tianjin, then end of 1951 in Shanghai. 1954: vice-minister of the *Gonganbu*. Ambassador to Rumania (1959), then Albania (1964). Disappears during the Cultural Revolution. 1983: director of the National Import–Export Packaging Company.

XU Dunxin 徐敦信

Head of the secret services, *Guoanbu*, in Tokyo in 1986. Officially minister/counsellor to the embassy. 1983: director of the Japanese affairs division at the Ministry of Foreign Affairs. 1984: under-director of the department of Asian affairs. Replaced in 1988 by Tang Jiaxuan.

XU Sheng 徐生

1983: director of the *Gonganbu* in the province of Liaoning in 1983.

XU Shiguang 許士光

Official in Detachment 8341. 1988: becomes Liaoning's Provincial Seventh People's Congress Chief Procurator, replaced as head of Public Security Department (*Gonganting*) by Guo Dawei.

XU Zicai

1966: Chinese engineer assassinated in The Hague by his *Diaochabu* compatriots, which led to the expulsion of the chargé d'affaires, LI Enqiu, in July.

XU Zirong 徐子榮

Born 1908 in Henan. 1949: senior official of the *Gonganbu*.

YAN Youmin 严佑民
Born 1918 in the Shaanxi region. 1964: vice-minister of the *Gonganbu*: 1968: accused by the Red Guards of being a supporter of LUO Ruiqing. 1979: secretary of the municipality of Shanghai.

YANG Dezhong 楊德中
1964: director of a department in the *Gonganbu*. Secretary in charge of protecting Zhou Enlai. 1969: president of the Revolutionary Committee of the University of Beijing. Visits Korea with Zhou. A protégé of WANG Dongxing, he becomes his assistant at the General Affairs Bureau of the CC of the CCP. October 1979: accompanies Hua Guofeng and LING Yun to France, West Germany, Great Britain and Italy. Identified as head of the Guards department of the *Gonganbu*. 1983: assistant director of the Bureau of General Affairs.

YANG Fan 楊帆
Assistant-director of the *Gonganbu* in Shanghai, expelled from the Party with Pan Hannian in July 1955. Condemned in 1959 as a 'counter-revolutionary' and disappears, during the purges following the Gao Gang affair.

YANG Jinren 楊靜仁
Member of the Hui minority. 1941: chief-of-staff of a muslim cavalry brigade. 1978: assistant director of the UFWD. 1982: director of the same department.

YANG Jiqing 楊奇清
Born 1908 in Hunan. Specialist in security. In 1949: director of the Bureau of Public Protection (*Zhengzhi Baohuju*) part of the *Gonganbu*. Vice-minister of Public Security until his arrest in March 1968 as a 'revisionist'. (In 1955, adviser to Zhou Enlai at the Bandung Conference, and in 1962, head of the special delegation to the fortieth anniversary of the Mongolian Ministry of Public Security). Resurfaces in 1974, becomes a member of the Praesidium of the CC of the CCP.

YANG Qiqing (1911–1978) 楊奇清
1954: vice-minister of the *Gonganbu*. Disappears during the Cultural Revolution. Resurfaces in 1978, as a member of the *Gonganbu* Party Committee.

YANG Shangkun 楊尚昆
Born 1905 in Sichuan. 1926: studies at the Sun Yat-sen University in Moscow. One of the 'Twenty-eight Bolsheviks' 1945–66: head of the General Affairs Bureau of the CCP (specialist in phone-tapping). Close to Liu Shaoqi. In August 1966, accused of having 'spied on Mao Zedong for the USSR'. Rehabilitated in 1978.

1987: member of the Politburo of the CCP and secretary general/ vice president of the very important Military Commission of the CC. April 1988: elected President of the Republic of China.

YANG Xiaonong 楊效農
1957: director of the Xinhua press agency in Paris and Berne. Directs a number of secret operations in Africa, notably in the Congo in the 1960s. Considered by Western counter-espionage as one of the main *Tewu* agents in Europe. 1983: member of the press and publications circle of the CC of the CCP.

YANG Yuheng 楊玉衡
1970: official of the ILD (June: in the company of Kang Sheng, receives Kadri Jabiu, official of the Albanian Interior Ministry and its Secret Services).

YANG Zhihua (1900–1973) 楊之華
Wife of Qu Qiubai. With Kang Sheng in USSR in 1935. Represents the International Red Cross in China. 1966: arrested and accused of committing treason in Xinjiang in 1941 by Kang Sheng. Dies in prison.

YAO Lun 姚伦
1979: assistant director of the *Gonganbu*. 1984: adviser to the same ministry.

YU Lei 俞雷
November 1983: vice-minister of the *Gonganbu*.

YU Qiaqing (1865–1951?) 虞洽卿
Born near Ningbo (Zhejiang), director of the Sanpeh Steam Navigation Company in Shanghai and of a number of enterprises. 1925: elected president of the Chinese General Chamber of Commerce. 1929: elected municipal councillor for Shanghai. Assistant to DU Yuesheng in the secret society of the Green Gang (*Quingbang*) which controls the opium trade and prostitution, and linked to the Guomindang secret services. In 1931, Kang Sheng becomes his private secretary.

YU Sang 于桑
Specialist in counter-espionage. 1951: travels to Rumania and East Germany with Marshal Zhu De. 1961: leading member of the China-Latin America Association. 1964: vice-minister of the *Gonganbu*. 1969: elected member of the CC of the CCP at the Ninth Congress. 1971 and 1972: responsible for the protection of the Kissinger and Nixon visits to China. At the same time, is part of the special commission on the Lin Biao affair. 1975: attends Kang Sheng's funeral. 1982: elected deputy to the CC. Disappears.

YU Xiusong (1898–1937) 俞秀松
Born in the Zhejiang province, communist from the very beginning. Studies in 1925 at the Sun Yat-sen University, then at the Comintern's Leninist School, head of the Moscow section of the CCP. Sent to Siberia, at the request of Wang Ming and Kang Sheng. November 1937: assassinated by the same in the Xinjiang.

YU Zhensan 俞真三
Head of the Bureau of External Affairs of the *Guoanbu*. Adoptive son of Kang Sheng. Defects to the West at the beginning of 1986.

YUE Xin 岳欣
1963: head of an office of the *Gonganbu*. Accompanies Liu Shaoqi on a trip around Asia in the spring. 1965: ambassador to Finland. 1974: ambassador to Togo. 1984: vice-president of the China-Korea Friendship Association.

ZENG Sheng 曾生
Born 1910, in the Guangdong. Real name: Zen Zhensheng. Studied in Hong Kong and Australia. 1935: the CCP gives him the task of organising the Hong Kong Seamen's Association. 1937–47: organises various guerrilla movements. From 1950: high-up civil and military responsibilities in Guangdong (in particular supervises the opium trade in the Rivers of Pearls region). Appointed deputy admiral; disappears for seven years, severely criticised during the Cultural Revolution (1967–74). Becomes Minister of Communications in 1979.

ZENG Tao 曾涛
1960: head of the Xinhua office in Havana, negotiates diplomatic relations with Cuba. 1962–6: first ambassador to Algeria. Several times head of the Western section at the Ministry of Foreign Affairs.

ZENG Wei 曾威
1973–5: vice-minister of the *Gonganbu*.

ZENG Zhaoke. 曾昭科 (alias John TSANG)
Teaches at the Hong Kong Police School. Ruling official of the *Tewu*. Expelled in 1964. Professor at the University of Jinan (Shandong). Vice-president of the executive committee of the Canton Popular Congress in 1985. Continues his intelligence work on Hong Kong.

ZHANG, Nikolai Petrovich
Chinese of Soviet nationality, recruited in May 1971 by the GRU (intelligence service of the Far East military region of the USSR), arrested on 20 June 1974 by Chinese border guards in the Aihui region. Sentenced to seven years' imprisonment for espionage on 20 July 1980.

ZHANG Guotao (1897–1979) 張国燾

Born in the Jiangxi. Founder of the CCP, member of the leadership. Opposes Mao in 1935 and goes over to the Guomindang in 1938. Becomes one of the experts in the special anti-communist political section of Dai Li's special services. In exile in Taiwan, Hong Kong and Canada, where he dies. The archetypal traitor in the CCP historiography.

ZHANG Hanzi 張漢滋

1985: director of the *Gonganbu* in Shanghai, replaced in 1986 by LI Xiaohang.

ZHANG Li 張立

Kang Sheng's granddaughter. Head of the Red Guards during the Cultural Revolution. Deputy for Henan at the Fifth National Congress in 1978. Disappears . . .

ZHANG Nansheng 張甬生

Born 1908, Fujian. 1934–5: first political commissioner of intelligence and public security in the Political Security Bureau (*Zhengzhi Baohuju*). 1978: member of the National Committee of the Fifth CC of the CCP.

ZHANG Pi 張玉

Director of the *Gonganbu* of the Anhui and political commissioner of the Armed Police Corps, 1983.

ZHANG Qirui 張其瑞

1975–6: *Gonganbu* leader.

ZHANG Songsheng 張崧生

Leader of the Red Guard. Arrested in August 1931 by the Guomindang.

ZHANG Tong 張彤

Born 1919. 1959–60: military attaché in India. 1961: chargé d'affaires in Congo, supports the Gizenga guerrillas. 1974: ambassador to Egypt; 1977: to West Germany. 1982: head of Bureau of Foreign Affairs at the Ministry of Defence.

ZHANG Weilin 張蔚林

Agent of the communist secret services who organises at the beginning of the 1940s a network within the listening station of Dai Li's intelligence service, responsible for intercepting communist transmissions.

ZHANG Xiufu 張秀夫
Director of the Zhejiang *Gonganbu*, 1983. 1985: political commissar, Headquarters of Chinese People's Armed Police.

ZHANG Yaoci 張耀詞
Member of the Praesidium of the Ninth Congress of the CCP in 1969. Member of Zhou Enlai, Zhu De and Mao Zedong's funeral committee in 1976. Ruling member of the Guards division of Detachment 8341. WANG Dongxing's assistant at the General Affairs Bureau of the CC in 1978.

ZHANG Youheng 張友恒
1981: director of the *Gonganbu*. Becomes director of the Canton office of the new *Guoanbu*, whose task it is to spy on Hong Kong in 1983. Replaced by YE Jinmei in 1987.

ZHANG Zishi 張子石
Son of Kang Sheng and CAO Yi-ou. Born in Shandong. 1967: leading member of the Shandong Revolutionary Committee. July 1975: first secretary of the CCP in Hangzhou, Zhejiang, and vice-president of the provincial revolutionary committee. Disappears in April 1978. In his speech of 9 November 1978 in front of the Party School, concerning the Kang Sheng affair, Hu Yaobang utters strange words: 'We should take care of and provide for Kang Sheng's children, family and friends, who were proved by the enquiry to have had no connection with the Gang of Four. One exception: Cao Yi-ou who persists in her errors. Death is to be the road taken by Zhang Zishi (Kang Sheng's son) who persists in his errors and refuses to be reeducated.'

ZHAO Cangbi 趙蒼壁
1950: assistant director of the *Gonganbu* for the administrative and military committee of South-west China. 1956: director of the *Gonganbu* for Sichuan. 1979–83: minister of the *Gonganbu*. 1983: member of the consultative commission of the CC.

ZHAO Fu 趙夫
Head of the security service for the Chinese embassy in Sweden, went over to the CIA in 1962.

ZHAO Yaobin 趙耀斌
Cabinet chief and Kang Sheng's secretary in the *Shehuibu*, in Yan'an in the 1940s. Sent into the 'white zone' to carry out clandestine work, went over to the Guomindang in 1947 (or 1949?). Subsequently becomes head of the research division of Military Intelligence (*Qingbao Ju*) in Taiwan where he dies in 1984.

ZHENG Zoukang (Tcheng Tsou-K'ang) 鄭祖康
1950: director of the Bank of Communications, Saigon, linked with Lucas Pun in the piastres affair.

ZHOU Xing 周興
In the 1930s, head of the Political Security Bureau (*Zhengzhi Baoweiju*). 1967: political commissioner for the military district of Yunnan.

ZHU Bingliang 朱炳亮
1970: head of Lin Biao's security forces.

ZHU Entao 朱恩濤
Assistant director of the Bureau of International Cooperation of the *Gonganbu*, member of the Interpol executive in 1986.

ZHU Jiayao 祝家犾
1975–6, leader of the *Gonganbu*.

ZHU Liang 朱　朱良
1981: assistant director of the ILD. 1985: director of the ILD and vice-president of the Chinese People's Association for Peace and Disarmament.

ZHUO Xiong 卓雄
Born 1916 in Manchuria. 1949: *Gonganbu* director, in charge of Bureau 81955, vice-minister for geology until the Cultural Revolution. 1978: Resurfaces as vice-minister for civil affairs.

ZOU Dapeng (1902–1966) 鄒大鵬
1941: section head of the CCP's Military Commission department. 1948: mayor of Zhanzhun. 1949: general secretary of the *Shehuibu*. 1952: head of the Third Bureau of the CC of the CCP and assistant director of the *Shehuibu*, directed by LI Kenong. 1956: vice-president of the Commission for Cultural Relations with foreign countries. On the death of Li Kenong in 1961, the *Shehuibu*, the central intelligence organ, becomes the *Diaochabu*, and Zou becomes its head. 1966: assassinated. LUO Qingchang takes his place.

Notes and Sources

CHAPTER 1
A CHILD OF SHANDONG

p. 11 Cit. 'Revolutionary Democracy' in Lenin, *Pravda*, no. 100, 6 May 1913.

p. 16 *Le Rêve dans le Pavillon Rouge (The Dream of the Red Chamber)*, Ed. Guy Le Prat, Paris, 1982. Hua Kun, in his article 'Expert de la Chambre de l'Ouest' ('Expert of the Chamber of the West') (*Spring & Autumn*, Hong Kong, no. 63, 1957), states that Kang Sheng has published comparative studies of the various accounts of the 'Chamber of the West'.

p. 18 Quotation 'Although he was about thirty' in Peng Shuzhi in his memoirs published by Claude Cadart and Cheng Xingxiang, *L'Envol du communisme en Chine (The Rise of Communism in China)*, Gallimard, Paris, 1983.

CHAPTER 2
RED SHANGHAI, WHITE SHANGHAI

p. 23 Quote from Boris Pilnak, *Journal de Chine*, Paris, L'Obsidiane, 1986.

CHAPTER 3
BIRTH OF THE *TEWU*

p. 45 Extract from a CCP pamphlet seized on 15 September 1928 at Amoy, quoted in police records from the French Concession, October 1928. An astonishing collection of brochures, leaflets and records have been discovered in the private museum of Taiwanese counter-espionage which is used in particular for the instruction of future officers.

CHAPTER 4
A MATTER OF BETRAYAL

p. 66 According to certain versions, Gu Shunzhang was betrayed by Kang Sheng. As far as we can make out, it was a version of events that both Beijing and Taipei endorsed later in order to demonstrate that for a long time Kang had yearned for the post of head of secret services. This theory is hardly credible, since it means that Kang Sheng had helped the Guomindang to destroy the services which he intended to manage and above all that he would have taken the risk himself of being caught. Nevertheless, some independent observers share this theory.

p. 71 Report by Louis Fabre, 1932, records of the Ministry of Foreign Affairs.

p. 72 The links between Du Yuesheng and the French, note of 16 June 1931 to the French consul in Shanghai, Mr Koechlin, to the Minister of Foreign Affairs, Aristide Briand. Letter of 19 February 1932 from Étienne Fiori, head of the police department of the French Concession of Shanghai. The constant ministerial reshuffles certainly benefited Koechlin and Fiori. At the time Fiori wrote his report, Briand had been replaced by Pierre Laval. But when the letter arrived in France, Laval gave his portfolio at the Quai d'Orsay up to André Tardieu.

p. 77 The commander Louis Fabre, depressed on account of being unable to join the free French in London, himself shot at the time of the invasion of the French Concession by the Japanese. Robert Jobez and his wife had already reached London by 1941 together with twenty-four policemen from the Concession. Under the pseudonym of Robert Magenoz, he is the author of two works – *De Confucius à Lénine* (*From Confucius to Lenin*), Saigon, Editions France-Asie and *L'Expérience communiste en Chine (De Confucius à la nouvelle démocratie) (The Communist Experience in China (From Confucius to the New Democracy))*, Paris, Les Iles d'Or, 1954.

p. 82 In the interview which she gave to the sinologist Roxane Witke (*Comrade Chiang Ch'ing*), Mao's wife omits to mention Yu Qiwei, but hints at the existence of Yu Shan, his sister. All her life, Jiang Qing glossed over this period of her life. Long Yucan was an official in the political police of the Guomindang, and heard the confessions of Yu Qiwei and Jiang Qing at the time. Later, under the pseudonym of 'The Old Dragon' (Lao Long), he published an extremely detailed biography of Jiang Qing (*Jiang Qing Waizhuan*). In the 1970s, Long Yucan was an analyst at the Taiwanese investigations bureau (*Fawabu Diaochaju*).

Australian sinologist Ross Terrill's version of the story differs slightly from the testimonies that we have put together, principally from Europe. However, his book, *The White-boned Demon*, New

York, William Morrow, 1984, basically reinforces the information gathered by the authors on the subject of the relationship between Kang Sheng and Jiang Qing (testimonies of Ding Wang, Lu Keng, James Yi and Hsia Chih-yen).

CHAPTER 5
A CHINESE IN RUSSIA

p. 86 The arrest of Liao Chengzhi. Under the false name of He Liuhua, Liao was arrested with one of his comrades Luo Denxian, one of the few communists with a working-class background. He was immediately shot by the Guomingdang. He was also a friend of Kang Sheng, as demonstrated in the long biographical piece which he dedicated to him in 1936 in a book published in Moscow, namely, *Biographies de martyres (Zhongguo Gongchandang Lieshizhuan)*.

p. 88 The presence of Kang Sheng in Moscow around 1928 is still much debated. There is reason to believe that the OGPU, who organised the Chinese Party's Sixth Congress in the outskirts of Moscow prevented the appearance of their protégé for reasons of security.

p. 99 Quotation from Pieck, in Ypsilon, *Pattern of a Worlds Revolution*, La Table Ronde, 1948.

p. 101 Quotation from Nguyen Thi Minh Kai in *La Femme au Vietnam (The Woman in Vietnam)*, Hanoi, Editions Langues Etrangères (Foreign Language Editions), 1976.

CHAPTER 6
THE KIDNAPPING OF CHIANG KAI-SHEK

p. 109–10 Quotation from Chiang Kai-shek, *Les Origines du drame chinois*, (*Origins of Chinese Drama*), Paris, Gallimard, 1938.

p. 111 The Liaison Office. Among the communist heads of the Xi'an Bureau was Li Tao, a specialist in military information (and moreover head of this section after 1949). He was, with General Xuan Xiafu, an old pupil of the Huangpu Military Academy and a colleague of Chiang Kai-shek. Dai Li's secret service, the BIS, kidnapped, strangled and threw him into a dry well in spite of the Xi'an agreements.

P. 113–14 The Sheng Shicai incident. The principal protagonist wrote his memoirs: Allen S. Whitting, General Sheng Shih-ts'ai, *Sinkiang, Pawn or Pivot*, Michigan, 1958. In his fascinating book, *Setting the East Ablaze – Lenin's Dream of an Empire of Asia* (London, John Murray, 1984), *Times* reporter Peter Hopkirk dedicates several pages to the Sheng Shicai affair (although he does so without mentioning either Kang Sheng or Chen Yun). This book, on the strategy of the Comintern in Asia at the beginning of the 1920s, is particularly invaluable since the author had access to the British colonial archives as well as those of the Intelligence Service.

'The Bureau of the Eighth Route Army repeatedly asked Jiang Dingwen (local head of the BIS) for the return of Xuan Xiafu, and the Yan'an authorities made an official protest to Chiang Kai-shek, asking him to release Xuan Xiafu. Chiang Kai-shek admitted his part in Xuan's death: "Xuan Xiafu was my student. . . . Since he had betrayed me I had him killed . . ." '

p. 116 Discussions with Stalin, quoted in *Kang Sheng he Mao Zedong* in *Zhenming*, 1 August 1980, Hong Kong.

CHAPTER 7
KANG SHENG THE MATCHMAKER

p. 122 Meeting between Jiang Qing and Kang Sheng. Lao Long, *Jiang Qing Waizhuan*, op. cit. The wife of Wang Jiaxiang, who was in Moscow at the same time as Kang Sheng and Wang Ming, and after 1949 became Ambassador in the USSR, was from Yan'an. She was called Zhu Zhongli but she published a biography under the name of Zhu Shan, namely, *Jiang Qing Ye Shi* (less reliable than the above mentioned book).

Interview with Ding Wang, Hong Kong, June 1986 (namely the author of *Biographie critique de Hua Guofeng* [*Critical Biography of Hua Guofeng*] (*Hua Guofeng pingzhuan*, Tokyo, 1978)

Ross Terrill's *The White-boned Devil*, op. cit., is a good summary of the original information regarding the meeting and marriage of Jiang Qing and Mao. However, in the interview she agreed to give to Roxane Witke, Jiang Qing underplays Kang's role: 'Her close friend and confidant was Kang Sheng who was delighted at the marriage because this would give him access to the Chairman.'

p. 128 Speech by Luo Ruiqing, 3 December 1942.

CHAPTER 9
THE INVENTION OF MAOISM

p. 160–1 Quotations taken from the records of the French Deuxième Bureau, January 1935.

CHAPTER 11
CIVIL WAR IN CHINA

p. 187 Regarding Lin Biao and more generally the military structure of that period, it is worth referring to the works of General Guillermaz. French staff officers have made a particular study of these events. Note General L-M Chassin, *La Conquête de la Chine par Mao Tse-toung* (*The Conquest of China by Mao Zedong*), Payot, Paris, 1952 and the book written by an old specialist on the Communist world: Michel Garder, *Mao Tse-toung*, Paris, La Table Ronde.

It is not an accident that neither the historians of the Chinese Communist Party nor those of the Guomindang have been able to carry out much of a comprehensive study on the civil war. The passing from one camp to the other – very common at the time – the intrigues, the secret negotiations, the multiple acts of betrayal, the dubious role of the special services, the eliminations and massacres by one army on the march to victory and the other making its escape does little service to either Beijing or Taipei.

p. 192-4 On the death of Dai Li: several other causes are often mentioned. 1. He was murdered by his rival in the secret services, Chen Lifu, on Chiang Kai-shek's instructions. (Account of Pierre Laurin on the rumours circulating at the time in Hong Kong, July 1986.) 2. A bomb was placed in the plane. Account/evidence of Oliver Caldwell to the authors, July 1986, confirming his work: *A Secret War*, The Southern Illinois University Press, 1972. Constantin Rissov, author of *Le Dragon Enchaîné*, Paris, Robert Laffont, 1986, and who had a brush with Dai Li's secret services, states: 'According to books (in Chinese) by Shen Zui (one of Dai Li's lieutenants) published in Beijing in 1962 and 1984 under the titles *Wo suo zhidao de Dai Li* and *Juntong neimu*, Dai Li's plane crash was accidental and due to bad weather. However, it is necessary to mention that Shen Zui had changed sides and wrote what he was told to write by his new masters. If there had been an assassination attempt, I personally think that the guilty men were more likely to be Dai Li's enemies within the Guomindang itself.' (4 August 1986).

CHAPTER 12
LAOGAI, THE CHINESE GULAG

P. 206 Quotation from *People's Daily*, 25 March 1951.
P. 212 Quoted in Marius Magnien, *Au pays de Mao Tse-toung* (*In the Land of Mao Zedong*), Paris, Éditions Sociales, 1952.

CHAPTER 13
RED FLAG OVER ASIA

p. 235 Wilfred Burchett died in Sofia, Bulgaria, in 1983. The purpose of his last campaign was to demonstrate that the Bulgarian secret services were innocent in the assassination attempt of Pope John Paul II.

p. 235–6 Quote from Mao Zedong in *Selected Works*, vol. V.

p. 240 The engagement of Larry Wu Tai Chin by Liao Chengzhi is still open to debate – Asian and American sources differ. We will have to wait for access to CIA records at the beginning of the next millennium.

CHAPTER 14
KANG SHENG'S A-BOMB

p. 252–4 The reported remarks of Kang Sheng are pieced together in the account of the scholar Tang Pa Chek at the International Agency of Atomic Energy in Vienna, quoted in Michel Borri, 'La Chine et la Bombe' ('China and the Bomb'), *Le Figaro*, 12 May 1966.

p. 258 The Americans and most probably the Russians have several times attempted to destroy Chinese atomic bases. The 'Maple Syrup' operation planned by the CIA consisted of the massive bombardment of the Xingjiang by means of soporific gases followed by the dropping of parachutists charged with blowing up these plants, a strange account of which was published in 1981 in the United States. It was a book by Lawrence Gardella, *Sing A Song to Jenny Next*, New York, E. P. Dutton, 1981. Between 9 and 30 May 1952, Gardella had taken part in an ultra-secret CIA operation during the Korean War the aim of which was to blow up a Chinese atomic laboratory. His team parachuted down, six marines in all, into the Jilin in the north of China not far from Korea. Having attacked the planned targets and having lost his colleagues, Gardella crossed a part of China alone before boarding a submarine in Liayun, near to a port on the Yellow Sea south of Qingdao in Shandong . . . According to his publishers, Gardella never spoke about this adventure until he knew that he was dying of a terminal illness. It was therefore after his death from leukaemia that his book appeared. The CIA have always denied that this operation went past the planning stage. In any event, it has been proved that the American and Taiwanese secret services parachuted teams into communist China as from 1949. The SDECE itself managed to infiltrate a few small groups armed with radio equipment. A member of one of these groups, a Franco-Chinese, remained a prisoner of the *Gonganbu* until the end of the 1970s.

CHAPTER 15
THE GREAT RETURN

p. 269–70 Quotation: Harry J. Angslinger and Will Dursler, *Les Trafiquants de la drogue: l'extraordinaire organisation des gangs*, Paris, Fayard, 1963.
p. 272 The Gao Gang affair. Shortly after the disappearance of the Gao Gang group in Shanghai, Pan Hannian and Fang Yang, the two main people responsible for the repression, were dismissed and disappeared. According to certain sources, the *Gonganbu* leader, Fan Yang, was shot. Pan Hannian was imprisoned until recently – he was freed in 1979.

CHAPTER 16
THE BREAK WITH MOSCOW

p. 280 Speech by Kang Sheng in *People's Daily*, 6 February 1960.

CHAPTER 17
AFRICA: RIPE FOR REVOLUTION

p. 291 Abu Nidal and Abu Daoud, *People's Daily*, 31 March 1972.
p. 295 Quoted from Azzedin, *On nous appelait fellaghas* (*They Called Us Fellaghas*), Paris, Stock, 1976.
p. 309 Letter from Kang Sheng in 1966, quoted in *Rapport de Hu Yaobang* (*Hu Yaobang's Report*), 1978, op cit.

CHAPTER 19
THE CULTURAL REVOLUTION

p. 328 Kang Sheng, Chen Boda, Mao interviews in *Translations on Communist China*, Joint Publication Research Service, 12 February 1970.
p. 335–6 *Beijing Information*, 14 November 1967.
p. 336 Enver Hoxha, *Reflections on China*, volume 1, 1962–72, Tirana, Ed. 8 Nentori, 1979.
p. 341–2 See the investigation carried out simultaneously by John Penrose of the *Daily Mirror* and Duncan Campbell of the New Statesman. See Duncan Campbell, 'The Bent World of British Intelligence' in the *New Statesman*, 16 May 1980.

CHAPTER 20
THE GRAND INQUISITOR

p. 341 *Beijing Information*, 24 July 1967.

CHAPTER 21
WESTERN INTELLIGENCE AGAINST
KANG SHENG

p. 360 Quotation from Étienne Manac'h, *Mémoires d'Extrême-Asie*. The French security services, the SDECE and DST, basically held a gun to the head of the Asia–South Seas department in the Ministry of Foreign Affairs for sending back this Chinese man. The diplomats, however, fired their own bullet, blaming counter-espionage activities for having almost soured relations with Beijing by forcibly keeping a Chinese national who did not intend to stay in France. The actual identity of Zhang Shirong is still obscure. E. Ducoureau, for example, states that the DST knew 'later' that he was a top-ranking official of the *Tewu*.

p. 362 Quoted from an unpublished manuscript by Chan Hei Pun, alias 'Cipher Chen', an account of his experience as a coding officer in the 'Policia de Seguranca Publica' in Macao.

p. 364 The author of the book *The Prime Minister was a Spy* and its source have instituted many libel proceedings against those in the British and Australian press who have tried to disprove their argument. According to Anthony Grey, the current case should turn to their advantage. Moreover it was stated to the author that it was impossible to know whether Harold Holt still lives in Beijing or even whether he was still alive (telephone interview, January 1987).

P. 553 Roger Hollis in China. The founder of M15, Vernon Kell, was himself in China in 1900 during the Boxer Rebellion. More recently, another M15 chief, Howard Smith, was honoured by appearing in the biographical dictionary of foreign persons, the *Dangdai Guoki renwu cidian*. The book *Spycatcher*, by a former M15 member living in Australia, Peter Wright, who is at the centre of a controversy with the British government, sheds new light on Hollis's role. *Spycatcher* was published in both the People's Republic of China and Taiwan.

CHAPTER 22
THE SECRET OF MAOISTS IN EUROPE

p. 370 Document Plissonnier. The Section de Montée des Cadres (SMC), the political police of the French Communist Party, had organised an enormous file of actual or prospective pro-Chinese dissidents. Unfortunately for the Section, the secret was not well kept. An auxiliary member of the SMC, who was also a casual informer to the Party's press, was sympathetic towards the pro-Chinese. The secret records of the SMC were rediscovered in the hands of a Maoist who nowadays has completely abandoned politics (as have many of those whom the authors have met). However, the person leaking the information had a successful career in the FCP, rising to an important position. The authors have been able to ascertain the existence of these records and that they are not a fabrication on the part of the Chinese for the purposes of discrediting the French Communist Party thanks to accounts given by former heads of Service B – the secret arm of the French Communist Party during the war. The records of the SMC comprise close to a thousand pages (now in the hands of the authors).

p. 375 The Belgian Security against the pro-Chinese. Based on account of a former specialist in information services in Brussels. His experience of the Chinese world and encyclopaedic knowledge in the area of information has allowed the authors to gather much information and to take into consideration witnesses from both sides of the barricade, thus giving them an objective view. The sense of historical truthfulness of this former officer in charge of counter-espionage also encouraged the authors to interview Jacques Grippa and his friends.

CHAPTER 23
'DEATH TO LIN BIAO, LONG LIVE RICHARD NIXON!'

p. 387 There are several versions of the death of Lin Biao. The official one, transmitted in 1972 via overseas bases of the Chinese Communist Party in Hong Kong and then at the CCP Congress is the least likely: that Lin and his family escaped the wreckage of the plane and fled to Mongolia. A second version was published in various countries at the same time: Yao Ming-le, *The Conspiracy and Death of Lin Biao*, New York, Alfred A. Knopf, 1983. The author of this book, written like a thriller, is anonymous. It claims to be inspired by the private journal of a high-ranking CCP official in charge of the enquiry into the Lin Biao affair. He is given the name of Zhao Yanyi (the authors think that this pseudonym is intended to allude to Zhang Yaoci, an assistant to Wang Dongxing). In other words: the Lin clan, in particular Lin Biao's son, Lin Linguo, attempted to assassinate Mao. He was then persuaded to go to dinner with Mao and was executed with a bazooka by a Wang Dongxing unit. In his enquiry, 'The Death of Lin Biao' for *Yomiuro Shimbun*, Tobiari Haruo has clearly demonstrated the fanciful character of this account (*Yomiuri Shimbun*, 17 May 1983). Moreover, it is full of historical errors and specialists wonder whether it was written by Russian KGB or Taiwanese *Diachaju* forgers (whose interests often seem to coincide!). Alexei Antonkin, former correspondent of the news agency Tass in Beijing, who has since come over to the West and works as a journalist in Paris, gives ample information on the climate in which this episode took place as well as facts about the KGB enquiry. In any event, in his book, *Les Chiens de faience – témoinage d'un correspondant de l'Agence TASS à Pekin, The China Dogs – An Account by a Correspondent for the News Agency Tass in Beijing*) Paris, Ed. de l'Equinoxe, 1983, he tends to lean towards the assassination of Lin Biao and Ye Qun at Beidaihe theory. The definitive history of this episode with documents to support it has yet to be written. The authors think that the most credible version, told in this book, is that they were assassinated in a restaurant in Beijing. Hsia Chih-yen, whom the authors interviewed in Tokyo, is a very well-informed defector. His version, published in the Japanese review *Bungei Shunju* in 1978, has been quoted and 'confirmed' by numerous accounts, some of which have been gathered by the authors, including some by pro-Beijing journalists. (The meticulous knowledge of Hsia Chih-yen allowed him to write a spy novel entitled *Un hiver froid à Pekin* (*A Cold Winter in Beijing*), Paris, Ed. Alta, 1978, whose original version envisaged with accuracy the fall of the Gang of Four.) This version of the death of Lin Biao has been told by Emile Guikovaty in *L'Express* (16 December 1978) and then by one of the most efficient French China watchers, Patrick Sabatier, in collaboration with the sinologist Wojteck Zafanolli in *Libération*, 23 December 1980.

In all the versions of the death of Lin Biao, there is one crucial piece of evidence in common: Kang Sheng was at the centre of the decision-making with regards to his murder.

p. 392 Dialogue between Lin Bao and Qiu Huizuo on Kang Sheng, quoted in *Rapport de Hu Yaobang* (*Hu Yaobang, Report*).

p. 399 Speech by Kang Sheng at the time of his visit to Bodnaras, *Beijing Information*, 22 June, 1970.

p. 405 Quotation from *The Times of India*, January 1974.

CHAPTER 24
THE SHADOWS CLAIM THEIR MASTER

p. 407 *Beijing Information* no. 4, 28 January 1974: complaints about the spying activities led by members of the USSR Embassy. Complaints about the abduction of a Chinese diplomat by Soviet authorities. *Le Monde*, Alain Bouc, 'A Grey Volga in the Night', 25 January 1974.

p. 408 *Zhongfa* no. 24, 1976. Alongside this, Ross Terrill (in *The White-boned Demon*, op. cit.) presents a different version of these facts calling into question the role of Deng Xiaoping.

p. 408 An analysis of the list of officials present at the funeral of Kang Sheng (in *Renmin Ribao*, 17 December 1975) reveals a number of important officers in the secret services, often introduced as 'members of a certain department in the Central Committee'. The following are the names of those appearing in this book at Kang's side: Yu Sang, Feng Xuan, Liu Wei, Luo Qingchang, Geng Biao, Guo Yufeng, Liao Chengzhi, Liu Yufa, Zhang Chengdong, Li Xin, Ling Yun.

P. 413 Concerning Cao Yi-ou, authors' interview with Lu Keng. Another source: Bartke, *Who's Who in the People's Republic of China*, Harvester Press, 1981. Japanese source, 5 March 1980, Cao Yi-ou disappeared from the political scene. According to Fox and Butterfield (*China Alive in the Bitter Sea*), after Kang Sheng's death, she lost her seat as deputy but was never, unlike others, the object of attacks. The authors have written to Kang Sheng's widow to ask her simple biographical questions (for example, when did she marry Kang Sheng?) but in vain. Without doubt this missive is in the records of the Gonganbu.

p. 419 Bian Shi means to flagellate a corpse.

CHAPTER 26
THE 'SON OF KANG SHENG' DEFECTS TO THE WEST

p. 445 The VACRS, Vocational Assistance Commission for Retired Servicemen, was created by Chiang Kai-shek himself. Without being recognised officially, it was a 'super ministry' at the Council of Administration in which all the other ministries have to take part. The VACRS administers a great number of businesses in Taiwan and overseas and is renowned for its economic successes. Its chairman from 1957 to 1964 was Chiang Ching-kuo. A former chief of staff, former senior officer of the Marines (and thereby in charge of the naval frogmen who landed in Communist China in order to steal documents in the 1960s) General Cheng Wei-yuan today presides over the fate of the VACRS. He was very willing to talk to the authors of his experiences and to reply to their questions.

p. 449 *Zheng Ming*, October 1986. The author of the article, Luo Pote, doubts whether Yu Zhensan betrayed Jin Wudai. But the statement by US intelligence officers, according to which it was another Chinese renegade who betrayed the CIA 'mole', is thought by certain specialists to be disinformation designed to confuse Beijing. See 'The

Not So Secret Service—Peking Loses a Master Spy', *Newsweek*, 22 September 1986.

p. 449–50 The Beijing office of the AFP was the first to report the news of Yu Zhensan's defection, on 2 September 1986. The *Guojia anquanbu* did not forgive Lawrence MacDonald, head of the AFP bureau in Beijing, for making this public, and he was subsequently expelled from China.

Epilogue
THE SECURITY LOBBY AFTER TIAN AN MEN

p. 454 *New York Herald Tribune*, 31 December 1987.

p. 455 Tai Ming Cheung, 'State Secrets Redefined', in *Far Eastern Economic Review*, 3 November 1988.

p. 456 See Roger Faligot and Rémi Kauffer, 'Le chef des services secrets vise le fauteuil de Deng,' *Le Figaro-Magazine*, 1 July 1989, and Jacques de Golfiem, *Personalités chinoises d'aujourd'hui*, Paris, l'Harmattan, November 1989.

p. 456 For all the numerous changes in CP structures in 1989, see the most useful *China Directory* 1990 (Published by Radiopress, Inc. R-Bldg, Shinjuku, 33–8, Wakamatsu-cho, Shinjuku-ku, Tokyo 162, Japan), whom the authors thank again for their constant and friendly help).

Selected Bibliography

GENERAL

Wolfgang Bartke — *Who's Who in the People's Republic of China*, a publication of the Institute of Asian Affairs in Hamburg, Harvester Press, 1981.

H. L. Boorman & R. C. Howard — *Biographical Dictionary of Republican China*, 4 vols., New York 1967–71.

Donald W. Klein & Anne B. Clark — *Biographic Dictionary of Chinese Communism*, 1921–1965, Cambridge, Mass., Harvard University Press, 1971.

Warren Kuo — *Analytical History of the Chinese Communist Party*, 4 vols., published by the Institute of International Relations, 1968–71, as well as its Chinese version, Guo Hualun, *Zhongguo Gongchandang Shilun*.

Jean Maitron — *Dictionnaire biographique du mouvement ouvrier international: La Chine*. Under the editorship of Jean Maitron, Lucien Bianco and Yves Chevrier, Paris, Editions Ouvrières et Presses de la Foundation Nationale des Sciences Politiques, 1985.

Archives of the Deuxième Bureau/Information Service. Reports of its agents abroad between 1919 and 1939, series N: historical service of the Territorial Army (Vincennes); of the Municipal Police of the French Concessions in China, Ministry of Foreign Affairs (Paris).

China Directory. Annual publication of the Chinese State, appearing every year since 1971. Published by Radiopress Inc., Fuji Television, Tokyo.

Chinese Communist Who's Who, Institute of International Relations (IIR), Taipei, 1970–71.

Dangdai Guoji Renwu Cidian (biographies of foreigners), Shanghai, Cishu Chubanshi, 1980.

The Far Eastern Review, Hong Kong weekly.

Gendai Chugoku Jinmei Jitem (biographical dictionary of contemporary Chinese figures), Tokyo, Kasan Kai, 1986.

Issues & Studies. Historical magazine, Taipei.

Peking Information, weekly magazine now called *Beijing Information*.

Who's Who in Communist China, 2 vols., Union Research Institute, Hong Kong, 1969–70.

Zhonggong Dangshi Renwu Zhuan (historical biographies of public figures in the People's Republic of China), 30 vols., Shenxi Editions, 1980–86.

CHAPTER 1

David D. Buck

Issues & Studies, vol. V I, no. 6, Taipei, 1970.
'Educational Modernisation in Tsinan, 1899–1937' in *The Chinese City Between Two Worlds*, Mark Elvin & G. William Skinner (eds.), Stanford, 1974.

Claude Cadart &
Cheng Yingxiang

L'Envoi du communisme en Chine, Paris, Gallimard, 1983.

Lao Long

Jian Qing Waizhuan.

Guy Le Prat

Le Rêve dans le Pavillon Rouge (The Dream of the Red Chamber), Paris, 1982.

Philippe Robrieux

Histoire interieure du parti communiste, 1920–45, vol. 1, Paris, Fayard.

Ross Terrill

The White-boned Demon, New York, William Morrow, 1984.

Roxane Witke

Comrade Ch'iang Ch'ing, 1977.

CHAPTER 2

Soviet Volunteers in China, 1925–45, Articles and Reminiscences, Moscow, Progress Publishers, 1980.

Marie-Claire Bergère

L'Age d'or de la bourgeoisie chinoise (1911–37), Paris, Flammarion, 1986.

Jean-Marie Bouissou

Seigneurs de guerre et officiers rouges, 1924–7, Paris, Ed. Mame, 1974.

William R. Corson &
Robert C. Crowley

The New KGB, Engine of Soviet Power, New York, William Morrow, 1985.

Lu Dafang

Shanghai tanyi jiulu, Taipei, Shijie Shuju, 1980.

U. T. Hsu

The Invisible Conflict, Hong Kong, 1958.

Harold Isaacs

The Tragedy of the Chinese Revolution, 1951.

Pan Ling

Old Shanghai – Gangsters in Paradise, Hong Kong, Heinemann Educational Books (Asia), 1984.
In Search of Old Shanghai, Hong Kong, Joint Publishing Company, 1982.

Charles B. Maybon &
J. Fredet

Histoire de la concession française de Shanghai, Paris, Plon, 1929.

Elisabeth K. Poretski

Les Nôtres, Paris, Denöel, 1969.

Sterling Seagrave

The Soong Dynasty, London, Sidgwick & Jackson, 1985.

CHAPTER 3

Issues & Studies, vol. V I, no. 6, Taipei, 1970.

Brian Crozier

Chiang Kai-shek – The Man Who Lost China, New York, Charles Scribners', 1976.

S. Goliakov & V. Ponizovsky

Le Vrai Sorge, Paris, Fayard, 1967.

Jules Humbert-Droz

De Lénine à Staline, Neuchâtel, A la Baconnière, 1971.

H. S. Kai-Yu

Chou En-lai, eminence grise de la Chine, Paris, Mercure de France, 1968.

Pierre Laurin

Mes Chines, Langres, Ed. Dominique Gueniot, 1984.

Gordon W. Prange	*Target Tokyo*, New York, McGraw-Hill, 1985.
Edgar Snow	*Red Star Over China*, New York, Random House, 1938.
Charles A. Willoughby	*Shanghai Conspiracy (The Sorge Spy Ring)*, New York, E. P. Dutton & Co. Inc., 1952.
Zhang Guotao	*The Rise of the CP (1928–38)*, vol. I, The University Press of Kansas, 1972.
Zhou Enlai	*Oeuvres Choisies*, Vol. I, Beijing, Ed. de langues etrangères, 1981.

CHAPTER 4

Otto Braun	*A Comintern Agent in China 1932–9*, California, Stanford University Press, 1982.
Oliver J. Caldwell	*A Secret War – Americans in China, 1944–5*, Southern Illinois University Press, 1972.
Richard Deacon	*A History of the Chinese Secret Service*, London, Frederick Muller, 1974.
Gu Sengbian	*Dai Li Jiangjun yu kang Ri zhanzheng (The Army of General Dai Li and the Anti-Japanese Resistance)*, Taiwan, Huaxin Chu Banshi, 1965.
Hsi Huey Liang	*La Chine et la balance du pouvoir européen*, Nanterre, revue des Amis de la BDIC, 1986.
	The Sino-German Connection, Assen/Amsterdam, Van Gorcum, 1978.
U. T. Hsu	*The Invisible Conflict*, op. cit.
Albert Londres	*Mourir pour Shanghai* (preface by Francis Lacassin), Paris, 10/18, Union Générale d'Editions, 1984.
Shen Zui	*A KMT War Criminal in New China*, Beijing, Foreign Language Press, 1986. (Translation of *Wo zhe sanshi nian*, Hunan Renmin Chubanshi, 1983.)
Ross Terrill	*The White-boned Demon*, op. cit.
Roxane Witke	*Camarade Chiang Ch'ing*, op. cit.
Yuen Sheng	'Sun Yat-sen University', *Moscow and the Chinese Revolution, A Personal Account*, The University of Kansas Center for East Asian Studies, International Studies, East Asian Series, Research Publication no. 7, 1971.
Zou Lang	*Dai Li Xin Zhuan*, 2 vols., Hong Kong, Xin Shidai Chubanshi, 1985.

CHAPTER 5

Alexandre Bennigsen & Chantal Lemercier-Quelquejay	*Sultan Galiev, le père de la révolution tiers-mondiste*, Paris, Fayard, 1986.
E. H. Carr	*The Bolshevik Revolution (1917–23)*, London, Macmillan, 1952.
Richard Deacon	*A History of the Chinese Secret Service*, op. cit.
Milorad Drachkovitch & Branko Lazitch	*Biographical Dictionary of the Comintern*, California, Stanford University Press, 1973.
Sun Tzu	*L'Art de la guerre*, Paris, Flammarion, 1983.

Jan Valtin	*Out of the Night*, New York, Alliance Book Corporation, 1941.
Ypsilon	*Pattern of a World Revolution*, Paris, La Table Ronde, 1948.
Yuen Sheng	'Sun Yat-sen University', op. cit.

CHAPTER 6

Chiang Kai-shek	*Les Origines du drame chinois*, Paris, Gallimard, 1938.
Jacques Guillermaz	*Histoire du parti communiste chinois*, vol. 2, Paris, Petite Bibliothèque, Payot, 1975.
Peter Hopkirk	*Setting the East Ablaze – Lenin's Dream of an Empire of Asia*, London, John Murray, 1984.
Luo Ruiqung, Lü Zhengcao & Wang Bingnan	*Zhou Enlai and the Xi'an Incident*, Beijing, Foreign Language Press, 1983.
Shen Zui	*A KMT War Criminal*, op. cit.
Edgar Snow	*Red Star over China*, op. cit.
Arpad Szelpal	*Les 133 Jours de Beta Kun*, Paris, Fayard, 1959.
Wang Ming	*Cinquante histoires du PCC et la trahison de Mao Zedong*, Moscow, Editions du Progrès, 1984.
Allen S. Whitting & General Sheng Shih-ts'ai	*Sinkiang, Pawn or Pivot*, Michigan, 1958.

CHAPTER 7

Otto Braun	*A Comintern Agent in China 1932–9*, op. cit.
Tim Carew	*The Fall of Hong Kong*, London, Pan Books, 1969.
Roger Faligot	'Chinese Set Up Dublin Connection', *Hibernia*, Dublin, 27 March 1980.
Guotao Zhang	*The Rise of the CP (1928–38)*, op. cit.
Richard Harris Smith	*OSS The Secret History of America's First Central Intelligence Agency*, University of California Press, 1972.
Warren Kuo	*Analytical History of the Chinese Communist Party*, vol. 4, op. cit.
Lao Long	*Jian Qing Waizhuan*, op.cit.
Edgar Snow	*Red Star over China*, op. cit.
Ross Terrill	*The White-boned Demon*, op. cit.
Peter Vladimirov	*The Vladimirov Diaries*, New York, Doubleday, 1969.
Charles A. Willoughby	*Shanghai Conspiracy*, op. cit.

CHAPTER 8

Richard Deacon	*A History of the Japanese Secret Service*, London, Frederick Muller, 1982.
M. R. D. Foot & J. M. Langley	*MI9 – Escape and Invasion, 1939–45*, London, Futura Publications, 1980.
Milton E. Miles	*A Different Kind of War, The Unknown Story of the US Navy Guerrilla Forces in World War II China*, New York, Doubleday, 1967.

Pan Ling   *Old Shanghai*, op. cit.
Brian Power   *The Puppet Emperor – The Life of Pu Yi, Last
                            Emperor of China*, London, Peter Owen, 1986.
Curt Riess   *Total Espionage*, New York, G. P. Putnam's
                            Sons, 1940.
Constantin Rissov   *Le Dragon enchaîné*, Paris, Robert Laffont,
                            1986.
Richard Harris Smith   *OSS*, op. cit.
Peter Vladimirov   *The Vladimirov Diaries*, op. cit.
Herbert O. Yardley   *The Chinese Black Chamber*, Boston, Houghton
                            Mifflin Company, 1983.
Zou Lang   *Dai Li Xin Zhuan*, op. cit.

CHAPTER 9

John Minford Barme   *Seeds of Fire: Chinese Voices of Conscience*,
                            Hong Kong, Far Eastern Economic Review Pub.,
                            1987.
G. Fabre   *L'Affaire Wang Shiwei: genese de l'opposition en
                            Chine populaire* (unpublished thesis, EHESS),
                            Paris, 1980.
Merle Goldman   *Literary Dissent in Communist China*, Mass.,
                            Harvard University Press, 1967.
Warren Kuo   *Analytical History of the Chinese Communist
                            Party*, vol. 4, op. cit.
Mark Selden   *The Yenan Way in Revolutionary China*, Mass.,
                            Harvard University Press, 1971.
Peter J. Seybolt   *Terror and Conformity, Counterespionage Cam-
                            paigns, Rectifications and Mass Movement,
                            1942-3, in Modern China*, vol. 12, no. 1, January
                            1986.
Shen Zui   *A KMT War Criminal in New China*, op. cit.
Peter Vladimirov   *The Vladimirov Diaries*, op. cit.
Wang Ming   *Cinquante histoires du PCC et la trahison de Mao
                            Zedong*, op. cit.
Wang Shiwei   *Les Lys sauvages*, 1942 (trans. Tchao Chong in the
                            *Communist Programme for Literature and Arts in
                            China*, Hong Kong, 1955).

CHAPTER 10

Mohamed Amin &   *Malaya, The Making of a Neo-Colony*, London,
  Malcolm Caldwell (ed.)   Spokesman, 1977.
David Barrett   *Dixie Mission: The United States Army Observer
                            Group in Yenan*, Berkeley, Center for Chinese
                            Studies, s.d.
J. G. Beevor   *SOE Recollections and Reflections, 1940-5*,
                            London, Bodley Head, 1981.
Dennis Bloodworth   *The Tiger and the Trojan Horse*, Singapore,
                            Times Books International, 1986.
Chong Sik Lee   'Korean Communists and Yenan', *The Chinese
                            Quarterly*, no. 9, January–March 1962.
Chu Shai-hsien   *Chinese Communists' United Front Tactics
                            Against Japan and Their Ultimate Goal*, Taipei,
                            WACL, October 1979.

Milorad Drachkovitch & Branko Lazitch — *Biographical Dictionary of the Comintern*, op. cit.

Martin Elson — *World Communism Today*, New York, McGraw-Hill, 1948.

Institute of North Korean Studies — *The Red Dynasty*, Seoul, June 1982.

Alain Kervern — *La Lumière des bambous*, Romillé, Ed. Folle Avoine, 1986.

Jean Lacouture — *Hô Chi Minh*, Paris, Le Seuil, 1976.

Jean Maitron — *Dictionnaire biographique du mouvement ouvrier international*, vol. 2, Editions ouvrières, Shiota Shobei, Japan, 1979.

Reinhold Neumann Hoditz — *Hô Tsçhi Minh*, Hamburg, Rororo, 1971.

Nosaka Sanzo — *Fûsetsu no ayumi* (autobiography), Tokyo, 1971.

Paul Quinn-Judge — 'Vietnam – A Clone of the *KGB*?', *Far Eastern Economic Review*, Hong Kong, November 1984.

Richard Harris Smith — *OSS*, op. cit.

Peter Vladimirov — *The Vladimirov Diaries*, op. cit.

CHAPTER 11

Oliver J. Caldwell — *A Secret War*, The Southern Illinois Press, 1972.

Richard Deacon — *A History of the Chinese Secret Service*, op. cit.

Anthony Grey — *The Prime Minister was a Spy*, Weidenfeld & Nicolson, London, 1983.

Jacques Guillermaz — *Histoire du parti communiste chinois*, vol. 2, op. cit.

Raymond de Jaegher — *Tempête sur la Chine*, Paris, Plon, 1953.

Pan Ling — *Old Shanghai*, op. cit.

Yuen Sheng — 'Sun Yat-sen University', op. cit.

Zhou Enlai — *Oeuvres choisies*, vols. I & IV, Beijing, Ed. de Langues Etrangères, 1980.

CHAPTER 12

Dries van Coillie — *J'ai subi la lavage de cerveau*, Belgium, Mobilisation des Consciences, 1964.

Rene Dazy — *Fusillez ces chiens enragés . . . Le genocide des trotskistes*, Paris, Olivier Orban, 1981.

Jean Lefeuvre — *Shanghai: les enfants dans la ville*, Paris, Temoignage Chretien/Casterman, 1957.

Li Fu-jen & Peng Shu-tse — *Revolutionaries in Mao's Prisons*, New York, Pathfinder Press, 1974.

Costa de Loverdo — *Le Dossier Lotus (Tibet 1959)*, Paris, Ed. Ditis, 1960.

Robert Magnenoz — *Expérience communiste en Chine*, op. cit.

Mao Zedong — *Selected Works*, vol. 5., Beijing, 1969.

Pan Ling — *Old Shanghai*, op. cit.

Michel Peissel — *Les Cavalier du Khan, guerre secrète au Tibet*, Paris, Robert Laffont, 1092.

Ratne Deshapriya Senanayake — *Inside Story of Tibet*, Beijing, Afro-Asian Writers Bureau, 1967.

CHAPTER 13

Mohamed Amin & Malcolm Caldwell (eds.)	*Malaya*, op. cit.
Andrew Boyle	*The Climate of Treason*, London, Hutchinson, 1979.
Wilfred Burchett	*At the Barricades, Forty Years on the Cutting Edge of History*, London, Times Books, 1981.
Kirill Chenkin	*Andropov, Portrait of a Czar*, Milan, Ed. Rizzoli, 1983.
Fred J. Cook	*The FBI Nobody Knows*, New York, Macmillan, 1964.
E. H. Cookridge	*Soviet Spy Net*, London, Frederick Muller, s.d.
Roger Faligot	*Les Services speciaux de Sa Majesté*, Paris, Temps Actuels, 1982.
Roger Faligot & Pascal Krop	*La Piscine, The French Secret Service since 1944*, Oxford, Basil Blackwell, 1989.
Alfred W. McCoy	*The Politics of Heroin in Southeast Asia*, New York, Harper & Row, 1972.
Mao Zedong	*Selected Works*, vol. V, op. cit.
William J. Pomeroy	*The Forest*, New York, International Publishers 1963.
Asoka Raina	*Inside RAW*, New Delhi, Vikas Publishing House, 1980.
Sterling Seagrave	*The Soong Dynasty*, op. cit.
Michael Tregenza	*Espionage*, London, Hamlyn, 1974.
John Baker White	*Sabotage is Suspected*, London, Pan Books, 1957.

CHAPTER 14

Pierre Biquard	*Frédéric Joliot-Curie et l'énergie atomique*, Paris, Seghers, 1961.
Pierre Broué	*Révolution en Allemagne*, Paris, Editions de Minuit, 1971.
Richard Deacon	*A History of the Chinese Secret Service*, op. cit.
	A History of the Russian Secret Service, London, Grafton Books, 1987.
Roger Faligot & Rémi Kauffer	*Service B*, op. cit.
Alexander Foote	*Handbook for Spies*, London, Museum Press Ltd, 1949.
Lawrence Gardella	*Sing A Song to Jenny Next*, New York, E. D. Dutton, 1981.
Mao Zedong	*Selected Works*, vol. IV.
Viktor Suvorov	*Soviet Military Intelligence Operations*, London, Hamish Hamilton, 1984.
Nigel West	*MI6, British Secret Intelligence Operations, 1909–45*, London, Weidenfeld & Nicolson, 1983.
Charles A. Willoughby	*The Shanghai Conspiracy*, op. cit.

CHAPTER 15

Peter Huang	'Chinese Communist Production and Sales of Narcotics', *Issues & Studies*, Taipei, March 1971.

Walter Kolarz	*Les Colonies russes d'Extrême-Orient*, Paris, Fasquelle, 1955.
Alfred McCoy	*La Politique de l'heroïne en Asie du Sud-Est*, op. cit.
Harrison Salisbury	*Chine-URSS, la guerre inevitable*, Paris, Albin Michel, 1970.
Edouard Sauvage	*Dans les prisons chinoises*, author's own edition, Provins, 1957.
Ross Terrill	*The White-boned Demon*, op. cit.
Roxane Witke	*Comrade Ch'iang Ch'ing*, op. cit.

CHAPTER 16

Francois Fejtö	*Chine-URSS, la fin d'une hegemonie (les origines du grand schisme communiste, 1950–7)*, Paris, Plon, 1964.
	Chine-URSS, de l'alliance au conflit, 1950–72, Paris, Le Seuil, 1973.
Klaus Mehnert	*Pékin et Moscou*, Paris, Stock, 1962.
Oleg Penkovsky	*The Penkovsky Papers (The Russian Who Spied for the West)*, New York, Doubleday, 1965.

CHAPTER 17

Yaacov Caroz	*The Arab Intelligence Networks*, 1978.
Yves Ciampi, Pierre Accoce & Jean Dewever	*Le Monde parallele*, Paris, Fayard/Chantrel, 1968.
Richard Deacon	*The Israeli Secret Service*, London, Sphere Books, 1979.
	The History of the Chinese Secret Service, op. cit.
Ludo Martens	*Pierre Mulele ou la seconde vie de Patrice Lumumba*, Anvers, EPO, 1985.
Philippe Richer	*La Chine et le Tiers-Monde*, Paris, Payot, 1971.
Michael Tregenza	*Espionage*, op. cit.
Roland Vezeau	*L'Afrique face au communisme*, Paris, Edimpra, 1967.
Gordon Winter	*Inside BOSS*, London, Penguin Books, 1981.
David Wise & Thomas Ross	*The Espionage Establishment*, 1968.
Fulbert Youlou	*J'accuse la Chine*, Paris, La Table Ronde, 1966.

CHAPTER 18

Philip Agee	*Inside the Company*, London, Penguin, 1975.
Martin Elson	*World Communism Today*, op. cit.
Roger Faligot & Rémi Kauffer	*Service B*, op. cit.
Cecil Johnson	*Communist China and Latin America, 1957–67*, Columbia University Press, 1970.
Gilles Perrault	*Un homme à part*, Paris, Bernard Barrault, 1984.
Philippe Richer	*La Chine et le Tiers-Monde*, op. cit.
Ross Wise	*The Invisible Government*, New York, Vintage Books, 1974.

CHAPTER 19

David Bonavia & John Byron — *The China Lovers*, Hong Kong, South China Morning Post, 1985.

Jacques Guillermaz — *Le Parti communiste chinois au pouvoir (1949–79)*, op. cit.

Enver Hoxha — *Reflections on China*, 1962–72, Tirana, Ed. 8 Nentori, 1979.

New World Press — *A Great Trial in Chinese History*, Beijing, 1981.

Ross Terrill — *The White-boned Demon*, op. cit.

Dick Wilson — *The Story of Zhou Enlai*, London, Hutchinson, 1984.

Roxane Witke — *Comrade Ch'iang Ch'ing*, op. cit.

CHAPTER 20

David Bonavia & John Byron — *The China Lovers*, op. cit.

Pierre Broué — *Le Parti bolchevique*, Paris, Ed. de Minuit, 1963.

Maurice Ciantar — *Mille Jours a Pékin*, Paris, Gallimard, 1969.

New World Press — *A Great Trial in Chinese History*, op. cit.

CHAPTER 21

Alexander Foote — *Handbook for Spies*, op. cit.

Anthony Grey — *The Prime Minister was a Spy*, London, Weidenfeld & Nicolson, 1983.

Etienne Manac'h — *Mémoires d'Extrême-Asie*, op. cit.

Pierre Faillant de Villemarest — *GRV, Le plus secret des services soviétiques, 1918–88*, Paris, Stock, 1988.

Nigel West — *MI5: British Security Service Operations, 1909–45*, London, Granada, 1983.

CHAPTER 22

Simone de Beauvoir — *La Longue Marche*, Paris, Gallimard, 1957.

Marcel Buttex & Daniele Martin — 'Les "Cordonniers" suisses du KGB', *Espionnage*, no. 6, December 1970.

Roger Faligot & Rémi Kauffer — *Service B*, op. cit.

Rémi Kauffer — *L'OAS, histoire d'une organisation secrète*, Paris, Fayard, 1986.

Patrick Kessel — *Le Mouvement 'maoïste' en France*, vols. 1 & 2, Paris, UGE 10/18, 1972 & 1978.

CHAPTER 23

Alexei Antonkin — *Les Chiens de faïence - temoignage d'un correspondant de l'Agence TASS à Pékin*, Paris, Ed. de l'Equinoxe, 1983.

Dennis Bloodworth — *Heirs Apparent, What Happens When Mao Dies*, New York, Farrar, Straus & Giroux, 1973.

David Bonavia & John Byron — *The China Lovers*, op. cit.

Richard Deacon — *A History of the Chinese Secret Service*, op. cit.

Yao Ming-le   *The Conspiracy and Death of Lin Biao*, New
                               York, Alfred A. Knopf, 1983.

CHAPTER 24

Serge Thion & Ben Kiernan   *Khmers rouges*, Paris, J.-E. Hallier/Albin
                               Michel, 1981.
Ross Terrill   *The White-boned Demon*, op. cit.
Nien Cheng   *Life and Death in Shanghai*, London, Grafton
                               Books, 1986.

CHAPTER 25

David Bonavia   *Hong Kong 1997 – The Final Settlement*, Hong
                               Kong, South China Morning Post, 1985.
Emily Lau   'The Rising Tide', *Far Eastern Economic Review*,
                               August 1983.
                               'Shadow in the Wings', *Far Eastern Economic
                               Review*, 9 January 1986.

CHAPTER 26

Sterling Seagrave   *The Soong Dynasty*, op. cit.
Edgar Snow   *Red Star over China*, op. cit.
Ross Terrill   *The White-boned Demon*, op. cit.
Tiziano Terziani   'China's Heart of Darkness', *Far Eastern Eco-
                               nomic Review*, 12 April 1984.

Index